Events Management

Second Edition

Events Management

Second Edition

Glenn A. J. Bowdin
Principal Lecturer, UK Centre for Events Management,
Leeds Metropolitan University, UK

Johnny Allen
Foundation Director, Australian Centre for Event Management,
University of Technology, Sydney, Australia

William O'Toole
Managing Director, EPMS.net, Member of the Project Management
Research Group, University of Sydney, Australia

Robert Harris
Director, Australian Centre for Event Management,
University of Technology, Sydney, Australia

Ian McDonnell
Senior Lecturer, School of Leisure, Sport and Tourism,
University of Technology, Sydney, Australia

AMSTERDAM • BOSTON • HEIDELBERG • LONDON • NEW YORK • OXFORD
PARIS • SAN DIEGO • SAN FRANCISCO • SINGAPORE • SYDNEY • TOKYO
Butterworth-Heinemann is an imprint of Elsevier

Butterworth-Heinemann is an imprint of Elsevier
Linacre House, Jordan Hill, Oxford OX2 8DP, UK
30 Corporate Drive, Suite 400, Burlington, MA 01803, USA

First published in Australia by John Wiley & Sons Australia Ltd
33 Park Road, Milton Q 4064
© John Wiley & Sons Australia Ltd 2004

First published in Great Britain 2001
Second edition published in Great Britain 2006
Reprinted 2006 (twice), 2007 (twice)

Permissions may be sought directly from Elsevier's Science & Technology Rights
Department in Oxford, UK: phone (+44) (0) 1865 843830; fax (+44) (0) 1865 853333;
email: permissions@elsevier.com. Alternatively you can submit your request online by
visiting the Elsevier web site at http://elsevier.com/locate/permissions, and selecting
Obtaining permission to use Elsevier material

Notice
No responsibility is assumed by the publisher for any injury and/or damage to persons
or property as a matter of products liability, negligence or otherwise, or from any use
or operation of any methods, products, instructions or ideas contained in the material
herein. Because of rapid advances in the medical sciences, in particular, independent
verification of diagnoses and drug dosages should be made

British Library Cataloguing in Publication Data
A catalogue record for this book is available from the British Library

Library of Congress Cataloging-in-Publication Data
A catalog record for this book is available from the Library of Congress

ISBN: 978-0-7506-6533-9

For information on all Butterworth-Heinemann publications
visit our website at books.elsevier.com

Printed and bound in *Great Britain*

07 08 09 10 13 12 11 10 9 8 7 6 5

Contents

List of Figures

List of Tables

The Authors

Glenn A. J. Bowdin is Principal Lecturer in Events Planning at the UK Centre for Events Management, Leeds Metropolitan University, where he has responsibility for managing events-related research. He is co-series editor for the *Elsevier Butterworth-Heinemann Events Management Series*. His research interests include the area of service quality management, specifically focusing on the area of quality costing, and issues relating to the planning, management and evaluation of events. He is a member of the editorial boards for *Event Management* (an international journal) and *Journal of Convention & Event Tourism*, Chair of AEME (Association for Events Management Education), Charter Member of the International EMBOK (Event Management Body of Knowledge) Executive and a member of Meeting Professionals International (MPI).

Johnny Allen was Foundation Director of the Australian Centre for Event Management (ACEM) at the University of Technology, Sydney. He was event manager for the Darling Harbour Authority from 1989 until 1996, and has an extensive career in event planning. Prior to his position at the ACEM, he was the special event manager for Tourism New South Wales. Johnny has now retired but remains involved with event management and event education.

William O'Toole has been creating and managing events for over 30 years. He has developed courses in event project management for a number of universities, including his alma mater, the University of Sydney. He trains event managers in countries around the world, such as Malaysia, Bahrain, the USA, China and the European Union countries. His company, EPMS, has worked with organizations as diverse as the Australia Taxation Office and the Al Ain Economic Development Department (UAE) to develop their event management systems. Currently, he is the senior adviser to the International Event Management Body of Knowledge project based in the USA, the United Kingdom and South Africa.

Rob Harris is Director of the Australian Centre for Event Management (ACEM), and a Senior Lecturer in the School of Leisure, Sport and Tourism at the University of Technology, Sydney. He has been involved in event management, training, research and consultancy for over a decade, and has developed undergraduate, postgraduate and TAFE programmes in the area. Rob's expertise in the area of event management has resulted in his developing and teaching short course programmes throughout Australia, in South East Asia, China, the United Kingdom and New Zealand. He was a founding Director of the Festivals and Events Association of Australia and is currently a member of the editorial board of the academic journal, *Event Management*.

Ian McDonnell is Senior Lecturer in the Faculty of Business's School of Leisure, Sport and Tourism at the University of Technology, Sydney, where he teaches management and marketing of leisure and tourism services.

Series Editors

Glenn A. J. Bowdin is Principal Lecturer in Events Planning at the UK Centre for Events Management, Leeds Metropolitan University, where he has responsibility for managing events-related research. He is co-author of *Events Management*. His research interests include the area of service quality management, specifically focusing on the area of quality costing, and issues relating to the planning, management and evaluation of events. He is a member of the editorial boards for *Event Management* (an international journal) and *Journal of Convention & Event Tourism*, Chair of AEME (Association for Events Management Education), Charter Member of the International EMBOK (Event Management Body of Knowledge) Executive and a member of Meeting Professionals International (MPI).

Don Getz is a Professor in the Tourism and Hospitality Management Program, Haskayne School of Business, the University of Calgary. His ongoing research involves event-related issues (e.g. management, event tourism, events and culture) and special interest tourism (e.g. wine). Recent books include *Event Management and Event Tourism* and *Explore Wine Tourism: Management, Development, Destinations*. He co-founded and is a member of the Editorial Board for *Event Management* (an international journal).

Professor Conrad Lashley is Professor in Leisure Retailing and Director of the Centre for Leisure Retailing at Nottingham Business School, Nottingham Trent University. He is also series editor for the Elsevier Butterworth-Heinemann series on Hospitality, Leisure and Tourism. His research interests have largely been concerned with service quality management, and specifically employee empowerment in service delivery. He also has research interest and publications relating to hospitality management education. Recent books include Organisation Behaviour for Leisure Services, 12 Steps to Study Success, Hospitality Retail Management and Empowerment: HR Strategies for Service Excellence. He has co-edited, Franchising Hospitality Services, and In Search of Hospitality: theoretical perspectives and debates. He is the past Chair of the Council for Hospitality Management Education. He is a Chair of the British Institute of Innkeeping's panel judges for the NITA Training awards, and is adviser to England's East Midlands Tourism network.

Series Preface

The events industry, including festivals, meetings, conferences, exhibitions, incentives, sports and a range of other events, is rapidly developing and makes a significant contribution to business and leisure-related tourism. With increased regulation and the growth of government and corporate involvement in events, the environment has become much more complex. Event managers are now required to identify and service a wide range of stakeholders and to balance their needs and objectives. Though mainly operating at national levels, there has been significant growth of academic provision to meet the needs of events and related industries and the organizations that comprise them. The English-speaking nations, together with key Northern European countries, have developed programmes of study leading to the award of diploma, undergraduate and postgraduate awards. These courses focus on providing education and training for future event professionals, and cover areas such as event planning and management, marketing, finance, human resource management and operations. Modules in events management are also included in many tourism, leisure, recreation and hospitality qualifications in universities and colleges.

The rapid growth of such courses has meant that there is a vast gap in the available literature on this topic for lecturers, students and professionals alike. To this end, the *Events Management Series* has been created to meet these needs to create a planned and targeted set of publications in this area.

Aimed at academic and management development in events management and related studies, the *Events Management Series*:

- provides a portfolio of titles which match management development needs through various stages;
- prioritizes publication of texts where there are current gaps in the market, or where current provision is unsatisfactory;
- develops a portfolio of both practical and stimulating texts;
- provides a basis for theoretical and research underpinning for programmes of study;
- is recognized as being of consistent high quality;
- will quickly become the series of first choice for both authors and users.

Preface

Each year, events occur throughout the United Kingdom. They dominate the media, fill transport systems, hotels and venues, meet business objectives, motivate communities and create positive and negative impacts. For example, the Notting Hill Carnival can trace its origins back to 1964 when, established as a festival, it provided an opportunity for West Indians to celebrate and commemorate their ancestors' freedom from slavery. Over the years, the event grew slowly, from 200 visitors, to some 3000 in the early 1970s. The turning point for the Carnival came in 1975, when the Carnival was promoted by Capital Radio, resulting in 150 000 people from the West Indian community attending. In the last decade, the Carnival has boasted audiences up to 1.5 million people from all communities – attracting attention from Greater London Authority and other stakeholders who fear for the safety of visitors and wish to support its future development.

Until relatively recently, events have been seen as part of hospitality, tourism, leisure and recreation industries, or as a support service to businesses. However, the environment is changing and the events industry is emerging in its own right supported by a growing body of knowledge. The UK events industry is wide ranging, incorporating many different sectors from the smallest of exhibitions, conferences and parties, through to large-scale sport and entertainment events. Although definitive data are not available, due to the complex nature and diversity of the industry, figures suggest that the economic impact of business tourism alone (e.g. conferences, exhibitions, incentive travel) is over £20 billion. This suggests that the industry offers significant income to the UK economy, which has not gone unnoticed by local and national governments, regional development agencies, and other public sector bodies. Increasingly, they are using events as a means of serving a host of policy objectives – from delivering tourists, regenerating communities and celebrating moments in time (such as the extensive range of events during the Millennium) to arousing civic pride, inspiring the arts and stimulating regional economies, illustrated by the increasing number of events strategies across the UK and support for large-scale events, including the successful London 2012 Olympic Games bid. Alongside this, the industry is seeking to increase professionalism, illustrated by the development of qualifications, education and training programmes within the industry and academia, supported by a range of professional associations.

The UK has developed an enviable programme of events, including The Championships (known the world over as simply Wimbledon), Notting Hill Carnival, The Open Championships, Glastonbury Festival, Royal Ascot, Edinburgh International Festival, the British Grand Prix, Belfast Festival at Queen's, Eisteddfod and the FA Cup – together with many others that cover the full spectrum of business and community interests. These events and others, which are discussed in later chapters, illustrate in various ways the power of events to raise the profile of their host cities, attract visitors, deliver economic benefits and create jobs. They also show the various origins of events, ranging from community celebrations growing out of protest, to international events supported for political and economic needs. They raise issues of the costs, benefits and impacts on their host communities and serve as models for event management, development and marketing.

Events Management examines these and other aspects of events from a UK perspective. Specifically, the book aims to:

- Present the study of events management within an academic environment
- Introduce students and practitioners to the concepts of event planning and management
- Develop an understanding of key areas required for planning and managing events, including planning, project management, logistics, risk management, legal considerations, human resources, budgeting, staging, strategic marketing, promotion and evaluation
- Increase the students understanding of the events industry within its broader business context.

Section One deals with the context for events – the reasons human societies create events and the events culture that has evolved are examined, as are the range and types of events and their impacts on their host communities, environment, economy and tourism. Section Two illustrates a methodology for the strategic management of events by examining the processes involved in conceptualizing, developing, planning, implementing, marketing and sponsoring events. The section also examines the formation, leadership and training of event teams. Section Three looks at the event project in detail and focuses on the systems event managers can use to plan and manage events, discussing project management, control and budgeting, risk management and legal issues, logistics, staging and the process of monitoring and evaluating events and reporting back to stakeholders. Finally, Section Four explores current and emerging trends and issues in events management.

The book is conveniently divided into fifteen chapters, which may be used to structure teaching sessions. Each chapter commences with clear objectives and ends with review questions in order to assess the students understanding. The book is also amply illustrated throughout with case studies, which assist the reader to relate the theory of events management to the real world of events practice, with all its challenges, frustrations and rewards. The book provides the reader with both a tool for greater understanding of events management and a framework for planning and implementing events.

Events Management is supported by a website (http://em.worldofevents.net), which includes an online 'history of events', together with links to websites and other resources for both students and lecturers.

The events industry is emerging, supported by an increasing body of knowledge, education, research and industry professionals; hopefully, the second edition of *Events Management* will contribute to this evolution and to a better understanding of how events enrich our lives, and it is hoped that the reader will in turn contribute to the future of this young and exciting industry.

Acknowledgements

Glenn wishes to thank Johnny, Bill, Rob and Ian for collaborating on this exciting project and the publishing team at Elsevier Butterworth-Heinemann and Cepha for all their support, advice and professional guidance during the production of this text. Special thanks and appreciation to current and past colleagues and students from the UK Centre for Events Management and Tourism, Hospitality & Events School, Leeds Metropolitan University, for their ideas, advice and suggestions, together with members of the Association for Events Management Education (AEME) and event educators elsewhere for their feedback on the first edition. Finally, Glenn dedicates this edition to his wife Eileen and their sons Peter and Sean, for giving their time and support for the completion of this project, which meant a year of lost evenings, weekends and holidays.

The authors and publisher would like to thank the following copyright holders, organizations and individuals, for permission to reproduce copyright material in this book.

Figures

p. 47 (Figure 2.1): Xerox Corporation, *Guide to Waste Reduction and Recycling at Special Events*, 1998, reproduced with permission of Xerox Corporation, New York; p. 83 (Figure 3.5): © Events Tasmania 2003; p. 87 (Figure 3.7): Alexandra Redmond, Glasgow Convention Bureau, Glasgow; p. 119 (Figure 5.1), p. 146 (Figure 6.1): Adapted from Getz, D. (2005), *Event Management and Event Tourism*, reproduced by permission of Cognizant Communications Corporation, New York; p. 121 (Figure 5.2), p. 268 (Figure 9.1), p. 275 (Figure 9.3), p. 283 (Figure 9.6): William O'Toole, EPMS.net; p. 167 (Figure 6.10): California Traditional Music Society; p. 168 (Figure 6.11): Peach, E. and Murrell, K. (1995), Reward and recognition systems for volunteers. In: Connors, T. ed., *The Volunteer Management Handbook*, New York, John Wiley & Sons. Copyright © 1995 T Connors. This material is used by permission of John Wiley & Sons. Inc.; p. 168 (Figure 6.12): MOTIVATION AND PERSONALITY 2/E by Maslow, © 1954. Reprinted by permission of Pearson Education Inc., Upper Saddle River, NJ; p. 169 (Figure 6.13): Adapted and Reprinted by permission of Harvard Business Review. [Exhibit]. From 'One More Time: How Do You Motivate Employees?' by F. Hertzberg, 01/03, p. 90. Copyright © 2003 by the Harvard Business School Publishing Corporation; all rights reserved; p. 151 (Figure 6.2), p. 155 (Figure 6.4): Harrogate International Festival; p. 159 (Figure 6.6): School of Volunteer Management, 2004; p. 160 (Figure 6.7): Bradner, J. (1995) Recruitment, orientation, retention. In: Connors, T. ed., *The Volunteer Management Handbook*, New York, John Wiley and Sons. Copyright © 1995 T Connors. This material is used by permission of John Wiley & Sons Inc.; p. 162 (Figure 6.8): Buckler, B. (1998), Practical steps towards a learning organization: applying academic knowledge to improvement and innovation in business performance, *The Learning Organization*, 5(1), pp. 15–23, reproduced by permission of MCB University Press, Bradford; p. 163 (Figure 6.9): R. Stone (2002). *Human Resource Management 3rd edn*, John Wiley & Sons, Brisbane. This material is used by permission of John Wiley & Sons, Australia; p. 189 (Figure 7.5): Adapted with the permission of The Free Press, a Division of Simon & Schuster Adult Publishing Group from COMPETITIVE STRATEGY: Techniques for Analyzing Industries and

Competitors by Michael E. Porter. Copyright © 1980, 1998 by The Free Press. All rights reserved; p. 198 (Figure 7.6): Marketing for Leisure and Tourism by Michael Morgan, Pearson Education Limited. Copyright © Prentice Hall Europe 1996; p. 203 (Figure 7.7): Principles of Marketing by Frances Brassington and Stephen Pettitt, Pearson Education Limited. Copyright © Frances Brassington and Stephen Pettitt 1997 © Pearson Education Limited 2000, 2003; p. 208 (Figure 7.8): Reprinted by permission of Harvard Business Review. [Exhibit]. From 'Strategies For Diversification' by I. Ansoff, September–October, pp. 113–124. Copyright © 1957 by the Harvard Business School Publishing Corporation; all rights reserved; p. 210 (Figure 7.9): SERVICES MARKETING: PEOPLE, TECHNOLOGY by Lovelock and Wirtz Adapted and reprinted by permission of Pearson Education Inc., Upper Saddle River, NJ; p. 229 (Figure 8.1): Sponsormap.com; p. 232 (Figure 8.2): Adapted from Crompton, J. (1994), Benefits and risks associated with sponsorship of major events, *Festival Management and Event Tourism*, 2(2), pp. 65–74, reproduced by permission of Cognizant Communications Corporation, New York; p. 234 (Figure 8.3): Meenaghan, T. (2001). Understanding Sponsorship Effects. *Psychology and Marketing*, 18(2), pp. 95–122. Copyright © 2001 John Wiley & Sons Inc. This material is used by permission of John Wiley & Sons Inc.; p. 243 (Figure 8.4): Bank of Scotland Corporate; pp. 248–249 (Figure 8.5): Adapted from Crompton, J. (1994). Benefits and risks associated with sponsorship of major events', *Festival Management and Event Tourism*, 2(2), pp. 65–74. Reproduced by permission of Cognizant Communications Corporation, New York; p. 308 (Figure 10.8): Adapted from Burke, R. (2003). *Project Management: Planning and Control Techniques*. 4th edn. Chichester, John Wiley & Sons. © 2003 Johns Wiley & Sons Limited. Reproduced with permission; p. 320 (Figure 11.1), p. 330 (Figure 11.2): p. 339 (Figure 11.8): Crown copyright material is reproduced with the permission of the Controller of HMSO and the Queen's Printer for Scotland; p. 331 (Figure 11.3): Allen, K. and Shaw, P. (2001) *Festivals Mean Business: The Shape of Arts Festivals in the UK*, reproduced by permission of British Arts Festivals Association, London; p. 333 (Figure 11.4): Chris Hannam, Stagesafe Limited; p. 334 (Figure 11.6): O'Toole, W. and Mikolaitis, P. (2002). *Corporate Event Project Management*. New York, John Wiley & Sons. © 2002 O'Toole and Mikolaitis. This material is used by permission of John Wiley & Sons Inc.; p. 365 (Figure 12.8): Slice PR, London; p. 391 (Figure 13.3): Roger Foley, Fogg Productions; p. 422 (Figure 14.3), pp. 423–424 (Figure 14.4), p. 426 (Figure 14.5): © 1999 UK Sport; p. 428 (Figure 14.6): Media Release on Economic Impact of 1998 Network Q Rally. Reproduced by permission of the Motor Sports Association; p. 445 (Figure 15.2): © International EMBOK Executive 2005, reproduced with permission.

Text

p. 11 (Table 1.1): PSI (1992), Arts festivals, *Cultural Trends*, 15, reproduced by permission of Policy Studies Institute, London; pp. 31–33: Lisa Gudge, Access All Areas; pp. 33–35 2002 Manchester The XVII Commonwealth Games: Post Games Report. London, Commonwealth Games Federation, pp. 18–19. Reproduced with permission; p. 43 (Table 2.2): © 2004, The London Organising Committee of the Olympic Games Limited; p. 59: The NEC Group, Birmingham; p. 63: Glastonbury Festival of Contemporary Performing Arts; pp. 90–93: Crown copyright material is reproduced with the permission of the Controller of HMSO and the Queen's Printer for Scotland; pp. 93–94: Lars Blicher-Hansen, Danish Tourist Board, Copenhagen, Denmark; pp. 112–116: Jane Ali-Knight, Kath Mainland, General Manager, Amanda Barry, Marketing and PR Manager and all the staff at the Edinburgh International Book Festival for their kind support when putting this case study together; pp. 135–139: Randle Stonier, former Chairman, Euro RSCG Skybridge; pp. 139–143: DMG World Media; pp. 174–176: Manchester City Council's Games Xchange; pp. 176–178: World Event Management; pp. 179–226: Robyn Stokes; p. 202 (Table 7.2): Crown copyright material is reproduced with the permission of the Controller of HMSO and the Queen's Printer for Scotland; p. 202 (Table 7.3): Getz, D. (2005), *Event Management and Event Tourism*, 2nd edn. reproduced by permission of Cognizant Communications Corporation, New York; p. 204 (Table 7.4): © 2004 CACI Limited, London. All rights reserved; pp. 221–223: Katharine Jordan,

CMP Information Ltd; pp. 224–226: Imagination; pp. 255–259: Rachael Church, Editor, Sport and Technology; pp. 259–262: Cheltenham Arts Festivals Ltd.; pp. 287–291: Neil Timmins; pp. 291–293: Jack Morton Worldwide; pp. 314–317: Edinburgh International Festival; pp. 345–348: Logistik Ltd; pp. 348–51: Patrick Loy; pp. 377–379: Bill Egan, GE Energy Rentals Ltd; pp. 379–384: Belfast Festival at Queen's; pp. 406–407: David Jamilly, Theme Traders; pp. 408–411: Paul Milligan, AV Magazine; pp. 430–433: Scottish Enterprise Edinburgh and Lothian, City of Edinburgh Council and EventScotland; pp. 433–435: DF Concerts and Tennent's Lager; pp. 455–458: Claire Holder; pp. 458–461: Kristine Toohey and Sue Halbwirth. The publisher would also like to acknowledge Dr Robyn Stokes, Queensland University of Technology, for her work on chapters 7 and 8 for the third edition of the Australian version of this text, published by Wiley.

Every effort has been made to trace ownership of copyright material. Information that will enable the publisher to rectify any error or omission in subsequent editions will be welcome. In such cases, please contact Elsevier's Science and Technology Rights Department in Oxford.

Section One
Event context

The first part of this book looks at the history and development of events, and the emergence of the events industry in the United Kingdom. It examines the impacts of events, including their social/cultural, physical/environmental, political and tourism/economic impacts. This part also deals with the nature and importance of event tourism.

Chapter 1

What are events?

Learning Objectives

After studying this chapter, you should be able to:

■ define special events, mega-events, hallmark events and major events
■ demonstrate an awareness of why events have evolved in human society
■ describe the role of events in the UK, and the UK tradition of events
■ describe the rise and effect of the community arts movement and its affect on the development of festivals and public events
■ understand the growth and emergence of an events industry
■ distinguish between different types of events
■ discuss the attributes and knowledge requirements of an events manager
■ describe the consolidation of the events industry in the UK
■ list the types of organization involved in the delivery of event management training.

Introduction

Today, events are central to our culture as perhaps never before. Increases in leisure time and discretionary spending have led to a proliferation of public events, celebrations and entertainment. Governments now support and promote events as part of their strategies for economic development, nation building and destination marketing. Corporations and businesses embrace events as key elements in their marketing strategies and image promotion. The enthusiasm of community groups and individuals for their own interests and passions gives rise to a marvellous array of events on almost every subject and theme imaginable. Events spill out of our newspapers and television screens, occupy much of our time and enrich our lives. As we study the phenomenon of events, it is worth examining where the event tradition in the United Kingdom has come from, and what forces are likely to shape its future growth and development. As events emerge as an industry in their own right, it is also worth considering what elements characterize such an industry, and how the UK event industry might chart its future directions in an increasingly complex and demanding environment.

Events as benchmarks for our lives

Since the dawn of time, human beings have found ways to mark important events in their lives: the changing of the seasons; the phases of the moon; the eternal cycle of birth, death and the miraculous renewal of life each spring. In Britain, the early folk festivals were associated with Plough Monday, May Day, Midsummer Day and Harvest Home, the latter celebrating the final gathering of the grain harvest (Oxford Interactive Encyclopaedia, 1997). From the Chinese New Year to the Dionysian rites of ancient Greece and the European carnival tradition of the Middle Ages, myths and rituals have been created to interpret cosmological happenings. To the present day, scratch the surface of the archetypes of Old Father Time on New Year's Eve, Guy Fawkes on 5 November Bonfire Night, Hallowe'en, or Father Christmas on 25 December, and remnants of the old myths and celebrations will be found underneath.

Both in private and in public, people feel the need to mark the important happenings in their lives, to celebrate the key moments. Coming of age, for example, is marked by rites of passage, such as initiation ceremonies, the Jewish bar and bat mitzvahs and the suburban twenty-first birthday party.

At the public level, momentous events become the milestones by which people measure their private lives. We talk about things happening 'before the new millennium', in the same way that an earlier generation talked of marrying 'before the Depression' or being born 'after the War'. Occasional events – the 1966 World Cup, the new millennium and the Manchester 2002 Commonwealth Games – help to mark eras and define milestones.

Even in the high-tech era of global media, when people have lost touch with the common religious beliefs and social norms of the past, we still need social events to mark the local and domestic details of our lives.

The rich tradition of events

The UK, and the various countries and cultures within it, has a rich tradition of rituals and ceremonies extending over thousands of years. These traditions, influenced by changes within society, including urbanization, industrialization and the increasingly multicultural population, have greatly influenced many events as they are celebrated today. Palmer and Lloyd (1972) highlight that Britain has many customs and traditions that are tied in with the changing seasons and country life. In addition, they note that with developing immigration, particularly after the war, settlers brought their own customs and traditions that have now become part of Britain's heritage. In the cultural collision with the first migrants from the former colonies of India, Pakistan and the Caribbean, new traditions have formed alongside the old. However, many events which people take for granted today have been taking place in one form or another for hundreds of years. These include fairs, festivals, sporting events, exhibitions and other forms of public celebration.

The Lord Mayor's Show provides an example of this – originating from 1215 when King John granted a Charter confirming the citizens of London's right to choose their own mayor. One of the conditions of the Charter was that the man chosen as mayor must be presented to King John for approval and had to swear an oath of allegiance. This was the basis for the original show – literally the mayor has to go to Westminster to be shown to the Sovereign. The Lord Mayor's Show is now one of the largest parades of its kind in the world, with over 5500 participants, 2000 military personnel, 180 vehicles, 66 floats, 21 marching bands and 21 carriages inluding the State Coach involved in a procession that is nearly 2.8 miles long, yet travels a route of less than 2 miles (Lord Mayor's Show, 2005b).

The term 'festival' has been used for hundreds of years and can be used to cover a multitude of events. The Policy Studies Institute (PSI, 1992, p. 1) note:

A festival was traditionally a time of celebration, relaxation and recuperation which often followed a period of hard physical labour, sowing or harvesting of crops, for example. The essential feature of these festivals was the celebration or reaffirmation of community or culture. The artistic content of such events was variable and many had a religious or ritualistic aspect, but music, dance and drama were important features of the celebration.

The majority of fairs held in the UK can trace their ancestry back to Charters and privileges granted by the Crown. The original purpose of the fairs was to trade produce, much the same as exhibitions operate today. For example, the famous Scarborough Fayre dates back to 1161. The first recorded Charter granted to King's Lynn was 1204, with the Charter for the Valentine's Day fair granted by Henry VIII in 1537. Cambridge Fair dates back to 1211 and provides an excellent example of a fair that started out as a trade fair, run under the auspices of the local religious community, but continues today as a pleasure fair. Hull Fair, the largest travelling fair in Europe, dates back to 1278 and Nottingham Goose Fair to 1284 (Toulmin, 2002a).

Britannica.com (2005) notes that the term 'festival', as commonly understood today, was first used in England in 1655, when the Festival of the Sons of the Clergy was first delivered at St Paul's Cathedral, London. Established as an annual charity sermon, it assumed a musical character in 1698. Other examples of early festivals include the Three Choirs Festival (1713), the Norfolk and Norwich Festival (1789) and the Royal National Eisteddford of Wales (revived in 1880 although it originates from 1176) (PSI, 1992). Festivals of secular music started in the eighteenth century – the first devoted to Handel took place in Westminster Abbey in 1784 – with many of these continuing well into the twentieth century (Britannica.com, 2005).

Industrialization, festivals and the sporting event calendar

Exhibitions and trade shows have taken over much of the traditional purpose of the fairs. The Exhibition Liaison Committee (1995, pp. 2–3) noted:

Since pre-Biblical times producers and merchants have displayed their wares at fairs. However the present UK exhibition industry can trace its origin back to the first industrial exhibitions held in London in 1760 and 1791. These were organised by the Royal Society of Arts and culminated . . . in the Great Exhibition of 1851 which was housed in the impressive 'Crystal Palace' erected in Hyde Park.

Dale (1995) highlights that the Great Exhibition was a triumphant success, with over 6 million visitors – around 25 per cent of the population. It proved to be an excellent promotional tool for Britain, British industry and related trades, and was the first international trade show (Cartwright, 1995). The exhibition generated profits of over £180 000 (Exhibition Liaison Committee, 1995). The following years saw the development of many exhibition facilities that are in existence today, including

Alexandra Palace and the Royal Agricultural Hall (1862), Olympia (1886) and Earls Court (originally opened 1887, current structure from 1936).

Sport provides many of the UK's most significant and enduring events. As well as attracting large crowds and media attention, they help to create a national identity and are important to the country's tourism appeal. As the origin of most team sports, Britain has an international reputation for sport and stages many international world-class events each year, drawing in large numbers of visitors and providing major benefits for local economies (English Tourism, 1999). Many of the most famous UK sporting events have their origins in the eighteenth and nineteenth centuries, including equestrian events such as Royal Ascot (1711), the Epsom Derby (1780) and the Aintree Grand National (1839, name adopted 1847), water-based events such as the Oxford and Cambridge Boat Race (1829), Cowes Week (1826), Henley Royal Regatta (established 1839, named Henley Royal Regatta from 1851) and the first Americas Cup race off the Solent, Isle of Wight (1851). Other major events from this period include The Open Championship (Golf) (1860), the FA Cup (1872), The Championship (Wimbledon) (1877) and Test cricket (England vs Australia, 1882).

During the eighteenth and nineteenth centuries, mostly choral festivals were developed in cities across England, including Leeds. However, further trends included local singing competitions in taverns in the eighteenth century, and amateur singing and brass band competitions in the nineteenth century (Britannica.com, 2005).

Wood (1982) observed that due to the dual forces of industrialization and Christianity in the mid-nineteenth century, many of the traditional festivities that developed alongside folklore were lost. In the emerging climate of industrialization, the working classes had little time for traditional celebrations, with the new National Police Force disciplining the working classes through criminalizing many of the traditional festivities. The middle of the nineteenth century saw at least forty saint days per year, although not all were public holidays in all areas. However, the Victorians believed that it was uneconomical for workers to have so much free time and, as a result, they abolished a number of festivals and tidied up the public holidays to control this. Later, they introduced a week's paid holiday to replace the lost Bank holidays (Harrowven, 1980). Wood (1982, p. 13) noted:

> The assumed irrationality of festivity underlay the bourgeois social order of industrial life and for the working classes this meant that old ways of thinking about the future, steeped in folklore and superstition, were slowly obliterated. The emerging morality of industrialism insisted that personal security could only be gained by thrift, diligence and abstinence from the pleasures of the flesh. There was little place for riotous assembly in this code of ethics until far sighted [sic] commercial entrepreneurs began to discover in the frustrated needs of the working class a whole new sector of the industrial market. Celebration was then resurrected as the Leitmotif of the emerging leisure industry and has remained a key element of mass entertainment ever since.

Palmer and Lloyd (1972) acknowledged that weakening community life and the increasing pace of progress lead to folk festivities that had lasted hundreds of years being changed, a trend which they note will continue with the rapid change in civilization. However, they highlight that British resolve has prevented the complete extinction of these celebrations, with many too deep-rooted in communities to completely disappear. Although many do not take place as spontaneously as previously, the folk rituals continue to survive or be revived, with some of the modern revivals adding new energy to old traditions. They explain:

> It is said that if you scratch civilisation you find a savage. If you scratch the owner-occupier of a desirable semi-detached residence you will find a man who is unconsciously seeking something safe and familiar, something with roots deep in the forgotten past. He may call Morris dancers 'quaint' ... and refuse to appear as St. George in a mummer's play, but he will still eat hot cross buns on

Good Friday, hang up mistletoe at Christmas, and give a Hallowe'en party … Modern man is what history has made him, and one facet of history lies in the popular customs that have their beginnings in cults almost as old as man himself. (Palmer and Lloyd, 1972, pp. 9–10).

Records of amateur festivals taking place across Britain date from as early as 1872. The 1870s witnessed the spontaneous birth of local competition festivals alongside developments of intense competition in industry. The first recorded festival was Workington Festival, which is still running today (BFF, 2005). Perhaps one of the most famous music events in the world, the Last Night of the Proms, originates from this period, with the first Proms concert taking place in 1895.

Birth of an events industry?

Wood (1982) highlighted the birth of what is now becoming known as the events industry. She identified that commercializing popular celebrations required wealth for people to participate and therefore meant selecting suitable elements of the traditional festivities and adapting them for 'vicarious consumption'. Consequently, celebrations that were traditionally seen as indecent or immoral were restricted. The Hoppings, in Newcastle (now one of Britain's biggest fairs), provides a good example of one approach, founded in 1882 as a Temperance Festival, in conjunction with race week. The idea of using a fair to advise people to act morally and not drink was in contrast to the London Council and the Fair Act in 1871, which asserted fairs were places of ill repute and dangerous for residents. The purpose of fairs has changed over time to what are seen today as events that mainly operate for enjoyment, with rides, sideshows and stalls (Toulmin, 2002b).

With the increase in work through industrialization, the practicalities of celebration meant that people were too tired to celebrate as they had done previously. Thus, celebration, and commercial celebration, provided the opportunity to relax from working life and, from a government perspective, it provided the basis for ensuring that celebration and traditional pleasure culture did not interfere with work. Wood (1982, p. 15) noted:

In order to remove the guilty feelings attached to the pursuit of 'sinful pleasure' by the legacy of the Protestant Work Ethic, it became necessary to firstly earn the material means of acquiring product of the entertainment industry and secondly, to ornate the rituals of mass celebration with an aura of professionalism and beneficient spectacle strong enough to dispel the appeal of popular home-spun amateur entertainment and pleasure seeking.

In 1871 bank holidays were made lawful, with the days dictated by the government and the monarch. Since that time, the monarch has retained the power to proclaim additional holidays, with the approval of Parliament, as illustrated by the extra bank holidays given for the 1977 Silver Jubilee (Harrowven, 1980) and the 2002 Golden Jubilee celebrations.

Speak to any international visitor, and it is likely that comments relating to Britain's rich history will emerge. The monarchy and anniversaries of major historic events have played a key role in public celebrations and the traditions, image and culture of Britain for hundreds of years. Royal events encourage patriotic fervour and serve not only to involve the general public in celebrating the monarchy itself, they have also contributed much to the UK's position as one of the leading international tourist destinations, attracting millions of tourists each year. Judd (1997) notes that Queen Victoria's Diamond Jubilee celebrations in June 1897 were staged mainly to display the achievements of Britain and the British Empire. Patriotic sentiment, lavish receptions and balls, street parties with flags and bunting, shows, and military and naval displays marked the festivities – similar displays have been witnessed since, for example, at the Coronation of Queen Elizabeth in 1953, the Queen's Silver Jubilee in 1977 and Golden Jubilee in 2002.

According to Rogers (2003a), the origins of the UK conference industry lie in political and religious congresses, and trade and professional association conventions in America in the late nineteenth century, though recognition of an industry itself is more recent, dating from the middle to latter half of the twentieth century. Shone (1998) supports this and notes that although the emergence of the conference industry dates from the last thirty years, and to some extent, the past 250 years, this would ignore the development that took place for the preceding thousands of years. He goes on to discuss the development of meeting places for trade, supported by the growth in appropriate facilities, from public halls (first century AD), churches (tenth and eleventh centuries), market towns (thirteenth century) and guildhalls (fourteenth century), through inns and coffee houses (seventeenth century), assembly rooms, town halls and universities (eighteenth century), to the growth in specialist banqueting and assembly facilities such as the Café Royal and Connaught Rooms in London, and meeting rooms within hotels (nineteenth century).

Some of the leading exhibitions today have their origins in the early part of the twentieth century. The Daily Mail Ideal Home Show is a prime example. The show was launched in 1908. Since that time, it has mirrored changes in Britain's social and lifestyle trends. The show is dedicated to setting and reflecting trends, from the 1930s when plastics and stainless steel made their first appearance, through the 1960s with the introduction of American-style kitchens as an international dimension was introduced, to the twenty-first century when the exhibits continue to be at the forefront of innovation and still include the 'House of the Future' – one of the show's most famous features. Who would have thought in 1908 that technological concepts showcased at the exhibition as futuristic and innovative could become part of everyday life?

Significance of events established

In 1915, the British government realized the value of exhibitions to the country and held the first British Industries Fair at the Royal Agricultural Hall (now the Business Design Centre), London. The event proved to be a great success and grew rapidly over the following years, to the stage where it ran in Earls Court, Olympia and Castle Bromwich (Birmingham) simultaneously. However, due to the increasing demand from trade associations and exhibitors for more specialized events, the final British Industries Fair took place in 1957 (Cartwright, 1995). The period is also notable for the 1938 Empire Exhibition at Bellahouston in Glasgow, which attracted 12.6 million paying customers (Dale, 1995).

Following the world wars, the promotion of popular celebration became a thriving sector of the new industrial economy. The Policy Studies Institute (PSI, 1992) notes that, since 1945, arts festivals have become a prominent feature in the UK. It adds that over 500 festivals now take place each year, plus hundreds more one-day community festivals and carnivals. Some of the most famous festivals, including Cheltenham (1945), the Edinburgh International Festival (1947) and the Bath Festival (1948 – then named Bath Assembly), were developed by arts practitioners following the two world wars as a means of encouraging contact between European countries (PSI, 1992). Although some arts festivals have been in existence for hundreds of years, over half of all festivals have been established since 1980, with only six festivals within the PSI research established before the twentieth century and a small number held before the end of the Second World War. Those taking place before 1945 tended generally to be music festivals, for example, Glyndebourne Festival (1934) which focuses on opera, as arts festivals are more contemporary.

The 1951 Festival of Britain was held at South Bank Centre, London, to celebrate the centenary of the Great Exhibition and to provide a symbol for Britain's emergence from the Second World War. It proved to be a great success, yet it underlined the fact that Britain had lost its early lead in staging international exhibitions (Cartwright, 1995). As a result, in 1959 the Pollitzer Committee inquiry identified that the shortage of quality exhibition space was damaging the UK's ability to compete in the global marketplace and recommended that further developments were required. Rogers (2003a) identifies that since the 1960s significant investment has taken place in the infrastructure to support conferences, meetings and related events, with the 1990s showing the highest sustained growth in venue development illustrated, for example, by the developments in Birmingham (International Convention Centre) and Glasgow (Scottish Exhibition and Conference Centre).

Emergence of professional events

The 1950s and 1960s were also notable for other factors that shaped events as they appear today. First, the period saw the rapid increase in communities from the West Indies and South Asia, and the establishment of events to celebrate these cultures. For example, the Notting Hill Carnival was established in 1964 by the West Indian community to celebrate their ancestors freedom from slavery (see the case study in Chapter 15). Second, the period saw the emergence of festival culture that is still around today. McKay (2000) highlights that, contrary to popular belief, festival culture was established in the 1950s, rather than the 1960s. He states:

> *The early roots of British festival culture in the jazz festivals run by Edward (Lord) Montagu at Beaulieu (1956–1961) and in Harold Pendelton's National Jazz Federation events at Richmond then Reading (from 1961 on) indicate the perhaps surprising extent to which the trad and modern jazz scenes of the 1950s and early 1960s blazed the trail for the hippy festivals of the later 1960s and beyond.*

This period saw the appearance of a number of popular music festivals, including the Bath Blues Festival (1969), the Pilton Festival (1970, forerunner of the Glastonbury Festival), and the Isle of Wight Festival (1968, 1969, 1970). The Isle of Wight Festival 1970 is believed to be the largest ever UK festival, when over 600 000 people are believed to have attended. This event illustrated the need for professional organization and control, as the organizers ended up making the event free when they lost control of admissions. The promoters, Fiery Creations, are said to have made this their last festival on the island owing to concerns over the festival's size, claiming that it had become unmanageable.

The 1970s and 1980s saw a range of multipurpose venues being built, that were funded predominantly by local authorities, including the National Exhibition Centre (NEC) in Birmingham (1976) and the Wembley Exhibition Centre (1977) (Exhibition Liaison Committee, 1995). Since then, the pace of development has continued, with the addition of exhibition space alongside or within football stadia, an increasing number of multipurpose indoor arenas (e.g. Sheffield, Manchester, Birmingham, London, Newcastle, Cardiff and Belfast), additional exhibition space at the NEC and Earls Court (Greaves, 1999), plus the launch of Excel in London (2000), yet demand apparently still outstrips supply given the continuing development and redevelopment taking place.

The growth in community festivals in the 1970s allowed professional artists to measure their skills against ordinary working people, and provided a means of harnessing community spirit by focusing attention away from social deprivation and unrest. Funding for such celebrations came through art associations, with the events developed within an umbrella of social welfare and community development. Thus, community festivals and festivities were used by governments to provide a focus for society, in order to rejuvenate communities and provide the basis for social and economic regeneration (Wood, 1982). Festivals had become part of the cultural landscape, and had become connected again to people's needs and lives. Every community, it seemed, had something to celebrate, and the tools with which to create its own festival.

Closely allied to sporting events is the area of corporate entertainment and hospitality. Crofts (2001) observes that Britain has one of the most sophisticated corporate hospitality markets, due in part to the concentrated summer social season that includes many of the distinguished events highlighted earlier. Peter Selby, of Keith Prowse Hospitality, noted that corporate hospitality in the UK is believed to originate from the early 1970s, when the Open Golf Championship let Gus Payne erect a catering tent at the event. Other events saw this as a means of generating revenue and keeping control of their events, by limiting their reliance on sponsors, and quickly followed suit. Further, in the mid to late 1970s, Keith Prowse Hospitality was established. Initially selling incentive packages, clients began asking to use the facilities for entertaining their customers as well – at this point, it is believed, a new industry was born (Crofts, 2001). Greaves (1996, p. 46) notes:

> with the blip of the recession putting a stop to the spiralling extravagance of the 1980s, a more targeted and cost efficient display of corporate entertainment has had to step into the shoes of the last decade, refashion them and then carry on walking down a different path.

Through the 1980s and 1990s certain seminal events set the pattern for the contemporary events industry as we know it today. The Olympic Games in Los Angeles in 1984 demonstrated that major events could be economically viable, and blended the media mastery of Hollywood with sport and events in a manner that was destined to be prophetic. The production and marketing skills of the television industry brought the Olympics to a wider audience than ever before, and demonstrated the power of a major sporting event to bring increased profile and economic benefits. The 1980s saw a rapid increase in the use of spectator sports for corporate hospitality, with international sporting events such as the Open Golf Championship, Wimbledon, Royal Ascot, the British Grand Prix and rugby events at Twickenham still popular today. Roger de Pilkyngton, marketing director of Payne & Gunter, noted that the focus changed from entertaining for the sake of it, to a more strategic use of hospitality. The mid to late 1980s saw an expansion of teambuilding and multiactivity events (Greaves, 1996), the market growth continuing into the twenty-first century.

In 1985, Live Aid introduced the era of the telethon, followed by the BBC's Children in Need and Comic Relief's Red Nose days (Bear Necessities of Golf, 1998). Live Aid was a unique television event – it was a direct plea to the audience of 1.5 billion people in 160 countries to give Ethiopia famine relief. It resulted in £200 million being raised (Younge, 1999).

Table 1.1 illustrates the origin dates of arts festivals. It shows particularly that the 1980s benefited from significant expansion, due to success observed in established festivals, supported by increased funding from the Arts Council and regional arts associations (now boards). New Leisure Markets (1995) note that as a result of festival development and redevelopment in the 1970s and 1980s, the typical festivals are

Table 1.1 Year of origin of UK arts festivals

Year of origin	Percentage of total
Pre-1940	4
1940s	4
1950s	3
1960s	12
1970s	21
1980s	51
1990/1	5

Source: PSI, 1992, p. 14

modern events. Further, the 1980s saw increasing links with local authorities as they recognized the role of the arts in regeneration and tourism.

These festivals gave the cities and towns a sense of identity and distinction, and became a focus for community groups and charity fundraising. It is a tribute to their place in the lives of their communities that many of these festivals still continue a century later.

During 1995, extensive VE Day and VJ Day commemorations, parades and celebrations marked the fiftieth anniversaries of the end of the Second World War in Europe and Japan. A series of events was staged not only to celebrate victory and to thank those that fought for their country, but also to look forward to the future and meet former enemies in a spirit of reconciliation. The finale to the VE celebrations was the biggest celebration of reconciliation in European history. Taking place in Hyde Park, London, it was attended by the Queen and members of the royal family, leaders and representatives of fifty-four countries touched by the war, and a crowd of 150 000 people (Hardman, 1995).

The UK enjoyed success throughout the twentieth century, hosting some of the world's major international sporting events. These have become more than the particular sport – many are 'festivals of sport', reflecting the package of events taking place alongside the main event, and also the increasing crossover between sport, leisure, festivals and public events. These develop interest in the event, encouraging festive spirit and community involvement, and enhancing the image of the event in the host community. For example, during the past 100 years, the UK has hosted the 1908 and 1948 Olympic Games in London, the 1966 World Cup in London, the 1986 Commonwealth Games in Edinburgh, the 1991 Rugby Union World Cup in England, the 1975, 1979 and 1983 Cricket World Cups and the 1991 World Student Games. In the past ten years alone, the UK has hosted in quick succession the UEFA European Football Championships (1996), the Rugby Union World Cup (1999), the Cricket World Cup (1999), the Rugby League World Cup (2000), Ryder Cup (2002), the Commonwealth Games (2002) and the World Indoor Athletics Championships (2003). More recently, England spent £10 million bidding for the FIFA Football World Cup in 2006, a bid subsequently awarded to Germany and also bid for the 2007 Rugby Union World Cup, an event awarded to France, while a joint Scotland/Ireland bid for the 2008 UEFA European Football Championships was awarded to Austria and Switzerland. Wales (Celtic Manor) will be hosting the Ryder Cup in 2010 while Scotland (Gleneagles) holds this privilege in 2014. Finally, London successfully bid for the 2012 Olympic Games. The pursuit of major events such as these forms part of government strategy implemented through UK Sport (discussed further in Chapter 2). Since 1997 when the strategy was launched, UK Sport has supported over seventy events of European, World or Commonwealth status. They are also pursued by national event agencies such as Northern Ireland Events Company and EventScotland and regional or local authorities, for example North West Development Agency and Sheffield City Council Major Events Unit (discussed in Chapter 3).

The spirit of Live Aid was rejuvenated in 1999, with the NetAid fundraising concerts and again in 2005 for the Tsunami Relief Concert at Millennium Stadium in Cardiff (see case study at the end of this chapter) and Live 8. Using modern technology not available at Live Aid in 1985, the NetAid concerts took place simultaneously in London, Geneva and New Jersey, with a combined live audience of 110 000. However, the difference with this event was that 2.4 million people watched the live Internet broadcast of the event in one day, setting a new world record, and worldwide television, radio and Internet coverage has so far generated over 2 billion impressions on the NetAid.org website. NetAid illustrates the potential use of the Internet as a medium for social change, through using the Internet to provide a global resource against extreme poverty. NetAid has also been credited with helping to secure $27 billion in US debt relief by U2's Bono (NetAid.org, 1999). Live 8 took place in July 2005. Timed before the G8 Summit of world leaders (Canada, France, Germany, UK, Italy, Japan, Russia and USA) at Gleneagles Hotel in Scotland, Live 8 was developed not to raise money, which had been the aim of Live Aid, but to campaign for justice by putting pressure on the G8 leaders to end poverty in Africa by cancelling debt, increasing aid and delivering trade justice. What had originally been planned as five concerts (Berlin, London, Paris, Rome and Philadelphia) expanded to twelve, with events taking place in Barrie, Berlin, Cornwall (Eden Project), Johannesburg, London, Moscow, Paris, Philadelphia, Rome and Tokyo. The main concert took place in Hyde Park where over 200 000 watched acts including U2, Sir Paul McCartney, Robbie Williams, Cold Play, Madonna, Dido, Pink Floyd, The Who, REM and a host of other leading artists perform over the ten hour event. Live 8 was watched by an estimated three billion people worldwide with the event broadcast through television, radio, the Internet and mobile phones (Live8, 2005).

Into the new millennium

The trend in local authority funding for arts festivals has continued into the twenty-first century. Allen and Shaw (2001) found that, of the 137 festivals responding to their study, 82 per cent received part of their funding in 1998–99 from local authorities, with 51 per cent gaining grants from arts councils and 42 per cent from the English Regional Arts Boards. New Leisure Markets (1995) identifies that festivals are attractive to local authorities as they provide visitors/tourists, encourage commercial sponsorship, present cultural experiences for residents by taking arts to a wider audience, give staff a focus and can motivate involvement from the local performing arts community.

Commenting on their study (Allen and Shaw, 2001), Tim Joss, Chair of BAFA Trust highlights the modern role of festivals. He comments:

> *It's time for many people – in the arts, in national and local government, and elsewhere – to change their attitude to festivals. The old view that festivals are flashes in the pan contributing nothing to long-term development must go. This valuable research paints a very different picture. It makes an impressive case for arts festivals as flexible, efficient, contemporary enterprises rooted in their local communities. And thanks to their special freedom to collaborate with artists, venues, and artistic and other partners, they are proving themselves valuable catalysts for cultural, social and economic development (BAFA, 2001).*

Across the UK, the new millennium brought an unprecedented level of funding for community projects, including events, and firmly focused the spotlight on the events industry. North West Arts Board (1999) note that community festivals and events such as melas, Chinese New Year and carnivals are extremely important, providing not only the opportunity for communities to celebrate their identity and presence in the UK, but also a stage for creative expression within the context of their cultural heritage. The year-long Millennium Festival, supported with £100 million from the National Lottery funded Millennium Commission, saw communities take part in around 2000 events across the UK, including major celebrations in twenty-two towns and cities on New Year's Eve 1999, a further thirty-two events closing the year in 2000 and over 370 large-scale festivals. Steve Denford, Senior Festival Manager at the Millennium Commission Press Office (2000), noted:

> *The Millennium Festival is the largest programme of year-long celebrations ever mounted in the UK with an opportunity for all communities to come together and celebrate the year 2000. Throughout the year the diverse programme of events is offering something for everyone and something happening everywhere.*

One of the largest combined events was the Beacon Millennium Project, whereby 1400 beacons were lit across the UK on 31 December 1999, providing the focal point for community-level celebrations. Further initiatives included investment of over £1.3 billion in around 200 new buildings, environmental project, visitor attractions, and a total of £200 million provided as 40 000 grants, or 'Millennium Awards' for individuals to put their ideas into action for their communities (Millennium Commission, 2000).

The Millennium Festival caused communities across Britain to pause and reflect on identity and the past, and to look forward to the future. It also changed forever the nature of our public celebrations, as a new benchmark has been created against which all future events will be measured. The millennium also left a legacy of public spaces dedicated to celebrations and events, and government, both local and central, supportive of their social and economic benefits. For example, the Millennium Square in Leeds opened on 31 December 2000 as a multipurpose event and leisure space in the heart of the city – purpose-built to provide a relaxing leisure space for the people of Leeds, yet incorporating a range of services to reflect the needs of event organizers.

Major events are continuing into the 21st century with increasing recognition of the role that events can play beyond merely entertainment, linking in to cultural, arts, regeneration, education, tourism and other strategies. A series of festivals and events were planned as part of the SeaBritain Festival 2005, coordinated by the National Maritime Museum, 'to celebrate the ways in which the sea touches all of our lives'. The centrepiece of the festival was the Trafalgar Weekend in October to mark the 200th anniversary of Nelson's victory (National Maritime Museum, 2005). Liverpool was successful in securing the European Capital of Culture 2008. This has prompted a series of events before, during and after 2008 and significant investment in cultural infrastructure, revitalising the city (Liverpool Culture Company, 2005a). The other unsuccessful bidding cities, including Newcastle Gateshead and Bradford have capitalized on their bids to take forward cultural programme in their cities. For example, Newcastle Gateshead Initiative have begun an ambitious programme of events, festivals and initiatives under the culture[10] project (Newcastle Gateshead Initiative, 2005).

The business world was quick to discover the marketing and image-making power of events, and events became established through the 1990s and early this decade as an important element of the corporate marketing mix. Companies and corporations began to partner and sponsor major events, such as Microsoft and Adecco's involvement in 2002 Manchester Commonwealth Games. Other corporations created events as vehicles for their own marketing – for example, Sundae on the Common, a festival on Clapham Common in London (August 2005) developed for Ben & Jerry's ice-cream. By early this decade, corporate involvement in events had become the norm, so sponsorship was perceived as an integral part of staging major events. Companies became increasingly aware of the role that events could play in promoting their image and increasing their market share, but they also became more focused on event outcomes and return on investment. It became common for large companies to have an in-house event team, focused not only on the company's involvement in public events, but also on the internal role of events in staff training and morale building. Events became not only a significant part of the corporate vocabulary, but also a viable career option with employment opportunities and career paths.

This brief outline of the history of modern events relates primarily to the UK situation, but a similar story has been replicated in most post-industrial societies. The balance between more traditional festivals and contemporary corporate events changes according to the nature of the society in a given geographic area. Nevertheless, events are a growing phenomenon worldwide, suggesting they fulfil a basic need in human society. The UK is widely recognized as a leader in the event field, for example, with events such as Edinburgh International Festival and 2002 Manchester Commonwealth Games, and the opening and closing ceremonies of the 2004 Athens Olympics organized by Jack Morton UK, being regarded as international benchmarks for best practice in the field.

What are events?

Before exploring events in further detail throughout the following chapters, it is important to clarify the terms used. Many authors have discussed the definition of events and the various terms used to describe these, however, there is little agreement on standardized terms or categories to use. A useful starting point when looking at definitions and terminology is The Chambers Dictionary (1998, p. 560) which defines event as,

> *anything which happens; result; any incidence or occurrence esp a memorable one; contingency or possibility of occurrence; an item in a programme (of sports, etc); a type of horse-riding competition, often held over three days (three-day event), consisting of three sections, ie dressage, cross-country riding and showjumping; fortune or fate (obs); an organized activity at a particular venue, eg for sales promotion, fundraising.*

It can be concluded from this definition that the term event may be viewed in a variety of ways, with other texts and dictionaries offering similar definitions. The Accepted Practices Exchange (APEX) Industry Glossary of terms (CIC, 2003) defines an event as, 'An organized occasion such as a meeting, convention, exhibition, special event, gala dinner, etc. An event is often composed of several different yet related functions.' Getz (2005, p. 16) notes that a principle applying to all events is they are temporary and that, 'Every such event is unique stemming from the blend of management, program, setting and people'.

Special events

The term 'special events' has been coined to describe specific rituals, presentations, performances or celebrations that are consciously planned and created to mark special occasions and/or to achieve particular social, cultural or corporate goals and objectives. Special events can include national days and celebrations, important civic occasions, unique cultural performances, major sporting fixtures, corporate functions, trade promotions and product launches. Special events' is sometimes used to describe the industry, while events industry is increasingly used. The industry is now so vast that it is impossible to provide a definition that includes all varieties and shades of events. As an early pioneer in events literature, Goldblatt (2005, p. 6), highlighted the human aspect of events, defining special events as, 'a unique moment in time, celebrated with ceremony and ritual to satisfy specific needs'. In his groundbreaking work on the typology of events, Getz (2005, p. 16) suggests that special events are best defined by their context. He offers two definitions, one from the point of view of the event organizer, and the other from that of the customer, or guest:

1. *A special event is a one-time or infrequently occurring event outside normal programmes or activities of the sponsoring or organizing body.*
2. *To the customer or guest, a special event is an opportunity for a leisure, social or cultural experience outside the normal range of choices or beyond everyday experience.*

Among the attributes that he believes create the sense of 'specialness' are festive spirit, uniqueness, quality, authenticity, tradition, hospitality, theme and symbolism.

It is clear from the above discussion that whether an event is special or not depends to some degree on the viewpoint of the practitioner or person experiencing the event, or indeed the author, researcher or student in the field. However, it is clear that special event is again being used as a term that includes many other categories.

Jago and Shaw (1998, p. 28) express another view from a tourism context. Based on their research which explored and developed a definitional framework for special events, they suggested six core attributes of special events. These were that special events should attract tourists or tourism development; be of limited duration; be one-off or infrequent occurrence; raise the awareness, image, or profile of a region; offer a social experience; and, be out of the ordinary. In their summary definition of a special event they draw together a number of the above areas: 'A one-time or infrequently occurring event of limited duration that provides the consumer with a leisure and social opportunity beyond everyday experience. Such events, which attract, or have the potential to attract, tourists, are often held to raise the profile, image or awareness of a region' (Jago and Shaw, 1998, p. 29).

Types of events

There are many different ways of categorizing or grouping events, including by size, form and content, as discussed in the following sections. This text examines the full range of events that the events industry produces, using the term 'events' to cover all of the following categories.

Size

Events are often characterized according to their size and scale. Common categories are major events, mega-events, hallmark events and local/community events, although definitions are not exact and distinctions become blurred. Following an extensive review of classifications, typologies and terminology in use within the literature and published research, Jago and Shaw (1998) proposed mega-events and hallmark events as subcategories of major events, while other authors present these categories on a scale according to size and impact. This is illustrated in Figure 1.1.

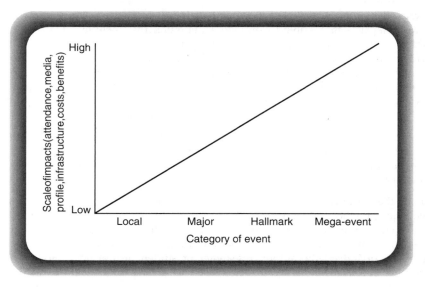

Figure 1.1 Categorization of events

Local or community events

Most communities produce a host of festivals and events that are targeted mainly at local audiences and staged primarily for their social, fun and entertainment value. These events often produce a range of benefits, including engendering pride in the community, strengthening a feeling of belonging and creating a sense of place. They can also help to expose people to new ideas and experiences, encourage participation in sports and arts activities, and encourage tolerance and diversity. For these reasons, local governments often support such events as part of their community and cultural development strategies. Janiskee (1996, p. 404) defines local or community events as:

> family-fun events that are considered 'owned' by a community because they use volunteer services from the host community, employ public venues such as streets, parks and schools and are produced at the direction of local government agencies or nongovernment organizations (NGOs) such as service clubs, public safety organisations or business associations.

Janiskee also comments that community festivals can become hallmark events and attract a large number of visitors to a community. Janiskee estimates that community celebrations in the USA have been increasing at an annual rate of 5 per cent since the 1930s, and anecdotal evidence suggests that it is reasonable to assume similar growth in the UK.

Major events

Major events are events that, by their scale and media interest, are capable of attracting significant visitor numbers, media coverage and economic benefits. The Isle of Man hosts the TT Races and Silverstone has the British Formula One Grand Prix, both significant annual major events. Cowes Week, hosted on the Isle of Wight each year, provides a focus on maritime pursuits as well as attracting international prestige and media. The Open Championship, staged at different links golf courses each year, attracts strong destination promotion around the world for the host region. Many top international sporting championships fit into this category, and are increasingly being sought after, and bid for, by national sporting organizations and governments in the competitive world of international major events. UK Sport (1999a, p. 4) consider that three elements are required to be classed as a major sporting event:

1. It involves competition between teams and/or individuals representing a number of nations.
2. It attracts significant public interest, nationally and internationally, through spectator attendance and media coverage.
3. It is of international significance to the sport(s) concerned, and features prominently on their international calendar.

Hallmark events

The term 'hallmark events' refers to those events that become so identified with the spirit or ethos of a town, city or region that they become synonymous with the name of the place, and gain widespread recognition and awareness. Tourism researcher Ritchie (1984, p. 2) defines them as: 'Major one time or recurring events of limited duration, developed primarily to enhance awareness, appeal and profitability of a tourism destination in the short term or long term. Such events rely for their success on uniqueness, status, or timely significance to create interest and attract attention'.

Classic examples of hallmark events are Carnival in Rio, known throughout the world as an expression of the Latin vitality and exuberance of that city, the Tour de France, the Oktoberfest in Munich, Germany and the Edinburgh International Festival in Scotland. These events are identified with the very essence of these places and their citizens, and bring huge tourist revenue as well as a strong sense of local pride and international recognition. Getz (2005, pp. 16–17) describes them in terms of their ability to provide a competitive advantage for their host communities:

> *The term 'hallmark' describes an event that possesses such significance, in terms of tradition, attractiveness, quality or publicity, that the event provides the host venue, community, or destination with a competitive advantage. Over time the event and destination can become inextricably linked, such as Mardi Gras and New Orleans.*

Examples in the UK might include the Notting Hill Carnival, the Grand National at Aintree, the FA Cup Final (until the recent redevelopment where it has taken place at the Millennium Stadium Cardiff, this was clearly associated w Wembley Stadium) and The Championships at Wimbledon, all of whic a degree of international recognition. Commenting on the val Championships, John Barrett, author, and Senior BBC Comm '"Wimbledon", as The Championships are universally know the years an established part of the fabric of British life. It is m more than just the world's most important and historic tennis a symbol of all that is best about sport, royal patronage, and so the British do so well, a subtle blend that the rest of the world fi (Jones, 2000).

Mega-events

Mega-events are those events that are so large that they affect whole economies and reverberate in the global media. These events are generally developed following competitive bidding. They include the Olympic Games, the Paralympic Games, the FIFA World Cup, the IAAF World Championships and World Fairs, but it is difficult for many other events to fit into this category. Getz (2005, p. 18) defines them as:

'Mega-events, by way of their size or significance, are those that yield extraordinarily high levels of tourism, media coverage, prestige, or economic impact for the host community, venue or organization.

Hall (1997, p. 5), another researcher in the field of events and tourism, offers this definition:

Mega-events such as World Fairs and Expositions, the World Soccer Cup Final, or the Olympic Games, are events which are expressly targeted at the international tourism market and may be suitably described as 'mega' by virtue of their size in terms of attendance, target market, level of public financial involvement, political effects, extent of television coverage, construction of facilities, and impact on economic and social fabric of the host community.

Finally, Jago and Shaw (1998, p. 29) define mega-events simply as, 'A one-time major event that is generally of an international scale'. In relative terms, by these definitions the Great Exhibition in London in 1851 was perhaps the UK's first mega-event. Although belonging to an era of less encompassing media, other early examples may include the 1908 and 1948 London Olympics, the 1938 Empire Exhibition in Glasgow, the 1951 Festival of Britain and the 1966 World Cup. Modern events such as the 1991 World Student Games in Sheffield and the Euro '96 football championships would struggle to meet all of Getz's criteria. More recently, the UK Millennium Festival in 2000, if taken as a national event, would probably qualify, as may the Manchester 2002 Commonwealth Games with the associated national Spirit of Friendship Festival, and the London 2012 Olympic Games.

Form or content

Another common means of classifying events is by their form or content. Cultural events, including festivals, are a universal form of events that pre-date the contemporary events industry and exist in most times and most societies. Sports events have grown out of similar roots to become a sizable and growing sector of the event industry. Business events, sometimes called MICE (Meetings, Incentives, Conventions and Exhibitions) events, are an established arm of the events industry, and generate considerable income for their host cities and, increasingly, for regional centres.

Cultural events

Cultural events can also be contenders as major events. For example, major musicals such as *Phantom of the Opera*, *Miss Saigon* and *Cats* reap considerable tourism revenue for London's West End. Edinburgh festivals are an important expression of human activity that contributes much to our social and cultural life. They are also increasingly linked with tourism to generate business activity and income for their host communities. Council and related organizations, supporting both private and public sector initiatives, have developed an enviable reputation and tourism bonanza through staging a wide range of festivals that cater to different market needs.

Cheltenham has developed the Cheltenham International Jazz Festival, Cheltenham International Festival of Music, Cheltenham Science Festival and the Cheltenham Festival of Literature, Bath and North East Somerset have developed the Bath International Music Festival and Glyndebourne has the developed the world-famous opera festival. Each has an eye to positioning itself in the tourism markets as well as in the arts world. Some local authorities and government/regional agencies are taking these initiatives one stage further, by developing an event-focused arts strategy (e.g. Bath and North East Somerset Council) (Arts Development Service, 2004), using events to deliver the cultural strategy (e.g. Brighton and Hove, Newham Council) or developing a specific events/festivals strategy (e.g. Edinburgh District Council, EventScotland, North West Development Agency). The value and role of carnival within cultural events has been recognized with the recently published National Carnival Arts Strategy (Nindi, 2005). Event tourism and event strategy are further discussed in Chapter 3.

Arts festivals share a number of characteristics, including intense artistic output, and a clear time-specific programme delivered with a clear purpose and direction (Rolfe, 1992). South East Arts (1998, p. 2) have developed seven categories for festivals within their region based on the overall purpose and size, which can usefully be applied to classify festivals in other regions. These are:

1. *High-profile general celebrations of the arts*: these address an ambitious agenda and a multitude of aims – to reach the highest standards, to achieve a high media profile, to reach a broad audience, to generate high levels of income.
2. *Festivals that celebrate a particular location*: from small villages to large towns, these festivals aim to bring people together to celebrate their local area, often featuring a large number of local groups. These festivals subdivide into those run by voluntary groups and those run by local authorities. Festivals run by voluntary groups tend to be smaller.
3. *Art-form festivals*: focused on a specific art form, offering unique opportunities for audiences to see particular kinds of work, and may also address the development of that artform by providing a focus for critical debate, master classes, commissions of new work, etc.
4. *Celebration of work by a community of interest*: these festivals highlight work by specific groups of people, e.g. disabled people, young people or women and often contain a large proportion of participatory workshops.
5. *Calendar*: cultural or religious festivals. Indigenous traditions of large-scale assembly have largely died away in England, but the Asian and Caribbean communities have brought carnival and melas to enhance the cultural mix of festivals in the UK.
6. *Amateur arts festivals*: a large but low-profile sector that involves thousands of people. Many of these festivals are competitive.
7. *Commercial music festivals*: a hugely popular phenomenon, some local authorities also run outdoor pop music festivals that adopt a similar model.

New Leisure Markets (1995) identify that UK festivals are divided between single-theme and multi-theme events. The main themes for single-theme festivals are folk (35 per cent), classical music (15 per cent), jazz (15 per cent), literature (5 per cent) and film (5 per cent). Mintel (2004) note that the music concert and festival industry, which includes commercial music festivals, was estimated to be worth £613 million in 2004, with pop or rock music focused events accounting for between 71 and 73 per cent of the market, followed by classical (24.8 per cent) and Jazz (2.8 per cent). It should be noted that opera was not included in the study. Further, AFO (2004) estimated that there are now over 350 folk festivals taking place in the UK.

Sports events

The testing of sporting prowess through competition is one of the oldest and most enduring of human activities, with a rich tradition going back to the ancient Greek Olympics and beyond. Sports events are an important and growing part of the event industry, encompassing the full spectrum of individual sports and multi-sport events such as the Olympic, Commonwealth and Masters games. Their ability to attract tourist visitors and to generate media coverage and economic impacts has placed them at the fore of most government event strategies and destination marketing programmes. Sports events not only bring benefits to their host governments and sports organizations, but also benefit participants such as players, coaches and officials, and bring entertainment and enjoyment to spectators. It is interesting to note that UK Sport (1999a) classify the sporting calendar into four groups within the overall umbrella of major events, including mega, calendar, one-off and showcase events. There is some duplication with the points discussed earlier. However, the categories are included, together with the elements above, in order to illustrate the need to clarify terminology before commencing a study into events or bidding, and provide a useful illustration of potential objectives and means of attracting these types of events.

1. *Mega events*: awarded after competitive bidding. Includes the Summer Olympics, the Paralympic Games, the FIFA World Cup and the IAAF World Athletic Championships.
2. *Calendar events*: no bidding required, commercially successful events, play a regular part in the international calendar for that sport, e.g. The Championships (Wimbledon), the British Formula One Grand Prix, The Open Championship, Test Series in cricket, Rugby Union Internationals.
3. *One-off events*: generally awarded after competitive bidding, substantial television rights interest nationally and internationally, e.g. the Rugby League and Union World Cups, the Cricket World Cup and European Football Championships.
4. *Showcase events*: generally awarded after competitive bidding, these events have the potential to boost sport development, provide the UK with a good chance of winning medals and can improve the UK's image overseas and/or involve regions in UK, e.g. the World Judo Championships, the World Disability Championships and the European Showjumping Championships.

Business events

Business events include conferences, exhibitions, incentive travel, and corporate events. These industries are sometimes grouped as discretionary business tourism, MICE (meetings, incentives, conventions and exhibitions/events) or a variety of other terms. Internationally, in April 2005 the Joint Meetings Industry Council recommended adopting the term The Meetings Industry as a unifying term at the launch of its 'Profile and Power' campaign which seeks to distinguish the activities from tourism and other industries (JMIC, 2005). This sector is largely characterized by its business and trade focus, although there is a strong public and tourism aspect to many of its activities. The following section provides an overview of some of the sectors. Market data should be viewed with some caution, as much is based on estimates and the methodologies used are not always comparable, however, it is useful in providing a general understanding of the market size.

The Business Tourism Partnership (BTP) suggests that conferences, exhibitions, incentive travel, corporate hospitality and business travel combined account for 28 per cent of overseas visitors in the UK and 29 per cent of all inbound tourism earnings. This equates to an estimated tourism income worth £20 billion, not including business transacted at the events estimated to be worth £100 billion (BTP, 2005).

Conferences can be very diverse, as revealed by the definition of the Convention Industry Committee in the APEX Industry Glossary (CIC, 2003):

1. Participatory meeting designed for discussion, fact-finding, problem solving and consultation.
2. An event used by any organization to meet and exchange views, convey a message, open a debate or give publicity to some area of opinion on a specific issue. No tradition, continuity or periodicity is required to convene a conference. Although not generally limited in time, conferences are usually of short duration with specific objectives. Conferences are usually on a smaller scale than congresses.

For the British Conference Venues Survey (BACD, 2004), a more succinct definition is used, 'an out-of-office meeting of at least four hours' duration involving a minimum of eight people' (Rogers, 2003a, p. 19). Conferences can be categorized according to their primary market focus, generally as corporate or association. The conference market is worth an estimated £11.7 billion per annum (BTP, 2005). Although many conferences are relatively small scale, for example, 77 per cent of association conferences have less than 500 delegates (Rogers, 2003b) and corporate events average 99 (Right Solutions, 2005), there are larger examples which may illustrate the scale of the sector. The Rotary International World Convention – brought 24 000 big-spending delegates to Glasgow in 1997, while the 1998 Lions International Convention at Birmingham NEC brought in 25 000 from 180 countries (The NEC Group, 2005a). Another example is when the Bournemouth International Centre hosted the biggest political conference so far in the UK – around 20 000 delegates, journalists, exhibitors and technicians attended the Labour Party Conference in September 1999 (Barnes, 1999). A further example from the Scottish Exhibition and Conference Centre (SECC) in Glasgow was when in September 2004 they hosted over 14 000 delegates for the 14th Annual Congress of the European Respiratory Society leading to a £10 million injection into the local economy (SECC, 2005).

Exhibitions are a considerable and growing part of business events. Exhibitions can be defined as, '. . . a presentation of products or services to an invited audience with the object of inducing a sale or informing the visitor. It is a form of three-dimensional advertising where, in many instances, the product can be seen, handled, assessed by demonstration and in some cases even smelt and tasted'. (Exhibition Liaison Council, 1995), or more recently and succinctly defined as 'an event that enables buyers and sellers to meet together in a market situation' (Exhibition Audience Audits Ltd., 2005). Internationally, the terms exposition, expo, (trade/consumer) show, trade fair are sometimes used by some interchangeably, though exhibition has been adopted in the UK as the overarching term. Research published by the Exhibition Venues Association (EVA) suggests that spend on exhibitions had reached an estimated £1.7 billion by 2003 (Exhibition Audience Audits Ltd., 2004). Exhibitions bring suppliers of goods and services together with buyers, usually in a particular industry sector. The British International Motor Show, the Ideal Home Show and the International Boat Show are three of the largest exhibitions in the UK, each generating tens of thousands of visitors. The Exhibition Liaison Committee (1995, p. 8) identified that there are four main categories of exhibition in the UK:

- *Agricultural shows*: held in the countryside on open sites (including purpose-built show grounds). Normally occur once a year, with attendance ranging from 5000 to 200 000 at the largest events within a period of one to five days. Examples include the Royal Show (180 000) and the Newbury and Royal Berkshire Show (70 000).

- *Consumer shows*: aimed mainly at the general public, although may have a trade element. Include subjects such as gardening, home interiors, motoring and fashion. Extensively promoted by the media, for example, the Ideal Home Show (established in 1908) or Clothes Show Live.
- *Specialized trade shows and exhibitions*: the product emphasis and target buying audience are generally defined and controlled by the organizer. These are sometimes referred to as business-to-business (B2B) events. For example, International Confex and PLASA (Production Light and Sound) at Earls Court, The National Venue Show/Event Services Show at NEC, The Event Show, RSVP and The Meetings & Incentive Travel Show at Olympia, and the Showmans Show at Newbury Showground all focus on various aspects of the developing events industry.
- *Private exhibitions*: includes product launches, in-store and concourse displays, which are exclusive to one or a defined group of manufacturers. The audience is normally by direct invitation.

A further category of show is one which combines trade and consumer markets, which Morrow (2002) refers to as the combined or mixed show, for example, the British International Motor Show or the London Boat Show (Rogers, 2003b). Finally, a new term to emerge over recent years is the confex – an exhibition and conference combined. These take one of two forms, either professional, scientific and medical conferences that offset their overheads from income generated by an associated trade show, or an exhibition that enhances visitor numbers by featuring linked conferences in their show (Exhibition Audience Audits Ltd., 2005).

Exhibitions can also be categorized according to the industry sector that they focus on or by size. The Exhibition Industry Research Group (Exhibition Audience Audits Ltd., 2005) agreed a new categorization system in 2001 using four categories:

- **Category 1:** Exhibitions held in qualifying venues (a qualifying venue is one offering more than 2000 m² of continuous covered space.
- **Category 2:** One day public exhibitions held at qualifying venues.
- **Category 3:** Exhibitions that are primarily outdoor held in qualifying and non-qualifying Venues (i.e. major agricultural and horticultural events attracting more than 50 000 visitors, trade/public and trade events that are held at non-qualifying primarily outdoor venues).
- **Category 4:** Exhibitions held at non-qualifying venues (venues that offer less than 2000 m² for indoor exhibitions).

The modern exhibition industry is clearly structured, taking in venue owners, exhibition organizers and contractors from the supply side, and exhibitors and visitors generating the demand. Major conference and exhibition centres in the main cities and many regional centres now vie for their share of the thriving business event market.

Another lucrative aspect is incentive travel, defined by the Society of Incentive Travel Executives (1998, cited in Rogers, 2003a, p. 52) as 'a global management tool that uses an exceptional travel experience to motivate and/or recognize participants for increased levels of performance in support of organizational goals'. The UK's unique locations and international popularity as a tourism destination make it a leading player in the incentive travel market, with the inbound incentive travel market estimated to be worth an estimated £165 million in 1996 (Rogers, 2003a).

A final category that may be included within business events is corporate events, which includes incentive travel, client entertainment, staff entertainment, meetings and conferences (Rogers, 2003b). Although definitive data does not exist, due to difficulties with definition and the cross-over with other sectors, the client and staff entertainment aspects may be reflected in data collected on corporate hospitality, which indicates that the sector was worth over £700 million (Tambe, 2004) and could be as much as £1 billion (BTP, 2005). In addition, a survey by the International Visual Communications Association (IVCA), found that audiovisual communications represented an industry sector set to be worth an estimated £2.8 billion in 2005, up from £2.62 billion in 2004, of which £578 million was attributable to business events (Anon, 2005a).

The structure of the events industry

The rapid growth of events in the past decade led to the formation of an identifiable event industry, with its own practitioners, suppliers and professional associations. The emergence of the industry has involved the identification and refinement of a discrete body of knowledge of the industry's best practice, accompanied by the development of training programmes and career paths. The industry's formation has also been accompanied by a period of rapid globalization of markets and communication, which has affected the nature of, and trends within, the industry. Further, it has been accompanied by an era of increasing government regulation, which has resulted in a complex and demanding operational environment. The following sections describe the key components of the event industry.

Event organizations

Events are often staged or hosted by event organizations, which may be event-specific bodies such as the Harrogate International Festival or the Glastonbury Festival of Contemporary Performing Arts. Other events are run by special teams within larger organizations, such as BBC Good Food Show organized by BBC Haymarket Exhibitions, or ITMA 2003 which was organized by a team within The NEC Group. Corporate events are often organized by in-house event teams or by project teams within the companies that are putting on the event.

Event management companies

Event management companies are professional groups or individuals that organize events on a contract basis on behalf of their clients. The BBC, for example, may contract an event management company to stage an event or organize inhouse through, for example, BBC Worldwide, or the Microsoft Corporation may contract an event manager to stage the launch of a new product. The specialist companies often organize a number of events concurrently, and develop long-term relationships with their clients and suppliers.

Event industry suppliers

The growth of a large and complex industry has led to the formation of a wide range of specialist suppliers. These suppliers may work in direct event related areas, such as staging, sound production, lighting, audiovisual production, entertainment and catering, or they may work in associated areas, such as transport, communications, security, legal services and accounting services. This network of suppliers is an integral part of the industry, and their increasing specialization and expertise assist the production of professional and high-calibre events.

Industry associations

The emergence of the industry has also led to the formation of professional associations providing networking, communications and liaison within the industry, training and accreditation programmes, codes of ethical practice and lobbying on behalf of their members. Because the industry is so diverse, the UK has a multitude of industry associations that represent the various sectors within the industry, with some serving more than one sector and others competing for members within the same sectors. Some are international associations with affiliated groups in countries such as the UK; others are specific to their region or country. Event managers should identify the association(s) that best suits their individual situation and the needs of their organization, as some associations promote individual membership, whilst others promote membership on an organizational basis. Some of the main trade and professional associations covering the events industry are listed below:

- *Associations*: European Society of Association Executives (ESAE).
- *Conference/meetings*: Association for Conferences and Events (ACE), Association of British Professional Conference Organisers (ABPCO), British Association of Conference Destinations (BACD), European Federation of Conference Towns (EFCT), International Association of Congress Centres (AIPC), International Association of Professional Conference Organisers (IAPCO), International Congress & Convention Association (ICCA), Meeting Professionals International (MPI), Meetings Industry Association (MIA) and Society of Association Executives (SAE).
- *Exhibitions*: Association of Exhibition Contractors (AEC), Association of Exhibition Organisers (AEO), Association of Shows and Agricultural Organisations (ASAO), British Exhibition Contractors Association (BECA), Exhibition Venues Association (EVA), National Exhibitors Association (NEA).
- *Incentive travel*: Eventia (formerly Incentive Travel and Meetings Association (ITMA)), UK chapter of the Society of Incentive Travel Executives (SITE).
- *Festivals*: Arts i.e. British Art Festivals Association (BAFA), Association of Festival Organisers (AFO), British Federation of Festivals for Music, Dance and Speech (BFF), International Festival and Events Association (IFEA) Europe.
- *Corporate hospitality*: Eventia (formerly Corporate Events Association (CEA)), Hotel, Catering and International Management Association (HCIMA).
- *Music events/event production*: Concert Promoters Association (CPA), Production Services Association (PSA), Professional Light and Sound Association (PLASA), United Kingdom Crowd Management Association (UKCMA).
- *Event (other)*: Institute of Leisure and Amenity Management (ILAM). International Special Events Society (ISES), International Visual Communications Association (IVCA), National Outdoor Events Association (NOEA), The Event Services Association (TESA), Society of Event Organisers (SEO).
- *Venues*: Association of Event Venues (AEV), National Arenas Association (NAA).
- *Miscellaneous/suppliers*: British Hospitality Association (BHA), Hotel Booking Agents Association (HBAA), Independent Street Arts Network (ISAN), Made-Up Textiles Association (MUTA), Mobile Outdoor Catering Association (MOCA), Society of Ticket Agents and Retailers (STAR).

It should be noted that although categorized above for convenience, in reality many of these associations work across sectors/categories. In addition, organizations representing the hospitality, tourism and leisure industries and the profession associated with these, for example, with the Tourism Alliance, British Hospitality Association and The Tourism Society, also have a role in events industry as the boundaries are not clearly defined.

There has been some discussion over whether there is a need for consolidation of associations to ensure that the industry can move forward and its needs be effectively lobbied to government. Although this has not happened across the board, there are a number of initiatives taking place where associations are effectively working together, including forming federations and alliances. The Business Tourism Partnership represents the leading trade associations (ACE, AEO, ABPCO, BACD, BHA, EVA, Eventia, ICCA, MIA, MPI, NOEA) and government agencies (UK Inbound, Northern Ireland Tourist Board), VisitBritain, Visit London, Visit Scotland, Wales Tourist Board) involved in conferences, exhibitions, meetings and incentives. Eventia, launched in January 2006 draws together the ITMA and CEA. The European Live Music Forum (ELMF) draws together eight national and European associations with an interest in the live music industry in Europe, including CPA and IFEA, with the aim of developing the market and working effectively with the European Union Commission. European Federation of the Associations of Professional Conference Organisers (EFAPCO), including ABPCO, has been formed to enhance the image of European for hosting meetings, promote European Professional Conference Organisers (PCOs) and to maintain standards. An extended list of national and international associations is available on the website Worldofevents.net.

External regulatory bodies

As noted, contemporary events take place in an increasingly regulated and complex environment. A series of local government and statutory bodies are responsible for overseeing the conduct and safe staging of events, and these bodies have an integral relationship with the industry. Councils often oversee the application of laws governing the preparation and sale of food, street closures, waste management and removal. In addition, events organizers have a legal responsibility to provide a safe workplace and to obey all laws and statutes relating to employment, contracts, taxation and so on. The professional event manager needs to be familiar with the regulations governing events and to maintain contact with the public authorities that have a vested interest in the industry.

Publications

In order to support the development of industry and education, an increasing number of books have been written, particularly over the last decade. A number of books focus on events planning and management, including Getz (2005), Goldblatt (2005), O'Toole and Mikolaitis (2002), Shone and Parry (2004), Silvers (2004b), Tassiopoulos (ed) (2000), Van Der Wagen and Carlos (2005) and Watt (1998), with Donald Getz and Joe Goldblatt generally acknowledged as the pioneers of the subject. Building on the growth in interest and number of courses studying the subject, two dedicated series of events books are available, The Wiley Event Management Series (edited by Dr Joe Goldblatt, published by John Wiley & Sons, Inc, Hoboken, New Jersey) and the Events Management Series (edited by Glenn Bowdin, Professor Donald Getz and Professor Conrad Lashley, published by Elsevier Butterworth-Heinemann, Oxford) – both series are beginning to address specific gaps in the events management literature, including the interaction with the range of disciplines, for both the professional development and higher education markets. The discipline is served by three dedicated journals, *Event Management* (formerly *Festival Management and Event Tourism*), *International Journal of Event Management Research* and the *Journal of Convention and Event Tourism* (formerly *Journal of Convention and Exhibition Management*), which aim to develop the research base to support the new professionals. Finally, this wealth of knowledge is enhanced with a range of periodicals providing contemporary articles and industry news, such as *Access All Areas, AV, Conference and Exhibition Factfinder, Conference and Incentive Travel,* Conference News, *Event, Event Organiser, Event & Venue Specialist, Exhibition Bulletin, Exhibition News, Lighting&Sound International, Live!, Meetings and Incentive Travel, RSVP and Total Production International.* For extensive links to event-related books, research journals, periodicals and publications, please visit WorldofEvents.net.

Event management education and training

As the size and needs of the event industry have grown, event management training has started to emerge as a discrete discipline. In the early years of the industry, the field was characterized by a large number of volunteers. Those event managers who obtained paid positions came from a variety of related disciplines, drawing on their knowledge gained from that discipline and skills learnt on the job. Many came from allied areas such as theatre and entertainment, audiovisual production and film, and adapted their skills to events. Others came from working for event suppliers such as staging, lighting and sound production companies, having discovered that they could expand and build on their existing skills to undertake the overall management of events. However, as the use of events by government and industry has grown, event budgets have increased, and the logistics of events have become more complex, the need has emerged for skilled event professionals who can meet the industry's specific requirements. Education and training at a number of levels have arisen to meet this need.

Identifying the knowledge and skills required by event managers

Research for the Institute of Management (Coulson and Coe, 1991) identified the qualities that future managers should possess. These included the ability to communicate, flexibility, adaptability, a broad perspective on organization goals, a balanced perspective overall and an understanding of the business environment. Further, nine out of ten believed that managers should have an ability to assume greater responsibility, contribute to teams, handle uncertainty and surprise, be aware of ethics and values, and have a commitment to ongoing learning. Research by Katz (1974, cited in Mullins, 2005, pp. 211–212) identified the qualities possessed by effective managers, which were grouped under the headings of technical competence (specific knowledge, methods and skills applied to discrete tasks), social and human skills (focus on interpersonal relationships, motivating staff, effective teamwork and leadership, sensitivity and style of management) and conceptual ability (ability to view complexity of situations, decision making, contribution related to objectives of the organization and strategy). Mullins (2005) notes that as managers' progress within an organization, more emphasis will be placed on conceptual ability and less on technical competence. In addition to generic management skills, Getz and Wicks (1994, pp. 108–109) specify the following event-specific areas of knowledge as appropriate for inclusion in event management training:

- History and meanings of festivals, celebrations, rituals and other events
- Historical evolution; types of events
- Trends in demand and supply
- Motivations and benefits sought from events
- Roles and impacts of events in society, the economy, environment and culture
- Who is producing events, and why?
- Programme concepts and styles
- Event settings
- Operations unique to events
- Management unique to events
- Marketing unique to events.

Limited research has been conducted within the events industry to identify the skills, qualities and attributes of successful event managers, particularly in the UK. The Business Tourism Forum and the Business Tourism Advisory Committee (1999, p. 36) found that the conference and event industries required enhanced negotiation skills, higher client management skills and a detailed knowledge of specific venues. In addition, the industry requires people with an informed understanding of, and ability to anticipate, client needs and to suggest solutions to problems and improvements to plans. Further research, conducted in Canada and Australia, provides a useful insight into the attributes and knowledge required specifically by event managers. While developing occupational standards for events managers, the Canadian Tourism Human Resource Council (CTHRC, 2005, p. 6) identified that an event manager is responsible for:

- determining the parameters, policies and procedures,
- planning, designing and producing,
- overseeing coordination,
- developing and implementing the marketing plan,
- preparing financial, business and evaluative reports,
- developing a risk management plan,
- overseeing financial management.

CTHRC group skills under six broad headings of administration, event planning and management, marketing, risk management, human resource management and professionalism. Goldblatt (2005) highlights six qualities of leading event management leaders, with integrity being highlighted as paramount, followed by confidence and persistence, collaboration, problem solving, communications skills and vision.

Perry, Foley and Rumpf (1996) described the attributes and knowledge required by event managers resulting from their survey of managers attending the Australian Events Conference in Canberra in February 1996. Seven attributes were frequently mentioned, of which vision was listed as the most important, followed closely by leadership, adaptability, and skills in organization, communications, marketing and people management. Knowledge areas considered most important were project management, budgeting, time management, relating to the media, business planning, human resources and marketing. Later studies by Harris and Griffin (1997), Royal and Jago (1998), Harris and Jago (1999) and Arcodia and Barker (2002) confirmed the importance of these knowledge/skill domains. In developing the Event Management

Body of Knowledge (EMBOK), the International EMBOK Executive, building on earlier work of Silvers (2004a), settled on five over-arching domains administration, design, marketing, operations and risk management (Silvers, Bowdin, O'Toole and Nelson 2005). Allen (2005) focuses on the skills of time management and explores the techniques event managers can use for smooth event implementation. Despite occasional differing emphasis and nuances, the field is beginning to agree on the specific body of knowledge of best practice appropriate to the training of professional event managers.

People1st, the Sector Skills Council covering hospitality, tourism, leisure and related industries, was established in 2004 to replace the Travel, Tourism Services and Events National Training Organisation (TTENTO) and the Hospitality Training Foundation (HtF), in order to help support the industry and to further the agenda toward a fully trained workforce. Their remit includes producing industry research and labour market data and encouraging communication between education providers, employers and industry associations.

Training delivery

As training has become needed, it has been delivered in a range of formats by a variety of institutions.

Industry associations

The major event industry associations have all been involved in the delivery of training and certification programmes and are beginning to recognize the benefits that these, together with the developments in formal education, can have to address the shortfall in qualified professionals that some areas of the industry are experiencing. These programmes typically involve a points system whereby accreditation can be gained from a mix of participation in the association, contribution to the industry, attendance at conferences and seminars, and often a written paper or examination. Pre-requisites often include membership of the association, industry experience and allegiance to a written code of conduct or ethics. Accreditation programmes are usually supported by educational provisions such as seminar training programmes, online training courses and self-directed learning resources. For example, ISES offers an examination-based accreditation as a Certified Special Events Professional (CSEP), MPI offers examination-based accreditation as a Certified Meetings Manager (CMM) and supports the Convention Industry Council's Certified Meeting Professional (CMP), together with a range of education opportunities; while MIA, Eventia, PSA, AEC/AEO/AEV and other associations provide training courses, focusing on topics including health and safety, sales and procurement. Thus, each area of industry is increasingly investing in training and education in order to ensure that there is a sufficient qualified staffing base to support the developing industry.

Universities and colleges

Universities and colleges have become involved in event education, with many offering events management or marketing subjects as part of tourism, hospitality, leisure, recreation or sport management courses. The George Washington University in Washington DC was an early pioneer in offering a concentration in event management within a graduate programme; in 1994 it commenced a complete certification programme in event management (Getz and Wicks, 1994).

Dedicated, or combined, courses in events management are being delivered at colleges and universities across the UK at foundation degree, diploma, degree and masters level. These courses focus on providing education and training for future event professionals. Generally built around a management core, they cover areas such as and management, marketing, human resource management, finance and operations together with event specific modules such as event planning, production and risk management. Universities & Colleges Admissions Service (UCAS, 2005), the organization responsible for processing applications to higher education in the United Kingdom (UK), currently list 41 colleges and universities offering undergraduate events courses in the UK, with anecdotal evidence suggesting that this figure is likely to be on the low side when taking into account additional courses already being offered or in development. In addition, six universities are known to be offering postgraduate masters courses in the UK. For example, the UK Centre for Events Management (Leeds Metropolitan University) launched the first events management degree in 1996. This has now been established in the market and has been joined by a range of specialized one-year (top-up) degrees in conferences and exhibitions management, sport events management, managing cultural and major events and fundraising and sponsorship, and an MSc Events Management. Further research undertaken in development of WorldofEvents.net, an online directory, indicates that these developments are being mirrored internationally, with dedicated event-related courses being offering in Ireland, Germany, France, Australia, Canada, USA and elsewhere.

In order to recognize these developments, AEME (the Association for Events Management Education) was formed in 2004 in order to further develop events education and best practice and to act as the events management subject association particularly within the UK. Featuring many of the UK providers of events education together with trainers, associations and educators from Ireland, US, Australia and elsewhere among its members, AEME hosts an annual Events Management Educators Forum to further the association's aims. For further information about AEME, please visit www.aeme.org.

For links to events-related courses and qualifications offer by training companies, associations and further/higher education internationally, please visit WorldofEvents.net and Learn Direct (www.learndirect-advice.co.uk).

Career opportunities in events

As demonstrated above, events are an expanding industry, providing new and challenging job opportunities for people entering the field. A successful career in events depends on applicants identifying their own skills and interests, and then matching these carefully with the needs of prospective employers. Areas of expanding activity – such as corporate events, conferences, local government and tourism – may be fruitful areas to examine. Employers often look for a mix of qualifications and experience, so intending job seekers may be advised to consider taking entry-level positions to take that important first step towards a satisfying and rewarding career. Although to date limited information has been developed about careers in events, this is beginning to change, with the Association of Graduate Career Advisory Services (AGCAS), associations (for example, ACE, AEO, BACD, MIA and

MPI) and other organizations producing career information, with much more likely to be produced in the near future.

Meeting Professionals International (MPI), one of the leading industry associations worldwide with around 20 000 members, have developed career pathways for meeting professionals as MPI Professional Pathways. The initiative identifies five levels of competence, covering college/university students, entry/novice level, experienced level, senior level and executive/advanced. As part of the initiative, they have defined standardized classification of competencies for meeting and event professionals as well as identifying critical knowledge, skills and abilities and job descriptions (MPI, 2005).

For links to events-related careers information, vacancies, recruitment companies and related resources, please visit WorldofEvents.net.

Chapter summary

Events perform a powerful role in society. They have existed throughout human history in all times and all cultures. British cultures have a rich tradition of rituals and ceremonies. The events tradition in modern Britain began to take off towards the end of the nineteenth century, with industrialization reducing spontaneous celebration and increasing professionally organized events. The ruling elite often decided the form and content of public celebrations, but an alternative tradition of popular celebrations arose from the interests and pursuits of ordinary people. Many nineteenth-century leisure pursuits such as race meetings have survived to the present day. Through the twentieth century, the changes in society were mirrored by changes in the style of public events. A tradition of city and town festivals evolved in the post Second World War years, and was rejuvenated by the social movements and cultural changes of the 1970s. Notions of high culture were challenged by a more pluralistic and democratic popular culture, which reinvigorated festivals and community events. With the coming of the 1980s, the corporate sector began to recognize the economic and promotional value of events.

The 1990s saw the events industry emerge, with various sectors, particularly those focused on business-related events, pushing forward the claim for an industry to be recognized, supported by dialogue with government and for an increase in training and support for the industry-related NVQs. Further, the period saw the growth in events-related education in colleges and universities, with dedicated courses and modules being developed to support the emerging industry. Events vary in their size and impact, with terms such as special events, mega-events, hallmark events and major events used to describe and categorize them. Events are also categorized according to their type and sector, such as public, cultural, festivals, sporting, tourism and corporate events. The business events sector (including meetings, incentives, conventions and exhibitions) is one of the fastest growing areas of events. With increasing corporate involvement, events are now seen as an industry with considerable economic and job creation benefits.

The emerging events industry with its needs, challenges and opportunities will be examined in the following chapters.

Questions

1. Why are events created, and what purpose do they serve in society?
2. Do events mirror changes in society, or do they have a role in creating and changing values? Give examples to illustrate your answer.
3. Why have events emerged so strongly in recent years in the UK?
4. What are the key political, cultural and social trends that determine the current climate of events in the UK? How would you expect these to influence the nature of events in the coming years?
5. Identify an event in your city or region that has the capacity to be a hallmark event. Give your reasons for placing it in this category.
6. What characteristics define an industry, and using these criteria do you consider that there is an events industry in the UK?
7. Do you agree with the attributes and knowledge areas required by events managers listed in this chapter? Do an inventory of your own attributes and skills based on these listings?

Case study 1.1

Tsunami Relief Cardiff

When Britain awoke to the news of the South Asia tsunami disaster on Boxing Day 2004, people quickly looked for ways to help. Some had more at their disposal than others. With the pitch at Cardiff's Millennium Stadium out in preparation for a New Year's Eve event, general manager Paul Sergeant saw an opportunity, and along with Pablo Janczur, director of Cardiff-based production company Push4, began to consider the feasibility of holding a 'Live Aid-style' fundraiser at the stadium.

Short lead time

With the pitch scheduled to go back on January 24, 2005 ahead of the first Six Nations rugby international on February 5, time was tight. Ignoring received wisdom that such an undertaking might be impossible in the time frame available, a small team began making calls to record labels and tour managers, while discussing crewing and equipment availability with contractors for a prospective date of January 22. 'For the first week we were like coiled springs', Push4's technical project co-ordinator, Matt Wordley, explains, 'One of the most frustrating things was having to ask so many people to be on standby for an event that might not even happen'.

Amid mounting speculation in the press, enough artists were able to confirm their support for the event in time for the team to meet a last-chance deadline with the local authorities two weeks ahead of the show date. Regular Nine Yards collaborators John Armstrong and Jane Kelly were production manager and site manager respectively, allowing Claire Sampson to effectively take on the role of event producer, and assist the venue and Push4 with various activities usually tackled by the promoter. 'I'm doing a lot of things I wouldn't as production manager', she agrees, before reeling off a variety of examples, not least the hours spent compiling last-minute video messages that morning, her role cuing presenters and VT clips during the show to allow stage manager Julian Lavender to focus entirely on the enormous movement of kit between changeovers and the need to manage the breadth of broadcast crews on site, not least a BBC documentary team.

Broadcast schedule

Balancing television requirements with the demands of running a smooth live show was an involved process despite the tight timescale. Agreeing times during sound check when the front of house PA would be turned down to allow various news anchors to deliver their pieces to camera a case in point. Flexibility, cooperation and goodwill was required from all involved. 'We've had wonderful support from the venue, the licensing team, police and fire services', Sampson continues. 'Everybody has listened and been realistic about the timescales. Because of the speed this has been put together we haven't had all the usual meetings in advance. The running order was still being finalized right up to the show and we're grateful to crew and artists alike for their co-operation'.

Production schedule

The need to minimize changeover times between the 21 acts on what remained a taut seven hour live broadcast meant guitar bands were strewn among acoustic sets and vocals to track throughout an unashamedly eclectic line-up, with Stereophonics frontman Kelly Jones, Goldie Lookin' Chain, Aled Jones, Charlotte Church and show-opener Katherine Jenkins among considerable local presence. Physical turnarounds were aided by a substantial upstage production area, with as much kit as possible staying set up on risers following soundchecks, while Brit Row operated a double desk system alternating between Yamaha PM1Ds for the live acts and PM5Ds for the presenters, video playback and vocals to track. Success was rooted in thorough pre-production, with both sets of desks programmed in advance to speed up the line checks. A final massive changeover for Jools Holland's Rhythm & Blues Orchestra took just nine minutes.

'Brit Row knows the acoustics of the venue very well and had enough first division engineers as well as the kit to do it,' Sampson reflects, while acknowledging the wealth of choice she had across the board following an outpouring of production support. In the end, a combination of experience at the venue, of working for live broadcast, and a familiarity with Nine Yards and each other, coupled in some cases with sheer speed out of the blocks, won through. Most organizations worked at cost, with others going further: McGuinness supplied free trucking, Energyst Cat Rental Power donated the 455 kVA and 250 kVA Twinpacks that enabled Power Logistics to supplement mains supply in order to run the PA, lighting and video screens, while Showsec and Imaginators were among companies whose employees donated wages.

Despite the venue's many plus points, notably the ability to unload articulated lorries directly onto the stage from the arena floor, it remains a sporting venue that requires significant augmentation for the handful of music events staged each year. Logistically, Tsunami Relief upped the ante even further, with any spare space hijacked for the cause, while in-house caterer Letheby & Christopher extended its remit to include artist and VIP hospitality. Eat To The Beat served 185 media representatives from its kitchen truck parked among the Outside Broadcast (OB) vehicles and took over facilities at the adjoining Cardiff Arms Park social club to cater for the 250 crew.

Summary

Tsunami Relief Cardiff demonstrates how a successful large scale event can be achieved at short notice. However, the event would not have been possible without the skills, experience and determination of a strong team of professional venue managers, event managers, producers, technicians, broadcasters, artists and other logistics organizations, together with support and cooperation of the appropriate authorities. Public response to the event was beyond expectations, with live Internet streaming and interest from international broadcasters extending its reach. James Dean Bradfield of crowd favourites Manic Street Preachers captured its essence, 'You've got three minutes to get your gear on and that's it. We got on stage, saw the people in the crowd and knew everybody had made the right decision'.

For further information on the organizations discussed in this case study, please visit www.millenniumstadium.co.uk (Millennium Stadium), www.push4.co.uk (Push4), www.britanniarow.com (Britannia Row), www.energyst.co.uk (Energyst), www.powerlog.co.uk (Power Logistics), www.crowd-management.com (Showsec), www.imaginators.co.uk (Imaginators), www.allleisure.co.uk (Letheby & Christopher) and www.eattothebeat.com (Eat To The Beat).

By Lisa Gudge, Deputy Editor, Access All Areas, www.access-aa.co.uk.

Questions

1. The Tsunami Relief concert was organized to raise money and awareness. How might that influence the packaging of the event?
2. Identify some of the management implications for organizing an event at short notice.
3. Charities are increasingly searching for new and innovative event ideas in order to achieve their objectives. In general terms, what objectives might a charity event have?
4. You have been tasked by a charity with developing some new event concepts for them. Select a charity with which you are familiar and outline what the objectives would be for this event. Brainstorm event concepts (at least five) that may be used to achieve their objectives.

Case study 1.2

Manchester 2002 The XVII Commonwealth Games – Key Lessons

Introduction

Every city bidding for a major sporting event, particularly one of the top multi-sport events in the world, spends considerable time, energy and resources assessing the financial, economic and social viability of the event. There is no right or wrong answer. Every city and every Games will deliver a different event, unique to its own place, time and cultural setting.

Following the Commonwealth Games, a Post Games Report was produced to pull together an overview of the challenges and questions involved, while a project (Games Xchange) implemented in Manchester manages the archive of documents and records and ensures that the knowledge is transferred to future events and projects. The report covers the questions that M2002 asked, the process the Organising Committee (OC) went through, and most importantly, the lessons learned during the planning and implementation of the Manchester 2002 Commonwealth Games. It is only through sharing this information that the Commonwealth Games (and indeed other multi-sporting events) can raise the bar and communicate through sport.

There are many lessons and recommendations contained throughout the Post Games Report; however, there are core fundamentals that are vital to all multi-sport events. These are summarized below.

Maximize potential

It is more than a sporting event. Whilst the sporting competition sits at the core, it is also the pebble that is thrown into a pond creating ever widening circles of opportunities that encompass more and more people and include ever increasing opportunities, activities and programmes that can use sport to develop host cities and communities and harness greater human values.

Partnerships

Partnerships provide not only funding but expertise and experience, which is priceless and should never be underestimated, particularly at every level of Government; from national to local and all key sporting bodies; from the crucial funding and strategic partners to operational stakeholders, such as transport and the Police; national and regional stakeholders to the critically important sponsors, partners and supporters.

Planning

Organizational and operational planning are the life blood of a successful event – from designing and building the venues, through to holding test events, planning risk management, timetabling reliable transport and other essential services.

Infrastructure

Infrastructure planning, construction and Games operations of venues, villages and transport not only provide the legacy, but form the stage upon which the sporting drama unfolds. It is the physical and visible manifestation of years of planning, the public face of the organization, the Games experience of both athletes and spectators.

Technology

With each major event sporting technology moves forward in leaps and bounds. It is important to remember that the technology landscape may well change over the planning and implementation period due to developments in timing and scoring devices, telecommunications, results services and even broadcast formats, such as the Internet. By way of example, Manchester 2002 (M2002) was the first multi-sport event to pilot delivery of results to PDAs (Personal Digital Assistant) over GPRS (General Packet Radio Service). This will be standard in forthcoming events. The technology infrastructure and operating platforms for any Games must be flexible as it is initially created so far in advance of many functional needs.

Human resource

People, (whether paid staff, volunteers or contractors), are the wheels that keep the Games moving forward both in the planning stages and during the event itself. The task of creating a workforce that is the equivalent of a FTSE 100 company and then disbanding the majority of staff post-Games is unique only to this type of event and takes great human resource skills and courage to meet both the needs of the Games and the needs of the individuals involved. Different skills are often required for planning and operational phases and individuals need to understand this and appreciate that their roles may evolve over time.

Financial

The financial and commercial requirements of an event of this scale provide the oxygen that keeps the organization alive. Transparency, accountability and exceptional corporate governance are critical to ensuring funds are received in a timely manner. It is also important to remember that plans for every Functional Area (FA) will need to be reassessed in the planning, testing and operational phases so having adequate contingency funds is vital to operational success.

Marketing and communication

No event can achieve its full potential without creative and impactful marketing and communication strategies. Whilst so much is being created in terms of infrastructure, venues and legacies it is sometimes easy to forget that the signature of an outstanding event is full venues and community support and involvement at Games time. The media, together with marketing campaigns play a decisive role in influencing the public to attend and in shaping their memories of the event itself. Much of this work needs to be done many months before the Games through community and educational campaigns, such as The Queen's Jubilee Baton Relay and the Spirit of Friendship Festival.

Summary

If there was a multi-sport mantra it would have to be plan, plan, plan, test, test, test, communicate, communicate, communicate.

These core fundamentals shaped the planning and implementation of the 2002 Commonwealth Games in Manchester. Many are lessons learned as the programme developed and grew. The Post Games Report illustrates in detail the points made above and give further details and recommendations that may assist future cities hosting multi-sport events. The report itself has been put together in sections, however, for ease of reference and for those who do not wish to go into great depth for every section you will find Executive Summaries of the key sections in Volume I.

For further information about the Commonwealth Games, please visit www.thecgf.com. For further detailed information on the legacy of the Manchester 2002 Commonwealth Games, and to access the Post Games Report online, please visit www.gameslegacy.com.

Source: 2002 Manchester The XVII Commonwealth Games: Post Games Report. London, Commonwealth Games Federation, pp. 18–19.

Questions

1. What type of event are the Commonwealth Games? Explain your answer.
2. Running festivals alongside sporting events is becoming increasingly popular. What can these bring to the event?
3. Using other materials at your disposal, for example, the official website, conduct research into the Manchester 2002 Commonwealth Games. What facts can be ascertained from this material regarding the size, nature and management of the event?
4. How would you expect the experience of organizing the Manchester 2002 Commonwealth Games to influence bidding for and management of large-scale events within the UK in the future? Explain your answer.

Chapter 2
The impacts of events

Learning Objectives

After studying this chapter, you should be able to:

- explain the role of the event manager in balancing the impacts of events
- identify the major impacts that events have on their stakeholders and host communities
- describe the social and cultural impacts of events and plan for positive outcomes
- describe the physical and environmental impacts of events
- discuss the political context of events
- discuss the tourism and economic impacts of events
- discuss why governments become involved in events
- describe the use of economic impact studies in measuring event outcomes.

Introduction

Events do not take place in a vacuum – they touch almost every aspect of our lives, whether the social, cultural, economic, environmental or political aspects. The benefits arising from such positive connections are a large part of the reason for the popularity and support of events. They are increasingly well documented and researched, and strategies are being developed to enhance event outcomes and optimize their benefits. The recent explosion of events, along with the parallel increase in the involvement of governments and businesses, has led to an increasing emphasis on an economic analysis of event benefits.

Understandably, governments considering the investment of substantial taxpayers' funds in events want to know what they are getting for their investment and how it compares with other investment options. This climate has given rise to economists' detailed studies of events and to the development and application of increasingly sophisticated techniques of economic analysis and evaluation. However, events can also have unintended consequences that can lead them to have public prominence and media attention for the wrong reasons. The cost of event failure can be disastrous, turning positive benefits into negative publicity, political embarrassment and costly lawsuits. An important core task in organizing contemporary events is the identification, monitoring and management of event impacts. In this chapter, we examine some of the main areas affected by events, along with the strategies that event managers can employ to balance event impacts.

Balancing the impacts of events

Events have a range of impacts – both positive and negative – on their host communities and stakeholders (Table 2.1). It is the task of the event manager to identify and predict these impacts and then to manage them to achieve the best balance for all parties, so that on balance the overall impact of the event is positive. To achieve this, all foreseeable positive impacts must be developed and maximized, and negative impacts countered. Often negative impacts can be addressed through awareness and intervention – good planning is always critical. Ultimately, the success of the event depends on the event manager achieving this positive balance sheet and communicating it to a range of stakeholders.

Great emphasis is often placed on the financial impacts of events, partly because of the need of employers and governments to meet budget goals and justify expenditure, and partly because such impacts are most easily assessed. However, local and national government policies commonly acknowledge the 'triple bottom line' of social, economic and environmental goals/yardsticks in relation to events. Event managers should not lose sight of the full range of an event's impacts and the need to identify, describe and manage them. It is also important to realize that different impacts require different means of assessment. Social and cultural benefits, for example, are vital contributors to the calculation of an event's overall impact, but describing them may require a narrative rather than a statistical approach. In this chapter we discuss some of the complex factors that need to be taken into account when assessing the impacts of events.

Social and cultural impacts

All events have a direct social and cultural impact on their participants, and sometimes on their wider host communities, as outlined by Hall (1997) and Getz (2005). This impact may be as simple as a shared entertainment experience, as is created by a sporting event or concert. Other impacts include increased pride, which results from some community events and celebrations of national days, and the validation of particular groups in the community. Some events leave a legacy of greater awareness and participation in sporting and cultural activities. Others broaden people's cultural horizons, and expose them to new and challenging people, customs or ideas. For example, the melas held in Bradford, Leeds, Manchester, East London (Newham) and Edinburgh each summer have introduced Asian tradition with its strong religious and cultural associations to wider audiences. The City of Bristol illustrated the benefits to be gained through social inclusion, from hosting the West Indies cricket team during the Cricket World Cup 1999. The council in partnership with Gloucester County Cricket Club and First Group developed a range of events targeted at schoolchildren and the local Afro-Caribbean community, including free access to warm-up sessions, coaching clinics and school visits (Select Committee on Culture, Media and Sport, 1999). In 1997, the ceremonies for the handover of Hong Kong from Britain to China had great symbolic importance for both countries. World media coverage of the ceremonies provoked emotions ranging from pride to sadness, jubilation to apprehension. On a different front, the installation of the Ice Cube outdoor ice-skating rink at Millennium Square in Leeds and similar events in Edinburgh and Somerset House in London illustrate the trend in finding innovative alternative uses for city centre space.

Events have the power to challenge the imagination and to explore possibilities. The Long Walk to Justice, a series of marches in Edinburgh and around the world to

Table 2.1 The impacts of events

Sphere of event	Positive impacts	Negative impacts
Social and cultural	• Shared experience • Revitalizing traditions • Building community pride • Validation of community groups • Increased community participation • Introducing new and challenging ideas • Expanding cultural perspectives	• Community alienation • Manipulation of community • Negative community image • Bad behaviour • Substance abuse • Social dislocation • Loss of amenity
Physical and environmental	• Showcasing the environment • Providing models for best practice • Increasing environmental awareness • Infrastructure legacy • Improved transport and communications • Urban transformation and renewal	• Environmental damage • Pollution • Destruction of heritage • Noise disturbance • Traffic congestion
Political	• International prestige • Improved profile • Promotion of investment • Social cohesion • Development of administrative skills	• Risk of event failure • Misallocation of funds • Lack of accountability • Propagandizing • Loss of community ownership and control • Legitimation of ideology
Tourism and economic	• Destinational promotion and increased tourist visits • Extended length of stay • Higher yield • Increased tax revenue • Business opportunities • Commercial activity • Job creation	• Community resistance to tourism • Loss of authenticity • Damage to reputation • Exploitation • Inflated prices • Opportunity costs • Financial management • Financial loss

Source: adapted from Hall (1989)

coincide with the G8 Summit at Gleneagles in 2005, served to draw attention to the plight of Africa due to debt and the Make Poverty History campaign and to bring this issue powerfully to the attention of the leaders of the G8 nations and the media. The start of the week of events was marked with the Live 8 concerts taking place in Hyde Park, London and eight other countries: France, Italy, Germany, USA, Japan, Canada Russia and South Africa. The estimated audience for the concerts was three billion people worldwide (Live 8, 2005). Research undertaken to assess the impact of the 2200 funded Millennium Festival events (Jura Consultants and Gardiner & Theobold, 2001, p. 55) found the following social benefits:

- Communities were mobilized and involved.
- There were high levels of community integration.
- Organizers and volunteers benefited from significant personal development opportunities.
- High numbers of volunteers were involved, giving significant amounts of creation of educational and recreational opportunities.
- Attracted a cross-section of the community to come and participate.
- Vast majority reported a strengthening of links in the local community and an increased sense of local pride.
- Provided entertainment in a friendly atmosphere.
- More likely that festivals will continue in some form in the future.

Events can also contribute to the political debate and help to change history, as demonstrated by the watershed United Nations Conference on Environment and Development ('The Earth Summit') in Rio de Janeiro, Brazil in 1992 and the World Summit on Sustainable Development in Johannesburg, South Africa in 2002. Further, they can promote healing in the community, as demonstrated by events dedicated to the victims and survivors of the terrorist attack in New York on 11 September 2001, the Bali nightclub bombing in October 2002, the South Asia Tsunamis on 26 December 2004 and the London transport bombings on 7 July 2005.

Events can form the cornerstone of cultural strategies. For example, Newham Council have developed a local cultural strategy, entitled 'Reasons To Be Cheerful', at the heart of which is the vision that people choosing to live and work in Newham by 2010. In order to achieve this, events are used in a number of key areas. The strategy includes the following themes, with selection key points from the action plan:

- *New governance arrangements*: work with the Mayor and the Greater London Authority (GLA) to ensure Newham plays a full part in London's Cultural Strategy and in bids for major events such as the Olympics.
- *Showcase developments and a strengthened economy*: establish Three Mills as a major centre for creative industries, a regional performance venue and a visitor destination.
- *An environment which supports a good quality of life*: establish mechanisms to attract major events to the area.
- *Local area strategies*: planning celebrations of local cultures which will increase community cohesion (Newham Leisure Services, 2000).

Research suggests that local communities often value the 'feel-good' aspects of hallmark events, and are prepared to put up with temporary inconvenience and disruption because of the excitement which they generate, and the long-term expectation of improved facilities and profile. The Flora London Marathon provides the opportunity each year for professional and amateur athletes to participate in a great international sporting event. For the professionals, this is an opportunity for them to prove their sporting excellence against the world's elite. For others, it provides an opportunity to prove to family, friends and relatives their endurance. However, for 76 per cent of the runners, it provides an opportunity to raise funds for their favoured charity. Charities benefit each year from the millions of pounds raised through sponsorship. A survey after the 2003 marathon found that £31.8 million had been raised for good causes (London Marathon, 2005), while an earlier achievement of £24 million in 2000 placed this as most lucrative charity sporting event in the UK resulting in an entry in the Guinness World Records (2005).

A study of Leeds residents' and visitors' views of Euro '96 for Leeds City Council, indicated that the success of the tournament nationally and regionally had impressed people who traditionally had little to do with football, leading to civic pride. For a proportion of Leeds residents, the football stadia would be associated with the spectacle of the France vs Spain game rather than the long-held association with hooliganism (Tourism Works, 1996). However, the same level of support was not received from Leeds residents for Leeds Love Parade or the Leeds Festival, with the result that the former did not gain approval for 2001 and later moved from Temple Newsam to Bramham Park near Wetherby.

The All England Lawn Tennis Club and The Championships attempt to take a socially aware attitude to the organization of the championships, using the event to encourage junior interest and participation in tennis. In addition to the proceeds of the tournament being ploughed back into tennis development each year, specific local benefits include:

- local schools and tennis clubs offered use of the covered courts
- financial assistance to Merton Borough's tennis development programme
- renewal of 15 tennis courts in Wimbledon Park in 1988 and again in 2003 and provision of floodlighting
- Raynes Park Sports Ground facilities (football, cricket, hockey, athletics and tennis) offered to schools and sports clubs
- Merton Youth Concert Band and Jazz Orchestra play on both semi-final days of the championships
- Ball boys and girls drawn solely from local schools since 1969 and 1977, respectively (All England Lawn Tennis Club, 2005).

A public opinion study by UK Sport (1998) found that 87 per cent of the public believe it important that the UK host major events, with 88 per cent believing that success on the world sporting stage creates a national 'feel-good' factor. In developing a UK strategy for major events, UK Sport highlight the role that events play in sport, and as a result, society as a whole. They state, 'Events matter ... because they are the heart and soul of the experience for everyone involved in sport – athletes, coaches, officials, volunteers, media, sponsors and fans. Our attitude to events is ultimately our attitude to sport: the hosting of major events should therefore be a key part of any sports system which aims to be a world leader' (UK Sport, 1999a, p. 4).

However, such events can have negative social impacts. Bath and North East Somerset Council conducted a resident survey to canvass opinion on the local impact of events staged at Royal Victoria Park. The survey found that of the 303 returned questionnaires (27 per cent response rate), a significant number (almost 25 per cent) said they had planned time away from home to coincide with events to avoid noise or disruption. Further, although over 75 per cent of the sample had attended some of the events in the last twelve months, including Bath Festival Opening Night, the Spring Flower Show and the Fringe Festival, respondents considered the Festival Opening Night, the Fringe Festival and the Funfair to be the most intrusive events in terms of both amplified music and general disturbance. As a result of these disruptions, most respondents considered that finishing times for events between 10.00 p.m. and midnight would be most appropriate (Howey, 2000).

The larger and more high profile the event, the more potential there is for things to go wrong, and to create negative impacts. A study into the impact of the Network Q Rally 1999 on Lanidloes and the forest of mid-Wales found that 48 per cent of respondents had a negative attitude towards spectators, with main reasons being the spectators driving recklessly, imitating rally drivers and their lack of respect for locals (Blakey, Metcalfe, Mitchell and Weatherfield (2000). In 1997, the bomb scare at the Aintree Grand National, one of Britain's most popular sport events, had an unforeseen impact on the local community, when 60 000 racegoers were evacuated. Due to the security alert, thousands of people were left stranded with 20 000 cars and hundreds of coaches trapped inside the grounds overnight. With all hotels fully booked, Merseyside Emergency Committee was convened and schools, leisure centres, church halls, together with generous local families, providing emergency accommodation (Henderson and Chapman, 1997).

Events, when they go wrong, can go very wrong indeed. Consider the impact of gatecrashers on Glastonbury 2000 – immediately, the pressure placed on facilities, food and other resources, and in the long term, the cancellation of Glastonbury Festival in 2001 amid worries of crowd safety and prosecution of the organizer for breach of the entertainment licence. More seriously, the tragic death of ninety-six Liverpool fans at Hillsborough in 1989, the bombing incident at the Atlanta Olympics in 1996, the death of eight fans at Roskilde Festival in 2000 and the death of over one-hundred people at a rock concert in Rhode Island, together with other disasters, shocked the world (for further data on crowd-related disasters, visit Crowd Dynamics – www.crowddynamics.com). Such events have far-reaching negative impacts, resulting not only in bad press but damage or injury to participants, stakeholders and the host community.

Managing crowd behaviour

Major events can have unintended social consequences such as substance abuse, bad crowd behaviour and an increase in criminal activity (Getz, 2005). If not managed properly, these unintended consequences can hijack the agenda and determine the public perception of the event. In recent years, English football clubs have successfully implemented strategies to manage alcohol-related bad crowd behaviour in order to protect their reputation, football's image and future. However, the image was tarnished by the alcohol-fuelled violence of fans abroad during the World Cup 1998 in France and European Championships in Holland and Belgium in 2000, which some believe to be a main factor in England losing their bid to host the World Cup in 2006. It should be remembered that football is not the only sport to suffer, with the 'yobbish' behaviour spreading into the summer Test cricket programme and Royal Ascot. For example, in the 1998 Test cricket series between England and South Africa, Old Trafford Cricket Ground banned non-members from bringing alcohol into the games and, bizarre as it would seem to some, the wearing of novelty clothing, as a result of 'rowdyism' at the previous match at Edgbaston. Deeley (1998) noted:

> At Edgbaston there were many complaints about the behaviour of groups of bizarrely dressed young men in the cheapest seating on the Rea Bank stand, chanting football fashion, shouting obscene remarks and dancing in the aisles. At Old Trafford people wearing dress deemed offensive and 'full body suits' (pelicans, teddy bears and the like) will be refused admission. The county say hats, wigs and head-dress restricting the view of others will not be tolerated.

He goes on to investigate the possible causes, as similar behaviour was not demonstrated at either Lords or The AMP Oval grounds. He found that availability of alcohol could have a significant affect if the grounds did not have an effective bar management policy (either leaving bars open or unnecessarily closing could influence the mood of the crowd). The other issue, so called 'rowdyism' could be managed through strictly limiting tickets to avoid large groups sitting together (for example, Lords limited tickets to four per person) and banning or ejecting those that turn up in eccentric costumes, or those causing a disturbance to others through chanting or taking part in congas. However, this may take away from the atmosphere at games. Other events such as the Notting Hill Carnival, the summer music festivals (e.g. Glastonbury and Reading) and dance events have in some years been tainted by a perceived drug culture, which some believe is encouraged by tolerant policing.

Crowd behaviour can be modified with careful planning. Sometimes this is an evolutionary process. Managing New Year's Eve in London and in Edinburgh have seen a series of modifications and adjustments. In 1999, at the launch of the Millennium Festival year, around 3 million people partied along the banks of the River Thames and around Trafalgar Square to witness one of the largest firework display ever staged in Britain. An estimated 2 million of these used the London Underground to access Central London between midday and midnight, with only a temporary closure of Underground stations to alleviate safety fears. Police made ninety-nine arrests (more than half for drunkenness) and three police officers were attacked in two separate incidents, but generally the celebrations passed off without serious incident (Harrison and Hastings, 2000).

However, Londoners were to be disappointed in 2000 when Greater London Authority cancelled celebrations due to a clash between crowd safety management and commercial viability. The main issue raised was a fear that the transport system would be dangerously overcrowded, as seen the previous year, which lead to Underground and train operators proposing a restricted service, and transport unions threatening industrial action unless safety concerns were addressed. A strategy proposed to manage this – restricting transport, cancelling the midnight firework display and moving an earlier display from 7 to 5 p.m. – proved unpopular with sponsors due to the reduced audience, leading to the largest sponsor, Yahoo, withdrawing their £350 000 offer and, ultimately, cancellation of the event (O'Neill, 2000). Subsequently, a review of major events in London by a Greater London Authority London Assembly Committee identified a number of conditions for successful major events in London, including sufficient lead time of at least 18 months, a dispersed event, sufficient resources, empowered leadership, a committed multi-agency partnership, effective project management and effective decision making (Major Events Investigative Committee, 2001). The Royal Bank of Scotland Street Party, Edinburgh's Hogmanay, had its capacity reduced from a record 200 000 in 1999 to 100 000 for New Year 2000 and onwards in order to increase safety. As a result of better crowd management and improved strategies, global celebrations of the New Millennium were largely reported as good spirited and peaceful.

Since the terrorist attack in New York on 11 September 2001, the threat of terrorism has resulted in increased security at major events worldwide. However, due to appropriate precautions, events such as the FIFA World Cup in South Korea and Japan in 2002 and the Rugby World Cup in Australia in 2003 were conducted safely without major incidents. Security for the Olympics was increased from 11 500 (including 4500 police officers) for the Sydney Games in 2000 to 45 000 (including 25 000 from the police force) for the Athens Games in 2004 (Kyriakopoulos and Benns, 2004). Further, security was a key theme of the successful London 2012 Olympic bid with the government taking ultimate responsibility through the Home Office and guaranteeing to make every effort to ensure a safe games. Estimates at the bid stage indicate that it will require 14 800 trained police together with 6500 private security staff and 10 000 volunteer for stewarding a marshalling (London 2012, 2004b). Table 2.2 provides an indication of the levels of security involved in previous major international events in London and England.

Table 2.2 Major international events

	Year	Event	Duration of event (days)	Number of participants	Number of dignitaries and VIPs	Number of attending spectators	Number of security personnel
London	Annual	Notting Hill Carnival	2	10 000	n/a	850 000	12 000
	Annual	London Marathon	1	34 000	n/a	26 000	850
	Annual	Wimbledon Tennis	14	960	56	539 000	11 900
	2002	Golden Jubilee Weekend	4	15 500	540	1 000 000	10 180
	2002	The funeral of the Queen Mother	9	5476	585	400 000	12 887
	2000	Millennium Celebrations (London)	1	2000	500	1 000 000	4500
England	Annual	Epsom Derby	2	1000	3000	100 000	1000
	Annual	Royal Henley Regatta	4	16 000	12	60 000	320
	2003	UEFA Champions League Final	1	30	10	67 000	700
	2002	Manchester Commonwealth Final	10	5717	30	900 000	22 500
	1996	UEFA European Championships	21	500	100	1 236 000	18 500

Source: London 2012 (2004b), p. 43

Community ownership and control of events

Events can also have wider effects on the social life and structure of communities. Traffic arrangements, for example, may restrict residents' access to their homes or businesses, as experienced for the G8 Summit at Gleneagles. Other impacts may include loss of amenity owing to noise or crowds, resentment of inequitable distribution of costs and benefits, and cost inflation of goods and services that can upset housing markets and impact most on low-income groups as outlined by Getz (2005). It follows that communities should have a major say in the planning and management of events. For example, the Mayor of London, Ken Livingstone, initiated an extensive review of the management, organization and funding of Notting Hill Carnival, together with longer-term trends and opportunities for the event's development. This included the views of stakeholders, including relevant community organizations and the general public (Mayor's Carnival Review Group, 2004). However, Hall (1989) concludes that the role of communities is often marginalized and that governments often make the crucial decision of whether to host the event without adequate community consultation. Public participation then becomes a form of placation designed to legitimize the decisions of government and developers, rather than a full and open discussion of the advantages and disadvantages of hosting events.

This makes it all the more important for governments to be accountable through the political process, for the allocation of resources to events. Hall (1997) maintains that political analysis is an important tool in regaining community control over hallmark events, and ensuring that the objectives of these events focus on maximizing returns to the community.

Allegations of corruption within the International Olympic Committee (IOC), the scandal over ticketing strategies by the Sydney Organizing Committee for the Olympic Games (SOCOG) and the outrage over a loan from the English Football Association to the Welsh Football Association, allegedly in return for their support of the England 2006 World Cup bid, are examples of the increasing pressure for transparency and public accountability in the staging of major events. Reviews of these issues have resulted in changes being made to policies, procedures and bidding processes to ensure that issues such as these do not arise again.

Physical and environmental impacts

An event is an excellent way to showcase the unique characteristics of the host environments. Hall (1989) points out that selling the image of a hallmark event includes the marketing of the intrinsic properties of the destination. However, host environments may be extremely delicate and great care should be taken to protect them. A major event may require an environmental impact assessment to be conducted before council or government permission is granted for it to go ahead. Even if a formal study is not required, the event manager should carefully consider the likely impact of the event on the environment. This impact will be fairly contained if the event is to be held in a suitable purpose-built venue, e.g. a stadium, sports ground, show ground, conference or exhibition centre. The impact may be much greater if the event is to be held in a public space not ordinarily reserved for events, such as a park, town square or street. For example, Birmingham city centre was brought to a standstill in 1993 when an unforeseen number of residents turned up to witness the relaunch of local radio station, BRMB, leading to a reprimand for organizers from police and the council. Another example is the 13 tonnes of litter left after the Oasis concert in the Haymarket, Roseburn and Murrayfield areas. Not only did Edinburgh Council arrange the cleanup from this event, which they acknowledged was only one-third of the litter created by New Year/Hogmanay celebrations, disturbingly, their cleanup staff came under attack from people throwing bottles and their vehicles had to be escorted off site by police (City of Edinburgh Council, 2000a). Aspects such as crowd movement and control, noise levels, access and parking will be important considerations. Other major issues may include wear and tear on the natural and physical environment, heritage protection issues and disruption of the local community.

Effective communication and consultation with local authorities will often resolve some of these issues. In addition, careful management planning may be required to modify impacts. In Liverpool, organizers of the John Smith's Grand National have worked over several years to progressively reduce the traffic impact of visitors to the event by developing a park-and-ride system of fringe parking and shuttle buses to the event area. A similar park-and-ride system is operated at the Royal Norfolk Show held at Norfolk Show Ground, Norwich. Many festivals and outdoor events have reduced their impact on the environment by banning glass bottles, which can break and get trodden into the ground, and implementing effective waste management strategies. Event managers are discovering that such measures make good financial as well as environmental sense, for example, by generating savings in the cost of the site cleanup.

When staging large events, the provision of infrastructure is often a costly budget component, but this may result in an improved environment and facilities. Many of London's landmark venues have been the legacy of major events, including Crystal Palace (1851 Great Exhibition), Earls Court/Olympia (1887 to 1890 American, Italian, French and German Exhibitions), Royal Festival Hall and South Bank (1951 Festival of Britain) and more recently the Millennium Dome (1999/2000 Millennium Festival) (Evans, 1996). Similarly, Sheffield profited from an investment of £139 million in the development of state-of-the-art facilities for the 1991 World Student Games, including Ponds Forge International Swimming Pool, the Sheffield Arena and the Don Valley Stadium (Select Committee on Culture, Media and Sport, 1999). Manchester benefited from investment in facilities for the Commonwealth Games 2002 and London will benefit from significant investment in facilities for the London 2012 Olympic Games for many years to come.

Waste management, recycling and sustainable events

Concern for sustainability and consideration of the environmental impacts of events is increasing, with a number of industry initiatives being developed. Governments are increasingly using public education programmes and legislation to promote the recycling of waste materials and reduce the amount of waste going to landfill sites. Events are targeted as opportunities to demonstrate best practice models in waste management, and to change public attitudes and habits. The Commonwealth Games 2002 provided Manchester with sporting facilities to take it well into the twenty-first century, as well as major infrastructure improvements in accommodation, transport and communications. However, the development of facilities for events such as this raises major environmental issues that are magnified by the scale and profile of the project. In order to address these concerns, UK Sport clearly identifies the need for environmental sensitivity in all aspects of bidding for and staging major events. It states:

> *Major events and the environment are inextricably linked, and without due care events can impact adversely on the environment, directly or indirectly. Major events also have a very positive role to play in fostering understanding of environmental issues, raising awareness and generating resources . . . Particular attention will be paid to the environmental issues raised by very large numbers of*

people coming together for a short period of time, with subsequent problems of safety, congestion, consumption, and waste. Areas of particular attention will include: access; infrastructure; energy consumption; energy renewal; sustainability; minimizing resource requirements; the use of natural products; and innovative design and technology that reduces both operating and maintenance costs and greatly extends the lifetime of sports facilities and new event venues. (UK Sport, 1999a, p. 10).

For the event manager, incorporating a waste management plan into the overall event plan has become increasingly good policy. Community expectations and the health of our environment require that events demonstrate good waste management principles, and provide models for recycling. The environmentally conscious event manager will reap not only economic benefits, but also the approval of an increasingly environmentally aware public. For example, Glastonbury Festival effectively reduce their impact on the environment through an effective waste management and recycling strategy, using hundreds of volunteers as part of their dedicated Recycling Crew. Their role includes collecting litter, separating recyclable items, giving out litter bags and working with the 'Reclammator' to help Glastonbury become the greenest festival (Glastonbury Festivals Ltd, 2000). With increasing concern for the atmosphere, events such as the Brit Awards and Glastonbury are also beginning to take part in schemes such as 'Carbon Neutral'. This involves an assessment of the energy used by the event – as a result, sufficient trees are then planted to absorb the carbon dioxide produced.

SEXI (Sustainable Exhibition Industry) was an 18 month project established to research the amount of waste produced by the exhibition industry, identify best practice and make recommendations for reducing this waste in the future. Now being taken forward by the AEO, EVA and BECA, the project resulted in an eight point action plan for the industry:

1. Measure, monitor and report
2. Raise awareness within the industry and with exhibitors, promulgate best practice and report bad practice
3. Improve environmental performance throughout the industry
4. Ensure that all areas of the industry are compliant with Duty of Care
5. Undertake research into how to improve applied practice and promote outputs and encourage adaptation throughout the industry
6. Reduce waste to landfill with zero as the ultimate target
7. Offset carbon dioxide emissions associated with exhibitions
8. Education and training (Midlands Environmental Business Club Limited, 2002).

Based on experience gained at the 1996 Summer Olympics in Atlanta, the Xerox Corporation (1998) present an eight-step model for waste reduction and recycling at events, illustrated in Figure 2.1.

The London 2012 Olympic Games, in partnership with World Wildlife Fund (WWF) and BioRegional have developed 'One Planet Olympics', based on the ten principles of 'One Planet Living', which has informed the London 2012 Olympics Environmental Management System. The aim is to achieve the first sustainable Olympic Games (London 2012, WWF and BioRegional, 2005). The principles and associated strategies are:

- **Zero Carbon** – Reducing carbon dioxide emissions by minimizing building energy demand and supplying from zero/low carbon and renewable resources.
- **Zero Waste** – Developing closed resource loops. Reducing the amounts of waste produced, then reclaiming, recycling and recovering.
- **Sustainable Transport** – Reducing the need to travel and providing sustainable alternatives to private car use.

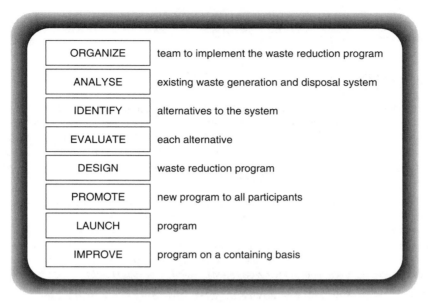

Figure 2.1 Eight-stage process for waste reduction and recycling
Source: Xerox Corporation, 1998, *Guide to Waste Reduction and Recycling at Special Events.*
New York, Xerox Corporation, p. 1

- **Local and Sustainable Materials** – Materials chosen to give high performance in use with minimized impact in manufacture and delivery. Using local materials can have further benefits to local economies and in supporting traditional solutions.
- **Local and Sustainable Food** – Supporting consumption of local, seasonal and organic produce, with reduced amount of animal protein and packaging.
- **Sustainable Water** – Reducing water demand with sustainable management of rain and waste water.
- **Natural Habitats and Wildlife** – Existing biodiversity conserved with opportunities taken to increase ecological value and access to nature.
- **Culture and Heritage** – Cultural heritage acknowledged and interpreted. Sense of place and identity engendered to contribute towards future heritage.
- **Equity and Fair Trade** – Create a sense of community. Provide accessible, inclusive and affordable facilities and services.
- **Health and Happiness** – Promote health and wellbeing. Establish long-term management and support strategies (London 2012, WWF and BioRegional, 2005, p. 4).

Further advice for sporting events is provided by UK Sport (2002), who have also identified seven steps for 'greening' events (UK Sport, 2005, p. 63). These are:

1. Adopt a green policy
2. Carry out an 'Environmental Scoping Review' of venues and operations
3. Establish environmental teams
4. Define programmes and set appropriate targets
5. Implement programmes
6. Monitor implementation and adjust
7. Evaluate and publicize results programme accordingly.

The principles identified in this section provide an excellent basis for the staging of major events in the future.

Political impacts

Politics and politicians are an important part of the equation that is contemporary event management. Ever since the Roman emperors discovered the power of the circus to deflect criticism and shore up popularity, shrewd politicians have had an eye for events that will keep the populace happy and themselves in power. No less an authority than Count Nicolo Machiavelli, adviser to the Medicis in the sixteenth century, had this to say on the subject:

> A prince must also show himself a lover of merit, give preferment to the able and honour those who excel in every art ... Besides this, he ought, at convenient seasons of the year, to keep the people occupied with festivals and shows; and as every city is divided into guilds or into classes, he ought to pay attention to all these groups, mingle with them from time to time, and give them an example of his humanity and munificence, always upholding, however, the majesty of his dignity, which must never be allowed to fail in anything whatever. (Machiavelli, 1962, pp. 112–13).

The Royal Family took this advice to heart, providing some of the most popular events of the last century with the Coronation of Queen Elizabeth II and the fairytale-like wedding of Prince Charles and Lady Diana Spencer. Following the tragic untimely death of Diana, Princess of Wales, in 1997, more recent royal events have attempted to reflect the modernization of the monarchy and the mood of the people, with the wedding of Prince Edward and Sophie Rhys-Jones in 1999, the one-hundredth birthday of the Queen Mother in 2000 and the wedding of Prince Charles to Camilla Parker Bowles in 2005. An extensive programme of events was organized for the Queen's Golden Jubilee in 2002 (BBC News, 2002a), which coincided with the Commonwealth Games in Manchester, with a year of events planned around six themes: celebration, community, service, past and future, giving thanks and Commonwealth, and an extra bank holiday to mark the occasion. The celebrations culminated in a concert in the grounds of Buckingham Palace for 12 000 people who had won a ticket by national ballot, while over one million people congregated on The Mall and in various London parks to watch the concert on giant screens and hundreds of street parties took place across the UK (BBC News, 2002b). Queen Elizabeth The Queen Mother's funeral in April 2002 marked a return to tradition, with over 200 000 people walking past her coffin during a period of Lying-in-State and over one million people lining the streets of London around Westminster Abbey for her funeral.

Successive British politicians have continued to use the spotlight of events to build their personal profile and gain political advantage. Commenting on the Great Exhibition of 1851, Asa Briggs noted how criticism of the project disappeared as the crowds flocked to see the event – crowds that were encouraged to attend through the equivalent of a Travelcard (Carling and Seeley, 1998). In 1951, Foreign Secretary Herbert Morrison received significant criticism due to his enthusiasm for the Festival of Britain project, leading an opposition MP to label him 'Lord Festival' a title that stuck (Carling and Seeley, 1998). Former Prime Minister John Major was frequently seen at major cricket matches during his term in office. In 1997, his first year in office, the Prime Minister, Tony Blair, continued with the Conservative government planned Millennium Dome project, attempting to use the Dome as a symbol of 'New Labour, New Britain', and of himself as a visionary and enlightened leader. When details of the Dome's contents were first published, he summarized the aim of the festival:

> *In this Experience I want people to pause and reflect on this moment, about the possibilities ahead of us, about the values that guide our society … It will be an event to lift our horizons. It will be a catalyst to imagine our futures … As we approach the Millennium we can boast that we have a richness of talent in this country that is unparalleled: the finest artists, authors, architects, musicians, designers, animators, software makers, scientists… so why not put it on display? (Carling and Seeley, 1998, p. 5).*

However, although the year-long exhibition, the Millennium Experience, achieved over six million visitors during its year of operation, this was significantly less than the predicted twelve million. In addition, the project was plagued by financial problems during the year due to the lower than expected visitor numbers, leading to additional funds being provided by the Millennium Commission (The Comptroller and Auditor General, 2000). Although to some extent a success, the Millennium Dome may be remembered more for the lack of legacy planning and the spiralling costs both during and after the Millennium Experience. Although the Dome has been used for a small number of events since 2001, it will not fully re-open until 2007 when it will become an entertainment venue including a 23 000 seater arena, a 2000 capacity music club and an ice rink. Following a £6 million per year sponsorship deal, the venue, now owned by Anschutz Entertainment Group (AEG), will be known as 'the O2' (BBC News, 2005).

Arnold, Fischer, Hatch, J and Paix (1989, pp. 191–2) leave no doubt as to the role of events in the political process: 'Governments in power will continue to use hallmark events to punctuate the ends of their periods in office, to arouse nationalism, enthusiasm and finally, votes. They are cheaper than wars or the preparation for them. In this regard, hallmark events do not hide political realities, they are the political reality'.

Governments around the world have realized the ability of events to raise the profile of politicians and the cities and areas that they govern. They have also realized the ability of events to attract visitors, and thus create economic benefits and jobs. This potent mixture has led to governments becoming major players in bidding for, hosting and staging major events. The UK government has undertaken two major inquiries into the staging of major events. In 1995, the National Heritage Committee ran an inquiry into 'Bids to Stage International Sporting Events' which identified how bidding for and staging international events could be improved. They found that, 'unless Britain does coordinate the multitudinous and sometimes apparently conflicting organizations that are involved, and is given a clear focus, then our country is unlikely to be successful in any bid for which there is fierce competition' (House of Commons National Heritage Committee Report, 1995, cited in UK Sport, 1999b, p. 5). This led to the GB Sports Council (the forerunner of UK Sport) being given the responsibility for sport event development in the UK (English Sports Council, 1999).

In 1998 a second Select Committee was established to investigate all aspects of staging international sporting events, from bidding through to economic, environmental and regeneration legacies of these events (Select Committee on Culture, Media and Sport, 1999). The committee took comprehensive evidence from associations and groups representing all major sports, government ministers and tourism bodies, together with information from organizations with experience of hosting major events (including fact-finding trips to Australia and Malaysia). The ensuing report detailed thirty-two principal conclusions and recommendations, including:

- the need for further research into economic benefits and impacts, and incorporation of an independent assessment as a requirement for future funding

- support for the proposed UK Sport Major Event Strategy
- the need to vet qualifications and ability of suitable candidates for committee posts of international sporting events, in order to ensure the effective representation of British interests
- the need for central government to partner local authorities in order to gain the national benefits from the event, including the Manchester 2002 Commonwealth Games
- the need for a 'Minister for Events' with responsibility for an events strategy incorporating sport and non-sport events (Select Committee on Culture, Media and Sport, 1999, s. IX).

The outcomes of the committee have been reviewed to monitor performance, with generally positive feedback gained (see Select Committee on Culture, Media and Sport, 2001).

Established in 1997, UK Sport includes the aim to, 'promote the UK or any part of it as a venue for international sports events and to advise, encourage and assist bodies in staging or seeking to stage such events'. It aims to provide a one-stop shop for event advice and support. In keeping with this, it established a Major Events Steering Group in 1999 which includes members with a range of experience including legal issues, media, marketing, sponsorship, event management, local authority involvement and the international politics of sport (UK Sport, 1999a). Elsewhere, the Northern Ireland Events Company and EventScotland have been established (discussed in Chapter 3). Edinburgh has built-up a strong international reputation as a festival city, with an extensive programme of major events including Edinburgh International Festival, Edinburgh Fringe, and Edinburgh's Hogmanay.

This involvement of governments in events has politicized the events landscape as pointed out by Hall (1989, p. 236):

> Politics is paramount in hallmark events. It is either naïve or duplistic to pretend otherwise. Events alter the time frame in which planning occurs and they become opportunities to do something new and better than before. In this context, events may change or legitimate political priorities in the short term and political ideologies and socio-cultural reality in the longer term. Hallmark events represent the tournaments of old, fulfilling psychological and political needs through the winning of hosting over other locations and the winning of events themselves. Following a hallmark event some places will never be the same again, physically, economically, socially and, perhaps most importantly of all, politically.

It is important to acknowledge that events have values beyond just tangible and economic benefits. Humans are social animals, and celebrations play a key role in the well-being of the social structure – the common wealth. Events have the ability to engender social cohesion, confidence and pride (Wood, 2002). Therein lies the source of their political power and influence, and the reason why events will always reflect and interact with their political circumstances and environment.

Tourism and economic impacts

A primary concern of an event entrepreneur or host organization is whether an event is within budget and, hopefully, results in a surplus or profit. This is a simple matter of whether the income from sponsorship, merchandise and ticket sales exceeds the costs of conducting and marketing the event. However, from the perspectives of the host communities and governments, a wider range of economic impacts is often of equal or greater significance.

Governments are increasingly turning to tourism as a growth industry capable of delivering economic benefits and job creation. They are also seen as image-makers, creating profile for destinations, positioning them in the market and providing competitive marketing advantage. One of the most important impacts is the tourism revenue generated by an event. In addition to their spending at the event, external visitors are likely to spend money on travel, accommodation, goods and services in the host city or region. This expenditure can have a considerable impact as it circulates through the local economy. Effective tourism promotion can result in visitors to the event extending their length of stay and visiting other regional tourism destinations and attractions. In addition to the tourism generated during the event, events may attract media coverage and exposure that enhance the profile of the host town or city, resulting in improved long-term tourism image and visitation. Chapter 3 discusses these and other aspects of the tourism impact of events.

Business opportunities

Events can provide their host communities with a strong platform for showcasing their expertise, hosting potential investors and promoting new business opportunities. The media exposure generated by the success of an event can dramatically illustrate the capacity, innovation and achievements of event participants and/or the host community. Advantage West Midlands secured European Union funding of £1.2 million to launch a major marketing campaign for the Birmingham International Motor Show with the objective of raising attendances and generating tourism revenue. In addition, with the automotive industry being a major provider of employment in the region, this was seen as a potential showcase for industry in the region (Advantage West Midlands, 2004).

Little research has been done on analysing business development strategies for events and quantifying the amount of business that these strategies generate. More work needs to be done so that event enhancement frameworks are better understood and their outcomes can be assessed.

Commercial activity

Whatever the generation of new business at the macro level, the suppliers of infrastructure, goods and services undoubtedly profit from the staging of major events. The construction industry – witness the construction boom resulting from the Commonwealth Games 2002 in Manchester and the redevelopment of Wembley National Stadium – is often stimulated by the need for new or improved facilities required to stage a major event. But do these benefits trickle down to traders and small business operators? A survey of 1000 tourism-related businesses was conducted in relation to the Rugby World Cup in Wales in 1999 (Anon, 2000). The accommodation sector fared best, with two-thirds of accommodation providers experiencing improvements in business performance, and a 7.5 per cent increase in room rates by operators in Cardiff and the south-east of Wales. Around half of food and drink outlets reported increased performance. This sector also reported having made considerable investment in promotional activities and small-scale product development. However, over half of those who responded from the retail sector thought that, despite improvements in average spend, the event had impacted negatively on their overall performance. As another example, the World Masters Athletics Championships 2000 in Gateshead were expected to lead to an estimated 150 000 additional bednights, adding a minimum of £12 million to the local economy (Select Committee on Culture, Media and Sport, 1999).

Muthaly et al. (2000) used a case study approach to examine the impact of the Atlanta Olympics on seven small businesses in Atlanta. The case study included:

- a wholesale restaurant equipment dealer, which expanded its existing business and current line of equipment, resulting in a 70–80 per cent increase in revenue as a result of the Games
- a one-person home rental business specifically started to provide bed-and breakfast housing for Olympic visitors, which lost US$23 000 due to lack of any significant Games business
- a frozen lemonade stand franchise that employed up to 50 people at four fixed and three roving locations, which failed due to problems with inventory, staffing, unanticipated and unregulated competition, and lower than expected attendance at the Games
- an established beverage distributor, who became an approved Games vendor and reported increased profits through additional sales to usual customers and a firm policy of not extending credit to new customers
- a craft retail location at Stone Mountain Park, a major tourist attraction for Atlanta and the south east where some Olympic events were located. The owner lost about US$10 000 on a special line of Olympic theme dolls, sculptures and so on, as a result of added costs and a lack of customers
- a UK-based currency service and foreign exchange business that established two locations downtown near the Olympic Park and two uptown near the retail and residential heart of the city. The principal felt that it was not a very successful business project, given the changing nature of the market (people using credit or debit cards in place of currency) and lack of communication with Olympic organizers
- an established sporting goods retail store that reported increased sales of established lines and regular merchandise, but not of Olympic merchandise stocked to sell in front of the store. The owner reported considerable staffing difficulties due to poor transport planning and absenteeism as a result of the Games.

The study team concluded that large businesses such as Delta Airlines, local constructions companies, local law firms associated with the Olympics, and niche players that watched their risk carefully fared very well. However, for many small operators, dreams of big profits turned into heartache. Visitors did not come in anticipated numbers, and those who did come did not spend the amount of money expected. Olympic visitors proved to be sports mad and tight fisted, and uninterested in traditional tourist attractions.

From these and other studies, the anticipated benefits of major events to traders and small business operators appear to be sometimes exaggerated, with the results often being sporadic and uneven. Benefits also seem more likely to accrue to those businesses that are properly prepared and that manage and invest wisely in the opportunities provided by events. More research needs to be done in this field to identify appropriate strategies to enhance the benefits of events to small business.

Employment creation

By stimulating activity in the economy, expenditure on events can have a positive effect on employment. Employment multipliers measure how many full time equivalent job opportunities are supported in the community as a result of visitor expenditure. However, as Faulkner (1993) and others point out, it is easy to overestimate the number of jobs created by major events in the short term. Because the demand for additional services is short lived, employers tend to meet this demand by using their existing staff more rather than employing new staff members. Existing employees may be released from other duties to accommodate the temporary demand or requested to work overtime.

However, major events can generate substantial employment in the construction phase, as well as during the staging of the event. The 2002 British Grand Prix at Silverstone was estimated to support 1150 full time equivalent jobs in the United Kingdom, including 400 full time equivalent jobs within 50 miles of the circuit (MIA, 2003). The 2002 Manchester Commonwealth Games was estimated to have generated 6100 jobs, of which 2400 are additional jobs in Manchester (Cambridge Policy Consultants, 2002). The America's Cup in Auckland in 2000 was estimated to generate 1470 new jobs in construction, accommodation, marine and related activities (Scott, 2003). The 2000 Oktoberfest in Munich generated employment for an estimated 12 000 people through the 0.7 billion euro that 5.5 million visitors to the event spent over 16 days (Munich Tourist Office, 2000, cited in Richards and Wilson, 2002).

Government's use of events as economic development strategies

The strong growth of the events industry is part of a general economic trend away from an industrial product base to a more service-based economy. Traditionally, communities and governments have staged events for their perceived social, cultural and/or sporting benefits and value. This situation began to change dramatically in the early 1980s when major events in many parts of the world began to be regarded as desirable commodities for their perceived ability to deliver economic benefits through the promotion of tourism, increased visitor expenditure and job creation.

Major events with international reputations have appeared on the sporting calendar in the UK for many years on an annual basis, however, their value has not always been recognized. Changes began to emerge in the mid to late nineties when the National Heritage Committee (1995) and the Select Committee on Culture, Media and Sport (1999, 2001) fully investigated the value of hosting major sporting events which gathered evidence on the value of events. As a result, events began to be recognized, for example, with UK Sport establishing a major events strategy in 1999 (UK Sport, 1999a).

As outlined elsewhere, various local and national governments have pursued vigorous event strategies since the 1980s, building strong portfolios of annual events and aggressively bidding for the right for their city, region or country to host major one-off events. Apart from international and regional rivalry and political kudos, what motivates and justifies this level of government involvement in what otherwise might be seen as largely commercial enterprises? According to Mules (1998), the answer lies in what he terms the 'spillover effects' of events. While many major events might make an operational loss, they produce benefits for related industry sectors such as travel, accommodation, restaurants, hirers and suppliers of equipment and so on. They may also produce long-term benefits such as destination promotion resulting in increased tourism spending. However, a single organization cannot capture this wide range of benefits. Governments thus sometimes play a role in funding or underwriting events so these generalized benefits might be obtained. For example, the UK government has underwritten the London 2012 Olympic Games

(London 2012, 2004b). A further example is the role that regional development agencies (RDAs) are playing in supporting events in their region which have the potential to promote the region or bring in tourists, for example, when a number of RDAs sponsored the 2004 Tour of Britain Cycle Race and together with other agencies sponsored the event again in 2005 (SIRC, 2005).

Economic impact studies

In deciding what events should be funded and what levels of funding are appropriate, governments need to obtain a full picture of the event's costs and the anticipated return on investment. To do so, they sometimes undertake economic impact studies, which seek to identify all of the expenditure involved in the staging of events, and to determine their impacts on the wider economy. According to Faulkner (1993), the impacts of an event derive from three main sources:

1. expenditure by visitors from outside the region
2. capital expenditure on facilities required to conduct the event
3. expenditure incurred by event organizers and sponsors to stage the event.

However, this expenditure has flow-on effects that need to be taken into account in calculating the economic impact of an event. For example, money spent on a meal by an event visitor will flow on to businesses that supply the restaurant with food and beverage items. The money spent on the meal is direct expenditure, while the flow-on effect to suppliers is indirect expenditure. The event may also stimulate additional activity in the economy, resulting in increased wages and consumer spending. Further, sales of goods at exhibitions result in jobs being supported elsewhere, for example, at the International Spring Fair at Birmingham NEC in 1997, it was estimated that over £1.6 billion of orders were taken. This is referred to as induced expenditure.

The aggregated impact on the economy of all of the expenditure is expressed as a multiplier ratio. Multipliers reflect the impact of the event expenditure as it ripples through the economy, and they vary according to the particular mix of industries in a given geographic location. The use of multipliers is controversial, and some studies prefer to concentrate on the direct expenditure of an event as being more reliable, although this does not give a true picture of the complex impact on the economy of the event expenditure.

Conducting economic impact studies that account for all of the myriad factors of the event expenditure and environment is quite complex and usually undertaken by specialist researchers with an economic background. However, a considerable body of literature is available to provide an insight for event managers into the process of conducting economic impact studies on events (see Burgan and Mules, 2000; Crompton and McKay, 1994; Giddings, 1997; Mules, 1999; Mules and McDonald, 1994).

An impact review commissioned by the Motor Sport Association on the Network Q Rally, one of the largest spectator sports in the UK with 134 921 paying spectators, found that it pumped £11.1 million into the local economy, 60 per cent of which was from outside the area. Those to benefit included local accommodation providers, restaurants, retail outlets and transport providers. They noted that the event also generates an additional £17 million from tourism stimulated by the television coverage (Lilley III and DeFranco, 1999a). Impacts could indeed be greater, as later research by Blakey et al. (2000) indicates that in 1999 there were over 1 million live spectators and 11 000 volunteer officials, which would make it the largest sporting event in the UK. The British Grand Prix 1996, seen by many to be one of the showcase UK events, had an economic impact of £28 million, £25 million from outside the local area (Lilley III and DeFranco, 1999b). In the most recent study of the 2002 FIA Foster's British Grand Prix, expenditure had risen to an estimated £34.7 million and income to the UK of £17.2 million (£5.6 to the region), equating to 1148 jobs, of which 403 were within the region (MIA, 2003). British International Motor Show, held at Birmingham NEC in June 2004 branded as The Sunday Times Motor Show Live, played host to an estimated 461 000 visitors, bringing an additional £61.4 million into the local economy with gross spending amounting to £105.5 million (SMMT, 2004).

Table 2.3 summarizes the economic benefits of a number of recent events in the UK. The results are not strictly comparable, as the methodologies for evaluating events vary widely. However, the table does demonstrate the considerable tourism and economic benefits that flow from major events. UK Sport is attempting to address comparability issues through proposing a standard methodology, discussed in Chapter 14.

Events have the potential to provide niche development opportunities for city and regional governments. Research conducted on behalf of the Society of London Theatre demonstrated that theatre can have a major impact on tourism and the economy, with the 1997 West End theatre season worth £1075 million to the city of London, supporting 41 000 jobs (Travers, 1998). A study on behalf of the London Development Agency (LDA, 2003) into Notting Hill Carnival found that it brought an estimated income of £93 million into London in 2002, supporting in the region of 3000 full time equivalent jobs. This study, together with a review of other aspects of the carnival (Mayor's Carnival Review Group, 2004) has lead to increased attention being paid to the carnival by the Mayor of London and other interested stakeholders.

Birmingham maximized the benefits of successfully staging the G8 Birmingham Summit, the Eurovision Song Contest and the Lions Clubs International Conference in 1998, which had a combined impact of £35.65 million additional spend and highlighted the city's ability to successfully stage international conferences. Following these high-profile events, a national telephone survey of 1000 people, by Birmingham Marketing Partnership (BMP), found that 68 per cent believed Birmingham had improved as a city, 55 per cent thought it was a friendly city and 70 per cent considered Birmingham to be a leading event city. Further research by the City Council and BMP established that the media impact was eight times greater than could be expected for major news stories, equating to approximately £1.8 million of media coverage (Notman, 1999). Birmingham NEC successfully hosted ITMA 2003 (the International Exhibition of Textile Machinery) – the world's largest exhibition. This was the first time the event took place in the UK since its launch in 1951. Taking over 200 000 square metres of stand space, with 1275 exhibitors from forty countries, the event attracted an audience of 125 500 from 129 countries. Independent research by KPMG estimated that the event resulted in £85 million additional expenditure in the West Midlands, equivalent to 1550 full-time equivalent jobs for the region or £110 million spending in the UK as a whole (The NEC Group, 2004). Birmingham has continued to capitalize on its image as a major event city, through promoting itself as 'Europe's meeting place' and expanding the NEC complex, the UK's largest exhibition space, which according to research in 1999 generated £711 million impact – supporting nearly 22 000 jobs (The NEC Group, 2005b) .

There is increasing interest in the impacts of festivals, illustrated by the recent completion of two large scale studies. For example, on a national level, a study conducted on behalf of The Association of Festival Organisers (AFO) by Morris Hargreaves McIntyre (AFO, 2004) discovered that folk festivals generate spending of over £77 million. In addition, their study found that festivals have a role in developing audiences and in training, launching and supporting artists and administrators.

Table 2.3 Examples of economic benefits of events

Event	Total attendance ('000s)	Total visitors from outside local area ('000s)	Total expenditure from outside local area (£M)	Total economic impact (£M)
European football championships (Euro'96), UK 1996		280	120	195
1st Cornhill test match England vs Australia 1997	72 700	66.9 (92 per cent)	4.6	9
World Badminton Championships and Sudirman Cup 1997	21 700	13.5 (62 per cent)	0.386	1.9
British Grand Prix 1997	170 000	136 (80 per cent)	25	28
Weetabix Women's British Open Golf Championship, Sunningdale 1997	50		207	2.1
Network Q Rally of Great Britain 1998	135	81 (60 per cent)	6.7	17
Leeds Love Parade, 2000	250	165 (66 per cent)		12.8
British Grand Prix 2002	160 000		5.6	17.2
ITMA 2003	125 500		85	110
Matthew Street Festival, Liverpool 2004	335 000			25
British International Motor Show 2004	461 000		61.4	105.5

Source: Lilley III & DeFranco 1999a, 1999b; Liverpool Culture Company, 2005b; MIA, 2003; The NEC Group, 2004; SMMT, 2004; The Tourism Works 1996; UK Sport 2000; Yorkshire Tourist Board 2000

Further, on a regional level, a picture begins to emerge of the potential scale of the impacts of festivals. A recent study of eleven festivals in the East Midlands (Maughan and Bianchini, 2003) found that the festivals spent just under £990 000 in the region with an additional £570 000 estimated due to multiplier effects, while money spent by audiences amounted to some £7 million, with an additional £4.16 million additional income for the region estimated. Developing a programme of festivals or events for a region can also pay dividends, as illustrated by the study commissioned for Cheltenham Borough Council into Cheltenham's Festivals (Brookes and Landry, 2002). This study found that the programme of thirteen festivals generated close to £34 million income to the town, sustaining some 300 jobs. In addition, as they note, the town receives a wealth of positive media coverage that adds to the town's image and attracts new investment and employment.

Cost-benefit analysis

Money spent on events represents an opportunity cost of resources that may have been devoted to other needs in the community. This has caused governments to look at the cost-benefit analysis of events, and has given rise to a specialized branch of economic study. As discussed earlier, Edinburgh has developed a year round strand of economic activity based on its positioning as the festival capital of Europe. For example, City of Edinburgh Council (2000c) note that Edinburgh's Hogmanay is now in the same league as the Edinburgh International Festival in terms of both its image and the impact it has on the city's economy. For an outlay of around £1.4 million the event generates an economic return in the region of £30 million.

An extensive evaluation commissioned in 1990 by the Department of the Environment of the Liverpool International Garden Festival (1984), Stoke National Garden Festival (1986) and Glasgow Garden Festival (1988) found that Liverpool and Stoke cost in the region of £40 million to stage, with an additional local impact of £21 million (1985 prices). Costs of staging the Glasgow festival were higher at around £69 million, due in part to the greater sponsorship and franchizing. Benefits generated fit under three broad headings of reclamation (increased speed and higher-quality reclaiming of the site), environmental gains (visual impact during and after the festival, image-building for the cities) and economic impact (1400–2500 jobs) (PA Cambridge Economic Consultants, 1990).

Monitoring long-term impacts

Impacts that are calculated during the actual timeframe of an event tell only part of the story. In order to form a full picture of the impact of the event, it is necessary to look at the long-term effects on the community and its economy. The case of the 1991 World Student Games give some indication of the aftershock of the event. Bramwell (1997) notes that there is a temptation to evaluate mega-events too soon after an event before the full impact can be assessed. He points out that, despite the debt incurred by the city during the event, five years after the games the city had been designated a City of Sport and had benefited from an extensive programme of national and international events, and the development of a further £20 million private leisure scheme next to the Arena. The city was left with a legacy of infrastructure and quality tourism developments that were either initiated or speeded up by the event. On a wider level, an event-led city strategy grew out of the games (Destination Sheffield, 1995). With a brief to attract or initiate events each year that would profile the city, it has already hosted 160 national, 19 European, 10 world championships and 48 other international events (KRONOS, 1997).

The methodology for evaluating the economic impact of events will be treated in more detail in Chapter 14.

Chapter summary

All events produce impacts, both positive and negative, which it is the task of the event manager to assess and balance. Social and cultural impacts may involve a shared experience, and may give rise to local pride, validation or the widening of cultural horizons. However, social problems rising from events may result in social dislocation if not properly managed. Events are an excellent opportunity to showcase the physical characteristics of a destination, but event environments may be very delicate, and care should be taken to safeguard and protect them. Events may involve longer-term issues affecting the built environment and the legacy of improved facilities. Increasingly, environmental considerations are paramount, as shown by the environmental guidelines that have been developed by UK Sport to be considered when bidding for and staging events, to manage their environmental impact.

Political impacts have long been recognized by governments, and often include increased profile and benefits to the host community. However, it is important that events fulfil the wider community agenda. Governments are attracted to events because of the economic benefits, job creation and tourism that they can provide. Events act as catalysts for attracting tourists and extending their length of stay. They also increase the profile of a destination, and can be designed to attract visitors out of season when tourism facilities are underutilized. In considering appropriate levels of funding for events, governments and organizations use economic impact studies to predict the likely impacts of events and then determine the wider outcomes. Large events also serve as catalysts for urban renewal, and for the creation of new tourism infrastructure. Events bring economic benefits to their communities, but governments need to weigh these benefits against costs when deciding how to allocate resources.

Questions

1. Describe some examples of events where the needs have been perceived as being in conflict with those of their host communities. As the event manager, how would you resolve these conflicting needs?
2. Describe an event with which you are familiar and which has been characterized by social problems or bad crowd behaviour. As the event manager, what would you have done to manage the situation and improve the outcome of the event? In your answer, discuss both the planning of the event and possible on-the-spot responses.
3. Select a major event that has been held in your region, and identify as many environmental impacts as you can. Evaluate whether you think the overall environmental impact on the host community was positive or negative, and recommend what steps could be taken to improve the balance.
4. Describe an event that you believe was not sufficiently responsive to community attitudes and values. What steps could be taken in the community to improve the situation?
5. Identify an event in your region which has a significant tourism component, and examine the event in terms of its ability to:
   (a) increase tourist visits and length of stay
   (b) improve the profile of the destination
   (c) create economic benefits for the region.

6. Select an event in which you have been involved as a participant or close observer, and identify as many impacts of the event as you can, both positive and negative. Did the positive impacts outweigh the negative?
   (a) What measures did the organizers have in place to maximize positive impacts and minimize negative impacts?
   (b) As the event manager, what steps could you have taken to balance the impacts and improve the outcome of the event?

Case study 2.1

ITMA 2003, The NEC, Birmingham
Introduction

ITMA (International Textile Machinery Exhibition) is one of the largest trade exhibitions – and the largest single sector trade show – in the world. Staged every four years, ITMA is a peripatetic exhibition – travelling around venues in Europe. Until recognizing the facilities on offer at The NEC, Birmingham, the only countries assumed capable of staging the event were France, Germany and Italy, who have shared the show for the past 30 years.

ITMA 2003 ran from 22 to 29 October 2003. Over the 8 days of the event, 1275 exhibitors took part from 40 countries, with the show having an overall attendance of 125 500 visits from 129 countries. To give some idea of the magnitude of the exhibition, the show used all 21 exhibition halls at The NEC and required every piece of mains cable, with extra supplies being brought in from London, Manchester and Glasgow, while more than 2500 articulated trucks were required to deliver all the exhibition stands and display material.

Why the NEC?

Co-ordination between The NEC, the Airport and Rail station ensured a seamless journey for visitors. An event like ITMA needs a massive supporting structure, which is where The NEC comes into its own. There are currently close to 75 000 bed spaces within 1 hour of The NEC (30 000 within 30 minutes), from 5 star to quality budget, guest houses, self catering accommodation and even some private homes. A specialist web site was created to assist visitors through online booking facilities, while a close partnership with the Birmingham Convention and Visitor Bureau meant that visitors were also able to reserve:

- a wide range of other services including shuttle bus services between The NEC and the main hotels
- air and rail tickets
- airport transfers to The NEC from all major UK airports
- coach and car hire
- sightseeing and social programmes
- events
- receptions
- theatre tickets.

More than 500 restaurants in the city provided a variety of culinary delights, and the new Mailbox and Bullring developments offered visitors a multitude of shopping options.

Uniquely, there were also some world-famous performers appearing at The NEC Arena, with pop superstar Christina Aguilera performing at The NEC Arena on Saturday, October 25 and Mariah Carey appearing three days later.

The organizer

ITMA 2003 was organized in-house by The NEC organising division Centre Exhibitions, on behalf of show the owners, industry body CEMATEX (Comité Européen des Constructeurs de Machines Textiles/European Committee of Textile Machinery Manufacturers). CEMATEX is made up of eight member associations from the UK, France, Germany, Italy, Switzerland, The Netherlands, Belgium and Spain. Other key markets represented at ITMA include Turkey and China.

The exhibitors

ITMA 2003 used the whole of The NEC site – 200 000 square metres of space. The tenancy covered 38 days – 22 build days, eight open days and eight breakdown days.

The exhibition was clearly international, including 1275 exhibitors from 40 countries, with the top 10 exhibiting countries (in order of space taken) being as follows:

1. Italy
2. Germany
3. Switzerland
4. Spain
5. Belgium
6. Turkey
7. UK
8. France
9. USA
10. Austria

In terms of space taken, 78 per cent of exhibitors came from the CEMATEX, with the greatest increase in exhibitor numbers (compared to ITMA 1999) from the following non-CEMATEX countries: Turkey (from 33 to 61 exhibitors); India (from 41 to 86 exhibitors) and China (from 10 to 28 exhibitors). The largest product sectors were Dyeing and Finishing, taking 33 per cent of the total space, followed by Spinning (24 per cent) and Weaving (17.7 per cent).

The visitors

Despite the perception of economic and political concerns, visitors to ITMA 2003 travelled from all over the world, with an average of over 15 600 each day of the show. Analysis revealed that 64 per cent of the visitors came from Europe, and over 24 per cent from Asia/SE Asia and the Middle East. The top visiting countries, after the UK, were Turkey, Germany and Italy, with the breakdown of visitors shown below:

1. UK 15 per cent
2. Turkey 7.82 per cent
3. Germany 7.49 per cent
4. Italy 6.55 per cent
5. Pakistan 6.03 per cent
6. India 5.09 per cent
7. France 4.82 per cent

8. Belgium 3.87 per cent
9. Spain 3.45 per cent
10. USA 2.78 per cent
11. China 2.69 per cent

Most visitors came for the Weaving Sector (18 per cent), followed by the Spinning Sector (15 per cent) then Dyeing and Finishing (12 per cent), although a large percentage of the visitors (20 per cent) were involved in more than one sector. For the first time, ITMA 2003 introduced a separate sector for non-wovens.

Unique features

Despite The NEC's wealth of experience, the demands of a show the size and scope of ITMA required a wealth of innovative approaches. This was the first ITMA, since the first show 52 years ago, to have an industry forum addressing the strategic issues that face the textile machinery field. It was also the first to fully embrace the opportunities presented by the Internet, and to endow the exhibition with an element of showmanship and 'pizzazz!'

Additionally, a radical approach was implemented for developing relationships with customers, with a decision to make the exhibiting process simpler by supplying as many services as possible through a single source, equipped with multi-lingual staff. Working alongside service suppliers, this dedicated team was able to liaise directly with exhibitors, presenting a 'one-stop-shop' for exhibiting queries. The feedback from exhibitors suggested that they welcomed this approach as a way providing cost-effective and simplified solutions.

Key moments

The 'Forum' (a conference that discussed the key business issues facing the industry) was a first for ITMA. Previous events had only run conferences addressing technical issues; never before had the event seen such high profile and significant presentations. The opening session was particularly interesting as the topic was the impact of China joining the World Trade Organization in 2005. The consequences will affect the whole business world not just the world of 'textiles'. The event was attended by the Chinese Government Minister for Textiles who engaged in a 'full and frank' debate with a high profile industry lobbyist from the USA, addressing such issues as 'dumping', tariffs, and unfair trading practices.

Remember John Betjamen's poem The Night train, which accompanied a famous film about the Royal Mail trains? Or those old films you see of Lancashire cotton mills all thundering away churning out fabric. Well, the same image was created within the exhibition halls used to display weaving equipment, where, for 20 minutes in every hour the dozens of huge looms all began operating at once. It was a powerful visual and audible experience that really did conjure up the industry at its most dynamic.

Watching the machines turning out a full Axminster carpet – 6 metres wide – at the rate of 2 metres a minute is really quite mesmerising. For the technical amongst you, that's 14 000 threads on the weft and a warp introduced with shuttles (mechanical, water jet or air jet) all moving so fast you cannot see it.

Business and economic impact

As the UK's largest ever international exhibition, ITMA generated an estimated £85 million for the West Midlands economy in visitor spending, according to research undertaken by KPMG, which also found that the show supported the equivalent of more than 1500 full-time jobs. To place these figures in context, this represents the largest impact of any single show ever staged in the UK – activities at The NEC Group each year generate spending of more than £1 billion, and ITMA alone represented an additional 8 per cent to the figure during 2003. Total spending within the UK, as a result of ITMA, is estimated at £110 million. The KPMG study also found considerable positive feedback about Birmingham and the West Midlands region as a destination, with almost half (45 per cent) of visitors surveyed said that they are likely to bring friends or family back to the area in the future.

ITMA helped Birmingham International Airport (BIA) break performance targets. In October 2003, the airport handled 881 709 passengers, an increase of 11.4 per cent on the previous year, and its busiest October on record. During the event, BIA also handled more than 100 special charter flights along with larger aircraft on scheduled routes to deal with the exhibition traffic. Most exhibitors (63 per cent) and nearly half of all visitors (47 per cent) flew directly into Birmingham International Airport as their gateway into the UK. ITMA was also the first major test for the Monorail link, which connects the airport directly with Birmingham International station and The NEC. It transported – without a problem – more than 22 000 people during the show.

As might be imagined, there were a few nerves amongst exhibitors at the thought of ITMA running in the UK for the first time, however, these proved to be completely without foundation. Feedback from exhibitors in every sector has been extremely positive, with reports of a considerable amount of business being done during the show. Indeed, 60 per cent of all visitors were of Director level and above, and this clearly was an important factor in the quantity of orders being placed during the show.

It is clear from the above case study that ITMA was successful on a number of levels. Major exhibitions, such as ITMA, clearly have a range of impacts which organizers have to manage effectively to maximize the positive effects and ensure that the exhibition meets all exhibitor, visitor and stakeholder requirements. ITMA demonstrated the ability of The NEC to organize and host exhibitions of this scale, while also demonstrating the positive benefits of working with a range of partners from across Birmingham and the West Midlands. After ITMA, The NEC was recognized for its work in bringing international visitors to the region for ITMA 2003, with The NEC Group also recognized for its commitment to language and communication at the National Language for Export Awards 2003. Knowledge, skills and experience developed from ITMA will help The NEC move forward as one of the major European exhibition centres and it has illustrated the potential of The NEC, Birmingham, the West Midlands and the UK as future host for large-scale international exhibitions.

For more information about The NEC Group, please visit www.necgroup.co.uk.

By The NEC Group.

Questions

1. From the case study, identify the main stakeholders in ITMA.
2. In evaluating the impacts, what are the long-term benefits to Birmingham of hosting the Show?
3. What factors contributed to the success of the Show?
4. The case illustrates the impact of the external environment on the event itself with rail disruption causing a reduction in target numbers and a change in transportation. What other issues from the external environment may impact on the Show? What strategies could event managers implement to minimize the impact of such issues?

Case study 2.2

Glastonbury Festival Environmental Policy

Glastonbury Festival of Contemporary Performing Arts (Glastonbury Festival) recognizes that running the event at Worthy Farm has a direct impact (both positive and negative) on the environment. The Festival is committed to enhancing the environment through our operations wherever possible, and minimizing any negative impact.

The Festival also commits to maintaining the rich and diverse environment that has evolved through alternative land usage. Holding a festival once a year in the middle of the growing season prevents the use of environmentally damaging conventional farming practices which would have a more intrusive impact on the ecology.

This statement will focus on litter management, sewage management, management of the general ecology of the site and environmental messaging to festival goers. The Festival is committed to working with the grain of nature, not against it, and complying with all environmental legal requirements.

Litter management

Any event with 150 000 attendees will generate significant levels of litter. The Festival is committed to minimizing the amount of waste, and managing the on site collection of that waste efficiently. The Festival works to the key environmental management principals of 'Reduce, Reuse and Recycle'. The Festival is equally committed to quickly and effectively clearing any litter caused by the Festival in the local community.

In 2003, 30 per cent of litter was moved off site during the event – in itself a 100 per cent increase from 2002. Over the next 5 years the Festival has set a target of increasing the amount of rubbish moved off site during the event to 50 per cent. This will be addressed by increasing the numbers of litter bins, of tractor teams and of dustcarts, while sustaining existing levels of skip clearance and litter clearing staff.

The Festival commits to continuing its policy of reducing waste. Significant reductions have been recorded in the last three years by placing controls on what is brought on-site by staff, contractors, sponsors and traders – and by emphasis on their responsibility to remove items brought on-site.

The Festival is also committed to continuing the composting initiative developed in 2004, to minimize the amount of waste that goes to landfill. It is Festival policy that all disposables provided to food traders by Festival wholesalers will be biodegradable, and manufactured in environmental friendly fashion. This is closely monitored and enforced.

The Festival will actively promote recycling to festival goers and will research further recycling options. The Festival achieved twice the 2004 MDC target and commits to exceeding the MDC target of 24 per cent of recycled waste in 2005. This is a demanding target for a one off event in a field, compared to domestic, industrial or commercial outlets with regular established collection practices. In 2004, in addition to the 110 tonnes of composted organic waste, the Festival recycled 150 tonnes of chipped wood, 26.8 tonnes of cans and plastic bottles, 10.3 tonnes of glass, 100 tonnes scrap metal and 13.3 tonnes of cardboard. The Festival commits to work with the statutory authorities on recycling and litter management issues.

Managing sewage and waste water

The Festival commits to transporting sewage and waste water offsite, with the use of the lagoon as a temporary holding facility, in full consultation with the Environment Agency and Wessex Water.

The Festival undertakes to provide containers for waste water and direct all employees and traders that there must not be any discharge of any contaminated water to surface or ground waters. This will continue to be closely monitored. All foul drainage from the market areas and traders will be collected and transported to the lagoon for subsequent disposal. The levels of the effluent collection lagoon will be continually monitored, with effluent being transported to approved sewage treatment works during the event. The lagoon will be thoroughly cleansed before it is returned to agricultural use. The Festival undertakes to commit to the standards set by the Environment Agency with regards to sewage disposal and to an ongoing process of consultation with the Environment Agency and Mendip District Council with regards to minimizing any environmental damage caused by the Festival.

The Festival will protect watercourses to minimize the potential of pollution during the event and undertakes to provide more urinals and toilets than recommended by the Event Safety Guide, siting the additional facilities at potential pollution hot spots. The Festival will also monitor the streams during the event. The Festival also is committed to investigating further developments in technology, which may result in minimizing the volume that needs to be transported off site, which in turn will reduce the impact from carbon emissions caused by the tankers. Any developments will only be progressed with the approval of the appropriate authorities.

Managing the ecology of the site

The Festival is committed to maintaining the high level of bio-diversity that was found on the festival site by the independent bio-diversity audit carried out by Liz Biron of Somerset Environmental Records Centre in 2003. The Festival aims to further increase this level by continuing its commitment to protecting vulnerable habitats, its new county wildlife sites, badger sets, ponds, streams, hedges and ditches, in nature reserves and non-public zones or by fencing them off.

The Festival will continue to try to increase both the abundance and diversity of wildlife, by:

- actively enhancing habitats on site by tree planting, hedge planting, coppicing and hedge laying, etc.;
- continuing to allow the process of succession from inherited improved grassland to more diverse unimproved grassland;
- allowing a significant level of agricultural weed species (docks and nettles etc.) to exist on its core site.

The Festival will continue to protect vulnerable species individuals by establishing, on a need basis, new temporary reserves. This was successfully achieved in 2003 and 2004 by creating a new reserve within the core site for three deer trapped within the site by the perimeter fence. This temporary reserve was so successful that the deer stayed in this locality long after the fence was removed. Indeed in 2004 the deer moved into the nature reserve of their own accord. This is a good example of area managers/workers and central management working together to resolve serious issues.

The practical reality of this commitment is that the Festival, for the fifth year running, will be enhancing the environment of its core site by more trees and hedge planting at three locations on-site. The planting to date has brought the total number of native tree and hedge plants planted to over four thousand since 2000.

Environmental messaging

The unique environment of the Festival brings together many Non-Governmental Organizations (NGOs) and environmental groups, and through participation in the Festival, the public are exposed to many positive influences highlighting environmental values – and hopefully influencing subsequent behaviour. Glastonbury Festival is committed to:

- having a 'Green' message central to future marketing campaigns, to dissuade festival goers from urinating in streams, ditches and hedges.
- including environmental messages in festival publications such as the Fine Guide, the programme, the daily paper and on the Festival web site, which has direct links to environmental and humanitarian organizations.
- using the screens at the main stages only to promote environmental and humanitarian messages.
- employing the services of environmental organizations in the running of the event, increasing the amounts these organizations can raise towards their objectives – and increasing their profile.
- maintaining the Greenfields, the largest area of its kind dedicated to environmental awareness. Many different environmental concerns that enhance the fabric of our society, from international organizations such as Greenpeace, to small woodland trusts, place a high value on this facility. The festival is the biggest single regular donor to Greenpeace and offers a fertile recruitment ground for members and for promoting environmental campaigns.
- continuing to give trading opportunities to green organizations, and making decisions on which traders to invite based on green credentials.

Additionally the Festival is committed to:

- creating awareness among its employees and subcontractors about the 'Reduce Reuse Recycle' mantra and about the importance of minimizing any negative impact on the environment.
- employing safe work practices, developing contingencies and implementing measures to prevent, eliminate or reduce pollution,
- encouraging festival-goers to use environmentally sound transport options, by promoting the use of public transport and lift share.
- continuing to work with Future Forests to be carbon neutral. Future Forests have planted over 6500 naturally occurring deciduous trees in the woods in the South West of England because of their involvement with the Festival. Since GF pioneered Future Forest's involvement in 1997 many other events have followed this lead. (When the trees planted at Worthy over the last five years are taken into account as well, there is now a significant carbon sink.)
- improving energy efficiency, seeking green alternatives where possible.

The Festival will review the effectiveness of implementation of the above on a regular basis and constantly seek to improve environmental performance according to the above criteria.

For further information on many aspects of the planning and management of Glastonbury Festival, including an extensive student information pack, please visit www.glastonburyfestivals.co.uk.

By Glastonbury Festival of Contemporary Performing Arts, Worthy Farm, Pilton, Shepton Mallet, Somerset, BA4 4BY.

Questions

1. Summarize the potential environmental impacts of Glastonbury Festival. How do these differ from an event taking place in a purpose built venue?
2. Based on the case study, identify examples of what you consider to be best practice approaches to environmental management. Discuss why you have chosen these.
3. What other practical measures could the organizers consider to ensure that the environmental impacts are minimized?

Chapter 3
Event tourism

Learning Objectives

After studying this chapter, you should be able to:

■ describe 'event tourism' and the destination approach to event tourism planning
■ conduct an event tourism situational analysis to create a foundation for goal setting and strategic decision making
■ describe the range of goals that a destination might seek to progress through an event tourism strategy
■ list and describe organizations that might play a role in a destination's efforts at event tourism development
■ describe generic strategy options available to organizations seeking to develop event tourism to a destination
■ list and discuss approaches to the implementation and evaluation of event tourism strategies
■ discuss the potential that event tourism has to generate positive outcomes in small communities.

Introduction

This chapter will explore the relationship between events and tourism from the viewpoint of destinations (cities, towns, counties, regions or countries) that are seeking to develop and implement strategies to increase visitation. The chapter begins with an overview of event tourism, before moving on to propose and discuss a strategic approach to event tourism planning. This approach involves: conduct of a detailed situational analysis; the creation of event tourism goals; the establishment of a structure through which event tourism goals can be progressed; and the development, implementation and evaluation of an event tourism strategy. It is argued in this chapter that the value of this process lies in its capacity to generate a coordinated strategic approach to a destination's overall event tourism efforts. The final part of this chapter seeks to redress the tendency in dealing with event tourism to focus on cities, regions and countries. It does this by briefly examining the significant, positive role that event tourism can play in the context of small communities.

Developing destination-based event tourism strategies

Government support at all levels has been integral to the expansion of event tourism. Not only have governments invested in the creation of specialist bodies charged with event tourism development, but many have also funded, or contributed significantly to, event-specific infrastructure, such as convention and exhibition centres and stadiums. For example, BACD's Investment Register (BACD, 2005) currently notes significant investment of over £4.68 billion in events-infrastructure projects funded from public and private funds. The willingness of governments to support event tourism through policy initiatives and legislation is also increasingly evident. Once the London 2012 Olympics bid was won, for example, the UK Government moved quickly to pass legislation to create organizing bodies, ensure Games security, and allow and expedite Olympic-related developments, including through the naming of an Olympics Minister to oversee the projects. Such willingness, however, can sometimes create problems due to the public's lack of participation in decision making, as Waitt (2003) noted in connection with the Sydney Olympics.

Responsibility for progressing event tourism efforts varies from destination to destination. In the context of smaller destinations, such as towns and regions, involvement may be limited to tourism promotional bodies, local government and the local chamber of commerce. Larger destinations (cities, regions, countries) are likely to have an expanded range of organizations involved in the event tourism area, including convention centres and visitor bureaus, tourism commissions/agencies, festival/public event bodies, major event agencies, government departments involved in areas such as sport and the arts, and event organizing companies.

The event tourism strategic planning process

A strategic approach to a destination's event tourism development efforts offers significant benefits. These benefits lie primarily in the areas of coordination and in the building of an event tourism capacity that represents the best strategic fit with the area's overall tourism efforts, and its current and projected business environment. This approach is presented in Figure 3.1 as a series of sequential steps, each of which is discussed in this section.

The timeframe in which event tourism strategic plans operate will vary from destination to destination, but 5–15-year planning horizons are not uncommon. For example, the Scottish Executive have employed a 13-year strategy with the vision of being 'one of the world's foremost event destinations by 2015' (Scottish Executive, 2002) (see the case study on page 90), and Events Tasmania employs a rolling 10 year events plan (Events Tasmania, 2003a).

Situational analysis

A detailed situational analysis should underpin the decisions made on what event tourism goals to set for a destination. This analysis should reflect the various perspectives of key stakeholders in the event area, such as tourism bodies, the

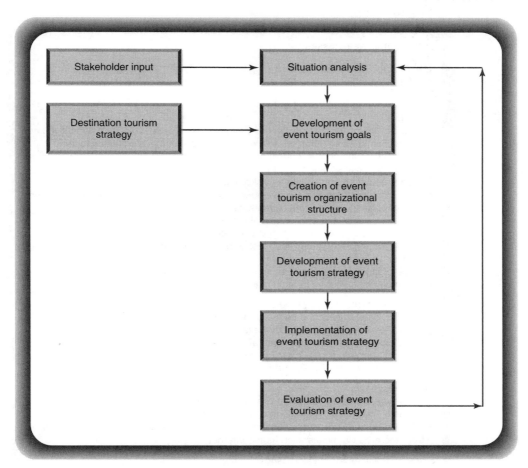

Figure 3.1 Event tourism strategic planning process

destination's community, government agencies associated with areas such as the arts and sport, and major event organizers. In preparing the major events strategy for Scotland, for example, the consultancy company charged with this task (Objective Performance Limited) spent 18 months engaged in research, including interviewing more than 80 individuals and organizations involved in major events in Scotland and overseas (Scottish Executive, 2002).

A strengths, weaknesses, opportunities and threats (SWOT) analysis (Chapter 5) is a useful way of assessing the situation that a destination faces in its efforts to develop event tourism. Figure 3.2 lists a range of factors that might feature in such an analysis undertaken as a precursor to developing a destination's event tourism strategy.

Development of event tourism goals

The role event tourism is required to play in a destination's tourism development efforts will vary according to the overall tourism strategy that is being pursued.

Strengths/weaknesses

Existing stock of events
- Type
- Quality
- Uniqueness/competitive advantage
- Number
- Duration/timing (for example, whether most events are scheduled at a particular time of the year, such as summer, and whether this clustering is advantageous/ disadvantageous from a tourism perspective)
- Current financial situation
- Image/reputation (particularly in visitor markets)
- Level of current demand from regional, national and overseas visitor markets and level of understanding of these markets
- Economic, social and environmental impacts
- Existing links between events and the destination's tourism industry (for example, level of packaging evident and level of partnering with tourism industry marketing bodies)
- Stage of individual events in terms of their 'product' life cycle
- Evidence of long-term strategic planning

Venues/sites/facilities/supporting services
- Number, type, quality and capacity of venues/outdoor event sites
- Capacity of local suppliers (for example, equipment hire, food and beverage services) to support various types of events
- Stock of supporting local tourism services (for example, accommodation suppliers, transport suppliers, tour operators)

Human resources
- Level/type of destination event venue/event management expertise
- Capacity to draw on volunteers to support event delivery
- Range/type of event-related training conducted in the area, or accessible to people from the area via means such as the Internet

Stage of event sector development
- Existence of organizations such as industry associations, convention and visitors bureaus and major event agencies

Destination location relative to major tourist markets
- Travel time and costs
- Types and frequency of public transport to the area

Degree of political support
- Level of available funding for event tourism
- Potential for legislative support
- Location of a major event agency inside local or national government

Level of community support
- Community perspectives on economic outcomes (for example, whether the community perceives it will benefit economically from the events staged or whether they think most benefits will be 'exported' from the area)
- Level of anticipated local patronage for events (necessary to underpin the economics of many events)

Figure 3.2 Possible factors for inclusion in a destination's event tourism SWOT analysis

- Level of willingness of the community to absorb short-term negatives, such as crowding and traffic congestion
- Willingness of a community to support events via volunteering, provision of home hosting services etc.

Extent and nature of existing relationships between events and the tourism industry
- Extent of event packaging evident
- Type/nature of links with tourism companies and organizations

Local weather patterns
- Rainy seasons or periods of extreme heat that may restrict the times in which events can be conducted

Opportunities/threats
Potential for partnering with selected organizations to progress one or more event tourism goals
- Possible partnering bodies:
  - Government departments
  - Cultural organizations
  - Tourism bodies
  - Chambers of commerce
  - Tourism businesses (to package events)
  - Environmental groups (to minimize impacts/maximize environmental outcomes)

Level and type of competition from other events in other destinations
- Direct competition from similar events
- Competition from dissimilar events conducted in the same time period

Market tastes/preferences for events
- Ability of an area to respond to market needs through existing and new events
- Impact on existing/planned events of changes in family structures, age of population, patterns of work/retirement and attitudes to health etc.

Availability of external funds
- Capacity to attract government grants or loans
- Likelihood of attracting sponsorship
- Potential to link events with overall destination branding efforts

Local cultural/environmental attributes that have the potential to be leveraged for event purposes (for example, unique flora or fauna, a strong and vibrant indigenous culture, history, ethnicity, architecture, local agricultural pursuits)

Level/type of links between local/regional sporting/business/cultural bodies and their national or international associations (for example, strong links between a regional sporting body and its national association may facilitate successful bids for regional/ national championships in the sports concerned)

Capacity of destination to absorb event tourism impacts without negative environ- mental or community outcomes
- Perspectives of community groups, such as non-government environmental organizations, on events of various types and scale

Figure 3.2 Continued

General economic conditions
- Employment levels
- Interest rates
- Inflation
- Consumer confidence levels

Other
- Changes in weather patterns due to global warming
- Security and health issues (for example, terrorism, SARS and Asian Bird Flu)
- Political climate (for example, the extent to which events involving particular groups or nations will be supported by key stakeholders, such as local or national governments)

Figure 3.2 Continued

An understanding of this strategy is important as it provides, for example, the basis for establishing event tourism visitation targets, as well as insights into destination branding and positioning efforts that an event strategy may be required to support. While each destination's event tourism goals differ, common considerations in setting such goals can be identified, and these are discussed below.

Leveraging events for economic gain

A key consideration in any event tourism strategy is the potential for events to bring 'new' money into a destination from outside visitors (Chapter 2). A single large-scale event, such as the Manchester International Festival, has the potential to contribute significantly to a destination's economy. When this event was proposed in 2004, research for the feasibility study suggested that it could initially bring in 160 000 visitors raising to 270 000 in future years, with an estimated economic impact of £34 million (Davidson, 2004).

Even in developing countries events can generate significant tourist demand (and therefore export income). In the Caribbean, for example, peaks in visitation in many countries often coincide with an event (Nurse, 2003).

Geographic dispersal of economic benefits flowing from tourism

When the destinations seeking to engage in event tourism are large geographic entities, such as regions or countries, it is not uncommon for them to use events as a means of encouraging travel to areas outside major tourism counties (see the EventScotland case study, page 90). In this way, the economic benefits from visitation are more widely spread.

Destination branding

A destination's 'brand' can be thought of as the overall impression, association or feeling that its name and associated symbols generate in the minds of consumers.

Events are an opportunity to assist in creating, changing or reinforcing such brands. According to a study by Jago, Chalip, Brown, Mules and Ali (2003) in Australia, such efforts depend greatly on local community support and on the cultural and strategic fit between the destination and the event(s) conducted there. This study also found, in the context of individual events, that event differentiation, the longevity/tradition associated with an event, cooperative planning by key players and media support were central factors in the successful integration of individual events into a destination's overall branding efforts.

The Edinburgh International Festival, one of the UK's best known events worldwide, is an excellent example of using an event for destination branding purposes. This event has been extensively leveraged to create a 'brand' for the city of Edinburgh. The city is now firmly established as the UK's festival city, a position it has sought to strengthen via a variety of means. These means have included drawing together a range of festivals into a programme of events, encouraging the development of new festivals, building a festival theatre and developing The Hub as Edinburgh's Festival Centre. Another example of 'identity' creation through events can be observed in Birmingham. This area claims to be 'Europe's finest event city' (Birmingham Convention Bureau, 2005) and conducts multiple events to reinforce this position, appealing to the business and leisure markets.

Many other examples of branding through events can be identified. The general category of food and/or wine festivals, for example, perform this function for a number of destinations, reinforcing to the broader market the destination's status in connection with these products. Ludlow Marches Food & Drink Festival and Abergavenny Food Festival are indicative of such events, showcasing quality food from the region.

Another aspect of the link between events and destination branding is the use of events by tourism marketing bodies as integral parts of broad 'theme' years. Liverpool Culture Company have developed a series of themed years in the build up to their hosting the European Capital of Culture in 2008 to reflect aspects of Liverpool culture, covering learning, faith, sea, performance and the city's 800th anniversary, with environment and innovation planned for the two years after 2008. The programme of events and activities is expected to attract 1.5 million people (Liverpool Culture Company, 2005a). Events are also sometimes used as the basis for theme years, an example being SeaBritain in 2005 coordinated by the National Maritime Museum. The goal of this themed year was to celebrate 'the ways in which the sea touches all of our lives' with the main event being a celebration of the Trafalgar Festival to mark the 200th anniversary of Nelson's victory (National Maritime Museum, 2005).

Destination marketing

Associated with the issue of destination branding is the more general one of destination promotion. Destinations often use the opportunity provided by events to progress their overall tourism promotional efforts, including a range of destination marketing organizations being established throughout the UK over recent years to further this aim, for example, Marketing Manchester, Marketing Birmingham, Marketing Leeds, Glasgow City Marketing Bureau and Experience Nottinghamshire.

The Wales Tourist Board undertook a major marketing and promotional campaign in relation to the Rugby World Cup in Wales in 1999. Its overall aim was to use the tournament as an opportunity to attract additional visitors, in order to raise the profile of the host nation and to secure lasting tourism benefits. Over 330 000 people were estimated to have visited Wales as a result of the event. In a survey of international rugby fans conducted before and after the Rugby World Cup, fewer than 20 per cent had visited Wales. Of those who had, almost 70 per cent thought it likely that they would return on holiday. Amongst those who had seen coverage of the event on television, 25 per cent thought that they would be much more likely to visit Wales on holiday as a result. Research indicated that around 135 000 trips may be generated from the UK over the next five years, potentially worth around £15 million (Anon, 2000).

If events are to be effective in positioning their destinations in the market, they must strive for authenticity and the expression of the unique characteristics of their communities. Visitors want to do what the locals do, and experience what the locals enjoy. The UK government report 'Tomorrow's Tourism' (DCMS, 1999, p. 7) argues that:

Tourism is based largely on our heritage, culture and countryside and, therefore, needs to maintain the quality of the resources upon which it depends. Tourism can provide an incentive and income to protect our built and natural environment and helps to maintain local culture and diversity. Where tourism is popular, it underpins local commercial activity and services and it can help to regenerate urban and rural areas.

Conversely, destinations that produce events for the tourists rather than events that have meaning for their own communities, run the danger of producing inauthentic, shallow events. Exploitative or badly run events with inadequate management or facilities can damage the reputation of a destination.

For example, Smith and Jenner (1998) point to the dramatic rise in visitation to Atlanta, Georgia (a 78 per cent rise in overseas visitors and a 35 per cent rise in domestic visitors) over the three-year period following its announcement in 1990 as the site of the 1996 Olympics. They attribute this increase in part to the publicity that Atlanta was able to obtain as a result of the Olympics. In the case of the Sydney 2000 Olympics, the Australian Tourist Commission (ATC) predicted an additional 1.7 million visits between 1997 and 2004, generating an additional $6.1 billion in foreign exchange earnings. It believes this event accelerated Australia's tourism marketing efforts by 10 years. This outcome was due in large measure to the additional $3.8 billion in media publicity obtained through specific ATC Olympic Games media relations activities, and the $300 million in exposure obtained through work with sponsors (Australasian Special Events Magazine, 2001).

Creating off-season demand for tourism industry services

Events have the capacity to be scheduled in periods of low tourism demand, when airline and accommodation providers often have surplus capacity, thereby evening out seasonal tourism flows. Skiing centres, for example, often use events as a means of generating demand during non-winter periods. Getz describes the way that events can overcome seasonality by capitalizing 'on whatever natural appeal the off-season presents, such as winter as opposed to summer sports, seasonal food and produce, and scenery or wildlife viewed in different places and under changing conditions'. He also notes that 'in many destinations the residents prefer the off-season for their own celebrations, and these provide more authentic events for visitors' (Getz, 2005, pp. 142–143).

Many UK destinations have developed events to enliven off-season periods. Within 'Achieving Our Potential: A Tourism Strategy for Wales' (WTB, 2000, p. 53) the Wales Tourist Board note the benefit that events can bring to Wales, highlighting that,

'Festivals and events, for example, can play a key role in attracting larger numbers of overseas visitors and in developing new markets within the UK throughout the year'. However, they go on to note that due to a previously uncoordinated approach to developing the event programme, the best known events within Wales are in the main summer months, which reinforces seasonality. As a result, the tourism strategy recommends the development of an events/festival strategy to distribute events throughout the year and a more coordinated approach to marketing in order to gain full benefit from business tourism (including meetings, incentives, conferences and exhibitions). A further example is Edinburgh, which in 2000 launched the new Capital Christmas winter festival to extend the traditional New Year Hogmanay celebrations and attract visitors in the off-season winter months. Donald Anderson, Leader of the Council, noted, 'Edinburgh attracts thousands of visitors all year round and our world renowned festivals play a major part in this. Capital Christmas and Edinburgh's Hogmanay together offer the best winter festival programme in the world and I know of no other city that hosts a full month of family entertainment throughout the festive season' (City of Edinburgh Council, 2000b).

Events can also be used as a means of extending the tourist season by conducting them just before or just after the high-season period.

Enhancing visitor experiences

Events add to the range of experiences a destination can offer, and thus add to its capacity to attract and hold visitors for longer periods of time (Getz, 2005). They also can provide newness, freshness and change, which sustain interest in the destination for locals, and enhance its attraction for visitors. Tourist attractions and theme parks incorporate events as a key element in their marketing programmes and use events to animate and interpret their products (Getz, 2005). Bradford Museum of Film, Television and Arts, Alton Towers in Staffordshire and Blackpool Pleasure Beach all use extensive event programmes to increase market profile and attract repeat visits. Getz (2005, p. 13) notes the use of events by a wide variety of tourism attractions.

Resorts, museums, historic districts, heritage sites, archaeological sites, markets and shopping centres, sports stadia, convention centres, and theme parks all develop programmes of special events. Built attractions and facilities everywhere have realized the advantages of 'animation' – the process of programming interpretive features and/or special events that make the place come alive with sensory stimulation and appealing atmosphere.

Extenders

Another important aspect to consider is the opportunity to keep visitors or tourists in the region when they have attended an event, in other words, to extend their stay. Davidson and Cope (2003) note that delegates or visitors to business events are generally being funded by their organization to attend at their employers expense. As a result, they may bring along partners or family, attend other business or social events, extend their visit either before or after the event to spend some of their leisure time (and money) in the area or return at a future date – this is particularly true of international delegates. As a result, it is important that organizers, tourism agencies and other stakeholders consider the opportunities that this may bring and ensure that delegates are provided with sufficient information before attending to influence their decision. VisitBritain and the Business Tourism Partnership provide useful guidance on ensuring that the benefits from business tourists are maximized (Davidson, 2002).

Catalyst for the expansion and/or improvement of destination infrastructure and tourism infrastructure

Events can enhance the quality of life, and thus add to the sense of place and the residential amenity of neighbourhoods. Events can also provide a significant spur to both public and private investment in a destination. Many writers (for example, Carlsen and Millan, 2002; Carlsen and Taylor, 2003; Hiller and Moylan, 1999; Jones, 2001, 2002; Mules, 1993; Ritchie, 2001; Roche, 2000) have highlighted the role that particularly large-scale events can play in urban renewal, and in the subsequent development of a destination's attractiveness and capacity as a tourist destination. For example, Millennium Square, a £12 million project funded by Leeds City Council and the Millennium Commission, is used for events but also provides traffic-free leisure space for residents to enjoy. Leeds' annual multicultural programme of events is the envy of many cities, ranging from Opera in the Park and Party in the Park, through to the Irish and Chinese festivals. Investment by the private sector in restaurants and tourist accommodation, for example, is often central to this process and may sometimes extend to the building of large-scale infrastructure items. The Sheffield World Student Games in 1991 provided major facilities, including Ponds Forge International Pool, the Sheffield Arena and the Don Valley Stadium that have contributed to Sheffield's reputation as a sporting city. The 2002 Manchester Commonwealth Games lead to the regeneration of East Manchester, including development of the City of Manchester Stadium, now home to Manchester City Football Club following the Games, to ensure a legacy and long-term after-use (see, for example, Carlsen and Taylor, 2003 for a discussion of the policies linking Commonwealth Games to regeneration). Other examples include the Millennium Dome and surrounding area in Greenwich (East London) as the focal point for the Millennium Festival celebrations, and the Festival Hall and South Bank Centre developed for the Festival of Britain in 1951, all of which gained infrastructure development stemming from hosting large-scale events. Hotel and facilities development, better communications and improved road and public transport networks are some of the legacies left by these events.

One of Edinburgh International Festival's founders, Henry Harvey Wood, noted in 1947 the role that the festival could play in regenerating the economy. He stated, 'If the Festival succeeds, Edinburgh will not only have scored an artistic triumph but laid the foundations of a major industry, a new and exciting source of income' (EIF, 2000, p. 2). The festival has succeeded and his prediction has come true. Edinburgh International Festival continues to be of substantial economic importance, as does the programme of events that have developed around it. In 2004 alone Edinburgh's summer festivals generated an estimated £135 million for the economy, sustaining the equivalent of 2900 full time equivalent jobs (SQW Ltd and TNS Travel and Tourism, 2005).

Progression of a destination's social, cultural and/or environmental agenda

A range of agenda may be pursued through the conduct of events – tourist visitation is one example. These other agenda may serve to condition how event tourism is approached, or may be independent of such considerations. It is not uncommon for major event agencies to also concern themselves with a range of non-tourism goals.

Government tourism and arts bodies often consciously use events to position their destinations in the market and deliver tourism, culture and art strategies. For example, Hampshire County Council noted that, 'festivals can provide high profile opportunities to celebrate communities, to promote artistic excellence and innovation, and to improve the image, identity and competitiveness of particular localities' (Fuller, 1998). The Events Unit within the Belfast City Development Department aims to 'promote and develop a high quality, sustainable, inclusive programme of public access events, in a safe enjoyable environment, in order to help raise the profile of Belfast in support of regeneration' (Belfast City Council, 2000a, p. 2). Key objectives of the Events Unit Strategy, mapped into the Development Department Strategy are:

- Develop and promote a high-quality, sustainable, inclusive programme of public access events to raise the profile of Belfast and utilize the common Belfast branding to ensure Belfast is an attractive and welcoming city.
- Work in partnership with the Tourism Development Unit and the Arts Unit to ensure the development, packaging and promotion of events which will enhance Belfast's reputation.
- Ensure that all promotional tools including literature, advertisements, press releases provide an appropriate range of information for residents and visitors to the city.
- Work in conjunction with the Tourism Unit and the Belfast Visitor and Convention Bureau (BVCB) to ensure that the common branding of the city is adopted appropriately (Belfast City Council, 2000b).

Another example is the key role that events play within the arts strategy of Bath and North East Somerset Council (B&NES) for 2005 to 2008 (Arts Development Service, 2004). The strategy aims 'to increase the number of residents and visitors to B&NES experiencing high-quality arts events and activities'. To achieve this, B&NES have set three strategic objectives:

- To build audiences by increasing the number of admissions and attendances to arts, events and activities
- To develop audiences by developing opportunities for audiences to access the arts
- To encourage the development of cultural and creative industries (Arts Development Service, 2004).

The increasing pursuit of cultural strategies may be achieved through events and festivals. For example, the Newcastle Gateshead Initiative launched a year of events as the next phase of their culture[10] cultural programme. Built around four themed festivals focusing on music, rivers and the sea, sport and visual arts, the ambitious £12 million programme, 2005 Alive, was used to promote attractions and the region around the world and draw together a range of world-class and community based events. Alan Clarke, Chief Executive of One NorthEast, noted:

> *This programme of events offers something for everyone; whether they are a resident of the region or a visitor. The scope of the campaign, which will take in events ranging from the Hexham Abbey Music Festival, to the Seve Trophy; the Stockton Riverside Festival to the Great North Run also means the entire region will benefit from the increased marketing activity and give tourists a real reason to stay longer and explore more widely in the North East (Newcastle Gateshead Initiative, 2005).*

The pursuit of broader outcomes from the conduct of individual events can also be observed. The Manchester Commonwealth Games, for example, were leveraged by the city's council as a catalyst for educational, skill-building and health improvement programmes, as well as a means of creating awareness and understanding of the various communities (from Commonwealth countries) that live in the Manchester area (Carlsen and Millan, 2002). Environmental agenda can also be progressed through events. The London 2012 Olympics are seeking to be the One World Olympics by focusing on sustainability and continue the positive initiatives started during Sydney 2000 with the 'Green Games'. One of the planned achievements is the regeneration and transformation of London's Lower Lea Valley (London 2012, 2004).

Whatever event tourism goals are set by a destination, specific benchmarks need to be established to assess progress towards those goals. For example, the Northern Ireland Events Company has the strategic task of supporting 2–3 World Class events, 4–6 International events and a number of smaller events (NIEC, 2005a).

Other areas of a purely tourist nature, where goals might be set and progress measured, include tourist income generated from events, changes in length of tourist stays, use levels of tourism services (particularly accommodation), the extent of geographic spread of tourism flowing from the conduct of events, the volume of event-related media coverage received by a destination, and changes in destination market position/image flowing from the conduct of events.

Creation of an event tourism organizational structure

To progress a destination's event tourism goals, it is necessary to allocate responsibility for achieving these to one or more organizations. In the case of towns or regions, such responsibilities often lie with the same body charged with overall tourism development. In the case of cities, regions or countries, multiple organizations may be involved, such as bodies responsible for festivals, business tourism, major events and overall tourism development (Figure 3.3). In Belfast, for example, significant organizations with major roles in event tourism development include:

- The *Northern Ireland Tourist Board* (the national tourism organization) has identified excellent events and business tourism as two of their winning themes with the potential to deliver competitive advantage for Northern Ireland as part of their tourism *Strategic Framework for Action 2004–2007*. They note for the Excellent Events theme, 'Research confirms that events are an effective tool for changing perceptions and attracting visitors – particularly off-season. Working with key strategic partners (such as the Northern Ireland Events Company and local councils), we will identify new opportunities to showcase excellence and plan investment requirements'. Further, for the Business Tourism theme they note, 'Business tourists spend on average three times more than leisure visitors, making this the most lucrative, high spend, high yield form of tourism. In 2002, 30 per cent of NI visitors came on business and generated £99 million. Our focus here will be on conferences, meetings and incentive travel, to allow more potential for discretionary spend' (NITB, 2003, p. 8).
- The *Northern Ireland Events Company* role is 'To contribute to improving the social and economic status of Northern Ireland, for the benefit of all the people, by supporting events, consistent with its aim, which would be unlikely to happen in Northern Ireland without the intervention of the Company' (NIEC, 2005a).
- The *Belfast Visitor and Convention Bureau* (BVCB, 2005) is, 'the lead organization responsible for the promotion of Belfast as a conference and leisure tourism

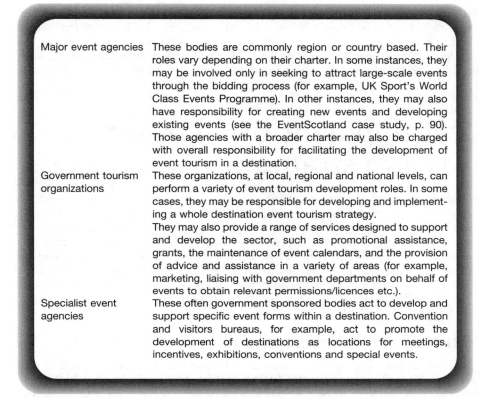

Major event agencies	These bodies are commonly region or country based. Their roles vary depending on their charter. In some instances, they may be involved only in seeking to attract large-scale events through the bidding process (for example, UK Sport's World Class Events Programme). In other instances, they may also have responsibility for creating new events and developing existing events (see the EventScotland case study, p. 90). Those agencies with a broader charter may also be charged with overall responsibility for facilitating the development of event tourism in a destination.
Government tourism organizations	These organizations, at local, regional and national levels, can perform a variety of event tourism development roles. In some cases, they may be responsible for developing and implementing a whole destination event tourism strategy. They may also provide a range of services designed to support and develop the sector, such as promotional assistance, grants, the maintenance of event calendars, and the provision of advice and assistance in a variety of areas (for example, marketing, liaising with government departments on behalf of events to obtain relevant permissions/licences etc.).
Specialist event agencies	These often government sponsored bodies act to develop and support specific event forms within a destination. Convention and visitors bureaus, for example, act to promote the development of destinations as locations for meetings, incentives, exhibitions, conventions and special events.

Figure 3.3 Major event tourism organizations

destination'. It exists 'to offer free and impartial advice to organizers considering holding an event in Belfast'.

- The *Belfast City Council Events Unit* has the aim to, 'promote and develop a high quality, sustainable, inclusive programme of public access events, in a safe enjoyable environment, in order to help raise the profile of Belfast in support of regeneration' (Belfast City Council, 2005a).

Belfast City Council have also recently established a new unit for promoting sport events in the city (Belfast City Council, 2005b).

The existence of multiple bodies charged with event tourism development at a destination, creates the potential for a loss of focus on its overall event tourism goals, as well as a less coordinated approach to their achievement, though this does not appear to have happened in Northern Ireland. For these reasons, there is a strong case for the creation of a single body, either within an existing organization (see the case study on Event Denmark, p. 93), or in the form of a new organization (see the case study on EventScotland, p. 90), with a charter to coordinate, assist and, if necessary, 'push' organizations towards the achievement of broader whole-of-destination event tourism goals. In the absence of such a body, alternative mechanisms need to be developed to try to produce such an outcome. These mechanisms might include shared board memberships between key event tourism bodies, clearly defined organizational missions to prevent overlapping efforts;

regular 'round table' meetings between key organizations and conditions on funding that require broader event tourism goals to be addressed. The Northern Ireland Tourist Board's support for Belfast and Derry Visitor and Convention Bureaus as key partners to help match the winning themes (in this case Business Tourism) with regions able to deliver them successfully is an excellent example of this (NITB, 2003).

Development of an event tourism strategy

In terms of general strategic options available to a town, city, county, region or country's event tourism body, several possibilities can be identified. These strategies concern the development of existing events, bidding to attract existing (mobile) events and the creation of new events. These three broad strategic options are not mutually exclusive – for example, event tourism bodies in any one destination may employ composite strategies involving two, or all three, of these options to achieve their destination's event tourism goals. Whatever strategy is selected, it needs to reflect the insights gained from the preceding situational analysis.

Existing event development

A range of possible approaches to using existing events to advance a destination's event tourism efforts can be identified. One option is to identify one or several events that have the capacity to be developed as major attractions for an area ('hallmark' events), with a view to using them as the foundation for image-building efforts. The previously cited examples of the Edinburgh Festivals are indicative of how events can be used in this way. A variant on this approach is to develop a single hallmark event that can then be supported by a range of similarly themed events. It may also be possible to merge existing smaller events to create one or several larger events, or to incorporate smaller events into larger events to add to their uniqueness and subsequent tourism appeal. Yet another approach is to develop one or several hallmark events, while at the same time maintaining a mix of small-scale events scheduled throughout the year, as a means of generating year-long appeal for a destination.

Event bidding

Many events are mobile in the sense that they move regularly between different destinations. Some sporting events and many business events (for example, association/corporate conferences) fall into this category. Some types of event tourism organizations (namely many national or region-based major event agencies, and convention and visitors bureaus) have been specifically established for the purpose of attracting new events to a destination via the bidding process. Bodies of this nature need to be able to identify events of this type – a task that convention and visitor bureaus undertake by maintaining representatives in other regions and overseas, and by directly communicating with meeting, incentive and exhibition planners. To attract such mobile events, it is necessary to prepare a formal bid (Chapter 5) that makes a persuasive case as to why an event should be conducted in a specific destination. Before doing so, however, it is necessary to ensure that a sound match exists between the event being sought and an area's capacity to host it. In this regard, the Northern Ireland Conference Support Programme (NITB, 2005), administered through Northern Ireland Tourist Board and Belfast and Derry Visitor and Convention Bureaus, note the following criteria for support:

- A minimum of 250 out of state delegates staying in the area for 1 night or 500 bed nights generated from out of state markets.
- Demonstrate a high prestige value, i.e. media coverage, high profile speakers.
- Demonstrate that the conference would not come to Northern Ireland unless support is provided.
- Benefit local businesses by providing opportunities for developing industry links, showcasing local products and by using local suppliers.
- Cover a subject area relating to local economic strategies or specific priority areas for Northern Ireland.
- Enhance Northern Ireland's international profile.
- Promote business extenders/partner programmes to include the rural hinterland of Northern Ireland.
- Show evidence of strict financial project management, cash flows and projected income.

The Northwest Conference Bidding Unit was launched in July 2004 and is administered through Marketing Manchester. Funded by the Northwest Development Agency and supported by other sub-regional tourist boards (The Mersey Partnership, Chester & Warrington Tourist Board, Lancashire & Blackpool Tourist Board and Cumbria Tourist Board) it aims to, 'combine the strengths of the region to carry out targeted sales and marketing activity to attract national and international association conferences to England's northwest'. The unit is one of the key elements of the North West tourism strategy and links into the major events strategy (Marketing Manchester, 2004).

New event creation

New event creation should be based around the activities and themes identified in the situational analysis as providing substantial scope for the development of tourist markets. It should also be the case that new events, as Northwest Development Agency (NWDA) (2003) points out, should be coordinated to bring maximum benefits to the region. Exactly what new events are created will vary with the strategic needs of each destination, with the range of generic options including active participant-based events, spectator-based sporting events, religious events, events with environmental/ cultural/heritage themes, music-based events, special interest events and business events. As with the development of existing events, event tourism organizations need to be mindful of the need to ensure that new events are adequately resourced if they are to have the best chance of long-term survival. This being the case, it may be desirable for organizations involved in event tourism to limit their support to only a few new events.

General considerations in event tourism strategy selection

In making decisions about what event tourism strategy pursue, it can be useful to think in terms of what 'portfolio' (or mix) of events (festivals, sporting competitions, business events, etc.) is likely to deliver the required benefits for a destination from event tourism. A useful first step in this regard is to rate events (existing, new and events for which bids are proposed) – using available data and professional judgement – against established criteria. A simple 1 (low) to 5 (high) rating system (Figure 3.4) could be employed for this purpose. If appropriate, a weighting could also be applied to each criterion, so the final numeric value associated with each event would be a product of the extent to which it was viewed as meeting each criterion, multiplied by the importance of that criterion.

A useful approach to thinking about the 'mix' of events at a destination is to view them from a hierarchical perspective. Using this approach, events with high tourism value and the capacity to progress many of an event tourism body's goals would appear at the top, while those with lower tourism value and limited ability to progress the organization's goals would be placed at the bottom. Such a hierarchy is commonly represented as a pyramid, as illustrated by the example of Events Tasmania's hierarchical model of events (Figure 3.5). Additionally, such models also provide insights into where 'gaps' may be in an area's current event portfolio. This model also notes the varying roles that Events Tasmania will play in different types of event.

Implementation of an event tourism strategy

Once an event strategy has been selected, the next step is for the organization(s) concerned to implement it by undertaking actions appropriate to its/their charter. This being the case, such actions may vary, from the provision of advice and marketing support up to the actual development and conduct of new events. The following section seeks to identify and broadly categorize the full range of actions that organizations directly involved in event tourism development might engage.

Financial support

Financial support can be in the form of grants, sponsorship and equity.

Event Name	Criterion 1	Criterion 2	Criterion 3	Criterion 4	Total
A	1	2	3	4	10
B	1	4	5	5	15
C	2	4	3	1	10

Figure 3.4 Event rating scale

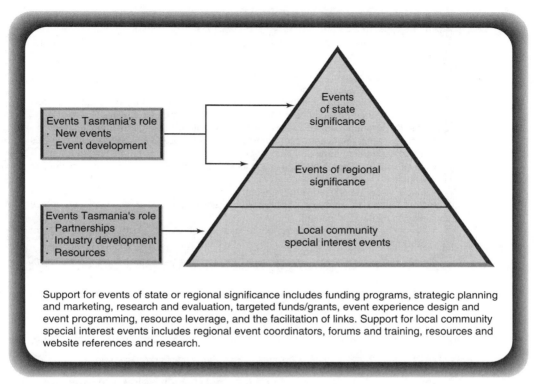

Figure 3.5 Events Tasmania hierarchical model of events
Source: Events Tasmania (2003b), p. 40

Grants

Grants are a common means of providing support for events that are deemed to have tourism potential. EventScotland, for example, operates two programmes, focusing on major and regional events. The Major International Events Programme can provide funding from one up to three years to support existing events with potential to grow into world-class events; identifies and bids for events that could be staged in Scotland; and helps create events that can take place annually or bi-annually, with the requirement that EventScotland's funding must add value to the event (EventScotland, 2005a). The Regional Events Programme aims to help develop a portfolio of events in towns and cities outside Glasgow and Edinburgh by providing funds to support additional elements to an event or new activities designed to help events to grow. The resulting portfolio of events should:

- generate economic benefits for specific regions of Scotland
- attract visitors to a region from other parts of the country
- inspire and involve local communities
- enhance the profile and appeal of the host region.

With funds of £500 000 annually, the Regional Events Programme provides grants between £2000 and £25 000 to events that can demonstrate confirmed financial support of the local agencies, local passion and leadership, viable budget and realistic planning, the opportunity to build legacy and sustainability,

Potential or demonstrated capacity to increase tourist visitation, yield per visitor and length of visitor stay

- Relationship between the event and area's overall tourism development strategy, including its branding efforts
- Level of evident community/local government/business/tourism industry support and associated capacity of event to grow and become self-funding
- Event's current tourism packaging efforts, or potential for tourism packaging
- Timing – does the event occur outside peak visitor seasons when tourism services are already being used at a high level?
- Level and quality of business, financial, operational and marketing planning in evidence
- Media value associated with the event
- Contribution to strategic social, cultural, environmental or economic outcomes sought by the destination
- Existence of processes designed to evaluate the event, particularly its tourism outcomes

Figure 3.6 Common Grant selection criteria employed by event tourism organizations

the capacity to grow spectator and participants and measurable outcomes (EventScotland, 2005).

An increasing number of other event support agencies that are emerging across the UK and elsewhere are beginning to have similar schemes in partnership with local councils and regional tourist agencies (for example, with funding from the Leader + European funding, Scottish Borders Tourist Board Events Innovation Scheme coordinated support for development of new festivals and events). Some local councils and tourist agencies have also moved to create event tourism grant schemes. For example, the Wales Tourist Board developed the Event Marketing Support Scheme (Event Marketing Support Unit, 2002) and Tyndedale Council administers the tourism events grants scheme (Tynedale Council, 2003). These grants are commonly based on a range of criteria, such as those in Figure 3.6.

Grants may also be provided by event tourism bodies in the form of seed money to allow new events to be established, or for specific purposes, such as the conduct of a feasibility study to determine the viability of a proposed event. Grants can also be used as a form of incentive to conduct an event in a specific destination. Northern Ireland Events Company, for example, operates a major events grants scheme that supports events where the organizers have secured at least 50 per cent of the funding, the event is likely to achieve significant out of state media coverage in relevant markets and provide significant economic benefits to Northern Ireland (NIEC, 2005b). Through Belfast City Council's Sports Events Unit, local government also provides funding support for organizations conducting major sports events that attract high number of visiting spectators and participants (Belfast City Council, 2005b).

Sponsorship

Some event organizations act to directly sponsor events as a way of financially assisting them, and/or as a way of leveraging the opportunity presented by the event to brand their destination through such means as signage and other visual identification, publicity and advertising. For example, regional development agencies (RDAs) were the principal sponsors of the 2004 Tour of Britain with Northwest Development Agency, Yorkshire Forward, East Midlands Development Agency and Welsh Development Agency each investing £150 000 and London Development Agency investing £200 000 to sponsor the event when the race passed through their region (SIRC, 2005).

Equity

To facilitate the conduct of an event, a tourism event organization may act to directly invest in it. For example, the Manchester International Festival, a major new festival launching in 2007 – will be operated by Manchester International Festival Ltd. With a planned budget of £5 million, this event is being funded £2 million from Manchester City Council with further funds coming from Northwest Development Agency and the private sector (Higgins, 2004).

Ownership

Some event tourism bodies develop and produce events to stimulate visitation to their destination. They act in this way for a variety of reasons, including ensuring their charter is progressed without the need to rely on the private sector; to address a lack of local event management expertise; and to recognize an unwillingness on behalf of the private sector to take the financial risk involved in event creation and delivery. This may involve the establishment of a subsidiary company to own and operate the events on the organization's behalf. For example, Liverpool Culture Company was set up by Liverpool City Council to deliver the European Capital of Culture 2008 including events and the cultural programme before, during and after 2008 (Liverpool Culture Company, 2005a). Other event tourism and destination marketing organizations have also acted to establish and develop new events, including Northern Ireland Events Company, EventScotland and NewcastleGateshead.

Bid development and bid support services

As noted, bidding is the major focus of a number of event tourism organizations. Such organizations act to research, develop and make bids, and/or work with bidding bodies (such as sporting or professional associations) to facilitate the making of a bid (including the creation of a bid committee). Once a bid is won, however, the event tourism organization commonly plays little, if any, further role other than perhaps assisting to stimulate event attendance or to create an organizing committee.

Event sector development services

Event sector development services include research, training and education, and the establishment of partnerships and networks.

Research

Some tourism event organizations commission or undertake research on a range of event-related matters as a way of gaining information that will aid the development of individual events or the sector in general. Matters explored include trends in event visitor markets, developments in competitor destinations, visitor perceptions of the quality of event experiences (particularly those supported by the event organization concerned), event sector stakeholder viewpoints, event economic impacts and overall sector management practices. Regarding this last point, research can be insightful in assisting event agencies to develop programmes designed to build the events sector. Evidence for this can be found in Goh's (2003) study, which highlighted weaknesses in this area in the context of Irish festivals, specifically:

- 47 per cent of festivals have no data on their audiences
- 59 per cent of festivals do not provide training for their volunteers
- 23 per cent of festivals have no presence on the world wide web
- 58 per cent of festivals have no strategic plan.

Training and education

To promote best practice and continuous improvement, and by doing so assist in creating events that are sustainable in the longer term, some event tourism organizations undertake – or commission outside bodies to undertake – training in areas such as event project management, event marketing and general industry best practice. Some also maintain a resource base (electronic or textual) on which event organizers can draw for educational/training purposes, as well as conducting industry events such as conferences.

Partnerships and networks

A range of opportunities exist for event tourism organizations to establish partnerships and networks both within the events sector, between the events sector and outside bodies. Forming links between individual events and other organizations that have the potential to enhance the attractiveness of events to visitor markets can be driven via the use of grants, for example. This can be done by explicitly favouring applications that demonstrate links with, for example, tourism bodies and cultural institutions, such as museums, heritage organizations, art galleries and community arts organizations. Other ways in which such links can be established include purposefully arranging formal and informal meetings and functions, involving members of the events industry, tourism organizations and the general business community. Once networks are established, they can serve a variety of purposes – for example, facilitating the sharing of information and expertise, expanding access to sponsorship opportunities and developing partnerships that will assist in the development of tourist markets.

Event tourism organizations may also find that they have much to gain by communicating their strategies to a range of public and private sector organizations, thus encouraging dialogue that may lead to the identification of opportunities to progress common agenda. Government departments associated with the arts, sport and regional development, for example, may all see opportunities to further their goals through an association with one or more event tourism bodies.

Coordination

Event tourism bodies can play a range of coordination roles. These roles include developing an event calendar to reduce event clashes and providing a 'one-stop shop' at which event organizers can obtain relevant permissions and clarify government policies and procedures of relevance. Given that a range of government bodies may be involved in the delivery of any one event, event tourism organizations can also act to establish coordination and consultation protocols between different government departments and agencies, as well as assisting events to 'navigate' their way through legislative and compliance issues.

Event/destination promotion services

To assist organizations (such as sporting bodies and professional associations) in their efforts to host specific events, event tourism organizations, depending on their charter, may provide a range of marketing collateral. Such collateral may include brochure shells, giveaways, videos/DVDs highlighting destination attractions, event facilities and services, and posters. Additionally, such organizations may seek to facilitate the conduct of events by, for example:

- providing information to organizations seeking to conduct events on a destination's event-related facilities and services,
- hosting familiarization tours and site visits (by event organizing committees),
- assisting with the preparation of event programmes and pre- and post-event tours,
- acting as a liaison between government and civic authorities,
- assisting in stimulating attendance at events via public relations activities and direct mail.

For example, Glasgow Convention Bureau offers a range of free services, outlined in Figure 3.7.

VisitBritain, as part of its promotional role, seeks to 'concentrate on those individuals within companies, organizations and specialist agencies who decide upon (or who have a strong influence upon), the choice of destination for business events such as corporate meetings, incentives and international conferences'. The second aim is 'to persuade business visitors to extend their stays, to bring partners or to visit the country again, as leisure visitors' (British Tourism Authority, 2005, p. 2). This second aim is referred to as business extenders, discussed later. To progress these aims, VisitBritain has developed promotional material for the business tourism industry, for example, including Meeting Britain newsletter, represents business tourism industry at major international trade shows and is an active member of the

- **Prepares** effective bid documents tailored specifically to your requirements, outlining essential and appropriate characteristics of the destination.
- **Works** closely with venues and hotels, checking availability and facility requirements and provides a conference accommodation booking service.
- **Arranges** site and familiarization visits to facilitate orientation and assessment and introduce clients to key personnel.
- **Offers** a free tendering service, collecting quotations and assisting in developing the conference package.
- **Sources** Professional Conference Organizers to service all your conference needs, from registration to programming.
- **Identifies** Destination Management Companies that will deliver pre- and post-tour itineraries and produce support materials.
- **Recognizes** the economic value of conferences by processing applications for civic recognition.

Figure 3.7 Services Offered by Glasgow Convention Bureau
Source: Redmond (2005)

Business Tourism Partnership (www.businesstourismpartnership.com), the organization drawing together the national tourism boards, and main industry associations.

Other

Other roles that event tourism organizations may play include: assisting in the development of business, marketing and risk management plans; providing advice on the negotiation of television rights and merchandizing strategies; and lobbying on behalf of the sector on matters relating to new infrastructure development, for example.

Evaluation of an event tourism strategy

Evaluation is fundamental to the success of any strategy. At the destination level, the broad goals that have been set for event tourism, and the objectives associated with those goals, will form the basis of any evaluation that takes place. The collection and interpretation of information is central to this process, with data on visitor flows associated with event tourism being of particular importance. In the context of business tourism in the United Kingdom, for example, data are available from a variety of sources, including STAR UK (drawing together data from VisitBritain and other national tourism bodies), regional tourism agencies/boards, and the Business Tourism Partnership. International bodies, such as the International Congress and Convention Association (ICCA), Union of International Associations (UIA) and the Meeting Professionals International (MPI) Foundation, also conduct research that relates to the UK's comparative performance in this area. ICCA (2004, 2005), for example, provides the following useful data on the UK's recent business tourism performance:

- In terms of association meetings per country, the United Kingdom is fifth in the global rankings in 2004, after occupying 3rd position in 2002. The USA is ranked number one, followed by Germany (up from 4th to 2nd), Spain (down from 2nd to 3rd), France (up from 6th to 4th) and the United Kingdom 5th in terms of the number of association meetings held in 2004.
- In terms of market share by continent, Europe remains number one with 60 per cent of the market, compared to all other regions. Asia's market share rose from 16 per cent in 2003 to 18 per cent in 2004.
- In terms of international association meetings per city, the market is lead by Barcelona, followed by Vienna, Singapore, Berlin and Hong Kong. London was down from 18th to 19th in the rankings in 2004 with only 44 meetings.

In addition to whole-of-destination assessments of event tourism performance in the context of specific types of event, or events in general, each organization involved in an area's event tourism development should have its own goals. To conform to the basic model of event tourism strategic planning used in this chapter, these goals should link directly to the destination's overall event tourism goals. Such individual assessments should also serve to 'build' towards an overall picture of a destination's event tourism performance, which can then be used to form the basis for future strategic decisions regarding event tourism development.

Tourism events and regional development

While the focus of discussion regarding event tourism is often on cities, regions or countries, many regions and towns have acknowledged the benefits that can potentially flow from event tourism, and have actively sought to engage in it. Local government in many regional areas is actively showing support for such efforts, being keen for communities to reap the economic and other benefits associated with events. Tynedale Council, for example, has recently established its own system of 'tourism event' grants (Tynedale Council, 2003).

Chapter summary

For destinations ranging in size from small towns to countries, event tourism is increasingly becoming a key aspect of their overall tourism development efforts. In this chapter, a basic event tourism strategic planning model has been proposed that seeks to bring a measure of structure and discipline to this process. This model is based on an understanding of both perspectives – that of event tourism stakeholders and that of a destination's overall tourism goals and strategy. The first step in the model is a detailed situational analysis, which leads to the establishment of event tourism goals. These goals are then progressed through an organizational structure created for this purpose. Ideally, such a structure would involve the establishment of a single organization with responsibility for the area, or the allocation of such responsibility to an existing body. In the absence of such a body, other options – such as regular meetings between key organizations in the area – can be used with similar intent. Once a structure is in place, strategic options need to be considered, and a strategy decided that is likely to involve multiple organizations. In the pursuit of this strategy, various tools and practices can be employed, including bidding, the provision of promotional and financial support, and activities designed to generally develop the event sector. How successful these practices are in progressing a destination's event tourism strategy and its associated goals needs to be assessed at both the destination level and the level of those organizations with a major input into the event tourism development process. Information gained from this process can then be used to refine future event tourism development efforts.

Questions

1. Discuss the value of having a clear understanding of a destination's overall tourism strategy before embarking on the process of creating an event tourism strategy.
2. List and discuss three goals that a destination may seek to progress through the development of an event tourism strategy.
3. What types of non-tourism goals might a destination seek to achieve by expanding its focus on event tourism?
4. In the absence of a single body with responsibility for directing a destination's event tourism efforts, what approaches might be used to ensure a coordinated response to this task?
5. Briefly discuss the three broad strategic options available to destinations seeking to expand visitation through the use of events.

6. What is meant by the term 'destination event portfolio'? What value does this concept have from an event tourism strategy perspective?
7. What types of action might bodies with a major involvement in event tourism consider taking to develop the event sector in their destination?
8. Briefly discuss how events can play a role in branding a destination.
9. Draw a basic event tourism strategic planning model. Briefly describe each step in this model.
10. Discuss the various forms that grants from event tourism bodies can take.

Case study 3.1

EventScotland

In 2003, Scotland released a major events strategy titled 'Competing on an international stage', with a vision of becoming a leading events destination by 2015. The strategy included establishing a central body, EventScotland, to provide coordination and leadership in securing major events. The following extract explains the strategy's background and aims.

Introduction

We announced in *Programme for Government* in 2001 that the Executive would seek to develop a major events strategy for Scotland. This builds on the work that we have done to secure the Ryder Cup for Scotland in 2014 and our bid to host the European Football Championships in 2008 (Euro, 2008).

Why develop a major events strategy?

Scotland is an event-rich country and these events serve to boost our international profile and image. World-class cultural and sporting events such as the Edinburgh Festivals or the Open Golf Championships (which we host on average at least every second year) are instantly associated with Scotland in many people's eyes. They demonstrate that we are a dynamic and modern country capable of making an impact – and delivering – on an international stage. They also serve to attract hundreds of thousands of visitors every year to our shores who come to experience events that are uniquely Scottish.

The staging of major sports events here also provides inspiration and ambition and encourages participation and competition at all levels. Governing bodies of sport and other sport organizations benefit from increased exposure and influence. Athletes, coaches, officials and volunteers benefit from preparation programmes and the competitions themselves. Our athletes have the opportunity to compete under home conditions in front of home support and young people in Scotland are inspired to participate and excel.

There are many organizations and agencies in both the public and private sectors responsible at present for delivering successful events in Scotland. Although each one can deliver success individually we have found overwhelming agreement with the view that, in order to fulfil our potential and compete on an international stage, Scotland must develop a coordinated and strategic approach to major events.

Proposals for Scotland's major events strategy

Based on (an) assessment of our current approach, we have identified the four key areas for action:

- building Scotland's international image by maximizing the benefits of our existing successes and our 'icon' events, including the Edinburgh Festivals and the Open Golf,
- developing a portfolio of sporting and cultural events to underpin Scottish tourism and Scottish brand messages, to strengthen our sporting and cultural environments and to attract visitors to areas of Scotland with spare accommodation capacity, particularly outside traditional high season,
- coordinating existing activity and exploring opportunities to enhance existing events being taken forward by public and private sector partners,
- building a centre of knowledge and expertise on securing, promoting and delivering events to secure Scotland's reputation as a premier events destination by 2015.

EventScotland

In order to deliver these objectives, a new body will be established to give central coordination and leadership to the drive to secure major events for Scotland. Called EventScotland, this will be a tight organization and its main task will be to work in partnership with public bodies, including those represented on the steering group and private sector events organizers, to deliver a portfolio of events in Scotland. This body would build on the success of existing events such as the Edinburgh Festivals and the Open Golf Championships and on the experience gained during the Ryder Cup and Euro 2008 bids, and it would seek out opportunities for hosting major events, working closely with other players. This new body will be small, flexible and arms length from [the] Government.

In detail, EventScotland's main tasks will be to:

(a) share information on the size, date and nature of existing and proposed events in Scotland. It will make available detailed information to partner organizations with an interest in events and provide information to the public through platforms such as visitscotland.com. As well as direct relationships with key players, an element of this function may include the establishment of a commercially secure 'extranet' available to partners. The provision of a centrally held events calendar for Scotland is an essential pre-requisite if we are to achieve our aim of becoming a foremost events destination by 2015. EventScotland will develop with partners the protocols necessary to ensure that this often commercially sensitive information can be gathered and shared appropriately to the benefit of all.

(b) assess, evaluate and determine which events EventScotland should support. This will include an economic, social and environmental appraisal of proposed events to determine whether they fit agreed priorities and how much – if any – EventScotland funding should be provided to it. EventScotland will work closely with public sector partners who already fund events to develop a common approach to event appraisal.

EventScotland will prioritize:

- events which highlight and capitalize on the unique visual appeal and landscape of Scotland,
- events which showcase Scottish culture and sport,
- events which Scotland can 'own', nurture, develop and (on occasion) export,
- events which require little or no infrastructure additions, or which tie to planned infrastructure development,

- events which underpin the priorities of the Scottish Executive and other public sector agencies involved in major event organization,
- events which have an intrinsic appeal to Scots,
- events which highlight and promote the unique appeal and proposition of individual destinations (city, town or rural),
- events which focus on quiet times of the year,
- events which offer a direct economic return on investment through tourism, promotion of Scottish business or other means,
- events which stimulate a sense of pride in the local population,
- events which are sustainable and which are accessible to a wide range of communities and groups,
- events which can secure favourable broadcast and print media coverage in key tourism/ investment markets,
- events of an international, prestige and leading status,
- events capable of generating new and/or complementary initiatives within the same sector at national, regional and grassroots levels,
- events which offer commercial and showcase opportunities for Scottish businesses,
- events which are available, achievable and affordable.

(c) stipulate conditions to govern use of the public money available to it. The role of EventScotland will be to add value to events rather than to replace or duplicate existing funding sources. It will require stringent evaluation of events to assess their success and it will develop these detailed criteria in conjunction with the other public sector organizations that already fund events. It will develop a methodology to ensure that these assessments and checks can happen quickly in order to maintain the commercial competitiveness of EventScotland.

(d) lead and support partners in securing new events for Scotland. This will involve identifying events available internationally which Scotland should bid for; building the appropriate partnerships to deliver successful bids; and interacting with event owners to bring these events to Scotland. Where appropriate, EventScotland will support other partners (local authorities, sports governing bodies or event organizers, for example) rather than lead a bid itself. This is some of the most commercially driven work which EventScotland would undertake, requiring it to put together quickly private/public sector funding or underwriting packages, contract hotel accommodation and sponsors and secures Ministerial endorsement where necessary.

(e) help to develop and improve existing events in order to maximize their benefits across the whole of Scotland. This again is commercially driven work involving, for example, identifying sponsors to work with existing event owners to extend their current activities, or working to develop satellite events in Scotland associated with existing successful events.

(f) develop and maintain a rolling portfolio of events in line with strategic objectives (increasing visitor numbers in areas/times of spare capacity; promoting Scottish tourism/Scotland the brand key messages; developing events to address health, education and closing the gap issues). This area of work will require in the first instance a close working relationship with the executive and other public sector partners in order to maintain a portfolio that closely reflects Executive objectives.

(g) develop a centre of knowledge and expertise to underpin and inform the above activity. It would learn from, codify and make available information about the funding, promotion and delivery of existing successful events. It would also learn from and make available information about the lessons learned from bidding for events including the Ryder Cup and Euro 2008.

(h) promote and communicate EventScotland as the hub of Scotland's major events strategy to partners, Ministers, the Scottish public and the international events audience.

(i) be accountable to Ministers and demonstrate an effective link to secure Ministerial endorsements as required. The clear and demonstrable support of Government is an essential element of a successful international events organization.
Source: Scottish Executive, 2002.

Questions

1. What was the rationale for the establishment of EventScotland by the Scottish Government?
2. Briefly describe the key roles that EventScotland is charged with performing.
3. Briefly discuss how EventScotland will determine which events it will support.
4. What criteria would you use to measure success of an organization such as EventScotland? Based on your criteria, how does EventScotland compare? Conduct research to obtain facts and figures to support your answer.

Case study 3.2

Event Denmark

At the end of 2003, the Danish Government announced five new steps designed to improve cooperation between business – including the tourism industry – and the nation's cultural life. Following on from this announcement, the Secretary of Culture (Mr Brian Mikkelsen) and the Secretary of Business and Economy (Mr Bendt Bendtsen) agreed on a plan designed to professionalize the development, management, marketing and evaluation of international events in Denmark. In support of seeking such an outcome, they claimed that:

The staging of many cultural and sports events is positive; it is profitable business, it supports the image of the region and the nation, and it is an asset for tourism, for the local society and commerce, as well as for the national economy (Blicher-Hansen, 2003).

Many other countries (for example, the Netherlands, Scotland and Australia) had made similar observations and subsequently created specialist event agencies as a way of focusing efforts on driving visitation through these means.

Responsibility for progressing this plan fell to the national Danish Tourist Board (DTB), which subsequently developed a strategy embracing both the cultural and tourism aspects of events, and created a separate event division within the DTB called Event Denmark. In developing this strategy, the DTB acknowledged that international air travel would continue to grow despite terrorist acts. Additionally, it was believed that in Europe the number of short holiday breaks taken was likely to increase, fuelled in large measure by airline competition. Such competition was making a long weekend city break trip a possible and regular monthly 'habit'. The DTB also acknowledged, since many Europeans were already seasoned travellers, that the value of simply promoting a destination might no longer be enough to attract visitors for a second or subsequent time. Events, therefore, and their associated one-off uniqueness had a significant role to play in driving future repeat visitor connection with people. This would be achieved through an association with an individual's cultural interests, whether a Magritte art exhibition in Paris, a unique production of Bizet's *Carmen i Sevilla* in Spain, or a performance of Hans Christian Andersen's fairytales in authentic surroundings in Denmark.

With these thoughts in mind, and with a desire to attract and develop more international events in Denmark, the DTB developed its event tourism strategy, giving responsibility for its implementation to the newly created Event Denmark. The following are the main aspects of this strategy:

- In the short term, generate a direct tourism effect – measured in terms of the number of visitors and their spending, level of immediate media exposure and awareness of the destination.
- In the medium term, support destination marketing in relation to the branding of Denmark. Branding themes that events could reinforce include the uniqueness of Danish culture (for example music, ballet, food, design and architecture), sporting opportunities (for example golf, football, sailing and cycling), historic traditions and the uniqueness of the natural environment.
- In the longer term, enhance the overall profile of Denmark as a unique visitor destination to position the country as a 'must go' destination — one that is on the cutting edge in many areas and one that offers unique experiences.

In working through its strategy, the DTB sought to identify existing events that embraced its requirements. Key considerations were that such events needed to be:

- open to the public,
- unique, not something that could easily be experienced elsewhere,
- high quality in content,
- appealing to an international audience,
- strongly associated with Danish traditions and/or national values,
- capable and open to marketing themselves internationally,
- accessible via such means as online ticketing facilities,
- able to use surplus tourism services (particularly accommodation) during periods of low seasonal demand,
- managed in a professional manner,
- designed to ensure that they were environmentally sustainable,
- preferably conducted on an annual basis.

Once these key considerations were identified, Event Denmark would arrange for these events to be promoted to international markets in a variety of ways – for example, via inbound tour operators, specialized tour operators, overseas travel agents and international online event booking agencies. Additionally, Event Denmark would aid their promotional efforts in such markets by advising them on how to gain exposure on global event listing websites, and by conducting public relations efforts through the DTB's overseas tourist offices and Denmark's embassy network around the world.

For further information about Event Denmark, please visit: www.eventdenmark.dk.

Source: adapted from Blicher-Hansen (2003).

Questions

1. What role do events play in achieving tourism strategy?
2. Discuss the criteria that Danish Tourist Board has developed to identify which events they will support. For example, are these clear and achievable? Are there other criteria that you would implement?
3. What lessons can be learned by from the Event Denmark approach by countries considering formalizing their event support at a national level?
4. What differences (if any) do you see between the responsibilities of Event Denmark and EventScotland?

Section Two

Event strategy

Event strategy begins with the event concept. Detailed planning, inspirational leadership, sound human resource management and dynamic marketing are all key elements of successful event management. This part of the book examines the conceptualizing and planning functions in some detail, and looks at the formation, leadership and training of event teams. It looks also at the event marketing process, and details strategic methods that event managers can employ to market their events competitively.

Chapter 4

Conceptualizing the event

Learning Objectives

After studying this chapter you will be able to:

■ identify the range of stakeholders in an event
■ describe and balance the overlapping and conflicting needs of stakeholders
■ describe the role of government, corporate and community sectors in events
■ discuss trends and issues in society that affect events
■ understand the role of sponsorship in events
■ develop partnerships with sponsors and the media
■ identify the unique elements and resources of an event
■ understand the process of developing an event concept.

Introduction

A crucial element in the creation of an event is the understanding of the event environment. The context in which the event is to take place will be a major determinant of its success. In order to understand this environment, the event manager must first identify the major players – the stakeholders and the people and organizations likely to be affected by it. The event manager must then examine the objectives of these major players – what each of them expects to gain from the event, and what forces acting on them are likely to affect their response to the event. Once this environment is understood, the event manager is then in the best position to marshal the creative elements of the event, and to shape and manage them to achieve the best outcomes for the event. This chapter examines the key stakeholders in events, and outlines some of the processes that event managers can use to produce creative and successful events.

Stakeholders in events

As discussed in the previous chapters, events have become professionalized and are increasingly attracting the involvement and support of governments and the corporate sector. One aspect of this

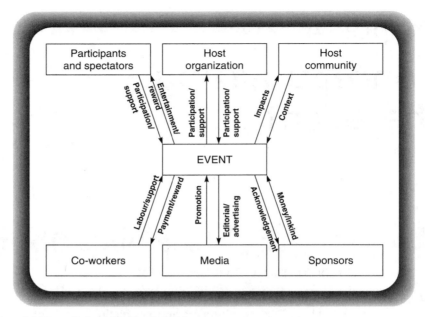

Figure 4.1 The relationship of stakeholders to events

growth is that events are now required to serve a multitude of agendas. It is no longer sufficient for an event to meet just the needs of its audience. It must also embrace a plethora of other requirements, including government objectives and regulations, media requirements, sponsors' needs and community expectations. People and organizations with a legitimate interest in the outcomes of an event are known as stakeholders. The successful event manager must be able to identify the range of stakeholders in an event and manage their individual needs, which will sometimes overlap and conflict (Figure 4.1). As with event impacts, the event will be judged by its success in balancing the competing needs, expectations and interests of a diverse range of stakeholders. For example, UK Sport (1998) identify that a list of key stakeholders for major sporting events would include athletes, the British Olympic Association, broadcasters, coaches, event organizers, the general public, international federations, local authorities, the media, national government, national sports governing bodies, officials, sponsors, sports councils and volunteers.

Mal Hemmerling, architect of the Australian Formula One Grand Prix in Adelaide and former Chief Executive of SOCOG, describes the task of the contemporary event manager as follows (Hemmerling, 1997):

> So when asked the question 'what makes an event successful?', there are now numerous shareholders that are key components of modern major events that are looking at a whole range of different measures of success. What may have been a simple measure for the event organiser of the past, which involved the bottom line, market share, and successful staging of the event are now only basic criteria as the measures by other investors are more aligned with increased tourism, economic activity, tax revenues, promotional success, sustained economic growth, television reach, audience profiles, customer focus, brand image, hospitality, new business opportunities and investment to name but a few.

The host organization

Events have become so much a part of our cultural milieu that they can be generated by almost any part of the government, corporate and community sectors, as illustrated in Table 4.1.

Government sector

Governments create events for a range of reasons, including the social, cultural, tourism and economic benefits generated by events. Some government departments have an events brief as part of their delivery of services, for example, the Department of Culture, Media and Sport. Others, including 'arms-length' government organizations, generate events as a means to achieve other objectives – VisitBritain to increase and extend tourist visits, the arts councils to preserve cultures and encourage tolerance and diversity, and Department for Trade and Industry (DTI) to assist industry and generate jobs. Many other departments are involved in one-off events to promote specific goods and services such as health promotions, Age Concern Week and National Science Week. Such events may celebrate special days such as Remembrance Sunday, St Patrick's Day or World AIDS Day. These events are often characterized by free entry and wide accessibility, and form part of the public culture.

Corporate sector

The corporate sector is involved in events at a number of levels. Companies and corporations may sponsor events in order to promote their goods and services in the marketplace. They may partner government departments in the presentation of events that serve common or multiple agendas. On other occasions, companies may create their own events in order to launch new products, increase sales or enhance their corporate image. These events, although they may still be characterized by free entry, may be targeted at specific market segments rather than at the general public.

Within the corporate sector there are also entrepreneurs whose business is the staging or selling of events. These include sports or concert promoters who present ticketed events for profit, and conference organizers/event management companies or industry associations mounting conferences or exhibitions for the trade or public, for example, wine shows, equipment exhibitions or medical conferences. Media organizations often become partners in other people's events, but also stage events for their own promotional purposes or to create programme content. Examples are radio stations promoting their identity through concerts, newspapers promoting fun runs or television networks presenting New Year celebrations live to air.

Community sector

Other events emanate from the community sector, serving a wide variety of needs and interests. These may include local sporting events, service club fundraisers, car club meets, local arts and craft shows – the spectrum is as wide as the field of human interest and endeavour. All these sources combine to create the wonderful tapestry of events that fill our leisure time and enrich our lives.

Table 4.1 Event typology

Event generators	Types of events
Government sector	
Central Government	Civic celebrations and commemorations
Public space authorities e.g. National Trust, National Park Authorities	Public entertainment, festivals, leisure and recreation events
Tourism e.g. VisitBritain, VisitScotland, Northern Ireland Tourist Board, Wales Tourist Board, regional tourism through Regional Development Agencies	Festivals, special interest and lifestyle events, destination promotions
Visitor & Convention Bureaus	Meetings, incentives, conferences and exhibitions
Arts e.g. Arts Council England, Scottish Arts Council, Arts Council of Northern Ireland, Arts Council of Wales, Regional Arts Councils	Arts festivals, cultural events, touring programmes, theatre, themed art exhibitions
Sport e.g. UK Sport, Sport England, Scottish Sports Council, Sports Council for Northern Ireland, Sport Council for Wales	Sporting events, hosting of national and international events
Economic development e.g. EventScotland, Northern Ireland Events Company, Regional Development Agencies	Focus on events with industry development and job creation benefits
Local government e.g. City Councils	Community events, local festivals and fairs
Corporate sector	
Companies and corporate organizations	Promotions, product launches, incentives, corporate hospitality, corporate entertainment and image building sponsorships
Industry associations	Industry promotions, trade fairs/exhibitions, seminars, training, conferences
Gaming and racing e.g. Racecourse Holdings Trust (owners of Aintree, Epsom, Newmarket)	Race meetings and carnivals
Entrepreneurs	Ticketed sporting events, concerts and exhibitions
Media	Media promotions e.g. concerts, fun runs, appeals
Community sector	
Clubs and societies	Special interest groups e.g. Flower festivals, car shows, traction engine rallies
Charities	Charity events and fundraisers

Types of host organization

Whether events emanate from the corporate, government or community sectors will determine the nature of the host organization. If the host is from the corporate sector, it is likely to be a company, corporation or industry association. The event manager may be employed directly by the host organization, or on a contract basis with the organization as the client. If the host is from the government sector, the host organization is likely to be a government or council department. Again the event manager may be a direct employee, or a contractor if the event is outsourced. If the host is from the community sector, the host organization is more likely to be a club, society or committee, with a higher volunteer component in the organization.

Whatever the host organization, it is a key stakeholder in the event, and the event manager should seek to clarify its goals in staging the event. These will often be presented in a written brief as part of the event manager's job description or contract. Where they are not, it will be worthwhile spending some time to clarify these goals and put them in a written form as a reference point for the organization of the event, and a guideline for the evaluation of its eventual success.

The host community

Event managers need to have a good grasp and understanding of the broad trends and forces acting on the wider community, as these will determine the operating environment of their events. The mood, needs and desires of the community will determine its receptiveness to event styles and fashions. Accurately gauging and interpreting these is a basic factor in the conceptualization of successful events.

Among the current significant forces acting on the community are globalization and technology, which are combining to make the world seem both smaller and more complex. These forces are impacting on almost every aspect of our lives, including events. Giddens (1990, p. 64) defines globalization as, 'the intensification of worldwide social relations which link distinct localities in such a way that local happenings are shaped by events occurring many miles away and vice versa'.

This process is speeded up by technology and the media, which have the power to bring significant local events to a worldwide audience, overcoming the barriers of national boundaries and cultural differences. This is exemplified by the global television coverage of major sporting events. World championships and mega-events such as the Olympic Games and World Cup Football, calendar events such as the Grand National, The Championships (Wimbledon) and the FA Cup Final, and even New Year celebrations and the result of bidding for mega-events are beamed instantly to live audiences throughout the world, giving them previously unimagined coverage and immediacy.

As global networks increasingly bring the world into our living rooms, the question arises of how local cultures can maintain their own uniqueness and identity in the face of global homogenization. International arts festivals increasingly draw from the same pool of touring companies to produce similar programmes. Local festivals and celebrations must increasingly compete with international product, and the raised expectations of audiences accustomed to streamlined television production. The challenge for many events is how to function in this increasingly global environment whilst expressing the uniqueness of local communities and addressing their specific interests and concerns.

Globalization is also impacting on corporate events as companies increasingly plan their marketing strategies, including their event components, on a global level.

This has resulted in some British event companies expanding internationally – for example, World Event Management – or taking over, merging with or being bought out by overseas companies in an attempt to create networks that can serve the international needs of their clients – for example, Jack Morton Worldwide, Euro RSCG Skybridge Group and United Business Media. This approach sometimes comes unstuck, as different markets in, say, New York, Sydney and Hong Kong reflect different event needs and audience responses. However, the forces of globalization are likely to lead to an increasing standardization of the corporate event product and market.

Simultaneously, the all-pervasive Internet and advances in information technology are increasing the availability and technological sophistication of events. For example, live broadcasts from music concerts and dance events are relayed instantly through the Internet to a global market. Madonna's concert at the Brixton Academy in November 2000 had a live audience of only 3500, but was 'webcast' to millions through the Internet, made possible by a £30 million sponsorship deal with Microsoft's MSN. Basing his forecast on projections by leading futurists and trends in the event management industry, Goldblatt (2000, p. 8) predicts '24 hour, seven day per week event opportunities for guests who desire to forecast, attend, and review their participation in an event'. He also predicts that events will eventually become 'totally automated enabling event professionals to significantly expand the number of simultaneous events being produced using fewer human staff' (Goldblatt, 2000, p. 8). As a counter-trend, Goldblatt (2000, p. 3) also points out that 'with the advance of technology individuals are seeking more "high touch" experiences to balance the high tech influences in their lives. Events remain the single most effective means of providing a high touch experience'.

Event managers must be aware of these trends, and learn to operate in the new global environment. Paradoxically, live events may increasingly become the means by which communities confirm their own sense of place, individuality and cultural uniqueness.

Involving the host community

In addition to the wider general community, events have a specific host community which impacts greatly on the success or failure of the event. This can be the geographical community where the event is located, or a community of interest from which the event draws its participants and spectators. Many researchers (Getz, 2005; Goldblatt and Perry, 2002; Jago, Chalip, Brown, Mules and Ali, 2002) have recognized the importance of the host community being involved in and 'owning' the event, which in turn emits positive messages to visitors. For example, the extensive involvement of volunteers during the Sydney Olympics developed community links and harnessed support for the event, which contributed to the positive atmosphere in the city during the games (Jago et al., 2002), with this experience similarly demonstrated at the 2002 Manchester Commonwealth Games (see case study in Chapter 6).

Many community members actively participate in events in their communities, and act as advocates on behalf of the event to potential participants. Pride London (formerly London Mardi Gras) and Manchester Pride, developed for the lesbian, gay, bi-sexual and transgender communities, are both examples of events that are fuelled by social activists committed to the goals of the event. Local participation and ownership of events is perhaps most visible in many local and regional events that continue to exist only because of the committed input of dedicated volunteers.

The host community may include residents, traders, lobby groups and public authorities such as council, transport, police, fire and ambulance services. The event manager should aim to identify community leaders and to consult them when planning of the event.

Councils may have certain requirements, such as licences (discussed in Chapter 11). For larger-scale events, the local authorities will generally call a meeting to include emergency services, environmental health, transport and the management team to discuss such matters as street closures, special access and parking arrangements (HSE, 1999).

If the event is large enough to impact significantly beyond the boundaries of the venue, a 'public authorities and residents' briefing may identify innovative ways to minimize the impact and manage the situation. Events held by Leeds City Council at Temple Newsam Park, Leeds, regularly attract upwards of 20 000 people to a wide programme of summer events, for example, Party in the Park (40–60 000 people) and Opera in the Park (40 000 people). Consultation with local community groups will ensure that the event is supported and its impacts minimized. With the increasing audience, the events have received some negative publicity in recent years due to the impact that these events have on the local community, including traffic disruption, but also the effect of litter, visitors trampling gardens and damaging the local environment.

Host communities have past experience of different events, and event managers can draw on this knowledge to ensure an event's success. In Manchester, local and sporting authorities consciously used major occasions and trial events, such as the Aqua Pura Commonwealth Games Trials and events across other venues as practice runs for the Commonwealth Games, with event organizers, public transport and public authorities working together to trial operations and venues and refine solutions.

In addition to formal contact with authorities, the event manager should listen out for the all-important rumour-mill that can often make or break the host community's attitude to the event, sometimes manifesting itself in commentary within local media. In the summer of 1999, many events established to celebrate the eclipse in and around Cornwall were not as successful as predicted. Two events to be worse hit were the high-profile failure of the Lizard Festival, at a cost of £1.5 million, and the Total Eclipse Festival, which led to the subsequent bankruptcy of the event organizer, Harvey Goldsmith's Allied Entertainment Group. These events failed, according to the organizers, due to the negative publicity generated by local authorities that claimed the area would not be able to cope with the anticipated large influx of visitors. This was only heightened by the negative reports by the media and, it could be said, a lack of counter-publicity by the promoters. As a result of this, and weather forecasts predicting cloud cover for the day, many events were not as successful as planned. Initial information had predicted an influx of 5 million extra visitors to the area, however, only 450 000 eventually arrived (Gartside, 1999).

Another high-profile example of the effect that public opinion can have on events is the Love Parade, hosted in Leeds for the first time in July 2000. The event, originally planned to take place in Leeds City Centre, was at short notice transferred to Roundhay Park due to police concerns over the expected audience being higher than initially predicted. An estimated 250 000 people attended the event which was generally seen as running without major incident. However, many residents did not appreciate the effect of this number of people in the area, with the litter, broken glass and general inconvenience they caused. Campaigning by local politicians and some residents led to the event not returning to Leeds in 2001.

Sponsors

Recent decades have seen enormous increases in sponsorship and a corresponding change in how events are perceived by sponsors. There has been a shift by many large companies from seeing sponsorship as primarily a public relations tool generating community goodwill, to regarding it as an important part of the marketing mix. Successful major events are now perceived as desirable properties, capable of increasing brand awareness and driving sales. They also provide important opportunities for relationship-building through hosting partners and clients. Major businesses invest large amounts in event sponsorship, and devote additional resources to support their sponsorships in order to achieve corporate and sales goals.

BDS Sponsorship Ltd (2005), define sponsorship as, 'a business relationship between a provider of funds, resources or services and an individual, event or organization which offers in return some rights and association that may be used for commercial advantage in return for sponsorship investment'.

In order to attract sponsorships, event managers must offer tangible benefits to sponsors, and effective programmes to deliver them. Large companies such as Coca-Cola, Vodafone and NTL will receive hundreds of sponsorship applications each week, and only those events which have a close fit with corporate objectives and which demonstrate the ability to deliver benefits will be considered.

Sponsors as partners in events

It is important for event managers to identify exactly what sponsors want from an event, and what the event can deliver for them. Their needs may be different from those of the host organization or the event manager. Attendance numbers at the event, for example, may not be as important to them as the media coverage that it generates. It may be important for their chief executive to officiate, or to gain access to public officials in a relaxed atmosphere. They may be seeking mechanisms to drive sales, or want to strengthen client relationships through hosting activities. The event manager should take the opportunity to go beyond the formal sponsorship agreement, and treat the sponsors as partners in the event. Some of the best ideas for events can arise from such partnerships. Common agendas may be identified which support the sponsorship and deliver additional benefits to the event.

Barclays Bank was a major sponsor of the Ideal Home Show held at Earls Court, London, in April 2000. The sponsorship was supported with a national advertising campaign in television, radio and print media, and through branches of Barclays' Bank, with customers offered discounted tickets. The show was retitled 'The Daily Mail Ideal Home Show in Partnership with Barclays Bank', with the logo, all signage, branding, promotional material and main entrance kitted out in Barclays' corporate colour, blue (Litherland, 1997). The sponsorship helped to promote sales of mortgages for Barclays, as well as increasing the profile of the event. Likewise, in 1999, Guinness supported its sponsorship of the Rugby World Cup with a major campaign in pubs and retail outlets, a national advertising campaign through television, print media and the Internet, competitions and street sampling. The sponsorship clearly identified Guinness with the celebrations, and provided the event with an additional promotional outlet – so much so, few can remember other sponsors involved in the event. The role of sponsors in events, along with techniques for identifying, sourcing and managing sponsorships, is treated in more detail in Chapter 8.

Media

The expansion of the media, and the proliferation of delivery systems such as cable and satellite television and the Internet, have created a hunger for media products as never before. The global networking of media organizations, and the instant electronic transmission of media images and data, has made the global village a media reality. The Olympic Games were first televised on a trial basis during the 1936 Berlin Olympics, when the audience peaked at an estimated 162 000 viewers. When the 1948 London Olympics were televised, the world still relied largely on the physical transfer of film footage to disseminate the images of the Games across the UK and overseas. An estimated 500 000 people watched the sixty-four hours of coverage, mostly within 50 miles of London. This event proved to be the starting point of what is now seen as a major source of revenue – television rights fees (IOC, 2005). Indeed, Children in Need and Red Nose Day feature multidirectional television link-ups that enable the British to experience the fundraising simultaneously from a diverse range of locations and perspectives. The Opening Ceremony of the Winter Olympic Games in Nagano in 1998 featured a world choir singing together from five different locations on five continents, with 200 singers each in Sydney, New York, Beijing, Berlin and Cape Town, singing along with a 2000-strong choir at the main stadium. Global television networks followed New Year's Eve of the New Millennium around the world, making the world seem smaller and more immediate. When the 2004 Athens Olympic Games began, a simultaneous global audience estimated at 4 billion people was able to watch the event tailored to their own national perspectives, with a variety of cameras covering the event from every possible angle. Events such as the funeral of Diana, Princess of Wales, have become media experiences shared by millions as they are beamed instantly to a global audience. In Britain alone, the Princess's death attracted record media coverage.

This revolution in the media has, in turn, revolutionized events. Events now have a virtual existence in the media at least as powerful, sometimes more so, as in reality. The television audience may dwarf the live audience for a sports event or concert. Indeed, the event may be created primarily for the consumption of the television audience, what popular media refer to as 'event television' (Goldblatt, 2000). For example, the London Weekend Television *Audience with . . .* events, which feature a prominent celebrity performing and involving the audience, or the more recent trend of music concerts, such as Boyzone and Phil Collins, allowing television audiences to request their favourite songs to be performed. Events have much to gain from this development, including media sponsorships and the payment of media rights. Their value to commercial sponsors is often increased greatly by their media coverage and profile. However, the media often affects directly how events are conceptualized and presented, as in the case of One Day Cricket or Super League, and can have a profound effect on the relationship of the event with its live audience. For example, note the effect on the scheduling of Premier League football matches since the increased involvement of Sky TV. So far sports events have been the main winners (and losers!) from this increased attention by the media. The range of sports covered by television has increased dramatically and some sports, such as basketball, have gone from relative obscurity in the UK to high media profile largely because of their suitability for television production and programming.

The available media technology influences the way that live spectators experience the event, for example, with instant replays available on large screens at major sporting events. Increasingly, spectators' viewing capabilities are technologically enhanced to parallel those of people watching at home. Media interest in events is likely to continue to grow as their ability to provide community credibility and to attract commercial sponsors is realized. Sporting events, parades, spectacles, concerts and major public celebrations are event areas of potential interest to the media, and where the need to make good television is likely to influence the direction and marketing of events. The role of the media can vary from that of media sponsors to becoming full partners, or even producers of the event.

Whatever the role of the media, it is important for the event manager to consider the needs of the different media groups, and to consult them as important stakeholders in the event. Once the media are treated as potential partners, they have much to offer the event. The good media representative, like the event manager, is in search of the good idea or unusual angle. Together they might just dream up the unique approach that increases the profile of the event and provides value in turn to the media organization. The print media might agree to publish the event programme as editorial or as a special insert, or might run a series of lead-in stories, competitions or special promotions in tandem with sponsors. Radio or television stations might provide an outside broadcast, or might involve their on-air presenters as compères or special participants in the event. This integration of the event with the media provides greater reach and exposure to the event and, in turn, gives the media organization a branded association with the event.

Co-workers

The event team that is assembled to implement the event represents another of the key stakeholders. For any event to be truly effective, the vision and philosophy of the event must be shared by all the team, from key managers, talent and publicist, right through to the stage manager, crew, stewards and cleaners. No matter how big or small, the event team is the face of the event, and each is a contributor to its success or failure.

Goldblatt (1997, p. 129) describes the role of the event manager in this process.

The most effective event managers are not merely managers, rather, they are dynamic leaders whose ability to motivate, inspire others, and achieve their goals are admired by their followers. The difference between management and leadership is perhaps best characterised by this simple but effective definition: managers control problems, whereas leaders motivate others to find ways to achieve goals.

Most people have experienced events that went well overall, but were marred by some annoying detail. There are different ways of addressing such problems, but team selection and management are always crucial factors in avoiding these problems. The Disney organization has a system where the roles of performer, cleaner, security, etc. are merged in the concept of a team looking after the space. The roles tend to ride with the needs of the moment – when the parade comes through, its all hands on deck! The daily bulletin issued to all staff members reminds them that customers may only ever visit Disneyland once, and their impressions will depend forever on what they experience that day. This is a very positive philosophy that can be applied to all events.

Participants and spectators

Last but not least are the 'punters' on the day – the participants, spectators, visitors or audience for whom the event is intended and who ultimately vote with their feet for the success or failure of the event. The event manager must be mindful of the needs of the audience. These include their physical needs, as well as their needs for comfort, safety and security. Over and above these basic requirements is the need to make the event special – to connect to the emotions. A skilled event manager strives to make events meaningful, magical and memorable. Hemmerling (1997) describes the criteria by which spectators judge an event:

> *Their main focus is on the content, location, substance and operation of the event itself. For them the ease with which they can see the event activities, the program content, their access to food and drinks, amenities, access and egress etc., are the keys to their enjoyment. Simple factors such as whether or not their team won or lost, or whether they had a good experience at the event will sometimes influence their success measures. Secondary issues, such as mixing with the stars of the show, social opportunities, corporate hospitality and capacity to move up the seating chain from general admission to premium seating are all part of the evaluation of spectator success.*

Current technologies can assist managers in involving and servicing event participants. The Internet now plays a major role in events, with participants using it to research the event before their arrival, keep track during an extended event and re-live the highlights of the event after they have departed. With the advances in technology it is possible to monitor the number of visitors to a website, what pages they have viewed and where they came from. For example, monitoring by WebTrends Ltd revealed that the 2002 Manchester Commonwealth Games website received 8.6 million 'hits' on 31 July 2002 (Manchester, 2002, 2003), which was perhaps conservative compared to figures reported for the Rugby World Cup (44.5 million hits during the 2003 final) (Kaless, 2003), Olympics (peak traffic of 53 million hits during Athens 2004 Olympics) (Vignette, 2004) and FIFA World Cup (1.75 billion hits during the 2002 tournament in Korea and Japan, averaging 6.2 million unique visitors per day) (Ayaya, 2002). By understanding how psychographics and the event audience influence the event concept, event managers can tailor their events more adequately to meet the needs of participants. As discussed in greater detail in Chapter 7, this understanding also helps to accurately direct the marketing efforts by using channels specific to the audience – for example, the marketing of National Chess Week to promote the playing of chess in schools and clubs and to raise money for Barnardo's.

Creating the event concept

Goldblatt (2005) suggests the 'five Ws' as important questions to ask in developing the event concept. These are:

1. *Why* is the event being held? There must be compelling reasons that confirm the importance and viability of holding the event.
2. *Who* will be the stakeholders in the event? These include internal stakeholders, such as the board of directors, committee, staff and audience or guests, and external stakeholders such as media and politicians.
3. *When* will the event be held? Is there sufficient time to research and plan the event? Does the timing suit the needs of the audience and, if the event is outdoors, does it take the likely climatic conditions into account?
4. *Where* will the event be staged? The choice of venue must represent the best compromise between the organizational needs of the event, audience comfort, accessibility and cost.

5. *What* is the event content or product? This must match the needs, wants, desires and expectations of the audience, and must synergize with the why, who, when and where of the event.

An important part of developing the event will be identifying unique elements and resources, which can make the event special, and contribute to its imagery and branding. Millennium event celebrations in 1999 had to be special, particularly with the eyes of the world focused on locations across the globe. In London, celebrations focused along the banks of the River Thames and around Trafalgar Square. At the stroke of midnight and to the chimes of Big Ben, a live audience of over 1 million, together with a worldwide television audience of millions, watched as the river turned to flames and what was claimed to be the largest firework display ever to take place in the world, illuminated the sky above London.

Brainstorming

Once the parameters of the event have been set, it is desirable to brainstorm the concept of the event, letting the imagination soar and consulting with as many stakeholders as possible. A good way to do this is to meet with them individually at first, establishing relationships with them and allowing them to become comfortable with their role in the event. In these discussions ideas will arise, but the process should be acknowledged as exploratory, not yet seeking to reach fixed conclusions.

Once the diverse stakeholders are brought to the meeting table, the ideas will start to flow. This is a time to ignore restraints of practicality – of cost, scale or viability. That time will come. The task is to create and to dream, and no idea should be dismissed as too wild or impractical to consider. The goal is to discover the right idea, the one that resonates so that everyone recognizes it and is inspired by the challenge and the potential that it offers. This is where the skills of an event director come to the fore – the ability to draw out ideas, to synthesize content and eventually to construct a compromise. No matter how good the idea or how strong the support, eventually it must serve the objectives of the event and be deliverable within the available resources. With some good fortune, this idea may be achieved in a single meeting, but most often the process will take several meetings and weeks or months of patience and hard work. But the results will be worthwhile if a strong vision for the event emerges, one that is shared and supported by all stakeholders and in which they all have confidence and are committed to achieve. This process is at the very heart of creative event planning, and when it works well it is one of the joys of being in the business.

Evaluating the event concept

The brainstorming process may occasionally result in a single exciting concept that matches the needs of the event. However, it is most likely that it will produce a range of possible concepts that will need to be carefully evaluated to select the best concept or, in some cases, to combine a number of distinct ideas into a single concept. To determine the practicality and effectiveness of the chosen concept, it will be useful to undertake an evaluation of the event concept by what Shone and Parry (2004) describe as the 'screening process', also known as a feasibility study. This involves using marketing, operations and financial screens to determine the extent to which the event concept matches the needs of the event and the resources available to the event manager to implement it. The basic question is to what degree does the event concept serve the purpose or the overall objectives of the event? If the concept does not serve the required purpose, then no matter how attractive or exciting it may seem, it should be stored away and left, perhaps for another occasion.

The marketing screen

The first screen suggested by Shone and Parry (2004) is the marketing screen. This involves examining how the target audience of the event is likely to respond to the event concept and whether the concept will be inviting and attractive to its audience. To determine this, an environmental scanning process needs to be undertaken. This will help to determine whether the event concept resonates with current tastes and fashions and whether it is likely to be perceived as innovative and popular, or as ordinary and predictable. A good barometer will be the media response to the concept. If media representatives consider it to be of current interest, they are likely to become allies in the promotion of the event. If the media response is poor, then it will be difficult to promote interest and engage the audience.

For much of this assessment, event managers will need to rely on their own instincts and on testing the response of friends, co-workers and stakeholders to the concept. An alternative, particularly if a large investment is involved in the event, is to undertake some form of market research. This can be done within the resources of the event management company or by employing marketing professionals to conduct a market survey or focus group research. Such research may reveal not only the likely market acceptance of the concept, but also additional information, such as how much the target audience is prepared to pay for the event, or how the event concept may be adapted to meet market expectations or requirements.

A further factor in the environmental scan will be to examine the competition provided by other events in the market. This step will examine whether there are other events of a similar type or theme in a similar timeframe, or major events and public holidays that are likely to impact on the target market. An investigation of the competition through a 'What's on' in the city listing, tourism event calendars, etc. will assist the event manager to identify and hopefully avoid, head-on collision and competition with other events.

The operations screen

The operations screen will consider the skills and resources needed to stage the event successfully, and whether the event manager has these skills and resources or can develop them or buy them in for the event. Specialized technical skills, for example, may be needed to implement the event concept. The event manager will need to consider whether event company staff members have these skills, or whether an external supplier needs to be engaged to provide them. Special licences, permits or insurance may be needed in order to implement the concept. If the event concept is highly innovative and challenging, the event manager may need to consider the degree of risk involved. It may be desirable to deliver an innovative event, but costly and embarrassing if the event is a failure because the skills and resources available to stage it are inadequate.

Another major consideration, as part of the operations screen, is staffing. This step will examine whether the event company has sufficient staff available with the right mix of skills and at the right time, place and cost to deliver the event effectively. If the event needs to rely heavily on volunteers, the operations screen will examine whether sufficient numbers are likely to be available, and whether the right motivation, training and induction procedures are in place.

The financial screen

The final screen suggested by Shone and Parry (2004) is the financial screen. This screen examines whether the event organization has sufficient financial commitment, sponsorship and revenue to undertake the event. The first step in this process is to decide whether the event needs only to break even, which may be the case if it is being staged as a company promotional event, or whether it is required to make a profit for the host organization.

The next step will be to undertake a 'ballpark' budget of the anticipated costs and income of the event. Breaking the event down into its component parts will allow an estimate to be formed of the costs for each component. A generous contingency should be included on the cost side of the ledger, as at this stage of the event there are bound to be costs that have been underestimated or not yet identified. Calculating the income may require deciding on the appropriate pricing strategy and identifying the 'breakeven' point of ticket sales. Other key revenue items to take into account may include potential government grants or subsidies, merchandising income and sponsorship support, both in cash and in kind. It is important not to overestimate the sponsorship potential, and professional advice or a preliminary approach to the market may be required in order to arrive at a realistic estimate.

Cash flow is an important aspect of the financial screen often overlooked by inexperienced event managers. It is important not only to have sufficient funds to cover the expenses of the event, but to have them available when they are required. If, for example, a large part of the revenue is likely to be from ticket sales on the day, then it may be necessary to chart out the anticipated expenditure flow of the event, and to consider whether credit arrangements need to be made.

Once the event concept has been screened and evaluated from the marketing, operations and financial aspects, the event manager is in a position to make an informed decision with regard to the conduct of the event. If the result is a 'go' decision, then the process of refining the event concept and developing the all-important event strategies and plans that are the subject of later chapters of this book can begin.

The synergy of ideas

Most good events emerge from a synergistic group process. Such a process was illustrated in 1999, when the Millennium Commission brought together a group of people to devise a programme of celebrations for the millennium.

The brief had some unusual features. The celebrations should capture the mood of the UK population, and reflect the multicultural communities within the country. It should provide an opportunity for all people, from all backgrounds, to take part. The Millennium Festival concept was born out of these discussions, with a plan for a whole year of National Lottery funded celebrations across the country. The highest profile element of the Millennium Festival was the Millennium Dome, opened on 31 December 1999. Although much criticized by the press, primarily due to the costs involved and not hitting projected attendance targets, it was still visited by over 6 million people throughout the year, with a high level of customer satisfaction achieved. With the theme 'Time to Make a Difference' and pulling on the creativity of professionals from across the country, the Dome included zones dedicated to mind, body, spirit, learning, skill and play. At the centre, a 10 000-seat auditorium hosted the Millennium Experience – a show developed by Sir Cameron Mackintosh and John Napier as a creative masterpiece, involving artists, circus acts, trapeze artists and stilt-walkers. The overall event experience, it is claimed, was to be a once in a lifetime experience, which people would talk about in years to come. Whether this was achieved, only time will tell, however, Culture, Media and Sport Committee (2000) and The Comptroller and Auditor General (2000) provide useful overviews and reviews of the project.

Although the above may have been the highest profile element, the Millennium Festival also included a wide range of events, from small community events to major city celebrations, on New Year's Eve in 1999 and again in 2000, and throughout 2000. The First Weekend, as the 1999 celebrations were known, enabled twenty-two towns and cities to develop the scale and creativity of their traditional New Year street parties. Many city councils chose to produce firework and music spectaculars, for example, with Edinburgh's Hogmanay attracting nearly 200 000 people, and Liverpool city centre attracting an audience of around 150 000 people to a laser show highlighting in the sky moments from the city's history.

Perhaps, one of the largest initiatives for the evening was the Beacon Millennium Project. Involving communities from across the UK, the project enabled 1400 beacons to be lit as the focal point of community celebrations, starting in the Scottish islands and moving down the country, taking in Edinburgh, Belfast, Cardiff and London along the way. The event included Her Majesty Queen Elizabeth II lighting the world's largest beacon, in London. With the beacon as the focal point, communities chose to celebrate in their own unique way. Some celebrated the evening in a traditional manner, focusing on the religious significance of the event with hymns, prayers and reflection, while others developed the evening into a major community occasion, with street parties, fireworks, food and drink, and a party atmosphere.

The millennium events served to illustrate festival and community celebrations not seen for some time in the UK, with events ranging from the professionally run council events, to community based, focused and organized events that allowed each to celebrate in their own unique way. The synergistic process started with funds being made available through the National Lottery funded Millennium Commission, and an underlying theme of time. Yet each company, council, committee and community chose to interpret the theme of the event and, as a result, a true sense of community spirit and celebration was developed. Jura Consultants and Gardiner & Theobold (2001) provide an extensive impact study of the Millennium Festival.

Chapter summary

With the increased involvement of governments and the corporate sector, events are required to serve a multitude of agendas. The successful event manager must be able to identify and manage a diverse range of stakeholder expectations. Major stakeholders will include the host organization staging the event, and the host community and its various public authorities whose support will be needed. Both sponsors and media are important partners, and can sometimes contribute much to the event in support and resources beyond their formal sponsorship and media coverage. The vision and philosophy of the event should be shared with co-workers, and the contribution of each should be recognized and treated as important. Ultimately it is the spectators and participants who decide the success or failure of an event, and it is crucial to engage their emotions.

Once the objectives of the event and the unique resources available to it have been identified, the next priority is to brainstorm ideas with stakeholders in order to shape and communicate a shared vision for the event. No event is created by one person, and success will depend on a collective team effort.

Questions

1. Who are the most important stakeholders in an event, and why?
2. Give examples in your region of government, corporate and community involvement in events and their reasons for putting on events.
3. Focusing on an event that you have experienced at first hand, list the benefits that the event could offer a sponsor or partner.
4. Using the same event example that you have discussed in the last question, identify suitable media partners and outline how you would approach them to participate in the event.
5. What are the means by which an event creates an emotional relationship with its participants and spectators?
6. What events can you think of that demonstrate a unique vision or idea? What techniques have they used to express that vision or idea, and why do you consider them to be unique?
7. Imagine that you are planning an event in the area where you live. What are its unique characteristics, and how might these be expressed in an event?
8. Name a major event that you have attended or in which you have been involved, and identify the primary stakeholders and their objectives.

Case study 4.1

Edinburgh International Book Festival – Festival of Ideas, Journeying and Imagining

Edinburgh's festivals are a vital part of Edinburgh's life, contributing major cultural, social and economic impacts as well as enhancing the city's civic profile. The economic impact of the festivals is well documented. Recent research by The City of Edinburgh Council and partners revealed that Edinburgh's 2004 summer festivals generated an estimated £127 m and supported up to 2500 FTE (full-time equivalent) jobs. The study reveals that there were 2.6 m festival attendees last year representing a 63 per cent increase in festival attendance since 1997 (SQW Ltd and TNS Travel and Tourism, 2005). The multiplier effect on tourism businesses in the city is also significant, with hotel occupancy rates typically soaring to 80–90 per cent in the capital during the festival period. Beyond economic impacts, the festivals also play an important role in the cultural life of the city with 36 per cent of festival attendees coming from the local community.

Edinburgh is host to 15 diverse national and international festivals annually, as well as several community and participative festivals. These range from the prominent and internationally known Hogmanay and the Edinburgh International Festival (EIF) to lesser known but equally important festivals, such as The Harp Festival and the Scottish International Storytelling Festival. Together with its counterparts, the International, Jazz, Fringe and Film festivals, the Edinburgh International Book Festival forms what is now widely regarded as the biggest and best arts festival in the world during the summer months in Edinburgh.

Background

The Edinburgh International Book Festival began in 1983 and is now a key event in the August festival season, celebrated annually in Scotland's capital city. Biennial at first, the book festival became a yearly celebration in 1997. Throughout its 20-year history, the festival has grown rapidly in size and scope to become the largest and most dynamic festival of its kind in the world. In its first year, the book festival played host to just 30 'Meet the author' events. Today, the festival programmes over 600 events, which are enjoyed by people of all ages.

In 2001, Catherine Lockerbie, the Book Festival's fifth director, took the Festival to a new level by developing a high-profile debates and discussions series that is now one of the Festival's hallmarks. Each year, writers from all over the world gather to become part of this unique forum, in which audience and author meet to exchange thoughts and opinions on some of the world's most pressing issues. Catherine also comments on how there appears to be little tension between the commercial and artistic in terms of the programming: 'in fact, we have an experimental and willing audience, and they appear willing to buy tickets and books for relatively uncommercial authors'.

Running alongside the general programme is the highly regarded Children's Programme, which has grown to become a leading showcase for children's writers and illustrators. Incorporating workshops, storytelling, panel discussions, author events and book signings, the Children's Programme is popular with both the public and schools alike and now ranks as the world's premier books and reading event for young people.

The festival also hosts a Schools Programme and a Schools Gala day, exclusively for schools the day after the mainstream festival. This four-day programme of author and arts events is the largest of its kind in the world, and is committed to enabling children to engage in 'the wonderful world of books ... with the focus firmly on participation, imagination and creation' (Karen Mountney, Children's Programme Director). The event is non-profit making, with a key aim being to improve access and contribute to education and lifelong learning for Scotland's school children. To encourage participation, the event is free for teachers and also provides a free bus fund bringing children to the festival from all over Scotland. Key events include the School Gala Day, when the book festival is open to schools only; the Outreach Programme, which tours some of the authors to libraries in Scotland; and focused events for teachers, such as 'Improving Children's Writing Skills' and 'Poetry in Primary Years'.

Since its inception, the Book Festival's home has been the beautiful and historic Charlotte Square Gardens, centrally located in Edinburgh's World Heritage listed Georgian New Town. Each year the gardens are transformed into a magical tented village, which welcomed 207 500 visitors in 2004.

The Book Festival is proud to run its own independent bookselling operation, with a strong publishers' presence. All proceeds from the sale of books are invested back into the running of the book festival, a not-for-profit charity organization that annually raises 80 per cent of its own funds.

Festival operations

Compared with their peers in the United Kingdom and internationally, Edinburgh's festivals provide extremely good value to the city. Festivals with the turnover of Edinburgh's would expect to receive more in local subsidy. Internationally, public support accounts for approximately 42 per cent of the major European festivals budget, with smaller festivals receiving about 35 per cent (the Edinburgh International Book Festival receives 14.9 per cent). The Book Festival, however, is largely funded privately: Sponsorship and Development 25 per cent, Book Sales 16 per cent and Box Office 41 per cent with key public funding bodies being the Scottish Arts Council and the City of Edinburgh Council (18 per cent). The book festival has developed a strong sponsor base, with the inaugural title sponsors being *The Herald/Sunday Herald*, five major sponsors and a series of smaller sponsors and supporters.

In terms of staff structure, the 9 senior staff are full-time, year-round staff, everybody below that is on a temporary contract ranging from 6 months to 3 weeks. At peak times there will up to 90 staff working on the festival, with 15 in the Box Office and 30 Front of House. The Festival has fought hard to retain its summer seasonal staff by paying them reasonably, offering discounts to the bookshop, catering and entrance to events, and instilling the feeling that they share ownership of the festival. Retention of staff offers the festival security and advancement, and increases the level of customer service at the event.

Target markets

Edinburgh residents, particularly those profiled as 'affluent city centre area' or' well off town and city area', represent the largest group of visitors to the book festival (46 per cent). In fact in 2003, 79 per cent of visitors were from Scotland, with the remainder from the United Kingdom and a small proportion (11 per cent) of international visitors. Market research has shown that 93 per cent of the audience are ABC1. In terms of demographics, 35 per cent of visitors fall into the 35–54 age category, 24 per cent in the 25–34 age group, 22 per cent in the 55 years plus group and 20 per cent in the 16–24 age category.

Within the local segment, there are several key target markets: the Friends of the Book Festival, who, as well as being keen supporters and lovers of the festival, also have a strong fundraising remit; families, who are avid supporters of the Children's Festival; and schools throughout the region.

Key issues

Maximizing quality and experience on site

A critical issue facing the book festival is managing capacity and visitor experiences on the site. The temporary nature of the site (which is erected yearly for the festival) can bring a host of problems, because all of the facilities have to be brought in and managed by the book festival. A key issue is obviously climate, because much of the site's ambiance is created through its outdoor nature and location. Extremely high rainfall in 2002 created problems of water logging and flooding. Thankfully, the main events were unaffected because they are held in huge staged tents, and 2003 thankfully experienced a return to sunshine.

Obviously, the site has fixed capacity and in 2004 experienced visitor numbers of around 11 500 a day and although over half of the events were sold out, the book festival sold only 63 per cent of tickets. A further increase in numbers, therefore, would have an effect on the provision of facilities such as toilets and food and drink outlets.

Managing author and customer expectations

Critical to the success of the book festival is the event satisfaction of both authors and customers. Authors are invited to participate in the festival and pay a nominal and, surprisingly, equal fee. Key benefits to them include the exposure to their work that the festival brings, the opportunity to meet with their readers and sign books, and have access to international media who are present at the festival. Also, because of the controversial nature of events such as 'East and West' and 'Imprisoned Writers' there are security and political issues around certain authors' presence. Thankfully due to sound relationships with the police and the presence of a security firm on site there have been no disruptions to the festival.

Customer expectations also have to be managed. 2003 was the first year that tickets could be bought online and in 2004, 21 per cent of tickets were sold via the Book Festival website, this was seen to be a key improvement in ticket purchasing. Customer feedback is sought from the event in the form of a questionnaire at the information desks and invited e-mail responses. Feedback from key stakeholders, such as the media and the sponsors, is also examined because they are invited to various corporate hospitality events throughout the duration of the festival.

Improving access

A key aim of the Festival is to improve access. Recent research found that the 18–25-year-old market was the most underrepresented and as these group would be the future lifeblood of the Festival research was undertaken in 2003 to examine strategies of how to increase the market share of this key market.

Another issue is improving access from more deprived areas of Edinburgh. The Schools Programme is aiming to do this for the family market. The move in 2000 to abolish the entry fee and make the site accessible to all is also a step nearer to social inclusion. The presence of more commercial authors such as Candace Bushnell of 'Sex and the City' fame, alongside more radical thinkers such as Susan Sontag, is also instrumental in widening audience participation.

Collaborative working

Pooling and maximizing resources has been seen as a critical way forward for Edinburgh's key festivals. Although informal networking and sharing of ideas and practices had commonly been practised, this was formalized in 2001 with the launch of the Edinburgh Festivals Strategy. The strategy recognized the need for a shared vision, which the City of Edinburgh Council, the various festivals and other interested parties could sign up to with a common plan of action. The Strategy Implementation Group holds responsibility for the implementation and monitoring of the Festivals Strategy Action Plan. The Action Plan is critical because it addresses recommendations, implementation partners, timescales and resource implications. Paul Gudgin, Director of the Edinburgh Festival Fringe, comments that 'it is helping to foster closer working relationships across many of their departments, and between all the festivals and a number of other key agencies' (Edinburgh Festival Fringe, 2002).

Cross-festival collaboration has resulted in improvements in the following areas:

- The inception of the Association of Edinburgh's Festivals
- Joint festivals website www.edinburghfestivals.co.uk
- The appointment of a Tourism Travel Press Officer for Edinburgh's summer festivals
- Production of a daily guide to the festivals, sponsored by *The Guardian* newspaper
- Production of an Advocacy document for the festival
- Multi-staffing of the festivals.

Conclusions

The Edinburgh International Book Festival is an excellent case study illustrating the process involved in creating and implementing the event concept. The world's largest celebration of the written word in 2004 featured more than 550 authors appearing at over 650 events, with contributors as diverse as Muriel Spark, Irvine Welsh and Michael Buerk. The Book Festival is increasingly being seen as a marketable commodity and there are obvious tensions between artistic programming and commercialisation. However, the continued success of the Book Festival is evident and, as Catherine Lockerbie, Director says, 'The Book Festival is bringing the rest of the world to us to engage in wider debate. A good thing'.

For further information about Edinburgh International Book Festival, please visit www.edbookfest.co.uk.

By Jane Ali-Knight, Lecturer in Festival and Leisure Management, Napier University, Edinburgh, based on Edinburgh International Book Festival 2005.

Acknowledgements to Kath Mainland, General Manager, Amanda Barry, Marketing and PR Manager and all the staff at the EIBF for their kind support when putting this case study together.

Questions

1. Tension between artistic programming and commercialization is a critical problem for many festivals and events, particularly those with a strong community base. How can festival and event organizers put in place strategies to counteract this?
2. What kind of activities can the Edinburgh International Book Festival engage in to increase participation from the market segment aged 18–25 years?
3. How can customer experience be measured at a festival and event? Discuss three different techniques that can be used, outlining the strengths and weaknesses of each approach.

Chapter 5
The planning function

Learning Objectives

After studying this chapter, you should be able to:

- understand the importance of planning to ensure the success of an event
- discuss the significance of the planning process in achieving desired event outcomes
- discuss the strategic planning process as it applies to events
- describe selected organizational structures evident in the events area
- construct objectives for an event which are specific, measurable, achievable, realistic and time specific.

Introduction

This chapter provides an overview of the concept of planning as it applies to the conduct of events. It begins by discussing the centrality of planning to the overall success of an event and then moves on to describing the strategic event planning process. This process is identified as comprising a number of sequential and interrelated steps, each of which is briefly described here. Additionally, this chapter examines the range of organizational structures from which an event manager must select to support and implement their planning efforts.

What is planning?

In its simplest form, the planning process consists of establishing where an organization is at present, where it is best advised to go in the future, and the strategies or tactics needed to achieve that position. In other words, the planning process is concerned with end results and the means to achieve those results.

Perhaps the value of planning is best summed up by the words of the famous American general, Douglas MacArthur, who observed: 'Without a plan you're just a tourist'. MacArthur's comments allude to the value of planning in focusing an organization (such as an event organizing committee) on particular objectives and in the creation of defined pathways by which these objectives can be achieved. Central to the establishment of such pathways is an understanding of internal (for example, available resources) and external (for example, current economic conditions) factors that will condition any decisions that are made. Other benefits associated with strategic planning include its capacity to: identify and resolve problems, generate a range of potential alternative strategies for consideration, employees gain a better understanding of the organization's strategies and may become more committed to achieving them, it clarifies roles and responsibilities and it reduces uncertainty about the future which may reduce resistance to change (Hannagan, 2005).

To engage productively in the planning process, an event manager needs to keep a range of matters in mind. Central among these matters are the need to monitor and evaluate progress, coordinate decisions in all areas so event objectives are progressed, and communicate with, inspire and motivate those responsible for carrying out the various elements of the plan. These matters are discussed in later chapters.

Event planning and management has been extensively discussed in an increasing range of texts, including Allen (2001), Hall (1997), Getz (2005), Goldblatt (2005), Masterman (2004), Shone and Parry (2004), Silvers (2004), Torkildsen (2005), Tum, Norton and Wright (2006), Van Der Wagen and Carlos (2005), Watt (1998) and Yeoman, Robertson, Ali-Knight, Drummond and McMahon-Beattie (eds) (2004) and has also formed the basis of management guides, including UK Sport (2005). While the power of planning as a management tool is acknowledged, actually engaging in planning involves some measure of discipline on behalf of the event manager. As Sir John Harvey-Jones, a past chairman of ICI, notes: 'Planning is an unnatural process: it is much more fun to do nothing. The nicest thing about not planning is that failure comes as a complete surprise, rather than being preceded by a period of worry and depression'.

Event managers also need to be mindful that plans, as Hannagan (2005) and Thompson with Martin (2005) note, need to be adapted to changing circumstances. Additionally, they need to be conscious of not falling foul of planning 'pitfalls'. These include:

- overplanning and becoming obsessed with detail as opposed to overall strategic considerations
- viewing plans as one-off exercises rather than active documents to be regularly consulted and adapted
- seeing plans as conclusive rather than directional in nature (Johnson, Scholes and Whittington 2005).

Planning for events

Where does the event planning process begin? The answer to this question depends on whether the event is being conducted for the first time or if it is a pre-existing event. In the case of a new event, the event manager may be required to first work through the broad concept of the event with key stakeholders and then undertake a feasibility study. If this study shows that the event is likely to meet certain key criteria (such as profitability), they would then move to develop a plan for its creation and delivery. In instances where an event is pre-existing and open to the bidding process (for example, a conference or sporting event), an initial decision needs to be made as to whether (after a preliminary investigation) it is worthwhile making a bid or proposal. If the answer is 'yes', a more detailed feasibility study might be conducted to identify such things as the costs and benefits associated with hosting it before preparing a formal bid. If a bid or proposal is prepared and it is successful, then detailed event planning would commence. The process associated with event planning in the context of new events and those attracted through the bidding process is shown in Figure 5.1 (page 119).

It should also be noted that event managers often find themselves in situations in which they are planning for recurring events such as annual festivals or exhibitions.

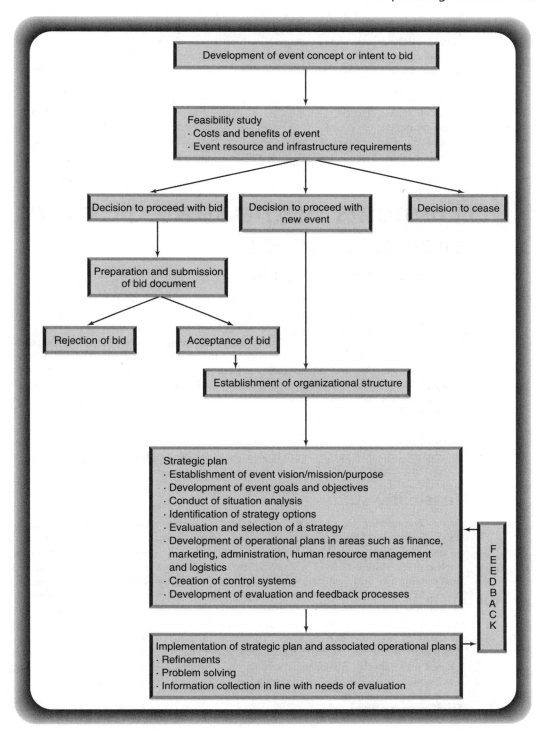

Figure 5.1 The strategic event planning process
Source: adapted from Getz (2005), p. 63

In this situation, the steps in Figure 5.1 (page 119) are not all relevant. In such instances, the event manager begins with an appraisal of the current situation faced by the event and also its previous plans. This process is likely to result in minor changes or refinements to existing vision statements, mission statements, goals, objectives and/or strategies, and the development of revised/new plans in areas such as marketing, human resources and finance. Also, on occasions, such reviews may result in major changes to the existing strategy and/or form of the event. Indeed, event managers need to keep in mind, as Mintzberg (2003) points out, the planning process tends to encourage incremental change, when what may be needed is a complete rethink of the current strategy.

Elements of the strategic event planning process

Concept or intent to bid

In the context of new events, this stage involves making decisions (often in consultation with major stakeholder groups) concerning such matters as the type/form of the event (for example, festival, parade), duration, location/venue, timing, and key programme elements that will serve to make the event unique or special. Once the event concept is sufficiently developed, it can then be subjected to more detailed analysis. (*Note*: Detailed discussion of developing event concepts can be found in Chapter 4). In instances where bidding is involved, events for which bids or proposals can be made need to be identified first. This may be as a result of requests for proposals (RFPs).

Once this is done, a preliminary assessment can be made as to their 'fit' with the capabilities of the event organizing body and the hosting destination. Events deemed worthy of further investigation may then be the subject of more detailed scrutiny via a feasibility study.

Feasibility study

Before committing to an event, its organizers need to determine how feasible or otherwise it would be to conduct that event. There are many considerations that may be taken into account in conducting a feasibility study. These may include (depending on the event) likely budget requirements; managerial skill needs; venue capacities; host community and destination area impacts; availability of volunteers, sponsors and supporting services (for example, equipment hire firms); projected visitation/attendance; infrastructure requirements; availability of public/private sector financial support; level of political support for the event; and the track record of the event in terms of matters such as profit. It should be noted that the level of detail and complexity associated with these studies will vary. An event such as the Olympic Games, for example, is likely to involve a more lengthy and detailed process than, say, a regional sporting championship or an association conference.

Bid preparation

This step is required in instances where it is decided to bid for an existing event based on the outcomes of a feasibility study. In a corporate event context, this may involve a formal proposal (Allen, 2002; O'Toole and Mikolaitis, 2002) in response to the RFP identified earlier. The bidding process involves a number of steps, specifically:

- identifying resources that can be employed to support the event (for example, venues and government grants
- developing a critical path for the preparation and presentation of a bid document to the 'owners' of the event
- developing an understanding of the organization conducting the event and the exact nature of the event itself
- identifying the key elements of past successful bids preparing a bid document
- presenting and/or submitting a bid to the 'owners' of the event, such as a sporting body
- lobbying in support of the bid.

In a corporate event context, the bidding process may involve submitting a formal proposal to the potential client, followed by a pitching process – a presentation of the idea to the client against competitors in order to secure the business. Each process and proposal will be developed to the client's specified requirements and therefore research will be required into the client organization. O'Toole (2004) produces a useful checklist for areas generally included in a proposal (Figure 5.2).

From the other perspective, the Communications Agencies Federation provides useful guidance to those wishing to put business out to tender/for proposals,

- Cover Letter
- Title Page
- Proprietary Notice – cautions about unauthorized disclosure
- Table of Contents (TOC)
- List of Abbreviations
- Executive Summary
- Body of Proposal
  - Profile of the Event Company:
    - General: including mission, background, credentials
    - Specific: including previous similar events and resources available
- Project partners and their profiles
- Event Specific information:
  - Objectives
  - Scope of Work
  - Stakeholders
  - Themes, design and ideas
  - Site/venue assessment
  - Resources required : AV, entertainment, catering, staff, suppliers.
  - Marketing and promotional services needed
  - Possible sponsorship
  - Budget – corresponding to functional areas of programme elements
  - Control management – reporting processes, organization structure responsibilities
  - Schedules – planning, transport, running order, promotion
  - Environmental impact – natural environment, traffic, transport.
  - Risk issues including insurance.
- Appendices

Figure 5.2 Contents of the event proposal
Source: O'Toole (2004)

including what should be included in a good client brief (CAF, 2003). This has also been developed an interactive tool for writing a client brief available at: www.clientbrief.info.

Only when a bid is successful does formal strategic planning for the event commence.

Decision to proceed or cease

In the case of new events, the outcomes of the feasibility study will directly determine if and when the event will proceed. In the case of events involving a bid, this decision will depend on whether a bid is accepted or rejected.

Establishment of organizational structure

Following the decision to proceed with an event, an organizational structure will need to be created through which the event can be delivered.

Simple structures

As the name suggests, a simple structure has a low level of complexity. As Figure 5.3 illustrates, all decision making is centralized with the event manager, who has total control over all staff activities. This is the most common structure in small event management businesses as it is flexible, adaptable to changing circumstances, easy to understand, and has clear accountability – the manager is accountable for all the activities associated with the event. The flexibility of this structure commonly means staff are expected to be multi-skilled and perform various job functions. This can mean individual jobs are more satisfying, and produce higher levels of staff morale. However, this structure has some potential limitations. As staff do not have the opportunity to specialize, they may not achieve a high level of expertise in any one area. Additionally, once an event organization grows beyond a certain size, decision making can become very slow – or even non-existent – as a single executive has to make all decisions and carry out all the management functions. Also, if the manager has an autocratic style of management, staff can become demoralized when their expertise is not fully utilized. There is also an inherent risk in concentrating all event management information in one person – obviously, sickness at an inappropriate time could prove disastrous.

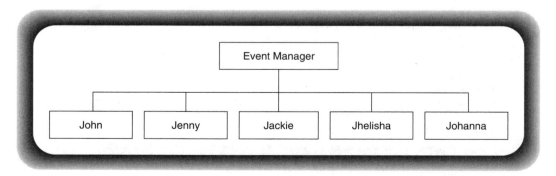

Figure 5.3 A simple organizational structure

Functional structures

As the name suggests, a functional structure departmentalizes (that is, groups related tasks) in a way that encourages the specialization of labour (paid/voluntary). Benefits of this form of structure are that individuals or groups (such as committees) can be given specific task areas, thus avoiding any overlap of responsibilities. Additionally, it is possible using this form of structure to easily add additional functional levels as the event requires them. In Figure 5.4 an example of such a structure is given. Potential limitations of this approach include problems of coordination due partly to a lack of understanding of other tasks, and conflict between functional areas as those doing the tasks attempt to defend what they see as their 'territory'. Various approaches can be used to prevent these problems arising. These approaches include employing multi-skilling strategies that require the rotation of staff through different functional areas, regular meetings between the managers/chairs of all functional areas, general staff meetings and communications (such as newsletters) that aim to keep those engaged on the event aware of matters associated with its current status (for example, budgetary situations or the passing of milestones). In Chapter 6, activities that are essential elements of the leadership function of the event manager are discussed.

Programme-based matrix structures

Another way of organizing committees or groups into an organizational structure is treating the various aspects of an event programme as separate (but related) entities. Organizers of a multi-venue sporting event, for example, may choose to have separate committees with responsibility for all tasks associated with event delivery at each location (Figure 5.5, page 124). In order to do this, each committee/group leader would be required to manage a team of people with a comprehensive range of event-related skills. If this structure is employed, it is sound practice, as Getz (2005) notes, to have some tasks, such as security, communications and technical support, cut across all programme areas to prevent duplication and enhance coordination.

A project-based matrix structure has several inherent advantages, including allowing groups/individuals to engage directly with the task (producing and delivering an event) and facilitating intergroup communication and cooperation. In using this structure, a high value must be placed on coordination so the event is presented as a unified whole.

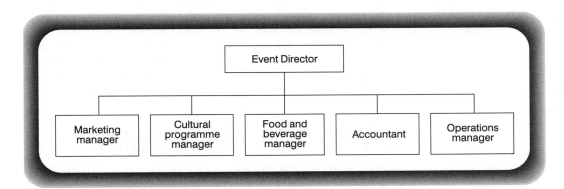

Figure 5.4 Functional structure

Event manager

Support systems	Venue teams (Each team would comprise people with a similar range of skills.)		
	Venue 1 team	Venue 2 team	Venue 3 team
Communications			
Transport			
Security			

Figure 5.5 Programme-based matrix structure for a hypothetical multi-venue sporting event

Multi-organizational or network structures

Most specialist event management companies are relatively small in size (fewer than 20 people), yet many conduct quite large and complex events. This is possible because these organizations enlist the services of a variety of other firms and organizations. In effect, they create 'virtual organizations' in order to conduct the event, which disappear immediately after it has finished. This process is represented in Figure 5.6, which shows various suppliers being enlisted by an event management firm to create a structure capable of creating and delivering an event. It should be noted that this process of growing an organizational structure quickly by contracting outside firms to perform specific functions is common in many forms of events, including public events such as festivals. Such an approach makes sense in situations where it is impractical to maintain a large standing staff when they can be used only for a limited period each year. Other advantages are that contracting specialist businesses with current expertise and experience on a need-only basis means there is no 'down time'. Budgeting can also be more exact because most costs are contracted and, therefore, known beforehand. This structure also allows for quick decisions because the core management group is made up of only a few people or one individual.

As with the other structures previously discussed, there are also possible disadvantages to be considered. These include issues associated with quality control and reliability of the contractors who are involved in performing tasks, and coordinating employees (from various other organizations) who lack a detailed understanding of the event. Nevertheless, the concept of the network structure is supported by contemporary management thinking on downsizing, sticking to core activities and outsourcing, and can be very effective for certain kinds of event.

Developing a strategic plan

Once it has been decided to proceed with an event, or a bid has been won, the event manager moves on to develop a strategic plan to guide their next stage of decision making.

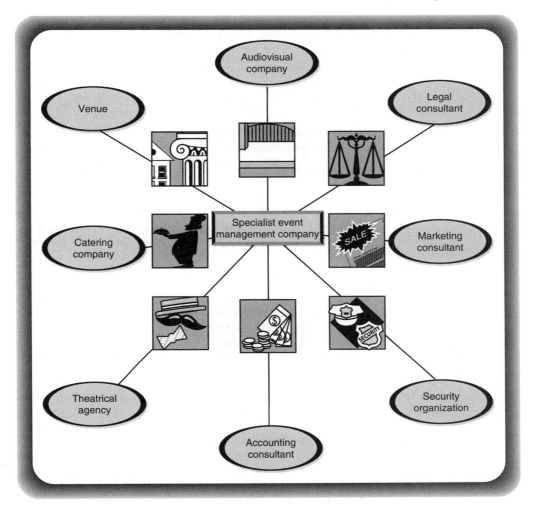

Figure 5.6 A network structure

The strategy process is about determining the current situation faced by an event (strategic analysis/awareness), considering the strategic options available to an event manager (strategic creation and choice) and the mechanisms for implementing and evaluating/monitoring the chosen strategies (strategic implementation) (Thompson with Martin, 2005). The context in which this process takes place is that of the purpose/vision/mission of the event. Each of the elements of this process is discussed in turn in this section.

Purpose, vision and mission statements

At a minimum, a clear statement of purpose and vision should underpin every event. This statement in turn will be conditioned by the needs of the various stakeholder groups with an interest in the event. Such groups may include client organizations, the local community, government at various levels, potential attendees and participants, sponsors and volunteers.

In the case of many events, particularly those of a corporate or public relations nature, a considered statement as to its purpose is all that is really required to provide sufficient direction and focus.

An example of a purpose statement is one developed for Brain Awareness Week, an annual international event coordinated by Dana Alliance (USA) and the European Dana Alliance for the Brain (2005), a non-profit organization that seeks to provide information about the personal and public benefits of brain research:

> *Brain Awareness Week is a worldwide celebration of the brain that grows more successful every year. It is an opportunity to let people know what is being done to diagnose, treat and prevent disorders of the brain, such as Alzheimer's, Parkinson's, stroke, schizophrenia and depression, which affect the lives of millions of people.*

For events that are more complex in nature (such as large public events) and involve a number of stakeholder groups, it can be beneficial to reflect more deeply on the matter of purpose. It is evident that many events are now doing this and, as a result, are creating vision/mission statements to guide their development and conduct.

A vision statement can be separate from an event's mission, or the two may be combined. Vision statements usually describe what the event seeks to become and to achieve in the longer term (Thompson with Martin, 2005). They are also often brief, precise and motivational in nature. The Windsor Festival (2005), for example, states, '... we offer a unique experience, which entertains and enhances the community, linking social, educational and commercial interests... Building on these foundations, we will increase the breadth and variety of the programme, increase accessibility to the arts and encourage wider recognition of the Festival'.

Some events use more expansive vision statements, which are really a combination of both vision and mission. The Liverpool Women's International Music Festival (WIMFEST, 2004) state their mission is to, 'be a festival that will celebrate diversity, tolerance, tradition, history and story telling; by women, through music and song. It will involve schools, young people, local communities, professional and amateur performers. The festival will encourage both individual and collective endeavour, empowering and enabling women to organize the event, produce, promote and perform'.

It should be noted that vision statements do not necessarily need to be written down (although it is often useful to do so), providing they are shared and understood by those involved with the event. It may be fair to say, for example, that while no formal vision statement may have existed at the time the Notting Hill Carnival began, those involved with it understood clearly that one of its long-term goals was about achieving equality and social acceptance.

A mission statement describes in the broadest terms the task that the event organization has set for itself. If the event has also established a vision statement, then the mission needs to be viewed in terms of fulfilling this vision. Such statements, at their most advanced, seek to define an event's purpose, identify major beneficiaries and customer groups, indicate the broad nature of the event and state the overall operating philosophy of the organization conducting it (for example, whether to be fully or partially self-funded). Several event mission statements that, to varying degrees, fulfil these criteria have been provided in Table 5.1.

Once established, a mission statement acts as the basis upon which goals and objectives can be set and strategies established. They also serve to provide a shorthand means of conveying to staff (either paid or voluntary) an understanding of the event and what it is trying to achieve. A coherent mission statement can be an invaluable

Table 5.1 Sample event mission statements

Event	Mission statement
Bath Festivals Trust	To enrich people's lives through participation in the arts
Boscombe Arts Festival	Boscombe Arts Festival works to promote participation, enjoyment and creativity for all Bournemouth residents through an annual Boscombe based festival.
Manchester 2002 Commonwealth Games	To deliver an outstanding sporting spectacle of world significance, celebrating athletic excellence, cultural diversity and the unique atmosphere of 'The Friendly Games'. To deliver a successful Games on behalf of all competitors, spectators and stakeholders. To leave a lasting legacy of new sporting facilities and social, physical and economic regeneration. To set a new benchmark for hosting international sporting events in the UK and the lasting benefit they can generate for all those involved.
Salford Film Festival	The Salford Film Festival will promote and raise the profile of Salford as an area of creative excellence in image media. The Salford Film Festival will focus on the community of Salford using moving image, still image and self-image. Through the production and screening of new productions the festival will encourage the development of links regionally, nationally and internationally and encourage and promote new media work.
Worcester Festival	The Worcester Festival is not a music festival, nor indeed an arts festival, but just … a festival. The Festival is for the people of Worcester and the surrounds. It is a series of partnerships between large cross-sections of the community, an umbrella for a huge range of activities. It is a coming together of people. It is an opportunity to stage an event, or to attend a large selection of both professional and community events. It is a celebration of life, and of Worcester and its people.

Sources: Boscombe Arts Festival (2005); Bath Festivals Trust (2005), Manchester 2002 (2003), p. 3; Salford Film Festival (2005); Worcester Festival (2005)

tool for establishing a common direction in a team, and promoting unity among its members.

Goals and objectives

Once an event's mission has been decided, the event manager must then move on to establish the event's goals and/or objectives. Goals are broad statements that seek to provide direction to those engaged in the organization of the event, as seen in Table 5.2. Objectives in turn are used to quantify progress towards an event's goals and as such set performance benchmarks and allow event organizations to assess what aspects of their planning have succeeded or failed. It should be noted that the terms 'goals' and 'objectives' are often used interchangeably but they are really distinct concepts. It should also be noted that for some forms of event (particularly those of a corporate nature) the step of creating goals prior to establishing objectives is

Table 5.2 Sample of event goals and objectives

Event	Goals
Salford Film Festival	To present a showcase of past present and future filmmaking in Salford alongside a range of relevant international film productions.
	To identify and raise the aspirations of emerging filmmakers primarily in Salford and its environs by developing sustainable partnerships with key stakeholders and sector champions.
	To develop pathways into image media partnerships with community groups, educational establishments and professional bodies.
	To increase the cultural and leisure opportunities and in doing so bring about a positive impact on the lives of young people
	To utilize culture and leisure to provide more opportunities to develop skills and improve esteem
SeaBritain 2005	To raise awareness of Britain's maritime and coastal heritage
	To encourage participation in maritime sport and leisure activities
	To promote the UK coast and its islands as a tourism destination, and travel by sea for European visitors
	To promote an understanding and involvement with the marine environment and marine conservation
	To raise awareness of the contribution made by the sea and seafaring to the UK economy and culture
	To develop maritime learning materials designed specifically to link with the National Curriculum
	To leave a legacy in 2006 and beyond
Windsor Festival	Continue to promote quality performances of music and the arts within the Royal Borough of Windsor and Maidenhead.
	Increase local access to the arts and music in the unique venues available with Windsor, Eton and Maidenhead.
	Encourage the development of young musicians and other artists.
	Provide opportunities for local performers.

Source: Salford Film Festival (2005); SeaBritain 2005 Press Office (2004); Windsor Festival (2005)

not usually necessary. The establishment of goals is useful when the event is complex in nature and involves a number of stakeholder groups. In such instances, they serve a useful role in building on the event's mission statement to provide direction and focus to the event organizers' activities.

Useful criteria that can be applied to the establishment of objectives are summed up by the acronym SMART, which refers to the fact that objectives should be:

- *specific*: focused on achieving an event goal (or, if no goals have been developed, its purpose)
- *measurable*: expressed in a way that is quantifiable
- *agreeable*: agreed on by those responsible for achieving them
- *realistic*: in terms of the event organization having the human, financial and physical resources to achieve them
- *time specific*: to be achieved by a particular time.

Each event will obviously vary in terms of the objectives it establishes. Examples of such objectives are as follows:

Economic objective

- Percentage return on monies invested or overall gross/net profit sought
- Financial value of sponsorship attracted
- Percentage of income to be raised from fundraising activities
- Percentage increase in market share (if the event is competing directly with other similar events)

Attendance/participation

- Total attendance/attendance by specific groups (for example, people from outside the area, specific age groups, professions)
- Size of event in terms of stallholders/exhibitors/performers/attendees
- Number of local versus outside artists
- Percentage of an area's cultural groups represented in a programme
- Number of community groups involved with the event

Quality

- Percentage level of attendee/exhibitor/sponsor/volunteer satisfaction
- Number of participants/speakers/performers of international reputation
- Number of complaints from attendees/exhibitors/volunteers

Awareness/knowledge/attitudes

- Percentage of attendees or others exposed to the event that have changed levels of awareness/knowledge as a result of the event
- Percentage of attendees or others exposed to the event who have altered their attitudes as a result of it

Human resources

- Percentage of staff/volunteer turnover
- Percentage of volunteers retained from previous year.

Wendroff (2004, p. 2) highlights seven goals for non-profit/charity events. These are to raise money, update the mission statement to educate the community, motivate board members and supporters, recruit volunteers and future board members, expand the organization's network, market the organization and solicity endorsements.

Situational analysis

A useful process that can be employed to gain a detailed understanding of an event's internal and external environment (or surroundings) is strengths, weaknesses, opportunities and threats (SWOT) analysis or, as it is sometimes called, a situational analysis. This process may involve referring to a range of existing information sources, including data collected previously on the event, census data and general reports on relevant matters such as trends in leisure behaviour. Additionally, it may be necessary to commission studies to fill information gaps, or to update event organizations on particular matters. A deeper understanding of the needs, wants, motives and perceptions of current or potential customer groups, for example, may be deemed necessary before changing an event in an effort to increase attendance.

The external environment consists of all those factors that surround the event and which can impact on its success. A thorough scanning of the full range of factors that make up the external environment should aid the event manager making decisions on such matters as target market(s) selection, programming, promotional messages, ticket pricing and when to conduct the event. Threats to the event (for example, proposed changes to legislation regarding outdoor consumption of alcohol) or the emergence of new competing events can also be identified through this process.

The external environment is usually assessed first, and consists of many factors. The main factors include:

- *Political/legal*: the decisions made by all levels of government become laws or regulations that affect the way in which people live in a society. The laws regulating the consumption of food and alcoholic beverages, for example, have changed radically in the UK since the 1950s, making outdoor food and wine festivals possible.
- *Economic*: economic factors such as unemployment, inflation, interest rates, distribution of wealth and levels of wages and salaries can impact on the demand for events. Declining living standards in a particular region, for example, may require an event to reduce its ticket prices and seek alternative sources of revenue (for example, grants or sponsorship) to subsidize the event costs.
- *Social/cultural*: changes in a population's ethnic/religious make-up or leisure behaviour can act to influence event demand. These changes can provide opportunities (for example, a demand for multicultural events) or pose threats (for example, an increased tendency to engage in home based leisure activities). Existing attitudes among a population towards a particular activity can also be a factor of interest to event managers. The love of sport possessed by many British, for example, was 'tapped' for the successful London 2012 Olympic bid, both to generate demand and to create a climate of tolerance for the various event preparation disruptions. The culture of a particular place can also provide a rich resource on which event managers can draw; for example, the architecture, traditions, beliefs, cuisine and artistic skills associated with a particular area can be embraced, selectively or collectively, by event managers.
- *Technological*: changes in equipment and machines have revolutionized the way people undertake tasks, including aspects of event management (Chapter 13). One example is using the Internet to promote festivals, exhibitions and events. Entering the word 'festival' into an Internet search engine will produce links to a multitude of events on all parts of the globe. Another example is the use of the Internet as a vehicle for conducting events such as conferences. Internet sites that support event professionals, students and educators by providing information, directories, and resources online are also appearing (for example, Domeresearch.com, EPMS.net and WorldofEvents.net).
- *Demographic*: the composition of society in terms of age, gender, education and occupation changes over time. A striking example is the entry of the baby boomers' generation (people born between 1945 and 1960) into middle age. The generation that gave the world rock 'n'roll, blue jeans and relaxed sexual morals is, and will continue to be, a large market for event managers, and will always have very different needs to the preceding and succeeding generations.
- *Physical/environmental*: concern over such matters as pollution and waste generation within the broader community is affecting the way in which events are conducted. Many councils and sustainable environmental groups are actively encouraging event organizers to 'green' their events (see, for example, Waste Awareness Wales, 2005). Another environmental consideration for event managers is the changing weather patterns caused by the impact of greenhouse gases. Such changes have the potential to impact on events, particularly when they are conducted outdoors.

- *Competitive*: other events that attract a similar audience need to be monitored. In this regard, comparisons relating to such matters as programmes and pricing are useful. Events do not necessarily have to be similar in nature to attract a similar audience. A consumer exhibition organizer in a port city, for example, suffered a significant decline in demand for an event they had organized when a visiting aircraft carrier decided to conduct a public open day at the same time.

A thorough scanning of the full range of factors that make up the external environment will reveal the event's target market(s), its range of activities, and opportunities for promotion, sponsorship and fundraising. Similarly, threats to the successful operation of the event can also be identified. Over a period of time, environmental factors can change, sometimes dramatically, necessitating adjustments to an event's objectives or design. For example, the ethnic composition of many areas within the UK has undergone marked change, and the resultant shifts in the social and cultural environments of those areas, have affected the demand for festivals celebrating particular cultures. In another example, a predicted reduction in government funding of cultural events would be a threat to an event organization dependent on such funding for much of its revenue.

When the analysis of the external environment is complete, the next step in the strategic planning process is to undertake an internal analysis of the event organization's physical, financial, informational and human resources in order to establish its strengths and weaknesses. Areas of strength or weakness associated with an event may include the level of management or creative expertise on which it can draw, the quality of its supplier relationships, ownership or access to appropriate venues and facilities (for example, stages and sound systems), the quality of event programme elements, access to appropriate technology such as ticketing systems, the level of sophistication of the event management software systems in use, access to financial resources, the event reputation, the size of the volunteer base and the strength of links with potential sponsors.

Identification of strategy options

The environmental scanning process gathers crucial information that can be used by the event manager in selecting strategies to achieve the event's vision, mission or purpose. Strategies must use strengths, minimize weaknesses, avoid threats and take advantage of opportunities that have been identified. A SWOT analysis is a wasted effort if the material gathered by this analytic process is not used in strategy formulation. Several generic strategies, which can be adopted by event managers, are summarized below.

Growth strategy

Many event managers have a fixation on event size and, as such, seek to make their events bigger than previous ones or larger than similar events. Bigger is often thought to be better, particularly by ambitious event managers. Growth can be expressed as more revenue, more event components, more participants or consumers, or a bigger share of the event market. It is worth pointing out that bigger is not necessarily better, as some event managers have discovered. An example of this is Streets Ahead (a Catalan festival which takes place in Manchester). It adopted a growth strategy from 1995 towards a street festival for the millennium, involving ten local authorities in and around Greater Manchester. In the first year, one authority was involved, the following year two, then four until, by 1999, all ten local authorities were taking part (Allen and Shaw, 2001).

It is important to recognize that an event does not necessarily have to grow in size for its participants to feel that it is better than its predecessors – this can be achieved by dedicating attention to quality activities, careful positioning and improved planning. However, a growth strategy may be appropriate if historical data suggest there is a growing demand for the type of event planned, or a financial imperative necessitates increasing revenue. The annual Reading Festival substantially increased attendance by incorporating contemporary pop acts into the event's line-up, thereby appealing to a market segment with a strong propensity to attend musical events.

Consolidation or stability strategy

In certain circumstances it may be appropriate to adopt a consolidation strategy – that is, maintaining attendance at a given level. Strong demand for tickets to T In The Park, for example, has allowed the event to sell tickets well in advance, cap attendance numbers and further enhance the quality of its programme. By capping ticket sales in a climate of high demand, this event has also created a situation in which it has greater pricing freedom.

Retrenchment strategy

An environmental scan may suggest that an appropriate strategy is to reduce the scale of an event but add value to its existing components. This strategy can be applicable when the operating environment of an event changes. Retrenchment can seem a defeatist or negative strategy, particularly to long-standing members of an event committee, but it can be a necessary response to an unfavourable economic environment or major change in the sociocultural environment. The management of a community festival, for example, may decide to delete those festival elements that were poorly patronized and focus only on those that have proven to be popular with its target market. Likewise, exhibitions may delete an accompanying seminar programme and focus on the core aspects of the exhibition.

Combination strategy

As the name suggests, a combination strategy includes elements from more than one of these generic strategies. An event manager could, for example, decide to cut back or even delete some aspects of an event that no longer appeal to their event target market(s), while concurrently growing other aspects.

Strategy evaluation and selection

Most management writers such as Thompson with Martin (2005) and Johnson, Scholes and Whittington (2005) consider that strategic alternatives can be evaluated by using three main criteria:

1. *Appropriateness/suitability* – strategies and their component parts should be consistent. That is, strategies selected should complement each other and be consistent with the environment, resources and values of the event organization.
2. *Feasibility* – the proposed strategy should be feasible. It should work in practice, considering the resources available (for example, finance, human resource, time). The strategy should also meet key success factors (for example, quality, price, level of service).
3. *Acceptability/desirability* – strategies should be capable of achieving the event's objectives. They should focus on what the environmental scan has identified as

important and disregard the unimportant. Event companies should, however, be careful not to overlook potential risks involved in the strategy; for example, financial or environmental risk, or the risk of the required skills not being available in the organization.

Once again, it is important to stress that the strategies chosen must be congruent with the findings of the SWOT analysis, or the environmental scan becomes a waste of time and intellectual energy and results in inappropriate strategy selection.

Operational plans

Once the strategic thrust of the event has been agreed, the implementation of the plan can commence. This process can be carried out by means of a series of operational plans. This application of project management practices and techniques (Chapter 12) is particularly useful at this point in the strategic planning process.

Operational plans will be needed for all areas central to the achievement of an event's objectives and the implementation of its strategy. Areas for operational planning will likely vary, therefore, across events. It would be common, however, for plans to be developed in areas such as budgeting, marketing, administration, staging, research and evaluation, risk management, sponsorship, environmental waste management, programming, transportation, merchandising and staffing (paid and volunteer).

Each area that develops operational plans will require a set of objectives that progress the overall event strategy; action plans and schedules; details of individuals responsible for carrying out the various aspects of the plan; monitoring and control systems, including a budget; and an allocation of resources (financial, human and supporting equipment/services).

Given that many festivals, exhibitions and events are not one-off, but occur at regular intervals – yearly, biennially or, in the case of some major sporting events, every four years – standing plans can be used in a number of operational areas. Standing plans are made up of policies, rules and standard procedures and serve to reduce decision-making time by ensuring similar situations are handled in a predetermined and consistent way.

Policies can be thought of as guidelines for decision making. An event may, for example, have a policy of only engaging caterers that meet particular criteria. These criteria might be based on licensing and insurance. Policies in turn are implemented by way of following established detailed instructions known as procedures. In the case of the previous example, procedures may require the person responsible for hiring caterers to inspect their licence and insurance certificates, check that they are current, and obtain copies for the event's records. Rules are statements governing conductor action in a particular situation. An event may establish rules, for example, regarding what caterers can and cannot do with the waste they generate on site, or on what they can or cannot sell.

Control systems

Once operational plans are implemented, mechanisms are required to ensure that actions conform to plans. These mechanisms take the form of systems that allow performance to constantly be compared to objectives. Performance benchmarks (such as ticket sales over a given period) are particularly useful in this regard. Meetings and reports are generally central to the control process, as are budgets. Budgets allow actual costs and expenditure to be compared with those projected for the various operational areas. A detailed discussion of the control and budgeting processes appears in Chapter 10.

Event evaluation and feedback

Evaluation is a neglected area of event planning; yet, it is only through evaluation that event managers can determine how successful or otherwise their efforts have been in achieving whatever objectives were set for the event. It is also through this means that feedback can be provided to stakeholders, problems and shortcomings of the planning process can be identified and improvements suggested if the event is to be repeated. Key considerations regarding evaluation from an event manager's perspective include when to evaluate, how to evaluate and what to evaluate. The answers to these questions are provided in Chapter 14.

Implementation of strategic plan and associated operational plans

Once implemented, a strategic plan and its associated operational plans are likely to require refinements to adapt them to changing circumstances. Additionally at this stage, information is collected to allow evaluation to occur.

Chapter summary

Planning is the basis for all successful events. To be successful, an event manager must gain a clear understanding of why the event exists (its vision/mission/purpose), what it is trying to do and for whom (its goals and/or objectives), and also decide on the strategies needed to achieve these goals and/or objectives. Additionally, an appropriate organizational structure is needed to 'steer' these processes. In this regard, the event manager can select from a number of options, depending on the assessment of the advantages and disadvantages of each. Strategies, in turn, need to be implemented through a range of operational plans developed within the context of an overall event budget. These plans need to be monitored and adjusted as appropriate in the light of changing circumstances, and evaluated against the objectives set for them and the overall objectives of the event.

Questions

1. Briefly discuss the value of setting vision/mission/purpose statements for events.
2. Undertake an Internet search of a particular event type (for example, festivals), identify four events that have established mission statements and compare these to the criteria given in this chapter.

3. Conduct an interview with the manager of an event of your choice with a view to identifying the key external environmental factors that are impacting on their event.
4. When might an event employ a retrenchment strategy *or* a growth strategy? Can you identify any specific event where one of these strategies is in evidence?
5. Identify several events, determine if they have established objectives, and assess these against the SMART criteria discussed in this chapter.
6. Select an event with a functional organization structure, and another with a network structure. Describe each of these structures, and discuss why you believe each event chose the organizational structure it did.
7. Explain the difference between a strategic plan and an operational plan.
8. Briefly discuss the difference between a policy and a procedure.
9. Explain why stakeholders are significant from the perspective of establishing vision and mission statements.
10. Critically examine the strategic planning process of a particular event in the light of the processes discussed in this chapter.

Case study 5.1

The Vodafone Ball by Euro RSCG Skybridge
An Event with History

Vodafone's continued programme of global acquisition had seen it become the world's largest mobile phone company, incorporating previously independent businesses in local markets under one brand. The company has historically thanked their employees and partners for their hard work and support on an annual basis. The vehicle for this has traditionally manifested itself in the form of a grand-scaled celebratory ball.

Vodafone wanted to find a refreshing way to invigorate the Vodafone Ball concept, whilst maintaining the employee excitement, expectation and enthusiasm that surround the annual ball.

Euro RSCG Skybridge utilized their in depth knowledge of Vodafone as a global company and its employees as individuals, to conceive, create, plan and produce a celebratory ball, designed to be the largest silver-service dinner party in the world and surpassing the previous years event and the expectations of a global audience.

Initial aims and objectives

Euro RSCG Skybridge looked to create a spectacular event to turn attitudes within Vodafone's newly created global corporation on their heads. Where there had been a belief that the business was stuffy and impersonal and big was bad, the event awakened employees to the personal dynamics, reconciling scale with intimacy and demonstrated that anything is possible when you are the biggest.

It was deemed important to understand exactly what fears the new business held for Vodafone employees to ensure any solution clearly targeted them, transforming negative beliefs into positives.

The brief

When considering the most impressive non-corporate benefit of being the biggest, a World Record and a place in The Guinness Book of Records, combined with the highly interactive and personal nature of a dinner party was seen as an exciting event at which to participate.

It was also important to move away from the traditional black tie event since we were trying to create a relaxed and casual environment, which shattered the myth Vodafone's size made them bureaucratic and unapproachable.

The remit of the brief was therefore to innovatively create, produce and manage a celebratory ball for Vodafone employees and their guests, on a scale a calibre befitting the growing stature of the organization and its corporate values and beliefs.

The required venue had to safely accommodate the required numbers of attendees, expected to be between 8000 and 12 000 people.

The brief covered pre-event planning, guest management and invitation process, total creative treatment including theming and entertainment, production and all logistical considerations relating to the proposed event.

For the ball to be a success, it had to exceed the expectations of those guests who had attended in previous years.

Response

The creative response leads with the main theme and event identity of a relaxed Beach Party. This was executed across all aspects of the event from the management approach to its tangible assets. The response included all pre-event guest management, overall creative theming and entertainment, production and all logistical considerations relating to the event.

London's Earls Court, was selected as the venue of choice due to its size, location, flexibility and reputation as an excellent entertainment venue. Earls Court provided the additional benefit and security of having staged the event previously.

Pre-event planning: logistics and production

The event requirements were assessed, based on the experiences of the previous year's event, the post-event evaluation, de-brief reports and the additional requirements derived from the increase in total guest numbers.

A Project Team was created to manage the complex Logistical and Production elements of the event. The necessity to have defined roles and responsibilities across the required key elements of the project would provide clear channels of communication and allow for areas of specialty to operate for the common stability of the event.

The Project Team developed a project plan complete with a critical path for each functional dynamic. The main functional responsibilities included:

- Overall project, venue and budgetary management
- Entertainment selection and management
- Main stage show production and direction
- Technical production
- Catering
- Health and Safety; including crowd control and security
- Creative execution; including theming, print and communications
- Transportation management
- Database and administrative management.

A series of status meetings were established with all stakeholders to continuously monitor and evaluate progress based on SMART principles, both internally within the agency and directly with the client's project coordinators, providing regular budgetary updates, status and contact reports.

The physicality and health and safety aspects of the event were examined in strict Risk Assessments, performed by the Project Team and specially commissioned professional Risk Assessors. All findings were documented and presented to the client and formed part of the essential event paperwork.

With the physical infrastructure in place, the other tangible elements were planned and executed to plan. The event was creatively teased to employees through a programme of internal communications, including posters, e-mails and a website, heightening awareness and expectation 6 months prior to the actual event.

The Beach Party theme was creatively incorporated into all aspects of the event from printed collateral, a specially designed website with online booking, the hotline, the invitation process through to the theming of the venue and the entertainment.

The logistics management of the event was a huge undertaking involving an invitation process where 6000 employees around the world were selected at random and invited to apply for two tickets to the event. Guests who accepted were directed to the dedicated website where they inputted all their required personal details including transport, dietary and medical requirements. A bespoke software tool created in house, provided the power behind every step of the party, including allowing guests to choose their place on the world's largest table plan for 11 500 people. Using a personal login, guests were also able to access all event details including detailed itinerary, up-to-date transport arrangements and even a friendly letter from the Chief Executive, emphasizing the personal nature of the initiative.

In total 136 coaches were sourced to transport 8500 guests. In addition 1420 car parking spaces were sourced, 300 VIP guests were chauffeured to and from the venue and approximately 700 domestic and international flight movements were booked.

Earls Court itself, was to be metamorphosized into a giant beach party occupying the whole of Halls 1 and 2, with the main hall being transformed into a huge dining and entertainment production arena split across levels one and two. A full sized funfair with side stalls and a 136 vehicle coach park occupied Earls Court 2, whilst most of the complex's satellite rooms were used for such activities as a comedy club, blues club, piano bar, karaoke, a huge gaming and amusement arcade.

The event: on-site operation

In the night the guests arrived by coach, car, public transport and foot. Strict marshalling and foot flow was managed around the perimeter of the building as well as dedicated movement channels within the buildings. This movement of people was formulated as part of the Standard Operating Plan derived from the Risk Assessment.

Prior to guests' arrival onsite, all personnel were fully briefed on the Standard Operating Plan and the Emergency Operating Plan by Heads of Departments. The 120 event crew, 150 production crew, 400 security staff, 2500 catering staff and 150 chefs were all made aware of their responsibilities during these briefings.

With the doors to Earls Court open for arrival, 11 500 guests made their way into the halls to be astounded by scale of their event. The format for the evening event included pre-dinner drinks, a sit down silver-service dinner and entertainment, pre- during and post-dinner.

Once seated, after a short introductory welcome and vote of thanks from the CEO, 2500 catering staff served a hot silver-service dinner to guests whilst they watched a full show of entertainment. The stage set was built like a beach bar and the ensuing stage show also included loud, upbeat music of song and dance specifically conceived, choreographed and uniquely performed for the event by a cast of over 100. During 'commercial breaks', a specially produced video montage highlighted the different international operating companies within the Vodafone extended family through a series of brand and product commercials.

Post-dinner guests were invited to explore all the entertainment areas within Earls Court, prior to a main stage concert. The main and sub-stages showcased numerous live bands and artistes such as the Corrs, Ronan Keating, Bjorn Again, Right Said Fred, Hear'say, Tony Hadley of Spandau Ballet and an Ibiza meets Handbag disco.

Control of the event was managed via a two-way radio system, with all communications and decisions being run through Event Control – this room contained 4 radio control personnel and the Event Director. The Event Director maintained control by reaching out through all the Functional Section Heads running Catering, Transport, Production, Entertainment and Security & Crowd Control.

Event challenges and statistics

The event required a continuous party atmosphere and seamless itinerary with heavy information technology (IT) and logistics support to provide one entertainment act after another whilst including motivational key messages, faultless hot catering and coping with the various health and safety issues as they arose. Interesting facts from the event include:

- 11 500 people
- 136 coaches all arrived and dropped off guests in a 45 minute window in addition to local shuttle buses
- Created specialist software to build a table plan for 11 500 guests
- Transportation organized for 8500 guests
- 1420 car spaces
- 300 VIP chauffeured guests
- 700 domestic and international flights
- 400 security staff
- 2500 catering staff
- 150 chefs
- 120 event crew
- 150 production crew
- 10 months of planning
- 2 tonnes of chicken
- 3 tonnes of vegetables
- 5700 bottles of wine
- 2400 litres of water
- 2000 litres of coffee
- 3 kilometres of tablecloth
- 65 000 pieces of crockery
- 78 000 pieces of cutlery.

Managing such a large number of guests provided an interesting challenge from the point of view of logistics management, crowd control, security, health and safety and subtle 'on-brand' messages.

The Ball became a reason for working at Vodafone and was so popular that it generated a 92 per cent response rate to invitations.

Euro RSCG Skybridge, Vodafone and its employees were awarded the Guinness World Record for the 'World's largest silver service dinner party' and the 'World's largest table plan', with the Financial Times and Daily Mail giving extensive, positive coverage and a delighted Chief Executive claiming it was 'the best party ever'.

Post-event evaluation and wrap up

Post-event evaluation highlighted the absolute appreciation and value by staff. In staff surveys, the event was cited as one of the reasons staff liked to work at Vodafone.

Detailed de-brief reports were written, along with de-brief meetings with the venue, key suppliers and importantly, the client during the post-event period. Great value is gained from the post event processes, which supports increased knowledge, understanding and identifies key action points for future events.

For further details about Euro RSCG Skybridge, please visit; www.eurorscgskybridge.com. By Randle Stonier, former Chairman, Euro RSCG Skybridge.

Questions

1. Identify the many stakeholders in the Vodafone ball, and list the likely benefits to each.
2. From the event description in the case study, what do you think was the likely process of conceptualizing the event?
3. Events of this size and complexity present many challenges for future years, including how to develop the event, while keeping it aspirational and tightly budgeted. Imagine that you are planning the above event again for next year.
   (a) If the numbers increase above the current level, the existing venue may not accommodate the large audience and the creative interpretation of the brief. Identify the strengths and weaknesses of the current venue. Suggest an alternative venue that could accommodate this event and list the benefits that your choice of venue would bring.
   (b) In order to keep the event aspirational in future, what vision or idea would you develop for this event? How would you conceptualize it? What are the unique elements in your event concept and how would this be expressed in the event?
4. Can you think of any other companies or organizations where a similar event model could be applied? List the potential stakeholders, and describe the steps that you would take in conceptualizing the event.

Case study 5.2

Daily Mail Ideal Home Show
Background

Maintaining a market leading position for a major exhibition may be a challenge for many organizers, but achieving this for a show that has been the biggest home event since 1908 is all the more remarkable. The Daily Mail Ideal Home Show, organized by DMG World Media at Earls Court in London, has reflected changes in society and home living since those early days, and continues to innovate in order to meet the needs of visitors.

The target audience for the Show is home owners and new home buyers who are in the market to refurnish their home, seeking products and services, advice and inspiring ideas in DIY, gardening and the lifestyles they provide to their families. Research undertaken at the 2004 show by Vivid Interface, on behalf of DMG World Media, identified that 82 per cent of visitors were from ABC1 social grades, over 30 per cent above the national average, with 66 per cent of the total visitors' female. Over the duration of the show, a total of £274 800 000 was spent (£10 569 230 per day), an average of £687 per visitor. As can be appreciated from these Figures, the show presents an excellent opportunity for exhibitors to showcase innovative new products, services and design ideas, but also to sell directly to a clearly defined target market.

Extensive research is conducted with visitors and exhibitors each year to ensure that the show continues to appeal to the target audience. A series of focus groups were conducted after the 2004 show which resulted in five key recommendations to be incorporated into the 2005 show:

1. Create features and attractions at the show that are more interactive.
2. Create a more visitor friendly experience.
3. Ensure value for money and added benefits for visiting the show.
4. Renew the media plan according to what the target customers respond to.
5. Target the messaging accordingly.

Innovations for 2005

For the 2005 Daily Mail Ideal Home Show (in association with npower), national research conducted on behalf of the organizers identified how an increasing number of British residents are investing in properties aboard, particularly in the Mediterranean, while this style of living is also increasingly being reflected in design ideas within their UK homes. The survey identified that an estimated 42 million people, or 70 per cent of British residents, would like to transfer from Britain to a continental life. As a result, the Daily Mail Ideal Home Show 2005 showcased simple through to sophisticated ways to bring the Continent home in style.

The show featured four authentic show homes including a stunning 'Property Keysol' Spanish Villa styled exclusively by Linda Barker, a beautifully designed Italian Merchant House styled Maggie Colvin, a French Chateau courtesy of Allied Carpets, and finally a 'Cave Home', one of the trendiest living spaces currently to hit the Mediterranean. Showcasing the latest interiors and forthcoming trends, the Cave home was styled and designed by interior experts Justin Ryan and Colin McAllister.

Each show home was positioned around a central Piazza, which was used to convey the passion and culture for each country using street performers, live entertainment, local produce and other features. This central area, the Mediterranean Village, depicted all aspects of Mediterranean living in partnership with Homes Overseas magazine.

For the first time ever visitors to the Show were given the chance to watch their favourite daytime television programme live from the Show, This Morning's Fern & Philip. Based in the stunning French Chateau within the Mediterranean Village, visitors were able to witness Fern and Philip broadcast live from the Show, on their very own sofa, for the entire week, from 7 to 11 March. In the true style of the Daily Mail Ideal Home Show, Fern and Philip also had their very own roomsets on display depicting their individual styles and design preferences.

In addition to the Mediterranean Village, the Daily Mail Ideal Home Show 2005 also featured a number of other innovations, including:

Ideal home magazine roomsets, incorporating the JJA ADA interior design clinic

Developed as a double-decker feature area, the downstairs showcased a series of 5 beautiful room designs and a stunning conservatory to inspire visitors with all the latest trends and glorious looks from around the world. The upstairs featured an interactive workshop area, courtesy of JJA ADA Interior Design Clinic, where visitors could meet a number of design experts who offered free help and advice on individual home designs and answered all those decorating questions and queries.

The Freestyle® men's Gadget Zone with T3 magazine

For the first time ever, the Show introduced an exciting area totally dedicated to the latest gadgets and gizmos on the market. The interactive Gadget Zone, sponsored by Freestyle® Mortgages and in association with T3 Magazine provided visitors with hours of fun as they got to experiment and witness a series of new, innovative and exciting products that have recently emerged into the market. The gadgets on display represented innovations in lifestyle and embraced ever changing technology to bring an assortment of gadgets and gizmos for everyday life, the home and the garden.

Crown town

Crown Town was a colour extravaganza packed full of interactive elements designed to give visitors a complete insight into the world of colour. This included visitors having their colour aura read and discovering what colours would be best suited in their homes, and getting expert advice with a personalized colour consultation from the experts at Crown Paints. A technology feature took this a stage further – visitors could see how a new room scheme might look by scanning in a photo of their own room and changing the colour of the walls at the click of a mouse!

Interactive show theatres

Celebrity appearances and expert advice were on hand for every type of home and lifestyle in the DIY Masterclass Theatre and the Sizzling Kitchen sponsored by Quality Standard Beef & Lamb. Celebrity guests including Justin Ryan and Colin McAllister, Anthony Worrall Thompson and Aldo Zilli hosted interactive demonstrations throughout the Show, giving visitors exclusive insights into the latest trends, designs and ingredients.

Roomsets with Justin Ryan and Colin McAllister

Celebrity designers and television personalities Justin Ryan and Colin McAllister demonstrated their design expertise and interior preferences in their fabulous roomsets. These stunning interiors showcased a much sought after and highly contemporary living space to give visitors an insight into their own interpretation of interior heaven.

Be a DJ competition

The popular 'Be a DJ Competition', in association with Heart 106.2 radio, returned this year. Every weekend at the Show the radio studio offered visitors the chance to try their hand at being a DJ, with prizes available to the winners including a tour of their studios.

The indulgence zone

Visitors were able to take time out from the wealth of attractions available on site to treat themselves to some free personal pampering courtesy of Color me Beautiful and the London College of Beauty Therapy. The Zone offered visitors a self-indulgent oasis where they could take time out from the bustle of the celebrity demonstrations and retail heaven of the Show, to put their feet up and pamper themselves with tailored beauty advice and the numerous beauty treats on offer. The Zone offered visitors complimentary hand massages, mini manicures, make up demonstrations and personal colour analysis.

Junior concept products

Due to the huge success of five years of Concept Products, the Show launched Junior Concept Products in 2005. This included the ideas of the youngest inventors and encouraged budding young designers (aged 8–11) to get creative and design a new product which could contribute to the quality of life and help make it better at home. Prizes were available for the individual best Junior Concept Products, each member of the winning team and, in addition, the winning schools received a monetary donation towards the purchase of Design Technology materials.

Garden ideas haven with magic 105.4

The Gardens feature showcased a series of unique and individual garden designs demonstrating the numerous different ways to make the most of and maximize all kinds of outdoor space. Each of the garden plots was uniquely designed to highlight the many different ideas available in developing visitors outdoor living space.

The Heart 106.2 makeover studios

A further innovation this year was the UK's first ever radio home make-over challenge. Heart 106.2 recruited ten of London's most willing and enthusiastic DIY 'wannabees' to take part in a fantastic two week challenge to design, build and style the exclusive Heart 106.2 makeover studios which dominated the entrance to Earls Court two throughout the duration of the show. Contestants received regular tips from specially brought in stylists and designers, with Heart listeners and visitors to the Show having the opportunity to make suggestions and text their decorating ideas and preferences. In addition, Show visitors and Heart listeners voted for their favourite room and the winning contestant. A webcam positioned within the studios showcased the work of each contestant and demonstrated their progress in conjunction with the contestant's personal online diaries. The winning contestant was awarded at the end of the week and presented with a cash prize by one of Heart's favourite DJ's. The following week saw the second group of five contestants competing for the prize.

New products

As a result of demand from the media for information on new products at the show, every exhibitor that had a new product at the show was promoted with a rosette on their stand to enable the media to easily identify them. In addition to this, a 'New Product Service' was introduced to highlight the top 20 products available at the Show. Finally, the organizers awarded some of the exhibitors with the Daily Mail Ideal Home Show Innovation Awards for the best new products to be launched at the show.

Summary

DMG World Media has maintained the position of the Daily Mail Ideal Home Show as the leading home lifestyle consumer show through continually innovating. Working effectively with exhibitors, sponsors, celebrity designers and the media ensures that creative new features are added each year, while incorporating interactive elements to the Show ensures that visitors have an enjoyable experience. This is clearly appropriate given the aim of the event and has proven to be a winning formula since 1908. Extensive research before, during and after the event, conducted with visitors, exhibitors and the wider target market, ensures that the Show reflects trends and styles in society and continues to meet the needs of attendees by delivering quality events, strong market opportunities for exhibitors and the best visitor experiences.

DMG World Media subscribe to Audit Bureau of Circulations (ABC) auditing of the show attendance data, which ensures that data are comparable with other exhibitions. In 2005, this data indicated that the Show was the largest consumer show in the UK. Taking place from 2 to 28 March 2005, over the three weeks 364 950 people attended the Show, including 345 148 visitors (291 005 paying, 54 143 complimentary visitors), 18 361 exhibitors, 672 organizer staff and 769 members of the press. The Show included 548 participating companies who took up 27 840 square metres of exhibition space, making it the sixth largest consumer show by net occupied stand space.

Building on the success of the Daily Mail Ideal Home Show, DMG World Media has grown and diversified its portfolio of Shows focusing on the home and garden markets and now has over 90 Shows throughout the UK, Canada, USA, Australia and New Zealand, including the Autumn Ideal Home Show at Earls Court, London and the Ideal Home and Garden Show and the Ideal Home Show Scotland at the SECC in Glasgow.

For further information on the Daily Mail Ideal Home Show, please visit www.idealhomeshow.co.uk.

By DMG World Media.

Questions

1. Write a purpose statement for the Daily Mail Ideal Home Show.
2. The case outlines the key recommendations from focus groups that were implemented for the 2005 Show. How could these be developed into objectives that correspond to the SMART principle?
3. Describe the strategies that DMG World Media uses for Daily Mail Ideal Home Show to achieve its objectives.
4. Explore the strategies adopted by DMG World Media with their portfolio of Shows. How do these compare to the Daily Mail Ideal Home Show?
5. Write a position description for the position of show director in the event organization.
6. Construct a policy document for the event that lists appropriate policies and procedures for producing the event.
7. Would you classify the process used for developing an event such as this as a single use plan or a standing plan? Explain your answer.

Chapter 6

Human resource management and events

Learning Objectives

After studying this chapter, you should be able to:

- describe the human resource management challenges posed by events
- list and describe the key steps in the human resource planning process for events
- describe approaches to determining human resource needs for events
- list areas, in the context of events, where human resource policies and procedures might be required
- describe event staff and volunteer recruitment and selection processes
- describe approaches to training and professional development relevant in an event context
- discuss staff supervision and evaluation practices in which an event manager might engage
- describe practices associated with the termination, outplacement and re-enlistment of event staff and volunteers
- describe approaches that can be employed to motivate event staff and volunteers
- describe techniques that can be used for event staff and volunteer team building
- describe general legal considerations associated with human resource management in an event context.

Introduction

Effective planning and management of human resources is at the core of any successful event. Ensuring an event is adequately staffed with the right people, who are appropriately trained and motivated to meet its objectives, is fundamental to the event management process. This chapter seeks to provide an overview of the key aspects of human resource planning and management with which an event manager should be familiar. It begins by examining considerations associated with human resource management in the context of events. It then moves on to propose a model of the human resource management process for events and to discuss each of the major steps in this model. Selected theories associated with employee/volunteer motivation are then described, followed by a brief examination of techniques for staff and volunteer team building. The final part of this chapter deals with legal considerations associated with human resource management. Issues associated with volunteer management receive significant coverage in this chapter, given the role volunteers play in the conduct of many types of event.

Considerations associated with human resource planning for events

The context in which human resource planning takes place for events can be said to be unique for two major reasons. First, and perhaps most significantly, many events have a 'pulsating' organizational structure (Hanlon and Jago, 2000; Hanlon and Cuskelly, 2002). This means they grow in terms of personnel as the event approaches, but quickly contract when it ends. From a human resource perspective, this creates a number of challenges, including obtaining paid staff given the short-term nature of the employment offered; working to short timelines to hire and select staff, and to develop and implement staff training; and needing to shed staff quickly. Also, volunteers, as opposed to paid staff, often make up the bulk of people involved in delivering an event. In some instances, events are run entirely by volunteers. The challenges presented by this situation are many, and relate to such matters as sourcing volunteers, quality control, supervision, training and motivation. Later parts of this chapter suggest responses to these challenges.

The human resource planning process for events

Human resource planning for events should not be viewed simply in terms of a number of isolated tasks, but as a series of sequential interrelated-processes and practices that take their lead from an event's vision/mission, objectives and strategy. If an event seeks to grow in size and attendance, for example, it will need a human resource strategy to support this growth through such means as increased staff recruitment (paid and/or volunteer) and expanded (and perhaps more sophisticated) training programmes. If these supporting human resource management actions are not in place, problems such as high staff/volunteer turnover due to overwork, poor quality delivery and an associated declining marketplace-image may result, jeopardizing the event's future.

Events will obviously differ in terms of the level of sophistication they display in the human resources area, given factors such as their access to resources in terms of money and expertise. For example, contrast a local community festival that struggles to put together an organizing committee and attract sufficient volunteers with a mega-event such as the Olympic Games. Nonetheless, it is appropriate that the 'ideal' situation is examined here – that is, the complete series of steps through which an event manager should proceed for human resource planning. By understanding these steps and their relationships to one another, event managers will give themselves the best chance of managing human resources in a way that will achieve their event's goals and objectives. As a way of introducing you to how this process can be applied to events, this chapter includes an event profile dealing with the successful volunteer programme at the Sydney Olympic Games.

While a number of general models of the human resource management process can be identified, the one chosen to serve as the basis of discussion in this chapter is based on that proposed by Getz (2005). This model (Figure 6.1) represents an attempt to display how this process works within an event context.

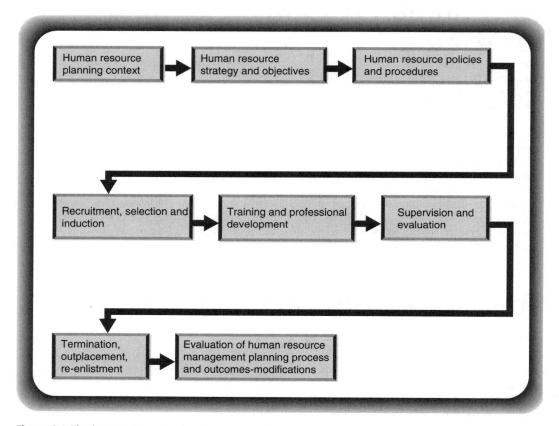

Figure 6.1 The human resource planning process for events
Source: adapted from Getz (2005), p. 221

Human resource strategy and objectives

This stage in the human resource management process for events involves a variety of activities, including establishing guiding strategies and objectives, determining staffing needs (paid and volunteer), and undertaking a job analysis and producing job descriptions and specifications. Each of these tasks is discussed in turn in this section.

Strategy

An event's human resource strategy seeks to support its overall mission and objectives. This link can be demonstrated by reference to the following examples that identify a few selected areas in which an organization might set objectives and the subsequent focus on supporting human resource management objectives and activities:

- cost containment – improved staff/volunteer productivity, reduced absenteeism and decreased staff numbers.
- improved quality – better recruitment and selection, expanded employee and volunteer training, increased staff and volunteer numbers, and improved financial rewards and volunteer benefits.
- improved organizational effectiveness – better job design, changes to organizational structure and improved relations with employees and volunteers.
- enhanced performance regarding social and legal responsibilities – improved compliance with relevant legislation, such as that relating to occupational health and safety at work, anti-discrimination and equal opportunities.

Whatever human resource management objectives are set for an event, they need to meet the SMART criteria discussed in Chapter 5.

Staffing

Staffing is the main strategic decision area for event managers in the area of human resources, because without staff there is nothing really to 'strategize' about! Event managers need to make decisions concerning how many staff/volunteers are needed to deliver the event, what mix of skills/qualifications/experience is required, and when in the event planning process these staff/volunteers will be needed (for example, the event shutdown stage only). Getz (2005, p. 222) suggests one way of undertaking this task in the context of events, involving a three-stage process:

1. Identify all tasks associated with event creation, delivery and shutdown. Site-related tasks, for example, might include site design and layout, setting up fencing, erecting tents and stages, positioning/building toilets, and placing signs and waste containers.
2. Determine how many people are needed to complete the range of tasks associated with the conduct of the event. Do all the tasks have to be done in order, by the same work crew, or all at once by a larger crew? What level of supervision will be required? What tasks can be outsourced and what must be done by the event team? Will more staff than normal be required to perform tasks (such as security) as a result of some specific circumstance (such as a visit by a celebrity to the event)?
3. List the numbers of staff/volunteers and supervisors and the skills/experience/qualifications needed to form the 'ideal' workforce for the event.

The most difficult task in this process is step 2, particularly if the event is new. Armstrong (2003) claims that managerial judgement is by far the most common approach used in business to answer this question. Such an observation is also likely to apply to the world of events. That is, the event manager, or various functional managers if the event is large enough, calculates how many, and what type, of human resources are needed to meet their objectives. In doing so, they are likely to account for factors such as prior experience, demand forecasts for the event, the number of venues/sites involved, skill/expertise requirements, previous instances of similar (or the same) events, the degree of outsourcing possible, the availability of volunteers and strategies adopted by the event.

In the case of some tasks associated with the conduct of events, it is possible to estimate staffing needs by engaging in some basic arithmetic. The number of people who can pass through a turnstile per hour, for example, can be easily calculated by dividing the processing time for an individual into 60 minutes. Assume the figure generated in this way is 240 – that is, 240 people can be processed in an hour through one turnstile. Next, an estimate of event attendance (including peaks and troughs in arrivals) is required. Now assume total attendance for the event has been fairly consistent at 5000 over the past three years, with 80 per cent (4000) of people arriving between 9 a.m. and 11 a.m. If this number of people is to be processed over a two-hour period, about eight turnstiles would need to be open (240 transactions per hour multiplied by two hours, divided by the number of attendees over this time, which is 4000). Based on these calculations, eight turnstile operators would be required for the first two hours; after this time, the number of operators could be dramatically decreased. However, care should be taken to ensure that sufficient staff are available at the event, particularly when considering stewards and security staff. The Health and Safety Executive (HSE, 1999) advise that the number of stewards should be based on the risk assessment, rather than precise mathematical formulas, in order to take into account the unique circumstances of the event.

Job analysis

Job analysis, sometimes referred to as job evaluation, is an important aspect of this stage of the human resource planning process. It involves defining a job in terms of specific tasks and responsibilities and identifying the abilities, skills and qualifications needed to perform that job successfully. According to Stone (2002), questions answered by this process include:

- What tasks should be grouped together to create a job or position?
- What should be looked for in individuals applying for identified jobs?
- What should an organizational structure look like and what interrelationships between jobs should exist?
- What tasks should form the basis of performance appraisal for an individual in a specific job?
- What training and development programmes are required to ensure staff/ volunteers possess the needed skills/knowledge?

The level of sophistication evident in the application of the job analysis process differs between events. Some small-scale events that depend exclusively, or almost exclusively, on volunteers may simply attempt to match people to the tasks in which they have expressed an interest. Even under such circumstances, some consideration probably should be given to factors such as experience, skills and physical abilities.

Job descriptions

Position, or job, descriptions are another outcome of the job analysis process with which event managers need some measure of familiarity if they are to effectively match people (both employees and volunteers) to jobs. The usefulness of this part of the planning exercise is well documented in the management literature. Beardwell, Holden and Claydon (2004) contend that position descriptions are helpful to managers in recruiting and selecting staff. In addition, they may be drawn upon for inducting and training of new employees, and development, job evaluation and performance appraisal of existing employees. Mullins (2005, p. 802) states that job analysis, leading to the job description and person specification is 'Central to a planned and systematic approach' of human resource planning. He goes on to stress that although valuable, it is important not to write job descriptions in a bureaucratic manner, which would imply 'a lack of flexibility, imagination or initiative on the part of the job holder'. Mullins highlighted criticism of job descriptions by Townsend, who described them as straitjackets, and Belbin, who suggested that they were an obstacle to progress in organizations as they lead to a lack of cooperation, claims for additional payment based on additional responsibilities or inflexibility with taking on team roles. Beardwell, Holden and Claydon (2004) report that problems can arise if job descriptions are not regularly updated, which may be the detrimental to the development of the staff and organization. In order to try to begin clarifying roles and develop career paths, MPI have developed a collection of standard job descriptions for positions at different levels in the Meetings Industry as part of their MPI Professional Pathways project.

Job descriptions commonly include the following information:

- Job title and commitment required – this information locates the paid or voluntary position within the organization, indicates the functional area where the job is to be based (for example, marketing coordinator), and states the job duration/time commitment (for example, one year part-time contract involving two days a week).
- Salary/rewards/incentives associated with position – for paid positions, a salary, wage or hourly rate needs to be stated, along with any other rewards such as bonuses. In the case of voluntary positions, consideration should be given to identifying benefits such as free merchandise (for example, T-shirts and limited edition souvenir programmes), free/discounted meals, free tickets and end-of-event parties, all of which can serve to increase interest in working at an event.
- Job summary – this brief statement describes the primary purpose of the job. The job summary for an event operations manager, for example, may read: 'Under the direction of the event director, prepare and implement detailed operational plans in all areas associated with the successful delivery of the event'.
- Duties and responsibilities – this information lists major tasks and responsibilities associated with the job. It should not be overly detailed, identifying only those duties/responsibilities that are central to the performance of the job. Additionally, it is useful to express these in terms of the most important outcomes of the work. For an event operations manager, for example, one key responsibility expressed in outcome terms would be the preparation of plans encompassing all operational dimensions of the event, such as site set-up and breakdown, security, parking, waste management, staging and risk management.
- Relationships with other positions within and outside the event organization – what positions report to the job? (An event operations manager, for example, may have all site staff/volunteers associated with security, parking, staging, waste management, utilities and so on reporting to him/her.) To what position(s) does the job report? (An event operations manager may report only to the event director/manager.) What outside organizations will the position need to liaise with to satisfactorily perform the job? (An event operations manager may need to liaise with local councils, police, roads and traffic authorities, and local emergency service providers.)
- Know-how/skills/knowledge/experience/qualifications/personal attributes required by the position – in some instances, particularly with basic jobs, training may quickly overcome most deficiencies in these areas. However, for more complex jobs (voluntary or paid), such as those of a managerial or supervisory nature, individuals may need to possess experience, skills or knowledge before applying. Often, a distinction is drawn between these elements, with some being essential while others are desirable. Specific qualifications may also be required. For example, some advertisements for event managers list formal qualifications

in event management as desirable. Personal attributes – such as the ability to work as part of a team, to be creative, to work to deadlines and to represent the event positively to stakeholder groups – may also be relevant considerations.

- Authority vested in the position – what decisions can be made without reference to a superior? What expenditure limits are on decision making?
- Performance standards associated with the position – criteria will be required by which performance in the position will be assessed. While such standards apply more to paid staff than to voluntary positions, they should still be considered for the latter. This is particularly the case if volunteers hold significant management or supervisory positions where substandard performance could jeopardize one or more aspects of the event. If duties and responsibilities have been written in output terms, then these can be used as the basis of evaluation.
- Trade union/association membership required with position.
- Special circumstances associated with the position – does the job require heavy, sustained lifting, for example?
- Problem solving – what types of problems will commonly be encountered on the job – routine and repetitive problems or complex and varied issues?

While job descriptions for paid positions often involve most, if not all, the information noted previously, voluntary positions are often described in far more general terms. This is because they often (but not always) involve fairly basic tasks. This is evident from Figure 6.2, which illustrates a job description for the volunteer steward position at Harrogate International Festival.

Job specification

A job specification is derived from the job description and seeks to identify the experience, formal qualifications, skills, abilities, knowledge, motivation and personal characteristics needed to perform a given job. As Mullins (2005) notes, care must be taken to ensure that legal requirements are considered. In essence, it identifies the types of people that should be recruited and how they should be appraised. The essential and desirable/preferred criteria shown in Figure 6.2 provides an example of how job specifications can be used in the recruitment process, with these elements used in job adverts to attract appropriate applicants.

Policies and procedures

Policies and procedures are needed to provide the framework in which the remaining tasks in the human resource planning process take place: recruitment and selection; training and professional development; supervision and evaluation; termination, outplacement, reemployment and evaluation. According to Thompson with Martin (2005, p. 758), 'Policies are designed to guide the behaviour of managers in relation to the pursuit and achievement of strategies and objectives'. He notes that they:

- guide thoughts and actions – for example, an event manager who declines to consider an application from a brother of an existing employee may point to a policy on employing relatives of existing personnel if there is a dispute
- establish a routine and consistent approach – for example, seniority will be the determining factor in requests by volunteers to fill job vacancies
- establish how certain tasks should be carried out and place constraints on management decision making – for example, rather than a manager having to think about the process of terminating the employment of a staff member or volunteer, they can simply follow the process already prescribed.

Volunteer Event Stewards promote and are ambassadors for the Festival; they are the first point of contact for members of the public when buying programme books, event merchandise and requesting general information. Volunteer Event Stewards are responsible to the Admin and Marketing Assistant.

The role of the Volunteer Event Steward is critical to the success of the Festival; stewards are advocates for our work, and support what we do. They are responsible for looking after, and being of service to, our most valued asset – our audience.

Responsibilities:
- Selling festival programmes at all events pre-performance, during the interval, and post-performance
- Providing good customer service to all audience members
- Cash handling during events
- To promote the work of the Festival and support Festival staff during events
- To carry out other duties, including merchandise sales, as required by Festival staff from time to time

Person Specification:
Essential: – Committed to the aims and objectives of the Festival
– Cash handling experience
– Ability to work as part of a team
– Smart appearance
– Ability to sell effectively
– Knowledge of and enthusiasm for the arts
Preferred: – Previous customer service experience
– Previous sales training or experience
– Knowledge of health and safety procedures

Personal Characteristics:
– Reliable, punctual
– Enthusiastic
– Hard-working
– Friendly and approachable
– Flexible attitude

Figure 6.2 Extract from volunteer event steward job description and person specification
Source: Harrogate International Festival (2004a)

Human resource practices and procedures for events are often conditioned or determined by those public or private sector organizations with ultimate authority for them. A local council responsible for conducting an annual festival, for example, would probably already have in place a range of policies and procedures regarding the use of volunteers. These policies and procedures would then be applied to the event. Additionally, a range of laws influence the degree of freedom that the management of an event has in the human resource area. Laws regarding occupational health and safety, holiday and long service leave, maternity and paternity, working hours, minimum wages, discrimination, dismissal and compensation all need to become integrated into the practices and policies that an event adopts.

If an event manager goes to the time and effort to develop policies and procedures, he or she also needs to ensure these are communicated to all staff and applied. Additionally, resources need to be allocated to this area so the 'paperwork' generated by those policies and procedures can be stored, accessed and updated/modified as required. Such paperwork may include various policy/procedure manuals and staff records such as performance evaluations and employment contracts.

Again, the larger (in terms of number of staff and volunteers) and more sophisticated (in terms of management) the event, the more likely it is that the event managers would have thought more deeply about policy and procedure concerns. Nonetheless, even smaller events benefit in terms of the quality of their overall human resources management if some attempt is made to set basic policies and procedures to guide actions.

Recruitment, selection and induction

The recruitment of paid and volunteer employees is essentially about attracting the 'right' potential candidates to the 'right' job openings. Successful recruitment is based on how well previous stages in the human resource planning process have been conducted, and involves determining where qualified applicants can be found and how they can be attracted to the event organization. It is a two-way process, in that the event is looking to meet its human resource needs at the same time as potential applicants are trying to assess whether they meet the job requirements, wish to apply for the position and perceive value in joining the organization. Figure 6.3 is a diagram representing the recruitment process.

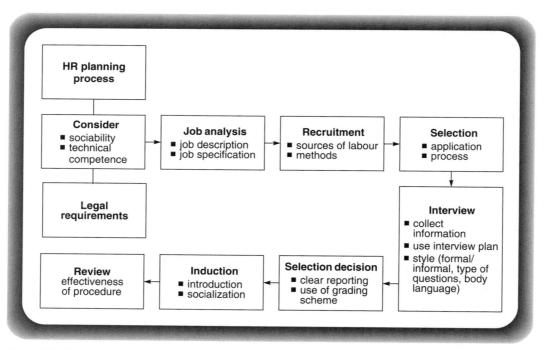

Figure 6.3 The recruitment and selection process for paid and voluntary employees
Source: adapted from Mullins (2005)

How event managers approach the recruitment process depends on the financial resources they have available to them. It may be appropriate, depending on the types of positions that need filling, to use recruitment agencies, for example, Anne Ellington Associates, Chess Partnership, Ellis Fairbank or ESP Recruitment for full-time staff, or the local job centre or employment agencies (for example, Adecco, Event-Staff.co.uk) to meet temporary staffing needs. With large events, a budget is likely to be set aside for this purpose, designed to cover costs such as recruitment agency fees, advertising, the travel expenses of non-local applicants and search fees for executive placement companies. However, because of the perceived attractiveness of working on events, it may be cheaper to recruit using advertisements in appropriate newspapers or trade journals, for example, *The Guardian* (national), *Manchester Evening News* (local) or *Event* (trade). In addition, there are an increasing number of Internet-based general recruitment services, for example, Stepstone (www.stepstone.co.uk), Topjobs.co.uk (www.topjobs.co.uk) and Monster.co.uk (www.monster.co.uk), or events industry specific sites, JobsUpdata (www.meetpie.com/jobs), Conference & Incentive Travel (www.citmagazine.co.uk/) or Event (www.eventmagazine.co.uk). Nevertheless, it must be recognized that the time spent by managers on this quite time-consuming process is also a cost, and therefore it may be more efficient to outsource to an agency. For links to event recruitment agencies and other resources, please visit WorldofEvents.net.

The reality for most events, however – particularly those relying heavily on volunteers – is that they will have few resources to allocate to the recruitment process. Nonetheless, they can still successfully engage in this process by:

- using stakeholders (for example, local councils, community groups, sponsors and event suppliers) to communicate the event's staffing needs (volunteer and paid) to their respective networks. McCurley and Lynch (1998), in the context of volunteers, call this approach 'concentric circle recruitment' because it involves starting with the groups of people who are already connected to the event or organization and working outwards. It is based on the premise that volunteers are recruited by someone they know – for example, friends or family, clients or colleagues, staff, employers, neighbours or acquaintances, such as members from the same clubs and societies.
- writing sponsorship agreements in a way that requires the sponsor, as part of their agreement with the event, to provide temporary workers with particular skills, such as marketing staff.
- identifying and liaising with potential sources of volunteers/casual staff, including universities and colleges (projects and work placements/internships may be specially created for these groups, particularly if they are studying festival, exhibition and events management or a related area such as film), religious groups, service clubs (such as Lions and Rotary), community service programmes, senior citizen centres and retirement homes, chambers of commerce, and community centres. The International Festival and Events Association maintains an internship 'bank' on its website (www.ifea.com/education/intern.asp).
- determining the make-up (for example, age, sex, occupations) and motivations of existing volunteers, and using this information as the basis of further targeted recruitment.
- gaining the assistance of local and specialist media (for example, radio, television, newspapers, specialist magazines) in communicating the event's human resource needs. This process is greatly assisted if one or more media organizations are in some way (such as through sponsorship) associated with the event.

- targeting specific individuals within a community who have specialist skills to sit on boards or undertake specific tasks, such as those tasks associated with the legal and accounting aspects of conducting an event.
- registering with a volunteer programme. In UK, these include Manchester Event Volunteer Programme (see case study at the end of this chapter), London Active Partnership, TimeBank, Community Service Volunteers and Volunteer to Win (programme for London 2012 and events before then).
- conducting social functions at which, for example, existing volunteers or staff might be encouraged to bring potential candidates, or to which particular groups/ targeted individuals are invited.

Once an appropriate pool of applicants has been identified, the next step is to select from among them those applicants that best fit the identified available positions. It is important to approach this process systematically, employing appropriate tools, to avoid the costs (financial and otherwise) that come from poor selection (increased training time, high turnover of staff/volunteers, absenteeism, job dissatisfaction and poor performance).

A useful starting point in the selection process is the selection policy. This policy should have been developed earlier in the policy and procedures stage of the human resource planning process. In constructing such a policy, thought needs to be given to:

- outlining how the event organization intends to comply with equal opportunities employment legislation
- approaches to measuring the suitability of candidates – for example, simple rating scales based on set criteria
- the source of people – for example, will the event organization promote from within where possible?
- the decision makers – that is, who will have the final decision on who to engage?
- selection techniques – for example, will tests be employed? Will decisions be made after one interview or several?
- the organization's business objectives – for example, do the candidates selected have the qualities and qualifications to progress the event's objectives?

The application process will vary based on the needs of the position, the number of applications anticipated and the resources of the event organization. In cases where a large number of applications are anticipated, it may be appropriate to consider screening applicants by telephone by asking a few key questions central to the position's requirements – for example, do you have a qualification in events management? Those individuals who answer these questions appropriately can then be sent an application. In the case of volunteers, applicants for positions in small-scale events may be asked to simply send in a brief note indicating what skills/qualifications they have, any relevant experience and the tasks they would be interested in doing. For larger events, volunteers may be asked to complete an application or registration form such as that developed by for Harrogate International Festival (Figure 6.4).

However basic, application forms for paid employees generally seek information on educational qualifications, previous employment and other details deemed relevant to the position by the applicant. The names and contact details of referees who can supply written and/or verbal references are also normally required. Additionally, a curriculum vitae (CV) is generally appended to these forms. Once received, applications allow unsuitable applicants to be culled; those applicants thought to be suitable for short-listing can be invited to attend an interview. Volunteers may simply be notified that they have been accepted and asked to attend a briefing session.

HARROGATE INTERNATIONAL FESTIVAL

VOLUNTEER APPLICATION

Title .... **Full name** ....

Address ....

....

Telephone number (daytime) .... **Telephone number** (evening) ....

The Festival is staffed by a full time team of four and one part time member of staff. However, as a registered charity (no. 244861) we rely on the help of volunteers to assist with various areas of work at different times of the year. Please indicate below which areas of work you would be able to assist with, and an outline of your availability.

I would be happy to help with the following (please tick all that apply):

☐   Distribution of Festival print material in Harrogate

☐   Distribution of Festival print material in Knaresborough

☐   Distribution of Festival print material in Ripon

☐   Distribution of Festival print material elsewhere (please specify) ....

☐   Stewarding at Harrogate International Festival events (21 July–5 August 2005)

☐   Stewarding at Harrogate International Sunday Series events (dates tbc – February–April 2005)

☐   Assisting with sticking and stuffing envelopes for Festival mailings

☐   Other (please specify) ....

I am available to help at the following times (please tick all that apply):

☐   Evenings

☐   Day time

☐   Weekends

☐   Weekdays

☐   Other (please specify) ....

Are you available for the period of this year's Festival, 21 July–5 August 2005?

☐   Yes – throughout

☐   Partially (please specify) ....

☐   No – not at all

Do you have any cash handling experience?

☐   Yes: if so, please give details: ....

☐   No

Do you have any basic First Aid knowledge?

☐   Yes: if so, please give details: ....

☐   No

Where did you hear about volunteering opportunities at the Festival?

....

Please give details of two referees:

Name   ....   Name   ....

Address   ....   Address   ....

          ....

          ....

Phone number   ....   Phone number   ....

Relationship to you   ....   Relationship to you   ....

Thank you for your time. Please return this to us at the following address:

Harrogate International Festival, 1 Victoria Avenue, Harrogate HG1 1EQ

If you have any queries, please telephone xxxxx xxxxxx

Figure 6.4 Volunteer application form
Source: Harrogate International Festival (2004b)

When selecting among applicants, Robertson and Makin (1986) (cited in Beardwell and Holden, 2001) suggest taking into account the following factors:

1. *Past behaviour*: The use of past behaviour can be employed to predict future behaviour. That is, the manner in which a person completed a task in the past is the best predictor of the way that person will complete a task in the future. Biographical data (obtained from the curriculum vitae or application form), references and supervisor/peer group ratings are commonly the major sources of such information.
2. *Present behaviour*: A range of techniques can be used to assess present behaviour, including:
   - tests, which may be designed to measure aptitude, intelligence, personality and basic core skill levels (for example, typing speeds)
   - interviews (see later discussion)
   - assessment centres, which conduct a series of tests, exercises and feedback sessions over a one- to five-day period to assess individual strengths and weakness
   - portfolios/examples of work, which are used to indicate the quality/type of recent job-related outputs. An applicant for the position of a set designer for a theatrical event, for example, may be asked to supply photographs of his or her previous work.
3. *Future behaviour*: If appropriate, interview information can be supplemented with observations from simulations to predict future behaviour. If the position is for a sponsorship manager, for example, applicants can be asked to develop a sponsorship proposal and demonstrate how they would present this proposal to a potential sponsor. Another common approach, according to Noe et al. (2003), is to ask, in the context of managerial appointments, for applicants to respond to memos that typify problems they are likely to encounter.

Interviews are likely to be the most common means of selection used by event organizations, so it is worthwhile spending some time looking at how best to employ this approach.

Interviews

According to Noe et al. (2003), research clearly indicates that the interviewing process should be undertaken using a structured approach so all relevant information can be covered and candidates can be directly compared. Mullins (2005) suggests using a checklist of key matters to be covered in the interviews. A sample checklist for a paid position associated with an event is shown in Figure 6.5. Checklists should also be used if interviews are to be conducted for volunteers. In such instances, answers might be sought to questions regarding the relationship between the volunteer's background/experience and the position(s) sought, reasons for seeking to become involved with the event, the level of understanding about the demands/requirements of the position(s) (such as time and training), and whether applicants have a physical or medical condition that may have an impact on the types of position for which they can be considered (keeping equal opportunities employment legislation in mind).

Applicant responses flowing from the interview process need to be assessed in some way against the key criteria for the position. One common means of doing this is a rating scale (for example, 1 to 5). When viewed collectively, the ratings given to individual items lead to an overall assessment of the applicant in terms of how he or she fits with the job, the event organization and its future directions.

INTERVIEWER'S CHECKLIST

Position title:_____ Candidate's name:_____ Date:_____

Interviewees:_____

Interview
1. Qualifications held
2. Employment history
3. Extent to which applicant meets essential criteria for the position
4. Extent to which applicant meets desirable criteria for the position
5. Organizational fit
   (a) To what extent will the position result in personal satisfaction for the applicant?
   (b) To what extent does the applicant identify with the organization's values and culture?
   (c) Can the applicant's remuneration expectations be met?

Assessment
Summary rating of applicant based on the above criteria. A simple scale of 'all, most, some, none' may be used for criteria 3 and 4. Additionally, some relevant summary comments may be made on each applicant.

Action
Follow-up action to be taken with applicant – for example:
• Advise if successful/unsuccessful.
• Place on eligibility list.
• Check references.
• Arrange pre-employment medical check.

Figure 6.5 Sample interviewer's checklist

Interviews may be conducted on a one-on-one basis or via a panel of two or more interviewers. The latter has some advantages in that it assists in overcoming any idiosyncratic biases that individual interviewers might have, allows all interviewers to evaluate the applicant at the same time and on the same questions and answers, and facilitates the discussion of the pros and cons of individual applicants.

Once the preferred applicant has been identified, the next step is to make a formal offer of appointment, by mail or otherwise. In the case of paid event staff, the short-term nature of many events means any offer of employment is for a specific contracted period. The employment contract generally states what activities are to be performed, salary/wage levels, and the rights and obligations of the employer and employee.

Under the Employment Rights Act, 1996, employees are entitled to receive a contract of employment within eight weeks of commencing employment. The legislation ensures that minimum conditions of employment are established in the contract. Armstrong (2003, p. 857) identifies the following areas typically to be included – details may either be discussed or referred to in separate documents (e.g. grievance procedure):

• a statement of job title and duties
• the date continuous employment commenced
• rate of pay, allowances, overtime, method and timing of payment
• hours of work including breaks
• holiday arrangements/entitlement

- sickness procedure (including sick pay, notification of illness)
- length of notice due to and from the employee
- grievance procedure
- disciplinary procedure
- work rules
- arrangements for terminating employment
- arrangements for union membership (if applicable)
- special terms relating to confidentiality, rights to patents and designs, exclusivity
- of service and restrictions on trade after termination of employment (e.g. cannot work for a direct competitor within six months)
- employer's right to vary terms and conditions subject to proper notification.

If large numbers of employees are used in an event, an enterprise agreement negotiated with employees can engender an atmosphere of trust and of working together to achieve a commonly sought objective.

In the case of volunteers, a simple letter of appointment, accompanied by details regarding the position may be all that is necessary. It is also appropriate to consider supplying volunteers with a statement about their rights and those of the event organization regarding their involvement in the event (Figure 6.6). Once an offer has been made and accepted, unsuccessful applicants should be informed as soon as possible.

Records of paid employees must also be kept. These should include:

- Name, address and telephone number
- Employment classification/employee number and national insurance number
- Whether full-time or part-time
- Whether permanent, temporary or casual
- Whether an apprentice or trainee
- Date when first employed
- Date when terminated
- Remuneration and hours worked
- Leave records
- Superannuation contributions.

McCurley and Lynch (1998) advise that it is also sound practice to keep records of volunteers. These may based on employee records, but will include as a minimum:

- Contract
- job description
- application/interview forms
- name and address
- role in the event and training received
- skills and expertise
- performance appraisal
- access to special equipment
- willingness to volunteer again.

This type of information facilitates human resource planning for future events.

Induction

Once appointees (paid or voluntary) commence with an event organization, a structured induction programme designed to begin the process of 'bonding'

Both the volunteer and the organization have responsibilities to each other. The volunteer contracts to perform a specific job and the organization contracts to provide the volunteer with a worthwhile and rewarding experience. In return, each has the right to some basic expectations of the other.

Volunteers have the right to:

- be treated as co-workers. This includes job descriptions, equal employment opportunity, occupational health and safety, anti-discrimination legislation and organizational grievance processes.

- be asked for their permission before any job-related reference, police or prohibited person checks are conducted

- a task or job worthwhile to them, for no more than 16 hours a week on a regular basis

- know the purpose and 'ground rules' of the organization

- appropriate orientation and training for the job

- be kept informed of organization changes and the reasons for such changes

- a place to work and suitable tools

- reimbursement of agreed expenses

- be heard and make suggestions

- personal accident insurance in place of workers compensation insurance

- a verbal reference or statement of service, if appropriate.

Organizations have the right to:

- receive as much effort and service from a volunteer worker as a paid worker, even on a short-term basis

- select the best volunteer for the job by interviewing and screening all applicants. This might include reference and police checks and, where appropriate, prohibited person checks for roles that involve working directly with children.

- expect volunteers to adhere to their job descriptions/outlines and the organization's code of practice

- expect volunteers to undertake training provided for them and observe safety rules

- make the decision regarding the best placement of a volunteer

- express opinions about poor volunteer effort in a diplomatic way

- expect loyalty to the organization and only constructive criticism

- expect clear and open communication from the volunteer

- negotiate work assignments

- release volunteers under certain circumstances.

Figure 6.6 Rights and responsibilities of volunteers and voluntary organizations
Source: School of Volunteer Management (2001)

the individual to the event organization needs to be conducted. Getz (2005, p. 227) suggests a range of actions be taken as part of an effective induction programme:

- Provide basic information about the event (mission, objectives, stakeholders, budget, locations, programme details).
- Conduct tours of venues, suppliers, offices and any other relevant locations.
- Make introductions to other staff and volunteers.
- Give an introduction to the organizational culture, history and working arrangements.
- Overview training programmes.

In addition to these actions, it is sound practice to discuss the job description with the individual to ensure he or she has a clear understanding of matters such as responsibilities, performance expectations, approaches to performance evaluation, and reporting relationships. At this time other matters associated with the terms and conditions of employment should also be discussed/reiterated, including probationary periods, grievance procedures, absenteeism, sickness, dress code, security, holiday/leave benefits, superannuation, salary and overtime rates, and other benefits such as car parking and meals. One means of ensuring mutual understanding of these matters is to have the staff member/volunteer read and sign their position description. Figure 6.7 gives an example of a position description that could be used for this purpose for volunteers.

The induction process can also be facilitated by the development of an induction kit for distribution to each new staff member or volunteer. Such a kit might contain:

- an annual report
- a message from the organizing committee chairperson/chief executive officer welcoming staff and volunteers
- a statement of event mission/vision, goals and objectives
- an organizational chart
- a name badge
- a staff list (including contact details)
- a uniform (whether a T-shirt or something more formal)
- a list of sponsors
- a list of stakeholders

Job title: _____

Supervisor: _____

Location: _____

Objective (Why is this job necessary? What will it accomplish?):
_____

Responsibilities (What specifically will the volunteer do?):
_____

Qualifications (What special skills, education, or age group is necessary to do this job?): _____

Training provided: _____

Benefits (parking, transportation, uniforms, food and beverage, expenses):
_____

Trial period (probation, if required): _____

References required (yes or no): _____

Any other information: _____

Date: _____

Signature of volunteer (to be added at time of mutual agreement):
_____

Signature of supervisor: _____

Figure 6.7 Example of a job description and contract for a volunteer
Source: Bradner (1997), p. 75

- any other appropriate items – for example, occupational, health and safety information.

A central outcome of the induction process should be a group of volunteers and staff who are committed to the event, enthusiastic and knowledgeable about their role in it, and aware of what part their job plays in the totality of the event.

Training and professional development

According to Armstrong (2003), learning, training and professional development should be considered in terms of meeting business needs and strategies. Training focuses on providing specific job skills/knowledge that will allow people to perform a job or to improve their performance in it. Professional development, on the other hand, is concerned with the acquisition of new skills, knowledge and attitudes that will prepare individuals for future job responsibilities.

Both training and professional development are significant in driving the success of an event, acting to underpin its effective delivery. For small and mid-sized events, much training is on-the-job, with existing staff and experienced volunteers acting as advice givers. This approach, while cheap and largely effective, has limitations. The major one is that it is not often preceded by an assessment of the event's precise training needs and how best to meet them within resource limitations.

A formal approach to training needs assessment serves to determine whether training taking place is adequate and whether any training needs are not being met. Additionally, such an assessment generates suggestions about how to improve training provided by the event. These suggestions might include:

- sending, or requesting stakeholder/government support to send, staff/volunteers on training programmes dealing with specific areas or identified
- training needs (for example, risk management, event marketing and sponsorship)
- identifying individuals associated with the event who would be willing to volunteer to conduct training sessions
- commissioning consultants/external bodies to undertake specific training
- encouraging staff/volunteers to undertake event-specific training programmes, now provided by some public and private colleges, universities and event industry associations – in return for certain benefits (for example, higher salaries, appointment to positions of greater responsibility/satisfaction).

When trying to identify what training is required to facilitate the effective delivery of an event, the central consideration is to determine the gap between the current performance of staff and volunteers and their desired performance. This can be achieved by:

- performance appraisals of existing staff/volunteers (what training do staff identify as being required to make them more effective)
- analysis of job requirements (what skills are identified in the job description)
- survey of personnel (what skills staff state they need).

Because of the infrequent nature and short duration of events, training of event volunteers usually takes place on the job under the direction of the event manager or a supervisor. For this to be effective it should be structured to include:

- *Defined learning objectives*: these outline what the trainee should be able to do at the end of the training.
- *Appropriate curriculum*: the content of the training is appropriate to the learning outcomes.

- *Appropriate instructional strategies*: these can take the form of discussion groups, lectures, lectures/discussions, case studies, role-playing, demonstrations or on-the-job training.
- *Well-conducting training*: the trainer is not an expert handing down instructions from on high but a facilitator who can identify, explain and model the skills, observe trainees' attempts and correct their errors.
- *Evaluation*: this is to assess whether the trainees have acquired the appropriate skills.

Buckler (1998, pp. 18–19) developed a simple model of learning from his research into learning organizations. The model is based on the premise that the involvement of leaders in the learning process is crucial for success, as learning cannot be effective if the manager does not understand the process. Buckler goes on to argue that effective learning requires interaction between managers (the teacher) and staff (pupils) in order to develop a shared vision of what is to be achieved, remove barriers to learning and encourage innovation/try new ideas in a safe environment. This process of learning can be modelled as shown in Figure 6.8. As can be seen from the typical comments made by learners, essential elements of the training process are reflection and feedback. That is, trainees think deeply about the connections between what they already know about the topic and the new data they receive by relating new knowledge to experience, and using theory to extend experience. Feedback, from trainer, supervisor or peers, or their own reflection, enables trainees to adjust their actions to enable the task to be correctly completed. It is unlikely that anyone has learnt any new skill without this process of reflection and feedback.

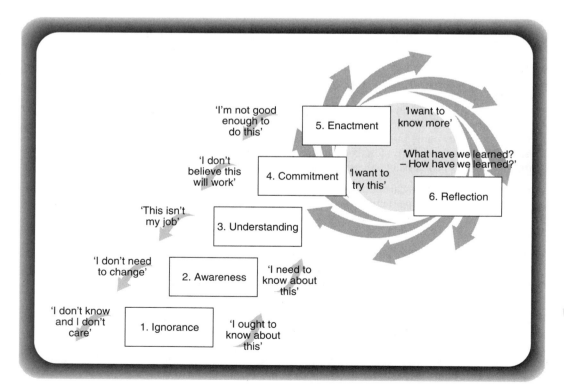

Figure 6.8 A simple model of the learning process
Source: Buckler (1998)

Supervision and evaluation

As a general rule, the bigger and more complex the event, the greater the need is for staff/volunteers to perform a supervisory function. This function may be exercised through a variety of means, including having would-be supervisors understudy an existing supervisor, developing a mentoring system or encouraging staff to undertake appropriate professional development programmes.

One of the key tasks of supervisors and managers is that of performance appraisal. This task involves evaluating performance, communicating that evaluation and establishing a plan for improvement. The ultimate outcomes of this process are a better event and more competent staff and volunteers. Stone (2002) proposes a dynamic performance appraisal programme (Figure 6.9) based on goal establishment, performance feedback and performance improvement.

According to Stone (2002), goals should be mutually arrived at by a supervisor and a volunteer or staff member. These goals, while specific to the particular job, are likely to relate to matters such as technical skills and knowledge, problem solving/creativity, planning and organizing, interpersonal skills, decision making, commitment to quality and safety, the achievement of designated results, attitudes and personality traits, reliability/punctuality, and professional development. It is important that measurements of progress towards goals are established, otherwise there is little point in setting goals in the first place. A person charged with overseeing waste management for an event, for example, may be assessed in terms of the percentage of material recycled from the event, levels of contamination in waste, the percentage of attendees (as determined by survey) that understood directions regarding the placement of waste in containers, and the level of complaints regarding matters such as full bins. Other areas for assessment might include those associated with personal development (enrolment and completion of a specific course),

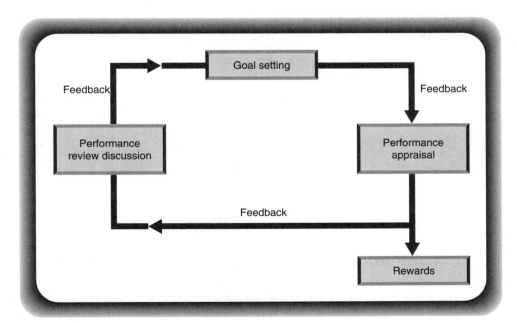

Figure 6.9 Dynamic performance appraisal system
Source: Stone (2002), p. 291

interpersonal relationships (opinions of supervisors/co-workers) and problem solving/creativity (approaches employed to respond to the unexpected).

Performance, in terms of progress towards the established goals, can be assessed in a variety of ways, including performance scales. According to Wood, Chapman, Fromholtz, Morrison, Wallace, Zeffrane, Schermerhorn, Hunt and Osborn (2004), irrespective of what assessment measures are used, responses to the following questions must underpin any efforts in this area: what does the job require? What does the employee/volunteer need to do to perform effectively in this position? What evidence from how work is undertaken would indicate effective performance? What does the assessment of evidence of performance indicate about future actions required?

Once an appraisal has been conducted, there should be a follow-up review discussion in which the supervisor/manager and the staff member/volunteer mutually review job responsibilities, examine how these responsibilities have been performed, explore how performance can be improved, and review and revise the staff members/volunteers short-term and long-term goals. The interview process should be a positive experience for both parties. To this end, it is worthwhile considering providing training to the managers/supervisors involved in this process so they adhere to certain basic practices such as preparing for the interview by reviewing job descriptions, previous assessments, being constructive not destructive, and encouraging discussion.

Integral to the appraisal system are rewards that paid staff receive in the form of salaries, bonuses, profit sharing, promotion to other jobs or other events and benefits such as cars and equipment use (for example, laptop computers). Options also exist to reward volunteers for their efforts. These include:

- training in new skills
- free merchandise (for example, clothing, badges, event posters)
- hospitality in the form of opening and closing parties, free meals/drinks
- certificates of appreciation
- opportunities to meet with celebrities, sporting stars and other VIPs
- promotion to more interesting volunteer positions
- public acknowledgement through the media and at the event
- free tickets to the event.

The 'flip side' to rewards – that is, discipline – also requires managerial consideration. It is useful to have in place specific policies and practices that reflect the seriousness of different behaviour/actions, and these should be communicated to all staff (paid and voluntary). These policies and practices are likely to begin with some form of admonishment and end with dismissal. Many of the approaches to disciplining paid employees (such as removing access to overtime) are not applicable to volunteers. Instead, approaches that may be applied to volunteers include re-assignment, withholding of rewards/benefits and suspension from holding a position as a volunteer.

Termination, outplacement and re-enlistment

Whether employing staff on contract or as permanent employees, event managers are occasionally faced with the need to terminate the services of an individual. This action may be necessary in instances where an employee breaches the employment contract (for example, repeatedly arriving at the workplace intoxicated) or continually exhibits unsatisfactory performance. This need may also arise when economic or commercial circumstances of the organization conducting the event require it to shed staff (such as when there is insufficient revenue due to poor ticket sales).

Various legal issues surrounding termination need to be understood by those involved in event management. In UK, these issues relate to unfair or unlawful dismissal, and are spelt out in employment legislation. Essentially, employers are required to give employees an opportunity to defend themselves against allegations associated with their conduct; in cases of unsatisfactory performance, they must warn and counsel the employee before terminating his or her service. These requirements do not apply to contracted or casual employees, or to staff on probation. A need can also arise to dismiss volunteers; for this purpose, Getz (2005) suggests a variety of approaches. These include making all volunteer appointments for fixed terms (with volunteers needing to re-apply and be subjected to screening each time the event is conducted) and using job descriptions and performance appraisals to underpin appropriate action.

Outplacement is the process of assisting terminated employees (or indeed volunteers), or even those who choose to leave the event organization voluntarily, to find other employment. By performing this function the event organization is providing a benefit to employees for past service, as well as maintaining and enhancing its image as a responsible employer. In the case of an event organizing company that decides to downsize, as many did after the 11 September 2001 (9/11) terrorist attacks, this process could lead to staff being aided to take up positions with, for example, other companies operating their own event divisions or large events that maintain a full-time staff year round. Even volunteers who are no longer needed can be helped into other positions by being put in contact with volunteer agencies or other events.

With recurring events, such as annual festivals, opportunities often exist to re-enlist for paid or voluntary positions. Many staff from the Sydney Olympic Games, for example, took up positions within the organization responsible for the Athens Olympics. To maintain contact with potential volunteers and past staff between events, a variety of approaches can be employed, including newsletters (see, for example, the Manchester Event Volunteers website, www.mev.org.uk), social events, the offer of benefits for re-enlistment, and personal contact by telephone between events.

Event managers should also keep in mind that staff will often leave of their own accord. The involvement of such staff in exit interviews can provide valuable information that could be used to fine tune one or more aspect of an event's human resource management process. A study of volunteers at a jazz festival (Elstad, 2003), for example, found the main reasons (in order) that volunteers quit were: (1) their overall workload, (2) a lack of appreciation of their contribution, (3) problems with how the festival was organized, (4) disagreement with changing goals or ideology, (5) wanting more free time for other activities, (6) a lack of a 'sense of community' among volunteers, (7) family responsibilities, (8) the festival becoming too large, (9) the inability to make decisions regarding their own position, (10) a dislike for some of their responsibilities, (11) lack of remuneration and (12) moving out of the festival's geographic area.

Evaluation of process and outcomes

As with all management processes, a periodic review is necessary to determine how well, or otherwise, the process is working. To conduct such a review, it is necessary to obtain feedback from relevant supervisory/management staff, organizing committee members, and paid and voluntary staff. The California Traditional Music Society, for example, uses a questionnaire to obtain feedback from volunteers (Figure 6.10, p. 167). A specific time should then be set aside, perhaps as part of a larger review of the event, to examine the extent to which the human resource management process as a whole (and its various elements) achieved the original objectives. Once the review is complete, revisions can be made to the process for subsequent events.

Motivating staff and volunteers

Motivation is a key, if implicit, component of the human resource management process. It is what commits people to a course of action, enthuses and energizes them, and enables them to achieve goals, whether the goals are their own or their organization's. The ability to motivate other staff members is a fundamental component of the event manager's repertoire of skills. Without appropriate motivation, paid employees and volunteers can lack enthusiasm for achieving the event's corporate goals and delivering quality service, or can show a lack of concern for the welfare of their co-workers or event participants.

In the context of volunteers, pure altruism (an unselfish regard for, or devotion to, the welfare of others) may be an important motive for seeking to assist in the delivery of events. Although this proposition is supported by Flashman and Quick (1985), the great bulk of work done on motivation stresses that people, while they may assert they are acting for altruistic reasons, are actually motivated by a combination of external and internal factors, most of which have little to do with altruism. As McCurley and Lynch (1998, pp. 11–13) point out: 'Motivation for the long-term volunteer is a matter of both achievement and affiliation, and often recognition is best expressed as an opportunity for greater involvement or advancement in the cause or the organization'. Further, short-term volunteers are motivated by recognition of their personal achievement, which can be achieved by simply thanking them for their contribution. The parameters of reward are discussed in this section.

Researchers from a variety of disciplines have done much work over many years on what motivates people, particularly in the workplace. Perhaps the most relevant and useful of these studies within the context of festivals and events are content theories and process theories.

Content theories

Content theories concentrate on what things initially motivate people to act in a certain way. As Mullins (2005) points out, they are concerned with identifying an individuals needs and relative strengths, and the personal goals they pursue to satisfy these needs. Figure 6.11 represents the essential nature of theories of this type.

Content theories assert that a person has a need – a feeling of deprivation – which then drives the person towards an action that can satisfy that need. Maslow's (1954) hierarchy of needs, illustrated in Figure 6.12, popularized the idea that needs are the basis of motivation.

In essence, Maslow's theory proposes that lower order needs must be satisfied before people are motivated to satisfy the next, higher need. That is, people who are trying to satisfy physiological needs of hunger and thirst have no interest in satisfying the need for safety until their physiological needs are satisfied. The first three needs are perceived as deficiencies; they must be satisfied to fulfil a lack of something. In contrast, satisfaction of the two higher needs is necessary for an individual to grow emotionally and psychologically.

Name: _____ Job: _____

CTMS VOLUNTEER SURVEY   Year _____

As in past years, we ask that you help by responding to these questions about your volunteer duties, so that we can continue to improve your entire volunteer experience. Please fill out this questionnaire and mail it back to CTMS in the return envelope provided. If you have any further comments or suggestions, please feel free to write or type your comments separately. Thanks again, and we look forward to seeing you again next year!

The Volunteer Coordination Committee

What shift(s) did you work?

Did you clearly understand, before the festival, what you were supposed to do, what **time** you were expected to work, and **where** you were going to work?

Was the printed training information you received at the training meetings thorough and complete? What would you change or add to it?

Do you think there were enough volunteers assigned to your job? Were you kept so busy that you could not do your job properly?

Do you think there were too many volunteers assigned to the same job as you were? Were you bored?

Was your job too difficult or strenuous for you in any way? Please explain.

Was there an extremely busy time during your shift? When was it? Do you feel you needed more help during this time?

Was there an extremely quiet time during your shift? When was it?

Did you run into any difficulties or situations that you didn't expect or didn't know how to handle? What were they? What did you do?

Is there anything you think CTMS should have provided or advised you to bring with you that would have made your job easier, more comfortable, or more efficient?

Were you able to get away during your shift to use a restroom if you needed one? If you were alone at your position, did someone come around and offer to relieve you temporarily so you could use a restroom?

Were there any problems that you were aware of that need correction for next year?

Would you volunteer for next year? If not, why not?

Thank you very much for completing and returning this questionnaire. Please write any comments specific to your volunteer job on a sheet of paper. Please write any other comments relative to the festival in general on a separate sheet of paper. Return both to CTMS.

Figure 6.10 Example of a volunteer survey
Source: California Traditional Music Society (2005)

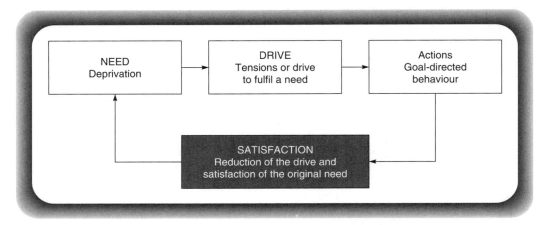

Figure 6.11 Basis of content theories of motivation
Source: Peach and Murrell (1995)

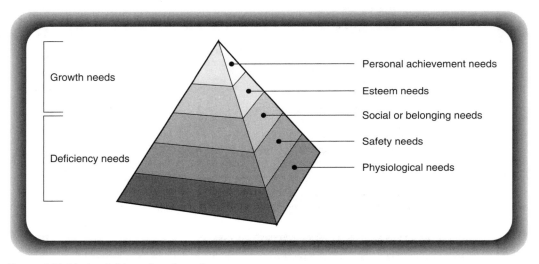

Figure 6.12 Maslow's hierarchy of needs
Source: MOTIVATION AND PERSONALITY 2/E by Maslow, © 1954. Reprinted by permission of Pearson Education, Inc., Upper Saddle River, NJ

Although little empirical evidence exists to support Maslow's theory, it can give insights into the needs people may be seeking to fulfil through employment. Some research, for example, indicates a tendency for higher level needs to dominate as individuals move up the managerial hierarchy.

Another researcher who falls within the ambit of content theory is Hertzberg (1968). He argues that some elements, which he calls hygiene factors, do not of themselves motivate or satisfy people. Among these factors are pay levels, policies and procedures, working conditions and job security. However, the absence or perceived reduction in these items can stimulate hostility or dissatisfaction towards an organization. Hertzberg further argues that other factors, which he calls motivators, of themselves lead to goal-directed behaviour. These elements include achievement, recognition and interesting work. Hertzberg's theory is illustrated in Figure 6.13.

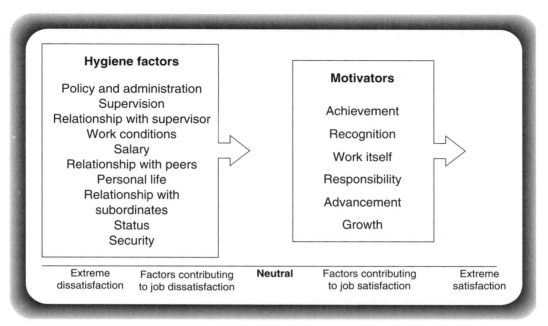

Figure 6.13 Hertzberg's two-factor theory
Source: Adapted and Reprinted by permission of Harvard Business Review. [Exhibit]. From "One More Time: How Do You Motivate Employees?" by F. Hertzberg, 01/03, p. 90. Copyright © 2003 by the Harvard Business School Publishing Corporation; all rights reserved

Hertzberg's theory suggests event managers can motivate staff and volunteers by:

- instituting processes of recognizing achievement
- empowering staff so they can take responsibility for the outcomes of their part of the event
- providing opportunities for them to grow in skills, experience and expertise.

It also suggests event managers need to be conscious of certain hygiene factors that can act as demotivators. These might include attitudes of supervisors, working conditions such as the length of meal/coffee breaks and hours of work, the status of one job compared with another (for example, waste management officer versus publicity coordinator), and policies such as the type/quality of uniforms provided to staff vs volunteers.

Content theories, such as those of Hertzberg and Maslow, provide managers with some understanding of work-related factors that initiate motivation; they also focus attention on the importance of employee needs and their satisfaction. They do not, however, explain particularly well why a person chooses certain types of behaviour to satisfy their needs (Wood, Chapman, Fromholtz, Morrison, Wallace, Zeffane, Schermerhorn, Hunt and Osborn, 2004). Process theories, the subject of the next section, take up this challenge.

Process theories

Representative of process theories of motivation are Adams's (1965) equity theory and Vroom's (1964) expectancy theory.

Equity theory

Equity theory is based on the reasonable premise that all employees (or, for that matter, volunteers) expect to be treated fairly. This being the case, if one employee or volunteer perceives a discrepancy in the outcomes that he or she receives (for example, pay or type of work allocated) compared with those of other employees or volunteers, that employee or volunteer will be motivated to do more (or less) work (Wood, Chapman, Fromholtz, Morrison, Wallace, Zeffane, Schermerhorn, Hunt and Osborn, 2004). This situation is represented in the equation below:

$$\frac{\text{Individual rewards}}{\text{Individual inputs}} \xleftrightarrow{\text{comparison}} \frac{\text{Others' rewards}}{\text{Others' inputs}}$$

What an employee or volunteer perceives as fair in terms of compensation (monetary or non-monetary) is subjective. The best way of maintaining an awareness of what an individual is thinking in this regard is to develop and maintain open lines of communication. If inequity is perceived and goes unnoticed, a number of outcomes are possible, including:

- a reduction in effort
- pressure to increase remuneration
- exit from the organization.

Expectancy theory

Expectancy theory holds that an individual's motivation to act in a particular way comes from a belief that a particular outcome will result from doing something (expectancy). This outcome will result in a reward (instrumentality). The rewards for accomplishing this outcome are sufficient to justify the effort put into doing it (valence). Motivation, under this theory, can therefore be expressed as:

$$\text{Motivation} = \text{Expectancy} \times \text{Instrumentality} \times \text{Valence}.$$

This being the case, whenever one of the elements in this equation approaches zero, the motivational value of a particular decision is dramatically reduced. Event managers need to be aware of this and, therefore, try to maximize all three motivational components. In other words, there must be a clear payoff if employees and volunteers are to perform at a high level. To understand what this payoff needs to be for each staff member and volunteer is difficult; however, the chances of doing so are greatly increased if lines of communication are kept open and if a genuine effort is made to understand each individual.

As an example of how expectancy theory works, take the situation of people who decide to work on their local community festival. They may have certain expectations:

- an expectation that by working on the event they will gain certain new skills
- an expectation that these new skills in turn will enhance their future employability, thus creating an instrumentality
- an expectation that the jobs for which they will be able to apply with these new skills are ones that they would find extremely rewarding, adding a strong degree of value to the circumstances.

If all three factors are strongly positive, then motivation will be high. It is from this theoretical framework that Peach and Murrell (1995, pp. 238–39) derive their reward and recognition techniques, which are shown in Table 6.1.

Table 6.1 Reward and recognition techniques

Reward systems that work	Recognitions techniques that work
Rewards that integrate the needs of the individual and the organization in a win-win understanding	Carefully constructed system that are built on the motives needs of volunteers – individualized need recognition for each person
Rewards based on deep appreciation of the individual as a unique person	Recognition integrated into task performance, where clear performance objectives are established
Rewards based on job content, not conditions – rewards intrinsic to the job work best
Assignment of the tasks that can be performed effectively, leading to intrinsic need satisfaction
Consistent reward policies that build a sense of trust that effort will receive the proper reward	Corporate growth and development objectives also become opportunities for recognition
Longevity and special contributions recognized frequently, not just every ten years
Recognition grounded deeply on the core values of the organization; what is recognized helps as a role model.
Rewards that can be shared by learns so that winning is a collective and collaborative experience	

Source: Peach and Murrell (1995)

Techniques for effective staff and volunteer team building

As noted at the outset of the chapter, event organizations often come together quickly and exist for short periods. This being the case, one of the greatest challenges faced by an event manager is creating a sense of 'team' with a strong desire to progress the event's objectives. In the context of volunteers, Nancy McDuff, (1995, pp. 208–10), an internationally recognized authority on volunteer programmes, proposes a 14-element formula for effective team building and maintenance:

1. Teams are a manageable size. Most effective teams are between 2 and 25 people, with the majority fewer than 10.
2. People are appropriately selected to serve on a team. Care and attention is paid to selecting people with the right combination of skills, personality, communication styles and ability to perform, thereby improving the chances of the team being successful.
3. Team leaders are trained. Leaders who find it difficult to delegate and want to do everything themselves make poor leaders. Try to ensure team leaders have training in supervision skills.
4. Teams are trained to execute their tasks. It is unrealistic to expect teams to perform effectively without appropriate training. The training should include the team's role in the activity and how that role contributes to the activity's overall success.
5. Volunteers and staff are supported by the organization. Teams must feel that the administration is there to support their endeavours, not to hinder them.
6. Teams have objectives. The purpose of the team is spelt out in measurable objectives. Having a plan to achieve those objectives helps build trust.
7. Volunteers and staff trust and support one another. People trust each other when they share positive experiences. When each team is aware of the organization's

objectives and how its role helps to achieve those objectives, it trusts co-workers and supports their efforts.

8. Communication between volunteers and the event organization is both vertical and horizontal. Communication, which means sending 'meanings' and under-standings between people, is a process involving an active and continuous use of active listening, the use of feedback to clarify meaning, the reading of body language, and the use of symbols that communicate meaning. Communication travels in all directions – up and down the reporting line, and between teams and work groups. Working together is facilitated by good communication.

9. The organizational structure promotes communication between volunteers and staff. The organization's structure, policies and operating programmes permit and encourage all members of the organization to communicate with their co-workers, their managers and members of other departments. This help builds an atmosphere of cooperation and harmony in the pursuit of common objectives.

10. Volunteers and staff have real responsibility. A currently fashionable concept of management is 'empowerment'. This means giving staff authority to make decisions about their work and its outcomes. Let us look at the example of a group of volunteers having the somewhat mundane task of making sandwiches. If they are empowered with the authority to decide what sandwiches to make, how to make them and where to sell them, their enthusiasm for the task will probably be enhanced and there will be a corresponding improvement in outcomes.

11. Volunteers and staff have fun while accomplishing tasks. Managers should strive to engender an atmosphere of humour, fun and affection among co-workers within the culture of the organization. Such actions as ceremonies to acknowledge exemplary contributions to the event, wrap-up parties and load-in celebrations can facilitate this atmosphere.

12. There is recognition of the contributions of volunteers and staff. Paid staff should express formal and informal appreciation of the work of volunteers, and volunteers should publicly recognize and appreciate the work of the paid staff. This mutual appreciation should be consistent, public and visible.

13. Volunteers and staff celebrate their success. Spontaneous celebrations with food, drink, friendship and frivolity should be encouraged by management of the event, to celebrate achievement of objectives. The event manager should allocate a budgeted amount for these occasions.

14. The entire organization promotes and encourages the wellbeing of volunteer teams. Everyone in the organization sees himself or herself as part of a partnership and actively promotes such relationships.

Once teams are in place and operating effectively, the event manager should monitor their performance and productivity by observing their activities and maintaining appropriate communication with team leaders and members. If deficiencies are noticed during the monitoring procedure, then appropriate action can be taken in terms of training, team structure changes or the refinement of operating procedures in a climate of mutual trust.

Legal obligations

Employment law regulates how employers deal with their employees in terms of pay and conditions, and prevents discrimination in relation to race, sex or disability. This legislation generally sets out minimum rates of pay, and conditions such as annual leave and working hours. Of course, there is nothing to stop an event manager from paying more than the minimum wage, as the labour market is not controlled, except by minimum conditions that must be met. Traditionally, the market has been based on the concept of free collective bargaining, however, in recent years, there have been increasing levels of legislation, including the impact of European Union directives. To ensure compliance with appropriate legislation, event managers who employ paid labour should consult the Department for Education and Skills (www.dfes.gov.uk/er), which undoubtedly can supply details of current labour legislation.

Many paid employees of events are employed as casual workers. To compensate for the irregular nature of their work, these employees may be paid rates above the normal full-time hourly rate. It is the responsibility, and in the best interests, of the event manager to ensure these employees are paid appropriately, particularly during the summer event season when there is increased competition for their services.

Event managers should also remember there are common law requirements regarding the duties of parties to an employment relationship. In the context of volunteers, common law precedents provide rights to damages if negligence can be shown on behalf of an event organizer.

Chapter summary

Event managers should approach the task of human resource management not as a series of separate activities but as an integrated process involving a number of steps, taking the event organization's mission, strategy and goals as their starting points. These steps have been identified in this chapter as: (1) the human resource strategy and objectives; (2) policies and procedures; (3) recruitment; (4) training and professional development; (5) supervision and evaluation; (6) termination, outplacement and re-enlistment; and (7) evaluation and feedback. These steps have application to the employment of both paid and volunteer staff, as well as to events of varying size and type. This chapter has also dealt with the issue of motivation, examining two broad theoretical perspectives on the matter, process and content theories. The final sections of this chapter dealt with mechanisms for developing task teams to conduct events, and with the legal considerations associated with human resource management.

Questions

1. Interview the organizer of an event of your choice and ask him or her what legal/statutory requirements have an impact on human resource management processes and practices.
2. In the context of a specific event, identify the policies and procedures regarding human resource management. Collect examples of forms and other material that support them.
3. Develop a job specification for the position of event manager for an event of your choice.
4. List the questions that you would ask a candidate during an interview for the position given in question 3.
5. Undertake a job analysis for an event of your choice.

6. Identify all voluntary positions involved in the event examined in question 5. Write brief job descriptions for each position.
7. Propose an induction and training programme for the event identified in question 5.
8. Critically review one stage in the human resource management process (as proposed in this chapter) employed by an event of your choice.
9. Discuss general approaches that you might employ to motivate the volunteer staff associated with an event. Which of these approaches would be most appropriate for an event such as the one you examined in question 8?
10. Construct a post-event evaluation questionnaire for volunteers involved in the event identified in question 5.

Case study 6.1

The XVII Commonwealth Games 2002 Manchester – A Volunteering Legacy

Introduction

In May 2001, a major recruitment programme was launched to fill the 10 000 volunteering roles needed to underpin the delivery of the 2002 Commonwealth Games in Manchester. In order to qualify applicants had to be available to work for at least 10 days, attend interview and training sessions, and have reached 16 years of age by 1 December 2001. In return they would have the opportunity to play an important role at the third largest sporting event in the world, an event which would occupy a unique place in the city's history.

Facing the challenge

Initially there was some concern expressed as to whether it would be possible to fill all the positions. A volunteer programme on this scale was unprecedented in peacetime Britain. Many predicted that the recruitment of 10 000 unpaid workers would prove difficult in a country in which the profile of volunteering was seen primarily in terms of charity shop workers and not part of the nation's wider cultural identity. However, these reservations proved to be totally unfounded as there was a tremendous response from the people of Manchester and the North West (around 80 per cent of those whose applications were successful originated from the North West of England).

In total 22 346 people applied for the 10 311 Games time roles of which 53 per cent were women and 47 per cent men. Over 56 per cent of applications were received over the Internet, with 70 per cent of people aged 20–24 filling in their forms on-line. Older people preferred the more traditional method of sending their application (around 80 per cent of people 65 and over applied by post). The oldest volunteer was 87 year old Desmond Pastore from Northenden Manchester who worked as an assistant on the statistics desk at the Rugby 7s tournament.

Aim of the programme

One of the aims of the volunteer programme was to encourage applications from the long term unemployed, ethnic minorities, people from disadvantaged areas and those with disabilities and special needs.

A Pre Volunteer Programme (PVP), part of the NW 2002 Social and Economic Legacy programme, had already been in operation in 23 regeneration areas around the North West since early 2000. The programme offered training, the chance to achieve a qualification in event volunteering, and enhanced opportunities for volunteering for the Games itself. During 2001 events and road shows were held across Manchester and the North West to recruit volunteers from the targeted groups.

Once appointed all volunteers were issued with the Crew 2002 Games uniform which was designed to be distinctive and easily identifiable. The uniform with its purple shell suit and northern style flat cap initially attracted negative comments, but the resulting national media attention, combined with the fact that Coronation Street's Norris Cole regularly donned his outfit during the popular TV show, helped to raise awareness of the Games across Britain.

By the end of the Games the volunteer uniform became a symbol of the huge contribution made to the event's success by the purple army.

Volunteer roles

The volunteers were perhaps most visible when directing spectators around the city centre or acting as stewards for the sports venues. However they were involved in many different aspects of the running of the Games in fields as diverse as logistics, medical services, catering and marketing.

The venue which employed the most volunteers was the Games Village (1247), followed by Sports City Plaza (1096) and the City of Manchester Stadium (967). In terms of the supporting infrastructure, transport required the most voluntary staff (2234), with event services next (1314) and security third (940).

City guides provided 281 volunteers to provide a warm welcome, signpost walking routes to the stadium and deliver front line visitor information. Road Events had the largest number of sports event volunteers (just over 200) followed by Athletics (just under 150) and Lawn Bowls (around 80).

The volunteer programme was certainly one of the major success stories of the Commonwealth Games. The friendliness and enthusiasm of the volunteers earned them high praise from athletes, spectators and national media alike, and there is no doubt that they can also claim some credit for the more positive image of Manchester that emerged from the Games.

Volunteer feedback

It is also clear from the testimony of the volunteers themselves that they found their time at the Games to be a most enjoyable and rewarding experience. Indeed comments such as 'the best time of my life' and 'amazing experience' are frequently repeated in their descriptions of how they felt to be part of 'Crew 2002'. For a few volunteers their Games experience proved to be the passport to longer term employment, whilst others were happy just to have been taken part in such a prestigious event. However the closing event at the City of Manchester stadium did not signify the end of the volunteer programme but rather the beginning.

Post games volunteer programme

After the games were over, volunteers from the North West and participants in the PVP scheme were given the opportunity to take part in the Post Games Volunteer Programme (PGVP). This project ran from January 2003 until March 2005.

The aim of this project was to respond to the upsurge in interest and the positive experience of volunteering. Games volunteers became involved in community projects as well as major events including the Salford Triathlon and Great Manchester Run. The project also offered support to volunteers who were seeking to gain new skills and experience, or looking for a route back into employment. The summer of 2003 saw the volunteers back on the streets as city guides providing a very northern welcome to the 70 000 Italians in Manchester for the UEFA Champions League Final at Old Trafford. More than 150 events across the region including the London Triathlon in 2004 and the World Paralympics in 2005 have benefited from the volunteers' continuing commitment.

In April 2005, the volunteering legacy continued to run as the project was mainstreamed into Manchester City Council's structure as Manchester Event Volunteers. Over 2500 volunteers are now registered on the database. Manchester Event Volunteering is open to both Commonwealth Games volunteers and new members.

For further details about the 2002 Manchester Commonwealth Games legacy, please visit www.gameslegacy.com. The Manchester Event Volunteer programme can be contacted on enquiry@mev.org.uk. The M2002 records and archive are now held at Central Library Manchester.

By Manchester City Council's Games Xchange, the information legacy programme.

Questions

1. How can the success of the Manchester 2002 Commonwealth Games volunteer programme be measured?
2. What role does recognition play in the success of the events volunteer programme?
3. What functions does a volunteer training manual perform?
4. Can you suggest any additional means by which the legacy of the volunteer programme can be continued?

Case study 6.2

Eurostar Forum by World Event Management

Introduction

This case study provides a powerful example of how World Event Management – a global player in corporate events and motivational, incentive and teambuilding programmes – provides effective communications, production, team building and on-site event management. The case study is concerned with the use of an event to motivate management teams and to communicate brand messages, based on the Eurostar Managers Forum, an annual meeting arranged for Eurostar Group.

The Eurostar Group, responsible for determining the communication direction and service direction of the overall Eurostar business, comprises three train operating companies from the UK (Eurostar UK), France (SNCF) and Belgium (SNCB). As a result of the geographical and cultural diversity, it is essential that management have a clear understanding of the organization. In order to facilitate this, Eurostar hold an annual two-day meeting of managers from all divisions of the three companies. For this year, the venue chosen for the event was The New York Convention Centre at Disneyland Paris, with the client managing their own travel, via the Eurostar, and their own logistics at the Sequioa Lodge Hotel, Disneyland Paris.

Diversity of the audience can present a significant challenge. The event was aimed at train operators, not marketeers, plus key distributors and contractors, and therefore the event had to be designed to ensure that the communication message was clear. As you can imagine, taking into account the requirements of 195 managers from three railway companies based in London, Paris and Brussels, speaking three different languages, and each having distinctly different cultures – required clear objectives to be formulated to ensure success. These were identified as follows:

- To understand the power of branding and the Eurostar brand
- To inform about performance and future developments and plans
- To encourage a very mixed group to get to know each other better
- To move the meeting format forward from the last meeting.

Based on these objectives, World Event Management developed a conference that involved and surprised the audience throughout the two days, based around a clear theme, and using a host/facilitator, video inserts, table challenges, breakout workshops and two very different team building activities.

The theme was developed around a key message – 'Making Our Marque' – to communicate the power of branding, the power of the Eurostar brand, and its relevant meaning to an audience of French and English speakers.

Event format

For the brand exercises, the audience was challenged to map out and present their current and future perceptions of the Eurostar brand. Real customer views were presented as video inserts – in three languages – to add the customers' perceptions into the discussion. During plenary sessions, simultaneous translation was provided in two languages.

The day ended in the early evening with a final team activity – 'Trading Brands' – which focused on using the power of brands to increase company value.

Day 1

For the first day, the audience was seated at round tables for the workshop and reporting back.

The delegates were divided into teams by badges with different famous brand names.

In order to keep the day informal, no lectern was used – instead all messages were presented in discussion format. A facilitator was used to introduce the theme, key messages, interact with audience and host discussions with all 5 speakers.

For the brand exercises, the audience was challenged to map out and present their current and future perceptions of the Eurostar brand. Real customer views were presented as video inserts – in 3 languages – to add the customers' perceptions into the discussion. During plenary sessions, simultaneous translation was provided in 2 languages.

The day ended in the early evening with a final team activity – 'Trading Brands' – which focused on using the power of brands to increase company value.

Day 2 (1/2 day a.m.)

On the second day, workshops were used where the audience, in mixed groups, were challenged to develop action plans to improve customer service and company performance. The findings from this were collated but not formally presented back to the group.

In the late morning, the audience took part in a final team activity – 'T-shirt Masterpiece'. The teams summarized the Eurostar brand and message on T-shirts, then each team in turn presented their message on stage.

Evaluating the results

As a result of the event, the following outcomes were achieved:

A better understanding of company service culture and future strategies Improved working relationships between delegates. Enthusiastic participation in both team activities.

World Event Management designed, produced and managed the theme, title and conference logo, the event format, running order, speaker support on screen, two team activities, customer interview films, simtran (simultaneous translation), set and staging, technical support and all stage management.

For further details about World Event Management, please visit www.world-events.com.

Questions

1. Why is this an 'event'? How is it different from and similar to other events that you know of?
2. Who were the event stakeholders?
3. What stakeholders' needs were satisfied by this event?
4. The case illustrates the use of events for motivational purposes. How can events such as this be used to motivate employees and managers? What other needs do they satisfy? On what basis can participants be selected to take part?

Chapter 7
Strategic marketing for events

Learning Objectives

After studying this chapter, you should be able to:

- describe how strategic marketing can be applied to festivals and events
- understand the consumer decision process for festival and events
- apply the principles of services marketing in creating strategies for event and festivals
- plan the event 'service–product' experience, including its programming and packaging
- develop event pricing strategies or other entry options
- create strategies for place/distribution, physical setting and event processes that respond to consumer needs
- establish relationships with event consumers and stakeholders through integrated marketing communication strategies.

Introduction

This chapter examines a strategic approach to festival and event marketing, and how the event manager carries out all of the marketing activities necessary to achieve the event's objectives, as set out in the strategic plan. Over the past few years, an increasing number of authors have demonstrated the importance of understanding the marketing domain applied to events (Allen, 2004; Hoyle, 2002; Masterman and Wood, 2005; Supovitz, 2005) in addition to the established marketing body of knowledge (Brassington and Pettitt, 2003; Dibb, Simkin, Pride and Ferrell, 2006; Jobber, 2004; Kotler, Wong, Saunders and Armstrong, 2005). To begin, it is useful to explore the concept of marketing as an event-management function.

What is marketing?

Marketing is a term often used, yet there is no standard universal definition. The Chartered Institute of Marketing (CIM, 2005) defines marketing as, 'the management process responsible for identifying, anticipating and satisfying customer requirements profitably'. In simple terms, marketing is concerned with satisfying consumer needs and wants by exchanging goods, services or ideas for something of value. More often, we are not just purchasing products, we are buying experiences (as we do with events and festivals) or adopting new ideas – for example, participation in extreme sports or new theatre forms. We might offer our pounds in exchange for a concert experience, but for some types of marketing exchanges – for example, community festivals – we could simply offer a coin donation.

Kotler et al. (2005, p. 6) suggest that marketing is 'A social and managerial process by which individuals and groups obtain what they need and want through creating and exchanging products and value with others'. In effect, marketing has evolved well beyond early views of the marketing concept (McCarthy and Perreault, 1987) as meeting customer needs through decisions about the four Ps – product, place, price and promotion.

While it is agreed that the consumer is the primary focus of marketing, changes over time have dramatically reshaped the marketing function. These include:

- growth in the number and diversity of services (including events) that require different marketing approaches from those for goods
- recognition of the unique marketing requirements of not-for-profit organizations (typical of many festivals)
- the increasing importance of stakeholders – for example, the community, government, investors/sponsors, media and others who can be as influential as consumers on organizational survival
- advances in technology such as the Internet, the linking of computers with telecommunications and other innovations that affect the marketing of services, including events
- internationalization, which has created global opportunities to enter new markets – for example, the touring and staging of events in offshore locations.

As a result of these changes, marketers of events and festivals have the benefit of new knowledge in services marketing, stakeholder and relationship management, and e-marketing to help shape their strategies. Increasingly, this knowledge helps the event or festival marketer to perform the marketing role defined by Hall (1997, p. 136) as:

that function of event management that can keep in touch with the event's participants and visitors (consumers), read their needs and motivations, develop products that meet these needs, and build a communication program which expresses the event's purpose and objectives.

At a practical level, the following list shows the marketing activities that an event marketing manager may undertake to produce a successful festival or event:

- Analyse the needs of the target market to establish the design of the event experience and the way in which it will be delivered.
- Predict how many people will attend the event and the times that different groups or market segments will attend.
- Research any competitive events that could satisfy similar needs, to devise a unique selling proposition.
- Estimate the price or value that visitors are willing to exchange to attend an event – for example, ticket price or donation.
- Decide on marketing communication, including the media mix and messages that will reach the audiences of the event.
- Consider how the choice and design of venue(s) and the methods of ticket distribution fit with the needs of attendees.
- Establish the degree of success of the event in achieving its marketing objectives.

All of these activities, vital for a successful event, are part of the marketing function. This chapter explores how event marketing managers seek insights into consumers of their festival/event and the event marketing environment before developing their marketing strategies and plans. It then discusses ways in which event managers can apply theories of strategic marketing, including services marketing and relationship management to develop their event marketing approach.

The need for marketing

Some critics of marketing argue that some cultural festivals and events should not be concerned with target markets and satisfying market needs, but should simply focus on innovation, creativity and the dissemination of new art forms. The argument is that consumers' needs are based on what they know, so consumers are less likely to embrace innovative or avant-garde cultural experiences. Dickman (1997, p. 685) highlights the reluctance of some administrators 'to even use the word [marketing], believing that it suggested "selling out" artistic principles in favour of finding the lowest common denominator'.

Erroneously, this view assumes that marketers, by adopting a consumer focus, respond only to the expressed needs of event visitors. In reality, sound marketing research can unveil the latent needs of consumers that only innovative events can satisfy. Often, a distrust of marketing is based on a misunderstanding of marketing principles and techniques. This attitude can be self-defeating for the following reasons:

- The use of marketing principles gives event managers a framework for decision making that should result in events that reflect innovation and creativity, but cater for market segments that seek novelty or the excitement of something new.
- Sponsoring bodies need reassurance that their sponsorship is linking their brand with their target markets. Sound marketing practices give marketers the ability to convince sponsors that a festival or event is the right marketing investment.
- Local and national government financially assist many festivals and events. Governments usually fund only those events whose management can demonstrate some expertise in marketing planning and management.
- Event stakeholders, such as the community, environmentalists and indigenous leaders, as well as consumers, are critical in today's societal marketing approach. A societal marketing approach (Kotler et al., 2005) emphasizes the importance of society's wellbeing alongside satisfaction of the needs and wants of event or festival markets.
- Consumers, particularly those who reside in major cities, have an enormous range of leisure activities on which to spend their disposable income. This means a festival or event, which, by definition, can be categorized as a leisure activity, will attract only those who expect to satisfy at least one of their perceived needs. Therefore, any festival or event needs to be designed to satisfy identified needs of its target market. Failure to do this usually results in an event that is irrelevant to the needs of its target market and does not meet its objectives.

All festivals and events, therefore, can benefit from understanding marketing principles and having some experience in applying those principles to satisfy the identified needs of a target market. Failure to understand the role of marketing, including its societal perspective, can lead to dissatisfied consumers and a weak relationship with stakeholders who strongly influence an event's long-term survival.

Events as 'service experiences'

The marketing concept is just as applicable to a leisure service such as an event as it is to any other product. In fact, it could be even more so, as a leisure service, like other services, is intangible, variable, perishable and inseparable. We are exposed to many well-known brand names in leisure services that have been marketing success stories, and some of these are special events – for example, the Moscow State Circus, the Edinburgh Tattoo, the Aintree Grand National and Glastonbury Festival.

Events as services differ from products in a number of ways. What is different about services is that we must experience them to consume them – the delivery and consumption of an event are inseparable, happening simultaneously in most cases. Given this immediacy of service consumption, the way in which an event is experienced can vary daily or each year the event or festival is staged. The challenge for event managers and marketers is to try to manage these variations in quality. Because people are central to the delivery of most services (including the staff or vendors at an event, as well as its visitors), managing the quality of an event experience depends on managing its human delivery and the behaviour of its consumers – that is, people who attend an event affect the level of enjoyment of other visitors.

Other key differences of services like events are that they are intangible and, unlike a product, cannot be owned – that is, we don't take the experience home with us. While a skateboard has search qualities (we can examine it for its shape, texture and colour), events or festivals have only experiential qualities. There is nothing tangible for us to pick up, touch, feel or try before purchasing tickets or after the event (other than event merchandise or mementos). Event marketers add some tangibility via promotional posters, event programmes or compact discs of the artists' work, but the primary purchase is an intangible experience. The marketer has the challenge, therefore, of providing potential visitors with advance clues about the nature of the event experience.

It is generally agreed that the intangibility of services makes them much harder to evaluate than goods, and this is also true for events. Many events also have some credence qualities – characteristics that we, as consumers, don't have enough knowledge or experience to understand or evaluate. For certain types of event, real-time interpretation (subtitles at the opera or expert commentary at a sports game) and post-purchase interpretation (views expressed by commentators or critics) enhance the consumer's experience.

For marketers, a further challenge is the perishability of the event experience – for example, seats unsold at today's football game or tonight's concert will not be available for sale again. While we can store an unsold product on the shelf, we cannot store today's unused opportunities for festival attendance until tomorrow or another date. Events are delivered in real time. If the weather is poor on the day of the festival, unsold tickets cannot be retrieved, and food and beverage sales for that day are lost. This means event demand and supply must be well understood, so seating, food and beverage, and other vital supplies to an event are not wasted.

The five key characteristics of services discussed here – inseparability, variations in quality, intangibility, lack of ownership and perishability – each have implications for an event's services marketing mix discussed later in this chapter.

The nexus of event marketing and management

Given the differences between services and goods, there is a need to understand the tight links between an events marketing, its people management (human skills and

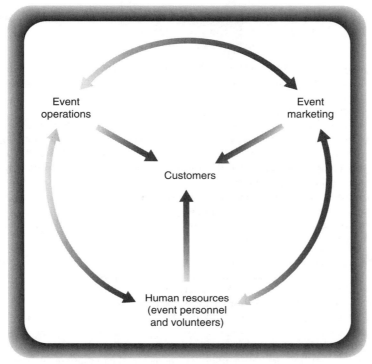

Figure 7.1 The event services trinity

expertise) and its operations management (for example, site layout, ticketing, queuing, sound and lighting, and other functions). While Chapters 6, 13 and 14 explore those topics, it is important to grasp just how closely the events marketer needs to work with other managers to ensure that consumer needs and expectations are fully met.

When we attend an event, our entire experience can be enhanced by the spectacle of stage design or lighting, special sound effects or ways in which the venue is designed to bring the performance to the audience. Our experience can also be marred by poor acoustics or incorrect advice from venue staff about parking or entry to the event. In their study of theatre event satisfaction, Hede, Jago and Deery (2003) used an expert panel to identify event attributes that consumers evaluate – for example, vision from the seats, theatre ambience, quality of the acting and singing, costumes and service at the theatre. It is important, therefore, to create a synergy between marketing, human resource and operations management – a relationship called the services trinity (Figure 7.1).

The role of strategic marketing

Before describing the strategic marketing process, it is useful to think about what 'strategy' means. In the world of business and in event management and marketing, strategy can be interpreted as how an organization (or event) marshals and uses its resources to achieve its business objectives, within its ever changing political, economic, socio-cultural and technological environment. Chapter 5 on event planning outlined this process. In this chapter, the strategy process is linked to the marketing function to show the framework in which event managers develop marketing objectives and strategies to satisfy consumer needs.

Some key points about strategy are that it is:

- longer term, rather than short term – once a marketing strategy is decided, it can be wasteful of resources and disruptive to an event to change the strategic direction. Careful thought is required before deciding on what marketing strategies to use to achieve event objectives.
- not another word for tactics – strategy is the broad overall direction that an event takes to achieve its objectives, while tactics are the detailed manoeuvres or programmes that carry out the strategy. Tactics can be changed as market conditions change, but the overall direction – the strategy – remains constant (at least for the planning period).
- based on careful analysis of internal resources and external environments – it is not a hasty reaction to changes in the market.
- essential to survival – well-considered thought out marketing strategies enable event managers to achieve the objectives of their event.

While the logic of deciding on a long-term strategy appears sound, festivals and events, like other organizations, vary in the extent to which their strategies are deliberate or emergent processes (Mintzberg, 1994). In particular, festivals that begin their life as community celebrations run by local volunteers are less likely to have a deliberate strategy process. It is unlikely that Glastonbury Festival, for example, commenced with a formal marketing vision and process that led to the strong brand image that the event enjoys today. It can be wrong, therefore, to assume failure will result from implicit (rather than explicit) strategies or those that simply emerge from the hundreds of decisions made by organizers in staging an event. However, a holistic vision of an event's direction and the fit between the marketing strategy and vision is a desirable starting point. The following definition reflects the essence of the strategy concept for the practising events marketer: 'Strategic event marketing is the process by which an event organization aligns business and marketing objectives and the environments in which they occur, with marketing activities that fulfil the needs of event consumers'.

Based on this definition, the starting points for any strategic marketing process should be the long-term objective(s) and mission or vision of the event organizers. Figure 7.2 shows the forces that influence these platforms of the strategic marketing process.

As shown in the figure, both the stakeholders of the event and the personal values of its organizers are critical influences. For example, Bath Festivals Trust was created in 1993 in order to develop Bath as a Festival City. The overall mission of the Trust is, 'to enrich people's lives through participation in the arts' (Bath Festivals Trust, 2005). The vision and values of festival organizers Imaginate have had a profound effect on all aspects of the Bank of Scotland Children's International Theatre Festival. Imaginate's vision is, 'That all children, by the age of 12, will have had a positive experience of performing arts' with the mission, 'To act as an advocate for the provision of high quality performing arts for children across Scotland' (Imaginate, 2005a). The festival in May 2005 attracted over 14 000 children aged three to fourteen, their teachers and families and is the largest performing arts festival for children and young people in the UK (Imaginate, 2005b). Other events present more of an event-focused mission – for example, the Scottish Traditional Boat Festival offers a festival where 'every member of the family can discover, enjoy and participate in the maritime and cultural heritage of the North East' (The Scottish Traditional Boat Festival, 2005). Some events and festivals also state the philosophical principles that underpin their

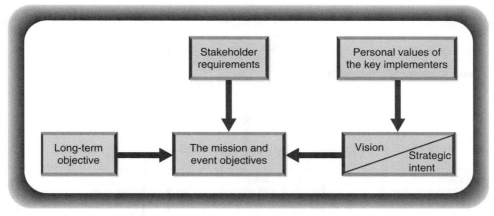

Figure 7.2 Constructing the mission

mission and guide event management and marketing. Harrogate International Festival's organizers express philosophies that recognize the role of arts in education and that by inspiring children and young people to enjoy arts and music will last them a lifetime (Harrogate International Festival, 2005). In effect, an event's philosophies and mission statement are an important foundation for determining the strategic marketing approach that best reflects the interests of its stakeholders and achieves its marketing objectives. Vision and mission are further discussed in Chapter 5.

Stages in the strategic marketing process for events include: research and analysis of the macro-environment, including the competitive, political, economic, social and technological (C-PEST) forces; research into the psychology of event consumers; segmentation, targeting and positioning (STP); the setting of marketing objectives; and decision making about generic marketing strategies and the event's services marketing mix. Figure 7.3 shows a recommended framework for developing the event marketing strategy.

Event marketing research

Before the marketing strategy is developed, research is usually conducted at (1) the macro-level, to understand external forces affecting the event and its markets, and (2) the micro-level, to gain insight into the event's existing and potential consumers and any strategies previously used by the organizers. A range of event marketing information can be obtained from primary and secondary sources to guide the strategy process.

To begin, a search of secondary data on macro-level trends affecting leisure consumption and the competitive environment for events can be drawn from on-line and off-line sources. Some useful information sources are:

- government statistics and reports (national and region statistics on the consumption of festivals and events, arts and sport)
- media coverage (about the events sector and particular events or festivals in the region)
- industry magazines such as Event (www.eventmagazine.co.uk) and Conference & Incentive Travel (www.citmagazine.co.uk).

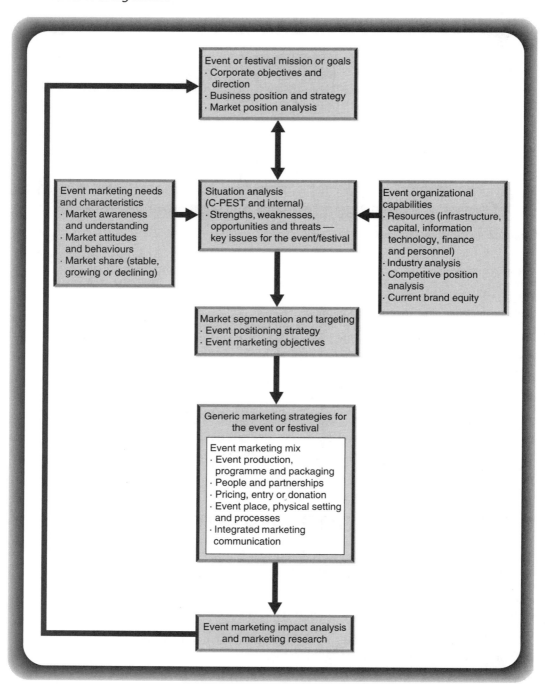

Figure 7.3 The strategic event marketing process

- historical and current data from other events, festivals and event organizers. A content analysis of the websites of festivals, events and event production agencies can be a valuable research technique. Jack Morton, which directed the opening and closing ceremonies of the 2004 Athens Olympics, Imagination and Euro RSCG Skybridge, the subject of case studies elsewhere in this text, are among many event companies whose websites offer a window to new and innovative event types.

A greater depth of understanding of macro-level issues such as event funding and the sponsorship environment, the seasonal saturation of events, the potential for oversupply of particular types of event and new technologies for event delivery can also be obtained through depth interviews with opinion leaders – for example, longstanding event directors or producers, public sector event agencies and academics.

At the micro-level, event marketers can use a mix of research techniques to gain insights into consumer segmentation and targeting. Past event reports that show vendor participation, event visitation, situational issues influencing past attendance and event satisfaction are desired resources, but not always available. Often, established members of the event organizing body (including volunteers) become a rich source of informal advice about the event's consumption trends. Further, more specific insights into existing event consumers can reliably be obtained from a mix of qualitative research (either depth interviews or a series of focus groups with eight to ten people across different segments of the market) and quantitative research (on-site intercept surveys or post-event research). For intercept surveys that are commonly undertaken at entry or exit points of the event, a randomly selected sample of at least 200 attendees (Getz, 2005) is recommended, to obtain meaningful marketing information. In this context, 'random' means all event customers have an equal chance of being selected for the survey. As customers exit the event, for example, every tenth customer could be asked to participate.

Data related to the visitors' demographics, motives, satisfaction and intention to revisit the event are generally sought. The data analysis can be manually performed for a small-scale survey that seeks only descriptive data about event consumers, but a statistical software package such as SPSS offers a deeper understanding of relationships between variables such as attendance motives and satisfaction. However, do not succumb to paralysis through analysis. Market research is an aid to competent event marketing, it does not replace it. Further guidance on conducting audience/visitor surveys is provided by the Arts Council of England (The Arts Council of England 1999, Verwey 1999).

Analysing event environments

Strategic marketing is a planning tool that emphasizes thorough analyses. The marketer's own sense of judgement is not enough to make good strategic decisions (Rao and Steckel, 1998). Astute marketing decisions emerge from a thorough analysis of competitor activities, the political, economic, socio-cultural and technological environments (C-PEST) in which the event occurs and an analysis of the event organization's internal resources.

The C-PEST analysis

Figure 7.4 depicts each of the analyses contained in the C-PEST framework. Note that the global entertainment environment is included because changes in the world of artistic or sporting endeavour need careful monitoring by event and festival managers. Such trend analyses are done for a good reason: to establish opportunities

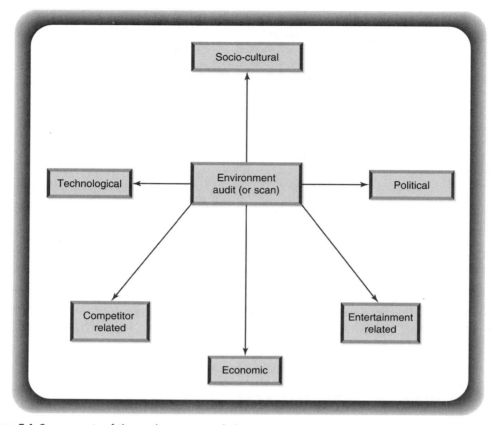

Figure 7.4 Components of the environment analysis

and threats for the festival/event and its management. Using this process, organizers can shape marketing strategies to capitalize on emerging entertainment opportunities and neutralize threats.

In conducting environmental analyses, it is easy to become overwhelmed by potential influences on the effective marketing of the event or festival. Stick to what is most critical to the event or festival in developing its marketing strategy in the current environment. To illustrate the C-PEST framework, the situation of the Edinburgh International Festival is considered. Now nearly 60 years old, the Edinburgh International Festival is a three-week celebration of dance, theatre, visual arts, opera and music, which energizes the city each year.

Competitive analysis

In describing competitor analysis and strategy, Porter's (1990) seminal work identified four elements that affect competition within an industry (Figure 7.5). This analytical tool is used to understand both industry-level and company-level competition, and it can also guide festival and event managers in their marketing decision making.

To begin, festival or event suppliers include the venues, artists and physical resources (such as lighting and staging) needed to produce a show. Unless other artistic festivals occurring at the same time depend on these suppliers, no major difficulties usually emerge with event supply. However, given that the mission of the

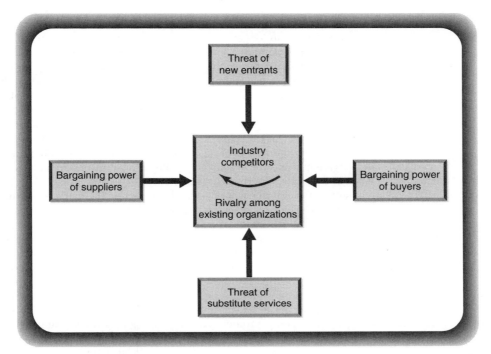

Figure 7.5 The four competitive forces
Source: Adapted with the permission of The Free Press, a Division of Simon & Schuster Adult Publishing Group from COMPETITIVE STRATEGY: Techniques for Analyzing Industries and Competitors by Michael E. Porter. Copyright © 1980, 1998 by The Free Press. All rights reserved

Edinburgh International Festival is to be the most exciting, accessible and innovative performing arts festival in the world, the organizers will liaise with suppliers of highly valued artists who have the power to increase talent costs or specify the conditions under which the artists will perform. Here, a relational strategy of building long-term alliances with agents and other festivals is important to ensure a continuity of supply at reasonable prices. This relational strategy could also be applied in forging close ties with venues such as King's Theatre, so the best venues for the festival's events are available and affordable. While some event suppliers such as venues and entertainment agents can wield considerable power, relationship marketing strategies help to address this power imbalance.

Because the buyers of the Edinburgh International Festival are large in number, little power is concentrated in their hands. Their only power is their price sensitivity to the festival's offerings. Given the festival's objective of providing arts of the highest possible standard, an end result could be higher ticket prices. If consumers decide a particular offering does not give value for money, and they stay away in droves, the festival organizers and sponsors could suffer embarrassment and a loss of money. Consequently, the role of the marketer is to carefully identify (through experience and market research) the price level at which this sensitivity could arise. In addition, with the mission of increasing accessibility, initiatives are also in place to encourage new audiences through tickets available at lower prices, for example with the Royal Bank £5 Youth Tickets, available to 16 to 26 year olds.

A threat of new entrants exists if there is some potential for market share to be lost to another festival or event offering similar experiences. The history of events within the UK is littered with examples of once hugely popular festivals or events that were once very popular and now no longer exist, or have been rejuvenated. For example, 1998 saw the end of the once popular Phoenix due to lack of ticket sales, and Reading Festival (established as an alternative to mainstream music events) has over the years broadened its musical appeal to incorporate mainstream music (Mintel, 2000). If there are few barriers to new entrants, this can be a real threat to the festival's viability. However, festivals such as the Edinburgh International Festival depend on grants and sponsors for much of their funding, so the barriers to entry are quite high. These entry barriers remain high while major sponsors (including government and corporate partners) are satisfied with the results of the festival – that is, so long as the funding agencies' objectives are met and the organizers' strategy for sponsorship management (Chapter 8) ensures their business results are achieved.

The notion of substitutes for an event or festival is based on the marketing premise that consumers are purchasing not a service, but a package of benefits – in this case, an array of stimulating entertainment. If a substitute experience provides entertainment that is more satisfying or just as satisfying in the same timeframe at a lower cost, then the threat of substitution becomes very real. A commonly cited strategy to avoid this threat is to offer a unique event experience to a well-defined target market that is not readily substituted. For the Edinburgh International Festival, the scale and sophistication of festival programming, together with the history and reputation of the festival, mean it would not be easily or quickly replaced by another event on the city's calendar. Yet, the ongoing proliferation of events and festivals, and the 'copy catting' that typifies services (including events), is a growing challenge for event marketers. 'Me too' events occurring on a smaller scale at other times of the year may have little short-term effect on attendance, but a gradual dilution of the existing event's unique selling proposition (the aspect that best distinguishes it in the marketplace) is one potential outcome of new entrants with similar event offerings.

Political environment   All levels of government can be active players in producing and sponsoring events and offering event development grants. For the Edinburgh International Festival, both the Scottish Parliament and City of Edinburgh Council, together with EventScotland and other agencies have played an active role in funding/ sponsorship and venue supply. Strategies to maintain this involvement are necessary, especially if a change of government occurs. As well as identifying the nature of government support, organizers need to take steps to understand new legislation or changes in the regulatory environment that affect event delivery – for example, rising public liability costs and regulations related to licensing, racing, gaming, lotteries and so on.

Economic environment   Some issues that have an impact on event marketing strategies are the buoyancy of the economy, foreign exchange rates, interest rates, employment rates, growth in household incomes and the government's fiscal policy. The value of the pound compared to the currency of other nations, for example, can raise or lower the cost of attracting foreign artists to the Edinburgh International Festival. Methods of combating economic challenges that affect the festival's mission are subject to continual review.

Socio-cultural environment   Factors of a social or cultural nature that affect event marketing strategies include the size and variety of cultural/subcultural groups in the event's target market; changes in lifestyle, including work–leisure patterns; changing demography; changes in entertainment demand and changes in education levels and household structures. For example, during the late 1980s/early 1990s the increase in popularity of dance music and its related culture lead to an increased demand for illegal dance events, commonly known as 'raves'. Interest in these illegal gatherings diminished after the mainstream nightclubs organized events to cater for this new market, including high-profile venues such as the late Hacienda in Manchester, that went on to enter the folklore and legend of dance music. These early developments led to the branded dance events and clubs, such as Ministry of Sound in London, Cream in Liverpool, Gatecrasher in Sheffield and the Back to Basics concept in Leeds. However, for some, illegal raves were and still are more popular as a response to commercialization of dance.

Organizers of the arts festivals might observe that women aged 18–30 years are more outwardly mobile, less tied to child rearing than ever before, and have more time and income to participate in events. A slightly higher proportion of females than males has been shown among attendees at various festivals – for example, research undertake for Arts Council Northern Ireland (Stephenson, 2005) found that 56 per cent of attendees at arts or cultural events were female. At the Town & Country Festival 2004 at Stoneleigh Park, the split was even more pronounced with 62 per cent female visitors (Haymarket Land Events LLP, 2005). A concentration of women in the workforce and increased travel by retirees has also contributed to a declining volunteer base for events and festivals (Cordingly, 1999).

Technological environment   Changes in technology present both opportunities and challenges for event organizers. In particular, the use of the World Wide Web, email marketing (including e-newsletters) and a mix of on-line and off-line event participation is now prevalent. The event website serves as a diverse branding tool for festivals and events, with opportunities for consumer interaction with event performers/players, up-to-the-minute event results and replays, and on-line recognition of event sponsors. For the Harrogate International Festival, organizers use web pages to provide previews of the events, promote major sponsors, provide news updates, local information, details about the education programme and give current news about recruitment for event volunteers. In analysing the technological environment, event marketers should evaluate the advantages and disadvantages of all forms of technology. Direct marketing via SMS messaging on mobile phones, for example, has become a popular event marketing tool, both before and during events. For those events with few resources and no permanent staff, the ability to build and maintain an effective website and stay abreast of new technology can be daunting. Yet, the failure to update a festival website on a regular basis or respond to on-line enquiries in a timely fashion can devalue the brand in the eyes of event visitors and sponsors. Marketers analysing their technological environment should note any opportunities for low-cost, technical support that could be available to their event or festival.

Entertainment environment   Entertainment is characterized by constant change as new ways of expression are developed, whether through new artistic forms or new types of sporting endeavour. The festival or event director generally tries to offer new experiences to consumers, to balance the familiar and novel event components. Trend analysis in the entertainment environment can be done via desk research and travel to centres of artistic innovation or places where emerging sports are practised (certainly a fun part of the job). While most events and festival organizers do not take an annual 'ideas tour' to exotic places to construct their marketing plan, they actively observe entertainment trends all year around. A good understanding of event innovations is also gained from reading professional and popular journals, networking with industry colleagues and travelling to trade fairs and exhibitions. Again, a key purpose of this analysis is to align the event's marketing strategies with opportunities and strengths, and to minimize the impacts of any threats and weaknesses.

Internal resource analysis

Another vital step in developing the marketing strategy is the assessment of the event's internal resources. Classic economists categorize the resources available to an entrepreneur as land, labour and capital. In event or festival organizations, the resources are human resources, physical resources and financial resources.

Human resources   The event strategist analyses the number and type of staff and volunteers available, the particular skill sets required to produce the event, the costs of employing people, and innovative ways in which people can contribute to the event's success. An analysis of the Edinburgh International Festival would show that the festival's directors have been individuals with a high profile since the festival's inception. As a result, a lynchpin of the marketing communication strategy is the use of the director as the public face of the festival who features strongly in media releases and interviews. Promoting a festival through its senior producers/directors and organized word-of-mouth by staff and volunteers also minimizes the cost of an event's marketing communication campaign. The Edinburgh Festival Fringe is an example of a festival that has capitalized on word-of-mouth marketing over the years through its participants and audiences. This was taken a stage further in 2005 by tapping into word-of-mouth of the loyal body of event-goers through implementing a show rating system using mobile phone texts, based on a unique number allocated to each of the 1800 shows (Ferguson, 2005).

Physical resources   For an event, physical resources can include ownership of a venue (although this is rare). More often, they include computer hardware and software, desktop publishing equipment, access to venues at competitive rates and the use of conference rooms in buildings of some significance. For example, the use of event management software capable of supplying timely data on all aspects of the festival would be a physical resource strength. A far less tangible resource is the festival's brand equity (public awareness and attitudes towards the event built over a longer period). It is fair to assume community goodwill towards the Edinburgh International Festival has become a valued resource.

Financial resources   Without access to suitable finance, no event marketing strategy can be put into place. Current access to funds or a demonstrated ability to acquire capital is an obvious strength for any event. This access includes the ongoing involvement of government and corporate sponsorship funds. With the involvement of local government through City of Edinburgh Council and the Scottish Arts Council, the patronage of Her Majesty the Queen, the inclusion of representatives of the City of Edinburgh Council on the festival board, and its corporate sponsors, the Edinburgh International Festival relies on a well established resource base, though this is not taken for granted as noted in the case study in Chapter 10. Adequate financial resources or backing for events and festivals often simultaneously depends on the strengths of its partnerships (a key reason for this element featuring in the event marketing mix).

The SWOT analysis

Once the C-PEST and internal resource audit is completed, an analysis of strengths, weaknesses, opportunities, threats (SWOT) can be conducted. This summary of the critical issues identified through the C-PEST and internal resources analyses (Tribe, 1997) enables the event marketer to marry opportunities and strengths, improve weaknesses, negate threats and, just as importantly, have a sound basis for establishing marketing objectives and strategies for the event. This task is made easier if all the data collected are summarized into no more than 10 bullet points for each section of the SWOT analysis.

The event consumer's decision-making process

Understanding the consumer decision-making process for events and festivals is aided by the following PIECE acronym:

- problem recognition – difference between someone's existing state and their desired state relative to leisure consumption
- information search – internal or external search; limited or extensive search processes for leisure (including event) solutions
- evaluation and selection of leisure alternatives
- choosing whether to attend an event and which optional purchases to make at the event or festival
- evaluation of the post-event experience.

Reflecting this PIECE process, the consumer identifies a need that may be satisfied by attending an event or other leisure experience, searches for information about such an experience in different media (the entertainment section of newspapers, the radio, magazines, friends and relatives), and then evaluates the alternatives available. Most of us then examine how the leisure experience compares with a list of the attributes we most desire. As event-goers, we may want to improve our family ties, so we attend a local community festival that all members of our family can enjoy. Alternatively, we may be looking for a novel or innovative event to satisfy our curiosity. After experiencing (or 'consuming') the event, we re-evaluate the experience for its quality of service and its capacity to satisfy our needs.

Problem recognition

For would-be event or festival consumers, problem recognition means a difference exists between what they would like to experience and what they have to do to satisfy that need (Neal, Quester and Hawkins, 2002). The central starting point for this problem recognition is the existence of one or more needs that may be satisfied by attending a festival or event. Events and festivals fulfil physiological needs (exercise, relaxation, sexual engagement), interpersonal needs (social interaction) and/or personal needs (enhanced knowledge, new experiences, fulfilment of fantasies) (Getz, 1991, 2005). How quickly we decide whether to attend an event partly depends on our event purchase involvement – that is, our level of interest in the purchase process, once it has been triggered (Neal, Quester and Hawkins, 2002). Some events are spontaneous, low-involvement decisions, such as when we visit a local park on the weekend, notice a small, cultural festival in progress, and wander over to join in. In contrast, attending events such as the Olympic Games in Beijing in 2008 or visiting New Zealand to follow the British Lions tour are high-involvement decisions.

Information search

In looking for information, most consumers try to determine (1) the relevant criteria on which to base their decision – the nature of event performers, the location, other attractions in the area, the ticket price and so on – and (2) the extent to which the event will satisfy their needs. As they compare different leisure experiences, event consumers engage in both external and internal searches for information.

External influences

Among the external influences on the potential event-goer are various social factors. These factors are described below in the context of event participation.

- *Family and household influences,* such as the desires of children, often influence the leisure behaviour of parents. The need for family cohesion and building familial ties is a strong leisure motivator for many people. It explains the large numbers of children and exhausted parents who congregate at agricultural shows around the UK, for example, the Great Yorkshire Show. Many festivals focus on children's entertainment for this reason.
- *Reference groups* are those groups that influence the behaviour of individuals. Groups in close contact with individuals (peers, family, colleagues and neighbours) are called primary reference groups. Those who have less frequent contact are called secondary reference groups. Most people tend to seek the approval of members of their reference groups. If attendance at a particular festival is perceived to be acceptable and desirable, then group members are more likely to attend. Showing examples of a typical reference group (for example, a nuclear family or a group of young people) enjoying themselves at a festival can be a persuasive communication strategy when those groups represent the festival's target market.
- *Opinion formers or opinion leaders* are those people within any group whose views about events and leisure experiences are sought and widely accepted. These opinion leaders are often media, theatrical or sports personalities (including critics and commentators) who are highly rewarded for their endorsement of products and leisure services. Often, the views of critics and commentators have a strong impact on attendance in sport and the arts.

The adoption of new leisure services tends to follow a normal distribution curve. Innovators (generally opinion leaders within a group) are the first to try the experience. Early adopters, who are a little more careful about adopting the innovation, follow them and act as opinion leaders for the majority. Laggards are the last to try something new; some may be loyal attendees of very mature events or events that are close to decline. It is logical that the marketing of new festivals or events begins by targeting the opinion formers or innovators within the market.

- *Culture* includes the 'knowledge, beliefs, art, morals, laws, customs and any other capabilities and habits acquired as a member of society' (Neal, Quester and Hawkins, 2002, p. 22). The UK is an example of a culturally diverse country in which Indigenous people and various ethnic groups with different patterns of living co-exist. Our culture can affect our buying habits, leisure needs, attitudes and values.

Culture has a profound influence on the design, marketing and consumption of events and festivals. In effect, events are simultaneously a celebration and a consumption experience that reflect our way of life. A growth of interest in events as diverse as London's Notting Hill Carnival, the Bradford Mela and the Eisteddfod, demonstrate the influence of, and interest in, culture.

An external search involving reference groups or other sources becomes especially important when event or festival attendance requires an extended decision-making process. Going to the Olympic Games, for example, is a high-involvement, extended decision, and event-goers will seek advice from websites, travel agents and other sources. Participating in some cultural events, such as the Shetland Folk Festival, could involve extended decision-making because it requires travelling by airplane or ferry to the island.

Internal influences

A range of *internal influences* also affect consumer decision making about events. These influences include perception (how we select and process information), *learning and memory, motives, personality traits and consumer attitudes*. If, for example, we have an existing preference (attitude) that steers us towards a classical music event, then we could deliberately select out information about competing leisure activities. Similarly, if we have information stored in our memory that helps to resolve a need (for example, a mental picture of spectacular fireworks at The Riverside Festival in Nottingham), then that event could quickly become the single, most satisfactory solution to our entertainment needs on a given weekend in August in Nottingham.

Personality, or an individual's characteristic traits that affect behaviour, is another influence on event or festival decisions (Brassington and Pettitt, 2003). People can be introverted/extroverted, shy/self-confident, aggressive/retiring and dynamic/sluggish. Although the effects of personality on consumer choice are difficult to measure, we can assume that festivals that celebrate adventure or sporting prowess will attract participants with 'outgoing' personalities. An awareness of particular personality characteristics among event consumers can help marketers to fine tune their strategies.

Among all of the internal influences, 'in developed economies, most consumer behaviour is guided by psychological motives' (Neal, Quester and Hawkins, 2002, p. 19). A body of empirical research on motives for event and festival attendance has emerged since the 1990s. Three theories of event motives, as summarized by Axelsen and Arcodia (2004), are:

1. the needs achievement hierarchy – a theory based on Maslow's original hierarchy, whereby motives change as each level of need – from the physiological through to self-actualization – is satisfied
2. 'push' and 'pull' motives – a theory that push factors (for example, escapism or curiosity) propel us towards an event, while pull factors (for example, aspects of events, such as wine and gourmet food) draw us to an event
3. intrinsic motives for leisure – a theory related to 'push' and 'pull' motives that we seek change from routine (escape) and intrinsic personal and interpersonal rewards from visiting/travelling to other environments. Example of these rewards might be the increased sense of endurance and friendships formed during a historic horse riding event (as described by Mannell and Iso-Ahola, 1987).

A set of common motives (or need satisfiers) for attending festivals has been cited in a wide range of studies (see, for example, Backman, Backman, Muzaffer and Sunshine, 1995; Crompton and McKay, 1997; Uysal, Gahan and Martin, 1993). A summary of motives for festival attendance that consistently emerge are:

- socialization or external interaction – meeting new people, being with friends and socializing in a known group
- family togetherness – seeking the opportunity to be with friends and relatives and doing things together to create greater family cohesion
- escape from everyday life, as well as recovering equilibrium – getting away from the usual demands of life, having a change from daily routine and recovering from life's stresses
- learning about or exploring other cultures – gaining knowledge about different cultural practices and celebrations
- excitement/thrills – doing something because it is stimulating and exciting
- event novelty/ability to regress – experiencing new and different things and/or attending a festival that is unique.

The above list tends to reflect the earlier three theories of event motives (Axelsen and Arcodia, 2004). These motives have been found in most festival studies and also among visitors to events and exhibitions. Both special event and gallery visitors during the Ilkley Autumn Arts Festival (staged at the Kings Hall and various venues around Ilkley each Autumn), for example, may seek relaxation, entertainment, education and a variety of other motives through their attendance at the different events. The order of importance given to the different motives appears to vary according to the type of festival or event. Visitors to a specialized festival, such as a hot air balloon festival, have been shown to be highly motivated by a desire to socialize with people sharing the same interest (Mohr, Backman, Gahan and Backman, 1993), while people attending a community festival have been shown to be motivated by 'escape' from day-to-day life (Uysal, Gahan and Martin, 1993).

Evaluating alternatives and making event choices

It is fair to assume that consumers rarely weigh up whether they will attend more than one or two events on a given day. Instead, they are likely to choose between an event/festival and the cinema, a private party or an entirely different leisure activity. For everyday products and services, evaluative criteria are often price, brand image and the contents of the market offer.

Services such as events that we have not previously attended are quite hard to evaluate, and we experience some uncertainty due to the financial, social, psychological, sensory, performance and time-related risks involved (Lovelock and Wirtz, 2004). Even if a festival has free entry, we may have travel costs, child care and other costs involved. Socially, we may think about the types of people we will encounter at an event, and the psychological costs and benefits of those encounters. We also evaluate the time that it will take to attend the event, and sensory risks such as our ability to see the stage or hear the music with clarity. The choice of whether to attend sports events can be linked to the stadium atmosphere, layout and facilities, rather than team performance. For example, Robertson and Pope (1999) found the atmosphere, the live action, stadium cleanliness and ease of getting seating were quite influential in the decision to attend Brisbane Lions (Australia Football League) games, while in their study of Minor League Baseball, Lee, Ryder and Shin (2003) found that cleanliness of facilities followed by quantity and convenience of facilities and parking were the three leading environmental motivation factors.

Any number of values may be applied in making different event consumption choices. Functional values, such as our perception of an event's price–quality relationship and ease of access, may dominate. Alternatively, emotional values may be more influential (the likely effects of a festival experience on our mood).

Other conditional values for a festival may be whether there is convenient transport, good quality classical music or nearby accommodation that suits our tastes.

Post-event evaluation

Once we have attended an event, we start to compare what we expected with what we experienced. Consumer expectations arise from a combination of marketing communications planned by the event or festival organizer, word of mouth from friends and family, previous experience with this or similar events, and the event's brand image. The exercise of comparing consumer's expectations with actual experiences of services is now commonplace. However, even when markets are tightly segmented into a group of people with a common characteristic, members of the same group can have different perceptions of the benefits they receive. Two close friends may attend City of Derry Jazz Festival: one may rate all of the event services very highly, yet the other may not be as enthusiastic, despite having experienced the same service. The relationship between event-goers' satisfaction, their perceptions of service quality and their intentions to revisit is very important to marketers who want to build a loyal visitor market.

Event satisfaction, service quality, repeat visits

Because leisure services are intangible, inseparable, variable and perishable, defining service quality is difficult. From the viewpoint of a festival or event consumer, quality service occurs when expectations of the event match perceptions of the service experienced. Understanding perceived service quality is thus a primary goal of marketers. Both existing and potential attendees can have a perception of event quality (formed from experience of the event, word of mouth and/or other marketing communication). However, perceptions of the event itself are based on the technical (performance outcomes) and functional (process related) qualities of the experience (Gronroos, 1990). Other external factors – for example, wet weather and personal factors such as an argument with a partner during the event – also affect consumer perceptions.

Because it is harder to evaluate 'technical' quality (such as the musical performance at the festival), much of the focus in measuring perceived service quality is on functional aspects, or ways in which service is delivered. For this reason, the five main dimensions of service quality in the commonly used SERVQUAL questionnaire (Parasuraman, Zeithaml and Berry, 1988; Zeithaml, Parasuraman and Berry, 1990) mostly reflect functional service aspects. These dimensions are:

- assurance – staff and/or volunteers give the appearance of being knowledgeable, helpful and courteous, and event consumers are assured of their wellbeing
- empathy – the event staff and/or volunteers seem to understand the consumers' needs and deliver caring attention
- responsiveness – the staff and volunteers are responsive to the needs of the consumer
- reliability – everything happens at the event in the way the marketing communication has promised
- tangibles – the physical appearance of the event equipment, artists' costume/ presentation and the physical setting meet expectations.

Using these five dimensions, the SERVQUAL questionnaire measures the difference between visitor expectations and perceptions of a festival or event. When the visitors' perceptions of their event experience match or exceed their expectations, a quality experience has been delivered, and the outcome is satisfied attendees who could decide to go to the event next time when it is held. The SERVQUAL instrument has also been used in a number of other event related studies. For example, Robinson and Callan (2001, 2002a, b, 2005) explored service quality in relation to venue choice of conference organizers, while O'Neil, Getz and Carlsen (1999) and Getz, O'Neill and Carlsen (2001) investigated service quality at a surfing event, and Thrane (2002) in the context of a jazz festival.

Event satisfaction is related to perceived service quality, but it is experience dependent. Satisfaction can be measured only among existing visitors to the event. Not every customer will be satisfied all the time; to maintain a competitive position, however, the event marketer should aim to achieve more than a basic level of satisfaction. A sense of delight or extreme satisfaction among event visitors is the ideal outcome (Lovelock and Wirtz, 2004). To this end, one objective in an event's strategic marketing should involve visitor satisfaction – for example, '95 per cent of event participants will give a satisfied or higher rating of the event'. Figure 7.6 shows how consumer dissatisfaction can occur based on some perceived gap in festival or event

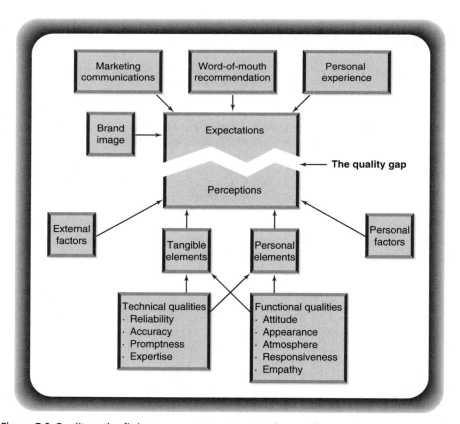

Figure 7.6 Quality – the fit between customer expectations and perceptions
Source: Marketing for Leisure and Tourism by Michael Morgan, Pearson Education Limited.
Copyright © Prentice Hall Europe 1996

quality. It is clear that customer satisfaction needs to be the focus when considering all aspects of event planning and management (Bowdin and Church, 2000).

Given the difficulty in understanding consumer expectations (with there being no clear set of expectations for each service setting), it is often argued that a 'perceptions only' measure of satisfaction (one that excludes expectations) is more useful. For festivals, various writers suggest consumer 'perceptions' are better indicators of the link between quality, visitor satisfaction and intentions to revisit (see, for example, Baker and Crompton, 2000; Thrane, 2002). Because musical performance has been highlighted as an important determinant of quality at a festival (Saleh and Ryan, 1993; Thrane, 2002), use of the SERVQUAL approach alone is probably not the marketer's best approach to research. Thrane (2002), however, also notes that aspects of quality measured by SERVQUAL do contribute to jazz festival patrons' satisfaction and intentions to revisit. A research instrument that adequately investigates both festival 'performance' and 'process' should be considered, therefore, in creating and evaluating festival and event marketing strategies.

Steps in the strategic marketing process

Strategic marketing involves distinct steps that event managers must understand to create a successful strategy. These steps include segmenting the market, targeting and positioning, setting measurable marketing objectives, choosing generic marketing strategies and designing an effective marketing mix.

Segmenting and targeting the event market

Most events do not appeal to everybody, so it is essential to identify those consumer segments whose needs most closely match the event experience. The market segments chosen should be:

- measurable – that is, the characteristics of the segment (socio-economic status, gender, age and so on) must be accessible to the event marketer
- substantial enough in size to be worth targeting
- accessible by normal marketing communication channels
- actionable by the event organizer, given the marketing budget and other resources (Morgan, 1996).

The segmentation process uses the concept of the buyer decision-making process as a guide. The process of identifying appropriate target markets is known as market segmentation. Segmentation can occur by geography, demography or lifestyle (psychography). The Pembroke Festival 2004, for example, had an extensive product range, categorized into arts, drama, music, dance, food, family and youth (Pembroke Festival, 2004). Each of these categories has different offerings, appealing to the buyer behaviour of different submarkets. The music category alone featured about 22 different offerings. By thinking about the potential visitors to the music programme the festival organizers can develop a mental snapshot of the overall target market for the music category and events within it. Actual segmentation of the markets could be based on geography, demography (including the visitors' life cycle phase) and/or behaviour (lifestyles, benefits sought and attendance profile – that is, first timers or repeat visitors).

Geographic segmentation based on the place of residence of event visitors is a commonly used method. Many community festivals are dominated by local visitors or daytrippers from the immediate county or region. For this reason, managers of community festivals often decide to focus on local residents as their major geographic segment. A key determinant of geographic segmentation is the potential 'drawing power' of the event as a tourist attraction. An event such as a capital city agricultural show (for example, the Great Yorkshire Show in Harrogate) would have a regional geographic segmentation and probably a national market segment for its more specialized event experiences. Although many event organizers have visions of creating tourist demand, few events develop the brand equity and 'pull' characteristics to succeed as independent tourist attractions. Many more events could succeed in attracting tourists if organizers improved their skills in packaging and marketing the event alongside other regional tourist experiences. If an event demonstrates its ability to draw external markets – for example, Notting Hill Carnival – then the potential geographic spread could be:

- local residents of the area
- day visitors from outside the immediate area
- regional domestic tourists
- international inbound tourists.

Demographic segmentation concerns the measurable characteristics of people, such as age, gender, occupation, income, education and cultural group. A demographic segmentation tool often used by marketers is a socioeconomic scale based on occupation (usually the head of the household, in family units). The traditional JICNARS classification, or social status/class, used by British marketers, used five categories based on occupation. These are summarized in Table 7.1 applied in an events context.

Although developed for the UK, these classifications are relevant to other developed countries. Media buyers in advertising agencies first used this method of classification, as the system is a very good predictor of reading and viewing habits. For example, ABC1 adults make up the majority of the readership for 'broadsheet' newspapers, such as *Financial Times* (91 per cent), *The Guardian* (90 per cent), *The Times*, *Daily Telegraph* and *Independent* (87 per cent), whereas they account for a minority of the tabloids readership (e.g. *Daily Star* 32 per cent, The *Sun* 35 per cent and *Daily Mirror* 38 per cent) (NRS, 2005).

However, these classifications are not always an accurate guide to income. For example, many Cs earn considerable incomes. The essential difference between As, Bs, C1s and the other categories is in the level of education. Research suggests that the higher the level of education, the higher the propensity of a person to participate in cultural activities including arts and community festivals (Torkildsen, 2005). Morgan observes that the age at which individuals terminate their formal education (16, 18 or after higher education at 21 or more years) can indicate their ambition, intelligence and, importantly for event managers, their curiosity about the world in which they live (Morgan, 1996, p. 103). For directors of festivals and events that include cultural elements, their target market is an educated one.

From 2001, new National Statistics Socio-Economic Classifications (NS-SEC) were adopted for the purposes of official statistics. This breaks the population down into seventeen operational categories based on occupation, size of employing organiza-tion, type of contract, benefits and job security. These may enable more clearly defined groups, particularly considering the trend towards the 'middle classes' within the

Table 7.1 A classification of socio-economic market segments for events

Group	Social status	Social grade	Head of household's occupation	Types of events group is likely to attend	Approx. % of England/Wales population
A	Upper middle class	Higher managerial, administrative or professional	Professional people, very senior managers in business or commerce or top-level civil servants, retired people (previously grade A), and their widows.	Cultural events such as fundraisers for the opera, classical music festivals	22
B	Middle class	Intermediate managerial, administrative or professional	Middle management executives in large organizations, (with appropriate qualifications), principal officers in local government and civil service, top management or owners of small businesses, educational and service establishments, retired people (previously grade B) and their widows.	Cultural events (but purchasing cheaper seats), food and beverage festivals, historical festivals, arts and crafts festivals, community festivals	
C1	Lower middle class	Supervisory or clerical and junior managerial, administrative or professional	Junior management, owners of small establishments, all others in non-manual positions. Jobs in this group have very varied responsibilities and educational requirements. It also includes retired people (previously grade C1) and their widows.	Most popular cultural events, some sporting events, community festivals	30
C2	Skilled working class	Skilled manual workers	Skilled manual workers, and those manual workers with responsibility for other people, retired people (previously grade C2) with pensions from their job and widows (if receiving pensions from their late husband's job).	Motor vehicle festivals/ shows, sporting events, community festivals	15
D	Working class	Semi-skilled and unskilled manual workers	Semi-skilled and unskilled manual workers, and apprentices and trainees to skilled workers, retired people (previously grade D) with pensions from their job, and widows (if receiving a pension from their late husband's job).	Some sporting events, ethnic festivals	17
E	Those at lowest level of subsistence	State pensioners, widows (no other earner), on benefit/unemployed, casual or lowest grade workers	Those entirely dependant on the state long-term, through sickness, unemployment, old age or other reasons; those unemployed for a period exceeding six months (otherwise classify on previous occupation), casual workers, those without a regular income. Only households without a Chief Income Earner will be coded in this group.	Very little, except occasionally free events	16

Source: adapted from Morgan (1996), National Readership Survey (2005) and ONS (2003)

UK population (Rose and O'Reilley, 1998). Depending on data analysis requirements, eight-, five- and three-class versions may be used, though the analytic version using eight overall classes is used for most analysis, with the 'Not Classified' including students, occupations not stated or inadequately described, and not classifiable for other reasons (Office for National Statistics, 2005) (see Table 7.2).

Other demographic variables are gender and age. Women and men occasionally have different needs and some events cater for these different needs. The years in which people are born can affect their outlook on life, their attitudes and values, and their interests. Depending on the event, one or several of these generations can be targeted, with event programme elements designed to cater for each segment. Table 7.3 shows the different generations born in the twentieth century.

Another method of age segmentation is by life cycle. This relies on the proposition that peoples' leisure habits vary according to their position in the life cycle. Wells and Gubar (1966) developed the original lifecycle model that reflected the life stages of the time (i.e. bachelor, newly married, full nester, empty nester and solitary survivors), however, due to changes in society this has now become outdated (Brassington and Pettitt, 2003). The family life cycle, illustrated in Figure 7.7, is reflective of the

Table 7.2 Socio-economic classification classes

Analytic class	Operational category	Percentage of population
1	Higher managerial and professional occupations	10.8
	1.1 Large employers and higher managerial occupations	
	1.2 Higher professional occupations	
2	Lower managerial and professional occupations	22.2
3	Intermediate occupations	10.3
4	Small employers and own account workers	7.7
5	Lower supervisory and technical occupations	9.4
6	Semi-routine occupations	13.3
7	Routine occupations	9.8
8	Never worked and long-term unemployed	16.5

Source: Labour Market Survey and Office for National Statistics (ONS, 2004)

Table 7.3 The generations born in the twentieth century

Generation	Born	Age in 2000	Formative years
First World War	Pre-1924	82+	Pre-1936
Depression	1924–1934	71–81	1936–1946
Second World War	1935–1945	60–70	1947–1957
Early boomers	1946–1954	51–59	1958–1966
Late boomers	1955–1964	41–50	1967–1988
Baby Bust (Gen. X)	1965–1976	29–40	1977–1988
Echo Boom (Gen. Y)	1977–1994	12–28	1989–2000

Source: US Travel Data Centre (1989) updated and cited in Getz (2005), p. 92

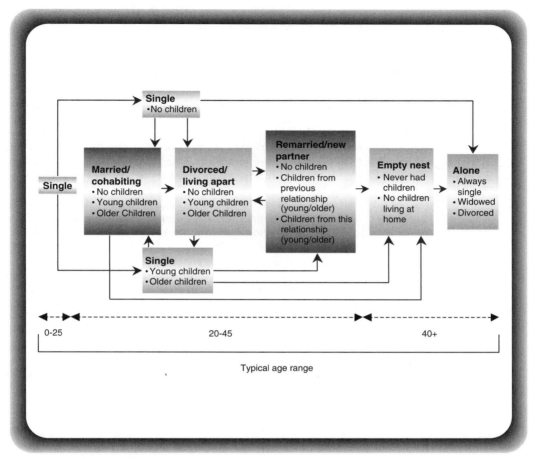

Figure 7.7 Modern family life cycle
Source: Principles of Marketing by Frances Brassington and Stephen Pettitt, Pearson Education Limited. Copyright © Frances Brassington and Stephen Pettitt 1997 © Pearson Education Limited 2000, 2003

modern family. For example, single or married/cohabiting people with children are equally the target market for community events that feature elements for both children and adults, whereas AB empty nesters are the perfect market for a cultural festival featuring quality food and drink and arias from well-loved operas.

Marketers sometimes employ a combination of age and lifestyle segmentation. 'Full nesters' are the target market for events that feature entertainment for both children and adults, for example, whereas 'AB empty nesters' are the perfect market for cultural festivals featuring quality food and drink, and arias from well-loved operas. However, care should be taken not to resort to age stereotypes. Many early baby boomers, in or approaching their fifties, are fit, active and interested in all types of culture, popular and contemporary, as well as high-culture festivals such as classical music or theatre. It could be argued that the most successful community festivals are those which are inclusive of all age groups, rather than focusing on just one age cohort. The group aged 35 years is a growing market segment, among whom food and wine festivals have become a popular leisure experience (with women marginally outnumbering men). Targeting the media-savvy, 18–34 years old market, which is not at all homogenous (singles, couples with and without children), requires a different approach.

Geodemographics – segmenting residential areas according to variables from population census data and additional sources including lifestyle databases – was initially developed as ACORN (A Classification of Residential Neighbourhoods) by the CACI Market Analysis Group (Kotler et al., 2005, p. 402). ACORN classifies residential areas into six main categories (see Table 7.4) with seventeen subgroups and fifty-six types, thus allowing areas to be linked to buying behaviour and lifestyle for more effective marketing. The new ACORN incorporates 2001 Census data and has been extensively revised to be more robust and not only classify postcodes but geographic areas to allow better discrimination. Registering on the CACI website (www.caci.co.uk) allows access to further information about ACORN and the ability to search specific postcodes.

The Office for National Statistics (ONS) publishes a great deal of data taken from each census that categorizes residential areas according to the demographics of the residents of that area. This information was traditionally published as paper-based documents, with a separate edition published for every region throughout the UK. However, it is now available in a range of other formats and is a valuable store of demographic information categorized by geographic area. Data shown include the demographic variables of sex, age, marital status, household member-ship and relationships, cultural characteristics, qualifications, employment, workplace and household accommodation. The launch of National Statistics in 2000 illustrated a shift toward more accessible official statistics, which includes census, other data and publications being freely available on line for not-for-profit end users (see www.statistics.gov.uk for further information). Directors of community festivals and other event managers should find this data very useful for product planning.

Table 7.4 ACORN consumer classification

Category		% UK pop.	Group		% UK pop.
1	WEALTHY ACHIEVERS	25.1	A	WEALTHY EXECUTIVES	8.6
			B	AFFLUENT GREYS	7.7
			C	FLOURISHING FAMILES	8.5
2	URBAN PROSPERITY	10.7	D	PROSPEROUS PROFESSIONAL	2.2
			E	EDUCATED URBANITES	4.6
			F	ASPIRING SINGLES	3.9
3	COMFORTABLY OFF	26.6	G	STARTING OUT	2.5
			H	SECURE FAMILIES	15.5
			I	SETTLED SUBURBIA	6
			J	PRUDENT PENSIONERS	2.6
4	MODERATE MEANS	14.5	K	ASIAN COMMUNITIES	2.5
			L	POST-INDUSTRIAL FAMILIES	15.5
			M	BLUE-COLLAR ROOTS	6
5	HARD-PRESSED	22.4	N	STRUGGLING FAMILIES	14.1
			O	BURDENED SINGLES	4.5
			P	HIGH-RISE HARDSHIP	1.6
			Q	INNER CITY ADVERSITY	2.1
			U	UNCLASSIFIED	0.3

Source: CACI (2004), p. 8

Table 7.5 Lifestyle dimensions

Activities	*Interest*
Work	Family
Shopping	Home
Holidays	Work
Social life	Community
Hobbies	Leisure and recreation
Entertainment	Fashion
Spots interests	Food
Club memberships	Media
Community	
Opinions	*Demographics*
Themselves	Age
Social and cultural issues	Education
Politics	Income
Educations	Occupation
Economics	Family size
Business	Life-cycle stage
Products	Geographic location
Future	

Source: adapted from Brassington and Pettitt (2003)

Psychographic segmentation – dividing a market according to its lifestyle and values, is another useful planning technique. This method involves measuring AIO (activities, interests, opinions) dimensions and demographics (Brassington and Pettitt, 2003; Kotler et al., 2005). Table 7.5 illustrates the primary lifestyle dimensions. Based on consumer research, classifications have been developed by various organizations.

However, like personality segmentation, psychographic segmentation of a market has some serious limitations for an event marketer:

> The main problem ... is that psychographic segments are very difficult and expensive to define and measure. Relevant information is much less likely to exist already in the public domain. It is also very easy to get the implementation wrong. For example, the organisation that tries to portray lifestyle elements within advertisements is depending on the audience's ability to interpret the symbols used in the desired way and to reach the desired conclusions from them. (Brassington and Pettitt, 2003, p. 192)

This type of segmentation offers, however, a better understanding of the types of experience and benefit that different 'lifestyle' groups seek in a leisure experience.

Positioning the event

How to position an event in the mindset of the market is an important strategic decision. Positioning represents the way in which the event is defined by consumers, or 'the place it occupies in consumers' minds relative to competing products' (Kotler et al., 2005, p. 432). Event positioning can be achieved in at least 10 different ways, as shown below:

1. The existing reputation or image of the event – for example, the Olympic Games and other longstanding events such as the Edinburgh Tattoo.
2. The charisma of a director or leader – for example, the Belfast Festival's director.
3. A focus on event programming – for example, Trafalgar Square Festival 2005, which was a three week festival programmed and positioned around the 'city rites' theme.
4. A focus on performers – for example major sports (such as the football and golf) and theatre that highlight the players/performers.
5. An emphasis on location or facilities – for example, Wimbledon, which is now synonymous with world-standard tennis.
6. Event users – for example, Bank of Scotland Edinburgh Children's Theatre Festival.
7. Price or quality – for example, a free civic concert series versus an operatic performance by the world's three best tenors.
8. The purpose or application of the event – for example, health awareness of SIDs or diabetes, or celebrations such as the United Kingdom's Trafalgar Weekend as the centerpiece of SeaBritain 2005.
9. The event category or 'product' class – for example, fashion events, food and wine festivals, and concerts.
10. Multiple attributes – for example, the London Fashion Week, which is positioned on its designers, reputation and image, as well as its purpose of bringing new fashion designers into the public eye.

Once decisions have been made about the event's segmentation, targeting and positioning, a platform is available to decide on event marketing objectives, strategies and tactics.

Developing event marketing objectives

Any successful development of a marketing plan is based on sound marketing objectives. Cravens, Merriless and Walker (2000, p. 272) make this important point: 'For marketing to be a beneficial business discipline, its expected results must be defined and measurable'. Hypothetical examples of marketing objectives for an event such as the Cheltenham International Music Festival might be to:

- increase box office receipts in 2007 by 10 per cent
- increase the percentage of seats sold in all ticketed events to 80 per cent in 2007
- retain 90 per cent of sponsors for 2007
- increase publicity generated in print and electronic media by a further 10 per cent from 2007.

It is important to stress again how marketing objectives, like all objectives, must be measurable and not expressed in vague terms that make measurement impossible. While many managers are tempted to state general aims rather than set objectives (making it harder to be accountable for whether event objectives have been achieved), this temptation must be resisted. Clearly defined and measurable objectives give the marketer the ends, while strategies and their supporting tactics are the means to those ends.

The dimensions of the objective thus have an impact on the choice of strategies. Consider the hypothetical objective for the Cheltenham International Music Festival of increasing box office receipts by 10 per cent in 2007. This increase is a substantial amount, much higher than the inflation rate, which implies that a business objective of the festival is to grow substantially each year to satisfy the entertainment and cultural demands of a more diverse audience base. The objective and the strategies to achieve it are chosen, therefore, only after careful analysis of the market needs, organizational capabilities and opportunities.

Choosing generic marketing strategies for events

Before events marketers begin the more precise task of deciding on marketing elements such as the programme, the ticket price and other variables, they should reflect on their overall strategies for the event's future. Is there a plan to grow or expand the event and/or its markets? Or is there a plan to consolidate the current programme and further penetrate existing markets? Any number of strategic options is available to the event/festival, depending on its resources, its competition and its objectives. (Chapter 5 explained a range of these strategies.)

The following discusses the application of Porter's (1990) generic strategies and the potential use of strategies of growth, integration and diversification (Kotler, Bowen and Makens, 1999) as they affect events marketing. First, Porter (1990) suggests most organizations have a choice of strategies of differentiation, focus or cost leadership. For the events marketer, decisions on these strategies are based on whether the aim is for the event to hold a leadership position in a region or city's leisure market or to have a narrower, yet well-defined market scope. The Henry Wood Promenade Concerts at the Royal Albert Hall appear to have established a cost leadership position with places guaranteed for those queuing on the day at £4 (ViewLondon.co.uk, 2005), with brand equity in diverse market segments and some economies of scale and efficiency in its management (including its branding and communication strategies). In contrast, the Greenbelt Festival at Cheltenham Racecourse draws a more specialized audience with a focus strategy, servicing a particular segment – that is, Christian music lovers – with a high-quality performance. A differentiation strategy means creating something that is perceived to be quite unique across the event/festival sector. Interesting examples of events that employed this strategy could include Beautiful Night, a concert that took place in Belfast and Dublin in 2004 using live broadcasting from BBC and RTE to link the two sites together to form one concert and broadcast on television. It also formed the finale to the 11 day BBC Music Live festival (BBC, 2004).

Other marketing strategy options arise from the overall event strategies of intensive growth, integration and diversification. Perhaps the most commonly cited tool in deciding on growth strategies is the product-market matrix (Ansoff, 1957, cited in Kotler, Bowen and Makens, 1999) shown in Figure 7.8.

An event that has a well-designed programme, but is not yet drawing large numbers, could consider a market penetration strategy – that is, concentrating on attracting more people from the same target market. If organizers consider that the event could reach a different target market without changing its programme, a market development strategy could be used. Finally, if consumer satisfaction studies show that the event is not satisfying its current visitor needs, new and different programme elements could be needed. The arena spectacular, Godskitchen's Global Gathering represents a good example of a new event being used to better satisfy the needs of contemporary visitors.

Integration strategies also present marketing opportunities for events. An event producer may decide to formally integrate with a venue provider (a festival that goes under the wing of a cultural centre) or integrate with other events or festivals. It has

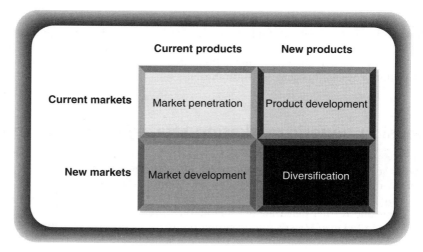

Figure 7.8 Ansoff's product-market matrix
Source: Reprinted by permission of Harvard Business Review. [Exhibit]. From "Strategies For Diversification" by I. Ansoff, September–October, pp. 113–124. Copyright © 1957 by the Harvard Business School Publishing Corporation; all rights reserved

been suggested that integration strategies have become more common in recent years among those events unable to cover excessive public liability fees. However, integration is also an opportunistic strategy: finding an event that complements the existing programme and brings new partnerships to a larger festival can be very attractive.

Diversification strategies can lead the marketer to add new events or support services to its stable of entertainment, or go into complementary businesses. A festival may develop an innovative range of merchandise for its existing market or it may market its software for visitor relationship management to other festivals. Such strategic options represent an important framework for deciding on the event's marketing mix, which is discussed next.

Selecting the event's 'services marketing' mix

Variations on the marketing mix have been made since the original four Ps of marketing were proposed (McCarthy, 1971). This chapter uses an adaptation of Getz's (2005) event marketing mix to present nine closely related components of events marketing. While each element is of considerable strategic importance, it is relatively easy to group them, as shown below:

- the event product experience (the core service), its programming (different event components, their quality or style) and its packaging (a mix of opportunities within the event or marketing of the event with other external attractions, accommodation and transport)
- the place (location(s) where the event is held and its tickets are distributed), its physical setting (the venue layout relative to consumer needs) and on-site event processes (queuing and so on)
- people (cast, audience, hosts and guests) and partnerships (stakeholders such as sponsors and media)

- price, or the exchange of value to experience the event
- integrated marketing communication (media and messages employed to build relationships with the event markets and audiences) (Getz, 2005).

Planning event 'product' experiences

Festivals and events, as service product experiences, contain three elements (Lovelock and Wirtz, 2004):

1. The core service and benefits that the customer experiences – for example, performing arts or sports event.
2. Supplementary features/augmented services that differentiate an event from its competitors – for example, its artists, service quality, the type of visitors, different modes of transport, and merchandise.
3. The delivery process – for example, the role of the customer in the experience, length of event, level and style of event.

As suggested earlier, an important characteristic of the marketing of leisure services is that people are also part of the product. In other words, much of the visitors' satisfaction comes from their interactions with other people attending the event. This means event marketers need to ensure (1) visitor segments within their audience are compatible and (2) there is an ease of interaction among people on-site.

Developing the event

The 'product' of an event is the set of intangible leisure experiences and tangible goods designed to satisfy the needs of the event market. The development of an event or festival can be easily modelled on the processes used to plan, create and deliver services (Figure 7.9).

The product life cycle concept suggests most events travel through the stages of introduction, growth and maturity to eventual decline or rejuvenation in a new form. Although there is no predictable pattern of life cycle transition for most products and services, we can find many examples of events that appear to have experienced all life cycle phases. Attendance at Notting Hill Carnival, for example, has waxed and waned over a number of years as the 'product' has been changed to reflect changing community, organizer and stakeholder needs and in no small part due to the weather and other external forces. Based on police estimates, in recent years attendances peaked at an estimated 1.4 million in 2000 and declined to hit a low of 500 000 in 2001, with attendances fluctuating again over recent years to an estimated 750 000 in 2004 (Cook and Morse, 2004). To avoid the decline, event managers need to closely monitor public acceptance of the content of their event product, to ensure it is still congruent with the leisure needs of contemporary society.

The creation of new service experiences usually ranges from major service innovations through to simple changes in the style of service delivery (Lovelock and Wirtz, 2004). These are evident in the event and festival sector:

- Major 'event' innovations – new events or festivals for previously undefined markets. Extreme sports events may represent one such innovation that emerged in

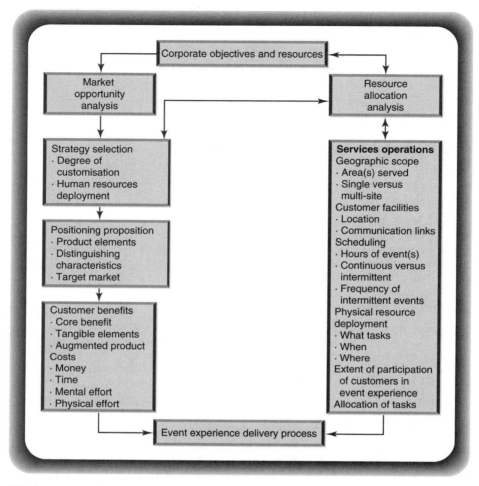

Figure 7.9 The process of creating an event 'product'
Source: SERVICES MARKETING: PEOPLE, TECHNOLOGY by Lovelock and Wirtz. Adapted and reprinted by permission of Pearson Education Inc., Upper Saddle River, NJ

the 1990s. However, major 'event' innovations are extremely hard to identify in an already crowded and innovative events sector, in which a wide variety of events serve existing, rather than new, leisure segments.

- Major process innovations – use of new processes to deliver events in new ways with added consumer benefits. The Internet has played a central role in innovating event delivery – for example, Live 8 gave people the chance to attend, watch on television, listen on radio and/or log on through the Internet (through the sponsorship by AOL) to participate in this major world event.
- Product (event) line extensions – additions to the current event programmes of existing events or festivals. This form of product development is very common. The Education & Community Programme, for example, is an initiative of the Harrogate International Festival which extends the festival's programme to include events year-round into the surrounding community.
- Process (event delivery) extensions – adjustments to the way in which existing events or festivals are delivered. The use of Internet ticketing agencies and on-line

booking of festival space by food and beverage vendors, for example, have enhanced event delivery processes.

- Supplementary service innovations – extra services that build on the event or festival experience. Examples are on-site childcare facilities, automatic teller machines and public telephones at event sites.
- Service improvements – modest changes that improve the event performance or the way in which it is delivered. Examples are a fashion festival featuring the work of a wider array of designers, and more outlets being provided for ticket purchase.
- Style changes – simple forms of product development for an event. Examples are improved seating arrangements, a new festival logo and improved costumes.

For any event, the decision to undertake any of the 'product' development strategies proposed must be based on market research. Although it is not possible to pre-test events as market offerings, new concepts or style changes (such as a new festival logo) are readily tested in the target market using qualitative research techniques such as focus groups. Some form of event concept testing is desirable before major changes are made.

Programming the event

A critical aspect of the event product that is not widely discussed is the development of an attractive event programme. For event managers, it is important to have an event portfolio that reflects (1) the mission, (2) the desired level of quality that satisfies artistic and market criteria, and (3) the revenue or profit objectives of event managers. The nature and range of market segments, and the ability to create thematic links between programme elements are the further considerations. Often, organizers need to balance the personal or artistic vision of event directors with the realities of market success criteria and the costs involved. The event programme may also reflect media broadcasting requirements, the availability of desired performers or players, and the practicalities of staging the event concept. In addition, the event manager must consider the programming of competing events, the event's life cycle phase (for example, more mature events may require some innovative programming to survive) and the duration of the event. An excellent example of event programming is the Trafalgar Square Festival 2005. Taking the theme, 'city rites', the festival explored energy, diversity, aspirations and dreams making full use of square with a range commissions, performances by artists and visiting companies over three weeks (Mayor of London, 2005).

Reflecting on their event programming experience at a Dublin discussion forum (The Theatre Shop Conference, 2002), producers pointed to at least four key elements in programming success:

1. The need for a distinguishing core concept in the programme – what is it that you're presenting that actually has meaning to the audience?
2. The need to marry the event programme with its physical environment or site – what kinds of performances will really be spectacular in this setting? What kinds of performers and stage structures (existing and created) will shine in this environment?
3. The role and operational approach of the artistic director/producer – the producers are both programme gatekeepers (selecting event participants from proposals submitted by performers) and poachers (travelling around to pick the best performers, just as sports clubs send out their talent scouts).

4. Established criteria for programme content – criteria include the compatibility of performers to a festival's market, the history of this type of performance at other events, and a performance's technical quality. Some producers of bigger festivals have a rule about (1) how many times an overseas act has performed within the country, and (2) a desired ratio of innovation and tradition in their event portfolio.

Programming is both an art and a science. The event manager considers the artistic or sport-related criteria that an event should achieve, as well as its marketing criteria. However, as with all successful entertainment, an intangible 'wow' factor also differentiates the truly successful event programme.

Packaging the event

Packaging is perhaps one of the most underdeveloped elements of the event marketing mix. Avenues for packaging include the opportunity to package different types of entertainment, food and beverage, and merchandise as a single market offer (a service bundle), and the opportunity to package the event with accommodation, transport and other attractions in the nearby region. Many festivals fail to tap into packaging opportunities that can be an effective means of better positioning the festival in its current markets and attracting tourists. In contrast, motor racing events such as the FIA British Grand Prix at Silverstone draw national and overseas tourists, demonstrating some sophistication with packaging. For example, packages are available including flights, hotel accommodation, grandstand tickets, return coach transfers, VIP parking, full hospitality much more depending on the price the customer is willing to pay. The ability to package an event goes back to its 'drawing power' discussed earlier. However, in the performing arts and sport, special package deals for existing subscribers or members represent another viable marketing use for the package concept.

People and partnerships

The principles of relationship marketing and management of key stakeholders and consumers now pervade the marketing literature. Many festivals and events start their lives on the basis of 'relationships and goodwill' between a dedicated group of people, so it is not unusual to find that successful events have solid partnerships and strong links with loyal supporters (attendees, volunteers, government and corporate representatives). For many festivals, a 'sense of sharing a common vision' often pervades the atmosphere, with a loose alliance between the types of people who run the festival and those who enjoy it. With large-scale events, it is hard to create that same sense of belonging, but strategies dedicated to building relationships with volunteers, sponsors and visitors are common. Partnerships are critical in attracting the resources to plan, manage and evaluate the event's marketing strategies.

The people of interest are not just event staff and volunteers (Chapter 6) and event attendees, but also the wider residential community. Community consultation and relationship building should be marketing concerns for an event from its inception. While organizers of the Glastonbury Festival worked to overcome negative reactions by local residents, local newspapers and other media annually reflect coverage of events that retain protestors. From a brand equity perspective, events need ambassadors internally and externally to fully capitalize on their competitive potential.

Pricing, free entry or donation

Given the diversity of leisure experiences offered to consumers, price can be a key influence on event demand. Contrasts in pricing strategy exist according to the type of event and its target markets. A mass-market event such as a lifestyle consumer show must keep its price at a level of affordability for its customers – middle income, middle Britain. On the other hand, a fundraising event such as the Barnardo's Firecracker Ball can ask a much higher price as its target market is much smaller (socioeconomic group AB who are supporters of the Barnardo's) but wealthier, and therefore willing to pay for a perceived quality experience. However, the high price can represent quality (or 'value for money') to the potential consumer and influence the decision to purchase.

While many special events are ticketed, a large number of festivals do not charge an entrance fee, and some simply seek a gold coin donation. However, a 'free' event still presents costs to the consumer and costs to the producer. Other key influences on ticket price or entry fees are competing opportunities and perceived value. The concept of 'net value' or the sum of all perceived benefits (gross value) minus the sum of all the perceived costs (monetary and otherwise) is useful for event marketers. The greater the positive difference between perceived benefits and costs, the greater the net value to the consumer.

With the Barnardo's fundraiser example, potential consumers compare the perceived benefits – dinner, drinks, entertainment, parking, opportunities to socialize, prestige and the novelty of an unusual night out – with the perceived costs. These costs could include money, time, the physical effort involved in getting to the venue, psychic costs (related to social interaction) and sensory costs (such as going out on a rainy night). If the organizer has adequately positioned the event and communicated its benefits, the target market is likely to perceive a positive net value and purchase tickets.

In establishing the pricing strategy for an event, an organizer will account for two cost categories:

1. Fixed costs – those costs that do not vary with the volume of visitors (for example, venue rental, interest charged on loans, lighting and power costs, the cost of volunteers' uniforms and artists' fees).
2. Variable costs – those costs that vary with the number of visitors (for example, the cost of plastic wine glasses at a festival, catering costs at a product launch and the cost of staff needed to serve attendees).

As well as analysing the above costs, the event manager should investigate the price of competing leisure experiences. If a similar leisure experience has a price of £x, the choices are: (1) match and charge the price £x, (2) adopt a cost leadership strategy and charge £x minus 25 per cent, or (3) adopt a differentiation strategy and use a price of £x plus 50 per cent, and use marketing communications to promote the value of the event.

Pricing strategies used to achieve event objectives may be revenue-oriented, operations-oriented or market based. A revenue-oriented strategy is designed to maximize revenue by charging the highest price that the target market will pay. Barnardo's Firecracker Ball is an example of a revenue-oriented pricing strategy. An operations-oriented pricing strategy seeks to balance supply and demand by introducing cheaper prices for times of low demand and higher prices at times of higher demand. Agricultural shows often use an operations-oriented pricing strategy. Finally, a market-oriented strategy uses differential pricing, which may be linked to alternate event packages. A clear link between packaging and pricing exists where a three-day music festival charges one price for those who participate for all three days (the fanatics), a day price to capture the first-timers or 'dabblers', and another price to see the headline act and enjoy a gourmet dinner package.

Key questions that the event marketer must resolve in determining the pricing strategy relate to both pricing levels and methods of payment. Figure 7.10 summarizes the decisions to be made by the marketer, along with some of the strategic options available.

Event 'place', physical setting and processes

'Place' refers to both the site where the event takes place (the venue) and the place at which consumers can purchase their tickets. Other decisions with marketing implications are (1) the design of the event setting, and (2) the processes used to deliver and experience the event.

The choice of a single venue or multiple sites for sports or cultural events should be made in the context of the event's overall strategy – for example, a strategy of market penetration or expansion. Increasingly, event marketers are recognizing that market expansion can be achieved by taking their events to new locations. For example, Euro

How much should be charged?
- What costs must be covered?
- How sensitive are customers to different prices?
- What are leisure competitors' prices?
- What levels of discounts to selected target markets are appropriate?
- Should psychological pricing (for example, £10.95 instead of £11) be used?

What should be the basis of pricing?
- Should each element be billed separately?
- Should one admission fee be charged?
- Should consumers be charged for resources consumed?
- Should a single price for a bundled package be charged?

Who shall collect payment?
- The event organization?
- A ticketing intermediary?

Where should payment be made?
- At the event?
- At a ticketing organization?
- At the customer's home? Using the Internet or telephone?

When should payment be made?
- When tickets are given out?
- On the day of the event?

How should payment be made?
- Cash – exact change?
- Credit card?
- Electronic point of sale (EPOS)?
- Token donation?

Figure 7.10 Pricing decisions for events marketers
Source: adapted from Lovelock and Wirtz, 2004, p. 173

RSCG Skybridge worked with Endemol, producers of Big Brother reality television programme to use the Big Brother House for corporate hospitality packages – an example of an innovative use of 'place'.

The physical setting, as noted in the discussion of programming, is crucial to the satisfaction of the event consumer. Most services marketers include it as a key element in the marketing mix, alongside processes of service delivery. As a result, you are encouraged to review the consumer implications of all facets of event design (Chapters 13 and 14).

In deciding the most appropriate place(s) for ticket distribution, organizers usually question whether to use a ticketing agency. Ticketing agencies widen the distribution network, ease the consumer's purchase process and speed up the entry of customers to a venue. While they also facilitate credit card purchases and telephone bookings, charges are incurred by both the event organizer and the customer. The benefits of using a ticket agency depend on the type of event, the availability of other ticket distribution options (such as the box office of a small theatre company and/or direct mail), the willingness of the target market to pay for a ticketing service, and the service's relative affordability.

Selling tickets via a ticketing agency or another distribution network such as the Internet has some advantages for the event producer. Ticket sales can be monitored, and the data collected can guide decisions on the level of marketing communication expenditure needed to attract the targeted visitor numbers. The security problems inherent in accepting cash at the door or gate are also alleviated. Because customers pay in advance, the cash flow to the event producer occurs well before the staging of the event, with obvious financial advantages for the event organizer.

The use of the Internet as a distribution medium for events is now widespread, with the key advantages of on-line ticket sales being:

- speed – consumers can purchase tickets without leaving their home, queuing or waiting for a phone operator to become available
- consumer ease – consumers can view the different experiences offered by the event or festival in their own time, selecting the events or shows that best suit their pocket and time constraints
- revenue – ticket revenue comes from the buyer's credit card, which facilitates security and ease of collection
- up-to-date technology – more and more consumers expect leisure services to be available for purchase on the Internet. An on-line presence is critical in establishing an event or festival brand.

An interesting example of the use of the WWW for distribution of tickets is the Leeds/Reading Festival (www.meanfiddler.com), a multi-show festival. The festival uses an on-line ticketing system – See (combining Really Useful Theatre ticketing, Ticketselect and Way Ahead – www.seetickets.com) – to provide an on-line booking system to support their physical box offices, ticket agencies and telephone box office. Consumers have a choice of booking on-line, by telephone, or from a box office or retail outlet. However, the booking fee remains even if the consumer chooses the on-line medium, with tickets available at face value if paying in cash at Mean Fiddler Box Offices.

Events and festivals rarely have their own on-line booking system that can accept bookings and credit card details electronically at no charge to the consumer. However, advances in technology are likely to result in increased efficiencies in on-line distribution over time.

Apart from ticketing, other operational processes have an immediate impact on the experience of event consumers. Visitors evaluate security checks on entry to the event, queuing for food, and the speed of access to services such as automatic teller machines and toilets. While later chapters address many of these event 'processes', the marketing implications of a smooth integration of 'front stage' and 'backstage' happenings at an event cannot be underestimated. The physical environment and processes that happen in that physical space directly contribute to the event's brand image – for example, mosh pits and crowd surfing at youth concerts are a logistical issue with significant implications for these events' ongoing market acceptance.

Integrated marketing communication for events

Where 'promotion' was once the primary term for the communication element in the marketing mix, the use of 'integrated marketing communication' (IMC) has all but overtaken it. With diverse changes in media technology, market expectations and competition, the traditional idea of promoting 'to' a market has been replaced by the need to form relationships 'with' the market. Integrated marketing communication 'considers all sources of contact that a consumer has [with the event] as potential delivery channels for messages and, makes use of all communication methods that are relevant to consumers' (Shimp, 2003, p. 8). The platform for creating IMC strategies for events and festivals is knowledge about the visitors – the consumer database that allows the event to establish a dialogue with the event's consumers. How an event manages its consumer relationships drives its brand value (Duncan 2002). When we think about an event brand such as Glastonbury Festival, we think of 'an integrated bundle of information and experiences that distinguish [it]' (Duncan, 2002, p. 13) from competing leisure experiences. Figure 7.11 offers an insight into the IMC process for an event, and the range of traditional and non-traditional media that create brand relationships.

Branding for an event is much more than a physical identity such as the five interlocking rings of the Olympics. The Olympics brand is based on perceptions, how we relate to that event and what it promises, as well as the physical logo and symbols (for example, the Olympic torch). However, clever use of the brand helps the event manager to make an intangible phenomenon more tangible for event consumers.

In developing an IMC strategy, an organizer should understand four sources of brand messages (Duncan, 2002):

1. *planned messages* (media releases, personal selling by the box office and/or ticket agency, advertising, e-newsletters, website)
2. *unplanned messages* (unexpected positive or negative impressions formed by word of mouth, media coverage, complaints)
3. *product messages* (implied messages of decisions about the event – programme, pricing, venue)
4. *service messages* (the nature of contact with festival or event staff or volunteers, the quality of event transport, other support services).

Given these message types, the event brand is shaped by more than its planned promotional tools; instead, there are many influences on the brand, some of which are more controllable than others.

Mirroring the strategy process, the development of an IMC plan hinges on an effective SWOT analysis, plus consumer and stakeholder research. The information from the analysis and research provides the platform for deciding whether objectives

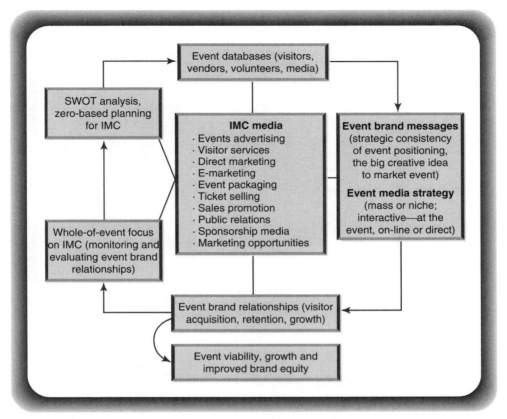

Figure 7.11 The IMC process model for events
Source: adapted from Duncan (2002), p. 9

and strategies for the IMC campaign should be informational, transformational (attitudinal), behavioural or relational in their focus. Figure 7.12 shows how these different approaches correspond with the 'think, feel, do' model of consumer behaviour.

Importantly, consumers do not react to marketing messages in any set order – they may feel, then act (local festival attendance) and later think about the experience, or they may go through a sequential processing of 'think, feel and act' (such as a decision to visit France to attend the next Rugby World Cup). It is important to consider these different decision-making patterns of market segments when deciding how to set out the objectives of a campaign.

The IMC strategy reflects the thrust of the chosen objectives and uses both message and media strategies to fulfil them. To illustrate, the Leeds Tykes rugby union team may have a behavioural objective of 'achieving a 10 per cent increase in attendance at home games at Headingley in 2007'. Their message strategy would be developed with reference to the psychological appeal – for example, motivators such as the responsibility of locals to support the home side, and the atmosphere and nostalgia attached to Headingley as a rugby venue.

Planning the IMC campaign requires 'one voice, one look' (Duncan, 2002) – that is, all direct marketing, advertising, publicity and event packaging must convey the same

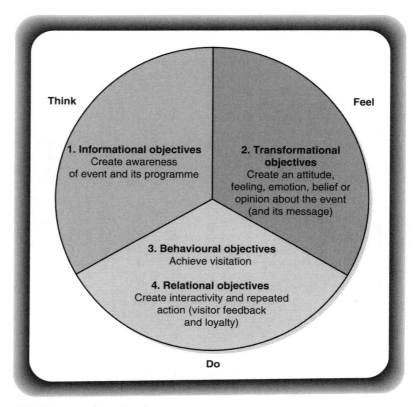

Figure 7.12 Event message objectives and strategies
Source: adapted from Duncan (2002), p. 320

message and look in its communication. At a national level, the 2002 Manchester Commonwealth Games successfully achieved 'one voice, one look' with its campaign for the games.

For the RBS 6 Nations Series for rugby union, the media strategy could involve choosing how the mix of planned advertising, e-marketing, publicity and/or other media will be used to best convey the message about packages to the games. As shown in Figure 7.11, the IMC mix can include a wide range of marketing communication functions. Public relations may involve the use of a celebrity spokesperson in the campaign – for example, rugby legend Martin Johnston could be used to boost interest in the games. A direct mail campaign and an e-newsletter to a database of corporate executives (a key market for rugby) could also feature Martin Johnston and give further strategic consistency to the campaign. Sales promotion in the form of a competition directed at the national supporters clubs might also bolster demand for the games.

Given the numerous marketing communication tools to include in an IMC mix, the event marketer needs to be familiar with their strengths and weaknesses, including their budgetary implications. An event with a mass market (for example, the Great Yorkshire Show) may use television advertising as a promotional device, whereas planned IMC for a community festival is more likely to concentrate on organized word of mouth, local media publicity and community service announcements.

A brief review of the more commonly used marketing communication mediums is offered here.

Advertising is any form of non-personal promotion paid for by the event organization. Radio, television, newspapers, magazines, the Internet, outdoor advertising (billboards, bus shelters and toilets) and mobile platforms such as buses and taxis are all channels for advertising. For most events and festivals, the expense of mainstream media (television, newspapers and radio) cannot be justified. Media partnerships (such as Cambridge Festival's sponsorship by BBC Radio 2 or Channel Four and Virgin Radio's partnerships/sponsorships at V Festival) can help to resolve this issue. However, the creative process of producing the messages can also be expensive, especially if done by an advertising agency. In creating advertising campaigns for events and festivals, it is vital to:

- provide tangible clues to counteract the intangible nature of the event – that is, show the artistic event or sports players in action, the event logo, the spectacle of the fireworks
- seek continuity over time by using recognizable symbols, spokespersons, trademarks or music – for example, football codes often use the tunes of famous artists, such as 'We are the champions' by Queen
- promise what is possible to foster realistic expectations – for example, show real-time action (it is necessary to take care with promises about ticket availability because they can become contentious)
- make the service more tangible and recognizable by showing members of the target market enjoying the event – for example, the roar and spectacle of a grand final crowd at the football is very persuasive.

Public Relations (PR) is used to build mutually beneficial relationships with stakeholders and consumers. It uses a wide range of tools, including publicity, special events, community consultation, e-publications and traditional newsletters. While all activities incur costs, media publicity is often favoured by festival organizers because it provides unpaid space in the media that reaches the event's market. An advantage to festival and event directors is that people generally enjoy reading about the sport, the arts and entertainment. However, marketers must be aware that the media will use a story only if it has news value (a unique angle or item of information of interest to readers, viewers or listeners). Journalists also carefully assess the structure and style of media releases, and the credibility of their source.

Sales promotion consists of those activities that use incentives or discounts to increase sales or attendance. Examples of sales promotion are family days at city shows or exhibitions, offering group discounts or a free ticket for one child. Alternatively, consumers may be offered free merchandise (T-shirts and posters) when purchasing several tickets or more.

Direct marketing communicates one-on-one with existing festival or event-goers via mail, the telephone or the Internet. It relies on organizers developing a list of people who previously attended the event and obtaining knowledge about their demographic profile and preferences. Incentives for consumers to provide information may include entry in a competition and the receipt of next year's event programme. Organizers can purchase lists of potential event consumers from direct marketing agencies. However, a key consideration in collecting information to build a database is the need to gain consumer permission and respect their privacy. An understanding of current regulations about direct marketing (including the use of e-newsletters) is now mandatory.

Many event directors find it difficult to determine a marketing communication budget. They sometimes use guides such as a percentage of ticket sales

(5 to 10 per cent), what competitors appear to be spending or what was spent last year. However, zero-based budgeting is the best approach, whereby the marketer works from a zero base to cost out the best mix of IMC strategies and tactics to achieve the set objectives. A marketing objective of selling 10 000 tickets could flow on to an IMC objective of educating a potential market of 100 000 people about the benefits of the event. A mix of advertising, direct marketing (on-line and off-line) and publicity might be considered. Yet, the IMC campaign cost must be realistic for that event or festival. In-kind support by website designers, graphic artists and printers, plus sponsored media space (television, newspapers and/or radio), can reduce a festival or event's financial outlay. However, for most events, the need to prioritize IMC strategies and tactics to trim down the financial outlay is inevitable. Wherever possible, the IMC strategies that move the event closer to a behavioural result must be preserved.

Chapter summary

A common misconception of many in the festival and event area is that marketing means nothing more than 'event promotion'. As this chapter has shown, marketing is a structured and coherent way of thinking about managing an event or festival to achieve objectives related to market/stakeholder awareness, event attendance, satisfaction and either profits or increased understanding of a cause.

The core of event marketing is the focus on existing and potential consumers – in this case, the event attendee. Successful marketing flows from a complete understanding of these consumers – who they are, where they live and the leisure needs they seek to satisfy. This understanding comes from primary and secondary market research and two-way communication with event stakeholders and consumers. From this knowledge, organizers can develop strategies and tactics that span the event product (including its programming and packaging), its place (venues, the physical setting and ticket outlets), its delivery processes, its people and partnerships, and integrated marketing communication.

Questions

1. Identify the five key characteristics of services. Offer examples of each characteristic in the event or festival context.
2. Discuss some technological challenges that have an impact on the marketing success of events managers.
3. Outline five key motives for festival attendance.
4. Identify the key steps in the consumer decision process. Offer examples of how each step affects the event consumer.
5. What considerations (other than monetary costs) influence decisions on pricing an event?
6. What are the four key criteria for successful programming identified by event producers?
7. Provide examples of three forms of product development in the event or festival context.
8. Why is the term 'promotion' less relevant than 'integrated marketing communication' (IMC) for events marketers?

Case study 7.1

International Confex

Background

Now in its twenty-fourth year, International Confex – the biggest event for people organizing events worldwide, organized by CMP Information Ltd – is recognized as Europe's leading annual forum for the meetings, events and corporate hospitality industries and support services. For exhibitors, it is a dedicated forum to showcase brands, products and services. For the visitor, it is more than just a trade show – it is the essential industry forum, where they can meet and network with key decision-makers face to face.

The event

International Confex is split into four industry sectors:

- *UK Venues, Destinations and Incentive Travel*: visitors planning to organize events within the UK recognize International Confex as the event where they can source the widest range of cities, regions, towns, venues and transport.
- *Overseas Venues, Destinations and Incentive Travel*: visitors with overseas budgets and attend International Confex to source the widest range of countries, cities, regions, towns, venues and transport.
- *Corporate Hospitality and Events*: visitors to International Confex are fully aware of the benefits of hospitality and motivation. They visit the show to source a full range of services such as participation, motivation and activity companies, as well as caterers, sporting venues and events, entertainers, theming and historical venues.
- *Exhibition and Conference Support Services*: International Confex is the leading forum for buyers who source contractual services to help create their meeting or event. These include audiovisual services, stand design and build, staging, lighting, security, production and new technologies such as virtual reality and video conferencing.

In total, main stand holders topped 416 in 2005, with around 1050 companies represented across the four different sectors – filling the ground floor of Earls Court 1. The exhibitors operate in 57 countries, presenting their venues, products and services to a predominately UK based visitors.

A conference runs alongside the exhibition designed for both experienced and new event organizers to develop their skills and learn about the latest developments in the industry. Speakers are experts in their field and present a programme of seminars and take part in panel debates on all aspects of conference organizing, incentive travel, corporate hospitality and events. Group Director, Ben Greenish said: 'People come to the exhibition for information. We plan to create added value by offering them the opportunity to fill in their skills gaps and increase their understanding of their own and related industry sectors'.

Visitor marketing programme

Visitors to International Confex can essentially be broken down into two key groups – specialists and generalists.

- *Specialists*: visitors whose core job function is an event organizer. These specialist visitors represent blue chip companies, major professional conference organizers, exhibition organizers, agencies and incentive motivation houses.

- *Generalists*: these visitors are responsible for meetings and events as part of a wider job remit. This group encompasses visitors including sales and marketing managers, public relations executives, training and personnel managers, executive PAs and association executives.

International Confex is known as the one show in the meetings and events industry that delivers. To ensure the quantity and quality of visitors at the show, CMP Information undertake a comprehensive marketing campaign. This includes advertising, inserts, direct mail, email, public relations (PR) and joint exhibitor promotions.

- Advertisements and inserts are placed in leading UK industry trade titles such as *Conference and Incentive Travel, Event, Conference and Exhibition Factfinder,* and generalist titles such as *Marketing* and *Marketing Week,* as well as key specialist trade titles across Europe.
- The direct mail campaign occurs about four months before the show. Using CMP Information's extensive databases and external lists, appropriate messages are sent to carefully targeted individuals. The direct mail campaign reinforces the advertising campaign to ensure the right messages reach the right people, at the right time.
- Marketing by email has increased over the last few years, with regular email news bulletins being sent to both the visitor and exhibitor databases. This is a cost-effective and quick way of communicating regularly with an audience who attend International Confex on an annual basis.
- PR for the event is achieved through editorial in over sixty worldwide publications. Around twenty industry magazines run previews of the event, detailing who is exhibiting and what they will be promoting at the show.
- Promotional opportunities offered to exhibitors include participation in the New Products Showcase or the Special Events Showcase, where they can present their products and services. There are also sponsorship opportunities to reinforce the exhibitors message at the show, such as branding of the visitor badges, carrier bags etc. Exhibitors are issued with visitor invitations and can request visitors to be qualified as a VIP (very important person), to identify key buyers to the show.
- The International Confex website offers exhibitors the opportunity to promote their company on the Web. Each exhibitor may include up to fifty words free of charge, and has the opportunity to add a hyperlink to their own website, or place a banner advertisement to promote their product.
- A training day takes place every year, with advice for exhibitors to get the most from the show.

Evaluation

International Confex is evaluated each year from a variety of perspectives, including extensive on-site visitor evaluation. The statistics from this provide useful information not only for the organizers and exhibitors, but also prove the success of the show for potential exhibitors and visitors. The show itself is ABC audited to ensure that the data produced is authentic, reliable, and verified by an external organization. This confirmed that International Confex 2005 was a highly successful, with a total attendance of 11 319, made up of 7198 registered visitor attendance and 4121 other attendance (press, exhibitor personnel etc).

In exhibitions, the quantity of visitors is important. However, it is the quality of these visitors that will continue to attract the leading companies to exhibit and as such the evaluation gathers this data. The ABC audit showed that:

- 70 per cent of visitors to International Confex 2005 approve or influence approval in the purchasing chain – attracting real buyers to the event.
- 61 per cent of visitors to International Confex 2005 were of managerial level or above.
- 54 per cent of visitors organize more than 10 events a year.
- Conferences for over 50 people account for 62 per cent of events the visitors organized.

Visitor surveys are used to evaluate the event overall, and the relative benefits of the four areas covered. In 2005, on-site visitor research showed that:

- 29 per cent of visitors held budgets of over £250 000 for organizing events.
- 78 per cent of visitors used the website to pre-register.
- 73 per cent attended to look for new ideas.
- 60 per cent said they were likely to make a purchasing decision as a result of visiting. Of those 79 per cent said it would be within 6 months of the show.
- 81 per cent of visitors hold events in the UK.
- 58 per cent of visitors attend to look for overseas venues.

Finally, from the organizers perspective, one of the ultimate measures of an events success is whether exhibitors book for the following year's event – International Confex 2005 exhibitors valued the show so highly that 68 per cent of the UK venue sector of the show rebooked a stand for International Confex 2006 by the end of the show.

Summary

As the 'international event for any event', International Confex is in the spotlight of fellow industry professionals and the industry media. CMP Information uses the results of visitor, exhibitor and other sources of evaluation to develop the exhibition on an annual basis to increase the quality and quantity of exhibitors and visitors. It is only through developing and refining the exhibition in the light of evaluation and the external environment that the International Confex will continue to the leading annual forum for the events industry.

For further details about International Confex, please visit www.international-confex.com.

By Katharine Jordan, Marketing Manager, CMP Information Ltd.

Questions

1. What are the advantages and disadvantages of the marketing campaign used by International Confex?
2. What visitor needs and wants does International Confex fulfil?
3. What alternative distribution strategies could International Confex utilize?
4. The International Confex product includes the opportunity to access an educational seminar programme. What other elements could be included in International Confex to develop the exhibition for the future?
5. Why do you think International Confex is successful in attracting the quality and quantity of visitors? What other strategies could be implemented to ensure that this quality is maintained and developed in the future?

Case study 7.2

Ford Thunderbirds by Imagination
Background

Having agreed to take responsibility for the main design execution of Lady Penelope Creighton-Ward's FAB 1- a 27ft, pink, 6-wheeled Thunderbirds car (as well as the provision of other vehicles, where required), Ford treated their association with the 'Thunderbirds' movie as more than just a 'product placement' opportunity. With this in mind, Ford invited design and communications company Imagination to think about ways to create an entertaining and engaging 'Thunderbirds' experience that would leverage their target family audience. Like FAB 1, it needed to be big, bold and larger than life, as well as make sure the essence of Ford came across – creativity, emotion and excitement.

The Solution

So, when it was announced that The Sunday Times Motor Show was to move to a slot in late May/June at Birmingham NEC, Imagination saw an opportunity to do something quite spectacular. The tagline 'Thunderbirds Powered by Ford', enabled Imagination to provide a good theme to direct and support Ford's technologies and, with this in mind, Imagination set to work designing a 'best in show' experience for the 7 400 square metre motor show stand, the largest European stand that Imagination had produced for Ford over its 30-year relationship together. The team worked on the interactive stand and live event performance for over 10 months with over 200 staff involved.

An entire themed experience was created, including the Ford design process (linking the original Ford Thunderbird to FAB 1), Brains' Lab (as a test bed for innovative futuristic ideas from Ford), and a style studio for Lady Penelope's pink StreetKa. The stand, nearly the size of a football pitch, was a recreation of International Rescue base, Tracy Island, complete with an 840 square metre 'lake', a 5-tonne sandy beach, a 16 metre long model of Thunderbird 2 (suspended from above the stand) along with a huge array of ground-breaking lighting and sound equipment. Props used in the Universal Pictures film 'Thunderbirds', which was to be released to the UK in July 2004, were also incorporated. The stand was divided up into over 11 different areas including a VIP upper deck, an International Rescue Vehicle Hanger and even a submerged Thunderbirds Submarine which appears within the live show. The Ford range of cars, including the FAB 1, Lady Penelope Creighton-Ward's stunning pink, six-wheel bubble canopy limousine, was also on full display to the public until the end of the motor show. Designed to create a 'family friendly' atmosphere, visitors could interact with the experience as well as being entertained. In addition to the core stand, Imagination created a fun, live-action show featuring audience participation, as well as a brand film, aimed directly at a family audience, that made the most of Ford's link with 'Thunderbirds'. This 'experiential' approach involving the whole audience is something which both The Ford Motor Company and the Birmingham Motor Show organizers, the Society of Motor Manufacturers and Traders (SMMT), were keen to establish at the 2004 show.

Ford's Public Affairs department also took advantage of the experience by asking Imagination to organize its eve-of-show press event, where invitees included design, TV, film and lifestyle press, as well as the core automotive media, together with writing, designing and producing a limited edition Press Pack about the making of FAB 1.

Results

Overall, the dramatic stand architecture, controlled walk-through experience, live show and merchandise helped to draw visitors through the entire product display. The whole experience was considered a huge success by public, press and clients alike and was visited by approximately 250 000–300 000 visitors over the course of the nine-day show.

Its success was also demonstrated in the sheer volume of press interest that it attracted. Ford's involvement in the show itself attracted column inches in local and national papers including the Sunday Times, Daily Telegraph, Birmingham Evening Mail and The Mirror, as well as TV and media coverage from ITV, BBC, five and Sky News. In addition, a host of industry and design magazines – including FX Magazine, Design Week and Events Magazine – were keen to concentrate on Imagination's role on the project. Thunderbirds Powered By Ford received a certificate of High Commendation in the 'Automotive' category and was shortlisted in the 'Best Brand Experience' category of the 2004 Marketing Brand Design Awards.

Acknowledging the project as an important part of their strategy to appeal to a wider, family audience, Ford achieved its goal to deliver a compelling, exciting and fantastic visitor experience. Mark Cameron Sponsorship and Events Manager, Ford of Britain noted:

Ford's Thunderbirds partnership with Universal Pictures provided an exciting and challenging project brief for Imagination to work with. The results are nothing short of amazing; providing a vibrant, engaging and unique experience for the huge numbers of expected visitors at the Ford stand. We want our customers to discover how fun and innovative the Ford brand is by creating much more than simply a display of the latest hot metal.

Imagination's Chris Marsh, Group Account Director, added,

Experiential design is all about developing a positive lasting customer engagement and to create an exhibition experience with this theme has been a design dream. The biggest challenge was not where to start, but where to stop in terms of letting the imagination run on the project. Creating the best ways to communicate, inform and have fun has allowed us at Imagination to become kids again and in the process deliver a win-win for Ford, Universal and the audiences directly in the 'live' spirit of this whole event.

Summary

It is clear that developing a live event, which reflected the ethos of Ford and engaged visitors in an interactive brand experience, was key to the success of the Thunderbird concept. Increasingly with the way that Shows are developing, organizers, exhibitors and their designers have to be increasingly creative in order to capture the imagination of visitors. The partnership with Universal Pictures, and the Thunderbirds film, provided a clear opportunity for the Imagination designers to use their talents to bring the brand alive and provided visitors with a memorable event.

For further information about The Imagination Group, please visit www.imagination. co.uk.

By Imagination, 25 Store Street, South Crescent, London, WC1E 7BL.

Questions

1. How does Ford Thunderbirds outlined above meet the definition of an event? How would you classify this type of event?

2. The case study discusses the concept of experiential design. What do you understand by this term? How is this applied in the Ford Thunderbirds event?

3. Identify the 'five Ws' of the Ford Thunderbirds event. What do you consider to be the prime 'wow' factor of the event?

4. Effective theming can add an additional dimension of attractiveness and impact to an event. Discuss this statement with reference to the above Ford Thunderbirds event.

Chapter 8
Sponsorship of events

Learning Objectives

After studying this chapter, you should be able to:

■ understand the use of sponsorship in the context of festivals and events
■ discuss trends that have led to the growth of sponsorship as a marketing communication medium in the private and public sectors
■ recognize the benefits that event managers can attract from reciprocal partnerships with sponsors
■ identify the key sponsorship benefits sought by events and sponsoring bodies
■ discuss the importance of sponsorship 'leveraging'
■ understand the need for sponsorship policies to guide decision-making by events and their sponsors
■ outline the sequential stages in developing and implementing an event sponsorship strategy
■ develop strategies and tactics to manage event–sponsor relationships and achieve positive and enduring relationships with sponsors.

Introduction

Sponsorship, either provided as cash or in-kind support such as products or services (often called 'contra'), is central to the revenue and resources of new and continuing events. Event managers and marketers are usually actively engaged in tasks such as identifying potential sponsors, preparing sponsorship proposals and managing their ongoing relationships with sponsors. Over the past five years, there has been a significant increase in the amount of guidance available related to sponsorship (Geldard and Sinclair, 2003; Grey and Skildum, 2003; Lagae, 2005; Masterman and Wood, 2006; Skinner and Rukavina, 2003). This chapter begins with a discussion of the role and growth of sponsorship as a marketing communication medium. It also explores the benefits that events and their sponsors seek, before explaining the policies, strategies and actions needed for successful event and festival sponsorship.

What is sponsorship?

Sponsorship has become a critical element in the integrated marketing communication mix (discussed in Chapter 7) of many private and public sector organizations. Among the different types of marketing communication (for example, public relations, advertising, personal selling, sales promotions and direct marketing), sponsorship is said to be one of the most powerful mediums now used to communicate and form relationships with stakeholders and markets (Grey and Skildum-Reid, 2003). Globally, expenditure on event sponsorship is escalating each year – from £18.1 billion in 2001 to an estimated £29.1 billion in 2005 according to research by consultants SponsorClick (Day, 2002). Drawing on data from Mintel and IPSOS UK/Sportscan, overall sponsorship spending in the UK each year is estimated to be around £816.3 million, made up of sport (£412.5 million), arts and business (estimated £129.8 million), broadcasting (estimated £205 million) and community (£69 million) (Sponsorshiponline.co.uk, 2005). Importantly, most spending estimates only take into account the sponsorship purchase itself, but it is generally accepted that many sponsors will spend at least equal to the cost of the event property itself on leveraging or maximizing investment impacts (Meenaghan, 2001a).

Although sponsorship may be attached to social causes and broadcast media such as television programmes as well as special events (De Pelsmacker, Geuens and Van den Bergh, 2004), just about every public event is now sponsored in some way (Kover, 2001). With the emphasis now on 'connecting with' rather than 'talking at' the marketplace, event and festival sponsorship can be an ideal way for marketers to create brand interaction with consumers and stakeholders. For example, the BBC Radio 2 Cambridge Folk Festival engages folk music-loving listeners of this established radio station with this internationally recognized festival. In contrast, Texaco has sponsored a range of events in the Pembroke areas to build good relationships with the local community where one of their refineries has been based for over 40 years.

In simple terms, sponsorship is the purchase (either with cash or in-kind support) of exploitable rights and marketing benefits (tangible and intangible) that arise from direct involvement with a personality/player, special event, programme, club or agency. The following definition from the International Chamber of Commerce International Code on Sponsorship (ICC, 2003, p. 2) also explains the concept:

> *any commercial agreement by which a sponsor, for the mutual benefit of the sponsor and sponsored party, contractually provides financing or other support in order to establish an association between the sponsor's image, brands or products and a sponsorship property in return for rights to promote this association and/or for the granting of certain agreed direct or indirect benefits.*

Importantly, sponsorship is a strategic marketing investment, not a donation (philanthropy) or a grant (a one-off type of assistance) which means events and festivals must view sponsorships as working business partnerships. Most sponsors are investors who expect to see a direct impact on their brand equity (enhanced awareness and imagery) as well as increased sales and profits. In the case of public sector sponsors, some kind of social marketing result is usually sought (for example, a greater awareness of water conservation or the dangers of drink driving). Tetley sought to maximize their image as 'The Beer' of Rugby League following their five year sponsorship of Tetley's Rugby Super League with signing up as 'Official Beer' partners of many of the league's clubs (Anon, 2005b), while in 2004 THINK! (the road safety campaign of the Department of Transport) boosted the awareness of their 'Save Racing for the Track' message to motorcyclists through sponsoring the British Superbikes Championship.

While long-term cash sponsors are highly sought after by events and festivals (for example, Coca-Cola's continuing long-term sponsorship of the Olympics), a mix of private sector cash and in-kind sponsorship, plus grants, can be vital for festivals. As discussed in the case study in Chapter 10, Edinburgh International Festival secured revenue from three main revenue streams: ticket sales (£1.74 million), sponsorship and donations (£1.73 million) and public sector grants (£2.56 million). Sponsorship may also take the form of in-kind sponsorship, for example, through a media partner in radio or television promoting the event or festival effectively rather than providing direct funds. Hence, creating a successful event or gaining festival sponsorship means establishing a reciprocal relationship between the organization providing the sponsorship (corporate, media and/or government) and the event. However, it also means an emotional connection must be made with those consumers targeted by both the event and its sponsors. This three-way relationship which underpins the success of sponsorship is illustrated in Figure 8.1.

Bank of Scotland's sponsorship of Edinburgh International Festival's Connecting to Music Workshops is a good example of the interplay between the event itself, its sponsors and the needs of the target market. The challenging and appealing workshops introduce 1000 children to a creative way of listening to classical music, culminating in live performance by a professional musician. For the sponsor and organizer, the workshops achieve their aims by increasing access to and enjoyment of the arts and inspiring children to learn about their responses to music (Bank of Scotland, 2005). This type of sponsorship illustrates how a mutually beneficial relationship can emerge when an event initiates opportunities that closely fit the sponsor's corporate or marketing objectives (Geldard and Sinclair, 2003). The Chapter now discusses a number of trends, including the need for more innovative and flexible marketing media, which underpin the rising popularity of sponsorship.

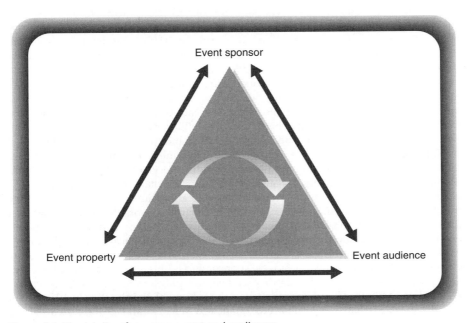

Figure 8.1 The trinity of sponsor, event and audiences
Source: adapted from SponsorMap (2004)

Trends influencing the growth in sponsorship

The worldwide interest in sponsorship as a form of integrated marketing communication stems from a range of sociocultural and business (including marketing and media) trends. Firstly, a growth in the popularity of events and festivals as leisure experiences has paralleled recognition that festivals and events offer unique social environments (at the event and on-line) to tap into niche markets. Creative sponsorship can reach consumers in environments when they are having 'a good time' and so they are more likely to accept a well-considered marketing message. It is no surprise that marketers are keen to tap into the kind of loyalty that festival-goers display – such as enduring primitive hygiene and severe sleep deprivation to see their favourite bands live (Blyth, 2003). There is also evidence that committed and loyal fans of a musical group or sport will attach themselves to those brands that support their interest; for example, Barclays, Coca-Cola and Vodafone are companies that have gained significant brand equity from UK sports sponsorships. Similarly, Virgin Mobile, as a major festival sponsor in the United Kingdom, considers that 'festivals offer a fantastic opportunity for brands to get close to consumers when they are excited and passionate. It's by harnessing that passion and adding to that experience that you benefit' (Blyth, 2003).

While sports have dominated the sponsorship market accounting for nearly 50 per cent of sponsorship expenditure in the UK (SponsorshipOnline.co.uk, 2005), evidence suggests that the corporate sector is seeking a greater balance of investment across the arts and sport. Despite Heineken's extensive involvement with the Rugby World Cup and the Heineken Cup, one of European rugby's leading events, it was reported in late 2003 that the company was shifting its global focus towards cultural events (Pearce, 2003). Most large brands now use a sponsorship mix within a wide-ranging brand marketing strategy. The Royal Bank of Scotland Group (RBS), for example, has attached its brand names to the RBS 6 Nations rugby tournament and NatWest Series of one-day international cricket, but also sponsor The Royal Bank Street Party (Edinburgh's Hogmanay), The Royal Bank of Scotland/Scottish Economic Society Annual Lecture and the Royal Highland Show.

Other influential trends on sponsorship are evident in the arenas of business, marketing and media. Companies expanding into international markets have harnessed the value of event sponsorship to create brand awareness in their new markets. Sports sponsorship has become a multibillion dollar business in Asia with companies, such as Samsung, becoming global brands and leveraging investment in global sports. Samsung, for example, made a $4.6 million sponsorship investment in a historic, one day cricket contest between India and Pakistan (Sudhaman, 2004).

The growth of sponsorship can also be attributed to changes in marketing itself – with the shift away from simple transactions to relationships (Gronroos, 1994). New trends in marketing communication media give event sponsors the chance to interact directly with their markets to create a brand relationship. Simultaneous brand exposure can be achieved through a range of on-site communication and alternative media. Sponsors are getting extra exposure, for example, as a result of live streaming events onto the Internet, text messages, sponsorship of live sites away from the event and giant screens at festivals that display text and photo messages from the crowd responding to billboard ads. Events such as the V Festival and the Rip Curl Newquay Boardmasters Festival use Jumbotrons (giant text screens) and posters inviting text responses for instant-win opportunities such as VIP access to the backstage area and free product samples (Blyth, 2003).

Sponsorship is also gaining leadership in most marketers' 'tool kits' because consumers are more cynical about traditional advertising – sponsorship is perceived to give 'more bang for the sponsor's buck'. When sponsorship is perceived to be a commercial activity with some benefit to society, consumers view advertising as being more manipulative with far less social value (Meenaghan, 2001b). The involvement in traditional media by marketers has also shifted as a result of:

- The rising costs of media space and the reduced effectiveness of advertising – many of us now simultaneously use multiple media, such as television, Internet, mobiles, text messaging etc (Duncan, 2002).
- A growth in the overall number of media outlets (including pay TV channels, radio stations, specialist magazines, direct mail pieces and the Internet) with media advertising becoming extremely cluttered (De Pelsmacker, Geuens and Van den Bergh, 2004; Duncan, 2002).
- The expansion of pay TV channels (satellite and cable) and their subsequent need for programme material. Events, especially sport events, have thus had more opportunity to be televised, enhancing exposure opportunities available to event sponsors (Lieberman, 2002).
- The globalization and commercialization of sport (Hinch and Higham, 2004) as both amateur and professional sports offer more opportunities for organizations to engage in sponsorship of events that have huge television audiences.
- A proliferation of brands, products and services offered by fewer manufacturers/ providers (Duncan, 2002). Companies, therefore, choose to improve their distributors' relationships with event-related entertainment and hospitality.

Sponsorship, especially through events and festivals, has been able to exploit these trends because it communicates in experiential environments, rather than one-way, persuasive media. Yet some events are also becoming cluttered with the diverse brands of multiple sponsors. As a result, sponsors must work closely with event organizers to achieve 'cut-through' with their own brands. Research by MEC MediaLab across 20 countries suggests that over 40 per cent of respondents believe sports events have become too heavily sponsored (Sudhaman, 2004). In this context, the event manager's task of making strategic decisions about an event's portfolio of sponsors (discussed later in this Chapter) will become even more critical as sponsorship matures as a marketing medium. Economic fluctuations will also continue to influence the sponsorship environment. The ratio of events and individuals seeking sponsorship to the overall sponsorship pounds available in the UK's corporate sector challenges the event manager's access to new, 'big money' partnerships. A number of other potential influences on the event manager's ability to attract sponsorship (De Pelsmacker, Geuens and Van den Bergh, 2004) that should be considered are:

- the changing expenditure patterns among marketers; for example, increased interest in radio and television programme sponsorship (Dolphin, 2003) and cause-related projects
- an increased diversity in the types of industries, firms and agencies using sponsorship (ranging from local florist shops to national financial institutions)
- a demand for more sophisticated (and innovative) sponsorships, tailored to a sponsor's needs, which produce a behavioural result (sponsorships that 'make the phones ring')
- the growing attachment of sponsors to events with broadcast coverage – events that are not televised or streamed to the audience via other channels are less attractive to corporate sponsors because the sponsors receive less exposure.

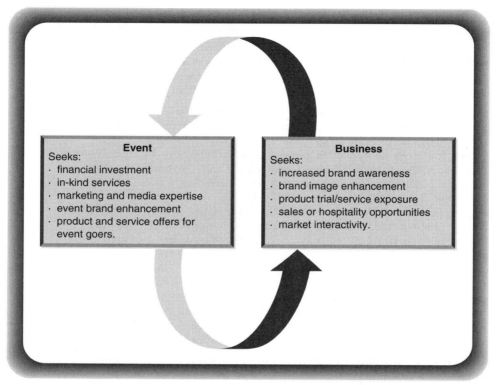

Figure 8.2 Mutual benefits sought by events and sponsors
Source: adapted from Crompton (1994)

All of these environmental trends underline the need for event managers to ensure their preliminary research and SWOT analysis (Chapter 7) includes a comprehensive analysis of the sponsorship environment. Part of ensuring the success of the event's sponsorship strategy is knowing the range of benefits that will attract sponsor partners – not just the benefits to be accrued by the event or festival.

Sponsorship benefits for events and sponsors

Sponsorships are pursued by events and festivals and purchased by corporations, media and government based on a thorough assessment of the benefits to be derived. Event managers must therefore obtain a good understanding of the full suite of potential benefits that a sponsorship will bring to their event/festival and their sponsors so they can customize their strategies. Figure 8.2 shows the relationship between events/festivals in terms of the benefits exchanged by each of the sponsorship partners.

Before embarking on a sponsorship strategy, the event manager should consider the sponsor-partnering benefits for the event and whether the event or festival is 'sponsorship ready'.

How events can benefit if they are 'sponsorship ready'

For many events and festivals, sponsorship (through cash and/or contra) brings a valuable opportunity for long-term business partnerships that not only grow the event, but also the audience numbers of a particular art form or sport. In the UK, Virgin Mobile's long-running sponsorship of the successful V Festival not only improved the brand equity of the festival, but it became a platform for Virgin Mobile to take 'ownership' of the festival audience and associate the Virgin Mobile brand with the youth market and music with the sponsorship selling a lifestyle and an image (Matheson, 2005). Virgin Mobile capitalize on the sponsorship at the event with a number of initiatives, including festival-goers being able to 'text the fest' to get their messages on the big screens, free kebabs and beer for their customers, and angels onsite to help put up tents or direct people back there at the end of the evening (Cake, 2005). For the event or festival, sponsorship is therefore much more than a means of boosting revenues. Wider objectives for having sponsor partners at an event could include sustaining an art form or developing a new sport (for example, note the growth in snowboarding over recent years), achieving issues-related objectives such as a sustainable environment or ensuring the survival of not-for-profit agencies; for example, the Air Ambulance Service.

Despite the obvious advantages of sponsorship, not all events and festivals understand the management implications of attracting business partners. Many event managers assume sponsorship is an appropriate source of income for their event and set about seeking to obtain it – later running into difficulties – not the least of which is being unable to attract any sponsors. Geldard and Sinclair (2003) identify a number of questions that an event manager should ask before seeking sponsorship as a revenue stream. These questions are as follows:

- *Does the event have sufficient rights or benefits that can be offered to sponsors?* Organizations must be able to recognize the potential of the event to achieve their marketing objectives, such as image enhancement or the development of stronger relationships with suppliers/buyers. If the desired benefits are not present, an event manager would be wasting his or her time in seeking income from this source. A better alternative in some instances may be to seek a donation which, by its nature, does not require strategic marketing benefits to be given in return. It is not uncommon for corporations, particularly large corporations, to provide an allocation of funds specifically for this purpose. Commonly, these funds are made available to events of a community or charitable nature.
- *Are the event's stakeholders likely to approve of commercial sponsorship?* It is not hard to imagine situations where some members of a particular association or the potential event audience might view commercial sponsorship negatively. A conservation body seeking sponsorship for its annual conference, for example, could find that its membership is against commercial involvement and at best, extremely selective about the companies with whom they will associate. In effect, broad support among the event's internal stakeholders is essential for sponsorship to be successful.
- *Are there some companies that are simply not suitable as sponsors?* Event managers need to identify organizations that are inappropriate as sponsorship partners. For example, a charity event aimed at raising funds for a children's hospital or another health-related cause, is unlikely to accept sponsorship from breweries. As another example, in the past tobacco has been accepted as a major source of sponsorship, particularly for sports events such as motor racing, snooker and darts. However, due to implementation of the Tobacco Advertising and Promotion Bill (Conway, 2000), events have been forced to identify other sources of sponsorship.

- *Does the event have the resources to market and manage sponsorship?* A considerable amount of time and effort is required to research, develop and market sponsorships to potential sponsor targets. Furthermore, sponsors must be 'serviced' after the contract is finalized, which means the event manager needs to ensure all promises made in the proposal are fulfilled. This involves allocating staff and other resources to building and sustaining the sponsor relationship.

Sponsors' benefits – links with the consumer response

An appreciation of the consumer effects of sponsorship helps to understand the engagement of corporate and government bodies with events and festivals. Knowledge and familiarity with a corporate or product brand, as well as attitudinal and behavioural effects have been linked with event sponsorship. The sponsor's investment assisting a sport or art form is believed to create goodwill among attendees, which in turn influences their attitude and behaviour towards the sponsor's brand (Meenaghan, 2001a). Although there is still a great deal of research to be conducted on sponsorship effects (most data has been gathered by private firms), it appears that sponsorship does stimulate goodwill (a positive attitude) which in turn influences consumer relationships with sponsors' brands.

According to Meenaghan (2001a, p. 102), the goodwill is generated for sponsors at three levels: the generic level (consumer feelings about their engagement in sponsorship as an activity), the category level (within sports audiences or arts) and at the individual activity level (fans of a football team such as Manchester United develop goodwill towards Vodafone as a team sponsor). Clearly, goodwill effects are achieved intensely for sponsors at an event category level (art or sport) and the individual event/activity level. Underlining the importance of fan/audience involvement with an event category in getting a sponsorship result, Performance Research (2001) has reported that over half of those with an interest in the arts said that they would almost always buy a product that sponsored cultural events. Figure 8.3 shows how sponsorship effects narrow at an individual event/activity

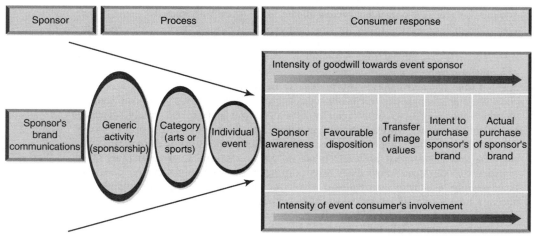

Figure 8.3 The sponsorship effects process
Source: adapted from Meenaghan (2001a), p. 115

level. It also demonstrates how the intensity of goodwill towards the sponsor moves in parallel with the intensity of fan or event consumer involvement.

Clearly, some additional benefits can be gained from leveraging a sponsorship in target markets with higher levels of event knowledge – 'involved' or 'highly active' event consumers are more likely to make an effort to process a sponsor's message (Roy and Cornwell, 2004). The more actively engaged a person is with what is being sponsored, the stronger the carryover effect and the link between the sponsor's brand and the event (De Pelsmacker, Geuens and Van den Bergh, 2004). However, this is not always the case. Euro 2000 was noted as being one of the most successful tournaments ever, however, only half of fans were able to identify any of the sponsors involved, and only 18 per cent reported that they would choose the sponsors product over others. The reasons for this lack of engagement are not known, but it was believed that television coverage on BBC meant that fans avoided many of the sponsors' messages. This illustrates that even high profile, big budget sponsorships need to be managed effectively to gain return on investment (Performance Research, 2000). This is a good reason why many companies try to sponsor festivals or events that have loyal and dedicated audiences.

The translation of a passion for the event itself into customer gratitude/goodwill and a commitment (SponsorMap, 2005) to use the sponsor's services or products is of interest to all existing and would-be sponsors. Emphasis is placed on consumers being in a positive environment at events as sponsoring brands are perceived in a favourable light. However, products that gain a stronger link to the event and its audience are often those that are demonstrated creatively in some way during the event (Cornwell, Roy and Steinard, 2001). For the 2005 V Festival, Virgin Mobile, the headline sponsors, capitalized on the sponsorship in a number of ways including urging the 130 000 festival goers to 'text the fest' to get their messages shown on large screens around the event (Matheson, 2005).

Based on consumer behaviour theories, various writers (De Pelsmacker, Geuens and Van den Bergh, 2004; Geldard and Sinclair, 2003; Meenaghan, 2001b) highlight an array of marketing benefits of event and festival sponsorship gained by corporate sponsors. These benefits include the following:

- *Access to specific niche/target markets* – mobile phone operators are using event sponsorship as a means of targeting potential customers in specific age brackets. For example, O2 sponsored music concerts to appeal to a youth market and establish itself as the biggest mobile network in the youth market (Carter, 2004), while Virgin Mobile sponsor V Festival as discussed elsewhere.
- *Corporate brand image creation/enhancement*: for major service providers like banks, the lack of a tangible product complicates the task of brand imaging. Sponsorship of festivals and events is therefore a valuable form of corporate image enhancement, illustrated by Royal Bank of Scotland's sponsorship of the Royal Bank Lates at Edinburgh International Festival – a series of 30 late night events over 20 days in 6 venues with a ticket price of only £5. Royal Bank of Scotland's rationale for the sponsorship is that they see this as an opportunity to raise their profile in their home city to locals and visitors, while continuing their support for the arts and Edinburgh International Festival (Royal Bank of Scotland, 2004). Renault sponsored Cirque du Soleil's Saltimbanco Season at the Royal Albert Hall in London in 2003. The partnership was seen as offering 'the perfect fit for two companies who insist on innovation in their own respective fields' while offering Renault the opportunity to promote their premium range of cars to an audience that met the profile of their target market (Renault, 2003).
- *Building brand awareness for an organization and its services/products*: Credit Expert, the online credit monitoring service from Experian, sponsored stand up comic

Bennett Aarron's show, 'It Wasn't Me, It Was Bennett Arron' at The Edinburgh Festival. The show focused on what it is like to become a victim of identity theft and how to prevent it and was therefore seen as a good opportunity to promote the online service which can notify subscribers of unusual activity on their accounts (Bold, 2005).

- *Influencing consumer attitudes about a product or service brand*: some companies use sponsorship as a strategy to change consumer perceptions about a longstanding brand. For example, Scottish Courage sought to change attitudes towards their Strongbow Cider brand as although this product had 63 per cent of the on-trade cider market, cider was seen as an uncool drink with a poor image. Recognizing music as a powerful medium with their target market of 18–35 year olds, and having been involved in festivals since 1999, they developed the Strongbow Rooms concept to add value to the festival experience. The programme of festival sponsorship include a spectacular Strongbow Rooms arena at 7 leading UK music festivals, exclusive tie-ins with world-class DJs, pre-event promotions in 450 pubs and 75 Students Unions, exclusive media partnerships with MTV and NME including a dedicated website, an extensive PR campaign and post-event loyalty programme (Scottish Courage, 2005).

- *Associating a product or service with a particular lifestyle*: makers of alcoholic beverages, for example, often sponsor or directly support youth-oriented events, such as rock music festivals, to develop an association between their product and a demographic that is young, fun seeking and keen to experiment. Bacardi Martini toured the 2003 summer festival circuit in the United Kingdom with BBar, a marquee that held up to 1000 people and featured 65 DJs and a small army of cocktail mixers. The aim was to create a memorable experience that tied in with Bacardi's brand values – an association with the party spirit (Wallis, 2003). Nokia took up headline sponsorship of the Prince's Trust event, Nokia Urban Music Festival, taking place at Earls Court. The festival for a crowd of 16 000 featured high-profile acts including Will Smith and Craig David. Aligning themselves with an 'edgy urban culture', Nokia were seen as a strong fit for the event as the brand (and therefore the event) appeals to the young people (which was the Prince's Trust aim) and for Nokia it was an opportunity to showcase latest handsets and technology (Bond, 2005).

- *Improving relationships with distribution channel members*: a corporation may be seeking to develop stronger relationships with agents or firms that currently distribute its products or services or to establish new distribution outlets. For example, Barclays sponsorship of the 2002 Scottish Open at Loch Lomond allowed Barclay's and Barclays Capital to treat clients to a range of experiences at the event including hospitality, meeting players and participating in golf clinics, in addition to the brand awareness opportunities offered by the event. Bob Diamond, head of Barclays Capital notes, 'We view our sponsorship relationships in the same way as client relationships. There is an incredible sense of partnership and working together towards a common goal' (Barclays Capital, 2005).

- *Achieving product sales and merchandising opportunities:* for companies with a product (rather than an intangible service), high sales targets can be set for an exclusive in-game presence at sporting events – for example, Heineken at the Rugby World Cup 2003 – or through having exclusive rights in their product category at a festival. Tiger Beer, for example, has targeted the Tartan Asian Extreme Festival for cult films. Their headline sponsorship included rolling out sampling of their beer as part of an integrated marketing campaign, which also includes the launch of The Tigers' awards to celebrate Asian films in the UK (Anon, 2005c). The Scottish Courage Strongbow Rooms concept resulted in an estimated increase in 12 per cent monthly sales gain, or 232 320 pints per annum, from those exposed to the brand at the seven festivals (Scottish Courage, 2005).

- *Demonstrating product attributes*: many festivals and events are primarily used by sponsors to demonstrate new products or technology. Through its sponsorship of events such as the Edinburgh International Festival and Brisbane's International Film Festival, the mobile phone distributor Nokia showcased the functionality of its handsets and educated people about new technologies such as MMS. Similarly, the telecommunications giant Orange uses its sponsorship of the Glastonbury festival in the United Kingdom, to offer free recharge points, provide e-top-ups and phone cards and to get people to experiment with technology like text alerts (Wallis, 2003).
- *Providing employee rewards and recognition*: organizations often perceive the sponsorship of a sporting or cultural event as a way of giving their employees access to a corporate box and/or tickets to reward or motivate them. For example, following on from their sponsorship, Royal Bank of Scotland's and Edinburgh International Festival secured New Partnership funding from Arts & Business which enabled the bank's staff to take part in 'Royal Bank Turn Up and Try It' workshops. Using arts for development purposes, the workshops focused on drama, theatre and music while linking in with festival events. The bank were keen to see a number of results from staff, including more creative thinking, dealing effectively with customers or colleagues, and looking at situations more laterally, while also involving staff in the arts sponsorship (Royal Bank of Scotland, 2003).
- *Creating goodwill and a climate of consent for an organization's activities*: companies as diverse as mining organizations, energy providers, banks and pharmaceutical manufacturers all support charity events to create an image in the community of being good corporate citizens. For example, NPower became headline sponsor for Macmillan Cancer Relief's flagship fundraising event, World's Biggest Coffee Morning, in 2004 (Anon, 2004).
- *Entertaining key clients with corporate hospitality*: corporate hospitality is an important drawcard for sponsors, especially those with business-to-business clients, Ellery (2004) comments, 'There is nothing quite like strawberries and cream washed down with chilled champagne at the Wimbledon Tennis Championships to woo potential business'. Where working relationships are quite intense, corporate hospitality events can break down the barriers and create social bonds that forge a better relationship between suppliers and clients.

In looking at the many benefits derived by sponsors, it should also be remembered that public sector bodies (for example, local councils, regional development agencies, authorities/commissions and agencies) engage in sponsorship. Many of the benefits illustrated in the corporate context are equally applicable to them. Most public sector agencies now employ marketing strategies to generate awareness of their products/services or issues and to influence community behaviour. For example, Glasgow City Council, Scottish Enterprise, European Regional Development Fund and other agencies are active partners in the Glasgow River Festival event with the aim of supporting the regeneration of the Clyde waterfront and attracting people back to the river (Richmond Event Management, 2005).

As noted in Chapters 2 and 4, local or national government or regional development agencies will normally support events through sponsorships, grants or contributions towards constructing the infrastructure needed to stage events because of the community benefits they bring. Events and festivals can also stimulate economic development in an area (for example, the 2002 Commonwealth Games in Manchester), create a greater sense of identity or cohesion and enhance the facilities available to local residents. To attract sponsorship, event organizers must think about how they can provide at least several of the benefits identified here.

Sponsorship leveraging – adding value to the investment

To fully capitalize on a sponsorship investment, most corporate and government agencies develop a leveraging strategy or a range of marketing activities that extend the sponsorship benefits well beyond the event or festival's promised offer. The 2004 IEG/Performance Research Sponsorship Decision Makers Survey of 110 corporate marketers found that sponsors are now spending at a ratio of around 1.3: 1 on leveraging their sponsorships, though this was down on previous years (Performance Research, 2004). Adidas as an official sponsor of the FIFA 2002 World Cup reportedly budgeted around $88 million to exploit their sponsorship with the cost of official sponsorships being somewhere between $20 and 28 million (Pickett, 2002).

When sponsors already have a high level of corporate brand awareness, leveraging is best focused on activities that achieve two-way communication with the market – for example, business-to-business customer hospitality or specific consumer offers either during the event or on-line. The need for sponsors to offer event consumers something they cannot obtain elsewhere is gaining importance. Beverage marketer Red Bull, for example, has set up a branded skate ramp at festivals in the United Kingdom, while the Walls company created a unique ice-cream beach to engage visitors at the 2003 V Festival in England (Wallis, 2003). In effect, the need to think of leveraging strategies that achieve 'cut-through' to a media savvy market without irritating them is the sponsor's challenge and also the event marketer's concern in order to add value for their sponsors.

The value of sponsorship policy

Just as most corporate and government agencies will establish a sponsorship policy to drive their decision making, Grey and Skildum-Reid (2003) strongly recommend that all events seeking sponsorship design a policy to guide their actions. They suggest that a sponsorship policy should state:

- the event's history of sponsorship and their approach to it, including some definition of what constitutes sponsorship versus grants and donations
- the event's objectives, processes and procedures for seeking sponsorship
- the rules for entering into sponsorship and the kinds of companies that will be excluded. It could be stated, for example, that no sponsorships are to be accepted from companies or individuals who are party to significant tendering processes for the event or companies with values that may be contrary to those of the event. A rationale for not including certain types of potential sponsors is useful as a later reference for event management.

Most policies will also indicate that sponsorships must be finalized through written agreements.

- the uniform approach adopted in seeking sponsorship, including whether all proposals are to follow a particular format and whether each sponsorship is required to have a management plan developed for it (see later discussion)
- the levels of accountability and responsibility, such as whether all sponsorships are to be signed off and overseen by a designated person
- the time at which the policy will be subject to review and evaluation.

For most events and festivals, involving the senior management of the event as well as staff and lead volunteers in the drafting of the sponsorship policy is a wise idea. Having a sense of ownership of the sponsorship policy becomes important if there are conflicts or disputes over decisions about sponsors. For larger events and festivals, the policy would also be presented to and approved by a board of directors.

Although there should already be an overall marketing strategy and plan for the event or festival (see Chapter 7), developing an event sponsorship strategy is a more defined task. Remember that it will have an interactive relationship with the event's marketing strategy because, whether it is venue design, ticketing, integrated marketing communications or even the programme itself, you will need to be creative about how you can integrate the sponsor's brand with the event's marketing plans. Accenture sponsored Total Meltdown, a concert featured as part of the London South Bank Centre's 50th anniversary celebrations in 2001 (Sponsorship Consulting Limited, 2005). Total Meltdown, a concert of contemporary music, was based on the concept of a well-known personality, such as Elvis Costello, programming their fantasy festival. Accenture aims for their sponsorship were:

- To create awareness of the new Accenture name and to achieve the transfer of values (youthful, dynamic, expressive) from the concert to Accenture.
- To deepen the Accenture impact on potential graduate recruits.
- To offer access to the event for existing staff and excite and motivate staff in the 22–44 year age bracket.
- To offer corporate hospitality for existing and potential clients.

To capitalize on the sponsorship, Sponsorship Consulting Limited worked with Accenture and South Bank Centre to create:

- An eye-catching visual identity for the sponsorship, which was used throughout the leveraging campaign.
- FreeCard promotions in restaurants, which achieved a 93 per cent pick-up rate
- London Underground 6 –sheet poster campaign across 62 stations
- Exciting private party room at the Royal Festival Hall
- A successful and memorable event
- Press advertising campaign and web banners
- Time Out ticket promotions
- Impactful venue signage
- Dramatic sponsorship of the lighting of the Royal Festival Hall for two weeks (Sponsorship Consulting Limited, 2005).

Stages in developing the event sponsorship strategy

As noted in Chapter 7, having a strategy means knowing the direction in which you are headed, which also applies to your event's sponsorship. For event managers, this involves thinking about event/festival visitors and the types of synergy they might have with corporate brands. It also involves thinking about the attributes and values of the event and companies that might share those values, and about the mix of sponsors who together might create a close-knit sponsor family, and brainstorming the kinds of partnerships that will grow the event.

Profiling the event audience

As a first step in creating your strategy, consider again the target markets of your event or festival. By adopting the market segmentation strategies outlined in Chapter 7, you will have a sound basis for matching potential sponsors to the consumers who frequent your event. Like all forms of integrated marketing communication, event sponsorship is most successful as a marketing medium when there is a solid database that profiles existing visitors and members/subscribers and their preferences. Sponsors will look for a reliable picture of the event audience to 'buy' the potential brand links you propose to develop, and to justify their investment.

In the case of T In the Park, research undertaken in 2003 by Hall & Partners showed that 98 per cent of consumers recognized Tennent's Lager as sponsor, with 35 per cent believing it was a perfect fit and 48 per cent believing that Tennent's Lager were supporting the Scottish music scene through this sponsorship and 23 per cent believed that the event would not happen without Tennent's support (Material Marketing & Communications Ltd, 2005) (for further information on T In The Park, please see the case study in Chapter 14). However, even for smaller events and festivals, steps to identify the market and demonstrate a fit between the event and sponsors' markets must be taken. This may be a more straightforward task for smaller festivals where links can be logically made with small to medium brands in their local market (Harrison, 2004). To obtain detailed market information to assist with sponsorship planning, some of the research tools noted in Chapter 7 (for example, on-site surveys and focus groups) can be especially useful.

Creating the event's asset register

Where the assets of a local festival may be relatively easy to identify, the inventory of assets available to a ruby league team like the Leeds Rhinos, or even a televised festival, are much more extensive. Despite the variation in the size and scope of different events and festivals, some common assets include the agreement to purchase product/services from a sponsor (for example, alcohol, transport, food), event naming rights, exclusivity (the capacity to lock out competition within a brand category), business and sponsor networking opportunities, merchandising rights, media exposure, including advertising opportunities during the event, venue signage, joint advertising with sponsors, the capacity to demonstrate product or technology at the event, corporate hospitality services and a volume of tickets for the sponsor's use.

In building their asset register, a sports team such as the Leeds Rhinos or Leeds Tykes, may take steps to group their assets (for example, in-game media exposure, player clothing), record the quantities and current availability of those assets (for example, 15 seconds of remaining in-game advertising) and build the sale value and cost of sales into the pricing of their marketable assets (Allsop, 2004). On a practical level, their website lists a number of opportunities including Big Match Sponsor, Associate Sponsor, Matchball Sponsor and Player Sponsorship among the many opportunities (Leeds Rugby, 2005). An overall asset register serves to tabulate the profits (the value minus the cost) for each of the individual sponsorships.

For a smaller event or festival, the process will be much less complex. Where the Leeds Rhinos could have a list of 100 saleable assets or more (over a series of games), a local festival staged annually has an inventory that is much easier to manage. Yet, with a little creativity, the festival or event marketer can also create new assets. Apart from identifying assets like signage not previously used for branding within the festival (for example, brand exposure at the front of a concert stage), some tailor-made assets for sponsors can be devised. Sponsorship of the Brit Awards, for example, paved the way for Mastercard to run a promotional campaign with British Airways. A video, 'A History of the Brit Awards' was shown on all in-bound UK flights with more than 500 000 passengers given the opportunity to enter a postcard into a competition to win tickets to the award show at Earls Court in London in February (Anon, 2004). It is fair to assume that many small- to medium-sized events and festivals with few sponsorship management staff will have untapped resources. However, in identifying and expanding the event's asset register, careful consideration must also be given to the time and personnel needed to effectively manage and market those assets.

Building the event sponsorship portfolio

In designing a sponsorship strategy, event managers will usually work out how a portfolio of sponsors can be established, given the bundles of festival or event assets that are available for purchase. Geldard and Sinclair (2003) identify strategies for this, such as sole sponsorship, hierarchical packages (for example, tiers of gold, silver, bronze), a pyramid structure (whereby each sponsor level below the principal sponsor jointly spends the amount invested by the top sponsor with proportional benefits), a level playing field (all sponsors negotiate and leverage their own benefits) and an *ad hoc* approach. For example, the Hay Book Festival 2005 had three levels of sponsorship, title sponsor, partner sponsors and event sponsors:

- The festival was branded as The Guardian Hay Festival, 2005 as the third year of a three-year title sponsorship deal.
- Partner sponsorship was available for between £10 000 and £50 000 for which sponsors received benefits, including branding on the website, in the main brochure, on site including flags around the site and in relevant tickets.
- The event sponsorship tier included over 60 companies and local businesses investing between £500 and £10 000 for which they received branding on all relevant tickets, accreditation on all listing in the main brochure, tickets and the opportunity to host receptions for writers and guests.

The Guardian Hay Festival 2005 sponsors listed on their website included: a broadcast sponsor (Channel 4), venue partners (Film Four, Copella, Arts & Business and The Elmley Foundation), festival bookseller (Pembertons), masterclass sponsor (Working Title), banker (HSBC), legal (RPC), accountant (Grant Thornton), streaming partner (Stream UK), communications partner (Orange), series sponsors (The Open University, illy, Simon Finch and Triodis Bank), furniture sponsor (Maskreys), print sponsor (AST Print Group Ltd), education sponsors (BUPA, Legal & General, The Foyle Foundation, The Headley Trust and Federation of Children's Book Groups) (The Guardian Hay Festival, 2005).

Although sole sponsorship of a festival may have the advantage of 'keeping it simple', the festival's survival is threatened if the sole sponsor is lost. For this reason, many events and festivals with a limited array of assets choose the tiered approach (different levels of investment for set benefit packages). However, as Grey and Skildum-Reid (2003, p. 97) point out, 'most events/festivals end up formulating their packages so that all of the levels get access to the best benefits, with the lower levels simply getting less of the supporting benefits'. For this reason, many events now tailor their asset packages for each sponsor using only broad categories, such as major/media, corporate and support sponsors. Using this approach, the sponsors are usually grouped according to their *type* (for example, naming rights, presenting sponsorship of a section, event, entry, team or particular day, preferred suppliers, etc.) and their *exclusivity* (among sponsors at any level, among sponsors at or below a given level, as a supplier or seller at the event or within event-driven marketing collateral) (Grey and Skildum-Reid, 2003). The purchase of other event assets such as merchandising rights, licenses and endorsements, hospitality, signage and database access by sponsors, to name just a few, serve to further differentiate the event sponsor packages. The use of tailor-made sponsorship packages is recommended for a number of reasons (Welsh, 2003):

- Packaged event properties are rarely a perfect fit for potential sponsors – most are either too broad or too narrow in their consumer reach and the rights available may be either more or less than the sponsor wants.
- Sponsors are often seeking more control over their sponsorship and its potential leveraging than packaged strategies offer – the simple transactional nature of buyer–seller arrangements is being replaced by partnerships and in some cases, the sponsor clearly has leadership in driving the relationship.
- Poor sponsorship packaging by events and festivals can lead to a greater instance of *ambush marketing* in certain industry/product categories (for example, banking and finance) or attempts by non-sponsoring companies to capitalize on an event's image and prestige by implying that they are sponsors (Andrews, 2001).
- Multiple layers of sponsorship introduced by events are causing some confusion – as the different sponsorship categories become more prolific, there is more potential for a loss of control by event organizers and sponsor conflicts (Shani and Sandler, 1998).

In light of these challenges, the appeal of determining sponsor partnerships on a case by case basis (with all sponsors informed of this practice) is growing. Cheltenham Festivals, discussed in the case study at the end of this chapter, is just one of many events shifting towards tailor-made sponsorships. Although an indication is given of the different levels of sponsorship that are typical and the potential costs associated with this, the opportunity is available for potential sponsors to discuss their specific requirements and how they support, or partner one or more of the Cheltenham Festivals.

Matching event assets with potential sponsors

Once the approach to building the sponsorship portfolio is determined, the business of identifying the right sponsor(s) begins. As noted, a first criterion is to find those organizations that want access to the same audience (or a significant component of it), or who have a specific problem that the event may assist in solving. Sponsorship managers for events use various research techniques to identify potential sponsors. By keeping track of business developments through industry associations, business and financial media and the web, a great deal of information can be gathered on the marketing direction of firms to guide sponsorship targeting. Which organizations are looking to enter new markets in your area or region? Which companies appear to have attributes and values that match those of your event/festival? The Reading and Leeds Festivals, branded as The Carling Weekend, are seen as an opportunity to attract young males aged 25–34 to the brand, as evidence suggests that people will grow with the brand. The V Festivals were originally launched to promote Virgin Cola but more recently have been sponsored by another Virgin Brand, Virgin Mobile, as they believe that the lifestyle and image associated with the brand matches the image portrayed by the festival (Matheson, 2005).

The event manager should also actively identify any government agencies or firms that are seeking to reposition themselves, regain market acceptance or introduce new products or services. Once identified, and depending on the nature of the event, such organizations can become a sponsorship target. An organizer of a garden festival, for example, may notice that a horticultural company has just launched a new range of fertilizers. This development could be a sponsorship opportunity if the company can be convinced that the event draws the right consumer audience to increase awareness and sales of its new product line. Event managers can also obtain insights into potential sponsors by reading their annual reports or viewing their websites. These sources often provide a good picture of the broad strategies the organization is pursuing. They also indicate the types of sponsorship they already have in place and whether they have any specific requirements for sponsorships (Figure 8.4). Another means of finding potential sponsors is to simply identify who has sponsored similar events or festivals in the past. This can be done by examining programmes/promotional material/websites of these other events, or directly contacting the event organizers (many festivals and events now see the value in some productive networking and information sharing). Finally, it is unlikely that you will be looking for all of your sponsors simultaneously, unless you are managing a brand new event. Therefore, the existing sponsors of the event or festival can be a very useful source of referral to other potential sponsors. This method of finding sponsors can be highly successful because the existing sponsor is presenting their company as a satisfied

Criteria

Bank of Scotland Corporate is committed to supporting business-to-business sponsorship activity across the UK that is of significance to the business community and of relevance to our customers, colleagues and industry.

We are unable to sponsor any of the following:

- Individuals requesting sponsorship
- Political organizations or fundraising events
- Charitable activity
- Overseas events
- Motorsport or any other high risk or extreme sporting activity
- Local team shirt sponsorships including junior football teams or golf teams
- Arts sponsorship
- Any events where a competitor within the banking sector is already a sponsor
- Any events or activity where there is no clear business benefit for the Bank.

If you can confirm that your request meets the above criteria, you should complete the downloadable request form which includes the following details:

1. **Company details**
   Contact name
   Company/organization name
   Company/organization address
   Telephone number
   E-mail address
   Are you a HBOS customer? Corporate/Business/Personal/No.
2. **Sponsorship details**
   Project name
   Brief description of opportunity
   Objective(s) of sponsorship
   Benefit to Bank of Scotland Corporate
   Amount requested

Figure 8.4 Bank of Scotland corporate sponsorship criteria and request form
Source: Bank of Scotland Corporate (2005a, b)

partner of the event in 'opening the door' and endorsing the event as a sponsorship property.

Once potential sponsors are identified, a more detailed examination of their business and marketing objectives and the types of asset that will meet their needs can be completed. Additional information that might be sought includes the types of event the organization is willing to sponsor, whether the organization is tied to particular causes (for example, charities) and the time in their planning cycle when they allocate their sponsorship budget (sponsorship proposals should be submitted to them some months before this time). Information such as this last item is likely to require direct enquiry to the company's marketing personnel.

The sponsorship approach

Once the potential sponsor(s) have been listed, the next challenge for the event manager is to determine the marketing or management person who will be the sponsorship decision-maker within the targeted company. In small companies, this person is likely to be the chief executive officer (CEO) or managing director. In companies of moderate size, the marketing or public relations manager may make such decisions, while in large corporations a dedicated sponsorship section could exist within the marketing, public relations or corporate affairs areas, as exists for Vodafone, Royal Bank of Scotland and other major sponsors of UK events.

Before developing any written proposal, it is customary to write a brief introductory letter to profile your event and the sponsorship opportunity. However, some sponsorship managers make direct contact by e-mail or telephone, especially if they have been referred by another sponsor or have some informal rapport with the company's personnel (which may be the case for a sports sponsorship property such as Leeds Rhinos or an arts property such as the Harrogate International Festival).

There are definite benefits in becoming acquainted with the company before preparing a proposal, simply because you need to fully understand their product/ brand attributes, their business objectives, their competition, how they use their current sponsorships and the ways in which sponsorship proposals need to be structured to satisfy their needs. If you can develop some preliminary rapport with those deciding on the value of your proposed partnership, you will have a better grasp of why they may be interested in sponsoring the event/ festival and how the proposal should be written to attract their investment. However, the ability to personally discuss your interest in a partnership may depend on the company's policy about written or verbal communication in the first instance. The most successful sponsorship approach is one where the event has put a lot of effort into planning before approaching the sponsor (much like going for a job). Certainly, you should start to think about how you can marry the event with the company's culture and explore some innovative ways in which to address the company's marketing objectives before you commence your final proposal (Harrison, 2004).

Preparing and presenting sponsorship proposals

A formal proposal document is commonly how sponsorship is negotiated and partnerships are formed. In broad terms, Geldard and Sinclair (2003) suggest that the sponsorship proposal should address the following questions:

- What is the organization being asked to sponsor?
- What will the organization receive for its sponsorship?
- What is it going to cost?

The length and level of detail a proposal uses to answer these questions depends on the value and cost of the sponsor partnership. However, a comprehensive treatment of these areas would mean the proposal would include:

- an overview of the event, including (as applicable) its mission/goals, history, location, current and past sponsors, programme/duration, staff, past or anticipated level of media coverage, past or predicted attendance levels, and actual or predicted attendee profile (for example, age, income, sex, occupation).
- the sponsorship package on offer and its associated cost. In pricing the sponsorship, it should be remembered that marketers have a range of alternative marketing media such as advertising, direct marketing and other tools that could achieve similar outcomes (depending on the sponsor's marketing objectives).
- the proposed duration of the sponsorship agreement.
- the strategic fit between the proposal and the business and marketing needs of the organization. Discussion here will be based on research conducted using the sources noted earlier.
- the event's contact details for the company's response and follow-up negotiation.

Many large corporations, to assist sponsorship seekers, have developed specific proposal guidelines or criteria. In Figure 8.4, an example of the criteria and areas required by the request form is provided for Bank of Scotland. Consideration is required to the time frame for sponsorship as time is required not only for the company to consider the application, but also for any successful sponsor to be able to capitalize on their involvement. Although for smaller scale sponsorships, a few months may be sufficient, most sponsors require at least a 12-month timeframe to maximize their sponsorship and around two years for a major sponsorship – for example, a Rugby World Cup. Sponsorships for events scheduled less than six months from the time of the initial approach have far less opportunity to be successfully leveraged by marketing personnel.

From the points discussed, it is possible to gain an insight into what makes a successful proposal. However, the failure rate with sponsorship proposals suggests that much more needs to be understood by event managers about their preparation. According to Ukman (1995), there are six attributes of a successful proposal:

1. *Sell benefits, not features*: many proposals describe the features of the event, such as the artistic merit of the festival, rather than the event's marketing assets and sponsor benefits. Sponsors buy marketing communication platforms so that they can reach their stakeholders and market(s) to form relationships or sell products/ services.
2. *Address the sponsor's needs, not those of the event*: many proposals emphasize the event's need for money, rather than the sponsor's needs such as market access, corporate hospitality or a better understanding of a new brand. Remember, event sponsorships should be seen as partnerships, not a means to patch holes in the event budget (Harrison, 2004).
3. *Tailor the proposal to the business category*: as noted, each of the event's assets will have a different level of importance to each potential sponsor. An insurance company, for example, might be interested in an event's database, while a soft drink marketer is likely to be more concerned with on-site sales opportunities. A tailored strategy should be worked out based on some research and head-to-head discussions among event personnel before laying out the sponsorship document.
4. *Include promotional extensions*: the two major sources of sponsor benefits are addressed here. First, there are the assets being purchased; for example, identification in marketing collateral and on-site signage that come with the deal

and only require action on the part of the event manager. The second set of benefits emerges from the sponsor's event leveraging discussed earlier – for example, trade, retail and sales extensions. Particular leveraging activities might include competitions, redemption offers (for example, free ticket offers for the customers of a sponsor's wholesalers) and hospitality. It is not enough to give sponsors a checklist of the direct benefits of the assets being purchased – a proposal should include the 'exploitation or leveraging menu' showing them how to leverage their investment.

5. *Minimize risk*: risk can be reduced through indicating some guaranteed marketing activities (including media space) in the package, listing reputable co-sponsors and showing the steps that will be taken to minimize the risk of ambush marketing by other companies. A clear indication of how the event/festival will service the sponsorship should also be given prominence in the proposal.

6. *Include added value*: the proposal should be presented in terms of its total impact on achieving results for the sponsor, rather than focusing on one aspect such as media. Generally, sponsors will be looking for an array of those benefits highlighted earlier in the Chapter – how the sponsorship will build relationships internally with staff, ways in which it will facilitate networking with other sponsors or potential business partners, and how it can build sales among consumer and business audiences.

Given that many of the organizations targeted by events as potential sponsors receive large numbers of proposals each week, an effort should be made to ensure the proposal provides sufficient information on which a decision can be made. If the organization has published guidelines for sponsorship seekers to follow, it should be evident from the contents page and a quick scan of the proposal that these matters have been addressed. Some attempt to make a proposal stand out can also be useful. A food and wine festival might print a brief version of the proposal on a good bottle of wine, for example, as well as submitting the fuller version. But be aware that glossy, printed proposals and presentations are usually not well accepted, because they do not suggest that the event is offering a customized partnership (Grey and Skildum-Reid, 2003).

Time is increasingly crucial in business. If a proposal is too long, has not been based on sound research, does not contain adequate information or it leaves out key elements (such as event contact details), the chances of the proposal being discarded are high. As a general rule, the length of a sponsorship proposal should be commensurate with the amount of money sought and must be as succinct as possible. If the value of the sponsorship is substantial and the proposal is over five pages (more than 10 pages could be too long), an executive summary should give a snapshot of its key elements along with a contents page.

Undertaking the sponsorship screening process

Commonly, organizations apply a screening process to sponsorship proposals as they seek to determine which relevant benefits are present. An understanding of this screening process is useful to the event manager as it assists in crafting sponsorship proposals. The framework for understanding the screening process developed by Crompton (1993) remains one of the most comprehensive developed to date. The framework adopts the acronym CEDAREEE to identify the major elements of the sponsorship screening process employed by corporations. The acronym is derived from:

- Customer audience
- Exposure potential

- Distribution channel audience
- Advantage over competitors
- Resource investment involvement required
- Event's characteristics
- Event organization's reputation
- Entertainment and hospitality opportunities.

These criteria are expanded in Figure 8.5.

Not all of these criteria are used in the assessment of each sponsorship proposal, or by every company, as a different range of desired outcomes or benefits will be specified. The required inclusions in sponsorship proposals such as those shown earlier for Country Energy, usually provide a good indication of the criteria that will be used to assess the sponsorship proposal.

An organization that has received a sponsorship proposal will act in several possible ways. After scanning the proposal, its management and/or marketing personnel may:

- dispose of it
- request further information
- seek to negotiate in an attempt to have the sponsorship offering
- improved to meet its needs
- accept the proposal as presented (it is more likely though that some adaptations will occur through negotiation).

Once sent, it is sound practice to follow up sponsorship proposals within a reasonable period (for example, two weeks afterwards) to determine their status (for example, yet to be considered, under review or rejected). On occasions, the proposed sponsorship package may be of interest to the organization, but they may wish to 'customize' it further. If this is the case, both the event and potential sponsor can negotiate to move the sponsorship towards a more mutually beneficial offer. Event managers should have a clear understanding of the minimum payment they are prepared to accept for the event assets on offer – to what extent can the event move in its negotiations to create a 'win-win' situation (particularly if multiple sponsors are being sought)? At this stage, it is vitally important not to undervalue the event's assets – a sponsorship sold below its potential market value will eventually need a price correction, which creates tension with event partners.

Event organizers also need to consider the time, effort and money that they devote to seeking sponsorship in determining their final 'price'. Harrison (2004, p. 8) suggests that 'the amount of money, or its equivalent value to you, that you raise in sponsorship should be (at least) double the amount that it has cost you to get it, otherwise you are going backwards'. When it is clear that both the event and sponsor have a sponsorship arrangement that offers the best possible outcomes for both partners, it is then usual for a written contract to be developed.

Negotiating event sponsorship contracts

It is sound business practice to commit the sponsorship agreement to paper to avoid misunderstandings about the event assets and benefits being offered, their costs, payment terms and the responsibilities of both parties. Where the contract was once just a reference for event organizers and sponsors, in the case of major sponsorship deals, the contract now establishes the ground rules for the ongoing working relationship between the sponsorship partners. Chapter 10 offers some more general guidelines about event contracts. With large-scale events, the document can be a 'saviour' for high-ticket sponsors, ensuring the ticketing obligations of the event

1. **Customer audience**
   - Is the demographic, attitude and lifestyle profile of the target audience congruent with the product's target market?
   What is the on-site audience?
   - Is sponsorship of this event the best way to communicate the product/service to this target audience?
2. **Exposure potential**
   - What is the inherent news value of the event?
   - What extended print and broadcast coverage of the sponsorship is likely?
   - Will the extended coverage be local, regional or national? Is the geographical scope of this media audience consistent with the product's sales area?
   - Can the event be tied into other media advertising?
   - Can the company's products/services be sold at the event?
   - What is the life of the event?
   - Are banners and signage included in the sponsorship? How many and what size? Will they be visible during television broadcasts?
   - Will the product's name and logo be identified on promotional material for the activity?
   - Event posters – how many?
   - Press releases – how many?
   - Point-of-sale displays – how many?
   - Television advertisements – how many and on what stations?
   - Radio advertisements – how many and on what stations?
   - Print advertisements – how many and in what print media?
   - Internet advertisements (on the event website, banner advertisements) – how many and on what sites?
   - Where will the product name appear in the event programme? Front or back cover? Number and site of programme advertisements? How many programmes?
   - Will the product's name be mentioned on the public address system? How many times?
   - Can the sponsor have display booths? Where will they be located? Will they be visible during television broadcasts?
3. **Distribution channel audience**
   - Are the sponsorship's advantages apparent to wholesalers, retailers or franchisers? Will they participate in promotions associated with the sponsorship?
4. **Advantages over competitors**
   - Is the event unique or otherwise distinctive?
   - Has the event previously had sponsors? If so, how successful has it been in delivering the desired benefits to them? Is it strongly associated with other sponsors? Will clutter be a problem?
   - Does the event need co-sponsors? Are other sponsors of the event compatible with the company's product? Does the company want to be associated with them? Will the product stand out and be recognized among them?
   - If there is co-sponsorship, will the product have category and advertising exclusivity?
   - Will competitors have access to signage, hospitality or event advertising? Will competition be allowed to sell the product on site?
   - If the company does not sponsor it, will the competitor? Is that a concern?
5. **Resource investment involvement required**
   - How much is the total sponsorship cost, including such items as related promotional investment, staff time and administrative and implementation effort?

Figure 8.5 Screening criteria used by businesses to determine sponsorship
Source: adapted from Crompton (1993)

- Will the sponsorship investment be unwieldy and difficult to manage?
- What are the levels of barter, in-kind and cash investment?
  Does the event guarantee a minimum level of benefits to the company?

6. Event's characteristics

- What is the perceived stature of the event? Is it the best of its kind? Will involvement with it enhance the product's image?
- Does it have a 'clean' image? Is there any chance that it will be controversial?
- Does it have continuity or is it a one-off?

7. Event organization's reputation

- Does the organization have a proven track record in staging this or other events?
- Does it have the expertise to help the product achieve its sponsorship goals?
- Does the organization have a reputation and an image with which the company desires to be associated?
- Does it have a history of honouring its obligations?
- Has the company worked with this organization before? Was it a positive experience?
- Does it have undisputed control and authority over the activities it sanctions?
- How close to its forecasts has the organization been in delivering benefits to its sponsors?
- How responsive is the organization's staff to sponsors' requests? Are they readily accessible?
- Is there insurance and what are the company's potential liabilities?

8. Entertainment and hospitality opportunities

- Are there opportunities for direct sales of product and related merchandise, or for inducing product trial?
- Will celebrities be available to serve as spokespeople for the product? Will they make personal appearances on its behalf at the event, in other markets, or in the media? At what cost?
- Are tickets to the event included in the sponsorship? How many? Which sessions? Where are the seats located?
- Will there be access to VIP hospitality areas for the company's guests? How many will be authorized? Will celebrities appear?
- Will there be clinics, parties or playing opportunities at which the company's guests will be able to interact with the celebrities?

Figure 8.5 Continued

organizer are met and that category exclusivity for the sponsor is protected to discourage ambushers. Closer event-sponsor relationships may technically be easier to establish in smaller-scale events and festivals, but the business practicalities of having a contract (approved by the lawyers of both parties) makes a lot of sense. If a prolonged period of negotiation is needed for a sponsorship (this is usual for a very large event sponsorship property), having a legal letter of agreement to confirm that the sponsorship will go ahead is important.

To help plan the content of an event sponsorship contract, various sponsorship agreement proformas are available, which can help draft the document for discussion with the sponsor and legal advisors. Grey and Skildum-Reid (2003) offer excellent support materials of this nature in their toolkit. The content of contracts would usually include: the objectives and responsibilities of both parties, benefits to be obtained by the event and the sponsor, termination conditions, ambush marketing protection, details of media, branding and leveraging, the promised exclusivity, marketing and sponsor servicing and insurance and indemnity requirements.

For small events and festivals, the scope and depth of the contract will be reduced (and the cost of legal advice is a key consideration), but often some in-kind (contra) support from a legal service can be obtained by a local community festival.

Managing and 'servicing' sponsorships

Once sponsorship has been secured, it must be effectively managed in order to ensure the benefits that were promised are delivered. Indeed, this is usually a requirement that is spelt out in some depth in sponsorship contracts for large events. However, a sponsorship management plan is critical for events and festivals of all types. This allows the event to show the steps it is taking to satisfy the sponsor's marketing needs listed in the sponsorship agreement and to build a quality relationship with its sponsors. Servicing sponsors can involve everything from maintaining harmonious relationships between a sponsor's staff and people within the event/festival to ensuring sponsor's signage is kept in pristine condition. Some festivals and events also tailor their servicing approach to the sponsor's needs. For example, as discussed in the Cheltenham Festivals case study, although there are a range of options available to potential sponsors, further benefits and approaches can be explored to maximize the sponsorship benefits for the sponsor (and the event). However, there should be no doubt about the level of servicing that a sponsor likes or expects if front-end negotiations have been well managed. Allsop (2004) suggests that at least 10 per cent (but preferably up to 50 per cent) of the sponsorship revenue should be set aside for actively servicing the sponsorship and this management budget needs to be spent wisely.

Communication, commitment and trust between partners

Great relationships between events and sponsors, like any other relationship, are built on a strong foundation of communication, commitment and trust. Smooth working relationships are going to have a strong impact on the sponsor's decision to renew their contract (Aguilar-Manjarrez, Thwaites and Maule, 1997). Research has also shown a link between having a market orientation (a customer-focused approach to doing business) and building commitment, satisfaction and trust between the sponsor partners (Farrelly and Quester, 2003). It appears that sponsors who don't see their event partner as being particularly 'market/consumer-oriented' often engage in less joint-marketing activities with that event. As a result, it is important to establish effective communication with sponsors so that they see the event as a serious marketer who will look for joint leveraging opportunities. Both the sponsor and the event need to have a reasonably equal input to how the sponsorship can be 'tapped', to achieve its full potential. Perceptions by the sponsor of an equitable contribution to the relationship could lead it to look for a more customer-oriented event (Farrelly and Quester, 2003) in its next sponsorship round.

A number of suggestions and actions (based on Geldard and Sinclair, 2003) can be adopted to ensure positive and enduring relations are developed with sponsors:

- *One contact*: one person from the event organization needs to be appointed as the contact point for the sponsor. That person must be readily available (a mobile phone helps), have the authority to make decisions regarding the event and be able to forge harmonious relationships with the sponsor's staff.

- *Understand the sponsor*: a method of maintaining harmonious relationships is to get to know the sponsor's organization, its staff, its products and its marketing strategies. By doing this, it becomes easier to understand the needs of the sponsor and how those needs can be satisfied.
- *Motivate an event organization's staff about the sponsorship*: keeping staff informed of the sponsorship contract, the objectives of the sponsorship and how the sponsor's needs are to be satisfied will help ensure the sponsorship will work smoothly and to the benefit of both parties.
- *Use of celebrities associated with the event*: if the event includes the use of artistic, sporting or theatrical celebrities, ensure sponsors have an opportunity to meet them in a social setting. Most people enjoy immensely the opportunity to tell anecdotes about their brush with the famous!
- *Acknowledge the sponsor at every opportunity*: use all available media to acknowledge the sponsor's assistance. Media that can be used include the public address system at a local festival, newsletters, media releases, the annual report and staff briefings.
- *Sponsorship launch*: have a sponsorship launch to tell the target market about the organizations and agencies that will sponsor the event or festival. The style of the launch depends on the type of sponsorship and the creativity of the event director. Finding an innovative angle to draw media coverage is valuable.
- *Media monitoring*: monitor the media for all stories and commentary about the event or festival that include mention of the sponsor (a media monitoring firm may be contracted to perform this task). This shows the sponsor that the event takes a serious interest in the sponsorship and is alert to the benefits the sponsor is receiving.
- *Principal sponsor*: if the event has many sponsors, ensure the logo of the principal sponsor (that is, the sponsor who has paid the most) is seen on everything to do with the event, including stationery, uniforms, flags, newsletters, stages and so on. Usually, this requirement will be spelt out in legal agreements, but it is important to add value for the principal sponsor wherever it is possible.
- *Naming rights*: if the event has given naming rights to a sponsor (e.g. John Smiths Grand National, Weetabix Women's British Open), it has an obligation to ensure these rights are used in all communications employed by the event organization. This includes making every endeavour to ensure the media are aware of, and adhere to, the sponsored name of the event. Sometimes this is difficult, but it must be attempted so the event holds up its side of the deal.
- *Professionalism*: even though volunteers manage many events, this does not mean that staff can act like amateurs. Sponsors expect to be treated efficiently and effectively, with their reasonable demands met in a speedy manner. Sponsorship is a partnership and loyalty to that partnership is often repaid with an ongoing investment.
- *Undersell and overdeliver*: do not promise what cannot be delivered. Be cautious in formulating your proposal and then ensure the expectations raised by the sponsorship agreement are met and, ideally, exceeded.

There is plenty of evidence of events who have found innovative ways to 'go that extra mile' with their sponsorship relationships. For example, the Wall's Beach at V Festival 2004, partnering Wall's and Virgin Radio, was designed as the 'ultimate festival experience' including sand, palm trees and deck chairs. It was billed as, 'the perfect place to chill in the day and soak up the festival vibe, and as the sun sets let yourself go at the coolest beach party this side of Ibiza!' (Virgin Radio, 2004).

Often, it takes only a little imagination to think of ways in which to prove to sponsors that the event or festival is an active business and marketing partner.

Management action plans to 'service' sponsors

In addition to the sponsorship contract, it is useful to prepare a sponsorship management plan. At its most basic, this *action plan* should identify what objectives the sponsorship will achieve for the sponsor, the benefits that have been promised, costs associated with providing specified benefits, review and evaluation approaches and the timeline for activities that need to be conducted to deliver on the sponsorship. These planning elements are discussed below.

Objectives associated with any given event sponsorship will be tailored to the needs of that partnership, but they should be realistic and measurable (as advised in Chapter 7). Lloyds TSB Scotland sponsored the children's programme at the Edinburgh International Book Festival from 1999 to 2004 (Lloyds TSB Scotland, 2005, p. 9). The rationale for the sponsorship was that they were supporting the premier event of its kind in the world for children bringing literature, language and ideas to a wide and diverse audience, while providing the opportunity to penetrate an audience which is difficult to reach. The key objectives were to provide product placement for the Young Savers account and continue Lloyds TSB Scotland's commitment to education by increasing the number and range of events. The event and sponsor set out some specific performance measures for evaluation. The outcomes from the sponsorship included:

- achieving 77 per cent sponsors recognition,
- increasing sales of the young savers account,
- doubling ticket sales since the start of the sponsorship,
- increasing exposure of visitors to the brand as visitor numbers to Edinburgh International Book Festival increased from 70 000 in 1999 to 207 000 in 2004,
- the 2004 Lloyds TSB Children's Programme included 185 events with 110 authors, over 40 workshops and 30 storytelling sessions,
- increasing the percentage of schools attending from outside Edinburgh from 15 per cent in 2002 to 60 per cent in 2003,
- attracting Arts & Business funding of £37 500 for Bus Fund and Schools Gala Day in 2002–03 and
- involving Lloyds TSB staff – assisting with the Bus and Schools Gala Day, staffing the Activity Corner and making more than 250 tickets available for hospitality and family use (Lloyds TSB Scotland, 2005, pp. 9–10).

Stakeholders affected by the sponsorship also need to be addressed in the management plan – these groups would include attendees, members of the broader community in which the event is taking place, staff of the sponsoring organization and media. All *benefits and associated actions* need to be clearly identified, along with the target group(s) to be reached and *costs* (financial or otherwise) that are associated with them. These costs might include signage manufacture and erection, supporting advertisements, promotional material, prize money, sponsor hospitality costs, professional fees, labour costs associated with hosting sponsors on-site, tickets, postage and preparation of an evaluation report. A budget needs to present all costs and show those costs in the context of the overall value of the sponsorship. Figure 8.6 provides a checklist of items to be included in a sponsorship budget (see Chapter 10 for more information on preparing budgets). It should also be remembered that sponsorship (both in-kind and cash) attracts tax, and this tax must be factored into any bottom line calculations.

Items that will incur cash outlays or person cost (£), hours to support the sponsorship
- Event programmes
- Additional printing
- Signage production
- Signage erection
- Support advertising
- Hospitality – food and beverage
- Telephone, Internet and fax
- Public relations support
- Tickets for sponsors
- VIP parking passes
- Cost of selling sponsorship (staff time at £ per hour)
- Cost of servicing sponsorship (staff time at £ per hour)
- Legal costs
- Travel costs
- Taxis and other transport
- Evaluation research/report
- Media monitoring

Total costs
Profit margin
Minimum sponsorship sale price

Figure 8.6 A checklist of items to be included in a sponsorship budget

A list of the *actions* necessary to fulfil the sponsorship should be made, specifying what is to be done and who is responsible. Mapping out all of the management and marketing activities on a spreadsheet or other form of graphic display can be a useful exercise.

An *evaluation and review* process needs to be built into the sponsorship management plan. The review process should be ongoing and act to identify and address any problems that could affect sponsorship outcomes. Evaluation is concerned with providing a clear understanding of how the sponsorship performed against the objectives that were set for it. Evaluation seeks to answer questions such as: Did the promised media coverage eventuate? Did the attendee profile of the event reflect the market profile described in the sponsorship proposal? What was the overall quality of the sponsorship's delivery and management? Evaluation also gives the partners the chance to fine tune the sponsorship arrangements, so both parties are well placed to renew the partnership. In general terms, the development of the sponsorship business plan can be a creative and rewarding task that simply serves to communicate to the sponsor that its investment is being managed professionally.

Measuring and evaluating the sponsorship

A shared responsibility of the event or festival and its sponsor is the measurement of the overall impact of the partnership. There are two components to measurement and evaluation: first, the evaluation of the effectiveness of the partnership and how the sponsor and event have contributed to it and, second, the measurement of the consumer-related marketing objectives set by the sponsor. While most events seek some feedback from their sponsors about the effectiveness of their sponsorship management, much more effort needs to be devoted to measuring the consumer effects of sponsorship. Many events have limited budgets for conducting sophisticated market research (and should consider some of the techniques suggested in Chapter 7), but many sponsors also do surprisingly little research to determine whether their investment in an event was warranted in terms of value for money. The IEG/Performance Research 2004 Sponsorship Decision-Making Survey found that 41 per cent of participating companies did not currently undertake any measurement of their sponsorships and 43 per cent spent 1 per cent or less of the rights fee on evaluation (Performance Research, 2004). This contrasts with advertising campaigns where pre- and post-testing of consumer effects is commonplace.

Some of the factors that complicate the measurement of sponsorship are that brand marketers often use a number of media, including sponsorship, to create brand relationships and there are often carry-over effects of previous media and marketing expenditure on brand awareness and image (De Pelsmacker, Geuens and Van den Bergh, 2004). Of particular importance in sponsorship measurement is the use of audience research that measures unaided and aided recognition of the event sponsor's name (sponsor awareness), attitudes towards the sponsor and any actions/behaviours that the sponsorship has caused in its target audience (this could be a signed contract on an important deal for a business-to-business bank client or a driver who has reduced their driving speed as a result of the sponsor's event messages).

While there is a need for more formal research (and publicly available findings) about the effects of sponsorship, it is clear that some sponsors of big budget event properties are becoming very rigorous about their measurement of the value of sponsorship.

Chapter summary

Overall, it is clear that there is a marked contrast in the effort and expenditure devoted to measuring sponsorship effects across different events and festivals and among sponsors themselves. What is clear is that marketing budgets and sponsorship expenditure are subject to tighter scrutiny as competition for funds increases – it is timely, therefore, for all events and festivals and sponsorship managers (who also compete for budgets in their companies) to review their measurement tools. Sponsorship has increasingly become a mainstream component of the marketing communication media of many corporations and public sector organizations. Influences on sponsorship growth worldwide can be found in the business and marketing environment and in the diversity of consumer and stakeholder benefits that sponsorships create.

From an event's perspective, sponsorship often (but not always) represents a significant potential revenue stream. Yet, sponsorships are fast becoming business partnerships that offer resources beyond money. To succeed in the sponsorship stakes, event organizers must thoughtfully develop policies and strategies, providing a clear framework for both events/festivals and sponsors to decide on the value and suitability of potential partnerships. Having an inventory of the event or festival assets available for sale is an important starting point for those seeking sponsorship.

The sponsorship approach should be based on comprehensive research at the front end before a formal proposal is written and submitted to potential sponsors. Event managers need to embrace the full range of benefits that organizations seek through their sponsorship, and formalize and manage their agreements so that commitments made to sponsors are met. This Chapter has provided critical insights into how to manage communication with sponsors as the event's business partners, how to maximize joint marketing opportunities and how to gain the long-term trust and commitment of sponsoring firms and agencies.

Questions

1. What is the difference between looking at event sponsorships as transactions versus business relationships?
2. Identify at least five trends that explain the expanded use of sponsorship as a marketing medium.
3. Identify a public sector organization that is sponsoring one or more events and contact the person responsible for sponsorship. Ask them what they are trying to achieve through their sponsorship strategy and how they assess the outcomes.
4. Name an event or festival for which sponsorship may be inappropriate and discuss why you have formed this conclusion.
5. Obtain several non-current sponsorship proposals from event organizers/corporate sponsorship managers. Critically evaluate the content and presentation of these documents in the light of what you have read in this chapter.
6. Identify a festival or event of interest to you and state the steps that you would follow in identifying potential sponsors for this event.
7. Investigate a specific recurring event with a view to identifying the potential assets and benefits it might be able to offer sponsors. Are all of these assets currently being offered to sponsors? If not, what reasons could exist for these assets being untapped?
8. Select an event and contact its organizers with a view to determining whether they have developed sponsorship policies or sponsorship business plans. Establish why they have, or have not, done so. If they have developed one or both of these documents, investigate how the content was decided.

Case study 8.1

Microsoft UK's Sponsorship of the 2002 Commonwealth Games

Introduction

At the end of 2000, Microsoft UK was approached by the Manchester 2002 Commonwealth Games Organising Committee, M2002 Limited, to become a sponsor following the demise of Atlantic Telecom which had been signed up previously. Prior to the approach, Microsoft UK had never undertaken sponsorship before of any kind. Sarah Fasey, the Commonwealth Games project director for Microsoft UK, takes up the story, 'Our local office supplied software to the original M2002 organizing committee as a community giving project. What became clear was that it was a much bigger and more complex project and after a series of meetings we saw it as a fantastic opportunity for Microsoft UK and that we should be there'.

The activity was weighed up against other marketing activities and it was considered that the Games gave Microsoft a broader opportunity not only to support image and reputation objectives but to showcase technology and entertain customers. Microsoft UK therefore became the official software and technology partner of the 2002 Commonwealth Games. Susan Hunt, who was general manager of sponsorship for M2002 Limited, is clear in defining the objectives from the event perspective at that time, 'We wanted a leading edge approach but not a bleeding edge approach. The Games are very risk adverse so we needed be sure we could absolutely deliver what was the minimum standard excellently. So we wanted solidity and a company that could make it happen'. She continues, 'We had to have delivery. We also sought companies that could pick up our brand values and run with them as well. We were lucky in Microsoft that we could deliver the two. But the priority in this instance was being able to deliver'.

Objectives and target audiences

Microsoft UK provided the first ever single technology platform for a major multi-venue sports event. Fasey explains, 'M2002 wanted the simplicity of one single platform. In the past, such as in previous Olympics, you had lots of different IT companies involved and then you had to spend a bunch of money on systems integration because of the different systems and then you needed a whole bunch of people to help you integrate them all. They [M2002] didn't want to be forced down the road of having to involve lots of different consultants to make the system work'. M2002's Hunt expands, 'To be able to deal with one partner with the size, clout and capacity of Microsoft UK was a definite advantage. There is no better IT company that we could have worked with'.

Financial details

So did any money change hands or did Microsoft UK just supply peoplepower and kit? According to Betty Maitland, who is a sponsorship consultant to Microsoft UK and was involved in the M2002 sponsorship, 'The majority was in value in kind. However, it is generally known that top tier sponsors paid $3million'. Microsoft UK's Fasey adds, 'They needed comprehensive infrastructure to run the games on, multiple sports, athlete tracking, managing the athletes' village, media centre, etc. They needed a lot of support from the hardware and software perspective so it was largely a value in kind deal'.

Marketing

According to Microsoft UK's Fasey the company wanted to get three things out of the games. 'One was to showcase our technology which we did. It was the first ever single multisports event to run on one platform – in this case Windows – and it was very successful. Secondly we wanted to exploit hospitality and we got fantastic feedback. We took 1400 customers during the course of the 10 days'. Post event research carried out by the Event Marketing team showed 89 per cent gave top scores for the experience and 100 per cent would attend similar hospitality. 'The third thing was to demonstrate that we were good guys really and that we are a business in the UK and contribute to the UK', adds Fasey.

Fasey feels that prior to the Games, 'the general public was quite cynical I think and the Games didn't have a lot of noise around them. But the minute they started everyone got behind them and we got good feedback internally largely due to the fact that we'd done something visible that our employees could be proud of'.

Execution and exploitation

Technology

The technology platform involved a team from Microsoft UK working as a partner to M2002 during the 18 month build up to the Games. Fasey explained, 'We had some of our people there helping design, build and make sure it was working. Then there were support people on site to sort out any bugs or faults so that there weren't any problems from the users' perspective. So we had a team of around 20 supporting staff there during the Games on site 24/7'. And further help was never far away if needed adds Fasey, 'We had our people on site but if something had happened that they couldn't fix then they would have been calling on the bigger teams in Reading, London and the US. They would have had access to whatever resources were needed to fix it'.

Awareness/image and reputation

Awareness of the sponsorship was promoted to achieve several image and reputation objectives. Microsoft supported UK athletics events in the build up to the Games which gave opportunities to promote Microsoft's involvement in the Commonwealth Games to the TV audience and also to gain a greater understanding of the way major sports events worked out. In terms of internal promotion Microsoft UK had great fun according to Fasey. 'We had a relationship with Tanni Grey Thompson as part of our marketing programme and she came to our head office a few times, she came to our charity day and sports day which got people engaged. She also spoke at our company conference which was very inspiring. We also had competitions to win tickets to go to the event and looked for volunteers to be involved on site. We also put an Internet Cafe into the athletes village and we had our own people there to show people how to use e-mail and Xboxes, etc.'.

Managing the sponsorship process

According to M2002's Hunt, the event's modus operandi was inspired by the Olympics and was aimed at teaching sponsors to leverage an involvement 'without the branding and the easy stuff such as signage and hospitality. It's more about what are the things that are going to help you fulfil your marketing objectives through this property. It's more of a marketing proposition'.

Regular sponsor workshops were held in the build up to the Games. Hunt says, 'In retrospect we would have made them less process-driven and more inspirational/ ideas-driven. The problem was that there were so many first time sponsors that we had to make the workshops very prescriptive in terms of timing, ticket applications, etc, the basic stuff. That took up so much time that we didn't have enough time to inspire them on how they could leverage their sponsorships. We did provide case studies and encourage them to do various things and most of them did'.

The workshops were combined rather than aimed at individual sponsors explains Hunt, 'For example, Cadbury spoke about what they did during the Olympics in Sydney and we had various speakers from time to time to inspire all the sponsors. Regular work in progresses ended up being held monthly'.

There were two camps of sponsors according to Hunt, 'Those involved from a marketing perspective and those who were also suppliers such as Asda supplying food and Microsoft providing IT. There were therefore dual work in progresses – ones where we treating them as a client and ones where we treating them as a supplier. Contact reports were all circulated so everyone knew where everyone was up to. There was regular phone contact too'.

Outcome and evaluation

M2002 and Microsoft UK are proud that a single technology platform was achieved. Says Microsoft UK's Fasey, 'It [the single platform] made it a much simpler process. In terms of cost it was 10 times cheaper than the previous Winter Olympics at Salt Lake City which is a comparable size'.

In terms of measuring the success of the sponsorship Hunt believes there are lessons to be learned: 'Because Microsoft and many of the sponsors came on relatively late in the piece, there was a scramble towards the end in terms of measurement. There could have been more benchmarking and we did try and encourage them but there wasn't much time. We did everything we could to facilitate that but it something we could have done better'.

Research of Games spectators by Intrepid showed 32 per cent perceived Microsoft much more positively and 48 per cent slightly more positively. Microsoft's involvement was positively received as respondents did not expect a large US company to be a sponsor. Overall there was a 13 per cent shift in attitude with 84 per cent of this positive.

Microsoft's infrastructure successfully demonstrated scalability to major enterprise customers and provided a valuable case study. Xbox became the official console and provided an onsite consumer experience resulting in 45 000 trials. Xboxes were also well received in the Athletes Villages resulting in 13 000 visits. An MSN dedicated Games channel received 240 000 hits and 6000 competition entries.

Lessons to be learned

According to Microsoft UK's sponsorship consultant Maitland, 'As a first time sponsor, valuable lessons were learnt about the amount of budget needed to support any future sponsorship; the commitment by all parts of the company and the need for technology partners to fully exploit the technology category'.

M2002's Hunt believes the sponsorship couldn't have gone more smoothly as far as the operations were concerned. 'The biggest success was that the Games imposed a personality on Microsoft and showed people the fun side through hospitality and gaming. It wasn't all clinical IT stuff, it was showing how technology can impact people in day to day life and put a relaxed informality on everything they did'. Nothing was ever a problem with Microsoft UK adds Hunt, 'They were terrific friends and neighbours. We were amazed how friendly an organization they are and that they really are a separate company to the US one and driven by the values of this country [the UK]. They proved themselves to be relaxed and competent. It was a really good partnership'.

Maitland comments, 'The Commonwealth Games provided the first sponsorship to really work as integrated marketing. Sport was seen to be a highly visual way of demonstrating Microsoft's products'.

But would Microsoft UK do it all again? Fasey wouldn't rule it out, 'We are certain that we would do something similar again. It was a new experience and a lot of hard work but we are glad that we did it and learned a lot'. Microsoft UK has no other sponsorships planned at the moment, but according to Fasey, 'We are feeling our way through a couple of proposals at the moment'. And one can't help but think that an Olympics hosted by London in 2012 would be high up on Microsoft UK's wish list.

For further information on the impact of technology on the business of sport, please visit www.sportandtechnology.com.

By Rachael Church, Editor, Sport and Technology.

Questions

1. Discuss how well Microsoft's evaluation of its sponsorship reflects the sponsorship effects process shown in Figure 8.3.
2. Select five key benefits of event sponsorship and briefly explain how Microsoft achieved those benefits from its sponsorship of the 2002 Manchester Commonwealth Games.
3. Using Ansoff's product–market matrix, discuss the strategies that Microsoft appeared to achieve from its sponsorship. In your discussion, use examples from the above case study.

Case study 8.2

Cheltenham Arts Festivals
Background

Cheltenham's festivals and entertainment programme is organized and promoted by the Festivals & Entertainments Division of Cheltenham Borough Council (CBC), in conjunction with Cheltenham Arts Festivals Ltd (CAF), a registered charity, which is administered from within the Division, sharing resources, staffing and office space. CAF is responsible for the organization and promotion of four annual festivals: Cheltenham Jazz Festival (May), the Cheltenham International Festival of Music (July), the Cheltenham Festival of Science (June) and the Cheltenham Festival of Literature (October). Also included in the season is the Cheltenham Folk Festival (February) and a year round programme of events at the Town Hall and Pittville Pump Room.

The Cheltenham Festival of Science is the newcomer among the festivals – launched in 2002, this five – day festival includes topical debates, talks, workshops, an interactive science space (the Discover Zone) and a mix of live art installations, experiments and cinema. Since 2002 the festival has attracted over 100 000 to the Discover Zone and sold over 50 000 tickets to over 400 events.

The Cheltenham Jazz Festival – since starting in 1996 the festival now attracts an audience of over 17 000. A five-day event, the festival hosts an array of popular international jazz stars alongside the best new and more adventurous artists. With a varied and adventurous programme, the Festival has successfully made its mark in the UK's music calendar, challenging the stylistic boundaries set by other festivals and developing new audiences in jazz.

The Cheltenham International Festival of Music is the longest running of the festivals and was also the first of the post-war festivals in the UK. Beginning in 1945 as a showcase for British contemporary music, in recent times Michael Berkeley (Artistic Director until 2004) expanded the festival's repertoire to include contemporary music from across Europe. In addition to presenting orchestral, chamber, choral and solo music alongside contemporary music-theatre and opera, the seventeen-day festival boasts an afternoon series, which features the very best in young and local musical talent, as well as a late-night strand of programming, commencing at ten in the evening. The new director, Martyn Brabbins, has succeeded in making the event even more accessible, with increasing attendances at the family events. The 2005 festival was a huge success, with ticket sales reaching 17 000 and hundreds more taking advantage of the free events programmed throughout the Festival, 19 events completely sold-out and an impressive 15 world premieres and 8 UK premieres performed.

The Cheltenham Literature Festival, with The Times as headline sponsor in 2005 in association with Ottaker's, began in 1949 when Gloucestershire writer John Moore organized a gathering of writers to celebrate the written word in Cheltenham. Over the last decade the festival has grown rapidly, with annual ticket sales now in the tens of thousands. At the heart of the festival is the love of literature and the art of the book, with additional strands including *Book It!*, all taking place in venues all over Cheltenham. The established ten-day Autumn Festival is complemented by a three-day Spring Events Weekend in April.

Sponsorship

The festivals seek funding for events, concerts and projects within the Education and Outreach Programmes from a wide range of sources including public funding bodies, commercial organizations, foundations and trusts and sponsorship. Sponsorship of the Festivals offers:

- a partnership with an important international brand
- a method of increasing brand awareness and raising company profile
- an opportunity for corporate hospitality and client entertaining
- an association with excellence and creativity
- a way of demonstrating commitment to the community

Benefits

There are a range of benefits to be gained through sponsorship of each of the Festivals. These are tailored to suit individual requirements but can include the following:

- branding and product promotion initiatives
- corporate hospitality
- networking and business development opportunities
- on-site sampling
- accreditation in 100 000 colour brochures, the main print vehicle
- opportunity to meet artists
- complimentary tickets in prime seat locations
- staff discount schemes
- website links
- priority booking

Each of the Cheltenham Festivals also offers its own unique benefits to sponsors:

- *Jazz*: Cheltenham Jazz Festival is acclaimed as one of the leading festivals of its kind. The audience, largely young professionals, enjoys its leisure time and the Jazz Festival offers excellent opportunities for highly targeted reach with brand promotions and product sampling.
- *Science*: The phenomenally successful Cheltenham Science Festival is winning praise from the science community for its innovation and pioneering ethos. The Festival features many

exclusive benefits for its sponsors, including opportunities for business to business marketing, brand promotion and corporate entertainment. The Festival achieves a perfect balance between accessibility and integrity, featuring debates, lectures, interactive family events, schools workshops and more.

- *Music*: The Cheltenham Music Festival is renowned for showcasing the very best of international contemporary music alongside a well established traditional programme. The core audience is extremely loyal – over half are mature professionals with high levels of disposable income. The Festival provides exceptional opportunities for corporate hospitality, so why not entertain your clients with a champagne lunch after a morning recital, or dinner after a concert?
- *Literature*: The Times Cheltenham Literature Festival is not only one of the oldest and largest literary events in Europe, it is also one of the most accessible, offering a rare chance to listen to debates and lectures, meet authors and see beyond the written word. The audience is diverse and sponsors can be carefully matched to individual events, providing companies with excellent opportunities for both niche marketing and relationship building.

Types of sponsorship

There are six types of sponsorship associated with Cheltenham Festivals:

1. **Association:** An association with the Cheltenham Festivals brand is sure to raise the profile of any organization, and above all we are interested in working with our sponsors to build mutually-rewarding, long-term relationships.
2. **Fees:** The sponsorship fees reflect the status of the performers, profile of the event, place in the programme, how much visibility the sponsoring organization requires and organizational costs. Shared sponsorship packages between two or more sponsors are available by arrangement. Fee levels vary between Festivals based on specific sponsorship opportunities, but the following gives a general indication:

   - Title Sponsorship £50 000 – £60 000
   - Principal Sponsors £15 000 – £35 000
   - Major Sponsors £8000 and above
   - Festival Partners £3000 and above
   - Festival Sponsors £1000 and above
   - In Kind and Co-sponsoring are also considered.

3. **Title Sponsorship:** Title Sponsorship packages are built around the sponsoring organization's requirements, but a key benefit is the profile achieved by incorporating the company logo within the Festival logo on all literature and banners erected at Festival venues and throughout Cheltenham prior to and during the Festival.
4. **Principal Sponsors:** Principal Sponsorship is most suited to organizations requiring high level exposure and a flexible package. At this level we provide ideal opportunities for product and brand promotion, such as named sponsorship and full branding of a key venue like the Festival Marquee and Arena or branding of the Festival Bags (5000–10 000 units per Festival). Further brand awareness can be generated by being named sponsor of a series of headline events, or even a series co-programmed with the sponsor, for example, the Swan Hellenic's Better to Travel series at the 2004 Literature Festival.
5. **Leaving a Legacy:** Individuals can make a positive contribution to the Arts by leaving a legacy to the Cheltenham Festivals. This could be used in a number of ways including sponsorship of a concert / event, supporting the education strands or commissioning new works in your name. A will is a chance to help the organizations that have been important in their lifetime.

6. **Patrons of the Festivals:** The support of Patrons makes a real difference to the quality of the Festival programme. Benefits of the Gold and Festival Patrons' scheme include a dedicated booking line, information about Festival events from the Festival Directors in advance and invitations to Festival Parties and receptions throughout the year.

A sponsorship launch is held in advance of each festival with the purpose of releasing programme information to potential sponsors and supporters. A sponsorship pack is collated for the launch, containing an overview of the festival themes, an outline of the benefits to be gained through sponsorship and full details of all events, print sponsorship opportunities and Education and Outreach projects available. Packs are also distributed to those unable to attend the launch. The CAF also produces a corporate sponsorship brochure, intended for distribution to potential new, and predominantly national, commercial sponsors, and a quarterly newsletter which contains news and information about the festivals with particular emphasis on sponsorship and the benefits it brings. This newsletter is targeted mainly at a local and regional audience in the business sector.

Summary

Sponsorship provides a source of funding and offers a range of other benefits to the festivals. As a result, a professional team are in place to attract and manage the sponsorship, which currently comprises a Head of Sponsorship and Science Festival Fundraiser, Trusts and Individual Giving Manager, Jazz Festival Fundraiser, Sponsorship Officer, Sponsorship Coordinator, and a Database and Research Coordinator. In August 2005, the website was re-launched in order to provide a clearer image for the Cheltenham Festivals brand and increase access to information about the festivals including news, sponsorship and education and outreach. The programme of festivals and events in Cheltenham has developed over the years to gain an enviable reputation for some of the most prestigious cultural events, which bring significant benefits to Cheltenham and the surrounding region, including an estimated economic impact of £34 million (Brookes and Landry, 2002). The challenge for the team is in attracting appropriate sponsors for the Cheltenham Festivals brand, which will continue to provide some of the funds necessary for the festivals to develop now and in the future.

For more details about the Cheltenham Festivals, please visit www.cheltenhamfestivals. com.

By Cheltenham Arts Festivals Ltd.

Questions

1. Focusing on one of the festivals, describe the target market in demographic and socioeconomic terms.
2. What factors would a potential sponsor look for when considering whether to sponsor the festival identified in question 1?
3. How would you break down the festival in order to maximize income from sponsorship for the festival, and the benefits gained by the sponsor?
4. Based on what you have read within the case study, and your identified target markets, what companies would find sponsorship of the festival a worthwhile investment of their marketing resources? Briefly explain the appropriateness of each sponsor to the festival.
5. Construct a sponsorship pack for the sponsorship launch.
6. Design a corporate sponsorship brochure.

Section Three

Event management

This part of the book looks at the systems that event managers can use to put the event plan into action. The chapter on project management looks at how to integrate the various event plans. The following chapter looks at controlling events and, in particular how the budget process can be used as a controlling mechanism in the implementation of an event. The chapter on legal and risk management describes the legal factors that event managers need to be aware of, and how to identify, minimize and manage the risks inherent in an event. This section also looks at the staging of events, and the evaluation and reporting process.

Chapter 9
Project management for events

Introduction

The production of a festival or event is a project. There are many advantages in using project management techniques to manage the event or festival. Project management oversees the initiation, planning and implementation of the event, in addition to monitoring the event and the shutdown. It aims to integrate management plans from different knowledge areas into a cohesive, workable plan for the entire project.

This chapter examines how the project manager fits into the event management structure. There are specific tools and techniques used by project managers, the chapter then explores the most common of these. It moves onto examine how evaluation of a project can build on the project management knowledge base to improve future project performance. Finally, some limitations of the project management approach to event management are outlined.

Project management

According to the leading textbooks on project management, world business is moving towards the accomplishment of business objectives through separate projects. Gray and Larson (2000, p. 3), quoting *Fortune Magazine* and the *Wall Street Journal*, call it 'the wave of the future'. Due to the changing nature of modern business, products and services now have to be managed as projects as a response to this change. A product in the modern world is continually evolving. Software upgrades are an example of this, and they create an environment that is constantly evolving. Authors such as Burke (2003). Lock (2003) and Slack, Chambers and Johnston (2004) have extensively discussed project management, while O'Toole and Mikolaitis (2002), Shone and Parry (2004) and Tum, Norton and Wright (2005) have explored this specifically within the events context.

O'Toole and Mikolaitis (2002), in their text on corporate event project management, note that the expansion of the event industry is a result of this change. New events are needed to launch products: new conferences and seminars are needed to educate the market and new festivals are needed to reposition towns and regions in the marketplace as the national economy changes. Government departments are not immune from this. The UK Government organized a number of conferences and meetings during the 2005 UK Presidency of the European Union, for example, the UK Presidency Better Regulation Conference targeted at senior business leaders, ministers of EU countries with an interest in regulation, European Commission representatives and members of the European Parliament.

As project management is used to manage these developments, the events industry appreciates that these techniques can be successfully employed in events. Events and festivals can been seen as a response to a constantly changing business and cultural environment and that they are projects – they can import increasingly pervasive management methodology.

What is a project?

Gray and Larson (2000, p. 4) provide a succinct definition:

> *a project is a complex nonroutine one-time effort limited by time, budget, resources and performance specifications designed to meet customer needs.*

According to this definition, special events and festivals are projects. The project produces an asset such as a building, film, software system or even a man on the moon – or a special event or festival. The asset is the ultimate deliverable of the project. The management is the planning, organizing, leading and controlling of the project.

The project management of events concentrates on the management process to create the event, not just what happens at the event. Many texts and articles confuse the event with its management. The event is the deliverable of a management process. A bridge, for example, is the deliverable of a series of processes called engineering and construction. The event may take place over a period of hours or days. The event management process may take place over many months or years. Project management is a system that describes the work before the event actually starts, the event and finally the shutdown of the event.

Project management is called the 'overlay' as it integrates all the tasks of management. Event management is made up of a number of management areas, including planning, leading, marketing, design, control and budgeting, risk management, logistics, staging and evaluation. Each of the areas continuously affect each other over the event life cycle. Project management can be regarded as integrating all of these disciplines; thus it covers all the different areas of management and integrates them so they all work towards the event objectives.

O'Toole and Mikolaitis (2002, p. 23) describe the advantages of using project management for events:

1. It is a systematic approach that can be improved with every event. Project management describes the management system. Once something is described it can be improved. If it remains hidden there is nothing to improve.
2. It avoids the risk that the event's success relies on one person. By having a system with documentation, filing and manuals, as well as clear communication and teams, the event is understood by anyone with the right experience.
3. It uses a common terminology and therefore facilitates clear, timely communication.
4. It ensures accountability to the stakeholders. Stakeholder management is a fundamental knowledge area of project management.
5. It makes the management of the event apparent. Too often the management is hidden by the importance of the event.
6. It helps train staff. Project management provides a framework for step-by-step training of the staff.
7. It is used in all other areas of management, not just events. The management methodology used for the event can be transferred to any project. Once the event is over the staff will find they have learned a useful transferable skill.
8. It is common to other businesses. Many of the event stakeholders will already be familiar with the terminology.

Points 4 and 5 are related to the event itself being mistaken for the management. Clear and timely accountability to numerous event stakeholders is a requirement for event managers. The accountability cannot wait until the event is delivered. Stakeholders, such as the police, sponsors and government may want a series of reports on the progress of the management. It is too late to find out that the management company was incompetent during the event. Clients are demanding a work in progress (WIP) report. A project management system has this reporting facility as a part of the methodology.

Project management comprises basic concepts that are not necessarily found in ongoing management. As described in Gray and Larson's (2000) definition of a project, it has a specific completion date, budget and product. This product or deliverable cannot be improved except by commencing on another project. Unlike ongoing management, such as a company continually producing a product and adapting it, a project has to produce the best product the first time. There is no time for improvement. In the words of the music industry 'you are only as good as your last gig'. The management of the project passes through phases. The management has to be aware of the knowledge areas and the way they change over the project life cycle.

Phases of the project management of events

A project will pass through a series of phases or stages. Figure 9.1 illustrates these phases.

A project phase is a series of related tasks, performed over a period of time and under a particular configuration of management to produce a major deliverable.

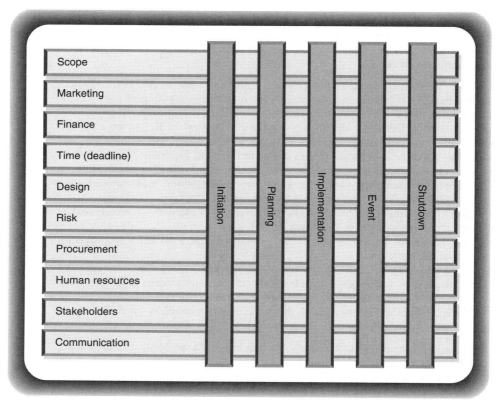

Figure 9.1 The phases of project management
Source: O'Toole (2004)

The end of a phase is often characterized by a major decision to begin the next phase. There are a number of different views on project phases. Some texts on project management for software development describe up to seven phases. Civil engineering texts have four phases of project management described in the *Guide to the Project Management Body of Knowledge, 2000 (PMI, 2000)*. Event and festival management is accurately portrayed as having five phases. The phase approach to describing the management is purely descriptive – as with any description, it approximates reality. The aim is to provide clarity to the confusing tasks involved in event management. Some project phases overlap – planning and implementation can take place at the same time in different areas of management. The promotion schedule, for example, may be happening at the same time as aspects of the programme are being redesigned. This chaos, however, does have a pattern and the five-phase approach is a useful tool to help the reader to understand it.

Initiation

The first phase of initiation is characterized by the idea of the event being developed and setting the objectives. It may be a vague idea, for example, that a town should organize a heritage festival or a promoter decides to organize a rock concert. As well as this event concept, the initiation phase may include a feasibility study.

In corporate events, this stage may be characterized by producing an event proposal and pitching for the client's business. The project feasibility study will report on the viability of the event and the management required to deliver it. It may include site and date suggestions, possible sponsors and supporters, a draft budget, possible risks, required management for the event and event logistics. The feasibility study or proposal may incorporate a number of alternative configurations of the event, so that the sponsor or client can choose the best options that will suit them. The initiation phase interfaces and overlaps with the process of conceptualizing the event as discussed in Chapter 4 and with the strategic planning process as set out in Chapter 5. The project objectives will relate to the objectives of the host in sponsoring the event.

The business case for the project is often used as a form of feasibility study. It describes the reason for the event in terms of the return on investment to the host community or company. The end of the initiation phase is characterized by a 'go/no-go' decision – whether to proceed with the event or not.

Planning

The second phase is the project planning. Planning is characterized by working out what is needed and how it will fit together. Chapter 5 discusses this phase in detail from a strategic point of view. Each of the knowledge areas on the left side of Figure 9.1 will produce a separate plan. A major role of project management is to integrate all these plans; that is, to make sure they all work together. For this reason the plans are often called baseline plans. They are regarded as a starting point rather than a finished plan. Once the plans have been formulated they need to be implemented.

Implementation

Implementation is the third phase. The characteristics of this phase in project managing events are:

- the application of all the plans, such as hiring staff, sending out requests for tender, confirming contractors and carrying out the promotional schedule
- monitoring and controlling – testing the plans and confirming how relevant they are as the organizing progresses
- making decisions based on the comparison between the plans and reality
- work in progress reporting to the key stakeholders
- active risk management.

The beginning of this phase is a time of high activity with meetings to discuss specific issues, decisions to be made and communication between various parties. The management may need to visit the planning phase when there are major changes and the plans need to be revised. At this time, the team has to be focused on the project scope and ensure all the plans are compatible with each other and with the overall objectives of the event.

In traditional project management, this third phase is the final phase and involves handover of the deliverable. Events are not a tangible asset that can be handed over in the same way as a building. For this reason, it is wise to add an extra phase into the project phases and call this 'the event'.

The event

Unlike civil engineering project management, the project event manager is working during the deliverable; that is, the event. Although this is not seen as a separate phase by traditional texts on project management, it fits into the definition above. During the event, the tasks and responsibilities tend to roll on regardless of what the management wants to have happen. The staff numbers during the event, including volunteers, may increase dramatically. The short-time period, attendance of the major stakeholders, the audience and the participants, means that the management cannot rely on the same management techniques used during the lead-up to the event. This is recognized in all events, when the operations manager, artistic director or the stage manager takes over the running of the event. In the theatre, at an agreed time before the show, the stage manager is regarded as the ultimate authority. At a certain time before the event the management team will move into 'operations mode', which might mean getting out of the office and into their costumes for the event. The monitoring and controlling at this point will be devolved to other teams and the management will run the event by looking for errors and making on-the-spot decisions. The tools and techniques used by management during this phase are found in Chapter 13 on staging.

Shutdown

The event manager will be responsible for the shutdown of the event. It is the last phase and requires a separate series of tasks and responsibilities. Management will be scaled down and return to their pre-event formation. Chapter 12 describes the processes use in event shutdown. This phase includes the on-site shutdown and the management closure. The shutdown plans will be created during the planning phase, and the shutdown ideally is the implementation of these plans. However, in an industry beset by major changes, the shutdown will rarely go exactly to plan. Monitoring and decision making from management will be needed. The shutdown phase can take the event from a seeming success to a failure if the management does not make the right decisions at this time. Shutdown includes preparation for the next event. On-site, this includes packing for the next event; Off-site, the management will be archiving the documents and assessing their management. It is during this phase that the success of the management system is evaluated and the baseline plans or templates created for future events.

In summary, the best way to describe the event management process from a project management perspective is in terms of five phases: initiation, planning, implementation, the event and shutdown. These phases comprise the life cycle of the project. Each of the phases will require different management techniques and tools. Different areas of knowledge will be used. During the event, the event management team will be monitoring the event for any changes, rather than initiating any major new actions.

Knowledge areas

The management of any festival or special event will be concerned with the areas illustrated on the left side of Figure 9.1. The relative importance of each of these management areas will change and evolve over the phases. From this figure, the event itself is seen as a small part of the whole management process.

As mentioned in the planning section, management will produce a number of deliverables in each of these knowledge areas. In the finance area, for example, management will produce a financial plan and budget. The marketing area will produce a marketing plan and a promotion plan. The design area will produce the site plan and the actual event programme. These deliverables are used throughout the management process to organize the event. They focus the staff in each individual area and become the documentation of the event. The areas correspond to the departments of an ongoing business organization. The project management approach seeks to integrate the plans from each separate knowledge area into a cohesive, workable plan for the project.

PMBoK 2000™ (the *project management body of knowledge*) lists nine areas of knowledge for traditional project management areas: scope, cost, time, integration, procurement, quality, human resources, communication and risk (PMI, 2000). Event management is slightly different. It will also be concerned with marketing and designing the event. In the construction industry, the project manager would rarely be involved in designing the building, finding the money to build it or making decisions on the building's marketability. These are major concerns for the event and festival manager. These areas of project management knowledge can be explained as follows:

- *Scope* encompasses all the work, including all the plans, and is defined further in this chapter. The scope, therefore, helps to integrate the many plans. Controlling the scope is a fundamental responsibility of the project manager.
- *Marketing* is a combination of processes that help define the event and, therefore, the scope of the event. Marketing is described in Chapter 7. Marketing the asset is not a traditional separate function of project management; however, some of the modern texts on civil engineering and software projects are teaching aspects of marketing. As described in Chapter 10, marketing may be regarded as a feed-forward control mechanism for events and as a risk management tool to minimize uncertainty.
- *Finance* would be called 'cost' in traditional project management. In some industries, the project management would not be concerned with the source of funds. However, in events and festivals, the funding – or revenue – is often a basic responsibility of the event or festival management. These issues are dealt with in Chapters 7, 8 and 10.
- *Time management* in the form of schedules and milestones is primary to all project management. For events and festivals the deadline takes on a higher significance. Project management has developed numerous techniques to manage time.
- *Design* and creation of the asset is found in the project management of software and product development. The event or festival may be changing design right up until the day it starts. Event project management, therefore, must incorporate design under its integration of the event planning. Chapters 4 and 13 describe the processes involved in event design. Within the design area of knowledge resides the PMBoK heading of 'quality'.
- *Risk management* is seen as one of the knowledge areas of project management. Although it is a recent phenomenon in event management, managing risk is a fundamental function of project management. It covers all the other areas of management, is constantly undertaken and produces up-to-date reports, which is why it has been adapted for the project management of many events. Projects do not see risk management as an arduous exercise. It is regarded as a way to improve the quality of the project and the deliverable. Chapter 11 describes event risk management in detail.

- *Procurement* includes the sourcing and managing of supplies and the management of contracts. This is described in Chapter 11. It is closely linked to sponsorship, finance and risk management.
- *Human resources* could be seen as a part of procurement, but the special conditions of dealing with people, such as team building and leadership, are indispensable to all projects, and so human resources is considered a separate area of knowledge. Chapter 6 describes this aspect in relation to events in detail.
- *Stakeholder management* is an important responsibility of the event manager. Some large public events will have more than 70 stakeholders; therefore, it is an important area of management for the event team. Finding and servicing sponsors is one of the areas of stakeholder management. Sponsorship was examined in detail in Chapter 8.
- *Communication* includes external communication with the stakeholders and internal communication with the event team. It changes as event organizing progresses. The external communication is linked to marketing and stakeholder management. On-site communication is linked to the staging and logistics of events as described in Chapters 12 and 13.

Role of the project manager

Project management can be seen as a collection of skills and knowledge that allows the integration of various contractors to deliver the project. The old term for a project manager was a contract manager. What is the role of the event manager, given that this is also his or her job? There are three solutions to this problem:

1. Expand the skill base of the event manager to include project management.
2. Reduce the responsibilities of the event manager and hire a project manager.
3. Train existing project managers in events management.

Each of these solutions is being undertaken for different events and festivals. Event managers are being trained in project management at a variety of courses around the world. Project management is now a core subject in these courses. Figure 9.1 illustrates all the areas of responsibility of the event manager trained in project management. Solution 2 is found in public events where the event management is split between the event director and the producer in charge of the creative aspects of the event, and the event project manager is in charge of the contracts, communication, compliance and other management areas. The event producer and event project manager have equal status in the organization and report to the client. Originally, for large events, the roles would have been event director and operations or logistics manager; however, the operations manager could not take on the responsibilities of legal compliance, management integration and accountability, hence the pressure to create a new position of event project manager. In Figure 9.1, the event director would be mostly concerned with the event design.

Solution 3 is used for very large events such as the Olympics and Grand Prix. In Figure 9.1, the project company is responsible for all the areas of management. Their primary task is the integration and contract management. Most of the areas, such as marketing and finance, would be outsourced.

Key competencies of a project manager in events

Education providers and project managers' employers are moving towards a competency approach to training and employment. Project managers employed by events and festivals are expected to prove their skills in the application of project management to events. This is often expressed in terms of key performance indicators, competency levels or education benchmarking.

An informal survey of recent project management job descriptions for events and festivals has these competencies or skills as essential to the position:

- develop and work in a team and provide leadership
- successfully define tasks and deliver on time and to quality
- integrate the project plan with the strategic, marketing and artistic plan of the event
- undertake risk management according to the standards of the industry
- use financial controls, indicators and reports effectively
- develop a procurement plan and manage contracts
- demonstrate high level communication skills in presentation and negotiation
- liaise and manage a wide range of external stakeholders, including public and private organizations
- produce management progress reports for senior management and clients, including project evaluation and project closure
- possess knowledge of the event and similar events in this field
- have the ability to employ and assess project software and management systems related to events.

Other areas that may come under the responsibilities of the event project manager are:

- site design and management
- defining client requirements
- sponsorship management
- event concept development.

The three areas of event management often missing from the project management areas of responsibility are: the event concept creation, sponsorship development and marketing. In the more traditional application of project management, the finance of the project and the design of the asset are not in the domain of the project manager. In civil engineering, for example, the client will provide the finance and the architect will provide the asset design. However, these are increasingly becoming the roles of project management. Software project management will have a large influence on the design of the product; therefore, an event project manager may be required to expand their competencies to include design, marketing and finance.

Many universities offer courses on project management, while providers of events management education, for example, Leeds Metropolitan University, include project management in their events courses.

Project management techniques

Numerous techniques have evolved in project management through live testing in areas as diverse as information technology, product development and engineering. Many techniques originally come from other disciplines such as operations, research and logistics. Most of these techniques are useful to event management. The scope and work breakdown structure are used to delineate the event and provide a management framework for planning and control. The techniques are not used in isolation and they form a process or a series of tasks that overlap. The process is outlined as a cascade model in Figure 9.2. The description of project management as

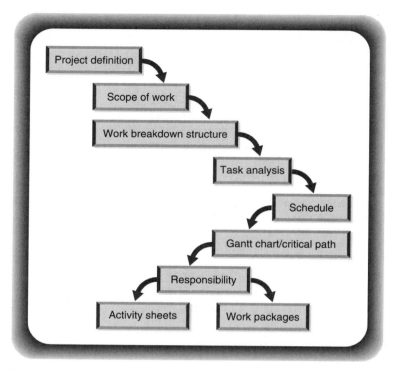

Figure 9.2 Project management cascade

a linear process is only an approximation, as each stage of the process will influence the early stages.

Defining the project and scope of work

The indispensable technique in project management is defining the project and, therefore, defining the scope. Misunderstandings over what is involved in the management of an event are common. Most project management literature stresses that the time spent on clearly defining a project in the initiation phase is time well spent. What is involved in the management? Who will do what? What will be the responsibilities of the client and the event company? These are some of the questions that assist project definition. Note that project definition is not the same as defining the event. A simple event may still be a complex project.

The scope – or scope of work – refers to the amount of work required to get the event up and running and then to shut it down; it is all the work. To define the scope is to gain an understanding of the event and its management. Often the event is described in terms of what is happening at the event. The scope definition captures the work necessary to deliver the event, as well as what is going on at the event.

The scope definition may be contained in the brief from the client or primary event sponsor; however, the client brief may be too simple and eventually lead to misunderstandings. Often the brief will only describe the deliverable, that is, the event and the work required to create it will be hidden. This has been a common problem in project management and the clarity and detail of the brief is identified as essential in the initiation period. For this reason, the event brief may be clarified by an

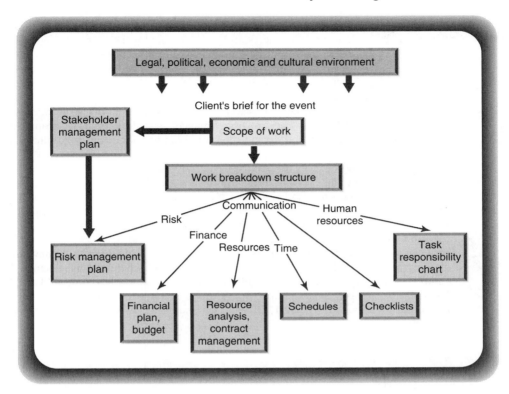

Figure 9.3 Plans and documents created from the work breakdown structure (WBS)
Source: O'Toole (2004)

addition of a statement of work (SOW). O'Toole and Mikolaitis (2002) describe the statement of work as 'a document that sets out the event objectives, lists the stakeholders, draft budget, scope, schedule and an outline of responsibilities'.

An important part of defining the scope is listing and understanding the requirements of the event stakeholders. In project management, a stakeholder is an organization or an individual who has an interest in the project. Under this definition, the list will include negative stakeholders, such as competing events and organizations opposed to the event. The primary stakeholders will include sponsors and the organizing committee. Secondary stakeholders include organizations that have an interest in the event if some action is not completed, or an unexpected incident occurs. For many events the Police and Emergency Services are secondary stakeholders. The deliverable of the stakeholder analysis is the stakeholder management plan. A good example of a stakeholder management plan in events is the sponsorship plan, as the sponsors are key stakeholders in events. The number of stakeholders in a simple event is large when compared to other projects. For this reason, Figures 9.1 and 9.3 show stakeholder management as a major function of the event project manager.

Creating a work breakdown structure

The next step in the cascade is the 'work breakdown structure' (WBS). Once the scope has been decided and defined, it needs to be categorized, documented and communicated. The creation of the WBS is a technique that focuses management on the work required to deliver the event. The creation of a visual display of all the work that needs to be done can assist the staff in understanding the scope of the work.

To deliver the event there will be an extensive number of tasks that have to be completed. These tasks can be complex and a long list of them may not be very helpful. A way to get this under control is to 'aggregate' the tasks under headings. All the tasks concerning the venue, for example, could be grouped under the heading 'venue' or 'on-site'. The tasks that concern finding the money and working out the cost could be listed under the heading 'finance'. Deciding on task groups and headings should be completed during the initiation phase or at the beginning of the planning phase.

Alternatively, another way to describe task grouping is breaking down all the work required to deliver the event into manageable units. These management units will require common resources and skills. As O'Toole and Mikolaitis (2002) point out, the work breakdown structure often parallels the folder system used on the computer or in the filing cabinet. For a public festival, the work breakdown structure may parallel the sub-committees' set up to organize the event. A festival may have four systems: committee, file folders, e-mail folders and paper folders. It makes sense to have them all integrated under the names of the headings in the work breakdown structure. The committee, the paper folder, the e-mail folder and the file folder should all be called 'venue', for example. It is a simple procedure to standardize the names of folders, but often overlooked. A local festival, for example, may have the following sub-committees:

- finance
- marketing (or promotion)
- finance
- legal or risk
- human resources, such as volunteers
- administration.

Note that each of these correspond to the knowledge areas illustrated in Figure 9.1. This is an example of the work breakdown structure where the sub-committees represent the work needed to organize the event.

Once the work breakdown structure is created it can be used for the next stage in planning the event. Figure 9.3 illustrates the plans and documents that can be created from the WBS. These plans and documents are often called the deliverables. They are proof that the tasks have been carried out and they are used by other areas of event management; that is, they are delivered to the event management team.

Analysing the resources

The resource list is developed from the WBS. The WBS is fundamental to resource analysis. The resources may be services, such as security, or goods, such as tents and chairs. Resources may also be a mixture of both, such as catering and sound. Resource analysis allows the event management to decide on what services and goods are:

- outsourced to suppliers
- sourced from the client or sponsor
- specially created or constructed for the event.

These are major decisions as they will impact on the budget. The resources may be grouped together and given to the one supplier. In project management this is called creating a work package. On large events, the supplier may need to submit a tender to supply these goods or services. An example of this is the supply of sound. From the

WBS it appears that sound equipment will be needed in various areas of the event, including the different stages and the entrance. These requirements are grouped together and given to a number of sound companies to supply a quote for the work.

One of the outputs or deliverables of the resource analysis is a list of suppliers. This deliverable is the input into the contract management process. Chapter 11 on risk management explains this process in detail.

Perhaps, the most important output of the resource analysis will be the human resource plan. This plan will be linked to the tasks and responsibilities described in the next section. In project management, the tasks are matched to the skills found in the pool of human resources available for the project. This process is outlined in Chapter 6. A straightforward measurement of hours required for the event and the cost per hour can give the overall cost of this resource; however, many events use volunteers. A cost-benefit analysis of volunteers is difficult, as there are so many intangible benefits and hidden costs.

Identifying tasks and responsibilities

The decomposition of event management into the WBS may identify all the tasks that need to be completed to deliver the event; however, this is highly unlikely as there are myriad tasks for even the simplest of events. One only has to think of the many tasks involved in organizing a wedding. The WBS will classify the tasks in manageable units. Each manageable unit will have groups of tasks associated with it. A WBS, for example, may have 'promotion' as a heading. Promoting the event will include the tasks of identifying the media, contacting the media, creating a schedule, creating a press release and many more. Each task has to be completed by a certain time and by a person or group of people; hence the task analysis is the beginning of assigning responsibilities. Chapter 6 on human resources goes into this area in more detail.

In project management practice it is common to map the WBS on the organizational structure. Each organizational unit corresponds to an area of the WBS. The management structure of a community event, for example, will be made up of a number of sub-committees. Each will have a clearly defined group of tasks assigned to it. An output of this process, often called task analysis, is the task responsibility chart or document. On this document are the tasks listed, who is responsible or what company, when the tasks should be completed and how the completion of tasks will be communicated. A task/responsibility list can also be put together at the end of meetings. Sometimes these are called action lists. Project managers prefer a task/responsibility list to the minutes of the meeting, because they are a 'call to action'. They are direct and the task is not hidden in other information, which is not relevant to the required actions.

Scheduling

Project management can be loosely defined as planning the who, what, where and when. The schedule represents the when. Almost all events have a fixed date or a deadline. Completed tasks take on an importance not found in other types of management. The schedule is a vital control tool allowing the project to progress. A mistake in scheduling can have a widespread affect to the other areas of management – leading to blowouts in costs, thereby compromising quality. The deadline is so important that most event managers work back from the date of the event. The schedule can be clearly represented by a Gantt chart.

Gantt chart

Gantt charts are bar charts named in honour of the management science theorist Henry Gantt who applied task analysis and scheduling to the construction of Navy ships. The Gantt chart is simple to create and its ability to impart knowledge quickly and clearly has made it a popular tool in project management. The steps in creating a Gantt chart are described as follows:

- *Tasks*: break down the work involved in the area of event management into manageable tasks or activities. One of the tasks, for example, of the security team for the event is the erection of the perimeter fence around the site. This can be further broken down into the arrival of the fencing material, the arrival of volunteers and equipment, and the preparation of the ground. As discussed above, this work is usually done as part of identifying tasks and responsibilities.
- *Timelines*: set the time scale for each task. Factors to consider are the starting and completion times. Other considerations in constructing a time scale are availability, hiring costs, possible delivery and pick-up times and costs. A major factor in the arrival time and day of large tents, for example, is their hiring costs. These costs can depend on the day of the week on which they arrive, rather than the amount of time they are hired for. Note that the schedule for many aspects of the event management will work back from the date of the event.
- *Priority*: set the priority of the task. What other tasks need to be completed before this task can start? Completing this priority list will create a hierarchy of tasks and identify the critical tasks.
- *Grid*: draw a grid with the days leading up to the event across the top and a list of the tasks down the left-hand side of the grid. A horizontal bar corresponding to each task is drawn across the grid. The task of preparing the ground for the fencing, for example, depends on the arrival of materials and labour at a certain time and takes one day to complete. The starting time will be when the prior tasks are completed and the length of the timeline will be one day. The horizontal bars, or timelines, are often colour coded so each task may be easily recognized when the chart is completed for all activities.
- *Milestones*: as the chart is used for monitoring the progress of the event, tasks that are of particular importance are designated as milestones and marked on the chart. The completion of the security fence, for example, is a milestone as it acts as a trigger for many of the other event preparation activities.

Figure 9.4 shows an example of a simplified Gantt chart. This chart is common to most small regional festivals.

In his work on project management, Burke (2003) stresses that this display provides an effective presentation which conveys the activities and timing accurately and precisely, and can be easily understood by many people, what Dinsmore (1998) refers to as high communication value. It forestalls unnecessary explanations to the staff and sponsors and gives a visual representation of the event. Timelines are used in all events, regardless of their size. The on-time arrival of goods and services even at a small event can add significant value.

The advantages of a Gantt chart are that:

- it visually summarizes the project or event schedule
- it is an effective communication and control tool (particularly with volunteers)
- it can point out problem areas or clashes of scheduling
- it is readily adaptable to all event areas
- it provides a summary of the history of the event.

For the Gantt chart to be an effective tool, the tasks must be arranged and estimated in the most practical and logical sequence. Underestimating the time needed (length of the timeline) can give rise to cost blow-out and render any scheduling ineffective. As Lock (2003) points out, extended schedules can lead to budgetary excess.

Network analysis: critical path

One important aspect of any project is the relationship of tasks to each other. This can be difficult to show on a chart. With larger events, the Gantt chart can become very complex, and areas where there is a clash of scheduling may be obscured by the detail of bars and colours. A vital part of event management is giving tasks a priority.

Assigning a priority to a task is essential as the event must be delivered on time. The arrival and set-up of the main stage at an event, for example, is more important than finding an extra extension cord. However, on a Gantt chart all of the listed tasks are given equal importance (or weight). The network analysis tool was developed to overcome these problems.

Network analysis was created and developed during defence force projects in the USA and United Kingdom in the 1950s and now has widespread use in many project-based industries. The basis of network analysis is its critical path analysis, which uses circles to represent programmed events and arrows to illustrate the flow of activities, thus the precedence of programmed tasks is established and the diagram can be used to analyse a series of sub-tasks. The most efficient scheduling can be derived from the diagram; this is known as the critical path. Figure 9.5 illustrates a network derived from the Gantt chart shown in Figure 9.4. The critical path is shown as an arrow. This means if the generator did not arrive on time, everything along the critical path would be directly affected. The lights would not be put up and, without evening light or electricity to run the pneumatic hammers, the tents could not be erected. Without the protective cover of the tents, the stage could not be constructed and so the sound system could not be set up. The critical path is indeed critical.

There are a number of software packages available to help create the Gantt chart and critical path. These are project management programs, which are usually used in the construction industry. Unfortunately, most of these packages are based on a variable completion time or completion within a certain time. In the events industry,

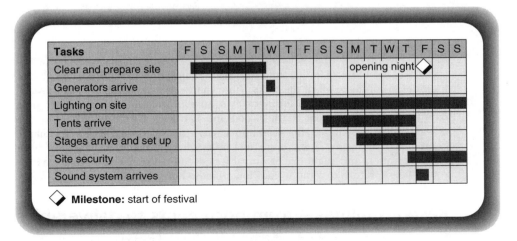

Figure 9.4 Simplified Gantt chart of a small festival

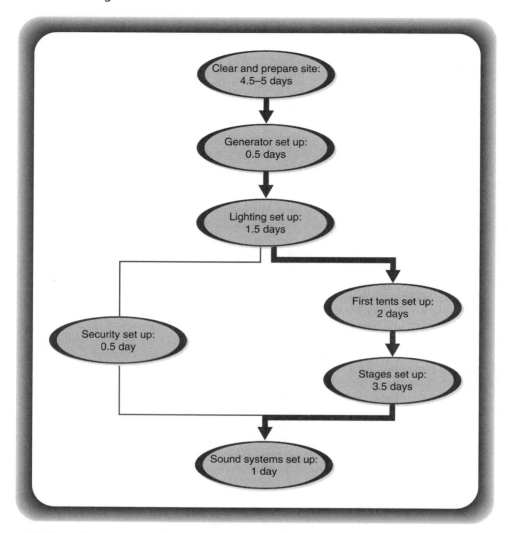

Figure 9.5 Gantt chart represented as a network

the completion time (that is, when the event is on) is the most important factor and every task has to relate to this time. The event manager cannot ask for an extension of the time to complete all of the tasks. Time charts and networks are very useful as a control and communication tool; however, like all project management techniques, they have their limitations. Catherwood and Van Kirk (1992) describe how the Los Angeles Olympic Organizing Committee gave up on the critical path chart as it became too unwieldy. There were 600 milestones. Rather than assisting with the communication and planning, it only created confusion. The solution was for the committee to return to a more traditional method of weekly meetings.

Responsibilities – from documents to deliverables

In managing a large event, the staff will be made up of various teams, volunteers and sub-contractors. If they are together only for a single event, they may not have a history of working together. This unfamiliarity with each other may lead to confusion in communication. There must be a way of communicating to the management team and stakeholders when tasks are completed, without creating unnecessary data information. The concept of deliverables is one way to control this complexity. The event itself is the major deliverable of all the tasks that make up the event management. A deliverable within the management of the event is the map of the site showing the layout of the event. To create this map the person responsible has to complete the design of the event and consider its logistics; therefore, the map is one of the outputs of the design process. The map is then delivered to other members of the event management team for use in her or his areas. A contract with a supplier is also a deliverable. It is proof that the negotiations have been completed. The deliverable of time planning is the schedule. As seen from these examples, the deliverables are often documents or files. They are developed by one group and passed on to another. After the event, these documents are also used to evaluate the management and may be used to prove the competence of the management. Figure 9.3 shows some of the event documentation. Some project management theory suggests that the project should identify all the deliverables and work backwards from these to discover the tasks necessary to create them. This working back from the deliverables allows the construction of the project's WBS.

The event documents can be compiled into an event manual. The manual can then be used for future events, as these documents may be used as templates.

The deliverables include:

1. *WBS*: a deliverable of the planning scope
2. *Task responsibility chart*: a result of analysing all the tasks that need to be completed and assigning them to the relevant people
3. *Checklists*: an indispensable tool for the event manager (these are created across all areas of the event)
4. *Schedules*: these range from the Gantt charts to production schedules used on the day of the event
5. *Resource analysis*: list all resources required and the contracts needed
6. *Financial plan and budget*: an output of the financial planning process
7. *Stakeholder management plan*: includes the sponsorship plan and the various communication plans, such as the promotion plan, as well as the reporting plan for the secondary stakeholders; for example, the local police
8. *Risk management plan*: a deliverable of the risk management. It may take the form of a risk register and a procedure for updating the register.

The deliverables from points two to eight emanate from the WBS and they help to refine the WBS. There are other documents used in events, including the contact list and site/venue layout map.

Payback period and return on investment

A term that is increasingly used in the event industry is the return on investment (ROI). It is a financial measure of the return to the event's key stakeholders as a result of its outcomes. The effects of the event can be multiple and include an increase in sales, community goodwill, increase in tourism and a change of behaviour. These outcomes should relate to the event objectives – a reason that the objectives should be measurable. In project management, it is expressed as the payback period. The payback period is the length of time needed to pay all the costs of the event. After the payback period, the consequences of the event produce a surplus. A music concert payback period may occur during or before the concert, as the ticket sales will cover the event costs. The payback period for a local car rally may be measured in years after the event. There are a number of payback problems found only in events (and not other project-based industries). To establish the payback period, the real costs of the event have to be estimated. Some events, such as those that have in-kind sponsorship or use volunteers, will have difficulty achieving this. The benefits of many events are intangible and difficult to measure in financial terms; however, there are economic tools to assist this process. The most common tool for measuring the intangible benefit of community well-being, is to establish the consumer surplus. The consumer surplus is the amount that the attendee would have paid to attend the event. Using this tool the cost/benefit of an event can be estimated and therefore so can the payback period.

Work in progress report and earned value

The client or major sponsor of an event cannot afford to wait until the event to know if it will be a success. Often, they require a report on how well the management is doing. This form of report is called a WIP, or work in progress. Using a project management methodology means that these reports are easily generated. The Gantt chart should give the client an idea of how the tasks are going. Earned value is a project technique that places a value on the percentage of the task completed. If the £10 000 promotion campaign for the event is 50 per cent complete at a certain date, for example, it is said to have an earned value of £5000.

Part of the WIP report is the risk register outlined in Chapter 11. The register describes the risks that have been identified and the actions taken to treat them. The register is a 'live' document. The WIP report is one of the control mechanisms for event management. Further discussion of control issues is found in Chapter 10.

Project evaluation

The evaluation of an event is generally concerned with its impact and level of success. Chapter 14 goes into this in detail. Project evaluation concerns the evaluation of the management of the event. The term that is common in other areas of project management is the acronym 'PEIR': project evaluation, implementation and review. This evaluation process is performed after the project is completed.

One of the attractions of using a project management system is that it enables this type of evaluation and subsequent improvement in management. By setting up a WBS the management can assess the tasks, responsibilities, schedules and risk management systems and improve upon them.

Project evaluation includes comparing the actual progress of the project against the planned project plan. As a result, the evaluation can suggest areas for improvement in the management. This is different to evaluating the event. It may be part of an event evaluation process, however, it is often forgotten. Figure 9.6 illustrates the project management system used by various events. One essential part of this system is the evaluation and archiving. Whereas PEIR occurs after the project is complete, the event plan, archive and review system is a description of the whole project management system from an evaluation point of view. Understanding the way a management system is evaluated creates a system that can be evaluated. The evaluation in this case is evaluating the validity of the system itself. As EPARS – the event, plan, archive and review system – in Figure 9.6 illustrates, one event is used as the baseline plan for the next event.

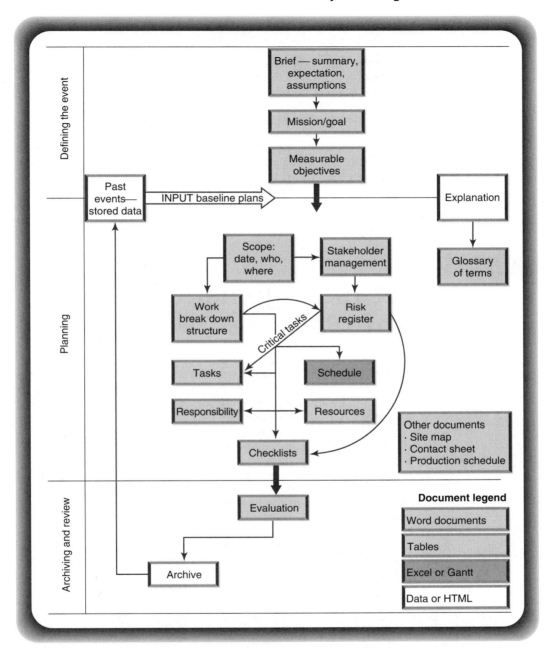

Figure 9.6 The event plan, archive and review system
Source: O'Toole (2004)

Event project evaluation includes:

- comparing the task descriptions and planned timelines with their actual performance
- assessing the ability of the system to respond to change; that is, its flexibility
- evaluating the timeliness of reports

- assessing the effectiveness of management decisions
- comparing planned milestones with the reality.

Each of these areas should indicate a fault or success in the management system. This feedback system can be used for each event to improve the management of the events. In this way, the event or festival is far more than a temporary and intangible affair. It is a way to improve the management of events in general. The event or festival can be regarded as a test of the management system.

An interesting offshoot of using such a system as EPARS, is that events can be used as a training model. By having a repeatable and improvable management system, a local festival can be used to train people in the skills of project management. Without a describable management system, the skill learned by working on a project cannot be assessed and, therefore, certified. Certification is basic to proving competency. This issue is taken further in Chapter 15. A number of countries, such as South Africa, are assessing this as a way to train their unemployed youth in business and organizational skills.

Project management systems and software

As project management is an integrated system, it appears to be easily translated into a software system. There are a number of project management software systems available to assist the practising project manager. Whether any of these can be directly and simply applied to events is a point for further discussion. Much of the project management software is excellent for planning the event management, as it imposes a discipline on the event team and demands a common language. Each of the systems is similar but due to the fluid nature of event management is limited in its usefulness. The 'Kepner-tregoe' and 'Prince 2' are two examples of highly developed and tested project management systems. The event plan, archive and review system, shown in Figure 9.6, is a visual display of the project management system used to structure the management of the event and, at the same time, assist in knowledge management. By creating templates the company or organization can save this information to be fed back into the next event. EPARS represents the adaptation of the traditional project management process, as illustrated in Figure 9.2, to the event environment. The inclusion of the stakeholder management as a basic function of event management, is an example of this. EPARS includes the use of checklists in the event management process. Checklists are used continually by event managers as they are easy to create and change.

Of the software systems, the most popular for event management is Microsoft Project. It is easy to buy and is readily set up. It can construct a Gantt chart quickly and is a useful tool for explaining the event to clients. The progress of the event management can be quickly ascertained by the percentage of tasks completed. The limitation of any project management software application to event management is a result of the variability of events themselves. Changes happen all the time. Venue changes, airline cancellations, different performers, more finance, new sponsors and new opportunities to promote the event are just some of the common changes in the event environment. In particular, a special event – that is, one not attempted before – will have a new configuration of suppliers and supplies. In such a situation, using current project management software to manage the event will be inadequate.

Using software for events is limited by its ability to work in a complex, changing and uncertain environment. Most event software currently employed is found in the more predictable and stable parts of the event industry; repeat exhibitions, conferences, meetings and seminars have a wide choice of software – special events and festivals do not have this software choice.

An important aspect of the project management process is that it is scalable. It can be applied to small events or large festivals. It can also be applied to any one area of an event, such as the promotion, or to the whole of the event. Chapter 13 on staging an event shows the tools associated with this. These correspond to the outputs of the project management process. The production schedule is a combination of task/schedule and responsibility documents. Project management software may be successfully applied to a part of the event; for example, a predictable section of the event, or a promotion schedule.

Limitations of the project management approach to event management

The limitations of the direct application of traditional project management have been analysed by O'Toole (2000). Traditional project management depends on a solid definition of the asset during the initiation phase and on a stable management environment. All the management tasks can then be measured against the defined asset. Festivals and events are not as clearly defined. Often they become more defined as the management of the project progresses, new marketing information comes to hand and new promotion ideas and programming openings arise. A large part of event managing is taking advantage of new opportunities which can mean that events can radically change, right up until the morning of the event. Project management, therefore, has to be flexible. Increased documentation, plans, written procedures and rules can easily lead to a management inertia unsuitable to this industry. It can destroy the core characteristic of special events and diminish the 'wow factor', the surprise, the vibe, or the theatre of events – essentially what makes the event 'special'. One solution to this problem used by major events (described in the previous section) is to appoint an artistic director and an event project manager. The former represents the innovative and creative aspects of the event content, while the project manager looks after the management responsibilities. Other areas that limit the use of project management are:

1. Using volunteers – the work of the volunteers is difficult to quantify and yet, as shown in Chapter 6, they are vital to the success of many festivals. To measure key success factors is an imperative task in a traditional project management system.
2. Stakeholders number – more stakeholders mean more objectives the event has to meet. Given that some stakeholders will change during the lead-up to the event, there is a more uncertainty in these objectives. This leads to a fluid management environment, with the event company continually keeping an eye on any change to the stakeholders. When this is combined with the intangible outcomes of an event, clearly defining stakeholder requirements can be almost impossible. In one sense, each individual audience member may have an array of expectations.
3. Marketing – the ability to respond to market changes is a fundamental principle of marketing. This is in opposition to a management system that relies on

the definition of the deliverable to stay the same. In project management, thinking about marketing can be regarded as a risk management strategy. The aim of marketing from this point of view is to increase the predicability of management. Using marketing tools such as consumer decision profiling, marketing segmentation, promotion and optimizing the market mix can reduce uncertainty.

4. Finance – finance may be found right up to the day of the event, during the event and after it is over. Extra sponsors may 'come on board', more tickets may be sold, or, for example, the auction may be a great success. This is another area of uncertainty that makes project planning difficult. Most project management theory assumes a fixed and defined source of funds, therefore, it tends to concentrate on the control of costs.

5. Event design – many events are supposed to have a large element of surprise – called the 'wow factor'. This is not an easy element to quantify or describe. At many events and festivals the right 'wow' can be the difference between success and failure. Traditional project management depends on the asset or deliverable being defined during the initiation phase. The surprise aspect of the event is often difficult, if not impossible, to describe. For some events, describing the 'wow' or surprise may lessen its value. It would be similar to describing the plot of a 'who-dunnit' mystery before reading the book.

6. Infrastructure and resources – usually of a temporary nature. Events and festivals can have notoriously short timelines. Other projects may take years to complete, whereas the event project may be over in a month. Short-term logistics, temporary structures and short-term contracts do not allow the luxury of detailed analysis that is recommended by many project management books. Overall, the event management is under the cloud of the deadline. Every aspect of the management, therefore, must be continually assessed according to its affect on the deadline.

Chapter summary

An event or a festival has all the characteristics of a project. The traditional tools of project management can assist the event team integrating all the areas of management. Each of these areas of management produces deliverables. The deliverables are the result of a number of tasks (proof of good management) and are communicated to the event team. Project management can supply management structure of the event. It concentrates on this management, whereas the event itself is often the focus of event studies. Event managers can benefit by using techniques such as scope definition, WBS, scheduling and critical path analysis. The WBS describes the work and generates other plans, such as the tasks, resource analysis and the risk register. By using project management, the event manager can easily produce the progress reports on the management. It provides a professional methodology and the language of modern business, that can be adapted to the event management environment. As events grow in scope, the project management becomes the most important aspect of the management. In such cases, an event project manager will be appointed. The event project manager's role is to integrate all the event plans and produce an accountable management system. Although project management is increasingly seen as a solution to compliance and management accountability, it has its limitations. These arise from the intangible nature of the event and the ever-changing event environment.

Questions

1. Construct a work breakdown structure for these events:
   (a) a rock concert
   (b) a wedding
   (c) a regional festival
   (d) an award ceremony.
2. Construct a schedule of key tasks for the events listed in question 1.
3. List the milestones for the events listed in question 1.
4. What are examples of tasks that can clash? What techniques can be put in place to recognize these clashes in time to enable the event management to fix them?
5. List the types of events and their characteristics that would suit the project management approach.

Case study 9.1

Project managing The Dream

On the GamesForce 2000 T-shirts adorning the (debatably) more fashionable staff buzzing around Sydney 2000 headquarters was the slogan, 'Delivering The Dream'. The successful delivery of this dream (the Olympic and Paralympic Games) to the customers and project stakeholders such as the competing athletes, the International Olympic Committee (IOC), national organizing committees, spectators, media and the great Australian public depended totally on the seamless integration and project management of the 'big five' Sydney 2000 organizations: the Sydney Organising Committee for the Olympic Games (SOCOG) (including sponsors and service providers), Sydney Olympic Broadcast Organization (SOBO), Olympic Coordination Authority (OCA), Olympic Roads and Transport Authority (ORTA) and Olympic Security Command Centre (OSCC). SOCOG's Project Management division had the central responsibility for understanding, scoping, integrating, recording and reporting the sub-projects of all four key organizations to the SOCOG Board and executive sub-groups, plus the IOC Executive Board and IOC Coordination Commission. In essence they had the responsibility for coordinating the master project – project managing *The Dream*.

Getting across the Games

Understanding the relationships (or dependencies) between organizational subprojects demands a willingness to work away from your desk; this is essential for building relationships. Initially, many of the venue teams with which I interacted showed a reluctance to share key information and project direction, naturally triggering my suspicion. I felt like a private detective hired by SOCOG to report venue management shortfalls and critical issues (which was not wholly true!) and not their achievements.

The difficulty in translating micro-level detail into macro-level reporting is in maintaining the meaningfulness of summarized information, without misrepresenting the accountable party. For instance, a summary bar may roll up 20 activities – 15 may have been achieved by the deadline, and five may be either pending completion or require an extension of time.

The summarized status on completion is 75 per cent – in work management terms it may be 99.9 per cent – with five signatures required from a single source on five outstanding documents! It became increasingly important to maintain a regular presence within the venue teams – to be proactive, but not too obtrusive. The key to gaining trust was to provide a range of services that benefited the venue teams (for example, providing user-defined reports, chasing problematic programme areas on their behalf, sharing information) – in essence, becoming a part time extension of their team.

To give you an understanding of the complexity of the SOCOG project management task, you only have to look at the key statistics pertaining to SOCOG's organizational breakdown structure, which are listed below.

- Six 'groups' – for example, games coordination
- Nineteen 'divisions' – for example, project management and special tasks
- Eighty-four 'programmes' – for example, project management
- Thirty competition venues
- Five major non-competition venues
- Three villages – Olympic, Media and Technical Officials
- Training venues, hotels, arts festivals and so on
- A Games-time workforce of 110 000 (paid, volunteers and contractors)

The sheer size of the multi-organizational Sydney 2000 with its multiple projects and multiple dependencies made managing and reporting the status of the master project at varying (hierarchical) levels extremely challenging.

Thoughts into action

There was no blueprint for the Olympic Games (as for many other unique events) and, although when I joined SOCOG we had on board many people who had experienced the highs and lows of Olympic Games, World Cups and other large events, the need to speed up the 'conceptual' phase and turn thoughts into structured directives and future actions became the immediate objective. Working hand-in-hand with operational integration programme area project management, the concept of the 'Games coordination timeline' was devised to communicate the importance of project managing the events while continually focusing Sydney 2000 on the delivery of the two final stages of the Games project delivery. The strategy behind the two-stage approach was to bring the Games closer in the minds of the organization ('only two stages to go!') and make the achievement of these stages more tangible to the responsible delivering parties.

The two stages of the Games coordination timeline can be seen in Table 9.1.

Table 9.1 The two stages of the Games coordination timeline

Stage	Name	Date	Focus
One	Venue project plan	01-01-99–31-01-00	'How we're going to get there', off-site activity planning, documentation and approvals
Two	Day-by-day plan	01-08-00–31-11-00	'What we're going to do when we get there', on-site activity installation, training, rehearsal, operation space-specific – CPA

'Venuisation' – building the team

The promotion of the Games coordination timeline was strategically launched in line with Sydney 2000's arguably most important organizational restructuring. This organizational metamorphosis was referred to as *venuisation.*

Venuisation, in basic terms, is the shift of organizational focus from programme-based delivery to venue-based delivery. The venue structure was created, multi-organizational venue teams began to develop, and Sydney 2000 organizations began to interact with each other on a day-to-day, face-to-face basis in a singular office environment.

Venuisation immediately began to improve communications between formerly remote organizations, and instil an empathy in each organization's individual agendum, an empathy which was previously either unrecognized or, in some cases, not acknowledged.

Project managing the event managers

In my humble and biased opinion SOCOG recruited well. The knowledge, professionalism and dedication of the Games workforce was quite astounding. However, in many organizations positive personal attributes do not always guarantee the possession of project management focus and skills. A good event operations manager, for example, may not necessarily make a good event project manager. The key management issues SOCOG project management had to successfully overcome with the implementation of the Games coordination timeline are briefly outlined in Table 9.2.

Table 9.2 Key management issues

Issue	Definition	Solution	Outcome
Technofear	Fear of the autonomous use of SOCOG's adopted project management software – Primavera P3	Use of a spreadsheet approach – deemed more use-friendly. Facilitated by P3's email-friendly post office system. Centrally managed by SOCOG project management.	Excellent response record to deadlines imposed by the monthly project management cycle; clarity and ownership of information; online ownership and updates
Empathy	Lack of understanding of the dependencies inherent in the delivery of the venue-based project	Pilot project developed before global release – evolution of the 'pilot' communicated to the venue teams.	Consistency in information reported: – level of content– activity descriptions– project structure
Multiple definitions	Key words and project phases that meant different things to different people	Joint OCA and SOCOG definitions of overlay, logistics and operations phases developed by project management/OCA, adopted by Sydney 2000 organizations.	Clear and global understanding of delivery phases, dependencies and project documentation; improved understanding of project management principles
Adoption	Lack of/fear of ownership of the plan – fear of incriminations through transparency and subsequent elevation of information	Venue readiness meetings organized on a monthly basis as part of the project management cycle – chaired by the venue manager. Plan owned by the team.	Venue team ownership of information

Another 'positive' problem SOCOG project management had to overcome in establishing the Games coordination timeline was Sydney 2000's focus on test events. Although a distraction from developing the plans, the lessons learnt and the essential team building gained through working on these high-profile, international-standard events added a greater integrity to the information being reported for the Games.

Managing the software

SOCOG consciously adopted Primavera P3 software as its primary project management tool for controlling the delivery of the Olympic and Paralympic Games. P3 is a high-end software application which is more than capable of managing multiple projects with multi-level sub-projects. By comparison with its off-the-shelf competitors it has an advanced suite of standard functions, including EVR (earned value report), user-defined reporting, post office and remote data entry. For an experienced project manager, this tool has the flexibility and 'grunt' to generate scenarios and reports reliably and speedily. SOCOG, for example, has extracted information from the core day-by-day project plan to generate the logistics 'bump in' and the site management 'overlay transition' schedules, setting the parameters for programme area task-level activity. In my opinion, another plus for P3 is the fact that it is a code-driven application, which encourages the project manager to scope the project and subprojects prior to developing the plan. The work breakdown structure becomes the framework and control mechanism for the project, as shown in Table 9.3.

Table 9.3 The games work breakdown structure

Level	Code-Field	Description
1	Master project (1)	The Games coordination timeline
2	Project (2)	Venue project plan and day-day plan
3	Event (2)	The Olympic Games and the Paralympic Games
4	Precinct (4)	Geographical areas – for example, Sydney West
5	Venue (30)	Specific venues allocated to precincts – for example, Sydney International Equestrian Centre, Sydney West
6	Space (multiple)	Specific (predominantly) room locations within the venue
7	Cluster (multiple)	Logistical delivery and resupply area within the venue – cluster of spaces
8	Activity/task	Action description
9	Responsibility	Notification of who is delivering the action and who is receiving the action
10	Reporting	Activities tagged to user-defined reports

The drawbacks for P3 as an event project management tool are few, as long as the event manager understands the software and project management principles that drive the creation of the work breakdown structure, coding structure and interdependencies.

For medium-level projects P3 might be considered a bit expensive (about $7000 off the shelf), but if you believe Primavera is the way to go there is an offspring of the parent product called Suretrak which has most of the 'whistles and bells' without the sting in the pocket.

You do not have to manage all aspects of a project or multiple projects through a single software application. SOCOG project management did not fully utilize the P3 suite. For instance, cost planning and analysis and resource levelling is owned by the venue manager but controlled via a quantity surveyor/finance manager and venue staffing manager respectively. The quantity surveyor uses specially developed in-house software, and the venue staffing manager uses an off-the-shelf spreadsheet package.

Project managing a 'medium-size' event

Many of the principles discussed in this chapter can be applied to a medium-sized event. Whatever the scope and budget of your project I would encourage you to do the following:

- Adopt a two-stage (off-site and on-site) focus.
- Project manage space-specific, on-site activities using CPA.
- Use mid-range PM software, such as Primavera Suretrak or MS Project.
- Be proactive – work away from your desk.
- Regular PCGs are essential – the key players are the event manager, quantity surveyor/finance/commercial manager, architect and local government agencies.
- Establish common project terminology.
- Develop your deployment and recruitment plans early – evolve the plan.
- Use the project plan in a positive way, highlight achievements and incorporate key performance indicators.
- If inexperienced or constrained by time, use the services of an experienced project management consultant to set up and administer the project.

For further information about the Sydney Olympic Games, please visit www.gamesinfo.com.au.

By Neil Timmins, Manager, Programming and Planning, Sydney Olympic Park Common Domain

Questions

1. Construct a lexicon of event terms that may cause confusion at events. This would include terms such as bump-in, shutdown, set-up and staging.
2. Why did the Olympics organization structure change from programme-based to venue-based? Was there an alternative way to organize the Olympics?
3. Why did the author use the term 'autonomous' in describing the fear of software?
4. Discuss the constraints of webcasting the Olympics. Some of these will be technical, political and financial.

Case study 9.2

Opening and Closing Ceremonies of Athens 2004 Olympics

With a collective audience of 4 billion television viewers worldwide and 140 000 live attendees, Jack Morton Worldwide delivered breathtaking Opening and Closing Ceremonies for Olympiad XXVIII, working in collaboration with Artistic Director, Dimitris Papaioannou. The Games marked a milestone in Olympic history, as they marked the return of the modern Games to Athens for the first time since their revival there in 1896. This was also the first time a non-indigenous company had produced the ceremonies for a host city. As a result, expectations were high and the pressure to deliver – especially given widely reported scepticism about the Greek hosts' ability to 'pull it off' and lingering security concerns – was on. However, Jack Morton was prepared for the challenge, drawing on its experience of producing the ceremonies for previous similar events such as the Manchester Commonwealth Games in 2002, the Salt Lake 2002 Paralympic Winter Games and the Hong Kong Handover in 1997. Lois Jacobs President International at Jack Morton said, 'The celebration of the Olympic Games in their ancient place of birth really is an historic event – one that Jack Morton Public Events is honoured to have been asked to produce'.

Opening ceremony

The Olympic Stadium was transformed from a world-class sporting venue into the world's largest theatrical stage. The dynamic Opening Ceremony celebrated the spirit of the Olympics and their homecoming and, at the same time, provided a global branding platform for Greece itself. The challenge was to create an event that would broadcast a positive image of the country to the entire world, an event that would redress stereotypes and influence perceptions about the country and its people. The ceremonies were held on a world stage, and Jack Morton's job was to make Greece its star.

Athens played host to one of the most beautiful and moving Opening Ceremonies in Olympic history. Jack Morton utilized the latest technologies to produce the event including a laser 'comet' igniting Olympic rings lying within a 500 000-gallon 'sea' on the stadium floor representing the beautiful seas that surround the country; a 60-foot, 22-ton Cycladic head that emerged from the sea's center, rose from its surface and broke apart into Greek statuary and a 370-metre rolling stage, and many other magical visual displays. A further feature was a performance by Bjork, who sang an original composition, her 'dress' blanketing the entire stadium floor. The audacious performance painted a dramatic picture of a country steeped in pride for its remarkable cultural heritage; a country, which has made an almost incalculable contribution to contemporary civilization. At the same time, the Ceremony captured the Greek joy of life and the emotional spirit of a newly transformed, modern city, and celebrated Olympic ideals.

David Zolkwer of Jack Morton commented, 'For us, the greatest achievement has been to bring form to such an intelligent and ambitious creative narrative, with apparent elegant simplicity. Our combined team of production and technical experts has harnessed their talent, innovative thinking, passion and the very latest technology to present to the world a story steeped in ancient culture but which conveys a totally contemporary message that resonates in the hearts and minds of all of us across the world'.

Closing ceremony

Just hours after the conclusion of the much heralded Opening Ceremony, and whilst the world became engrossed in the greatest sporting event on the planet, rehearsals for the Closing Ceremony continued apace on the outskirts of Athens. An exuberant celebration of the Games and Greece, the closing ceremony featured a spectacular 'ethnic collage' of dance, music and celebration, revelling in the diverse Greek folk culture of dance, music and ritual still very much alive and beloved in Greece today. In yet another incredible transformation of the Olympic stadium, where once a giant lake representing Greece's relationship with the sea that surrounds it took centre stage for the Opening Ceremony, for the Closing a huge beautiful spiral 45 000-stalk wheat field was 'planted' to represent the fertility of the earth and Greece's affinity with and dependence on the land.

Drawing on Greek custom and tradition a colourful and vibrant mosaic of dance and celebrations, all of which thrive today despite many of them originating from ancient times, punctuated the ceremony. The dance extravaganza included a troupe of men dressed in sheep and goat skins carrying heavy bells to wake nature and frighten away evil spirits; satyrs – wood-dwelling creatures with the head and body of a man and the ears, horns and legs of a goat – gathering grapes and pressing wine; the Tsamikos – a tough dance performed by muscular men; the Tsakonikos – where women dance closely in a row in spiral patterns; Greece's favourite dance the Kalamatianos; table dancing and fire leaping, all culminating in a dance to the famous music of Zorba.

Summary

In January 2003, seventeen days after winning a demanding and competitive bidding process that took over a year to complete, just three Jack Morton staff members opened the doors to a small Athens office to begin work on the ceremonies. Jack Morton's UK office led the ceremony production with a team of over 850 in Athens as well as international expertise drawn from its London, Los Angeles, Sydney and Hong Kong offices. To bring this enormous undertaking to life required Jack Morton to recruit and manage an army of over 8500 volunteers both performing and supporting the backstage effort. The vast majority were Greek, but the volunteer team also included ceremonies' 'enthusiasts' representing 15 other countries working alongside Jack Morton's technical crew. To produce and execute the ceremonies required a significant level of project planning including over 50 000 telephone calls to recruit volunteer performers, 6600 cast bus trips to and from rehearsal sites, five miles of audio and data cable, 7000 in-ear audio monitors, 11 000 yards of costume fabric and hundreds of hours of music recording. By the time both ceremonies were over, more than 700 000 bottles of water had been consumed by cast and crew.

The Opening and Closing ceremonies and Jack Morton's work received extensive major media coverage worldwide. In September 2004, a nationwide survey conducted in Greece showed that the public majority believes that the success of the Olympic Games enhanced the perception of their country on an international level; they identified the Ceremonies as the top two most memorable moments of the entire Olympics experience. In June 2005, the Independent reported that tourism to Greece increased 10 per cent in the ten months following the Olympics; the National Bank of Greece estimated 13.5 million tourists in 2005 and 14 million in 2006 as a result of the games' popularity – in no small part due to the flawless execution of the Opening and Closing ceremonies.

For further information about Jack Morton Worldwide, please visit www.jackmorton.co.uk.

By Jack Morton Worldwide.

Questions

1. What was the scope of the project for the events identified in this case study?
2. What challenges were faced by the organizers?
3. What project management tools and techniques could the organizers have used to help manage these challenges?
4. Conduct further research into the 2004 Athens Olympic Games and identify other examples of project management in practice.

Chapter 10
Control and budgeting

Learning Objectives

After studying this chapter, you should be able to:

- understand the use of control by management
- identify the control systems used in events and festivals
- analyse the factors that create successful control mechanisms
- identify the key elements of budgetary control and explain the relationship between them
- understand the advantages and shortcomings of using a budget.

Introduction

After planning the festival or event, the central function of management is controlling. Without a management system, such as project management, control becomes impossible. This chapter, therefore, should be read in conjunction with Chapter 9. This chapter introduces the various methods the festival or event management can use to recognize that the event is going to plan and respond to any changes. The event budget is perhaps, the most important control plan. This chapter then outlines tips on increasing revenue and decreasing expenditure.

What is control?

Control consists of making sure that what happens in an organization is what is supposed to happen. The control of an event can range from the event manager simply walking the site and discussing daily progress with staff, to implementing and monitoring a detailed plan of responsibilities, reports and budgets. The word 'control' comes from the Latin *contrarotulare*, meaning 'against the roll': in ancient Rome it meant comparing something to the official records, which were kept on paper cylinders or rolls. In modern times, the word has retained some of this meaning, and the control of any business involves comparing the progress of all key functions against a management plan to ensure that projected outcomes are met.

Event planning can be effective only if the execution of the plan is carefully controlled. To do this, it is necessary to develop proper control mechanisms. These are methods which are designed to keep a project on course and return the project to the plan if it wanders. Control affects every element of the management of events including project management logistics, human resources and administration, and its basic nature remains the same in every area.

Slack, Chambers and Johnston (2004, p. 771) define control as 'the process of monitoring operations activity and coping with any deviations from the plan; usually involves elements of replanning'. It is the process of coping with changes that affect plans. Control may mean a plan is revised or it may require intervention in the project to bring it back on track. The nature of control is described by Beniger (1986), who identified two complementary activities:

1. *Information processing*: this is necessary for all planning. When it is goal-directed, it allows the continual comparison of an organization's stated goals against reality.
2. *Reciprocal communication, or feedback*: there must be a constant interchange between the controller and the areas being controlled.

These activities depend on an effective communication system.

This chapter explores control in the context of events. It will demonstrate that the choice of workable control mechanisms is central to the success of an event, and discuss budgets, which are the main control systems used in events.

Elements and categories of control

The process of control involves establishing standards of performance and ensuring that they are realized. This can be a complex process, but consists of three main steps:

1. *Establishing standards of performance*: this can come from several sources, including standard practices within the event management industry, guidelines supplied by the board of management of the event, specific requirements of the client and sponsors, and audience or guest expectations. Standards must be measurable.
2. *Identifying deviations from standards of performance*: this is done by measuring current performance and comparing it with the established standards. Since the event budget is expressed in measurable terms, it provides an important method of highlighting areas that are straying from the plan and which require attention.
3. *Correcting deviations*: any performance that does not meet the established standards must be corrected. This can entail the use of many types of problem-solving strategies, including renegotiating contracts and delegating.

These three steps are also called the control cycle (Burke, 2003) and are central to the successful delivery of an event. Such a cycle would be applied with varying frequency, depending on the size and complexity of the event itself.

Generally, events are characterized by two types of controls – operational and organizational. Operational controls are used for the day-to-day running of the event. Organizational controls relate to the overall objectives of the event organization, for example, whether the event is profitable and satisfies the client's brief. Hicks and Gullet (1976) suggest a further category of controls according to when the controls are applied:

- *Predictive control* tries to anticipate and identify problems before they occur. Predicting cash flows for an event is an important area because expenses are not concurrent with income. For example, venue hire is usually paid for in advance of the event. Similarly, for an event with a small budget, briefing a lawyer is another example of predictive control. Some companies, for instance, may be less likely to pay promised fees to a small company than they would to a larger, more powerful company. Also, the organizers of a small one-off event are not in a position to threaten a defaulting company with withdrawal of further work opportunities. In these, and similar situations, a swift letter from a solicitor who has been briefed beforehand can often hasten payment. Another term for predictive controls is 'feedforward'.

- *Concurrent control* measures deviation from the standards as they occur. The event manager's informal question of 'How's it going?' falls into this category. For example, the monitoring of food stalls during an event is essential to ensure that food safety regulations are being followed. It may be difficult to predict just how a caterer will deviate from the guidelines. At one festival, for example, tea and coffee urns were placed against a canvas dividing wall. On the other side, a children's play group was in operation.
- *Historic controls* are mostly organizational controls and can include analysis of major deviations from an event plan so that the next event runs more closely to plan. Such controls review the concluded event and are concerned with the question: 'How were objectives met?'

In order to compare actual and planned progress in managing an event, points of comparison are necessary. These include the following:

- *Benchmarks* are identifiable points in the organization of the event where a high standard is achieved. Benchmarks emphasize quality and best practice. For example, catering of a given high standard could be a benchmark for a corporate party. Attaining a benchmark is often a cause for celebration by the event company.
- *Milestones*, or key dates, are intermediate achievement dates that stand as guideposts for monitoring an event's progress. They mark particularly critical completion times. For example, the arrival of the headline performers at the venue is a critical time, and the submission date of a client proposal is a key date. A milestone trend chart is a graphic illustration of the milestones and includes whether they have been met or delayed. It is a sophisticated technique used for large events. By tracking the milestones, a trend may be discovered. If all the milestones are late, for example, it may indicate a problem with the management. Schedule slippage is another term for this.
- *Identification of deliverables* is a method used by project management, as set out in Chapter 9. A deliverable is the tangible result of one of the areas of project management. This tangible result may be documents such as a report, a contract, a site map or a contact list. To use the budget as an example, the budget is a document that is a result of planning the event finance. It enables staff to be focused on the job of creating the budget and is proof that the task of financial planning has been completed. The budget is then passed on to other areas of the event management. Therefore, the deliverable encapsulates a part of the management and is proof that it has been performed. A more obvious deliverable would be the arrival of sound equipment at an event. Using this system, the event manager identifies all the deliverables from the work breakdown structure (WBS). These are given dates for completion and used to control the progress of the event management.

Figure 10.1 illustrates the control process and how each element fits into the planning process.

Event control can be expensive in time and money. Its cost and effectiveness depend on the choice of the control mechanisms that make up the control system.

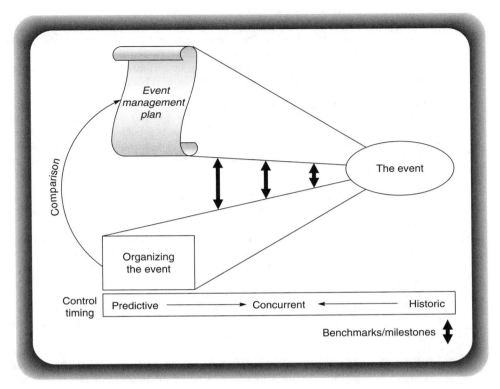

Figure 10.1 The control process

Control mechanisms must be:

- *Meaningful and efficient*: they should be directed only at those areas that contribute to the success of the event. These significant areas have to be identified in advance, and addressed in the event plan. A limited amount of time is available for measuring and comparing – this process must be streamlined so that it does not become an end in itself.
- *Simple*: controls should not be any more complicated than is necessary. Their aim is practical and they have to be able to be communicated to many levels within an event. For example, an excessively complicated system of controls can alienate a broadly based festival committee.
- *Relevant*: controls must be prepared to match each area of event management and they should be distributed to those who have the responsibility of carrying them out. For example, there is no point in the publicity section having data that concern the budget of the performers.
- *Timely and flexible*: deviations from the plan should be identified early and addressed before they develop further. Concurrent controls should allow sufficient time to correct any gaps with the plan. Flexibility is essential, as the controls may need to respond to revision of the event plan up until the last moment. Sometimes, milestones must be moved to accommodate changes in the event. For example, a benchmark may be an attendance of 1000 people, but if only 800 chairs were delivered, it is no longer a best practice benchmark and must be dropped in case it creates a logistical problem.

- *Able to suggest action*: the most useful control mechanisms provide corrective actions to be taken when members of the event team find a gap between the plan and reality. Without these suggestions for action, inexperienced staff or volunteers can become confused and the event manager can be swamped by problems that could readily have been solved by others if guidance had been provided.

When deviations or gaps are identified, the event manager can make a reasoned choice – either to close the gap, or leave it alone and revise the plan. Historic organizational controls, for example, may show a gap between the event objectives and what actually happened. The event manager can choose to change the objectives himself or herself or change aspects of the event. Examples of gaps that can be measured include:

- *Ticket sales targets vs actual sales:* For the entrepreneur, the sale of ticket is the 'make or break' of the event. Any deviations from the schedule may cause a cash flow problem.
- *Supplier compliance vs contract:* In the fluid situation of setting up an event there can be many deviations from the plan. In particular, supplier may not send the exact goods as described in the contract. This needs to be anticipated and pre-empted.
- *The 'buzz' or event awareness vs the marketing/promotional plan:* If the promotion of the event is not creating at least an interest then the plan may have to change. The level of press coverage or community support may indicate the 'buzz'.
- *Percentage of task completed:* from the Gantt chart, the expected completion time of the tasks can be compared to the actual progress.
- *Level of sponsor support vs sponsorship objectives*: the sponsorship may be lagging behind the initial expectations of the event company. This may be a result of changes within the sponsor's business, a situation that could result in a lack of funds or support as the event draws near.
- *Actual logistics vs the operation plan*: A small deviation from the plan can create major problems throughout the event. If the delivery trucks to an exhibition arrive in the wrong docks, the delay and confusion can be magnified in a short space of time.
- *Entertainment vs crowd response*: If the crowd is not responding as expected, it may be time for quick management action.

Control methods

Some of the control methods used in events are very straightforward, whilst others can be complex and require a high level of financial reporting skills. However, they all have the same aim – to highlight areas that have strayed from the plan so that management can take appropriate action.

Reports and meetings

Reports that evaluate the progress of an event are perhaps the most common control method. The reports are presented at the management or committee meetings. The frequency of these meetings will depend on the proximity of the event date. Many event management companies hold weekly meetings with reports from the teams (or subcommittees) and individuals responsible for particular areas. The meetings are run using standard meeting rules, such as those described in Comfort (1996), with a time for team/subcommittee reports. The aim of these reports is to assist the meeting in making decisions.

Typically, an annual community festival may have monthly meetings throughout the year leading up to the event, and increase these to weekly meetings two months before the festival. The weekly meetings may alternate between the festival committee and the general community (which discuss major decisions by the festival committee). In this way, the public can be given some control over the planning of the festival. At the committee meetings, the subcommittees dealing with publicity, sponsorship, entertainment, youth and community relations can report their actions. The reports expose any gaps so that the event coordinator can take action to close them. This is also called management by exception, because it assumes everything is flowing well, that the subcommittee handles routine matters and the event coordinator need only step in when significant deviations from the plan demand it.

Project status report

The status report is a 'snapshot' of the progress of the project. These are described in Chapter 9 under the heading of 'Work in progress (WIP) reports'. The WIP is the common term used for a project status report in the event industry. The headings often found in a WIP report for a large or complex event include:

- *WBS*: areas filled in according to their progress
- *funds committed*: the commitment of funds may be informal (such as by verbal agreement) but will have an effect on the amount of funds available
- *risk register*: a list of the risks and the status of their treatment
- *variances or exceptions*: any changes to the original plans.

Delegation and self-control

The use of subcommittees at a festival is an example of delegating activities to specialist groups. Part of the responsibility of each subcommittee is to solve problems before they report. Since it is impossible for the event manager to monitor all the areas of an event, this method is valuable because it allows delegated groups to control their own areas of specialization. However, the subcommittee must confine its actions to its own area and the event manager must be aware of possible problems arising across different subcommittees. For example, solving a problem in the entertainment part of an event could give rise to problems in the sponsorship areas.

Quality

There are various systems to control the quality of an event and the event company itself. In particular, quality control is dependent on customer feedback, and on the role played by event personnel in delivering quality service. Integrating the practical aspects of controlling quality with the overall strategy of an event is called total quality management (TQM). It seeks to create an event company that continually improves the quality of its services. In other words, feedback, change and improvement are integral to the company's structure and operations. Event companies use various TQM techniques. One technique is finding and rewarding quality champions – volunteer programmes often have awards for quality service at an event. Different professional organizations, such as the Association of Exhibition Organizers (AEO), Eventia, International Festival and Events Association (IFEA), International Special Events Society (ISES), Meetings Industry Association (MIA), Meeting Professionals International (MPI) and The Event Services Association (TESA), share the same aim: to improve the quality of festivals and events within their respective sectors of the industry. They do this by disseminating information and administering a system of event evaluation through awards for quality, for example, the annual ITMA Awards. Further quality initiatives taken up by event, include Hospitality Assured Meetings, Investors in People and BS EN ISO 9001, with an increasing number of event companies achieving accreditation over recent years.

The breakeven chart

This simple graphic tool can highlight problems by finding the intersection of costs and revenue. Figure 10.2 shows a simple but effective breakeven chart for an event that is dependent on ticket sales. For example, the Proms in the Park in Birmingham would have fixed costs of stage, pyrotechnics and administration costs. However, the greater the attendance, the larger are the costs of security, seating, cleaning, toilets and so forth. However, at one point the revenue from ticket sales exceeds the costs. At this point, the breakeven point, the event would be making a profit. If a fixed cost such as venue hire is increased, the extra number of people needed 'through the door' can quickly be calculated. How would the organizers attract the extra people to the event? One means might be increased promotion.

Ratio analysis

There are several ratios that can be used to identify any problems in the management of an event. These can also be used for predictive control as in the earlier example. Their main function is as indicators of the health of the event organization. Dyson (2004) identifies two simple ratios as a useful starting point – known as liquidity

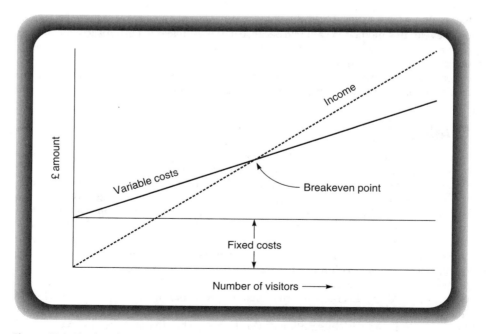

Figure 10.2 The breakeven chart

ratios, they measure the extent to which assets can be turned into cash. The current assets ratio is calculated as:

$$\frac{\text{Current assets}}{\text{Current liabilities}}$$

It indicates the financial strength of the event company or organization. The second liquidity ratio is known as the acid test ratio. Based on the premise that stock cannot always be turned into cash in the short term, or it may be unwise to do so, this removes stocks out of the equation. The acid test ratio is calculated as:

$$\frac{\text{Current assets} - \text{Stocks}}{\text{Current liabilities}}$$

However, calculation of assets can be difficult, since events by their nature have few current assets except those intangible qualities: goodwill and experience. In a similar way to a film production company, an event company may be formed to create and manage a one-off festival where every asset is hired for the duration of the event.

Return on capital employed (ROCE), sometimes referred to as return on investment (ROI), is a significant ratio for any sponsors or investors in an event, as it assesses the profitability of an event. This is expressed as:

$$\frac{\text{Net profit}}{\text{Capital}} \times 100 = \text{X per cent}$$

The net profit for a sponsor may be expressed in advertising pounds. For example, media exposure can be measured by column centimetres for newspapers, or time on air for television/radio, and approximated to the equivalent cost in advertising. This ratio is most often used for events that are staged solely for financial gain. An entrepreneur of a major concert performance must demonstrate a favourable ROCE to potential investors to secure financial backing.

Other ratios can provide valuable data. As Brody and Goodman (1988) explain in their text on fundraising events, the ratio between net and gross profit is important in deciding the efficiency of the event for fundraising and in comparing one event to another. This ratio is called the percentage of profit or the profit margin. Another example of an effective ratio is that of free publicity to paid advertising, particularly for concert promoters.

By performing a series of appropriate ratio analyses, an event management company can obtain a clear picture of the viability of the organization and identify areas requiring more stringent control.

Management system

Perhaps, the most thorough way of developing control methods is to establish a management system. Project management is such a system that is suitable to events and festivals. A system is similar to the blueprint in designing a house. It enables the house to be built so that all the parts fit together and tells the builder if there are any discrepancies.

WBS, combined with the schedule and task/responsibility list, is the blueprint for the event. Without this blueprint the event manager will not know if there are any problems until it is too late. The system will sort out the important problems needing immediate attention from the minor problems. It establishes a management environment in which it recognizes that each area of the event management mutually influences the other areas. Using a project management system means a thorough contracting process is employed. The contract, with its penalties and rewards, is often the critical part of the control system.

Management incentives and staff rewards

The management of an event can be financially tied to its success. Staff bonuses and rewards are a common control method in other industries. In the music industry, for example, staff bonuses are common for large concerts if they are successful. Keeping the event restricted to the budget is another common reason for rewarding the management of an event. Chapter 6 describes these reward systems under the heading of 'Staff motivation'.

The budget

A budget can be described as a quantified statement of plans (in other words, the plan is expressed in numerical terms). The budget process includes costing and estimating income and the allocation of financial resources. The budget of an event is used to compare actual costs and revenues with projected costs and revenues. In particular, maximum expenditure for each area of the event's operation is estimated. To achieve this efficiently, a budget can take many forms. For instance, it may be broken into sub-budgets that apply to specific areas of a complex or large event such as the staging, logistics, merchandising and human resources. Budgets are of particular importance to the management of events because most aspects of the event need payment before the revenue is obtained. Cash flow needs special attention. Most funding or sponsorship bodies need a budget of the event before they will commit their resources. This second part of the chapter expands on these points and provides an example to illustrate them.

Constructing the budget

Two types of budget process can be used in event management. The *master* budget, as the name suggests, focuses on each cost and revenue item of the total event (or event company) and the *functional* budget is constructed for a specific programme element, costs centre or department (Dyson, 2004). An example of the latter is a budget devised for a festival that concerns only the activities of one of the performance areas or stages. Such a budget effectively isolates this area of the event from the general festival finance. In this way budgets can be used to compare all the performance areas or stages. The master budget is illustrated in Figure 10.3. It includes box office, marketing, artist fees and staging.

The construction of a budget has the advantage of forcing the event management to allocate resources and financially plan the event. It imposes a necessary financial discipline on an event no matter how informally it is organized. In a similar way to the Gantt chart, it can be used for review long after the event is over.

Preparing a budget is illustrated by Figure 10.4. The process begins by establishing the economic environment of the event. The economy of the region and the country (and even European or world economy) may impinge on the event and significantly change the budget. For example, the effects of the rise in value of sterling against other world currencies, in particular those in the European Union using the Euro. This has

Festival Trust Financial Plan 2006/07 – 2008/09			
	Year 1 2006–7	Year 2 2007–8	Year 3 2008–9
INCOME	£	£	£
Ticket Sales	297 330	311 080	322 190
Other Sales	92 290	100 650	103 180
Private Sector Fundraising	345 840	372 020	381 260
Council Grant	347 600	345 290	331 870
Arts Board Grant	150 700	155 430	159 280
Other public sector fundraising	69 630	72 600	73 370
TOTAL	1 303 390	1 357 070	1 371 150
EXPENDITURE			
Artists & Staging	606 980	621 500	622 820
Marketing	125 950	123 200	126 280
Merchandising	24 860	25 520	26 180
Box Office	29 150	29 920	30 690
Salaries	349 030	360 470	369 490
Overheads	134 090	137 280	140 690
Contingency	33 110	37 070	37 950
TOTAL	1 303 170	1 334 960	1 354 100
SURPLUS/(DEFICIT)	220	22 110	17 050

Figure 10.3 Festival Trust 2006–09 Financial Plan

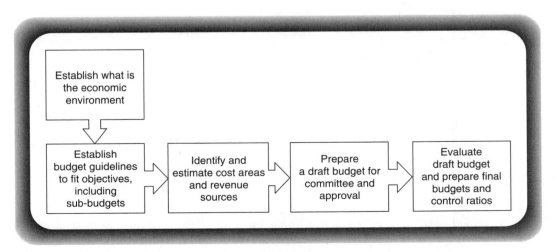

Figure 10.4 The budget process

made it more expensive for companies to place business in the UK, and made it more difficult to sell events within other countries. However, the benefit is that it has made it cheaper for UK residents to holiday and to buy equipment from abroad. To determine the economic environment, it is useful to ask the following questions. What similar events can be used as a guide? Will changes in the local or national economy affect the budget in any way? If it involves international performers or hiring equipment from overseas, will there be a change in the currency exchange rates? These, and many more, questions need to be answered before constructing a budget that will result in reasonable projections of costs and revenue.

The next step is to obtain the guidelines from the client, sponsors or event committee. For example, a client may request that only a certain percentage of their sponsorship be allocated to entertainment, with the rest to be allocated to hospitality. Guidelines must fit with the overall objectives of the event and may require constructing sub-budgets or programme budgets. This is both an *instructive phase*, in that the committee, for example, will instruct the event manager on the content of the budget and a *consultative phase*, as the event manager would ask the advice of other event specialist and the subcontractors.

The third step is to identify, categorize and estimate the cost areas and revenue sources. The categories become the items in the budget. A sample of the categories is given in Figure 10.5. This is a summary, or a first-level budget, of the cost and revenue areas. The next level down expands each of these main items, shown in Figures 10.6 and 10.7. The use of computer-generated spreadsheets enables a number of levels in the budget to be created on separate sheets and linked to the first-level budget. Cost items take up the most room on a budget and are described below.

Income	£	Expenditure	£
Grants		Administration	
Donations		Publicity	
Sponsorship		Venue costs	
Ticket sales		Equipment	
Fees		Salaries	
Special programmes		Insurance	
Concessions		Permits	
Security			
TOTAL		Accounting	
		Cleaning	
		Travel	
		Accommodation	
		Documentation	
		Hospitality	
		Community groups	
		Volunteers	
		Contingencies	
		TOTAL	

Figure 10.5 Generic budget – first level

	£		£
Administration	Office rental	Insurance	Public liability
	Fax/photocopy		Workers comp.
	Computers		Rain
	Printers		Other
	Telephone		SUB-TOTAL
	Stationery	Permits	Liquor
	Postage		Food
	Office staff		Council
	SUB-TOTAL		Parking
Publicity	Art work		Children
	Printing		SUB-TOTAL
	Poster leaflet distribution	Security	Security check
	Press kit		Equipment
	Press ads		Staff
	Radio ads		SUB-TOTAL
	Programmes	Accounting	Cash and cheque
	SUB-TOTAL		During
Equipment	Stage		After
	Sound		SUB-TOTAL
	Lights	Travel	Artists
	Transport		Freight
	Personnel		SUB-TOTAL
	Toilets	Accom.	
	Extra equipment		SUB-TOTAL
	Communication	Documentation	Photo/video
	First aid		SUB-TOTAL
	Tents	Hospitality	Tent
	Tables and chairs		Food
	Wind breaks		Beverage
	Generators		Staff
	Technicians		Invitations
	Parking needs		SUB-TOTAL
	Uniforms	Community	Donations
	SUB-TOTAL		SUB-TOTAL
Salaries	Co-ordinator	Volunteers	Food and drink
	Artists		Party
	Labourers		Awards and prizes
	Consultants		SUB-TOTAL
	Other	Contingencies	
	SUB-TOTAL		SUB-TOTAL

Figure 10.6 Generic budget – second level

Once the costs and possible revenue sources and amounts are estimated, a *draft budget* is prepared and submitted for approval to the controlling committee. This may be the finance subcommittee of a large festival. The draft budget is also used in grant submissions and sponsorships. The funding bodies, for example, UK Sport, Arts Council England, Scottish Arts Council, Arts Council of Northern Ireland,

Income	£		Ticket sales	£
Grants	Local government		Ticket sales	Box office
	Central government			Retail outlets
	Millennium Fund			Admissions
	Arts Council			SUB-TOTAL
	Other		Merchandise	T-shirts
	SUB-TOTAL			Programmes
Donations	Foundations			Posters
	Other			Badges
	SUB-TOTAL			Videos
Sponsorship	In kind			SUB-TOTAL
	Cash		Fees	Stalls
	SUB-TOTAL			Licences
Individual contributions				Broadcast
	SUB-TOTAL			SUB-TOTAL
Special programmes	Raffle		Advert sales	Programme
	Auction			Event site
	Games			SUB-TOTAL
	SUB-TOTAL		Concessions	
				SUB-TOTAL

Figure 10.7 Generic budget – third level

Arts Council of Wales, and Awards for All, have budget guidelines and forms that need to be filled out and included in the grant application.

The final step is the preparation of the budget and financial ratios that can indicate deviations from the plan. An operating business has a variety of budgets including capital expenditure, sales, overheads and production. Most events will only require an operation budget or cash budget.

Note the similarity between the classification system used for the budget and the WBS described in Chapter 9 ('Project management'). The WBS is often used as a basis of a budget. The costs of the lower levels are added to give the overall costs – called 'rolling up'. This means many aspects of the event can be coded. A simple coding system can be used to link the WBS, the budget, the task sheets and risk analysis – for example, the artwork (A) and the publicity (P) can use the code PA. This can be cross-referenced to the company, person who is responsible, possible risks or the amount budgeted.

With regard to estimating amounts within the budget, Watt (1998, p. 45) suggests that although it must be, 'as accurate as possible . . . it is always advisable to *overestimate expenditure* and *underestimate income*. To do the opposite is a recipe for disaster'.

Cash flow

The special nature of events, exhibitions, conferences and festivals requires close attention to the flow of cash. Catherwood and Van Kirk (1992), Getz (2005) and

Goldblatt (2005) all emphasize the importance of the control of cash to an event, which Goldblatt (2005) goes on to stress is imperative for the goodwill of suppliers. Without prompt payment the event company faces immediate difficulties. Payment terms and conditions have to be fully and equitably negotiated. These payment terms can ruin an event if they are not given careful consideration beforehand. To obtain the best terms from a supplier, Goldblatt (2005) suggests the following:

- Learn as much as possible about the suppliers and subcontractors and the nature of their business. Do they own the equipment? What are the normal payment terms in their business? Artists, for instance, expect to be paid immediately, whereas some information technology suppliers will wait for thirty days.
- Be flexible with what can be offered in exchange – including sponsorship. Try to negotiate a contract that stipulates a small deposit before the event and full payment after it is over.
- Suggest a line of credit, with payment at a set time in the future.
- Closely control the purchasing.
- Ensure that all purchases are made through a purchase order that is authorized by the event manager or the appropriate finance personnel. A purchase order is a written record of the agreement to supply a product at a prearranged price. All suppliers, contractors and event staff should be informed that no purchase can be made without an authorized form. This ensures that spending is confined to what is permitted by the budget.
- Obtain a full description of the product or service and the quantities required. Itemize the price to a per unit cost.
- Calculate any taxes or extra charges.
- Determine payment terms.
- Clarify delivery details.
- Consider imposing penalties if the product or service delivered is not as described.

As Figure 10.8 shows, the ability of an event coordinator to affect any change diminishes rapidly as the event draws closer. The supply of goods and services may, of necessity, take place close to or on the actual date of the event. This does not allow organizers the luxury of reminding a supplier of the terms set out in the purchase order. Without a full written description of the goods, the event manager is open to all kinds of exploitation by suppliers and, as the event may be on that day, there may be no choice but to accept delivery.

When considering cash flow, the advantage of the ticketing strategies of events such as T In The Park is obvious. As tickets are sold months before the event, the management is able to concentrate on other areas of planning. Event companies that specialize in the corporate area obtain a similar advantage. Generally they are paid upfront. This allows the event manager or producer the freedom to negotiate terms and conditions with the suppliers without having to worry about the cash flow. A cash flow timing chart similar to the Gantt chart is often helpful in planning events. This shows the names of the suppliers and their payment requirements. It includes deposit dates, payment stages, payment on purchase, monthly fixed cost payments and thirty-, sixty- or ninety-day credit payments.

Costing

The cash flow at an event is heavily dependent on the cost of goods and services. These are estimated for the construction of the budget. The prediction, categorization and allocation of costs is called the costing. In relation to the breakeven chart (see Figure 10.2), two types of costs have been identified. These are described in the following text.

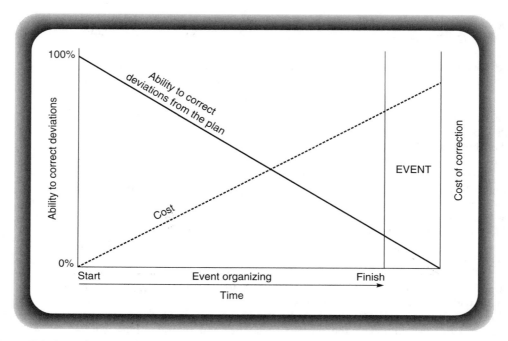

Figure 10.8 Control, cost and time
Source: adapted from Burke (2003)

Fixed costs or overheads are costs associated with the event that occur no matter how many people come to the event. They include the unchanging expenses concerned with the operation of the event management company, for example, rent, staff salaries, telephone and other office expenses. At a large festival these may include rates and interest on loans. When deciding on a budget these costs need to be apportioned reasonably to the various event areas. This process is called absorption of the overheads by the cost centres. Cost centres, for example, include entertainment, catering, staging or travel. If the fixed costs are incorrectly absorbed the cost centre will be wrongly described. For a correct financial picture of the future event, the overheads have to be reasonably spread to all areas. The aim of an event company is to reduce the fixed costs without effecting the quality of the event.

Variable costs are expenses that purely concern the event and are directly related to the number of people who attend the event. Food and beverage costs are related directly to the number of people at an event. The more people at an event the more tickets need to be printed, possibly more staff and certainly more food.

This division is not as clear-cut in the event industry as in other industries. It is sometimes clearer, instead, to talk in terms of *direct costs* (the costs directly associated with the event, whether variable of fixed) and *overheads* (costs associated with the running of the event company). In this case the direct costs are the major costs and the aim of the event company is to control these costs. Figure 10.7 lists the detailed budgeted costs of a one-off event.

Catherwood and Van Kirk (1992) divide the costs of an event into four main categories:

1. operational or production costs including event staff, construction, insurance and administration
2. venue/site rental

3. promotion – advertising, public relations, sales promotion
4. talent – costs associated with the entertainment.

To obtain the correct cost of each of the elements contained in the budget categories (sometimes called cost centres) there is a common costing process involved. The steps are listed below:

1. *Conceptual estimate* or 'ball park figure': this would be used in the conceptual development stage of the event to give management an idea of what costs are involved. Generally this would have an accuracy of plus or minus 25 per cent.
2. *Feasibility study*: this includes comparing costs in similar events, e.g. the cost of a headline speaker varies according to their career and popularity. Asking other event managers what was paid for the speaker gives the event producer a basis for negotiating a fair price and a more realistic budget estimation.
3. *Quote or definitive estimate*: this is the cost quote in reply to the tender. The larger festivals will put out to tender many of the elements of the event including sound, lights and security. A near correct estimate can be made on this basis. For small events, the quote may be obtained by ringing a selection of suppliers and comparing the costs. However, it is rarely the case that the costs are comparable, as there are so many unusual features or special conditions. Once an event company has built-up a relationship with a supplier, it tends to stay with that supplier.

Tips on reducing costs

With careful and imaginative planning, costs can be reduced in a number of areas:

- *Publicity*: an innovative event may need a large publicity budget that is based on revenue from ticket sales. The event manager's aim should be to reduce this wherever possible. Established festivals may need very little publicity as 'word of mouth' will do all the necessary work. For example, Bradford Festival, 2000, with a budget of £684 511, spent relatively little on publicity (8 per cent of total expenditure) because it had built-up such a reputation with its target audience and has developed an extensive collection of media partners for the event (Bradford Festival, 2000). The more innovative the event the greater the possibility for free publicity. The 1999 Rugby World Cup, for example, gained an enormous amount of free publicity due to the efforts of one of the main sponsors, Guinness.
- *Equipment and suppliers*: suppliers of products to events have down times during the year when their products may be hired cheaply. In particular theatrical productions at the end of their run are a ready source of decoration and scenery. Annual events like the summer festivals may have equipment in storage that can be hired.
- *In-kind gifts*: many organizations will assist events to achieve cross-promotional advantages. Entertainment can be inexpensive if there is a chance that they can promote a performance or product at the event. For example, a supplier may agree to supply their beer freely to the party for the media and guests prior to the event in exchange for the rights to sell it at the concert. A contra deal may be achieved with a radio station, with on air publicity achieved in return for displaying the radio station logo.
- *Hiring charges*: hire charges of large infrastructure components such as tents and generators and headline acts can be reduced by offering work at other festivals and events. Large cultural festivals around the UK, including the Edinburgh International Festival and the Harrogate International Festival, can offer a festival circuit to any overseas performer. Costs can therefore be amortized over all the festivals.
- *Priorities cost centres*: at some time it will be necessary to cut costs. This must be planned by knowing beforehand the effect on the overall event if one area or part

of it is significantly changed or eliminated. In project management this is called sensitivity analysis (Burke, 2003). Estimates are made of the effect of cost changes on the event and the cost centres are placed in a priority list according to the significance of the effect. For example, a sensitivity analysis could be applied to the effect of imposing a charge on a programme that was previously available free. While this could significantly increase revenue, it may produce a negative effect in sponsorship and audience satisfaction, which may well be translated into the reduction of revenue.

- *Volunteers*: costs can be reduced using volunteers instead of paid staff. It is important that all the skills of the volunteers are fully utilized. These skills should be continually under review as new skills may be required as the event planning progresses. For charitable functions, volunteers will often absorb many of the costs as tax deductible donations.

Revenue

Anticipating potential sources of revenue should be given as much attention as projecting expenses. The source of the revenue will often define the type of event, the event objectives and the planning. A company product launch has only one source of revenue – the client. Company staff parties, for example, are paid by the client with no other source of revenue. The budget then has only one entry on the left-hand side. A major festival, on the other hand, has to find and service a variety of revenue sources such as sponsors and participants. This constitutes a major part of festival planning.

Revenue can come from the following sources:

- ticket sales – most common in entrepreneurial events
- sponsorship – common in cultural and sports events
- merchandising advertising in-kind broadcast rights – an increasingly important source of revenue in sport events
- grants – local government, national government, Arts Councils, UK Sport
- fundraising – common in community events the client – the major source for corporate events.

Figure 10.8 features an expanded list of revenue sources. For many events, admission fees and ticket prices need careful consideration. It will impact on the cash flow and the breakeven point. One or more of three methods can decide the ticket price:

1. *Covering costs*: all the costs are estimated and added to the projected profit. To give the ticket price, this figure is then divided by the expected number of people who will attend the event. The method is quick, simple and based on knowing the breakeven point. It gives a 'rule of thumb' figure that can be used as starting point for further investigations in setting the price.
2. *Market demand*: the ticket price is decided by the prevailing ticket prices for similar or competing events. In other words, it is the 'going rate' for an event. Concert tickets are decided in this way. In deciding on the ticket price, consider elasticity of demand. For instance, if the ticket price is increased slightly will this affect the number of tickets sold?
3. *Perceived value*: the event may have special features that do not allow a price comparison to other events. For instance, for an innovative event the ticket price must be carefully considered. By its nature this kind of event has no comparison. There can be variations in the ticket price for different entertainment packages at the event (at many multi-venue events the ticket will include admission only to

certain events), for extra hospitality or for special seating. Knowing how to grade the tickets is an important skill in maximizing revenue. There are market segments that will not tolerate differences in pricing, whereas others expect it. It can be a culturally based decision and may be part of the design of the event.

Tips for increasing projected income

Income can be increased using a number of methods.

Ticket scaling

There are many ticketing strategies that strive to obtain the best value from ticket sales. The most common strategy is to vary the pricing with seat position, number of tickets sold and time of sale. Early-bird discounts and subscriptions series are two examples of the latter. Another strategy involves creating a special category of attendees. This could include patron, special clubs, 'friends of the event', people for whom the theme of the event has a special meaning or those who have attended many similar events in the past. For example, for a higher ticket price, patrons are offered extra hospitality, such as separate viewing area, valet parking and a cocktail party.

In-kind support and bartering

One way to increase income is to scrutinize the event cost centres for areas that could be covered by an exchange with the supplier or bartering. For example, the advertising can be expanded for an event with a programme of 'give-aways'. These are free tickets to the event given away through the press. Due to the amount goodwill surrounding a fundraising event, bartering should be explored as a method of obtaining supplies. Bartering may have tax implications. It should not be undertaken without close scrutiny of this risk.

Merchandising

The staging of an event offers many opportunities for merchandising. The first consideration is, 'Does the sale of goods enhance the theme of the event?' The problems of cash flow at an event, as stated earlier in this chapter, can give the sale of goods an unrealistic high priority in event management. It is easy to cheapen a 'boutique' special event with the sale of 'trinkets'. However, the attendees may want to buy a souvenir. For example, a large choir performing at a one-off spectacular event may welcome the opportunity to sell a video of their performance at the event. This could be arranged with the choir beforehand and result in a guaranteed income. As a spin-off the video could be incorporated into promotional material for use by the event management in bidding for future events.

Broadcast rights

An increasingly important source of revenue, particularly in sport events, is the payment for the right to broadcast. Live television broadcast is a lucrative area for potential – but it comes at a price. The broadcast, rather than the needs and expectations of the live audience, becomes master of the event. Often the live audience becomes merely one element in the television entertainment. As a result, the audience may include 'fillers' – people who fill any empty seats so that the camera will always show a capacity audience.

If the entire event is recorded by high-quality video equipment, future broadcast rights should also be investigated. For example, in many countries there is a constant demand for worthwhile content for pay television (cable or satellite). At the time of writing, Internet broadcast is in its infancy. There have been a number of music and image broadcasts but they have been limited by the size of the bandwidth. There can be no doubt that this will become an important medium for the event industry.

Sponsorship leverage

Leverage is the current term for using the event sponsorship to gain further support from other sponsors. Very few companies or organizations want to be the first to sponsor a one-off event. However, once the event has one sponsor's support, sufficient credibility is gained to enable an approach to other sponsors. For example, gaining the support of a major newspaper or radio station allows the event manager to approach other sponsors. The sponsors realize that they can obtain free publicity.

Special features

When an event is linked to a large population base, there are many opportunities for generating income. Raffles, for example, are frequently used to raise income. At a concert-dance in Bath, all patrons brought along a prize for a raffle drawn on the night. Each received a ticket in the raffle, as part of the entry fee to the event. The prizes ranged from old ties to overseas air tickets. The raffle took two hours to get through, but every person received a prize and it became part of the entertainment of the evening.

Holding an auction at an event is also an entertaining way to increase event income. For example, the Childline Next St Clements Ball (held in October 2000) included auction items such as a trip on a Sunseeker powerboat, a football signed by the England team and a pair of British Airways Club Class return tickets. The sale of the football shirts after a major match, complete with the mud stains, has been a way of raising revenue.

Reporting

The importance of general reporting on the progress of the event planning has been described in this chapter. The budget report is the means to highlight problems and suggest solutions. It is an efficient way to communicate this to the event committee and staff and should be readily understood. It is important that appropriate action is taken in response to the report's suggestion. Figure 10.9 is a list of guidelines for a straightforward report.

The most common problem in an event is the cost 'blow out'. Event managers often encounter unforeseen circumstances that can cost dearly. For example, the subcontractor that supplies the sound system can go bankrupt; the replacement subcontractor may prove more expensive. One of the unwritten laws of project management is that the closer the project is to completion the more expensive are any changes. Appropriate remedial action may be to go for the cheaper catering or to find extra funding. This could be a raffle to pay for the extra sound. Figure 10.7 shows graphically how the cost of any changes to the organization of an event escalates as the event date nears.

The main problem of a budget, particularly for events, is blindly sticking to it without regard for changes in the plan. It is a tool of control and not an end in itself. The elegance of a well laid out budget and its mathematical certainty can obscure that

- The report should relate directly to the area of the event management area to which it is addressed.
- It should not contain extraneous information that can only obsure its function. Brevity and clarity are the key objectives.
- The figures in the report must be of the same magnitude and they should be comparable.
- It should describe how to take remedial action if there is a significant problem.

Figure 10.9 Reporting guidelines

it is a slave to the event objectives, not its master. A budget is based on reasonable projections made within an economic framework. Small changes in the framework can cause large changes in the event's finances. For example, extra sponsorship may be found if the right products are added to the event portfolio or if there is demand from customers and venue capacity, increased tickets may be made available. A complicated, highly detailed budget may consume far more time than is necessary to make the event a success.

Time is a crucial factor in event management. Keeping rigidly within budgetary standards can take up too much time and energy of the event management, limiting time for other areas.

Finally, a budget that is constructed by the event management may be imposed on staff without adequate consultation. This can lead to losing valuable specialist staff if they find themselves having to work to unreasonable budgetary standards. In particular, an innovative event requires the creative input of all the staff and subcontractors. At these events, informal financial control using a draft budget is often far more conducive to quality work than strict budgetary control.

It needs to be remembered that a budget is only an approximation of reality, and not reality itself. It will need to be adjusted as the event changes and new information comes to hand. However, it is a vital part of the control mechanism for events.

Chapter summary

There is little point in expending effort in creating a plan for an event if there is no way to closely monitor it. The event plan is a prerequisite for success. The control mechanisms to keep the project aligned to the plan need to be well thought out and easy to understand by the management team. When the event strays from the plan there needs to be ways to bring it back into line or to change the plan.

An estimate of the costs and revenues of an event is called the budget and it acts as the master control of an event. With a well-reasoned budget in place, all sections of an event know their spending limits and can work together. The cash flow of an event needs special considerations. When is the cash coming in? Moreover, when does it need to go out? An event that does not have control mechanisms, including a well-thought-out budget, is not going to satisfy its stakeholders. Not only will it fail, but also organizations will never know the reason for its failure. A sound budget gives management a solid foundation on which to build a successful event.

Questions

1. Can the use of control and monitoring overwhelm the creative aspects of event management?
2. List the milestones for management of a fun run event of 10 000 people.
3. What are other gaps that can be measured to indicate a deviation from the event plan?
4. The budget is often perceived as the most important part of event management. What are the limitations of running an event by the budget? Do many events such as the arts festivals always come in under budget? What can lead to drastic changes in the budget?
5. Identify the cost centres and revenue sources for:
   (a) a celebrity poetry reading for a charity
   (b) a rural car auction with antique cars
   (c) a corporate Christmas party
   (d) a hot air balloon festival.
6. Staging, logistics, risk management and project management all have their techniques for monitoring and controlling. Compare them. Can they all come under the method used in risk management?
7. Why is cash flow of such importance to event management? Can an event be run on credit?

Case study 10.1

Edinburgh International Festival

The Edinburgh International Festival was founded in 1947 in the aftermath of a devastating world war. The founders believed that the Festival should enliven and enrich the cultural life of Europe, Britain and Scotland and provide a platform for the flowering of the human spirit. The programmes were intended to be of the highest possible standard, presented by the best artists in the world. The achievement of many of those aims over the years has ensured the Edinburgh International Festival is now one of the most important cultural celebrations in the world.

Both the political world and the world of the arts are now very different from the immediate post-war years and the Festival has developed significantly in the interim. However, the founders' original intentions are closely reflected in the current mission and objectives of the Festival. The mission is 'to be the most exciting, innovative and accessible Festival of the performing arts in the world, and thus promote the cultural, educational and economic well-being of the people of Edinburgh and Scotland' through:

- Presenting arts of the highest possible international standard to the widest possible audience
- Reflecting international culture in presentation to Scottish audiences and reflecting Scottish culture in presentation to international audiences
- Presenting events which cannot easily be achieved by any other UK arts organization through innovative programming and a commitment to new work
- Actively ensuring equal opportunities for all sections of the Scottish and wider public to experience and enjoy the Festival

- Encouraging public participation in the arts throughout the year by collaborating with other arts and festival organizations.

The Festival brings to Edinburgh some of the best in international theatre, music, dance and opera and presents the arts in Scotland to the world. Around the International Festival, a number of other festivals have grown, the largest of which is the Fringe. There is also the Military Tattoo, a Jazz & Blues Festival, Film Festival, Mela, Science Festival, Children's Festival and Book Festival. All of these are administered separately from the International Festival. A recent survey showed that the summer festivals generate £135 million for the economy of Edinburgh and sustain nearly 2900 jobs across Scotland.

Festival finances

All artists and companies in the annual three-week event appear at the invitation of the Festival Director. The Festival's budget covers all of the costs associated with delivering the programme including artists' fees, travel, venue hire and promotion of the event. The Festival has three main revenue sources: ticket sales, sponsorship and donations, and public sector grants.

- **Ticket sales:** The Festival raised £1.74 million of income through the sale of tickets, representing 27 per cent of total income. It is not possible to generate significant additional ticket sales revenue without abandoning the current accessible pricing policy. EIF continued developing wider access through a series of late night inexpensive events (£5 per ticket) and Turn-Up-and-Try-It tickets throughout the festival at £5. The success of these initiatives had an impact on some of the full-priced events.
- **Sponsorship and donations:** The Festival is Scotland's most successful arts organization at generating income from this area. The total of £1.73 million raised in 2004 represents 27 per cent of the Festival's total income and continues to be a strength at a time when many organizations are reporting a fall in income from the corporate sector.
- **Public sector grants:** In 2004, grants from the City of Edinburgh Council were £1.47 million and the Scottish Arts Council £1.09 million, with further grants obtained from SAC Lottery and Scottish Executive's National programme for Mental Health and Well-being. Grants account for 34 per cent of total income.

The development of The Hub, the new home for the Edinburgh International Festival, means that there is potential for growth. However, given that The Hub is not a purely commercial resource, but has an educational and artistic remit, it is expected to cover running costs from commercial income, thus enabling a year round programme of education activities. The total income and expenditure are summarized in Figure 10.10.

Revenue grants from the local authority and from central government have been at the core of the Festival's finances since 1947. This public subsidy helps define the style and tone of the Festival presented, enabling a subsidized ticket pricing policy that ensures access to the widest possible audience.

Public sector support for the Festival has declined in cash terms. The benefit of restoring 1994 levels of funding in 2002 has been eroded over the past two years as the grants have not risen with inflation. Whilst costs have been kept rigorously under control, the effect of rising costs and shrinking grants has been recognized. Positive discussions with funding bodies have resulted in a study, 'Thundering Hooves', being commissioned by the Scottish Executive, Edinburgh City Council, Scottish Arts Council and EventScotland, to look at how to support and develop Edinburgh's Festivals in the light of increasing competition worldwide. In addition, the Association of Edinburgh's Festivals has been established to encourage sharing of best practice.

EDINBURGH INTERNATIONAL FESTIVAL SOCIETY
Report and Financial Statements
For the eleven months ended 31 October 2004

Consolidated Revenue Account

	Notes	11 months ended 31 October 2004 £000s	£000s	12 months ended 30 November 2003 £000s	£000s
Operating income					
Ticket sales		1745		2237	
Sponsorship and donations	2	1731		1988	
Publications and other earned income		224		245	
Trading subsidiary sales	3	1199		1409	
Grant income			4899		5879
City of Edinburgh Council		1470		1444	
City of Edinburgh Council Youth Development		–		38	
Scottish Arts Council		1090		1090	
Scottish Arts Council Lottery		68		71	
Scottish Executive Health Department		30		–	
City of Edinburgh Council deficit grant		–		400	
Scottish Executive deficit grant		–		400	
			2658		3443
Total income			7557		9322
Operating expenditure					
Productions and performances			(4484)		(5256)
Marketing and public affairs		576		541	
Fundraising and sponsorship		235		278	
Administration		623		638	
Depreciation		112		137	
			(1546)		(1594)
Trading subsidiary costs	3		(1695)		(1798)
Total expenditure			(8089)		(8648)
Operating (deficit)/surplus for financial year	5		(532)		674
Bank interest receivable		35		23	
Bank overdraft and other interest payable	6	(34)		(53)	
			1		(30)
(Deficit)/surplus for the financial year			(531)		644
Allocated from restricted funds	14		116		124
General fund (deficit)/surplus for financial year	14		(415)		768

Figure 10.10 Edinburgh International Festival Consolidated Revenue Account

In summary, it is no longer possible to undertake the Festival without an increase in resources. The Council of the Edinburgh International Festival Society is working with a range of stakeholders, including the City Council and the Scottish Arts Council, to assist these bodies and the Scottish Executive to come to a satisfactory decision about future levels of support. All of the various stakeholders in the Festival now face hard choices about how much money they are prepared to invest in its future, and what kind of Festival they want. It is only through re-instating funding that the Edinburgh International Festival will continue to maintain and develop its role in Scotland's cultural future.

For further information about Edinburgh International Festival, please visit www.eif.co.uk.

By Edinburgh International Festival, The Hub, Castlehill, Royal Mile, Edinburgh, EH1 2NE Tel: 0131 473 2099.

Questions

1. Edinburgh International Festival is one of the largest internationally known festivals in Britain. What factors do you think have led to its growth and success?
2. Edinburgh International Festival is reliant on public funding for 34 per cent of its funds, yet this area has been in decline. From what you have been told in the case study, what affect will this reduction in funding have on the event?
3. In the long-term, various options exist for the organizers, including a shift in income streams to other areas, such as corporate sponsorship, or reducing the size of the event.
   (a) Evaluate the stated alternatives in the light of what is known from the case study.
   (b) How would a shift in income stream change the style of the festival and programming?
   (c) What effect would this change have on the image portrayed by the festival?

Chapter 11

Risk management and legal issues

Introduction

A working definition of event risk is any future incident that will negatively influence the event. Note that this risk is not solely at the event itself. In many texts on events, risk is taken to mean safety risk or financial risk, but this definition ignores problems in other areas of event management that may harmfully influence the success of the event. Fraud, for example, is a risk that has surfaced at many events. Misrepresentation of the event by marketing or overpromotion is another risk. Each of these risks may result in safety and financial troubles at the event. Risk management can be defined as the process of identifying these problems, assessing them and dealing with them. Fortunately, risk management may also uncover opportunities. In the past, this may have been done in an informal manner; however, the current management environment demands that the process be formalized. The event team must be able to show that risk management is being employed throughout the project. This chapter outlines the process of risk management. The process is made up of understanding the context of risk, risk identification, evaluation and control. This process can be applied to all the areas of event management. The second section of the chapter describes the legal issues. Some of these issues are complex, involving permits, licences and legislation. They are different across countries within the United Kingdom and implementation varies slightly between councils. One of the fundamental concepts common to all is the duty of care, and this is defined later in the chapter. Contracts are essential to all event management, and the process of contract management is also described in this chapter. Many of the event risks are transferred to a third party via an insurance contract.

In this chapter, two areas of event management often included in the risk area are considered in detail: legal compliance and contract management.

Risk management process

Events are particularly susceptible to risks. Risk, in the event context, may be formally defined as the likelihood of the event or festival not fulfilling its objectives. A unique venue, large crowds, new staff and volunteers, movement of equipment and general excitement are all a recipe for potential hazards. The event manager who ignores advice on risk prevention is courting disaster and foreshortening his or her career in the events industry. The sensible assessment of potential hazards and preventative action is the basis of risk management, and is a legal requirement under the Management of Health and Safety at Work Regulations 1992. According to the Health and Safety Executive (HSE, 1999, p. 7) risk may be defined as 'the likelihood that harm from a hazard is realised and the extent of it'.

Risk is not necessarily harmful. One reason, among many, that an event company wins the job of organizing an event is that competing companies perceive the event to be too risky. The successful company can manage all the risks with its current resources. Risk is the basis of the entrepreneur's business. Without risk, there can be no competitive advantage. Without the appearance of risk, there can be no tightrope walking or extreme games. Part of what makes an event special is the uncertainty – it has not been done before.

The British Standards Institution (BSI, 2002a, p. 7) defines risk management as the:

systematic application of management policies, procedures and practices to the tasks of establishing the context, identifying, analysing, evaluating, treating, monitoring and communicating risk.

Every part of event management has potential risks. Various publications exist to assist the event manager in managing risk, including general publications offered by the Health and Safety Executive (HSE, 1998) and guidance developed for exhibitions (AEO, BECA and EVA, 2002), music events (HSE, 1999), outdoor events other than pop concerts and raves (NOEA, 1993; 1997), sporting grounds (Department of National Heritage and the Scottish Office, 1997) and crowd safety (HSE, 2000). BSI (2004) has been developed to provide practical guidance for organizing all outdoor events and cross references to existing publications/regulations that event organizers should be aware of. Further, a number of additional publications have been developed specifically for events (Berlonghi, 1990; Hannam, 2004; Kemp and Hill, 2004; Tarlow, 2002). Possibly the best known out of these publications, sometimes referred to as the Purple Guide, is *The Event Safety Guide* (HSE, 1999). Designed to provide advice for the safe management of music events, concerts and festivals, the guide separates events into five phases where risk can be assessed:

- *Build-up*: this involves planning the venue design, selection of competent workers, selection of contractors and subcontractors, and construction, for example, of the stage, marquees, and fencing.
- *Load in*: this involves planning for the safe delivery and installation of equipment and services which will be used at the event, for example, stage equipment used by performers, lighting and sound systems.

- *Show*: this involves planning effective crowd management strategies, transport management strategies and welfare arrangements and planning strategies for dealing with fire, first aid, contingencies and major incidents.
- *Load out*: this requires planning for the safe removal of equipment and services.
- *Breakdown*: this includes planning to control risks once the event is over and the infrastructure is being dismantled, including disposal of waste-water and rubbish.

Berlonghi (1990) categorizes the *main areas* of risk as follows:

- *Administration*: the organizational structure and office layout should minimize risk to employees.
- *Marketing and public relations*: the promotion section must be aware of the need for risk management. By their nature, marketeers are optimistic about the consequences of their actions and tend to ignore potential risks.
- *Health and safety*: a large part of risk management concerns this area. Loss prevention plans and safety control plans are an important part of any risk management strategy. The risks associated with food concession hygiene and sanitation require specific attention.
- *Crowd management*: risk management of crowd flow, alcohol sales and noise control (see Chapter 12 on logistics).
- *Security*: the security plan for an event involves careful risk management thinking.
- *Transport*: deliveries, parking and public transport contain many potential hazards that need to be addressed.

A good risk management strategy will also cover any other operational areas that are crucial to the event and that may need special security and safety precautions, such as access control, ticket sales and other cash points and communications.

In Chapter 9, the areas of event project management are introduced and risk is one of those areas, but it is not an isolated area. The risk management process cuts right across all the other areas. In any one of the areas of knowledge and management, the risks must be identified and pre-empted, and their management fully integrated into the event plan. By using a project management approach to the event, risk management becomes an underlying process that is employed continuously in every area of the management. Figure 11.1 identifies nine steps that need to be taken to assess the risks associated with staging event.

Step 1	Understanding context: Consider event type, management, stakeholders and general environment
Step 2	Identifying risks: Look for the hazards
Step 3	Decision: Decide who might be harmed and how
Step 4	Evaluating the Risk: Evaluate the risks and decide whether the existing precautions are adequate or whether more should be done.
Step 5	Control: Control problems that may arise
Step 6	Mitigating actions: Consider mitigating actions
Step 7	Specific event risks: Consider specific event risks
Step 8	Recording: Record your findings
Step 9	Review: Review your assessment and revise it if necessary

Figure 11.1 Nine steps to risk management
Source: adapted from HSE 1998, p. 3

Understanding context

The context of risk management includes the type of event, the management structure, the stakeholder analysis and the general risk environment. Throwing white powder, for example, was considered a major danger at events a few years ago due to the publicity about the anthrax scare, as an incident could cause a stampede if any crowd member thought it was anthrax. Today, throwing white powder might not rate a mention in the press. Terrorism is a major concern for some events. While the attacks on the World Trade Center and Pentagon in 2001 increased the perceived threat in countries previously thought safe from terrorism, it must be remembered that terrorism at events has been a concern since the Munich Olympics. It is an ongoing concern in many countries. The 2001 attacks in the USA, 2004 attacks in Madrid and the 2005 attacks in the UK increased the public perception in western countries of this risk. Some nations deal with terrorism as part of their day-to-day security. Large events, as they attract global media interest, can be a terrorism target. The conclusion is that the surrounding environment has to be taken into account in the risk management process. The organization culture of the client and the event company are also part of the context to be considered.

Some companies or organizations are highly risk averse and would prefer a predictable event that has been tried and tested for many years. These clients prefer the 'franchised' event. A large part of the risk will originate with or involve the stakeholders. A comprehensive stakeholder analysis is a pre-requisite for thorough risk management. The stakeholders may also provide the support to deal with the risks. The legislation on duty of care and public liability are further examples of the event environment that will impinge on the risk management process. The financial risk is an example of an ever changing context. The currency exchange rate, the financial state of the sponsors, fraud and the demands of the shareholders are some of the external developments that can affect the financial viability of the event. A comprehensive risk assessment cannot be performed without understanding the context of the event, the risk environment and the stakeholder's requirements. One must remember this context is changing and therefore needs to be reassessed as the event management progresses.

Identifying risks

The next stage in the process is identifying the risks. Pre-empting problems requires skill, experience and knowledge. Something that appears safe to some of the event staff may contain hidden dangers. A sponsor's sign at an event may look securely mounted when examined by the marketing manager, but it will require the specialist knowledge of the stagehands to ensure it is secure. As the event manager cannot be an expert in every field, it is best to pool the experience of all the event staff and volunteers by convening a risk assessment meeting. Such a meeting should aim to gather risk management expertise. For large or complex events, an event risk consultant may be hired. The meeting is also an opportunity to train and motivate event staff in the awareness, minimization and control of risks.

Identification techniques

A range of techniques is available for event managers to assess and manage the risks involved in an event:

- *Work breakdown structure* – breaking down the work necessary to create an event into manageable parts can greatly assist in the identification of risks. It provides a visual scheme as well as the categorization of the event into units associated with specific skills and resources. An example of the work breakdown structure (WBS) is found in Chapter 9. Isolating the event areas in this way gives a clear picture of the possible problems. One of the areas of the WBS for an award night, for example, is the work associated with the Master of Ceremonies (MC). One of the authors has posed this question at many event workshops: 'What could go wrong with the MC?' Some of the problems identified by event managers' experience include: being inebriated, not turning up, leaving early, not reading the script, using inappropriate language, having a scruffy appearance, believing they are the main act, being unable to use a microphone and insulting the sponsor. This does not imply that these are common problems; however, an event manager would be foolish to ignore the experience of others. The construction of a work breakdown structure assists another area of management – the creation of a risk management plan – and thus illustrates the importance of the project management system to event management. Although the work breakdown structure is a necessary tool for risk management, it may not reveal the problems that result in a combination of risks. A problem with the ticketing of an event, for example, may not be severe on its own. If it is combined with the withdrawal of a major sponsor, the result may require the event to be cancelled.

- *Test events* – large sporting events often run smaller events to test the facilities, equipment and other resources. The Commonwealth Games test events were effectively used to iron out any problems before the main event. A test is a self-funded rehearsal. The pre-conference cocktail party, for example, is used to test some aspects of the conference. Many music festivals will run an opening concert on the night before the first day of the festival, as a means of testing the equipment.

- *Internal/external* – to assist risk analysis it is useful to have a classification system according to the origin of the risk. Internal risks arise in the event planning and implementation stage. They may also result from the inexperience of the event company. These risks are generally within the abilities of the event company to manage. External risks arise from outside the event organization and may need a different control strategy. This technique focuses on mitigating the impact of the risk – dealing with the consequences. The impact of a star football player cancelling, for example, may be minimized by allowing free entry to the event. For this reason, the SWOT analysis is a risk identification technique. The strengths and weaknesses correspond to internal risks, and the opportunities and threats correspond to the external risks.

- *Fault diagram* – risks can also be discovered by looking at their impact and working backwards to the possible cause. This is called a result-to-cause method. A lack of ticket sales at an event, for example, would be a terrible result. The fault diagram method would go back from this risk through the various event aspects to postulate its cause. The list of causes is then used to manage the risk.

- *Incident report* – almost all large public events have an incident report document. These may be included in the event manual and are to be filled out by the event staff when there is an incident. The incident data can then be used by agencies to give an event risk profile. This is not to be confused with an accident report book, which is a legal requirement for all events under the Reporting of Injuries, Diseases and Dangerous Occurrences Regulations 1995 (RIDDOR). The ambulance service may have data on medical incidents for events. By giving the ambulance service key characteristics of an event, such as audience number, alcohol availability, age group and type of event activity they can predict the type of medical incidents most likely to occur.

- *Contingency plan* – an outcome of the risk analysis may be a detailed plan of viable alternative integrated actions. The contingency plan contains the response to the impact of a risk and involves a decision procedure, chain of command and a set of related actions. An example of contingency planning was the response to the extreme weather conditions on New Year's Eve 2000. As a result of heavy snow and wind, followed by a quick thaw and heavy rain, many events were cancelled. However, the event at Belfast City was transferred from the outdoor venue to Belfast Waterfront (indoors) and the event was a success.

- *Scenario development and tabletop exercises* – the use of a 'what if' session can uncover many risks. A scenario of problems is given to the event team and interested stakeholders. They work through the problems and present their responses. This is collated and discussed. These tabletop exercises are surprisingly effective. One tabletop exercise used the scenario of an expected fireworks display, not happening at a major New Year's Eve event. All the agencies around the table then responded, describing the consequences as they saw it and their contingency plans. The problems included disappointed crowds, a rush for the public transport and other crowd management issues. Would the event company be able to announce to the crowd of 500 000 what had happened? The fireworks went off as planned in the following year. Two years later, however, the fireworks did not occur. A number of the agencies such as police, emergency service and railways were able to use their contingency plans. Major sponsors and government clients may send an event company a number of scenarios and ask for their response. This is a way of testing the competence of the event management.
- *Consultation* – part of due diligence in planning events is the concept of consultation. The event management team should consult with the various suppliers on their safety plans for the event. It is slightly different for different regions; however, consultation can also be used to strengthen the risk identification and analysis. Suppliers have a wealth of information on what can go wrong. Consultation does not imply just asking questions, the event manager must provide relevant information so that the other party can give a considered opinion. This opinion must be taken into account in the planning of the event and risk management. An essential aspect of risk identification is a way to accurately describe them. The risk for an outdoor event is not 'weather'. A beautiful fine day is still 'weather'. Heat or rain may be the risk descriptor. However, this is still not accurate enough. Extreme heat or rain before the event is getting closer to describing the actual risk. The process of describing the risk accurately also enables the event team to think the risk through.

Decision

Decide on who may be harmed. This may include, for example:

- people particularly at risk, e.g. young workers, trainees
- people not familiar with the site, e.g. contractors, visitors, members of the public.

Evaluating the risk

It is clear that there are an infinite number of things that can go wrong and a finite number that can go right. Identifying risk can open a Pandora's box of issues. Risk assessment meetings often reveal the 'prophets of doom' who can bring an overly pessimistic approach to the planning process. This is itself a risk that must be anticipated. The event team must have a method of organizing the risks so they can be methodically managed. Once the risks are accurately described, they should be mapped according to:

- the likelihood of them occurring (for example, on a five-point scale from rare to almost certain)
- the consequence if they do occur (for example, on a five-point scale from insignificant to catastrophic).

An accurate way of describing the risks is essential to clear communication. At a recent risk meeting, for example, the risk of providing *incorrect information to the media* was identified as 'likely' and the consequence was 'moderate' to 'major'. It was assessed as needing attention and requiring a solution. At another meeting it was found that the decision to possibly cancel the event was being left to the event's general manager (GM). However, during the event, the GM would be in a high security area with politicians, and difficult to contact. The risk of *GM impossible to contact* was rated 'certain' and 'catastrophic'. The solution was simple: have security clearance for a 'runner' to be able to communicate between the event team and the GM.

A risk meeting with the staff and volunteers is often the only way to uncover many risks. It is important that the meeting be well chaired and focused, since the time needed for risk assessment must always be weighed against the limited time available for the overall event planning. An effective risk assessment meeting will produce a comprehensive and realistic analysis of the potential risks in a risk register. The risk register is the document output of the risk management process and is further explained in the documentation section later in this chapter.

Control

Once the risks have been evaluated, the event management team needs to create mechanisms to control any problem that can arise. In *Five Steps to Risk Management*, the Health and Safety Executive (HSE, 1998) suggest that managers ask the following questions: can I get rid of the hazard altogether? If not, how can I control the risks so that harm is unlikely? The decisions include:

- changing the likelihood that a problem will occur – this can include avoiding the problem by not proceeding with that aspect of the event. A recent water-ski event, for example, was unable to obtain insurance. The management identified the part of the event that was high risk and cancelled it. This enabled the event to go ahead with the necessary level of insurance.
- changing the consequence if the problem does occur – such as contingency planning and disaster plans
- accepting the risk
- transferring the risk to another party.

Insurance is an example of changing the consequence by transferring the risk and accepting a smaller risk. The risk that is now accepted is:

- the insurance contract will be honoured (for example, the insurance company could go bankrupt)
- the event makes enough money to pay for the insurance.

The risk management process can be defined, therefore, as transferring the risks to a part of the event management that has the resources (including skills, experience and knowledge) to handle it. This is an important point because the risk is rarely, if ever, completely eliminated, except by cancelling the event. Once a risk has been identified and a solution planned, its likelihood of occurring and its consequences are reduced.

In his comprehensive manual on risk management for events, Berlonghi (1990) suggests the following risk control strategies:

- *Cancel and avoid the risk* – if the risk is too great it may be necessary to cancel all or part of the event. Outdoor concerts that are part of a larger event are often cancelled if there is rain. The major risk is not audience discomfort, but the danger of electrocution.
- *Diminish the risk* – risks that cannot be avoided need to be minimized. To eliminate all possible security risks at an event, for example, may require every patron to be searched. This solution is obviously unworkable at a majority of events and, instead, a risk minimization strategy will need to be developed – for example, installing metal detectors or stationing security guards in a more visible position.
- *Reduce the severity of risks that do eventuate* – a major part of safety planning is preparing quick and efficient responses to foreseeable problems. Training staff in elementary first aid can reduce the severity of an accident. The event manager cannot eliminate natural disasters but can prepare a plan to contain the effects.
- *Devise back-ups and alternatives* – when something goes wrong, the situation can be saved by having an alternative plan in place. In case the juggler does not turn up to a children's party, for example, the host can organize party games to entertain the children. On a larger scale, back-up generators are a must at big outdoor events in case of a major power failure.
- *Distribute the risk* – if the risk can be spread across different areas, its impact will be reduced if something does go wrong. One such strategy is to widely spread the cash-taking areas, such as ticket booths, so that any theft is contained and does not threaten the complete event income. This does not eliminate the risk, it transfers it to an area that can be managed by the event company – such as security and supervision. Having a variety of sponsors is another way to distribute risk. If one sponsor pulls out, the others can be approached to increase their involvement.
- *Transfer the risk* – risk can be transferred to other groups responsible for an event's components. Subcontractors may be required to share the liability of an event. Their contracts generally contain a clause to the effect that they are responsible for the safety of their equipment and the actions of their staff during the event. For example, performing groups may be required to have public liability insurance before they can take part in an event.

Mitigating actions

The following examples of mitigating actions are based on recommendations of the USA Emergency Management Institute.

At every event, people will leave some items unattended. Event officials must decide beforehand how to handle unattended packages and have a written plan for all personnel to follow. The issues to consider include: Who will respond? Are dogs trained to identify explosives available? Will the area be evacuated?

Concealment areas are areas where persons may hide or where someone may hide packages or other weapons. The best way to avoid problems in these areas is to map the event venue and identify the areas that could be used as hiding spots. Venue staff can assist in this matter.

Venue and security personnel should work together to conduct a security sweep of the venue. A few areas to address in advance are: How often is security going to go through the event site? What are they looking for? How do they handle incidents? Who is going to do the sweep? Once a sweep of the area has been done the area must be secured. Each of these mitigating actions, in addition to Berlonghi's strategies, can be reduced to the management of two risk dimensions: likelihood and consequence. A back-up generator is an example of reducing the *consequence* of a blackout. Checking the capacity of the electricity supply is an example of reducing the *likelihood* of a power failure.

Risk communication

Effective risk communication includes the following:

- *Understanding the terminology of risk* – the risk needs to be accurately described and understood by all the event staff and volunteers.
- *Open communication channels* – it is a well-known problem at events that staff are hesitant to tell event management that a task has not been completed. If they identify problems there must be a way that this can be communicated to the event management in a timely manner. A system of team leaders may be used with part of their role to collect this data.
- *Informal methods of communication* – management theorists, such as Drucker (1973), stress how important these informal methods are to the success of a company. This is true for events. The dinners, chats over coffee or just a friendly talk can greatly assist the communication process. Walking the site is a time-honoured way to find out what is going on.

The formal process of communicating risk includes the distribution of the risk plan. It is the output or deliverable of the risk management process. The plan contains a list of identified risks, their assessment, the plan of action, who is responsible and the timeline for implementation. In the fluid event management environment, a fixed plan may be quickly out of date. A risk management plan of a parade, for example, will have to be revised if there are any additions to the parade, such as horses. For this reason, it is recommended by most project management texts that a live risk register be established. The risk register is a plan that is constantly updated and revised. As new risks are identified they are added to the register. The register has a number of functions:

1. It is a live management tool.
2. It can be used to track risks so they are not forgotten.
3. It is proof of actions for a work-in-progress report.
4. It can be used after the event to help prove competent management.
5. It can be used for the next event to assist risk identification and planning.
6. It can have various levels of access to allow staff and senior management a role in risk management.
7. It can communicate the main issues, simply and clearly.

A live risk register can be put on the Intranet or Internet, and is therefore accessible to all members of the event team. At any time, it can be printed off and placed in a report to the various stakeholders. The risk register thus provides a snapshot for the event management process.

Specific event risks

Many of the risks that are specific to the event industry happen at the event itself. The risks associated with these will vary according to the nature of the event (HSE, 1999). Issues with crowd movement are an obvious area of risk. The consequences of a crowd-related incident can lead to duty of care and criminal liability issues, so they are a high priority in the event manager's mind. However, the risks at the event may be a result of ignoring the risks before the event. For this reason, the risk management must be tracked across all areas of event management. Many of the risks at the event can be tracked back to a lack of time in management. The lack of time is, in reality, an inability to scope the event management. The conclusion is that a systematic method must be used. Due to the temporary nature of events, there are numerous risks. For example, Upton (2004) highlights a number of examples of dangerous crowd behaviour at music events, including crowd surges, slam dancing/moshing (where people slam into each other while dancing), crowd surfing (where an individual is lifted above the heads of the crowd and swims or rolls towards the stage) and stage diving (where someone, either a member of the band or audience, jumps off the stage into the crowd and is then supported above their heads, possibly turning into a crowd surf. Another example is using volunteers at events, which can result in many kinds of risks. Some of the risks listed at a recent workshop relating to volunteers include: don't listen, don't turn up, complain and form subgroups, can't control, no accountability and deplete the asset. The latter refers to a problem with repeat events, when the volunteers are set in their ways and the event needs to change. The discussion is not exhaustive. It highlights some of the areas specific to events.

Crowd management

The two terms often confused are crowd control and crowd management. As Abbot (2000, p. 105) points out:

> *Crowd management and crowd control are two distinct but interrelated concepts. The former includes the facilitation, employment and movement of crowds, while the latter relates to the steps taken once the crowd has lost control.*

The concept of crowd management is an example of pre-empting problems at the event by preparing the risk management before the event. Many crowd control issues arise from inadequate risk management by the event company. However, there can still be unforeseen risks with crowds. There are many factors that impinge on the smooth management of crowds at an event. The first risk is correctly estimating the number of people who will attend the event. No matter how the site is designed, too many attendees can put enormous strain on the event resources. For example, gatecrashers at Glastonbury Festival 2000 doubled the licensed capacity to an estimated 200 000 people on-site. This led to the cancellation of Glastonbury 2001, due to increased safety fears in the wake of the Roskilde tragedy and prosecution of the organizer for alleged breach of the licence. Even at free events, too few attendees can significantly affect the event objectives. For example, the launch of Millennium Square in Leeds on New Year's Eve 2000 saw only hundreds, rather than the anticipated thousands, of visitors attend due to the extreme weather conditions on the evening. Crowd risk management is also a function of the type of audience and their standards of behaviour. A family event will have different priorities in risk management to a rock festival. The expectations of the crowd can be managed with the right kind of information being sent out prior to the event. The HSE guide, *Managing Crowds Safely* (HSE, 2000), provides general guidance for managing crowd safety in a systematic way, covering the areas of planning, risk assessment, putting precautions in place, emergency planning and procedures, communication, monitoring crowds and review. Crowd management for large events has become a specialist field of study, and there are a number of consultancies in this area. Excellent resources on the study of crowds can be found at www.crowdsafe.com, www.crowddynamics.com and www.safety-rocks.org.

Alcohol and drugs

Events can range from a family picnic with the audience sipping wine while watching a show to a New Year's Eve mass gathering of youths and the heavy consumption of alcohol. Under the law, both events are treated the same. The responsible service of alcohol provision in many countries is a method of reducing the likelihood of this risk. Some annual events have been cancelled due to the behaviour problems that arise from selling alcohol. The alcohol risk management procedures can permeate every aspect of some events, including limiting ticket sales, closing hotels early, increasing security and roping-off areas. The European Football Championships 2000, hosted jointly by the Netherlands and Belgium, illustrate the negative impact that alcohol can have, with violence, civil disruption, arrests, restaurants and bars closed, and the threat of England team being expelled from the tournament.

A worthy mention is the risk of drugs at events. Many modern events, in particular rave parties, involve risks arising from the drug use. Emergency and first-aid services are faced with the quandary of treating the problem and reporting the incident to police. Some rave or dance parties are secret – which is part of the allure – and first-aid services have to decide whether to inform the police of these parties and, therefore, risk the possibility of not being contracted again by the organizers. Another risk related to drug use is the presence of syringes and their safe handling by the staff.

Communication

The risks involved in communication are varied as it concerns the event organization and reporting any risks. Setting up a computer and filing system for the event office can prevent future problems. Easy access to relevant information is vital to good risk management. A standard, yet customized, reporting procedure can also reduce the risk of ineffective communication. Communication can include: how the public is informed of the event, signage and keeping the attendees informed when they are at the event site. The event manual is an excellent communication device for the procedures, protocol and general event information for staff and volunteers. There can be a risk of too much data obscuring the important information; therefore, it needs to be highly focused.

Stewarding and security

An important consideration for event organizers is how the crowd will be managed and controlled, or more importantly, who. This may range from event stewards and security staff through to volunteer stewards. Stewards are primarily responsible for crowd management, while security may be responsible the protection of performers, premises or equipment (HSE, 1999). This requires careful thought and planning to ensure that there are sufficient numbers of trained and/or qualified staff performing this role. In addition, as a result of the Private Security Industry Act 2001, paid security and stewards are regulated by the Security Industry Authority. Licences have been implemented to raise standards in the profession by ensuring security staff are trained and meet minimum requirements (including not having a criminal record). As a result of this act, all staff working as door supervisors or security guards, or the management of these services, will require a Security Industry Association licence. Unpaid volunteers do not currently require a licence. For up to date information about the implementation of this act please visit the Security Industry Association (www.the-sia.org.uk). BSI (2003) provides a useful code of practice and recommendations for the infrastructure, staffing, operation and management or safety and stewarding at indoor and outdoor events, while BSI (1999) provides guidance for door stewards and security and BSI (2002b) provides a code of practice for static security guards.

Environment

The risk to the environment posed by modern businesses is of increasing concern to the general community. There are dangerous risks such as pollution, spills and effluent leakage and the more indirect risks minimized by waste recycling, water and energy conservation. The impacts and therefore the priorities for their control will vary over the event project life cycle.

Emergency

An awareness of the nearest emergency services and their working requirements is mandatory for the event management. The reason for using outside emergency services is that the situation is beyond the capabilities of the event staff and needs specialist attention. It is important to understand the chain of command when emergency services arrive. They can be outside the control of the event management staff, who would act purely in an advisory capacity. They may be called in by any attendee at an event. Commenting on the potential consequences of a major incident, the HSE (1999, p. 31) advise that a multi-agency approach will generally be required, including the event management, policy, fire authority, National Health Service (NHS) including ambulance service, local authority, local emergency planning officer, stewards and first-aiders. As a result, procedures, demarcation of duties and responsibilities should be agreed in writing with all relevant parties within the planning stage.

Recording

It is advisable that all hazards and action taken are recorded by all organizations, however, by law only those employing more than five employees are legally required to do so. Records should be suitable and sufficient to demonstrate, should the need arise, that the risk assessment took place, the people affected were identified, significant hazards were dealt with, precautions were taken and the remaining risk was low. Accurate records can assist the event manager in monitoring hazards and provide evidence should this be demanded, for example, in a compensation claim (HSE, 1998).

Review

Evaluating the successes and failures of the risk control strategy is central to the planning of future events. The event company must be a 'learning organization'. The analysis of, and response to, feedback is essential to this process.

The *Event Safety Guide* provides advice within thirty-three chapters on specific arrangements for health and safety at music and similar events. The chapter headings, presented in Figure 11.2, can provide organizers with a useful basis for planning their requirements (HSE, 1999, p. 2).

Legal issues

Underpinning all aspects of an event are the legal issues. The actual laws relating to events and their management are different for each country. As events grow in

- □ Planning and management
- □ Venue and site design

- □ Fire safety

- □ Major incident planning (emergency planning)
- □ Communication
- □ Crowd management
- □ Transport management
- □ Structures
- □ Barriers
- □ Electrical installations and lighting
- □ Food, drink and water
- □ Merchandising and special licensing
- □ Amusements, attractions and promotional displays
- □ Sanitary facilities
- □ Waste management
- □ Sound: noise and vibration

- □ Special effects, fireworks and pyrotechnics

- □ Camping
- □ Facilities for people with special needs
- □ Medical, ambulance and first-aid management
- □ Information and welfare

- □ Children
- □ Performers
- □ TV and media
- □ Stadium music events
- □ Arena events
- □ Large events

- □ Small events
- □ Classical music events

- □ Unfenced or unticketed events, including radio roadshows
- □ All-night music events
- □ Unlicensed events
- □ Health and safety responsibilities

Figure 11.2 Checklist for planning risk assessment requirements
Source: HSE (1999), p. iii

number and importance to the economy, there will be more laws relating to them. There are some common principles. This chapter now introduces the concepts of event ownership and the crucial duty of care of the event management. The contract is the documentation of the relationship between the event and the various stakeholders. It is important, therefore, that event and festival management be familiar with the key terms used in the contract.

A key question in event administration is 'who owns the event?' The legal owner of an event could be the event coordinator, the committee, a separate legal entity or the sponsors, but it is important to recognize that the ownership of the event entails legal responsibility and therefore liability. The members of an organizing committee can be personally held responsible for the event. This is often expressed as 'jointly and severally liable'. The structure of the event administration must reflect this, and the status of various personnel, such as the event coordinator, the subcontractors and other stakeholders, must be clearly established at the outset. Likewise, sponsorship agreements will often have a clause as to the sponsor's liability, and therefore the extent of their ownership of the event. All such issues need to be carefully addressed by the initial agreements and contracts.

The organizing committee for a non-profit event can become a legal entity by forming an incorporated association. Such an association can enter into contracts and own property. The act of incorporating means that the members have limited liability when the association incurs debts. It does not grant them complete exemption from

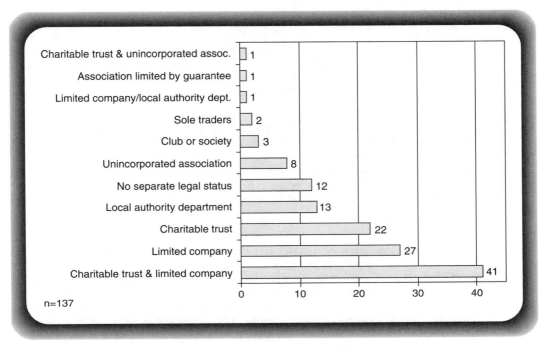

Figure 11.3 Legal structure of festivals
Source: Allen and Shaw (2001), reprinted with permission, British Arts Festivals Association

all liability such as negligence. By law, an association must have a constitution or a list of rules, which state the procedures and powers. These include auditing and accounting matters, the power of the governing body and winding up procedures. Community and local festival events often do not form a separate incorporated association as they can come under the legal umbrella of a body such as a local council. This gives the event organizing committee a good deal of legal protection as well as access to administrative support. For a one-off event, this administrative support can save time and resources because the administrative infrastructure, such as fax machine, phone lines, secretarial help, legal and accounting advice, is already established.

Establishing an appropriate legal structure for an event management company is an exercise in liability minimization. Several structures are possible for an event company, which could operate as a sole trader, partnership, charitable trust, or a company limited by liability. Figure 11.3 illustrates the legal structure of a sample of festivals, with just over half limited companies and just under half registered as charities (Allen and Shaw, 2001). Each of these legal structures has different liability implications. Legal advice may be required to determine the most appropriate structure for a particular circumstance.

Contracts

A contract is an agreement between two or more parties that sets out their obligations and is enforceable by law. It describes the exchange to be made between the parties.

A contract can be a written or an oral agreement. In the world of event management, an oral contract is of little use if problems occur in the future. Therefore, it is appropriate to put all contractual agreements in writing. This may frequently take the form of a simple letter of agreement, no more than a page in length. However, when large amounts of money and important responsibilities are involved, a formal contract is necessary. As Goldblatt (2005) explains, a typical event industry contract will contain:

- the names of the contracting parties, their details and their trading names
- details of the service or product that is offered (e.g. equipment, entertainment, use of land, expert advice)
- the terms of exchange for such service or product
- the signature of both parties indicating understanding of the terms of exchange and agreement to the conditions of the contract.

To make this mutual obligation perfectly clear to all parties, the contract would set out all the key elements. These would consist of: financial terms (including a payment schedule), a cancellation clause, delivery time, the rights and obligations of each party and an exact description of the goods and services being exchanged.

Contracts and contract terms have been subjected to scrutiny over recent years, due to event management, suppliers, performers and venues being caught out with hidden terms. In order to address this, Chris Hannam (of Stagesafe) developed a sample contract, terms and conditions and notes for the Production Services Association (PSA) for use between service companies, artist management agencies, freelancers and self-employed contractors. The sample contract is presented as Figure 11.4. The terms and conditions that accompany this include areas such as payment terms, insurance requirements for both client and supplier, health and safety commitment and confidentiality. This is accompanied by a schedule that outlines what both the supplier and the client will provide. Although developed in this specific context, it serves to illustrate a format that could be applied in other areas.

Event management companies may need a wide range of contracts to facilitate their operation. Some of these are shown in Figure 11.5 (page 334).

An event of medium size would require a set of formal contracts covering:

- the event company or coordinator and the client
- the entertainers
- the venue
- the supplier (e.g. security, audiovisual, caterers)
- the sponsor(s).

For smaller events these may be arranged by letters of agreement.

Contract management

It is surprising that so little is written on event contracts. Like other projects, contracts are the bedrock of the management. Originally, project management was called contract management. The process of managing the contracts is illustrated in Figure 11.6 (page 334). A common mistake by inexperienced event management companies is to assume that once the contract is set up it does not require reviewing. Event contracts need to be reviewed. Changing conditions, a common feature of event management, can lead to many contract problems. In some areas of an event, particularly large sporting events, contracts are frequently renegotiated. They can be described as 'an agreement frozen in time'. For this reason they provide a certainty in management.

THIS AGREEMENT is made the < *Date* > day of < *Month*................................>

BETWEEN < *Insert your name or Co name* > of:

< *Insert your address* .... > (The Supplier)

AND < *Insert your customers name* > of:

< *Insert your customers address* .... > (The Client)

CONTRACT DETAILS   **CONTRACT NO:** < *Insert your job No* >

EVENT, PRODUCTION OR TOUR: < *Insert name of job/tour* >

DURATION OF THE AGREEMENT: From: < *Insert Start Date* > To: < *Insert Finish Date* >

1. The Supplier agrees to supply goods/services in accordance with the Schedule attached here to or as subsequently agreed in writing by the parties hereto.

2. It is hereby agreed that prior to the signing hereof The Client has had ample opportunity to examine The Supplier's Terms of Business attached hereto and shall be deemed to have unequivocally accepted them.

3. The total contract price shall be < *Insert price and currency* > plus VAT (if applicable)

4. The terms of payment are: < *Insert Payment Terms* >

5. In the event of cancellation of this Agreement by The Client and without prejudice to any rights hereunder or under the Terms of Business attached hereto, The Client will indemnify The Supplier as a result of such cancellation for < .... >% of the contract price. Interest at a rate of <   >% per month is liable to be charged on any outstanding balances.

6. It is a fundamental term of this agreement that the stipulations as to payment contained be fully adhered to by The Client (including an absolute requirement of payment to be made within the times stipulated but subject to the proviso contained in Condition 4) and if for any reason The Client shall be in breach of such stipulations The Supplier shall have the right at its absolute and sole discretion and without prejudice to its other rights hereunder forthwith and without notice to dismantle remove or otherwise bring to an end any works service goods or other things supplied by the supplier hereunder and to terminate forthwith this agreement and be under no further liability hereunder to provide any of the services or goods herein agreed.

Signed for and on behalf of   )

The Supplier   )

Date

Signed for and on behalf of
The Client)

Date

IN ADDITION TO SIGNING THE AGREEMENT, THE CLIENT IS REQUESTED TO INITIAL ALL PAGES OF THIS AGREEMENT, THE TERMS OF BUSINESS AND SCHEDULES, IN THE TOP RIGHT HAND CORNER

Figure 11.4 A sample contract
Source: Hannam (2000)

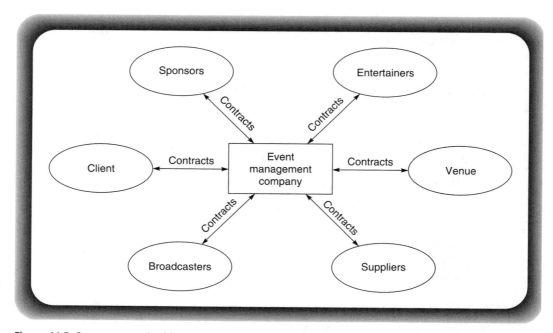

Figure 11.5 Contracts required by an event management company

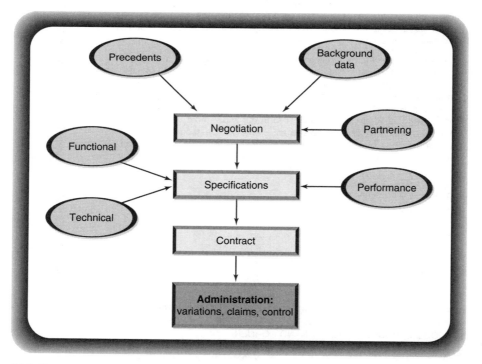

Figure 11.6 The contract management process
Source: O'Toole and Mikolaitis (2002)

Different contracts have different 'styles' and the event manager must be familiar with them. Some of these contracts are discussed in the following text.

Entertainment

A common feature of entertainment contracts is the 'rider'. This is an attachment to the contract, usually on a separate piece of paper. Hiring a headline performer may necessitate signing a twenty- to thirty-page contract. The contract often contains a clause requiring the event company to provide the goods and services contained in the rider, as well as the performance fee. The rider can include such things as a technical specification (e.g. size of PA system required, microphone, technician requirements, lighting), hospitality specification (e.g. food, drink, relaxing accommodation), and venue specification (e.g. payment terms, insurance requirements) (Kemp, 2000; Vasey, 1998). The event company ignores this at its peril. The rider can be used by the entertainer's agent as a way of increasing the fee in real terms, which can have serious consequences for the budget of an event. For example, a university students union that employs a well-known rock group at a minimal fee for a charity function would find its objectives greatly damaged by a rider stipulating reimbursement of food, accommodation and transport costs for thirty people.

Another important clause in the entertainment contract is exclusivity. For example, a headline act may be the major attraction for an event. If the act is also performing at a similar event in the same period, for example the summer festival season, this could easily detract from the uniqueness of the event. A clause to prevent this is therefore inserted into the contract. It indicates that the performer cannot perform within a specified geographic area during the event or for a certain number of days prior to and after the event. The intricacies of an entertainment contract, together with the expense, led Stayte and Watt (1998) to suggest that event managers obtain legal advice from a solicitor experienced in dealing with entertainment/music contracts.

The contract must contain a clause that stipulates the signatories have the right to sign on behalf of the contracting parties. An entertainment group may be represented by a number of agents. The agents must have written proof that they exclusively represent the group for the event.

Venue

The venue contract will have specialist clauses, including indemnifying the venue against damages, personnel requirements and provision of security staff. The contract can also contain the following elements:

- *Security deposit*: an amount, generally a percentage of the hiring fee, to be used for any additional work such as cleaning and repairs that result from the event.
- *Cancellation*: outlining the penalty for cancellation of the event and whether the hirer will receive a refund if the venue is rehired at that time.
- *Access*: including the timing of the opening and closing of the doors, and actual use of the entrances with controls to ensure only access to authorized areas.
- *Late conclusion*: the penalty for the event going overtime.
- *House seats*: this is the reserved free tickets for the venue management.
- *Additions or alterations*: the event may require some changes to the internal structures of the venue.
- *Signage*: this covers the signs of any sponsors and other advertising. Venue management approval may be required for all promotional material.

When hiring a venue, it is important to ascertain exactly what is included in the fee. For example, just because there were chairs and tables in the photo of the venue does not mean that they are included in the hiring cost.

Sponsor

The contract with the sponsor would cover issues related to quality representation of the sponsor such as trademarks and signage, exclusivity and the right of refusal for further sponsorship. It may specify that the sponsor's logo be included on all promotional material, or that the sponsor has the right to monitor the quality of the promotional material. Korman (2000) highlights that sponsors will generally ask for exclusivity within their own brand sector or may demand sole rights to gain full benefit from the event. He further identifies that minor sponsors should be managed to ensure that they do not establish a portfolio of rights that may damage public perception of the major sponsorship, and that sponsors are kept to a minimum to ensure that the message is clearly projected. As a result of these issues, the level of sponsorship – sole sponsor, headline sponsor, minor or major sponsor, or supplier – needs clearly stating in the contract. The contract would also describe the hospitality rights such as the number of complimentary tickets supplied to the sponsor.

Broadcast

Broadcast contracts can be very complex, due to the large amount of money involved in broadcasting and the production of related merchandise, such as videos and sound recordings. The important clauses in a broadcast contract address the following key components:

- *Territory or region* – the broadcast area (local, national or international) must be defined. If the attached schedule shows the region as 'World', the event company must be fully aware of the rights it is bestowing on the broadcaster and their value.
- *Guarantees* – the most important of these is the one stating that the event company has the rights to sign for the whole event. For example, some local councils may require an extra fee paid for broadcasting from their area. Also, performers' copyright can preclude any broadcast without written permission from their record and publishing companies. Comedy acts and motivational speakers are particularly sensitive about any broadcasts and recordings.
- *Sponsorship* – this area can present difficulties when different levels of sponsorship are involved. Sometimes the rights of the event sponsor and the broadcaster's sponsors can clash.
- *Repeats, extracts and sub-licences* – these determine the allowable number of repeats of the broadcast, whether the broadcaster is authorized to edit or take extracts from the broadcast and how such material can be used. The event company may sign with one broadcaster, only to find that the rights to cover the event have been sold on for a much larger figure to another broadcaster. In addition, a sub-licence clause may annul many of the other clauses in the contract. The sub-licenser may be able to use its own sponsors, which is problematic if they are in direct competition with the event sponsors.
- *Merchandising* – the contract may contain a clause that mentions the rights to own products originating from the broadcast. The ownership and sale of any of the recordings can be a major revenue source for an event. A clause recently introduced found in these sorts of contracts concerns future delivery systems. Multimedia uses, such as DVDs, CD-ROMs, cable television and the Internet are all relatively recent,

and new communications technologies continue to be developed, for example, the launch of WAP and 3G mobile phones. It is easy to sign away the future rights of an event when the contract contains terms that are unknown to the event company. It is wise to seek out specialist legal advice.

- *Access* – the physical access requirements of broadcasting must be part of the staging and logistical plan of the event. A broadcaster can easily disrupt an event by demanding to interview performers and celebrities. It is important to specify how much access the broadcaster can have to the stars.
- *Credits* – this establishes, at the outset, the people and elements that will be listed in the titles and credits.

The broadcaster can offer all kinds of assistance to the event company. They have an interest in making the area presentable for television and will often help decorate the site. The level of assistance will depend on its stake in the event. For example, Channel Four's involvement in Party in the Park (Hyde Park, London), through their T4 youth brand, has led to many kinds of synergies between the event, the sponsors and the broadcaster.

Constructing a contract

The process of constructing a contract is illustrated in Figure 11.7 and comprises five main steps: the intention, negotiation, initial acceptance, agreement on terms,

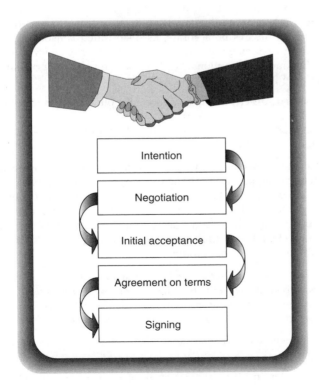

Figure 11.7 The process of constructing a contract

and signing. This process can be facilitated if the event management has standard contracts, where the name of the supplier and any special conditions can be inserted. This saves the event company going through unfamiliar contracts from sponsors, suppliers and entertainers, which can be very time consuming.

For large events and more complex contracts a 'heads of agreement' is sent after the negotiations are completed. This is a summary of any important specific points, listing the precise service or product that is being provided. The contract can be renegotiated or terminated with the agreement of all parties. The final version should contain a clause that allows both parties to go to arbitration in the advent of a disagreement.

Trademarks and logos

Another kind of ownership issue for event management is its ownership of trademarks and logos. Protection of trademark ownership is generally covered within legislation, including the Trade Marks Act 1994, the Copyright, Designs and Patents Act 1988 and anti-counterfeit regulations. However, specific legislation has been drawn up to protect the Olympics through the Olympic Symbol Etc. (Protection) Act 1995, which specifically prevents the use of their logo, motto and related word by any other party without the permission of the British Olympic Association. This protection will be enhanced to cover games related marks and symbols in relation to the London 2012 Olympics and Paralympics (London 2012, 2004c). This illustrates the importance of the ownership of event symbols.

The event company has to be aware of the risks of misrepresenting their event. There is a danger, when promoting an event, to exaggerate the benefits. Descriptions of the product must always be accurate, as disgruntled consumers may take legal action to gain punitive damages when they feel that advertising for an event has made false claims. The Trade Descriptions Act 1968 can be used to argue such cases. This makes it an offence if a trader:

- applies a false trade description to any goods supplies or offers to supply any goods to which a false trade description is
- applied makes certain kinds of false statement about the provision of any services
- accommodation or facilities.

In the events context, this may involve a music festival advertising that a certain performer will be taking part or implying the support of associations or organizations when this is known not to be true. It may also include a company implying sponsorship approval or affiliation with an event when it is not, for example, through ambush marketing. Couchman and Harrington (2000, p. 2) identify that ambush marketing, sometimes referred to as 'parasitic marketing', can take many forms, but will usually fall into two distinct groups:

(A) Activities traditionally considered piracies – these will usually have a clear-cut remedy in law. They are activities which clearly constitute infringements of the proprietary rights in an event, for example unauthorised use of a registered event logo on merchandise, false claims to be official suppliers to a particular team or use of copyright broadcast material on a website; and

(B) Other activities – more subtle practices for which the remedy is less clear-cut or may not even exist.

They go on to identify that typical examples of type (B) activities include: unauthorized or unofficial merchandise; unauthorized or unofficial publications;

unauthorized sales promotion activity or publicity stunts; unauthorized broadcasts/ virtual advertising/Web advertising of sports content/live screenings/ films/video/ photography/telephone commentary/'sponsored'; on-line text and audio commentary information lines/pager services; and unofficial corporate hospitality. London 2012 (2004c) indicated that the Secretary of State for Culture, Media and Sport had guaranteed that ambush marketing would be specifically addressed by legislation in relation to London 2012 Olympics.

Duty of care

A fundamental legal principal applied to events is that of taking all reasonable care to avoid acts or omissions that could injure employees, contractors, users, participants and visitors. This is called duty of care and is covered by the area of law known as torts. A tort is a breach of duty owed to other people and imposed by law, and in this it differs from the duties arising from contracts, which are agreed between contracting parties. Unlike criminal law, which is concerned with punishment and deterrence, the law of torts is concerned with compensation. Within the UK, duty of care is enshrined within legislation, including the Occupiers Liability Act 1957 and 1984, Supply of Goods and Services Act 1982 and the Health and Safety at Work etc. Act 1974 (HSE, 1999; Stayte and Watt, 1998). This is summarized in Figure 11.8.

> The Act sets out the general duties which employers have towards employees and members of the public, and employees have to themselves and to each other.
>
> These duties are qualified in the Act by the principle of *'so far as is reasonably practicable'*. In other words, an employer does not have to take measures to avoid or reduce the risk if they are technically impossible or if the time, trouble or cost of the measures would be grossly disproportionate to the risk.
>
> What the law requires here is what good management and common sense would lead employers to do anyway: that is, to look at what the risks are and take sensible measures to tackle them.

Figure 11.8 The duty of care
Source: Health and Safety Executive (2003), p. 2

For event management, duty of care means taking actions that will prevent any foreseeable risks of injury to the people who are directly affected by, or involved in, the event. This would include the event staff, volunteers, the performers, the audience or spectators and the public in the surrounding areas.

Disability discrimination act

Another area for consideration by event managers is to ensure that events are accessible to all members of society. Considering that over 10 million people within the UK have some form of disability, it makes business (as well as legal) sense to ensure that events are accessible. The Disability Discrimination Act (DDA) 1995 aims to ensure that disabled people are not treated less favourably than other customers (DRC, 2004). The Act makes it unlawful for a service provider to discriminate against a disabled person by refusing to provide (or deliberately not providing) any service which it provides (or is prepared to provide) to members of the public; or in the standard of service which it provides to the disabled person or the manner in which it provides it; or in the terms on which it provides a service to the disabled person (DRC, 2002, p. 5). The act includes reference to ensure fair treatment for employees with disabilities. For service providers, including event managers, venues and others involved in the events industry, this means not treating disabled people less favourably than non-disabled people and making reasonable adjustments to services and premises so that disabled people can access them (DRC, 2004, p. 8). Generally, consideration of the needs of disabled people from the very early stages of planning an event will ensure that not only are they accessible for disabled customers but service may also be improved for non-disabled people as well as the event will have been thought through.

There is a wealth of information available for the events industry to assist in ensuring that legal requirements are met. For example, the Disability Rights Commission (DRC) produces a range of materials, many of which are available through their website, www.drc-gb.org. This includes an excellent handbook, *Organising Accessible Events*, which has been developed with the input of events industry associations and other stakeholders. It offers advice on areas to consider in all aspects of organizing events, from transportation, venue design and layout, through promotional materials, ticketing and bookings, to use of technology and training staff. The Belfast Festival at Queen's case study in Chapter 12 provides a useful example of how one event has approached this.

Insurance

Central to any strategy of liability minimization is obtaining the correct insurance. Event Assured, one of the leading UK providers of insurance to events, provide helpful suggestions regarding insurance. These include the following, focused on legal liabilities:

- The contract with the venue – are you assuming any additional responsibilities beyond Common Law?
- Are you providing adequate security for your exhibitors property left at the venue? You could be held liable for theft if you have not taken reasonable precautions.
- Are you assuming liabilities or entering into contracts that may be outside the scope of your existing liability insurance? Make sure that your insurance contains the correct definitions of your business activities and geographical extent of cover. There is a continuing duty of disclosure under insurance contracts, so it is important to advise your insurers of any new, additional or unusual activities that may be undertaken at the event.
- If the contract states that certain minimum levels of cover are required, do you need to arrange extra cover for this event?
- Unless there is a specific limitation of liability in the contract, assume the worst could happen, and buy as much liability insurance as you can afford. It sounds far-fetched, but your liability could extend to the value of the whole building, and all the people inside it, and even adjoining premises!

- Are you accepting responsibility for the negligence of other parties such as the venue owners, contractors or event exhibitors? Ideally you should resist accepting responsibility for the actions of any other party unless you are in control of what they do. Avoid waiving any rights against other parties.
- If a main contract makes you responsible for the actions of subcontractors, or exhibitors, make sure that your contracts with subcontractors and exhibitors require them to indemnify you in like manner.
- Check the insurances of bona fide subcontractors – limits of liability and wordings. Make sure they contain a clause, which indemnifies you for their negligence.
- If possible, exhibition organizers/owners should control the insurance held by exhibitors by setting up a block policy, and making booking insurance part of the booking form. You can then offer an insurance, which offers the right clauses and limits. Exhibitors will benefit from knowing that there is a standard cover available designed to meet their obligations under their stand agreement.
- For labour only subcontractors, make sure that your insurers are aware of who they are, what they are doing, and what you are paying them. You are likely to be in an 'employer–employee' relationship with such persons, and need to make sure that Employers Liability Insurance operates.
- Are you responsible under equipment hire contracts for liabilities arising out of the use of the plant and for operators? If so, tell your insurers and arrange additional cover if necessary.
- If you are a professional event organizer (i.e. organizing the event for a client), then what are your professional liabilities? Even if the contract makes no mention of this, you will have a liability for negligent acts, errors or omissions, which arises at Common Law under a contract for the provision of professional services. Public liability insurance does not cover this – you may need professional indemnity insurance.
- Think also about the following: libel, slander, breach of copyright, breach of confidence, plagiarism (Event Assured, 2005).

There are many kinds of insurance that can be taken out for events. These include: weather insurance; personal accident insurance for the volunteer works; property insurance, including money; workers compensation insurance; public liability; employers' liability. The choice of the particular insurance cover is dictated by the risk management strategy developed by event management, based on legal requirements.

The increase in premiums in all insurance areas has been a shock to the industry. Some events have been cancelled. A number of strategies have been implemented to manage this situation:

- *Bulk buying* – through membership of some associations, for example, British Arts Festivals Association, events and event companies are able to access discounted insurance premiums through group purchasing.
- *Analysing the activities of the event into levels of risk* – the high premium may be the result of one aspect of the event. By changing or eliminating this from the event programme it may reduce the event risk seen by the insurance company.
- *Creating a comprehensive risk management procedure* – many events that previously ignored risk management have turned to the formal risk management process. This is one positive outcome of the insurance issue. The risk management plan becomes a document used to communicate with the insurance company. Given the experience of insurance companies, it is wise to seek their input on this document.

- *Holding harmless clauses or forfeiting the right to sue* – the attendee signs a contract to the effect that they are voluntarily assuming the risk inherent in the event activity. This requires legal advice to ensure that contracts are enforceable.

Regulations, licences and permits

There are long lists of regulations that need to be satisfied when staging events. The bigger, more complex or innovative the event, the larger the number of these regulations. The correct procedure in one local authority or county within the UK may be slightly different in another. The principal rule is to carry out careful research, including investigating similar events in the same area and seeking advice on what permits and licences are necessary to allow an event to proceed.

It is always the responsibility of an event company to find out and comply with all pertinent rules, regulations and licensing requirements. For example, in reviewing the Public Entertainment Licence for Glastonbury Festival 2005, the report from the Environmental Health Manager to the licensing authority at Mendip District Council includes input from a wide range of authorities including Mendip District Council, Avon and Somerset Police, Somerset Fire Authority, Westcountry Ambulance Services NHS Trust, Somerset Health Protection Unit, Mendip Primary Care Trust, Environment Agency, Somerset County Highways Authority, Emergency Planning Authority and the local Parish Councils (Kirkwood, 2005). Many local authorities apply environmental noise control protocols to control the impact of noise on communities, with guidance available from the Noise Council (Noise Council, 1995; HSE, 1999), while the recently updated *2005 Noise at Work Regulations* will reduce the sound levels at which action must be taken to ensure that employees and those exposed to excess noise (for example, sound checks and performances at concerts) (Howden, 2004). Not only that, but event managers must make it practice to pay particular attention to workplace health and safety regulations.

AEO, BECA and EVA (2002, p. A1) identify some of the relevant regulations with which an exhibition must comply during build-up, break-down and while the exhibition is open:

- Electricity at Work Regulations 1998 / EVA Regulations For Stand Electrical Installations
- Environmental Protection Act 1990 / Environment Act 1995
- Health & Safety (First Aid) regulations 1981
- Health & Safety at Work, etc., Act 1974
- Management of Health & Safety at Work Regulations 1999
- Manual Handling Operations Regulations 1992
- Noise at Work Regulations 1989 (updated 2005)
- Personal Protective Equipment at Work Regulations 1992
- Provision and Use of Work Equipment Regulations 1998
- Reporting of Injuries, Diseases and Dangerous Occurrences Regulations (RIDDOR) 1995
- The Building Regulations
- The Building Standards (Scotland) Regulations
- The Fire Precautions (Workplace) Regulations 1997 as amended 1999

- The Health & Safety (Signs and Signals) Regulations 1996
- The Lifting Operations and Lifting Equipment Regulations (LOLER) 1998
- Workplace (Health, Safety and Welfare) Regulations 1992.

It is evident that an exhibition or event manager may need to seek legal, professional or business advice to ensure that all relevant regulations are taken into account, particularly as these are not fixed and may be updated, replaced or additional regulations added – organizations such as industry associations, the Health and Safety Executive (HSE) and Business Link can prove to be a useful source of information in this respect.

The Performing Right Society (PRS) and Phonographic Performance Ltd (PPL) issue licences for the performance of their members' works. They function as a collection society, monitoring and collecting royalties on behalf of their members (music composers and their publishers). So when an event company decides to set fireworks to music, it is not just a matter of hiring a band or pressing 'play' on the sound system.

Permits and licences are required for many events to take place and for activities associated with this, including the handling of food, entertainment, pyrotechnics, sale of alcohol, street trading and road closures. For example, in England and Wales the Licensing Act 2003 (HMSO, 2003) has established a single integrated system for licensing premises used to supply alcohol, provide regulated entertainment or provide regulated late night refreshment. This new act has been designed to cut down on red tape by bringing together six existing licensing regimes (alcohol, public entertainment, cinemas, theatres, late night refreshment house and night cafes). Three types of licence available are: premises licence, temporary events notice and club premises certificate. Regulated entertainment includes the performance of a play, an exhibition of a film, an indoor sporting event, boxing or wrestling entertainment, a performance of live music, any playing of recorded music, a performance of dance, or entertainment of a similar description to live music, recorded music or dance. The key principles underpinning licensing are to prevent crime and disorder, public safety, prevention of public nuisance and the protection of children. As a result, many events where an audience or spectators are being entertained will be covered by the regulations and will require a licence, even if the audience is not paying for the entertainment. Applications for licences must be made with the appropriate local authority. There are exclusions for some types of event; however, it is advisable to review the specific requirements of the licences to identify these. The Live Music Forum, including representatives of industry, government, local authorities, the Arts Council, small venue operators and others, was established in 2004 to maximize take-up of the reforms relating to live music, promote live music and monitor and evaluate the impact of the Licensing Act 2005 (DCMS, 2005). Detailed guidance on the Act and the process to follow is available from the Department for Culture, Media and Sport (www.culture.gov.uk) or from the local authority where the event will take place.

This complex area needs the close attention of event management. Companies must undertake detailed research into all regulations affecting their event and should allocate time to deal with the results of that research. Government agencies can take a long time to respond to requests. Therefore it is imperative to begin early in seeking any permits or licences, and to factor delays and difficulties with obtaining them into the time frame of the event planning process.

Chapter summary

Risk management is a modern, formal process of identifying and managing risk. It is one of the functions of any event management and the process should be part of the event's everyday organization. There are risks that are specific to events, and to particular events. To correctly identify these risks, knowledge of the unique risks is essential. The risk is more than risks at the event itself. The output of this process is a live risk register that shows the risks and their management schedule. As part of this risk strategy, the management has to understand their legal requirements. They have a duty of care to all involved in an event. Any reasonably foreseen risks have to be eliminated or minimized. The process of doing this is central to a risk management strategy. Liability minimization is part of this strategy. This includes identifying the ownership of the event, careful structuring of the event management, taking out insurance and adhering to all the rules and regulations pertaining to events. Specific legal issues of concern to the event management include contracting, trademarks and trade practices. Legal matters can be complex and interpretation can differ from council to council and between countries including within the UK, particularly between England/Wales and Scotland or Northern Ireland. The information discussed within this chapter provides a brief overview of issues to consider, however, as regulations and guidelines are subject to constant change, it is highly recommended that any event company seek legal advice when unsure of these matters.

Questions

1. List the risks to a regional festival arising from these areas:
   (a) local organizing committee
   (b) sponsorship
   (c) volunteers
   (d) council politics
   (e) participants in the parade
   (f) computers
   (g) experience of organizing group.
2. List the areas covered by the contract between the event company and supplier of audiovisuals.
3. Event management has been described as 'just solving problems'. Can risk management replace all the other methods of management, such as marketing, logistics and project management, to create an event?
4. What are two methods of minimizing liability?
5. Contrast the risks involved in staging an outdoor concert to those involved in producing an indoor food fair. What risk management strategy could be used to reduce or eliminate these risks?
6. What actions can be taken to reduce the cost for overall liability insurance? Should the event company be insured for patrons to be covered after they leave the event?
7. Investigate what licences and permits are needed for a street party?

Case study 11.1

Radio One Love Parade, Leeds by Logistik
Background

The Love Parade ran for the first time in the United Kingdom in Leeds in July 2000. Following discussions with the Berlin Love Parade organizers, Radio One undertook to organize the dance music based event in the UK. The event concept involved a parade of 20 floats, sponsored by the leading dance music clubs in the UK, leading to a large, free open-air dance music event. Radio One signed an agreement to use the name 'Love Parade' in the UK and financially underwrote the event – they also promoted it and stimulated interest in the event. Logistik were ultimately tasked with putting together the event, managing it, staging it and running it. A third party was contracted to get support from all the big dance clubs in the UK who bought floats. Leeds City Council's role was as host and to help ensure the event went off well.

The concept

The mission was initially to establish and run a Love Parade in the UK, in association with the German event. Historically, there has been a lot of animosity between Germany and England and events such as this are positive in developing cultural links. The Love Parade in Berlin is well documented – it was established to celebrate the fall of the Berlin Wall, which proved to be an excellent stimulant for running an event. The underlying principle for both the German and UK events was that everybody, regardless of class, money, background, or status, had an equal opportunity to attend, join in with the event, and they could do that regardless of their financial position in life. Radio One supported this event wholeheartedly as it was an event open to everyone, clearly relating to their ethos of One Love.

The aims were to hold a free, safe and well attended event. These were clearly achieved. In addition, the objective, from an organizer's point of view, was to develop the event in such a manner that it could be developed and move on to another city – in 2001 the event moved to Newcastle.

Audience size

In order to determine the potential audiences for the Love Parade, a number of previous events were researched, including the Road Shows, the Big Sundays, and other events organized by Radio One, together with experience at previous dance events. The resulting audience was estimated at being 250 000 (based on Ariel photography and working out the number of people per square meter). This unprecedented audience resulted from two areas. Firstly, there was a high level of support from the youth press as it was unique and it caught the youths' imagination. Secondly, Radio One succeeded in their promotion of it – the event itself caught people's imagination, with a worldwide fellowship of people who love music, love to party, love to have a good time, behave themselves and to link up with Berlin.

The venue, facilities and staff

The venue for the event changed from the City Centre to Roundhay Park in Leeds four weeks before the event, due to concerns expressed by the police over the growth in anticipated audience. Roundhay Park is basically a big open field and as a result, the event site was built from scratch, including a large volume of toilets, food franchises, drinks franchises, bars and standpipes with free water. West Yorkshire Ambulance Service and the Drugs Advisory Group in Leeds provided first-aid stations and counselling. Transport was provided with a bus service running up to Roundhay from the City Centre. Onsite, three free stages and twenty free floats were provided for the audience to watch.

The management structure included a parade manager, site manager, production manager, stage manager, float managers, float stewards, event managers, and an event director. The team also included approximately 500 stewards from ShowSec International, a health and safety team, plus 600 police officers, West Yorkshire Ambulance Service, Drugs Advisory Services, and Leeds City Council Cleansing Services. In addition to this, contracts for services were signed with many suppliers.

The licensing and planning process

Planning commenced a year in advance where tacit agreement for the event was obtained from Leeds City Council, followed by the normal system of multi-agency discussion. Within the licensing framework, there was a fairly well understood set of steps that you go through to get a public entertainment licence. The basis is that a meeting is organized with the multi-agency group where the concept and aims are explained, from which will come hundreds of questions. Following this, a number of sub-meetings follow with environmental health (sound and toilets), the highways department (road closures), and the police (public order). The process involves risk assessments, safety plans, crowd control statements, and mission statements.

Documentation is refined to incorporate the above items and this is then built into the event plan. In this respect, simple is best. Whilst you can write reams of documentation, which can be as detailed as you want it to be, it has to be broadly understood by all those that are involved with the event, not just a key group of people who happen to be in a meeting. All the people involved in the event from the management team, to the stewards and the medics, have all got to have a good understanding of what's drawn from these meetings, understand what is being aimed for, and what to do in the event of x, y and z. Regardless of the size of the event, you still need a simple plan that everyone understands and can work to. This is the normal process for organizing events – clearly it was a lot more complicated for Love Parade due to the scale of the event. Because of the nature of this event, it was very difficult to stick to any sort of well-understood and pre-agreed formulas for getting permissions for the event through Leeds City Council and other agencies. Very quickly people realized that the event that they'd agree to had changed somewhat, because Radio One were the promoters and it was going to be a lot bigger. There was concern in some quarters that they were hosting the equivalent of the Notting Hill Carnival for dance music and peoples' attitudes changed. There was debate within Leeds City Council and with the multi-agency group, led by the police, about how the event could best be licensed and whether it should be licensed at all. The debate went on right up until the actual event – ultimately it had a public entertainment licence at Roundhay Park (and a drinks licence), however this was only resolved a few weeks before the event.

As a company, Logistik have insurance for employees, public, professional and hired in plant insurance. In addition, specific insurance was taken out to cover the Love Parade and increased the amounts on the other insurance to cover this size of event. The insurance indemnified everyone involved.

Consultation

Consultation with the local community was limited and not as it should have been due to the short time that was available following the move to Roundhay Park. As organizers, it can be problematic keeping the balance between canvassing opinion and planning the event, when some communities clearly object to events taking place near them, particularly at this scale. Although there was only a short time available before the event, meetings were arranged with a number of community groups, followed by further meetings and correspondence after the event to listen to people's views. Some of these were irate and unreasonable, but a lot of them were good meaning and contributed constructively. The city council also put together a questionnaire that was distributed to the local community to gain feedback. There was a fair amount of consultation afterwards but this didn't make up for the fact that there wasn't enough time to conduct effective consultation beforehand.

Evaluation

Generally, whether the event was a success depends on who is asked – it has to be looked at on balance and in the context of what was achieved. You could ask three different people 'was the event a success?' and, depending on their age, outlook on life, and geographical position (where they lived), they would give you three completely different answers. If you were under thirty and came to the event specifically to enjoy yourself, you would say it was an absolutely phenomenal success with 250 000 people, no major incidents in terms of injury, people had a really good time, it was a friendly atmosphere and there were no public order problems. If you talked to people who own shops in Leeds, the majority would think it was a success because it brought a huge amount of income into the city – an economic impact of around £15 million was reported purely in relation to the Love Parade. However, if you were resident, living near Roundhay Park, who doesn't like dance music and doesn't like their normal every day life being interrupted, then you would have a completely different view on the success of the event. They probably believe that it was not right for two reasons. Firstly, clearly such a huge event has a massive impact and disrupts people's lives – no matter what you do, that is a consequence of holding this sort of event. Secondly, culturally a lot of older people have a great distrust and dislike of dance music, even the type of people and their motivation for coming along. If you look at it from those people's point of view, they would say it was a terrible event and it shouldn't have been allowed. They were supported by some journalists in the very conservative local press who were outspoken about their opposition to the event and the problems that it caused.

In our view, the event was a success – it went off predominantly well and safely (against a huge amount of opposition) and it showed that if you give young people something to do and put together something that is meaningful to them, they will come along in huge numbers, enjoy themselves and behave themselves. However, Logistik learned a lot from developing this event and there are a number of areas where we can improve for the future. Firstly, we now fully understand the differences between the cultures of the police and the cultures of people who they perceived would be coming to the event. The Leeds Love Parade illustrated that many of the initial fears were unfounded. Secondly, the well-documented funding issue should be resolved with the police at the start of the process. With the experience of Leeds Love Parade, issues raised, including the size of the event, together with the concerns of residents and other stakeholders, will be addressed within the planning stages for future events to ensure that they meet the increasingly stringent requirements of the multi-agency groups.

For further details about Logistik events, please visit www.logistik.co.uk.

By Logistik Ltd.

Questions

1. What characteristics of Leeds do you think lead to it being chosen as the location for the first Love Parade in the UK?
2. What contracts and licences were considered necessary for the event? From what you know of the event, do these measures seem adequate? If not, what other areas of the event might usefully have been covered by written agreements?
3. The increased size of the event affected the perceived risk involved in staging it, leading to the move to Roundhay Park. What could organizers do to control the size of the event?
4. What lessons can be learned regarding the planning of the event, and how would you apply these lessons if you were organizing a Love Parade in the future?

Case study 11.2

Event Risk Management at Leeds New Year's Eve 2003

Most major cities in the UK, since the turn of the century, have staged some kind of New Year's Eve event for their residents and visitors. These events range in scale from a simple fireworks display to, what is probably the world's largest New Year's Eve party, Edinburgh's Hogmanay.

Such events offer the organizer some unique challenges in the staging of these events, particularly with regards to risk management:

- Staged in the middle of winter, with nighttime temperatures normally below or only just above freezing. NB: In 2000 and 2003 New Year's Eve events in Edinburgh, Liverpool and Newcastle have had to be cancelled due to extreme weather.
- They are large events, almost exclusively staged in city centres, as opposed to greenfield sites.
- The demographic of the audience is predominantly made up of 18–35 year olds; as such the consumption of alcohol is widespread, as people seek to 'toast the New Year'.
- Events normally feature a countdown, followed by a 'midnight moment' which can involve anything from fireworks and confetti to the singing of Auld Laing Syne'.
- The event organizer will need to consider all of the above and incorporate various control measures, which will need to be put into place as a part of the event risk management process.

Background

Prior to New Year's Eve 2000, the city of Leeds had not staged a major New Year's Eve event. Revellers seeking a 'gathering point' to see in the New Year, used to congregate in City Square, a small Square not that suitable for events. This was due to the Square technically being a roundabout, bordered on 3 sides by a busy road and the fact that it contained numerous statues and other street furniture, which in the run up to midnight soon became a vantage point for revellers. During the mid 1990s, things got so bad at City Square that a Medical and Police Unit were positioned on the Square, as effectively the gathering of revellers had become an 'un-managed' event.

Having been widely criticized by the press and the public for the largely low-key community-led celebrations laid on during at Millennium Eve (1999), and the fact that Leeds had a brand new public square, Millennium Square, in which to stage large-scale events, the decision was taken to create an event for New Year's Eve 2000.

Unfortunately, the weather was so bad across much of Northern England on 31 December 2000 that the Leeds event, which incorporated the opening of the Millennium Square, had to be curtailed, with only fireworks being successfully staged due to widespread blizzards. New Year's Eve events were then successfully staged in 2001, 2002 and 2003. The events quickly became very successful, with a number of interesting issues coming about, due to the staging of the event, as revellers were encouraged to join in the celebrations in a managed, rather than un-managed environment as previously.

- City Square was no longer seen as the gathering point for revellers in the City Centre.
- West Yorkshire Police reported a dramatic reduction in arrests made across the city centre, whilst West Yorkshire Ambulance Service reported a reduction in city centre casualties.
- Public transport was laid on to all areas of the city until 02.30 hours, which made the event more accessible and reduced the pressure on taxi services, as prior to 2000, bus services stopped at 19.00 hours or before.
- Images of the event were used widely in local media, and the event became billed as 'Yorkshire's largest New Year's Eve Party', which as a result saw audiences attending the event from across the region, staying overnight in the city's hotels.
- The city centre attracted a much wider demographic, including families and children as opposed to just being the preserve of 18–35 year olds. This was further encouraged through the programming of entertainment, such as street performers and the use of tribute acts with wide appeal such as 'Robbing Williams' or 'Beatlemania' and the development of a fun fair adjacent to the event, which added to the celebratory atmosphere. Alcohol and food were also widely available at the event.
- By making the event free and no ticket required, it increased accessibility, and prevented the problem encountered when giving free tickets away of potential capacity not being reached due to people deciding not to attend the event due to a change in plans or bad weather for example. This also results in non-ticket holders and visitors to the city not being frustrated by their lack of ticket, enabling them to still experience the event.

The risk management process

The event was becoming a victim of it's own success, as more and more people sought to join in the celebrations. The licensed event capacity was increased each year to a maximum in 2003 of 12 000, which included the use of adjoining streets to maximize capacities. In addition, given the nature of the event, organizers were experiencing a significant ingress of people to the Square from 23.30 hours – until just before midnight, as people left neighbouring bars and clubs to join the celebrations and see the fireworks display.

The issue of potential over-crowding is just one of the many issues the event management team had to consider in the development of their risk assessments for the event. The risk assessment ended up being a 36-page document, excluding the fireworks display, which due to its specialist nature was provided by the fireworks display provider.

In managing and recording the risk of over-crowding, the first stage is to identify that the potential hazard of overcrowding exists, and identify what the risk, so in this case the risk would be potential crushing, pushing, crowd collapse, ultimately resulting in serious injury or potential death.

The next stage is to rate the risk, first by estimating potential numbers involved, which for an incident as serious as overcrowding could be as high as 500. Then a further rating of the risk is calculated by grading the severity × the probable frequency. Table 11.1 illustrates the severity and frequency scales used.

Table 11.1 Severity and Frequency Scales

Severity		Probable Frequency	
Trivial	1	Improbable	1
Minor	2	Unlikely	2
Major – single	3	Possible – happens	3
Major – multiple	4	Happens occasionally	4
Hospitalization	5	Happens periodically	5
Fatality	6	Happens frequently	6

Therefore, using the example of over-crowding the maximum score would be 36 (the chance of fatalities (6) × happening frequently (6)). This alone, or in reality any score over about 20, would tell the Event Manager that the activity should not be staged. Some risk assessments just stop here, as risk assessments can adopt many different styles. However best practice has identified the need to then introduce 'Control Measure(s)'. For example, control measures put into place for New Year's Eve to prevent over-crowding included:

- The use of video screens to increase visibility of the stage and key elements of the event – the use of screens can also greatly assist in letting the audience know when the midnight moment actually is, all it takes is one group of people with a watch 3 or 4 minutes fast and the spontaneity of the moment can be lost.
- The use of barrier dumps and stewards at key ingress points to the Square to block the roads if there is a danger of capacity being reached. Such a plan was actually put into place at the 2002 event.
- The identification of possible vantage points, anything from bus shelters to walls and to control access to such points to prevent climbing, by either stewards or barriers/fencing.
- The use of event communications such as CCTV and radios to inform the Event Manager of crowd density and spread across the site. For example Millennium Square normally fills from the East, as this is the area where most pubs and bars are. This can result in the east of the Square being full, whilst to the west, the crowd is less dense. This information can then be relayed to stewards who would close certain approach routes and advise audience goers of alternative routes to the event.

After you have considered Control Measures such as these, you then rate the risk again, which should come up with a much lower figure thanks to the control measures you have put into place. A table can be used to assist this process (Table 11.2).

Table 11.2 Example of headings used in an event risk assessment

Hazard	Risk	Potential numbers	Severity rating × likelihood = primary risk based on no controls	Control measures	Severity rating × likelihood = primary risk based on no controls	Comments

Whilst this formula might appear simple and to some extent common sense, it is the recording of the potential for risk and the measures put into place that the risk assessment is designed to cover.

Risk assessments should also be used to consider issues throughout the 'on-site' period for example, such as how to manage the use of plant and machinery in a public space, or issues to consider such as the use of electricity in the open air. Therefore, risk assessments should ideally be broken down into sections for ease of use, for example Build and Breakdown, Venue, Audience, Performance.

Individual risk assessments should be obtained from each supplier providing equipment or services at the event (in some cases alongside a method statement, which actually details how they will undertake the task). This therefore allows the Event Manager to then cross refer documents in the completion of the event risk assessment.

Summary

Although risk assessments are time-consuming documents to produce, particularly when the event manager has many other tasks to complete prior to an event, they should never be generic (i.e. not off the shelf, being specific to the event being staged in each venue they are performed at). They should also be considered a 'working document' with amendments being included up to show day in some instances, although the licensing authority normally require at least a draft version several weeks before the event.

When dealing with a large commercial event, such as a festival, if the Event Manager or licensing authority does not feel competent in the writing or reviewing of risk assessments, or in undertaking the role of Event Safety Officer (the person who implements control measures and oversees event safety on-site), then several companies now independently offer such a service such as Capita Symonds who can independently provide such services to the event organizer.

For further information about events in Millennium Square, please visit www.leeds. gov.uk/millenniumsquare.

By Patrick Loy, former Events Manager at Leeds City Council (2000–2004). Currently working for Events for London, managing a wide variety of events on Trafalgar Square (including London's New Year's Eve celebrations), whilst also lecturing in events management at Leeds Metropolitan University.

Questions

1. What were the unique features of this event and how did this contribute to the risk assessment?
2. Draw the risk management process in a step-by-step diagram. Describe how this was applied to the New Year's event.
3. Identify what other management techniques could be used to control crowds at events such as this.

Chapter 12
Logistics

Learning Objectives

After studying this chapter, you should be able to:

- define logistics management and describe its evolution
- understand the concept of logistics management and its place in event management
- construct a logistics plan for the supply of customers, event products and event facilities
- use event logistics techniques and tools.

Introduction

This chapter adapts the science of business and military logistics to events. The management of an event is divided into supply, setting up and running the event on-site, and the shutdown process of the event. Communication, flow and supply are the three elements of event logistics treated in this chapter. Various checklists that can assist in the management of event logistics are outlined.

What is logistics?

One of the hardest tasks, for logisticians and non-logisticians alike is to look at a list and spot what's not there.

(Pagonis, 1992, p. 73)

Placing the word 'logistics' into its historical context provides an understanding of its use in present event management. Logistics stems from the Greek word *logistikos*, 'skilled in calculating'. The ancient Romans used the term for the administration of its armies. The term evolved to refer to the practical art of the relocation of armies. Given the complexity of modern warfare, logistics became a science that included speed of operations, communications and maintenance of the armed forces. After the Second World War, modern business applied the experience and theory of logistics as they faced similar problems with transport and supply to those faced by the military.

The efficient movement of products has become a specialized study in the management discipline. Within large companies, especially international companies, a section can be devoted to coordinating the logistics requirements of each department. Logistics has become a discipline in its own right. This has lead to consolidation into a separate independent function in companies, often called integrated logistics management. The Chartered Institute of Logistics and Transport (CILT (UK)) define logistics as, 'The time-related positioning of resources to meet user requirements', where resources may be transport, storage, or information (Supply-Chain Inventory Management Forum, 2003). Canadine (2001) notes that logistics is generally being used to operate the supply chains in order to satisfy a customer. He also highlights that an alternative definition of logistics is, 'The detailed organization and implementation of a plan or operation', where the plan or operation is to satisfy customer needs. The benefit of efficient coordination of logistics in the event company is that a company's product value can be improved.

For a complete understanding of event logistics, this chapter is divided into sections dealing with the tasks of event logistics and the role of the logistics manager.

The elements of event logistics

The various elements of event logistics can be organized into a system, illustrated in Figure 12.1. This system is used to organize the logistic elements of an event.

Whereas most logistics theory concerns the supply of products to the customers, event logistics includes the efficient supply of the customer to the product, and the supply of facilities to and from the event site. In this sense, it has more in common with military logistics than modern business logistics. Business logistics is an on-going activity and is part of the continual management of a company. Military and event logistics often concern a specific project or campaign rather than the continuing management. There is a definite preparation, lead up, execution and shutdown.

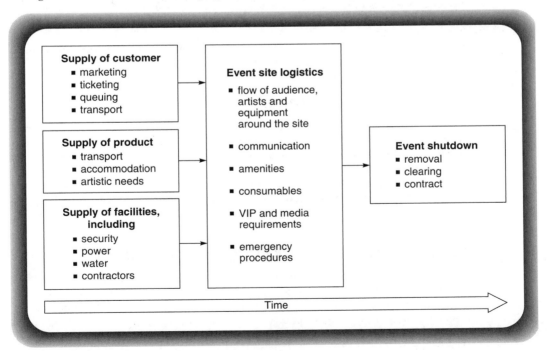

Figure 12.1 Elements of the logistics system

As well, issues such as inventory control and warehousing that are the basis of business logistics are not as important to a one-off event.

The areas of importance to event logistics can be categorized as:

- *Supply*: this is divided into the three areas of customer, product and facilities. Supply also includes the procurement of the goods and services.
- *Transport*: the transport of these goods and services can be a major cost to an event and requires special consideration.
- *Linking*: logistics is part of the overall planning of an event and is linked to all other areas. With large multi-venue events, the logistics becomes so complex that an operations or logistics manager is often appointed. The logistics manager functions as part of the overall network management structure outlined in this chapter.
- *Flow control*: this refers to the flow of products, services and customers during the event.
- *Information networks*: the efficient flow of information during the event is generally a result of efficient planning of the information network. This concept is expanded in the section about on-site logistics.

All these areas need to be considered when creating a logistics plan. Even for small events, such as a wedding or a small product launch, a logistics plan needs to be incorporated in the overall event plan. For these sorts of events, logistics comes under the title 'Staging', which is described in Chapter 13.

Given that the major elements of logistics are supply and movement, logistics play a large role in some types of event, including:

- events that have a large international component, such as major sporting events and overseas corporate incentive programmes
- complex events in foreign countries, such as trade exhibitions and conferences
- events that occur in remote locations and need most of the supporting resources transported to the site
- exhibitions of large or complex products, such as mining or agricultural exhibitions
- events that are moving, such as travelling exhibitions and races.

Supply of the customer

The customers of the event are those who pay for it. They can be the audience (concerts and festivals), spectators (sport), visitors (exhibitions), delegates (conferences) and the sponsors or the client (corporate events). The customers have expectations that have to be met for a successful outcome. In addition, there are legal requirements under DDA (as discussed in Chapter 9) to ensure that events are accessible to people with disabilities. These expectations for all customers will include aspects of logistics.

Linking with the marketing and promotion

The supply of customers is ultimately the responsibility of marketing activities. The numbers, geographical spread and expectations of the customers will affect the logistics planning. The targeting of specialist markets or widespread publicity of an event will require a logistics plan with very different priorities. For example, the transport requirements of the customers will vary according to the distance travelled. The majority of the audience of Party in the Park either drives from the surrounding area, or uses the shuttle bus service. Therefore, vehicle access, parking and the availability of an effective bus service are a priority at the event site. The British International Motor Show, until 2004 in Birmingham and from 2006 at Excel London, uses a nationwide publicity campaign, which attracts a large audience from all corners of the UK. This offers opportunities for special negotiations with coach operators, train companies and hotels. If the publicity of an event is spread nationwide the logistics will be different to a product launch that only concerns the staff and customers of a company. In this way the logistics are closely linked to the marketing of an event.

Ticketing

Ticketing is important to events whose primary income is from the entrance fee. Most corporate events, including office parties and product launches, and many public events are free. However, for other events, such as sport events, the extent of ticket sales can determine success or failure (Graham, Neirotti and Goldblatt, 2001). Ticket distribution is regarded as the first major decision in event logistics.

The pricing and printing of the tickets is generally not a logistics area. However, the distribution, collection and security are of concern, and with free events, form an effective means of controlling numbers. In the UK, tickets for events can be sold through various distributors like Ticketmaster for a fee, or they can be sold by mail or through the Internet, for example, through Aloud.com. Glastonbury Festival has always traditionally sold out of tickets, months in advance, however, in recent years they have sold out within hours of going on sale. Selling tickets at the gate gives rise to security problems in the collection, accounting and depositing of funds. The ticket collectors need training to deal with the public, as well as efficiently moving the public through the entrance and ensuring that access is controlled to appropriate areas. The honesty of the staff may also be a security concern. Events that have successfully managed this include, for example, The Open Championship, which each year have support through sponsorship from the Royal Bank of Scotland to provide cashiers/ticket staff. In larger venues, an admission loss-prevention plan is used to minimize the possibility of theft.

It is not unusual to sell tickets through retail outlets. The Millennium Dome attempted this on a grand scale by using National Lottery outlets as a distribution channel to sell tickets. Inventory control and cash receipts are two areas that require special attention when using retail outlets for ticket distribution. Numbering of the tickets and individual letters of agreement with each outlet are the most efficient methods of control. The letter of agreement would include the range of ticket numbers, level of the tickets (discount or full price) and the method of payment. Depending on the size of the event, the ticketing can be crucial to the event's success and take up a significant amount of the event director's time. Figure 12.2 is a checklist of the logistics of ticketing an event.

An innovative method of ticketing for festivals is to use the hospital-style wristbands, called crowd control bands. These are colour coded to indicate the level of the ticket – a day ticket, a weekend ticket or a special performer's ticket. The use of these wristbands introduces a visual method of control during a large event, as the sale of food and drinks is only allowed if the wristband is shown. In this way, the food vendors become part of the security for the event.

The Internet is increasingly used for the distribution of tickets for large events, concerts and conferences. This use of the Internet illustrates the linking of logistics and marketing, as discussed in Chapter 7. Originally the World Wide Web was used in the marketing of events by means of advertising them through a website. The introduction of encrypted data enabled the increase in the privacy and security

Does the artwork on the ticket contain the following?
- number of the ticket
- name of the event
- date and time of the event
- price and level of the ticket (discount, complimentary, full price, early bird)
- seating number or designated area (ticket colour coding can be used to show seating area)
- disclaimer (in particular, this should list the responsibilities of the event promoter)
- event information, such as a map, warnings and what to bring/not to bring
- artwork so that the ticket could be used as a souvenir (part of the ticket could be kept by the patron)
- contact details for information
- Security considerations, such as holograms to prevent copying

Printing schedule
- When will the tickets be ready?
- Will the tickets be delivered or do they have to be collected?
- If there is an error or a large demand for the tickets, will there be time for more to be printed?

Distribution
- What outlets will be used – retail, Ticketmaster, Internet, mobile phone, mail or at the gate?
- Has a letter of agreement been signed with all distributors, setting out terms and conditions?
- What method of payment will be used (by both the ticket buyer to the distributor and in the final reconciliation) – credit card, cash, direct deposit?
- Are schedule of payment and reconciliation forms available?
- Does the schedule of communications refer to ticket sales indicate sales progress and if more tickets are needed?

Collection of tickets
- How will the tickets be collected at the gates and transferred to a passout?
- How experienced are the personnel and how many will there be? When will they arrive and leave?
- Is a separate desk for complimentary tickets needed site of ticket collection site?
- What security arrangements are in place for cash and personnel?
- How will the tickets be disposed of?

Reconciliation of number of tickets with revenue received
- What method of reconciliation will be used? Is an accountant being used?
- Is the reconciliation ongoing, at the conclusion of the event, or at the end of the month?
- Is the system robust to allow for independent auditing, such as ABC auditing of exhibition visitor numbers?
- Has a separate account been set up just for the one event to assist the accountancy procedure?

Figure 12.2 Ticketing – logistics checklist

of payment methods and the sale of tickets from a site. The site collaborates with the existing ticketing system, and can be connected to travel agencies, hotels, transport companies and a whole host of other related services.

A further development in technology is the use of mobile phones for ticketing. For example, Live 8 used a text lottery with the general public invited to text in for limited availability tickets.

Queuing

Often the first experience a customer has at an event is the queue for tickets or parking. This was illustrated in 2003 by the queues of traffic making their way to Knebworth for Robbie Williams' sell out concerts. With an estimated 375 000 fans attending the shows over three consecutive days, the largest audience in UK music history (BBC News, 2003), the concert will be remembered not only for the scale of the event but also the traffic and parking issues that made press headlines and lead to a number of fans not seeing the concert due to being stuck in traffic.

Once inside the event, customers may be confronted with queues for food, toilets and seating. An important aspect of queue theory is the 'perceived waiting time'. This is the subjective time that the customers feel that they have waited. There are many rules of thumb about diminishing the customers' perceived waiting time. In the catering industry, the queuing for food can affect the event experience. An informal rule is one food or beverage line for every seventy-five to a hundred people. Figure 12.3 lists some of the factors to consider in the logistics of queuing.

The Atlanta Olympics and the Millennium Dome successfully used entertainers to reduce the perceived waiting time at the entrance and exhibit queues. Exit queuing can be the last experience for the customer at an event and needs the close attention of the event manager. At London's New Year's Eve celebrations, the authorities planned to use 'staggered entertainment' to spread the exit time of the crowds and avoid overcrowding on the London Underground. Within football stadia it is common practice to keep fans of one team within the ground until the opposing team's fans have dispersed, to avoid confrontation. Nightclubs may employ similar tactics, by raising lights shortly before the end of the evening and circulating security staff to avoid customers all waiting until the final record has played.

The over-supply of customers at a commercial event can give rise to a number of security and public safety problems that should be anticipated in the logistics plan. Equally, free events can attract too many customers if not carefully controlled. Only pre-sale tickets, and ticketing free events, will indicate the exact number of the expected audience. When tickets are sold at the entrance to an event, the logistics plan has to include the possibility of too many people. Over subscription may be pleasing for the event promoter, but can produce a logistical nightmare of what to do with the excess crowd.

- How many queues and possible bottlenecks will there be?
- Have an adequate number of personnel, including greeters, crowd controllers, ticket collectors and security been allocated?
- Is signage (including the estimated waiting time) in place?
- When will the queues form? Will they form all at once or over a period of time?
- How can the perceived waiting time be reduced (for example, queue entertainers)?
- What first aid, access and emergency procedures are in place?
- Are the lighting, and sun and rain protection adequate?
- Are crowd-friendly barricades and partitions in place?

Figure 12.3 Queuing – factors to consider

Customer transport

Transport to a site is often the first physical commitment by the audience to an event. The method and timing of arrival – public or private transport – is important to the overall logistics plan. The terms used by event managers are *dump*, when the audience arrives almost at once, and *trickle*, when they come and go over a larger period of time. Each of these needs a different logistics strategy. This first impression of the event by the audience can influence all subsequent experiences at the event. For this reason, it is the most visible side of logistics for customers. Graham, Neirotti and Goldblatt (2001) comment on the importance of spectator arrivals and departures at sport events. They stress that arrival and departure is a part of the event hospitality experience. The first and last impression of an event will be the parking facility and the traffic control.

The organization of transport for conferences takes on a special importance. Shone (1998) emphasizes the linking of transport and the selection of the venue. The selection of the conference venue or site has to take into account the availability and cost of transport to and from the site. Also, the transport to other facilities has to be considered. A venue that involves a 'long haul' will increase overall costs of a conference or event as well as add to the organizational confusion. It can also make the conference less attractive to delegates and, therefore, impact on delegate numbers.

For large events, festivals and parades, further logistic elements are introduced to the transport of the customer to the event. In particular, permission (council, highways department, police) and road closures need to be part of the logistics plan. Another requirement would be to plan sufficient signage to the event to ensure that customers, and equipment, arrive quickly and with the minimum of disruption to the local community. Events such as The Open Championship have signage commencing on main routes miles from the site as part of a coordinated transport plan to ensure that people are directed to the appropriate car parks. A leaflet, The Provision of Temporary Traffic Signs To Special Events, is available from the Department of the Environment, Transport and Regions to assist event managers in planning this aspect of the event. Guidance can also be gained from professional signage companies, such as Royal Automobile Club (RAC) signs service or Automobile Association (AA) signs. Figure 12.4 lists the elements of customer transport that need to be considered for an event.

Solving logistics problems (e.g. transport and parking) can become a significant issue for event organizers and will form part of the license requirements for the event. For example, for Glastonbury Festival 2000, wheel-wash and road-sweeping facilities were put in place as a contingency against poor weather, to ensure that mud was not deposited on the roads, which would cause a safety hazard.

Supply of product – product portfolio

Any event can be seen as the presentation of a product. Most events have a variety of products and services – a product portfolio – all of which go to create the event experience for the customer. The individual logistic requirements of the various products need to be integrated into a logistics plan.

For a large festival the product portfolio may include over 200 performing groups coming from around the UK and from overseas. For a small conference the product may be a speaker and video material. For an exhibition the product may include not only relevant exhibition stands focused on the theme of the event, but also displays and an educational seminar programme. It should be remembered that the product could also include the venue facilities. This is why the term 'the event experience'

- Have the relevant authorities (e.g. local council, police) been contacted for information and permission?
- Has adequate signage to the site been implemented?
- What public transport is available? Are timetables available?
- Has a backup transport system been organized? (in case the original transport system fails)?
- Is the taxi service adequate and has it been informed of the event? (Informing the local taxi service is also a way of promoting the event).
- What quality is the access area? Do weight and access restrictions apply? Are there any special conditions that must be considered (e.g. underground sprinkler systems under the access area).
- Is there adequate provision for private buses, including an area large enough for their turning circle, driver hospitality and parking?
- Is there a parking area and will it be staffed by trained personnel?
- Is a towing and emergency service available if required?
- Has transport to and from drop off point been organized (e.g. from the car park to the site or venue entrance and back to the car park)?
- At what rate are customers estimated to arrive (dump or trickle)?
- Is there adequate access and are there parking facilities for disabled customers?

Figure 12.4 Customer transport checklist

is used to cover all the aspects of the customers' experience. It can include, for example, the audience itself and just catching up with friends, in which case, the people become part of the product portfolio.

Transport

If the product portfolio includes products coming from overseas, the logistics problems can include issues such as carnet and customs clearance. A licence allows the movement of goods across an international boarder with an ATA Carnet, issued by Chamber of Commerce for exporting goods temporarily, or TIR Carnet, issued by the Road Hauliers Association or Freight Transport Association for importing goods temporarily. A performing artist group coming to the UK is required to have clearance for all its equipment, and needs to pay any taxes on goods that may be sold at the event, for example videos, DVDs or compact discs (CD)s.

A large account with an airline company can allow the event manager an area of negotiation. In exchange for being the 'preferred airline' of the event, an airline company can grant savings, discounts, free seats or free excess charges.

The artistic director would forward the transport requirements for the performers to the logistics manager well before the event. This one aspect of logistics illustrates the linking of the various functional areas of a large event.

Importing groups from overseas provides the logistics manager with an opportunity to communicate with these groups. The 'meet and greet' at the airport and the journey to the site can be used to familiarize the talent (i.e. the artists) with the event. Such things as site map, rehearsal times, accommodation, dressing room location, equipment storage and transport out can be included in the artist's event or festival kit.

Accommodation

The accommodation requirements of the artists (such as performers, keynote speakers or competitors) must be treated separately from the accommodation of the audience. The aim of the event manager is to get the best out of the 'product'. Given that entertainers are there to work, their accommodation has to be treated as a way of increasing the value of the investment in entertainment. Substandard accommodation and long trips to the site are certain ways of reducing this value. Often these requirements are not stated and need to be anticipated by the logistics manager.

Artists' needs on-site

A range of artists' needs must be catered for, including transport on-site, storage and movement of equipment, stage and back stage facilities, access, food and drink (often contained in the rider), sound and lights. All these have a logistic element but are described in detail in Chapter 13.

As with accommodation, an efficient event manager will anticipate the on-site needs of the artists. Often this can only be learned from experience. In multicultural Britain, the manager needs to be sensitive to requirements that are culturally based, such as food, dressing rooms (separate) and appropriate staff to assist the performer.

Supply of facilities

The supply of the infrastructure to an event site introduces many of the concepts of business logistics. The storage of consumables (food and drink) and equipment, and the maintenance of equipment become particularly significant. For a small event taking place over an evening, or conferences and exhibitions in permanent venues, most of the facilities will be supplied by the venue. The catering, toilets and power, for example, can all be part of the hiring of the venue.

Larger or more innovative events require the sourcing of many of the facilities. Some of these are discussed in detail in Chapter 13. An inaugural outdoor festival will need to source just about all the facilities. To find the best information about the availability and cost of the facilities, the event manager should look for a project in the area that required similar facilities. For example, toilets, generators, fencing, earth moving equipment and security are also used by construction and mining companies. Some facilities can be sourced through film production companies. Many of the other facilities travel with the various festivals. Large tents and sound systems need to be booked in advance. The Made-Up Textiles Association (2001, 2005) provides useful guidance on marquee hire including a code of practice for hiring, use and operation.

Innovative events, like a company-themed Christmas party in an abandoned car park, will require a long lead time to source the facilities. For example, it may take months to source unusual and rare props and venues for an event. These lead times can significantly affect the way the event is scheduled.

On-site logistics

The site of an event may vary from an old warehouse for a dance event to an underground car park for a Christmas party, to a 50-acre site for a festival.

Logistic considerations during the event become more complex with the size of the event. The flow of materials and people around the site and communication networks become the most important areas of logistics.

Flow

With larger festivals and events, the movement of audience, volunteers, artists and equipment can take a larger part of the time and effort of the logistics manager than the lead-up to the event. This is especially so when the site is physically complex or multi-venued, and the audience numbers are large. During the lead up time to an event, the subcontractors can take care of many of the elements of logistics. For example, the movement of the electricity generators to the site would be the responsibility of the hire company. However, once the facilities are on-site, it becomes the responsibility of the logistics manager for their positioning, movement and operation.

Something is being moved around on most events sites. The logistics must take into account the potential for flow of equipment and people during an emergency.

The access roads through a large festival and during the event would have to accommodate: artist and equipment transport; waste removal; emergency fire and first aid access and checking; stall set up, continual supply and removal; security; food and drink supplies; staging equipment set up, maintenance and removal; and site communication.

For operational and security reasons, an accreditation system is required to ensure that only appropriately authorised people can gain access to some areas of the event site. The movement of these people can be controlled, for example, through clearly identifiable coloured wrist bands or laminated badges (Access All Areas) to identify their clearance to security staff.

As illustrated by Figure 12.5, even during a straightforward event, many factors of the traffic flow must be considered. The performers for an event will need transport from their accommodation to the stage. Often the performers will go via the equipment storage area to the rehearsal rooms then to the stage. At the conclusion of the performance, the performers will return their equipment to storage then retire for a well-earned rest in the green room. For a community festival with four stages, this toing and froing can be quite complex.

At the same time as the performers are transported around the site, the media, audience and VIPs are on the move. Consideration also has to be given to accessibility for people with disabilities. Figure 12.5 does not show the movement of the food vendors' suppliers, water, security, ambulances and many more. When any one of the major venues empties there is further movement around the site by the audience.

> 0 Performers' accommodation → equipment storage area → rehearsal area →
>   stage → equipment storage area → social (green room)
> 1 Media accommodation → media centre → stages → social area
> 2 VIP accommodation → stages → special requests
> 3 Audience pick-up points → specific venue

Figure 12.5 Some of the traffic patterns to consider when planning an event

This results in peak flow times when it may be impossible, or unsafe, to move anything around the venue except the audience. These peaks and lows all have to be anticipated in the overall event plan. For example, movement of catering from the main production kitchens to the various hospitality units around Lord's Cricket Ground could only take place before spectators arrived and at set times when crowd density would be lighter, for example, avoiding morning coffee, lunch and afternoon tea service. Getting the timing wrong could lead to a thirty-minute journey, from what would normally take ten minutes.

Each event contains surprising factors in traffic flow. For the Brit Awards, taking place at Earls Court, for example, coordinating thousands of limousines, mostly containing celebrities, together with taxis and other traffic, could cause significant logistical problems on this main route through London. However, getting the limousines to set down customers at local hotels solves this. The case study of the Vodafone Ball, organized by Euro RSCG Skybridge Group, also illustrates the point as it requires meticulous planning, with 11 500 guests sitting down to a silver-service meal at the same time, and 2500 catering staff to coordinate. This earned a place in the Guinness Book of Records for the largest silver-served sit-down meal in the world, which recognizes the success of the planning involved.

Communication

On-site communication for the staff at a small event can be via the mobile phone or the loud- hailer of the event manager. With the complexity of larger events, however, the logistics plan must contain an on-site communications plan (Figure 12.6). The size of the communications plan will depend on the size of event – at one end of the scale, this may simply be a list of names, positions and mobile telephone numbers; at the other, it may also include fax, pagers, radio assignment numbers, on-site locations, extension numbers and lines of responsibility illustrating who is responsible to whom in the organization structure. Contractor contact details may be included on the main plan, however, on larger or more complex events, each contractor or service area (e.g. security, stewarding and catering) may be assigned a separate radio channel.

Name	Position	Location/base	Contact mobile number	Radio number	Reporting to	Responsible for
Jane Smith	Event Director	Roving	07771 XXX XXX	001	Board	Event Manager
Jackie Brown	Event Manager	Main Office	07771 XXX XXX	002	Event Director	Overall
Alan White	Assistant Event Manager	Area 1	07771 XXX XXX	003	Event Manager	All staff in area 1
Caroline Black	Assistant Event Manager	Area 2	07771 XXX XXX	004	Event Manager	All staff in area 2

Figure 12.6 Simple communication plan

It may be preferable for all communications to be directed through a main communications control centre, rather than via mobile phones, to ensure that operational issues are not confused and lines of communication remain clear. Policies should be implemented on radio usage to guarantee professionalism is maintained at all times.

The communication of information during an event has to work seamlessly with the other functions of event management. In particular, the immediacy of the information is important. The information has to be highly targeted and timely enough for people to act on it. This immediacy of information is unique to events because they must meet a deadline and generally involve large numbers of people. For this reason, event management tends to involve a variety of communication methods and devices, including:

- *two-way radios* – very common at large events, where the channels are reserved for emergency and police
- *mobile phones and text messages* – although limited by capacity, possibly becoming overloaded in an emergency. For this reason, some large venues acquire additional coverage
- *signage* – a common form of communication. Its placement and clarity are important issues (dealt with later in this chapter)
- *runners* – people whose job is to physically take the information to the receiver. Runners are indispensable if there is a power failure. Some large public events have bicycles ready for this purpose
- *news sheets* – paper news sheets used to inform the exhibitors of daily programme changes and updates on the attendee numbers and types
- *loud hailer* – surprisingly useful devices at some events such as parades
- *a sound system* – useful for announcements. The event team should know how to use it correctly
- *flags* – often used at sports events such as car racing
- *visual and audio cues* – used to communicate the start or finish of an action. Whistles, horns, flashing lights can all be used in this way. Artistic lighting can be used to move an audience around a venue
- *closed circuit television and web cams* – used in venues such exhibition and entertainment centres
- *short-range FM radios* – used to broadcast information during the event
- *WiFi and Bluetooth* – two recent technologies that are employed at some events, conferences and exhibitions to send and receive information
- *bulletin boards* – a humble and often effective way of contacting the volunteers and performers on-site.

The movement around the event site or venue of equipment, suppliers and people – that is, the logistics during the event – needs an efficient communication system. For this reason, events often have levels of redundancy or backups for any one type of communication. The test of good communication planning is a power failure or emergency when the system will stop or be overloaded, and the event management team will be swamped with decisions to be made. Communication planning has to account for such a situation, so it must be a fundamental part of the project management and undergo a thorough risk assessment.

Signage

On-site signage is an important part of communicating to all the attendees of the event. It may be as simple as messages on a whiteboard in the volunteers' dining area, or involve large on-site maps showing the public the location of facilities. Two important issues in on-site signage are position and clarity. A direction sign that is obscured by such things as sponsors' messages diminishes its value. For large events the signage may need a detailed plan. The issues to consider are:

- Overall site placement of signs – at decision points and danger spots, so that they are integrated into the event.
- Types of signs needed such as directional, statutory (e.g. legal and warning signs), operational, facility and sponsor.
- The sign literacy of attendees – what sort of signs are they used to reading?
- Actual placement of signs – entrance, down the road, height.
- Accessibility of signs – are they accessible to people with disabilities?
- Orientation of signs (i.e. when a customer is looking at the sign does it reflect the direction that they are facing?).
- Supply of signs, their physical maintenance and their removal.
- Maintaining the credibility of the signs. If a facility is moved, then the signs will need to be amended.

The most effective way of communicating with the audience at an event is to have the necessary information in the programme. Figure 12.7 shows the type of essential information that can be included in the programme for the audience, spectator or visitor.

Accommodation – whether accommodation is provided onsite or available nearby? May include contact details
Banking facilities – where are the nearest banking facilities? Are these onsite?
Cameras – are there any restrictions on camera usage? For example, some events may ban all cameras, others only commercial cameras.
Catering/bar facilities – what catering/bar facilities are available onsite? Where are they located?
Clothing – is there a compulsory or suggested dress code?
Directions – where is the event situated? Are there any special routes for getting there?
Disabilities – what extra facilities/services are provided for people with disabilities?
First aid – where are these situated? Assistance from the St Johns Ambulance or Red Cross may be acknowledged.
Information/meeting point – is there an area onsite where people can arrange to meet or have any queries answered?
Lost and found – where is office located for lost and found children or items of value?
Organizer/security – where are the organizer and security offices located?
Rules – are there any rules that visitors, spectators or the audience must observe?
Telephones – where are the nearest telephones located?
Tickets – remind visitors/audience of the requirement to bring their ticket to the event and of any restrictions (for example, is access restricted to certain areas?)
Toilets – where are toilets located?
Video/viewing screens – for sporting events and festivals, where are video screens located? For greenfield sports (e.g. golf), where will scores be posted?
Website – what is the address of the event website? What type of information may be found there?

Figure 12.7 Event programme information

Amenities and solid waste management

For large festivals, events and exhibitions, the layout of the amenities is always included in the logistics site map. Figure 12.8 is an example of a large festival logistics site map that shows the layout of amenities.

The site map is an indispensable tool for the event manager, and is described later in this chapter. The schedules for the maintenance and cleaning of the amenities are part of the plan. For smaller events, these areas may be the sole responsibility of the venue management and part of the hiring contract.

Responsibility for cleaning the site and restoring it to its original condition is of particular importance to an event manager, as it is generally tied to the nature of the event. For example, Leeds Festival at Temple Newsam in Leeds attracted a huge audience to a delicate area. Merely the movement of the audience destroyed the grass

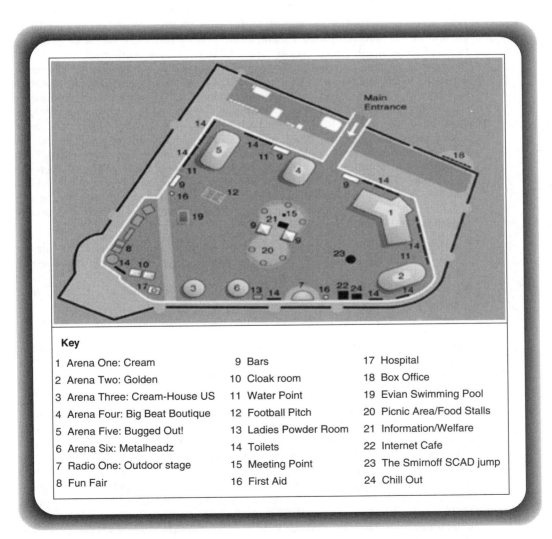

Key

1 Arena One: Cream	9 Bars	17 Hospital
2 Arena Two: Golden	10 Cloak room	18 Box Office
3 Arena Three: Cream-House US	11 Water Point	19 Evian Swimming Pool
4 Arena Four: Big Beat Boutique	12 Football Pitch	20 Picnic Area/Food Stalls
5 Arena Five: Bugged Out!	13 Ladies Powder Room	21 Information/Welfare
6 Arena Six: Metalheadz	14 Toilets	22 Internet Cafe
7 Radio One: Outdoor stage	15 Meeting Point	23 The Smirnoff SCAD jump
8 Fun Fair	16 First Aid	24 Chill Out

Figure 12.8 Creamfields 2000 Site Map
Source: Slice (2000)

and resulted in local residents being wary of any further events in their area. However, violence at the 2002 event, following trouble at previous years events, caused over £250 000 of damage and injuries. As a result, the event moved to Bramham Park near Wetherby from 2003 where the festival could be better managed to avoid disruption to local residents and the infrastructure could be invested in for the festival's long term future. If an event takes place in the countryside, such as an open–air concert, a motor sport event, a cross-country race or a corporate team challenge, extra care must be taken by the event manager to minimize the impact on the environment, particularly in protected areas, such as National Parks. An environmental impact assessment may generally assist the event manager in managing this. However, the National Parks may have their own specific guidelines and rules for such events. Lake District National Park Authority (1999) notes that although the impact of large events can be significant, for example, the Three Peaks Race, even small events can raise concerns and therefore size is not the major issue. They observe that, 'It is more important that the organizers of any event have taken account of the potential problems, and made every effort to avoid them, or reduce them to an acceptable level' (Lake District National Park Authority, 1999, p. 50). In order to be able to manage the events effectively, it is advised that the event manager effectively liaise with local bodies, local communities, and include areas such as transport, parking, toilet provision, marshalling (for sporting events) and safety within the plan. Guidelines provided by sporting bodies and user groups, for example, those developed by the Institute of Charity Fundraisers, can be a useful source of advice to event organizers, based on years of experience. Motor sport events are highlighted as causing particular concerns, and as a result, specific criteria have been developed to minimize the impact of this type of event. These relate to when the events can take place, which routes are allowed, restrictions placed on vehicle numbers and that all houses along the route are notified. Overall, the principles to consider when planning events in greenfield sites may form part of the licence conditions and include the following:

- traffic arrangements (e.g. planning effective routes to minimize traffic on narrow lanes, unsuitable routes, or local villages/towns, protecting verges and keeping routes clear)
- parking management (e.g. solid ground, plan for if vehicles get stuck, road cleaning)
- waste management (e.g. collection and minimization of litter inside and outside the site)
- drainage considerations for the site (including effective road surfaces for vehicle access)
- safety (e.g. uneven surfaces for audience/spectators)
- noise control.

Well-maintained toilets can be a very important issue with the audience, in particular, their number, accessibility and cleanliness. The HSE (1999) provides useful guidance in this respect. Requirements for minimum number of toilets for public entertainment buildings are outlined in BS6465: Part 1 1994, however, for licensed entertainment, the location and number of toilets should be agreed with the local authority and may be a term within the license. The number of units required will depend on the type of event, for example, those with higher fluid intake or where camping will take place. However, a general rule of thumb for a music event opening six hours or more is one toilet for every 100 females, and one toilet per 500 males plus one urinal per 150 males. Hand-washing facilities should be provided with no less than one per ten toilets, together with suitable hand-drying provision. The HSE (1999) also remind organizers of their responsibilities for people with special needs, for example, those requiring wheelchair access, and suggest a minimum of one toilet with hand-washing facilities per seventy-five people, although this should relate to anticipated numbers. One need only look at the press coverage of the summer festivals in the mid to late 1990s in order to recognize the importance to customers of clean toilets, which resulted in significant improvements over the past couple of years. The logistics manager has to be aware of 'peak flows' during an event and the consequences for vehicle transport of the waste and opening times of treatment plants.

The collection of solid waste can range from making sure that the venue manager has enough bins, to calling for a tender and subcontracting the work. The number of bins and workers, shifts, timelines for collection and removal of skips should all be contained in the logistics plan as it interrelates with all the other event functional areas. This is a further example of linking the elements of logistics. A plan for primary recycling – recycling at collection point – would include both the education of the public (signage) and specialist bins for different types of waste (aluminium, glass, paper). Effective management of the event, for example, by banning the audience from bringing in glass bottles, can not only reduce the physical impact on the environment and reduce clear up costs, but can also increase safety.

Consumables: food and beverage

The logistics aspects of food and beverage on a large multi-venue site primarily concern its storage and distribution. Food stalls may be under the management of a stall manager as there are regulations that need to be followed. The needs of the food stalls including transport, gas, electricity and plumbing are then sent on to the logistics manager. In particular the sale of alcoholic beverages can present the logistics manager with specific security issues.

At a wine and food fair, or beer festival, the 'consumables' are the attraction. The collection of cash is often solved by the use of presale tickets that are exchanged for the food, wine or beer 'samples'. The tickets are bought at one place on the site, which reduces possible problems with security, cash collection and accounting. Figure 12.9 lists some of the main factors to consider when including food and beverage outlets at an event.

As well as feeding and watering the public, logistics includes the requirements of the staff, volunteers and performers. This catering area, often called the green room, provides an opportunity to disseminate information to the event staff. A strategically placed large whiteboard in the green room may prove to be an effective means of communicating with volunteers.

Last, but not the least, is the catering for sponsors and VIPs. This generally requires a separate plan to the general catering. At some festivals a 'hospitality tent' is set up for the 'special guests'. This aspect of events is covered in Chapter 13 on staging.

The VIP and media requirements

The effect on event logistics by media coverage of the event cannot be overestimated. Even direct radio broadcasts can disrupt the live performance of a show – both in the setting up and the actual broadcast. The recording or broadcast of speeches or music often requires separate microphones or a line from the mixing desk. This cannot be left until just before the performance. Television cameras require special lighting, which often shines directly into the eyes of the audience. The movement

- Has a liquor license been granted?
- What selection criteria for stall applicants (including design of stall and menu requirements) will be used?
- What infrastructure will be needed (including plumbing, electrical, gas)?
- Does the contract include provisions for health and safety regulations, gas supplies, insurance and workers payment?
- What position on the site will the stalls occupy?
- Have arrival, set up, breakdown and leaving times been set?
- What cleaning arrangements have been made?
- Do stallholders understand the need for ongoing inspections, such as health, electricity, plumbing, waste (including liquids) disposal and gas inspection?
- Are there any special security needs that must be catered for?
- How and when will payment for the stall be made?
- Will the stallholder provide in-kind support for the event (including catering for VIPs, media and performers)?

Figure 12.9 Food and beverage – factors to consider

of production crew and television power requirements can be distracting to a live performance, and need to be assessed before the event.

Media organizations work on very short timelines and may upset the well-planned tempo of the event. However, the rewards in terms of promotion and even finance are so large that the media logistics can take precedence over most other aspects of the event. The event manager in consultation with event promotions and sponsors often makes these decisions. This is an area that illustrates the need for flexible negotiations and assessment by the logistics manager.

The VIP requirements can include special security arrangements. Once again it is a matter of weighing up the benefits of having VIPs with the amount of extra resources that are needed. This, however, is not the logistic manager's area of concern; the event manager or event committee should deal with it. Once the VIPs have been invited their needs have to take precedence over the publics'.

Emergency procedures

Emergency procedures at an event can range from staff qualified in first aid, to using the St John Ambulance or Red Cross service, to the compilation of a comprehensive major incident or disaster plan. The location of first aid should be indicated on the site map and all the event staff should be aware of this. The number of first-aiders, medical and ambulance provision will depend on the nature and size of the event. HSE (1999) recommends that a ratio of 2:1000 (for the first 3000 attending) may be appropriate for smaller events, with no less than two first-aiders on-site. However, exact requirements should be established as part of the risk assessment process and included within the event plan. HSE (1999) provide a method of estimating these. Large events require an emergency access road that has to be kept clear. These issues are so important that a local council will immediately close down an event that does not comply with their regulations that concern emergencies.

HSE (1999) and Home Office (2000) offer guidance in the preparation of a major incident plan. HSE (1999, p. 32) define a major incident as one 'that requires the implementation of special arrangements by one or more of the emergency services, the NHS or local authority' for treatment, rescue and transport of a large number of people, and associated issues, such as dealing with enquiries and the media. They suggest that the following areas are considered when planning the major incident plan:

- identify the key decision-making workers
- stopping the event
- identify emergency routes and access for emergency services
- requirements of people with special needs
- identify holding areas for performers, workers and the audience
- the script of coded messages to inform staff and announcements for the audience
- alert/communication procedures, including public warning
- procedure for evacuation and containment
- identify rendezvous points for emergency services and ambulance loading points
- locate nearest hospitals and traffic routes
- identify temporary mortuary facilities
- identify roles, contact list and communications plan
- location of emergency equipment and availability
- documentation and message pads.

The emergency plan must be developed for major incidents, with further plans covering minor incidents. The above provides a useful starting point for areas to consider, but you are strongly advised to obtain a copy of The Event Safety Guide (HSE, 1999) or other appropriate guidance notes currently available for exhibitions, outdoor events and sporting grounds (see references). The on-site emergency procedures are an example of the two functions of event management – risk and logistics – working together to formulate a plan. Overall, they come under the project plan. They are now mandatory for many events.

Considerations for creating the plan include: under whose authority is the plan being prepared? And what are the plan's aims and objectives? The emergency plan will influence the design of the site, particularly for large public events. Local councils require emergency access to all parts of the event, and the access route must be the correct width for an emergency vehicle and kept clear at all times. A mistake in this area can result in the event being closed immediately.

Emergencies can occur at any time during the event, and the planning has an effect on the evacuation procedures. These procedures should be different:

- while the audience is arriving, before they have entered the venue or site. The logistics involved are concerned with stopping the inflow.
- while some of the audience is already in the venue and others are arriving. This is a complex period of two directions of flow: people who are arriving and haven't heard that the event has been cancelled, and those who are eager to leave.
- during the event, when most of the audience is on-site.

The disaster plan stresses the lines of authority and necessary procedures. These procedures include the partial evacuation of the festival site in the event of a disaster (particularly prolonged heavy rain). It notes that rescuers should concentrate on personnel in immediate danger when conducting an evacuation.

Shutdown

As Pagonis (1992) points out, military logistics is divided into three phases: deployment, combat and redeployment, and it is often the case that redeployment takes the most effort and time. The amount of time and effort spent on the shutdown of an event are in direct proportion to the size of the event and its uniqueness. Repeated events, like many of the festivals mentioned in this chapter, have their shutdown schedule refined over many years. It can run quickly and smoothly. All the subcontractors know exactly how to get their equipment out and where they are placed in the order of removal. The event manager of a small event may only have to sweep the floor and turn off the lights.

Most difficulties arise in inaugural events, large events and multi-venue events. In these cases, logistics can be as important after the event as at any other time, and the need for planning most apparent. As illustrated in Figure 12.10, the management of event shutdown involves many elements. In project management terminology, this is called the asset handover and project closure. In event management, the most forgotten part is the closure of the project. The tools of project management can be used to manage the shutdown process. The shutdown plan should include a work breakdown structure, a task/responsibility list and a schedule with a critical path, and be subject to risk analysis. It forms part of the overall event project plan.

Crowd dispersal
- Exits/transport
- Safety
- Related to programming
- Staggered entertainment

Equipment
- Load-out schedule including correct exists and loading docks
- Shut down equipment using specialist staff (e.g. computers)
- Clean and repair
- Store - number boxes and display contents list
- Sell or auction
- Small equipment and sign off
- Schedule for dismantling barriers

Entertainment
- Send-off appropriately
- Payments – cash
- Thank you letters/awards/recommendations

Human resources
- The big thank you
- Final payments
- Debrief and gain feedback for next year
- Reports
- Celebration party

Liability
- Records
- Descriptions
- Photo/video evidence

Onsite/staging area
- Cleaning
- Back to normal
- Environmental assessment
- Lost and found
- Idiot check
- Site/venue hand-over

Contractors
- Contract release
- Thank you

Finance
- Pay the bills
- Finalize and audit accounts – best done as soon as possible
- Thank donors and sponsors

Marketing and promotion
- Collect press clippings/video news
- Reviews of the event - use a service
- Market research on community reaction

Sponsors and Grants
- Release grants: prompt reports
- Meet sponsors and enthuse for next time
- Government and Politics
- Thank services involved
- Reports to councils and other government organizations

Client
- Glossy report, video, photos
- Wrap up and suggestions for next time

Figure 12.10 Event shutdown checklist

The on-site issues initially involve the crowd. Whether for a sporting event, a conference or a concert, not much major work can be done until the crowd leaves. However, some tasks can be started, such as packing one stage while the crowd's attention is elsewhere. Crowd management at this time is vital because the event management is responsible for the crowd's safety as people leave the venue and make their way home. It is wise to include this issue in the risk management plan. If some members of the crowd want to 'party on', it is smart to plan this activity well ahead of time. Some of the local bars, restaurants, nightclubs and hotels may welcome the increase in patrons, if told beforehand.

The site may look empty after the event, but the experienced event manager knows that the work has only just begun. The equipment needs to be collected, repaired and stored, or immediately returned to its owners. Small equipment such as hand-held radios are easily lost, so many events have a sign-on/sign-off policy for these items. With large crowds, you can almost guarantee there will be an assortment of lost items. A member of staff needs to walk the site to check whether anything has been left behind – called the 'idiot check' in the music industry. At this point, the event manager realizes the value of a torch!

As the site is being shut down, it may also be prepared for the next event. This is a consideration for all the other resources. The equipment may be packed away so it can be easily found and used for the next event. Shutdown thus has a further element: preparation for the next event. Extensive site clean-up is also often required.

The shutdown of an event is the prime security time. The mix of vehicles, movement of equipment and general feeling of relaxation provides a cover for theft. The smooth flow of traffic leaving an event at its conclusion must also be considered. Towing services and the police may need to be contacted. Very large events may require the sale of facilities and equipment at a post-event auction. Some events find that it is more cost effective to buy or make the necessary equipment and sell it after the event. Finally, it is often left to the person in charge of logistics to organize the final thank-you party for the volunteers and staff.

Back at the event office, there will be at least a few weeks of project closure. This will include acquitting all the contracts, paying the bills and collecting all the records of the event, media clippings and any incident report sheets. These records will assist when all the reports have to be prepared and any funding is acquitted. Although the next step may not be the responsibility of the person in charge of logistics, the event logistics manager will have an important role.

The event is not over until the management of the event has been assessed (Chapter 9). The logistics plan is part of the overall event project plan, so has to be assessed for its effectiveness. It cannot be assessed unless there are written documents or files to compare against the reality of the event logistics. It will be difficult, if not impossible, to suggest real improvements for the next event without these. Too often, in the rush to the next event, the logistics problems are forgotten. The event management produces not just the event, but also a way in which to manage the event. Checklists are an example of a logistics management system. They represent the micro-management of the event. In the past, many events would have discarded these checklists after the event, yet the checklist is a portable tool – for example, the ticket checklist is common to all events, so it can easily be adapted to a checklist for invitations to a charity event. Checklists should be assessed after the event, along with the rest of the management system. Figure 12.10 (page 370) provides a checklist of points to consider when performing the shutdown.

Techniques of logistics management

The tools used in business and military logistics can be successfully adapted to event logistics. Because an event takes place at a specific time and specific place, the tools of scheduling and mapping are used. The dynamic nature of events and the way that the functional areas are so closely linked mean a small change in one area can result in crucial changes throughout the event. The incorrect placement of an electric generator, for example, can lead to a mushrooming of problems. If the initial problem is not foreseen or immediately solved, it can grow to affect the whole event. This gives initial negotiations and ongoing assessment a special significance in event logistics. The logistics manager needs to be skilled in identifying possible problem areas and needs to know what is not on the list.

The role of the logistics manager is now considered and their relationship with other functional areas and managers of an event.

The event logistics manager

As mentioned throughout this chapter, the logistics manager has to be a procurer, negotiator, equipment and maintenance manager, human resource manager, map-maker, project manager and party organizer. For a small event, logistics can be the direct responsibility of the event manager. Logistics becomes a separate area if the event is large and complex. Multi-venue and multi-day events usually require a separate logistics manager position.

Part of the role of the logistics manager is to efficiently link all areas of the event. Figure 12.11 illustrates the lines of communication between the logistics manager and various other managers for a multi-venue event. It is a network diagram because,

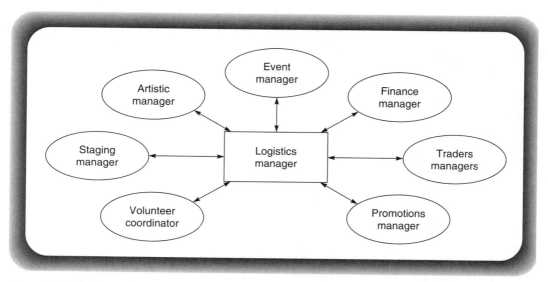

Figure 12.11 The lines of communication between the logistics manager and other managers for a multi-venue event

although the event manager or director has ultimate authority, decision-making authority is usually devolved to the various managers who work at the same level of authority and responsibility as the event manager.

The information required by the logistics manager from other festival managers is shown in Table 12.1. The clear communication within this network is also partly the responsibility of the logistics manager. Many of the tools and techniques of the logistics manager are discussed in Chapter 9.

Table 12.1 Information required by the logistics manager from the other festival managers

Position	General role	Information sent to logistics manager
Artistic director	Selection and negotiation with artists	Travel, accommodation, staging and equipment requirements
Staging manager	Selecting and negotiation with subcontractors	Sound, lights, and backstage requirements, programming times
Finance director	Overseeing budgets and contracts	How and when funds will be approves and released and the payment schedule
Volunteers coordinator	Recruitment and management of volunteers	Volunteers selected to assist Requirements of the volunteers (e.g. parking, free tickets)
Promotions manager Traders manager	Promotion during the event Selecting suitable traders	Requirements of the media and VIPs Requirements of the traders (e.g. positioning, theming, electricity, water, licence agreements)

Site or venue map

A map of the event site or venue is a necessary communication tool for the logistics manager. For small events, even a simple map can be an effective tool that obviates the need for explanations and can quickly identify possible problem areas. The map for larger festivals can be an aerial photograph with the logistic features drawn on it. For smaller events, it may be a sketch map that just shows the necessary information to the customer. The first questions to ask are 'what is the map for?' and 'who will be reading it?' A logistics site map will contain very different information than the site map used for promotion purposes. Of necessity, the map needs to filter information that is of no interest to the logistics plan. Monmonier (1996, p. 25) in his highly respected work on mapping summarizes this concept thus:

> *A good map tells a multitude of little white lies; it suppresses truth to help the user see what needs to be seen. Reality is three dimensional, rich in detail, and far too factual to allow a complete yet uncluttered two-dimensional scale model. Indeed, a map that did not generalize would be useless. However, the value of a map depends on how well its generalized geometry and generalized content reflect a chosen aspect of reality.*

The three basic features of maps – scale, projection and the key (showing the symbols used) – have to be adapted to their target audience. Volunteers and subcontractors, for example, need to clearly read and understand it. The communication value of the site map is also a matter of where it is displayed. Some festivals draw the map on the back of the ticket or programme.

The checklist for items to be included in a site map can be very detailed. Figure 12.12 shows a standard checklist of the logistics for a small festival.

- Scale and direction (north arrow)
- A list of symbols used on the map (key)
- Entrance and exits
- Roads and parking
- Administration centre
- Information booths
- First aid and emergency road access
- Lost children area
- Electricity and water outlets
- Toilets
- Lost property
- Food and market stalls
- Tents and marquees
- Equipment storage areas
- Off-limit areas and danger spots (e.g. creeks, blind corners)
- Green room
- Maintenance area
- Pathways
- Telephones
- ATMs
- Media area

Figure 12.12 Checklist for the logistics site map

With many sporting events, a sketch map on the ticket shows how to find the site, parking, and the location of seats and facilities. The back of tickets generally includes a list detailing the behaviour expected of event participants. The festival site shown in Figure 12.8 is a promotional map for the audience, originally presented in full colour with points of interest to the public displayed. For corporate events a simple map of the venue at the entrance – in particular showing seating, toilets, food areas and bar – can relieve the staff of a lot of questions! Further, the logistics map for volunteers, staff, performers and all other personnel would provide further details, including the placement of site offices, contractors compounds and service routes.

Negotiation and assessment

No matter what the size of the event, the mutual agreement on supply and conditions is vital. In particular, the special but changing nature of one-off events requires the techniques of dynamic negotiation to be mastered by the logistics manager. Marsh (1984, p. 1), in his work on negotiation and contracts, defines negotiation as 'a dynamic process of adjustment by which two parties, each with their own objectives, confer together to reach a mutually satisfying agreement on a matter of common interest'.

Logistical considerations need to be covered by the initial negotiations with subcontractors. Agreement on delivery time and removal times is an indispensable part of the timelines as they form the parameters of the critical path.

It needs to be stressed that the management of events in the UK is a dynamic industry. The special nature of many events means that many aspects cannot be included in the initial negotiation. Decisions and agreements need to be continually reassessed. Both parties to the agreement have to realize that the agreement needs to be flexible. However, all possible problems should be unmasked at the beginning, and there are logistics tools to enable this to happen.

Having prepared the schedules and site map, an important tool to use is what Pagonis (1992, p. 194) describes as the 'skull session':

Before implementing a particular plan, I usually try to bring together all of the involved parties for a collective dry run. The group includes representatives from all appropriate areas of command,

and the goal of the skull session is to identify and talk through all the unknown elements in the situation. We explore all problems that could emerge, and then try to come up with concrete solutions to those problems. Skull sessions reduce uncertainty, reinforce the interconnection of different areas of specialisation, encourage collaborative problem solving, and raise the level of awareness as to possible disconnects in the theatre.

Goldblatt (2005) calls this gap analysis. Gap analysis is studying the plan to attempt to identify gaps that could lead to a weakening in the implementation of the logistics plan. He goes on to recommend using a critical friend to review the plan look for gaps in your logical thinking.

The identification of risk areas, gaps and 'what ifs' is important in the creation of a contingency plan. For example, as Glastonbury Festival takes place during one of the hottest months of the year, the supply of water was identified as a priority area. For the 1997 festival, a permanent water main was constructed, supplemented by water carts, and drinking water made available to the general public through standpipes. On-site, there was also an attempt to encourage water conservation through an association with WaterAid.

Control of events logistics

The monitoring of the logistics plan is a vital part of the overall control of an event. An important part of the plan is the identification of milestones – times when crucial tacks have to be completed. The Gantt chart (Chapter 9) can be used to compare projected performance with actual performance by recording performance times on the chart as the tasks occur. It is a simple monitoring device, with the actual performance written on the chart as the tasks occur.

The aim of the logistics manager is to create a plan to enable the logistics to flow without the need for active control. The use of qualified subcontractors with experience in events is the only way to make this happen. This is where the annual festival with its established relationships to the suppliers has the advantage over the one-off, innovative event. The objective of the event director is to enjoy the event without having to intervene in any on-site problems!

Evaluation of logistics

The ultimate evaluation of the logistics plan is the success of the event and the easy flow of event supply and operations. However, the festival committee, event director and/or the sponsors may require a more detailed evaluation. The main question to ask is if the logistics met their objectives. If the objectives as set out in the plan are measurable, then this task is relatively straightforward. If the objectives require a qualitative approach, then the evaluation can become imprecise and open to many interpretations.

An evaluation enables the logistic manager to identify problem areas that enables improvement and therefore adds value to the next event. The term 'logistics audit' is used for a systematic and thorough analysis of the event logistics. Part of the audit concerns the expectations of the audience and whether they were satisfied. For very large events, the evaluation of the logistics may be contained in the overall evaluation undertaken by an external research company. Evaluation is discussed further in Chapter 14.

The logistics plan

Whether the event is a school class reunion or a multi-venue festival, a written logistics or operations plan needs to be part of the communication within the event. It could range from a one-page contact list with approximate arrival times, to a bound folder covering all areas. The folder for a large event would contain:

- general contact list
- site map
- schedules, including time lines and bar charts
- the emergency plan
- subcontractor details, including all time constraints
- on-site contacts, including security and volunteers
- evaluation sheets (sample questionnaires).

All these elements have been described and discussed in this chapter. These can make up the event manual that is used to stage the event. The manual needs to be a concise document, as it may be used in an emergency. An operations manual may only be used once but it has to be able to withstand the rigours of the event itself. Some organizations, particularly in the exhibition industry, have a generic manual on their intranet that can be adapted for all their events in any part of the world.

Although this text emphasizes the importance of planning, over-planning can be a significant risk, particularly with a special event, as there is often a need to respond and take opportunities when they arise. Artistry and innovation can easily be hampered by a purely mechanistic approach to event creation. The secret is to ensure that the plan is structured sufficiently well to ensure a safe event, whilst allowing creativity to shine through.

Chapter summary

Military logistics is as old a civilization itself. Business logistics is a recent science. Events logistics has the advantage of building on these areas, using the tools of both and continually improving on them as the events industry grows.

This logistics system can be broken down into the procuring and supply of customers, products and facilities. Once on-site the logistics system concerns the flow around the site, communication and the requirements of the event. At the conclusion of the event, logistics concerns the breakdown of structures, cleaning and managing the evacuation of the site or venue.

For small events, logistics may be the responsibility of the event manager. However, for larger events a logistics manager may be appointed. The logistics manager's role within the overall event management and his or her relationship with other managers was described. For both small and large events, the tools of business and military logistics are used. The logistics of an event need to be treated as any other area of management and have in-built evaluation and ongoing control. All these elements are placed in a plan that is a part of the overall event plan.

Logistics is an invisible part of events. It enables the customers to focus completely on the event without being distracted by unnecessary problems. It only becomes visible when it is looked for or when there is a problem. It enables the paying customer, the public, client or sponsor to realize and even exceed their expectations.

Questions

1. What are the logistics areas that need to be contained in initial the agreements with the suppliers to an event?
2. Set out an emergency plan for a small event.
3. List the logistics tasks for (a) a street parade, (b) a product launch and (c) a company party.
4. Create a list of types of event. For each type of event, rate the significance of logistics.

Case study 12.1

Electrical Services at Glastonbury Festival

GE Energy Rentals (absorbing Showpower Inc., who in turn acquired Templine Ltd in 1997) have been the main electrical power contractors for the Glastonbury Festival since 1990. This entails providing all the generators, the cabling, electrical distribution (to the highest standards of safety), and lighting, for the main site, all the stages and market. There are three distinct areas to the operation:

1. *The site*: this involves mainly lighting and the power sources for it. The site lighting performs much the same function as street lighting in a city, highlighting main routes and any obstacles, such as bridges or ditches, and for security. Another major part of this side of the job, is toilet lighting. It is a requirement of the council's licence for the event that all the toilets (there are about 1200 of them!) be adequately lit when it is dark. These toilets are clustered in small groups (of about forty toilets) all over the 550 acres of the site, so getting power to them is one of the most challenging parts of the job. There are also vital services such as the site medical centre, water pumps, etc. to be powered. The main site roadways and the vast circular perimeter fence are lit by seven to ten watchtowers, each with several floodlights, its own generator and an illuminated property lock-up. Approximately 4 miles of festoon lighting, with a bulb every 5 metres support this! The watchtowers, along with many other site functions, now require power for most of the week before the festival and a couple of days after it. The floodlights, stage lighting, and countless campfires make the festival site a huge, stunning feature on the Somerset landscape after dark.
2. *The stages*: for all the stages and performance areas GE Energy Rentals Ltd., provide generators and the cable and distribution. Large amounts of electrical power are needed for the stage lighting systems, PA systems, video screens, lasers, etc. For the main music stages this now also involves power for live television and radio outside broadcasts. These supplies are generally larger (400A three phase for main stage lighting) and the distribution much more complex than for site supplies. They are, however, clustered into smaller areas than the site wiring. Stage supplies are backed up with spare generators in case of failure. All the stages have extensive backstage villages of Portacabin dressing rooms, offices, hospitality and catering areas, and loading bays that also need power and lighting.
3. *Market*: the market power for the festival is a major undertaking, organizing and providing the power for most of the 600+ stalls. The timescale generally follows that of the site, except that the power is required for food storage (refrigeration) and security (lighting), twenty-four hours per day from the Monday before the festival to the Monday following. During the operational phase the markets are quite intensive as the large number of users

causes issues, with some attempting to use more than they have paid for (causing overloading of sections of the system) and others plugging in faulty equipment leading to tripping of sections. In bad weather conditions (such as the mudbaths of 1998 and 1999) these problems are amplified several times!

Timescale

To install, operate and then remove an installation of this size and complexity in the short time available, while meeting the very high standards of safety required, requires considerable planning and teamwork. The overall timescale is as follows:

Six months prior to event: power requirements for the markets are established. The process commences in January with forms sent out with the pitch applications for stalls at the festival. There then follows a process of collating the returned forms, chasing payments and attempting to anticipate those stall holders who will eventually require power, but are delaying informing us to delay payment! An outline plan is drawn up and the generators and major elements of the cabling and distribution allocated.

Three months prior to event: power requests are collated from the other festival area organizers and those who have not yet responded are chased up. Discussions commence with the main subcontractors regarding the supply of men and equipment. Plant is also booked at this stage (e.g. forklift trucks, accommodation and storage cabins).

Two months prior to event: detailed planning begins – each year's plan is based on the previous year, amended as the power requests come in. The site and performance areas are separated and described, power requirements ascertained and generators allocated. This is completed, in conjunction with the all-important site map, on computerized tables and schedules. About this time we usually have a meeting with Michael Eavis to discuss any special or new points and to agree a budget. With the plans taking shape it is possible to identify the number of generators required, usually about 200 units (including markets) with twenty-five, self-contained lighting tower units ranging from 600 to 6 kW. These are sourced from our fleet, especially the stage generators, and cross-hired from outside suppliers.

Four weeks before event: the first part of what will eventually grow into a crew of about thirty electricians and assistants arrive on-site to start erecting the watchtowers, floodlights and 4 miles of festoon lighting. Transport for plant and equipment to, around, and from site are finalized, using around 50 articulated lorries of equipment during the event. The main crew arrives on-site – all need to be accommodated and fed for five weeks in a bare field! Installation begins with site requirements, and the inevitable toilet-chasing as last minute changes to the plan occur. The on-site office is set up with all the plans and schedules on the walls to act as the nerve centre of the operation. Security commences on the gates, and site crew catering starts, requiring power and lights.

One week before event: the generators arrive on-site and have to be allocated, positioned with trucks and cranes, and wired up and tested for safety. Stage areas need to be made ready for the arrival of the lighting and PA rigs by about the Wednesday of show week.

Doors open! All site licence requirements must be met and are checked by local council staff.

Showtime! All systems are up and running. All the generators must be refuelled twice a day – each refuelling circuit takes about twelve hours to complete, so it is like painting the Forth Bridge. The generators will use about 200 000 litres of diesel fuel in the next four days. To reduce the risk of a major spillage, on-site storage is kept to about 1.5 days' supply – in separated bonded tanks – with regular tanker deliveries throughout the event. The on-call crew attends to any breakdowns or last minute additions. The other members of the crew get a chance to enjoy the festival, or just catch up on some sleep!

Post-event – the aftermath: immediately after the last band come off stage any generators wanted urgently elsewhere must be got away before the traffic builds up. Extra lighting is rigged up for the lighting and PA de-rigs. Another area requiring power is the litter recycling machinery. On Monday morning, the clear-up begins. All the wiring and distribution units have to be collected and loaded onto trucks. People who cannot tell the difference between cables and toilets can make this very unpleasant! The lights are taken down and the generators loaded onto a fleet of articulated trucks and returned to the hire companies. This phase of the operation usually takes about seven days. When the site is clear the crew leave site and on to the next job. Some power is left in situ for a week or two more for site crew catering, the fencing crew, etc. Following this, all that remains is to sort out of the paperwork, bills, hire return notes, payments and, of course, collect a cheque from Michael. At this point we look back at the event, take stock and start to plan for next year!

This all adds up to one of the largest jobs of the year for GE Energy Rentals Ltd. For all its size and complexity, the electrical system for the Glastonbury Festival would seem small beer compared to the engineer's responsible for the electrical system of a real city of 100 000. But then, they don't have to build it, use it, and remove it all within five weeks!

For further details about GE Energy Rentals Ltd., please visit: www.geenergyrentals.com.

By Bill Egan, GE Energy Rentals Ltd., Unit 7, io Centre, Cabot Park, Avonmouth, Bristol. BS11 0QL.

Questions

1. Create a Gantt chart that displays the electrical supply to Glastonbury Festival.
2. What aspects of electricity supply are 'sensitive' (i.e. a small change in one area of logistics will have a large effect on the electricity supply to the festival)?
3. Create a risk assessment list for the festival electricity supply that would be used as the basis of a 'skull session'.

Case study 12.2

Belfast Festival at Queen's

Introduction

The Belfast Festival at Queen's reached its 43rd anniversary in 2005. Every year, the largest festival of its kind in Ireland brings the best of international art to Belfast and brings international attention to the city's dynamic arts practitioners. The Festival covers all art forms including theatre, dance, classical music, literature, jazz, comedy, visual arts, folk music and popular music, attracting over 50 000 visitors.

Development

In the beginning, there was an enterprising young undergraduate, Michael Emmerson, who started running a small event based on the campus of Queen's University, Belfast.

The university, its students and the Belfast public saw that it was good and the infant Belfast Festival at Queen's was born. Ten years later and the Festival was ten times bigger and had already attracted such names as Dizzy Gillespie, Ravi Shankar, Sviatoslav Richter, Laurence Olivier and Jimi Hendrix!

In the 1970s, the Festival was a cultural oasis in a landscape dominated by political upheaval and it was to act as a catalyst for the city's future cultural renaissance. By the early '80s under the directorship of Michael Barnes, a former History lecturer, the Festival had expanded into a two week long arts extravaganza across the whole of the city and was hosting everything from Moscow State Ballet and the Royal Shakespeare Company to Dexy's Midnight Runners and the Flying Pickets! Billy Connolly and Rowan Atkinson had visited the Festival before they were famous and were welcomed back, while Michael Palin vowed never to take his one-man show anywhere else on earth such was his love of the event. The dusty archive files lurking in the caverns of the Festival House basement read like a who's who of prominent artists during the latter half of the 20th century.

By the 42nd Belfast Festival in 2004, 300 artists and events from over 20 countries travelled from all four corners of the globe to entertain, enthrall and excite audiences in venues across Belfast – including jazz from the USA, close-up theatre from Canada and Quebec, sensuous dance from Argentina, hip-hop from the Middle East and a bloodthirsty puppet show from Australia.

Accessibility

Drawing on the resources and coordinating events across 45 venues can present a number of challenges, particularly in ensuring that the events are accessible to all members of society, including those with a disability. Belfast Festival has introduced a number of initiatives to address these needs:

- *Venue Access*: An access information guide has been developed to help patrons find out about a venue's car parking facilities and what facilities there are for patrons with a disability. Alternatively, patrons can contact the Festival Box Office for information. Table 12.2 provides examples of the detail to be included, though it should be noted that available facilities may change and therefore either the website or Festival Box Office will provide current details.
- *Visually Impaired*: The Festival brochure is available in large print audiocassette, CD and Braille. Further, an audio description is available of selected theatre events.
- *Hearing Impaired*: Induction loops, a radio microphone system and portable induction loops are available at many of the venues and events. In addition, portable equipment can be booked in advance and Electronic Note Taking (ENT) and British Sign Language (BSL) are available upon request.

Summary

Events around the world are increasingly looking at their target markets and identifying how they can make their events accessible to all members of society. In addition, the implementation of the Disability Discrimination Act has provided fresh impetus for exploring this further and making reasonable adjustment to venues or programmes where required. The access information guide included with this case study provides an example of how event organizers can address many diverse needs and ensure that the audience are fully aware of what services and facilities are available at each venue.

For further information about Belfast Festival at Queen's, please visit www.belfastfestival.com.

By Belfast Festival at Queen's.

Questions

1. Belfast Festival at Queen's uses over 40 venues to stage the event. What are the logistical implications of using different venues?
2. The case study particularly demonstrates venue access for disabled visitors. What other aspects of the event would organizers of festivals such as this have to consider?
3. Identify and discuss what issues an event organizer would have to consider for the following events to ensure that they were accessible to all customers:
   (a) Large conference (250 delegates) within a hotel
   (b) Exhibition (200 exhibition stands, 10 000 visitors) within an exhibition centre
   (c) Festival (20 000) on a Greenfield site

Table 12.2 Example of access information guide

Venue	Wheelchair access/venue entry	Hearing and sight disabilities	Parking	Inside venue	Seating
Grand opera house	Mobile ramp (must know in advance)	Loop system and head-sets available No Tactile Signage	Parking next door or in Europa multi-storey	Adapted toilets No lift Guide dogs welcome	8 wheelchair spaces available p/evening.
Ulster hall	Ramps at side-doors	No loop system No tactile signage	Street parking only Lowered pavements outside building	Adapted toilet Chair-lift for balcony seats Guide dogs welcome	Recommended ground floor seats but balcony room is available for wheelchairs.
City hall	2 ramps at front and 1 at back	Loop system at reception and function rooms. Tactile signage.	Spaces are available within the grounds.	Lifts are available. Adapted toilets Guide dogs welcome. Wheelchairs available on-site	
Waterfront hall & NTL studio	Level access into main building and lift access into NTL Studio. Accessibility phone-line	Loop system, infra-red system in auditoriums and tactile signage	Badge holders phone in advance for parking. Multi-storey also has spaces	Wheelchairs available on-site. Lifts and adapted toilets available. Guide dogs welcome Lowered counters	Removable seating.
Clifton house	Level access into residential home.	No loop system No tactile signage	Spaces are available in the grounds.	Lift and chair-lift (do not need to get out of own chair). Adapted toilets in the Residential home (not in boardroom). Guide dogs welcome	Removable seating.
Elmwood hall	No ramps (steps only)	No loop system No tactile signage	Street parking only with a few possible places in the grounds	No adapted toilets Guide dogs welcome	Unfixed seating.

Lyric theatre	Ramp located at side of building.	Loop system available. No tactile signage.	Street parking	A lift and adapted toilets are available. Guide dogs welcome	Removable seating.
Empire music hall	Steps only	No loop system	Street parking	No lifts. Adapted toilet available. Guide dogs welcome	Loose seating.
Ulster museum	Wheelchair access at main entrance.	Loop system at reception. No tactile signage	Spaces available in the grounds but museum must be made aware a day in advance.	Lifts available. Adapted toilets. Guide dogs welcome	
Old museum arts centre	Steps only. Free entry for friends assisting those with a disability	No loop system or tactile signage.	Street parking	No lifts. No adapted toilets. Guide dogs welcome	
Ormeau baths gallery	Ramp located at side of building	No loop system. No tactile signage	Street parking	Lift and adapted toilet available. Guide dogs welcome	Loose seating.
Linenhall library	Level access	No loop system. No tactile signage	No parking within general area	Lift and adaptable toilets available. Guide dogs welcome	
Direct wine shipments	No wheelchair access. Steps to taster sessions held on 3rd floor.	No loop system. No tactile signage	Street parking	No lift. No adapted toilet	

(continued)

Table 12.2 Continued

Venue	Wheelchair access/venue entry	Hearing and sight disabilities	Parking	Inside venue	Seating
Belfast welcome centre	Level access	Loop system and mini-com system. Cassettes and large print brochures.	No parking within general area	Lift and adapted toilets available Guide dogs welcome Lowered counters	
Lanyon building	Level access	No loop system	Spaces available within the grounds	Lifts and toilets available. Guide dogs welcome Door controls	Loose seating.
Guinness spot	Level access	No loop system	Spaces available within the grounds	Adapted toilets available in the neighbouring Whitla Hall	Loose seating.
Whitla hall	Ramp access	Loop system	Spaces available within the grounds	Adapted toilets No lift Guide dogs welcome	Loose seating.
Students union	Ramp access	Loop system. No tactile signage	Street parking	Adapted toilets Lifts available Door controls Guide dogs welcome	Loose seating.
Harty room	Ramp access	No loop system	Street parking	Adapted	Loose seating.
QFT Drama studio	Ramp Access Info. – Phone for information.	Infra-red headsets	Street parking	Adapted toilets and lifts	Removable seating.
SARC	Ramp access	No loop system	Spaces available within the grounds	Adapted toilets Lift available	
St. Patrick's Church	Temporary ramp access	Loop system	Street parking	Adapted toilets	

Chapter 13

Staging events

Learning Objectives

After studying this chapter, you should be able to:

■ analyse the staging of an event according to its constituent elements
■ demonstrate how these elements relate to each other and to the theme of the event
■ understand the safety elements of each aspect of staging
■ identify the relative importance of the staging elements for different types of events
■ use the tools of staging.

Introduction – what is staging?

The term 'staging' originates from the presentation of plays at the theatre. It refers to bringing together all the elements of a theatrical production for its presentation on a stage. Most events that use this term take place at a single venue and require similar organization to a theatrical production. However, whereas a play can take place over a season, an event may take place in one day or night. Examples of this type of event are product launches, company parties and celebrations, awards ceremonies, conference events, concerts, large weddings, corporate dinners and opening and closing events.

Staging can also refer to the organization of a venue within a much larger event. A large festival may have performance areas positioned around the site. Each of these venues has a range of events with a distinct theme. At Glastonbury Festival of Contemporary Performing Arts (Pilton, Somerset), there are over fifteen performance areas, each with its own style. Because it is part of a much larger event, one performance area or event has to fit in with the overall planning of the complete event and has to fit in with programming and logistics. However, each performance area is to some extent its own kingdom, with its own micro-logistics, management, staff and individual character. On a larger scale, BBC Music Live 2000 involved concerts the length and breadth of the UK, each with its own event manager, stage manager and light and sound crews, together with the involvement of television production crews to broadcast a live performance of Lou Reed's song 'Perfect Day' synchronized from thirty-eight locations. This perfectly illustrated the interaction of event staging and television broadcast skills (Ball, 2000).

The main concerns of staging are as follows:

- theming and event design
- choice of venue
- audience and guests
- stage
- power, lights and sound
- audiovisuals and special effects
- catering
- performers
- crew
- hospitality
- the production schedule
- recording the event
- contingencies.

Silvers (2004a) refers to the six dimensions of an event experience which lead from the first impressions before arrival through to the last perception on departure, the dimensions being marketing materials, transport and entrance, atmosphere and decor, food and beverage, entertainment, and amenities and souvenirs. This chapter analyses the staging of an event according to these elements. It demonstrates how these elements revolve around a central event theme. The type of event will determine how important each of these elements is to the others. However, common to the staging of different events are the tools: the stage plan, the contact and responsibility list and the production schedule. Silvers (2004a, p. 2) uses the term professional event coordination to cover 'the integrated implementation of all the operational and logistic requirements of an event, based on the scope of event elements included in the event design'.

Theming and event design

When staging an event, the major artistic and creative decision to be made is that of determining what the theme is to be. The theme of an event differentiates it from other events. In the corporate area, the client may give the theme of the event. For example, the client holding a corporate party or product launch may want medieval Europe as the theme, or Hollywood, complete with actors and film set. Outside the corporate area, the theme for one of the stages at a festival may be blues music, debating or a children's circus. Whatever the nature of the event, once the theme is established, the elements of the event must be designed to fit in with the theme. This is straightforward when it comes to deciding on the entertainment and catering. With the medieval corporate party, the entertainment may include *jongleurs* and jugglers, and the catering may be spit roasts and wine. However, audiovisuals may need a lot of thought in order to enhance the theme. The sound and lights must complement the entertainment, as they do not fit in with the period theme. Figure 13.1 illustrates the elements of staging and it emphasizes the central role of the theme of the event. However, it should be remembered that, within events, these areas are not so clearly defined. For example, there is generally a close working relationship between audiovisual, special effects, light and sound staff in order to produce the event.

Theme Traders express the importance of staging in the following way:

At Theme Traders our mission is to create unique and unforgettable events. Funnily enough, meticulous planning and staging are crucial when trying to create a spontaneous and vibrant

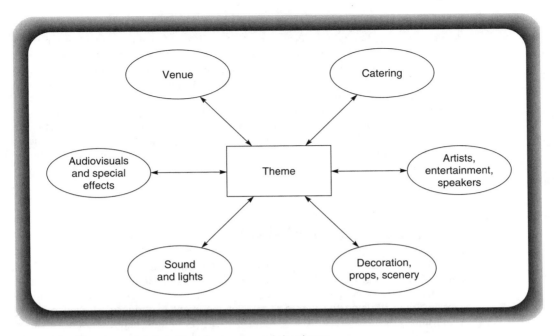

Figure 13.1 The elements of staging revolve around the theme

atmosphere. This can be understood in terms of 'staging' because things like lighting, space, noise and furniture are tools of 'mood' to be manipulated. Bad lighting, unwanted noise or bad use of space and access can make or break a party by affecting the response of guests to their environment. Similarly, responses to event features such as lighting and entertainment can help steer guests around a venue without them being aware of it. Stage managing their environment can often ensure that the guests do not have to be 'ferried' around and will 'naturally' go home at the right time! It is interesting that the most tightly staged environment will often inspire guests to feel a natural part of a very exciting party.

Programming

The program of the event is the flow of the performers, speakers, catering and the other elements of the event over time. It is the schedule of performance. As with all the elements of staging, programming is both an art and a science. The programme of the event depends on:

- the expectations of the audience
- the constraints of the venue and infrastructure
- the culture of the client and main sponsors
- the availability of elements of the staging, and their relationship to each other
- the logistics.

It is similar to the order in a street parade – the timeline or schedule of the programme is set out in a linear fashion. Far from this being a simple example, a parade is multifaceted, and there is little the event manager can do to change it, once it starts moving. Consider the music: the brass band cannot be performing near the highland pipe band; they perform at slightly different beats. An event programme also has a rhythm all of its own. The mix of entertainment, catering and speeches has to be well thought out so the event builds and the audience has times of intensity and times of rest. A New Year's Eve programme, for example, gradually lifts the audience to the moment before midnight.

A large festival's programme is a complex of activities. Many festivals use a form of a Gantt chart to map the various attractions and to help the audience navigate the event programme. If the event is broadcast, the event programme may have to be in sync with the television programming. This is a major consideration particularly for sport events.

Choice of venue

The choice of a venue is a crucial decision that will ultimately determine many of the elements of staging. Figure 13.2 lists the major factors in the choice of a venue. The venue may be an obvious part of the theme of the event. A corporate party that takes place in a zoo is using the venue as part of the event experience. However, many events take place within 'four walls and a roof', the venue being chosen for other factors. It can be regarded an empty canvas on which the event is painted. Events can be staged in a range of unusual spaces, from unused factories, parkland, car parks or shopping centres, to floating stages on water or using flat-back trailers from articulated lorries in a supermarket car park. The event manager can exploit the surroundings and characteristics of the venue to enhance the event experience. In these situations, the traditional roles of stage manager and event manager become blurred. When the audience and the performers mix together and where they and the venue become the entertainment package, the delineation between stage and auditorium is no longer appropriate.

An event that uses a purpose-built venue, for example, an arena or exhibition centre, will find that much of the infrastructure will be in place. Two documents

- Location
- Matching the venue with the theme of the event
- Matching the size of the venue to the size of the event
- Venue configuration, including sight lines and seating configuration
- History of events at that venue, including the venue's reputation
- Availability
- What the venue can provide
- Transport to, from and around the venue; parking
- Access for audience, equipment, performers, VIPs, staff and the disabled
- Toilets and other facilities
- Catering equipment and preferred caterers
- Power (amount available and outlets) and lights
- Communication, including telephone
- Climate, including microclimate and ventilation
- Emergency plans and exits

Figure 13.2 The factors in venue selection

that are a good starting point for making an informed choice about the venue are the venue plan and the list of facilities. However, because there are so many factors in an event that are dependent on the venue or site, an inspection is absolutely necessary. For music events, HSE (1999) suggest that main considerations for the site visit are available space for the audience, temporary structures, backstage facilities, parking, camping and rendezvous points, together with some idea of proposed capacity, concept for the entertainment and rough calculations of space requirements. For conference events, Shone (1998) identifies that location will be the key consideration, with the venue needing to be close to a main motorway and within an hour's travelling time of a major city and airport (if international delegates are expected). Further, Owen and Holliday (1993) recommend that the event manager makes a preliminary unannounced visit to the venue to check the ambience and courtesy of staff before making arrangements. Lyon (2004, p. 2) notes that a site inspection or familiarization (Fam) trip provides you with the opportunity to sample the destination or potential venue, with the aim of you being able to sell this back to your organization and recapture the experience for your delegates. He provides a useful handbook to assist this process.

Rogers (1998) suggests that there are a number of points to consider when shortlisting conference venues. These include:

- the type of venue (hotel, conference centre, university, football stadia or stately homes)
- the conference rooms and facilities available (including combination of room sizes and style of seating for the requirements of the event)
- accommodation and leisure options (depending on residential requirements and opportunities for social activities)
- an identifiable point of contact.

As with many aspects of supplier selection, the Internet has had a significant effect on venue choice. Using a search engine is often the first action in the investigation of a suitable venue. Some websites display a choice of venues once certain information (such as size of audience, approximate location and type of event) has been entered. The major hotels, conventions and exhibition centres, universities and purpose-built venues have websites to enable the matching of event requirements to venue characteristics. However, this method has the same limitations as those of using photos and brochures to assess a venue. The websites are a tool for selling the venue, not a technical description. In addition, many suitable venues may not have an Internet presence. An Internet search will show only venues that expect to host events. If the event is truly special, the event venue may be part of that theme. A car park or a rainforest, for example, will not appear in a search for event venues.

The final consideration when choosing an event is whether it requires a physical location at all. With the ongoing development of videoconferencing, and the extensive developments in the Internet, events can take place in 'cyberspace'. With some events, e.g. music concerts, the event takes place live in venue in the traditional manner, however, with the introduction of webcasting, a worldwide audience can view or experience the event simultaneously. In this instance, access to technological support and facilities, for example, a large bandwidth telephone line, will be a consideration. In other areas, for example, exhibitions and conferences, technology has been deployed in such a way that it may support the live event experience, through the website hosting supporting materials for visitors to view and in some cases interact with. Relatively recent advances in Internet technology, together with faster telecommunication infrastructure, have enabled conferences to take place solely on line, with delegates interacting, either visually through videoconferencing or through text with instant messaging. Exhibitions can take place in virtual exhibition venues, which can either be modelled on the live exhibition venue as a means of supporting the event experience or can take place solely in the virtual world without the boundaries of traditional venues and limited only by imagination and the available technology. The value of such developments is only just beginning to be realized, with some commentators predicting the death of live events, whilst other, more enlightened observers view these developments as a further medium to support or enhance the live event experience.

Audience/guests

The larger issues of audience (customer) logistics have been discussed in Chapter 12. The event staging considerations concerning the audience are:

- position of entrances and exits
- arrival times – dump or trickle
- seating and sight lines
- facilities.

Goldblatt (2005) emphasizes the importance of the entrance and reception area of an event in establishing the event theme, and suggests that the organizer should look at it from the guest's point of view. It is in this area that appropriate signage and meeting and greeting become important to the flow of 'traffic' and to the well-being of the guests. An example of a carefully planned entrance was the launch of Virgin Atlantic's service to Shanghai, where Terminal 3 of Heathrow Airport was transformed into a mini-Shanghai, with passengers leaving the departure lounge through a giant dragon's mouth (De Smet, 1999).

Once the guests have entered the event area, problems can occur that are specific to the type of event. In the case of conferences, audiences immediately head for the back rows. Interestingly, HSE (1999) mention the opposite problem at non-ticketed music events, where the area in front of the stage is rushed as soon as the gates are open. Graham, Neirotti and Goldblatt (2001) note a similar occurrence at sport events. The solution, therefore, is in the type of admission. For example, organizers can adopt reserved seating methods, by using ticket numbers or roping-off sections, and using a designated seating plan. The style of seating can be chosen to suit the event; theatre-, classroom- and banquet-type seating are three examples. Ultimately, the seating plan has to take into consideration:

- type of seating – fixed or movable
- the size of the audience
- the method of audience arrival
- safety factors including emergency exits and fire regulations
- the placement and size of the aisles
- sight lines to the performances, speakers or audiovisual displays
- disabled access
- catering needs.

The facilities provided for the guests will depend on the type of event. Referring to Figure 13.3, the corporate event will focus on audience facilities as they relate to hospitality and catering, whereas a festival event will concentrate on audience

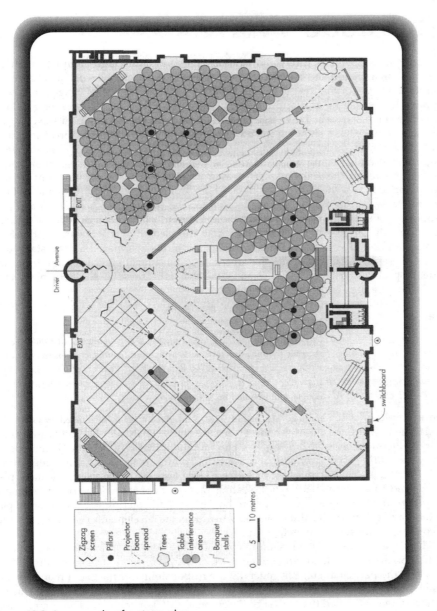

Figure 13.3 An example of a stage plan
Source: Roger Foley, Fogg Productions (www.fogg.com.au)

facilities as they relate to entertainment. For example, there are no chairs for the audience at the BBC Proms in the Park (Hyde Park, London), but because of the theme of the event, spectators are happy to bring their own or to sit on the ground on picnic blankets. At the other end of the spectrum, The DatebooK Ball at the Dorchester Hotel (London) has high-quality furnishings and facilities.

The stage

A stage at an event is rarely the same as the theatrical stage complete with the proscenium arch and auditorium. It can range from the back of a truck to a barge in a harbour. It is important to note that, in event management, the term 'stage' can also be applied to the staging area and not just to a purpose-built stage. However, all stages require a stage map called the stage plan. The stage plan is simply a bird's-eye view of the performance area, showing the infrastructure such as lighting fixtures, entrances, exits and power outlets. The stage plan is one of the staging tools (as shown in Figure 13.3) and a communication device that enables the event to run smoothly. For large events, the stage plan is drawn in different ways for different people, and supplied on a 'need-to-know basis'. For example, a stage plan for the lighting technician would look different to the plan for the performers. A master stage plan would contain a number of layers of these different plans, each drawn on separate layer of transparent paper. Other plans that are used in event design are the front elevation and side elevation. In contrast to the bird's-eye view that the stage plan gives, these plans show the staging area as a ground-level view from the front and side, respectively. They assist in establishing the sight lines, i.e. the audience's view of the staging area and the performers.

Catherine Sterry, Art director at Theme Traders, described the value of clear stage plans:

> *To create successful and memorable events it is absolutely essential to be both imaginative and have a precise understanding of planning techniques. Site visits to venues are essential as you need to create accurate technical plans which are both clear and easily understood by members of the installation and production team. This is imperative as members of the team may not have had the opportunity of a site visit and need clear visual and technical instructions.*

An example of when a large stage plan for a special event was used was for the Vodafone Ball at Earls Court, London (see case study in Chapter 5). The 11 500 guests were treated to a choice from zones of entertainment that reflected the theme, 'Beach Party', including a comedy club, a blues club, an arcade and a full scale fairground.

Where the staging of an event includes a large catering component, the stage plan is referred to as the venue layout, seating plan or floor plan. This occurs in many corporate and conference events where hospitality and catering become a major part of the staging. Figure 13.4 illustrates how the focus on the elements of staging changes according to the style of event.

The stage manager is the person in control of the performance and responsible for signalling the cues that coordinate the work of the performers. The scheduling of the event on the particular stage is generally the responsibility of the event manager. The stage manager makes sure that this happens according to the plan. The public face of the event may be called the Master of Ceremonies (MC) or compère. The compère and the stage manager work closely together to ensure that all goes according to the plan. The compère may also make the public announcements, such as those about lost children and programme changes.

The combination of electric wiring, hot lights, special effects, the fast movement of performers and staff in a small space that is perhaps 2 metres above ground level makes the risk management of the stage area particularly important. At the event, stage safety is generally the responsibility of the stage manager. Figure 13.5 lists a selection of safety considerations.

The backstage area is a private room or tent/marquee near the performance area set aside for the performers and staff. It provides the crew with a place to relax and the performers with a place to prepare for the performance and to wind down afterwards.

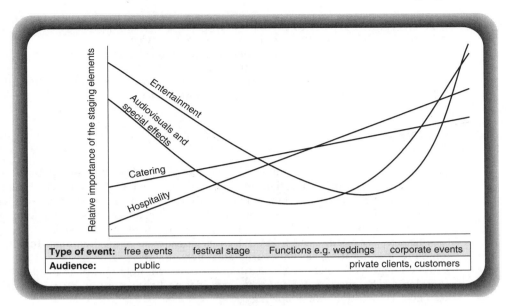

Figure 13.4 Relationship between type of event and the relative importance of the elements of staging

- There must be a well-constructed stage, preferably constructed professionally by a company with adequate insurance.
- There must be clear well-lit access points to the stage.
- All protrusions and steps should be secured and clearly marked.
- Equipment and boxes should be placed out of the way and well marked.
- There should be work lights that provide white lighting before and after the event.
- All electric cabling must be secured.
- A first-aid kit and other emergency equipment should be at hand.
- There must be a clear guideline as to who is in authority during an emergency.
- A list of all relevant contact numbers should be made.

Figure 13.5 Factors to consider in stage safety

It can be used for storage of equipment and for communication between the stage manager and performers, and it is where the food and drink are kept. Access is strictly controlled to ensure the safety of performers and security of equipment and other resources.

Power

Staging of any event involves large numbers of people, and to service this crowd electricity is indispensable. It should never be taken for granted. Factors that need to be considered concerning power are:

- type of power – three phase or single phase
- amount of power needed, particularly at peak times
- emergency power

- position and number of power outlets
- types of leads and distance from power source to device
- the correct wiring of the venue as old venues could be improperly earthed
- the incoming equipment's volt/amp rating
- safety factors, including the covering leads and the possibility of electricity earth
- leakage as a result of rain regulations regarding power.

Lights

Lighting at a venue has two functions. Pragmatically, lights allow everyone to see what is happening; artistically, they are central to the design of the event. The general venue or site lighting is important in that it allows all the other aspects of the staging to take place. For this reason, it is usually the first item on the checklist when deciding on a venue. Indoor lights include signage lights (exit, toilets, etc.) as well as lighting specific areas for catering and ticket collection. Outside the venue, lighting is required for venue identification, safety, security and sponsor signs.

Once the general venue or site lighting is confirmed, lighting design needs to be considered. The questions to ask when considering lighting are both practical and aesthetic. They include the following:

- Does it fit in with and enhance the overall event theme?
- Can it be used for ambient lighting as well as performance lighting?
- Is there a backup?
- What are the power requirements (lights can draw far more power that the sound system)?
- Will it interfere with the electrics of other systems? For example, a dimmer board can create an audible buzz in the sound system.
- Does it come with a light operator, i.e. the person responsible for the planning of the lighting with lighting board?
- What light effects are needed (strobe, cross-fading) and can the available lights do this?
- What equipment is needed (e.g. trees and cans), and is there a place on the site or in the venue to erect it?
- Does the building have permanent trusses available for rigging lighting?
- How can the lighting assist in the safety and security of the event?

The lighting plot or lighting plan is a map of the venue and shows the type and position of the lighting. As Reid (2001) points out, the decisions that the event manager has to make when creating a lighting plan are:

- placement of the lights
- the type of lights
- where the light should be pointed
- what colours to use.

Sound

The principal reason for sound equipment at an event is so that all the audience can clearly hear the music, speeches and audio effects. The sound system is also used to:

- communicate between the sound engineer and the stage manager (talkback or intercom)

- monitor the sound
- create a sound recording the event
- broadcast the sound to other venues or through other media, including television, radio and the Internet.

This means that the type of equipment used needs to be designed for the:

- type of sound to be amplified including, spoken work and music
- size and makeup of the audience, e.g. an older audience may like the music at a different volume to a younger audience
- acoustic properties of the room, e.g. some venues have a bad echo problem, so attaching drapes or material to the walls may alleviate this.
- theme of the event, e.g. a bright silver sound system may look out of place at a black tie dinner.

The choice of size, type and location of the speakers for the sound at an event can make a difference to the guest's experience of the sound. Figure 13.6 shows two simplified plans for speaker positions at a venue. The speakers may be next to the stage, which is common at music concerts, or distributed around the site. They may also be flown from supports above the audience. At a large site, with speakers widely distributed, the sound engineers need to take into account the natural delay of sound travelling from the various speakers to the members of the audience. A ducting system could also be installed above audience height to avoid tripping hazards caused by trailing cables.

For small events, a simple public address (PA) system may be used. This consists of a microphone and microphone stand and one or two speakers. It is basically the same

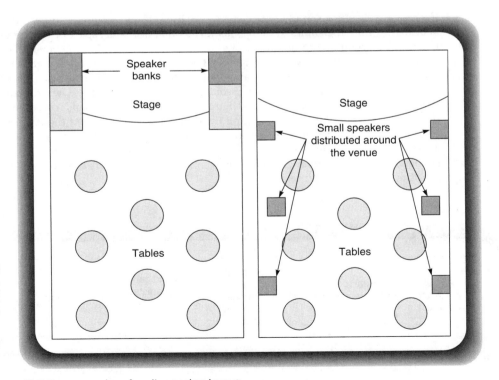

Figure 13.6 Two examples of audio speaker layout

as a home stereo system with a microphone added, and generally only has enough power to reach a small audience. The quality of sound produced makes them only suitable for speeches.

For larger events that have more complex sound requirements, a larger sound system is needed. This would incorporate:

- microphones, which may include lapel mikes and radio mikes
- microphone stands
- cabling, including from the microphones to the mixing desk
- mixing desk, which adjusts the quality and level of the sound coming from the microphones before it goes out of the speakers
- amplifier
- speakers, which can vary in the frequency of sound given out, from bass speakers to treble speakers that enhance the quality of the sound within a certain sound spectrum
- sound engineer
- sound technician, or front of house engineer, who looks after all aspects of the sound, in particular the sound quality that is heard by the audience
- backup equipment including spare leads and microphones.

The next step up from this type of system includes all of the above plus:

- monitor speakers (also called wedge monitors) that channel the sound back to the speaker or performer so they can hear themselves over the background sound
- monitor control/mixing desk
- monitor engineer, who is responsible for the quality of sound going through the monitors.

If an event needs a sound system managed by a sound engineer, time must be allocated to tune the sound system. This means that acoustic aspect of the venue is taken into account by trying out various sound frequencies within the venue. This is the reason for the often heard 'testing, one, two, one, two' as a sound system is being prepared. The sound engineer is also looking for any sound feedback problems. Feedback is an unwanted, often high-pitched sound that occurs when the sound coming out of the speakers is picked up by the microphones and comes out of the speakers again, thereby building on the original sound. To avoid the problem of feedback, microphones are positioned so that they face away from sound speakers. The tuning of a large sound system is one of the main reasons for having a sound check or a run-through before an event. Figure 13.7 shows a simplified sound run-through prior to an event.

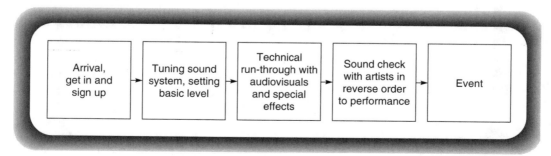

Figure 13.7 A simple flow chart for a sound system

Volume and subsequent leakage during an event can become a major problem. Local councils can close an event if there are too many complaints from residents. At some venues, for example, there are volume switches that automatically turn off the power if the sound level is too high. At multi-venue events, sound leakage between stages can be minimized by:

- thoughtful placement of the stages
- careful positioning of all the speakers (including the monitors)
- constant monitoring of the volume level
- careful programming of the events on each stage in a way that avoids interference.

Audiovisual and special effects

Many event managers hire lighting and sound from separate companies and integrate their services into the overall design of the event. However, there are suppliers that provide both lighting and sound equipment and act as consultants prior to the event. These audiovisual companies can supply a fully integrated system of film, video, slides and often special effects. However, most audiovisual companies are specialists in flat-screen presentations and the special effects area is often best left to specialists in this field. For example, pyrotechnicians require different skills and licences from ice sculptors. Complex events that use a variety of special effects and audiovisuals require a coordinator who is familiar with the event theme and knows how to link all the specialist areas to each other. This coordinator is called the event producer. Although the terms 'event manager', 'stage manager' and 'event producer' are confusing, they are terms that are used in the industry. The position of event producer is created when there are many different specialists involved in the event. Organizers of corporate events, including product launches and conferences, often subcontract the audiovisual elements, because the specialist knowledge required means an expert is needed to operate these systems effectively. The decision to use an audiovisual company for an event depends on:

- how the audiovisual presentation fits in with the overall event design
- the budget allocated to the event
- the skills of the audiovisual company, including its technical hardware and software
- the abilities of the audiovisual producer and writer.

For large-budget events, the audiovisual company will act as a consultant, with the producer and writer researching and creating a detailed audiovisual script.

According to Goldblatt (2005), special effects at an event are used to attract attention, generate excitement and sustain interest. In larger events, for example the Millennium Eve celebrations along the River Thames in London, the pyrotechnics become part of the overall logistics planning. Event managers and planners must fully realize the importance of event decoration, scenery and appropriate props as an enhancing tool for the staging of any event.

Because much of the audiovisual and special effects technology is highly complex, it is often 'pre-programmed'. This means that all lighting, audiovisual and sound 'presets' (technical elements positioned prior to the event), including the changing of light and sound levels and the cueing of video or slide presentations, can be programmed into the controlling computer. The computer control of much of the audiovisuals means that the whole presentation can be fully integrated and set up well in advance. Because these aspects are prearranged, including all the cue times, the advantage is that few technicians are needed to control these operations during the event. The disadvantages are that spontaneity can be taken from the event and, the more complex the technology, the more things can go wrong. Moreover, the technology becomes the master of the cue times and it is nearly impossible to take advantage of any unforeseen opportunities.

Props and decoration

Some events are similar to operatic productions in their use of scenery, stage properties (props) and decoration. Skilled use of these elements can make the attendees feel as though they are in an imaginary world. The audience can often enhance this by dressing the part and becoming part of the entertainment. Themed parties, festivals and dinners are a significant part of the event industry. The way in which these staging elements are combined and their relative emphasis at the event often reflects the personal style of the event company. Malouf (1999) devotes over two-thirds of her book to theming in events, particularly the use of flowers, lights and colour to create a sense of wonder, while Monroe (2006) provides a detail overview of designing and decorating events.

Catering

Catering can be the major element in staging, depending on the theme and nature of an event. Most purpose-built venues already have catering. For example, the Wembley Exhibition and Conference Centre has a contract catering company. The dinners that take place in the conference centre can only use the in-house caterers. Figure 13.8 illustrates some of the many factors to be considered in catering.

There are general principles that can be followed when planning the catering for events. For example, at a corporate function or formal dinner, a ratio of 1:10 (one member of staff to serve ten customers) is appropriate, whereas at a Christmas party, a ratio of 2:30 (two members of staff to serve three tables of ten customers) may suffice. Staffing numbers will be varied depending on the style of service being adopted, for example, whether silver served or plated, the complexity of the menu, the requirements of the client and the speed of service required. Another example would be, a formal dinner, where the top table dictates the serving of all other guests, may require more staff than if a rolling service can be operated, with tables cleared and the next course served as each table finishes. In this way, teams of staff can work together in order to ensure that all elements of the meal arrive in front of the guest at the same time. Theatre can play a large part in formal meals. For example, using an MC to call guests into the dining area, the top table entering to the synchronized clapping of all other guests, and through the tight coordination of waiting staff. For example, having all waiting staff entering the room in a formal line before 'breaking off' to take up their positions; upon the signal of the banqueting manager, usually involving the raising of an arm, the top table is served, followed immediately by the all the other tables. In this way, the status of VIP guests on the top table is maintained.

As Graham, Neirotti and Goldblatt (2001) stress, the consumption of alcoholic beverages at an event gives rise to many concerns for the event manager. These include the special training of staff, which party holds the licence (venue, event manager or client); and the legal age for consumption. The possible problems that arise from the sale of alcoholic beverages, for example, increased audience noise at the

In-house or contracted out?

The advantage of in-house catering is the knowledge of the venue. The advantage of contract catering is that the event manager may have a special arrangement with the caterer that has been built up overtime; the event manager can choose all aspects of the catering; and the catering can be tendered out and a competitive bid sought.

Quality control factors to consider

- Appropriateness and enhancement of the event theme.
- Menu selection and design, including special diets and food displays.
- Quality of staff and supervision.
- Equipment, including style and quantity, and selection of in-house or hired.
- Cleanliness.
- Culturally appropriateness - a major consideration in a culturally diverse society.
- Staff to guest ratio.

Costs

- Are there any guarantees, including those against loss and breakage?
- What are the payment terms?
- Who is responsible for licences and permits: the caterer, the venue or event management?
- What deposits and up front fees are there?
- What is the per capita expenditure? Is each guest getting value commensurate with client's expenditure?

Waste management

- Must occur before, during and after the event.
- Must conforming to food hygiene and food safety regulations and environmental concerns.
- Must be appropriate to the event theme.

Figure 13.8 Issues to be considered when arranging catering for an event

end of the event and general behavioural problems, can affect almost all aspects of the event. The decision whether to allow the sale or consumption of alcoholic beverages can be crucial to the success of an event and needs careful thought.

There are a variety of ways that the serving of alcohol can be negotiated with a caterer. The drinks service can be from the bar or may be served at the table by the glass, bottle or jug. A caterer may offer a 'drinks package', which means that the drinks are free for, say, the first hour of the catered event. A subtle result of this type of deal is that the guest can find it hard to find a drinks waiter in the first hour. Hansen and Thomas (2005) provide a detailed discussion of the catering aspects of events.

Performers

The 'talent' (as performers are often called) at an event can range from music groups to motivational speakers to specially commissioned shows. A performing group can form a major part of an event's design. The major factors to consider when employing artists are:

- *Contact*: the event's entertainment coordinator needs to establish contact with the person responsible for the employment of the group. This could be the artist, an agent representing the artist, or the manager of a group. It is important to establish this line of authority at the beginning when working with the artists.

- *Staging requirements*: a rock band, for example, will have a more detailed sound requirement than a folk singer. These requirements are usually listed on document called the spec (specification) sheet. Many groups will also have their own stage plan illustrating the area needed and their preferred configuration of the performance area.
- *Availability for rehearsal, media attention and performance*: the available times given by the artists' management should include the time it takes for the artists to set up on stage as well as the time it takes to vacate the stage or performance area. These times need to be considered carefully when, for example, scheduling a series of rehearsals with a number of performing groups. These are referred to as the time needed for 'set up' (load in) and 'breakdown' (load out).
- *Accompanying personnel*: many artists travel with an entourage that can include technicians, cooks, stylists and bodyguards. It is important to establish their numbers, and what their roles and needs are.
- *Contracts and legal requirements*: the agreement between the event manager and the performers is described in Chapter 11. Of particular importance to the staging are minimum rates and conditions, the legal structure of the group and issues such as workers' compensation and public liability. Copyright is also important as its ownership can affect the use of the performance for broadcast and future promotions.
- *Payment*: most performing groups work on the understanding that they will be paid immediately for their services. Except for 'headline' acts that have a company structure, the thirty-, sixty- or ninety-day invoicing cycle is not appropriate for most performers, who rarely have the financial resources necessary to wait for payment.

Performers come from a variety of performance cultural backgrounds. This means that different performers have different expectations about the facilities available for them and how they are to be treated. Theatre performers and concert musicians, for example, expect direct performance guidelines – conducting, scripting or a musical score. Street and outdoor festival performers, on the other hand, are used to less formal conditions and to improvising.

Supervision of performers in a small theatre is generally left to the assistant stage manager, whereas a festival stage may not have this luxury and it may be the stage manager's responsibility. Regardless of who undertakes it, supervision cannot be overlooked. The person responsible needs to contact the artists on arrival, give them the appropriate run sheets, introduce them to the relevant crew members and show them the green room (the room in which performers and invited guests are entertained). At the end of the performance, the artists' supervisor needs to assist them in leaving the area. Sonder (2004) provides a detailed insight into dealing with entertainment aspects of events.

The crew

The chapter on leadership and human resources (Chapter 6) discussed the role of staff and volunteers at an event. While a large festival or sport event will usually rely on the work of volunteers, staging tends to be handled by professionals. Dealing with cueing, working with complex and potentially dangerous equipment and handling professional performers leaves little room for indecision and inexperience. Professionalism is essential when staging an event. For example, the staging of a concert performance will need skilled sound engineers, roadies, security staff, stage crew, ticket sellers and even ushers (the roadies are the skilled labourers that assist with the set up and breakdown of the sound and lights). The crew is selected by matching the tasks involved with their skills and ability to work together.

The briefing is the meeting, before the event, at which the crew members are given their briefs, or roles, that match their skills. The name and jobs of the crew members are then kept on a contact and responsibility sheet. The briefing tends to be more informal than the later production meeting. The event producer should not forget that the crew comes with an enormous amount of experience in the staging of events. They can provide valuable input into the creation and design of the event.

It is also interesting to note that the changes in the events industry, particularly in the audiovisual area, are reflected in the makeup and number of crew members. As Lisa Proto, Operations Director at Theme Traders, points out:

> *In recent years development of new technology has eased the way for highly intelligent sound and lighting. This has resulted in a better use of resources and manpower as you will need less crew to run a highly technical console. Effects can be designed and programmed prior to the event, yet be flexible enough to adapt at the push of a button. Well programmed intelligent lighting and effects add to the drama and consistently create impact if planned effectively.*

Hospitality

A major part of the package offered to sponsors is hospitality (Catherwood and Kirk, 1992). What will the sponsor expect event management to provide for them and their guests? This can include tickets, food and beverage, souvenirs and gifts. As well as the sponsors, the event may benefit in the long term by offering hospitality to other stakeholders and VIPs. They can include politicians, media units, media personalities, clients of the sponsor, potential sponsors, partners and local opinion formers. They are all referred to as the guests of the event.

The invitation may be the first impression that the potential guest receives, and it therefore needs to convey the theme of the event. It should create a desire to attend as well as imparting information. Figure 13.9 is a checklist for making sure that the various elements of hospitality are covered.

In their informative work on sports events, Graham, Neirotti and Goldblatt (2001, pp. 85–92) describe ten strategies to achieve success in the provision of hospitality to guests:

1. Know the guests' needs and expectations.
2. Plan what the sporting event is expected to achieve for the guest, e.g. networking, incentive, promotional activity.
3. Understand arrival patterns of guests in order to plan, for example, staffing requirements.
4. Plan according to what has preceded or will follow the guests arrival, for example, meal requirements.
5. Create appealing invitations to capture the prospective guests attention.
6. Understand the protocol for the specific sport event, as most have specific guidelines.
7. Focus on first and last impressions to gain maximum impact.
8. Exceed the guest's expectations, particularly through providing extra amenities, for example, parking, welcome signs, and information desk in hotel lobby.
9. Be responsive to changes in the guests' needs during the event.
10. Evaluate the event so that it can be improved next time.

> **Invitations**
> - Is the design of high quality and is it innovative?
> - Does the method of delivery allow time to reply? Would hand delivery and e-mail be appropriate?
> - Does the content of the invitation include time, date, name of event, how to reply (RSVP), directions and parking?
> - Should promotional material be included with the invitation?
>
> **Arrival**
> - Has timing been planned so those guests arrive at the best moment?
> - What are the parking arrangements?
> - Who will do the meeting and greeting? Will there be someone there to welcome them to the event?
> - Have waiting times been reduced? For example, will guests receive a welcome cocktail while waiting to be booked into the accommodation?
>
> **Facilities**
> - Is there a separate area for guests? This can be a marquee, corporate box (at a sporting event) or a club room.
> - What food and beverage will be provided? Is there a need for a special menu and personal service?
> - Is there a separate, high-quality viewing area of the performance with good views and facilities?
> - Has special communication, such as signage or an information desk, been provided?
>
> **Gifts**
> - Have tickets to the event, especially for clients, been organized?
> - What souvenirs (programmes, pins, T-shirts, CDs) will there be?
> - Will there be a chance for guests to meet the 'stars'?
>
> **Departure**
> - Has guest departure been timed so that they do not leave at the same time as the rest of the audience?

Figure 13.9 A hospitality checklist

Corporate sponsors may have a variety of reasons to attend the event and these have to be taken into account in hospitality planning. Research conducted for Sodexho Prestige (2004) suggests that the main drivers for corporate hospitality, from a host perspective, are to keep client happy/generate good will, build relationships, an opportunity to meet with potential customers, raise profile of company, allow clients to relax/enjoy themselves, to say thank you, aid client loyalty/retention, boost staff morale, clients expect it, and it is an informal occasion to discuss business.

The hospitality experience is of particular importance at the corporate events. In one sense, such an event is centred around hospitality (see Figure 13.4). As it is a private function, there is no public and the members of audience are the guests. Most of the items on the hospitality checklist, from the invitations to the personal service, are applicable to staging these events. For the guests, the hospitality experience is fundamental to the event experience.

The production schedule

The terms used in the staging of events come from both the theatre and film production. A rehearsal of the event is a run through of the event, reproducing as closely as possible the actual event. For the sake of 'getting it right on the night', there may also need to be a technical rehearsal and a dress rehearsal. A production meeting, on the other hand, is a get-together of those responsible for producing the event. It involves the stage manager and the event producer, representatives of the lighting and sound crew or audiovisual specialists, representatives of the performers and the MC. It is held at the performance site or on stage as near to the time of the event as possible. At this crucial meeting:

- final production schedule notes are compared
- possible last minute production problems are brought up
- the flow of the event is summarized
- emergency procedures are reviewed
- the compère is introduced and familiarized with the production staff
- the communication system for the event is tested (Neighbourhood Arts Unit, 1991, p. 50).

The production schedule is the main document for staging. It is the master document from which various other schedules, including the cue or prompt sheet and the run sheets, are created. Goldblatt (2005, p. 204) defines it as the detailed listing of tasks with specific start and stop times occurring from set up of the event's equipment (also known as bump in or load in) through to the eventual removal of all the equipment (breakdown, bump out or load out). It is often a written form of the Gantt chart (see Chapter 9) with four columns: time, activity, location and responsibility. Production schedules can also contain a description of the relevant elements of the event.

Two particularly limited times on the schedule are the 'load-in' and 'load-out' times. The load-in refers to the time when the necessary infrastructure can be brought in, unloaded and set up. The load-out time refers to the time when the equipment can be dismantled and removed. Although the venue or site may be available to receive the equipment at any time, there are many other factors that set the load-in time. The hiring cost and availability of equipment are two important limiting factors. In most cases, the larger items must arrive first. These may include fencing, tents, stage, food vans and extra toilets. Next could come the audiovisual equipment and, finally, the various decorations. Supervision of the arrival and set up of the equipment can be crucial to minimizing problems during the event. The contractor who delivers and assembles the equipment often is not the operator of the equipment. This can mean that once it is set up, it is impossible to change it without recalling the contractor.

Load-out can be the most difficult time of an event, because the excitement is over, the staff are often tired and everyone is in a hurry to leave. Nevertheless, these are just the times when security and safety are important. The correct order of load-out needs to be on a detailed schedule. This is often the reverse of the load-in schedule. The last item on the checklist for the load-out is the 'idiot check'. This refers to the check that is done after everything is cleared from the performance area, and some of the staff do a search for anything that may be left.

The run sheets are lists of the order for specific jobs at an event. The entertainers, for example, would have one run sheet while the caterers would have another. Often the production schedule is a loose-leaf folder that includes all the run sheets. The cue sheets are a list of times that initiate a change of any kind during the event and describe what happens on that change. The stage manager and audiovisual controller use them.

Recording the event

By their very nature, events are ephemeral. A good quality recording of the event is essential for most event companies, as it demonstrates the ability of the organization and it can be used to promote the event company. It can also help in evaluating the event and, if necessary, in settling later disputes, whether of a legal or other nature. The method of recording the event can be on video, sound recording or as photographs. Making a sound recording can be just a matter of putting a cassette in the sound system and pressing the record button. With digital cameras now available at low prices, extensive photographs can be taken at minimal cost, which can then be used on the company website to provide cases of successful events. However, any visual recording of the event will require planning. In particular, the correct lighting is needed for depth of field. Factors that need to be considered for video recording are:

- What is it for – promotion, legal purposes or for sale to the participants?
- What are the costs in time and money?
- How will it effect the event? Will the video cameras be a nuisance? Will they need white lighting?
- What are the best vantage points?

Recording the event is not a decision that should be left to the last minute; it needs to be factored into the planning of the event as, for example, permission may be required from performers or members of the audience. Once an event is played out there is no going back.

Contingencies

As with large festivals and hallmark events, the staging of any event has to make allowances for what might go wrong. 'What if' sessions need to be implemented with the staff. A stage at a festival may face an electricity blackout; performers may not arrive; trouble may arrive instead. Therefore, micro-contingency plans need to be in place. All these must fit in with the overall event risk management and emergency plans. At corporate events in well-known venues, the venue will have its own emergency plan that needs to be given to everyone involved.

Chapter summary

The staging of an event can range from presenting a show of multicultural dancers and musicians at a stage in a local park, to the launch of the latest software product at the most expensive hotel in town. All events share common staging elements including sound, lights, food and beverage, performers and special effects. All these elements need to create and enhance the event theme. The importance of each element depends on the type of event. To stage an event successfully a number of tools are used: the production schedule, the stage plan and the contact and responsibility list, all of which are shown in Figure 13.10.

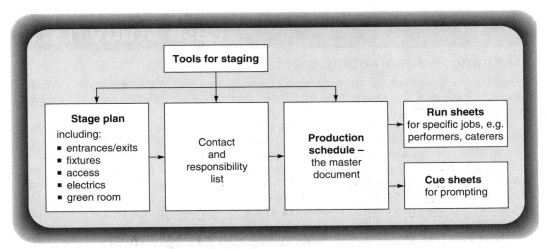

Figure 13.10 A summary of the tools necessary for staging an event

Questions

1. Break an event into its staging elements and discuss the relationship between each element.
2. Choose a theme for a company's staff party. How would you relate all the elements of staging to the theme?
3. Compile a stage plan, contact responsibility list and production schedule with the relevant run sheets for:
   (a) a corporate party for the clients, staff and customers of a company
   (b) a fun run with entertainment
   (c) a large wedding
   (d) one of the stages for a city arts festival.
4. Discuss the constraints on programming the following events:
   (a) a large musical concert in a disused open-cut mine
   (b) an association award dinner
   (c) a multi-stage arts festival
   (d) a surfing event
   (e) a mining exhibition conference
   (f) an air show
   (g) a tax seminar for accountants.
5. What is the case for contracting one supplier for all the staging elements? What are the disadvantages?

Case study 13.1

Theming – a marketing tool

Theming, styling, designing, creating, setting the scene and building an atmosphere are all areas covered on a day-to-day basis by Theme Traders – a specialist event management company based in Cricklewood, London.

Theming is similar to marketing. When a company plans the launch of a new product or service, all the Ps have to be considered – presentation, product, positioning and price. These are all the areas that have to be taken into account when planning and theming an event.

Through the 1980s and early 1990s, themes such as 'Wild West Ho Downs', 'Hawaiian Beach Parties', 'Arabian Nights', 'Science Fiction' and 'Bond Parties' were all the rage and these perennial 'themes' will never die. However, what event managers should always ask their clients is what they want to achieve – in a budget-driven world objectives are the name of the game. Heaven forbid that someone should have a party just for fun!

When a city bank asks for a party for 1300 people to be designed, the questions are endless – other than the standard issues (for example, age of guests, sex, venue and type of food), the most important enquiry for the event manager concerns what the client wants to achieve. In order to choose the 'style' and put a creative team to work, the event manager needs to know if this is a 'thank you' party, a celebration, or perhaps an event to 'schmooze' their top ten clients? Is there a need to create a moody mysterious scene, a fun and funky setting or is it to be a full on 'party party' with games and entertainment for the staff?

When one of those lovely 'ladies who lunch' comes to Theme Traders and asks them to arrange a top-notch summer party to celebrate her husband's fiftieth birthday, they might suggest a retro 1960s and 1970s evening, Austin Powers style – this could include bubble columns and lava lamps, animal print draping, a circular bed covered in fluffy pink material, psychedelic colours and glitter boots – or a night of rock 'n' roll where the birthday boy can go back to his teens, air guitar in hand and play to the strains of Pink Floyd and Deep Purple! But without asking the right questions the event manager could easily get it all horribly wrong – as the chief executive of a major blue chip company, he wants a sophisticated stylish party with a string quartet and a harpist!

In the summer of 1999, Theme Traders were asked to design the launch party for a new Internet company, cooldiamonds.com – now a highly successful Internet site where you can buy the best diamonds in the world or, alternatively, a cheeky diamond stud for your belly button! The brief was a mix of sophistication and fun. The directors wanted to invite a young sector of the press, trendy designers from Bond Street, clients from Knightsbridge and city business associates – including their bank manager!

It had to be somewhere central, so Theme Traders chose a beautiful room overlooking the Thames in a top London hotel. In essence, the event had to ooze sophistication but they wanted the youngsters to be able to party, the designers to be able to 'chill' and the Knightsbridge and city set to be able to enjoy deluxe dining in exclusive surroundings. The evening was to be special, unique, inviting and rich. After all, they were launching a luxury item!

One of the Theme Traders creative teams brainstormed the proposal, appointed an art director to the project and one of their senior event managers was assigned to make it all happen. At this stage, an illustration is often produced, which helps the client to focus on the creative team's ideas. Through experience, there is rarely any point in providing more than one illustration as the creative team have usually made a critical decision on how the party will appear through extensive brainstorming, therefore eliminating other second-rate ideas along the way. A crew from the showroom was assigned to the project and all the different departments worked together on the event. All events and parties at Theme Traders are the result of teamwork. Everyone employed is creative, not necessarily through his or her qualifications, but as people. It is essential for Theme Traders to be able to 'paint' a picture for their clients, and to bring that picture to life.

The result? The room was divided into two main areas blending one 'atmosphere' into the other. Using rich midnight blue velvet the entire area was draped with custom-made star cloths through which peeped twinkling silver white lights. At one end, low fluffy cloud-like tables were laid out with enormous soft pastel coloured cushions and beanbags around a starry dance floor. Lit with different shades of blue and white beams and gobos, the cooldiamonds.com logo shimmered everywhere! Over the dance floor hung rotating mirror balls that threw tiny diamond-like specs all around the room. In the 'champagne' area the tables were dressed to the floor with the same rich velvet material. In every centrepiece was a waterfall gently cascading over silver stones around the flicker of tiny tea-lights.

The mood of the whole room was changed as the evening progressed with creative use of lighting. Lighting designers had set the tone of the evening adding shades of blue and indigo, which highlighted and brightened the 'diamond' effect around the room as the evening progressed. All in all a cool but rich atmosphere was produced swimming in dreams and desires. The client was delighted!

What the client actually said after the event was that Theme Traders had solved their problem. They thought they would have to have two events, use different venues, incur double the expenses and basically could not see a way through their dilemma. Providing two very distinct arenas for two audiences in the same venue and at the same time could be considered a dilemma, but dilemmas like this are second nature to Theme Traders and they thrive on the challenge. Carefully mixing colours, fabrics and lighting to enhance moods, change atmospheres and make dreams come true – that is Theme Traders' speciality!

For further details about Theme Traders, and to view their website and image and event database, please visit www.ThemeTraders.com.

By David Jamilly, Director. Theme Traders, The Stadium, Oaklands Road, London NW2 6XN.

Questions

1. What process is involved in developing the theme for the event?
2. What benefit does theming bring to an event?
3. How do the elements of staging relate to the theme for the cooldiamonds.com event?
4. Based on the brief given, brainstorm alternative themes for the cooldiamonds.com event.
5. From the results of question 4, choose one theme for further development.
   (a) How will this theme deliver the clients requirements.
   (b) Referring to the elements of staging, describe how you would conceptualize and implement this theme. You may wish to illustrate your answer to focus your idea.

Case study 13.2

Live 8
Introduction

The Live 8 show on Saturday 2 July 2005, to help publicize the campaign to 'make poverty history' in Africa, was the biggest event in Hyde Park's history and the biggest ticketed event ever in the UK. Among those artists taking part were Coldplay, Elton John, Madonna, Paul McCartney, Robbie Williams, U2 and Pink Floyd.

Supplying the a–v for these shows was an enormous job, and four main contractors were assigned – Britannia Row Productions, which supplied the sound; Creative Technology, which supplied 12 giant LED screens; PRG, which brought in six articulated truckloads of lighting equipment; and Star Events Group, which provided the staging. The site and production areas for the Live 8 concert was constructed and operated by a crew of over 2000 and managed by Clear Channel Entertainment Group. The event overall was produced internationally by a number of people, including Richard Curtis, Sir Bob Geldorf, Harvey Goldsmith, John Kennedy and Kevin Wall with Ken Ehrlich, Larry Magid, Tim Sexton, Greg Sills and Russell Simmons (Live 8, 2005).

Screen technology

Due to the sheer numbers attending Hyde Park, over 200 000, the Live 8 concert in Hyde Park on July 2 was always going to rely heavily on large-screen video technology. It will come as no surprise that the show saw the biggest ever concentration of screens for an outdoor concert anywhere in Europe, with the equipment for both front and backstage supplied by Avesco companies, Creative Technology and MCL. The screen aspects of the production also included:

- Five LED screens positioned on stage; the main screen comprised 8×6 modules of Lighthouse 19 millimetre measuring 9.76×5.25 metre. Flanking it were two 6.4×4.8 metre, 25 millimetre Unitek screens, which were divided into four equal columns and arranged in a 90 degree arc either side of the main screen to visually 'wrap round' the performers. On each of the PA wings were 8.54×6.44 metre Lighthouse, 19 millimetre screens.
- Two relay screens one hundred metres from the stage, these were 44 metre square CT/ Screenco mobiles with Saco 15 millimetre screens, one of which is based in the UK and the other from CT's Dutch sister company JVR, which also supplied four Barco D-Lite 7 LED screens, each measuring 4.48×2.69 metre, to Screen Visions for the Berlin production. These were used as relay screens along Berlin's 'Straßeder 17 Juni', whilst two Barco G5 projectors with 300×225 projection screens and three 42 inch plasma screens were supplied to one of Dutch national television's studios for their broadcast of the event.
- Three further mobiles towards the back of the Hyde Park arena, two 40 metre square Lighthouse, 25 millimetre and one 30 metre square Panasonic, subcontracted by CT from Sweden's Massteknik. All the mobile screens were fed via digital video delays, allowing the timing on the video signal to be adjusted, to sync with the sound.
- 25 millimetre Unitek modules were deployed as a giant 1.2×35 metre LED banner panel across the top of the stage, a configuration more commonly seen at the side of football pitches. Driven by a dedicated text system, it was used to display slogans from Comic Relief, which provided much of the supporting visual material. The control system was operated by score board company Technographics.

- Video gear for the backstage area, supplied by CT and MCL – a Lighthouse 10 millimetre screen in the artist's garden and two of the new stand alone Lighthouse Pop Vision screens in the main hospitality area, as well as a number of plasma screens put in by MCL.

Avesco also had the massive logistical task of controlling the entire on screen video production and programming at Hyde Park. Outside broadcast supplier Bow Tie – which facilitated the main BBC system – provided a dedicated outside broadcast truck for screen production equipped with its own dedicated cameras and multi-channel VT record/playback facilities. Much of this equipment was supplied by another Avesco subsidiary, Presteigne Broadcast Hire. Graphic content for the main screens was managed using three Doremis and two channels of Arkaos. Further graphics-related services were provided for the SMS and MMS messaging facilities, which were available to the audience via sponsors AOL and Nokia. This enabled audience members to send images from camera phones via MMS. Montages of those pictures were then collated live on-site and put on to the screens during breaks between acts, alongside the SMS messages.

Lighthouse screens were also in use at the Berlin Live 8 concert, where two 5×4 R16, 16 millimetre pixel pitch screens helped relay the action to another huge audience. Meanwhile, 500 miles from Hyde Park in Gleneagles, Scotland, Lighthouse screens were also a key part of the G8 conference itself, where the leaders of the world's richest eight countries were meeting. Two 8×8 panel R16 screens were used to relay the conference to the gathered crowd supplied by Massteknik.

Sound

With 26 major artists, a scheduled turn round time between bands of less than five minutes and a large audience in Hyde Park, Britannia Row Productions, which provided the full PA system for the Live 8 show, certainly had its work cut out. 18 technicians and 25 sound engineers operated the PA system including:

- 200 Electrovoice X-Line loudspeaker cabinets, all powered by EV's Precision Series P3000RL remote controlled amplifiers.
- Six towers of EV X-Line, also powered by EV's Precision Series P3000RL, used as delays with additional L Acoustic V DOSC towers to ensure full coverage for the crowd.
- The entire sound system controlled by IRIS – Intelligent Remote Integrated Supervision – the software programme remotely controlling the P3000RL amplifiers from FOH.
- Stage monitors were Turbosound TFM-450 wedges with Turbosound Flashlight side fills and Turbosound TQ-440/TQ-425 drum fills powered by Pulse amplifiers.
- Several computers used to control and monitor the loudspeakers over 3 kilometre of signal cable.
- Over 500 Sennheiser microphones and 8000 metre of microphone cable used in order to keep the show running quickly from band to band. As well as providing a generic wireless radio and in ear monitoring system, Sennheiser also added its experienced technical support staff to Britannia's stage team.

Britannia enlisted both the assistance of the DiGiCo team and its D5 Live digital mixing console. In Hyde Park, three DiGiCo D5 Live digital mixing consoles were positioned at front of house, with a further three D5s at the monitor position. In front of house, one console was used for prepping, whilst the other two sat at the mix positions with the same arrangement for monitors.

Audio-Technica microphones were used extensively at Live 8 concerts around the world, in particular at the Philadelphia Museum of Art, in America, and at Live 8 Africa Calling at the Eden Centre, in Cornwall. The Philadelphia event in front of the Museum of Art, featured performances by leading artists such as Jay-Z, Linkin Park, and Def Leppard, all using Audio-Technica's Artist Elite 5000 Series UHF Wireless Systems. The Tokyo Live 8 concert featured Good Charlotte, performing on the Audio-Technica Artist Elite 5000 Series UHF Wireless System, and the Artist Elite AE6100 dynamic vocal microphone.

Lighting

PRG Europe supplied the lighting rig for the Hyde Park Live 8 event. The statistics for the event illustrate what a huge job it was to light such a show: six articulated truckloads of lighting equipment, 15 miles of cable, 47 tonnes of lights, suspended up to 10 metres above the stage from almost 180 metres of truss, 150 state-of-the-art moving lights, plus a further 120 other lights, Six follow-spots, a total of 295 000 kilowatt of light and 16 crew.

The lights had been on-site since June 22 in preparation for the July 2 event. Pete Barnes, UK lighting designer for Live 8 whose designs were also adapted as the basis for the Paris event, said: 'The challenge for this particular event is to provide lighting effects that meet the artistic values of a huge range of musicians, and at the same time make sure that the 150 000 people there can see what's happening as well as the billions watching on television'. James Thomas Pixel Fixtures were in use at Live 8. Peter decided on high impact LED fixtures with which to do this, and chose 120 PixelLine 1044 s and 14 of the new PixelLine 110 ecs. LED borders along the onstage trusses, used 72 1044 s units.

Staging

To give an idea of the size of the stage the Star Events group had to provide for Hyde Park, it was as high as five London double-decker buses stacked on top of each other and as wide as six buses lined up nose to tail, with an additional back stage area to accommodate equipment for the 26 bands that could have housed 29 London buses.

The stage for Live 8 had a 25 metre span by 20 metre deep main floor and the same area again as wing space. A raised floor area was built at the back, protected by a marquee and used for rolling risers to enable quick band changeovers. This was almost 5 metre above ground due to the slope on the site and was as big as the stage again. Another aid to the fast change-overs was a revolving stage, split into two, so one band could be setting up while the previous one was playing. It was hired in from the Revolving Stage Company.

The major challenge for the Star Events team was time. Whereas Party In The Park was due to happen on the Sunday July 3 (it was postponed to make way for Live 8) Live 8 took place a day earlier.

Production

The Live 8 shows saw the first ever relay of High Definition (HD) footage to the UK public by the BBC. The transmission was carried on satellite direct from Hyde Park to a BT downlink in the grounds of Cardiff Castle in Wales to a crowd of several thousand people. The BBC worked in partnership on the event with Shooting Partners.

The huge HDTV compatible LED display was supplied by Anna Valley Displays, which also provided a full HDTV projected picture on site. The high-definition screen was made up of 112 modules of Toshiba's 6 millimetre LED display in 16 × 9 format. For this project Anna Valley chose the Sanyo PLV-HD10 projector, capable of 5500 ANSI lumens, with a contrast ratio of 1000:1.

All the concert footage was filmed in HD, by 19 different HD cameras by the stage. Anna Valley's screen had to cope with changes in the footage from HD to Standard Definition footage, and to the text message services the Live 8 organizers were putting out. Blitz Charter Group (BCG) supplied a fully functional, true HD camera channel for the BBC's coverage of Live8. It was the UK's first transmission from an HD source camera. BCG supplied a camera channel, which included a Sony 750 HD Camera and a J11 HD lens, as well as a specially designed transmitter back-pack for the camera man who was out amongst the crowd, and a receiver desk, which was also designed by Charter.

Summary

Concerts of the size of the one at Live 8 happen all too rarely, the only comparable event in the UK was the original Live Aid event 20 years ago at Wembley Stadium. This case study has detailed the staging and audiovisual aspects of the event. It is testimony to the dedication of those involved that the Hyde Park show ran as smoothly as it did.

For further information about Live 8, please visit www.live8live.com. For further details about the suppliers discussed in this case study, please visit: www.audio-technica.com (Audio-Technica), www.avesco.co.uk (Avesco), www.britanniarow.com (Britannia Row), www.charterbroadcast.com (Charter Broadcast), www.clearchanneleurope.com (Clear Channel), www.digiconsoles.com (DiGiCo), www.lighthouse-tech.com (Lighthouse Technologies), www.pixelpar.com (Pixel), www.prgeurope.com (PRG Europe), www.shootingpartners.co.uk (Shooting Partners), www.stareventsgroup.com (Star Events), www.unitekdisplays.net (Unitek Displays).

By Paul Milligan, Assistant Editor, AV Magazine.www.avinteractive.co.uk

Questions

1. What key elements of staging are identified within the case study?
2. Identify the challenges faced by organizers of the Live 8 events. How may these differ between venues and countries?
3. Discuss what tools and techniques would be available to Live 8 producers to ensure the smooth running of the events?
4. Selecting one of the concerts, what skills would be required to organise this event?
5. From your understanding, what were the objectives of Live 8? How would success be measured for the Live 8 events?

Chapter 14
Evaluation and reporting

Learning Objectives

After studying this chapter, you should be able to:

- describe the role of evaluation in the event management process
- discuss when to evaluate an event
- understand and discuss the evaluation needs of event stakeholders
- identify and use secondary research sources
- create an evaluation plan for an event
- apply a range of techniques including the conducting of questionnaires and surveys in evaluating events
- describe and record the intangible impacts of events
- measure the expenditure of visitors to an event
- prepare a final evaluation report
- use event profiles to promote the outcomes of events and to seek sponsorship
- apply the knowledge gained by evaluation to the future planning of an event.

Introduction

Event evaluation is critical to the event management process. The events industry is still young and is struggling in some areas to establish legitimacy and acceptance as a profession. One of the best means for the industry to gain credibility is for events to be evaluated honestly and critically, so their outcomes are known, their benefits acknowledged and their limitations accepted. However, it serves a much deeper purpose than just 'blowing the trumpet' for events. It is at the very heart of the process where insights are gained, lessons are learnt and events are perfected. Event managers need to be aware of and utilize both primary and secondary research sources in the planning and evaluation of events. Event evaluation, if properly utilized and applied, is the key to the continuous improvement of events and to the standing and reputation of the event industry. As such, it should be a high priority for all event managers to properly evaluate their events and to disseminate this evaluation to their stakeholders and interested groups. If done well, this will not only enhance the reputation of their events, but also their own reputation as true professionals.

What is event evaluation?

Event evaluation is the process of critically observing, measuring and monitoring the implementation of an event in order to assess its outcomes accurately. It enables the creation of an event profile that outlines the basic features and important statistics of an event. It also enables feedback to be provided to event stakeholders, and plays an important role in the event management process by providing a tool for analysis and improvement.

The event management process, illustrated in Figure 14.1, is a cycle in which inputting and analysing data from an event enables more informed decisions to be made and more efficient planning to done, and improves event outcomes. This applies to individual repeat events, where the lessons learnt from one event can be incorporated in the planning of the next. It also applies to the general body of events knowledge, where the lessons learnt from individual events contribute to the overall knowledge and effectiveness of the events industry.

Edinburgh, for example, has learnt to cope with an influx of visitors that nearly doubles the population of the city for the Hogmanay celebrations, by applying the lessons learnt each year to the logistics planning for the next year's festival. Glastonbury Festival has been developed and refined over a period by intelligently feeding back information from one year's celebrations into the planning for the next.

Lessons learnt from one event can also be transferred to other events or to the whole events industry. The disaster at the FA Cup semi-final between Liverpool and Nottingham Forest at Hillsborough, Sheffield, in 1989, during which ninety-six fans were killed, led to a major review of the way that football grounds were designed, and improved crowd management techniques. The 1991 World Student Games in Sheffield left a legacy of event knowledge and experience, which has been applied to more recent events such as the European Football Championships in 1996, the Rugby Union World Cup in 1999 and informed development of the UK Major Event Strategy.

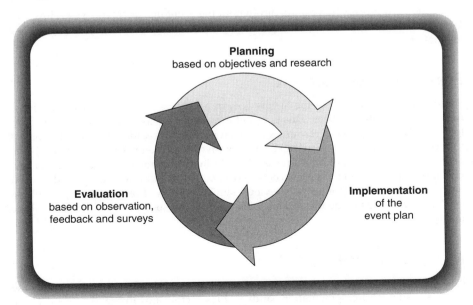

Figure 14.1 Evaluation and the event management process

Innovations in marketing, programming and staging, as well as improvements in operational issues such as crowd control, risk management and security, quickly ripple through the industry and become universally used and accepted. Sometimes this transfer of knowledge occurs through the movement of event personnel. Di Henry, who successfully organized the torch relay for the Sydney Olympic Games in 2000, went on to organize the torch relays for the Commonwealth Games in Manchester in 2002 and Melbourne in 2006. Andrew Walsh, who directed the opening ceremony for the Rugby World Cup in Sydney in 2003, went on to become executive producer for the opening and closing ceremonies of the Olympic Games in Athens in 2004.

The transfer of Olympic knowledge was formalized by the payment of $3 million by the International Olympic Committee to the Sydney Organising Committee for the Olympic Games (SOCOG) for the intellectual property of the Games, and the establishment of the Olympic Games Knowledge Service based in Lausanne, Switzerland. A further example of this knowledge transfer at a training level was a project funded by the Greek Government in 2000, where 70 Greek students undertook work placement at SOCOG during the preparation and conduct of the Sydney Olympic Games. This was supported by a sports management course at the University of Technology, Sydney. The knowledge and training gained was then applied to the conduct of the 2004 Olympic Games in Athens.

Innovations in terms of event communications, products and technologies are constantly spread and refined through the process of event evaluation leading to better event planning, implementation and further evaluation. It is an upward spiral leading to the improvement of individual events, and to an ever-growing and more knowledgeable events industry.

When to evaluate events

Evaluation is a process that occurs throughout the event management cycle. However, Getz (2005) and others have identified three key periods when it is useful to undertake evaluation.

Pre-event assessment

Some form of assessment of the factors governing an event usually takes place in the research and planning stage. This is sometimes called a feasibility study, and is used to determine what level of resources an event is likely to require, and whether or not to proceed with the event. Such a study may involve market research of the probable audience reaction to the event and is likely to involve some degree of research and prediction of attendance figures, costs and benefits. It will often compare the event with profiles and outcomes of previous similar events. The study may result in establishing targets or benchmarks against which, the success of the project will be measured.

Monitoring the event

Event monitoring is the process of tracking the progress of an event through the various stages of implementation, and enables factors governing the event to be adjusted. For example, ticket sales may be perceived as slow in the lead-up to an event, and this may result in increased advertising or publicity effort. Monitoring the budget may result in the trimming of expenses or the freeing up of money for other areas of expenditure. Observation during the event may lead to changes which improve the delivery of the event, such as adjusting sound volume, or altering the dispersal of security or cleaning staff to match changing crowd patterns. This process of monitoring is vital to quality control, and will also provide valuable information in the final evaluation of an event, and for future planning purposes.

Post-event evaluation

The most common form of evaluation, however, is post-event evaluation. This involves the gathering of statistics and data resulting from an event, and interpreting them in relation to its mission and objectives. Key Performance Indicators (KPIs) are sometimes used to translate the event objectives into measures that can be applied to gauge the success of the event. An important aspect is usually a debrief meeting of key participants and stakeholders, where the strengths and weaknesses of the event are discussed, and observations are recorded for future reference. Post-event evaluation may also involve some form of questionnaire or survey of the event participants or audience, which seeks to explore their opinions of the experience and to measure their levels of satisfaction with the event. It often involves the collection of data on the financial expenditure of the participants, so that the cost can be compared with the revenue generated by the event. The nature of the evaluation will be determined largely by the purpose of the event and audience for which it is intended.

Reporting to stakeholders

One of the prime reasons that event managers evaluate events is to report to stakeholders.

- The host organization will want to know what the event achieved. Did the event come in on budget and on time? Did it achieve its objectives? How many people attended, and were their expectations met? For future planning purposes it might be useful to know where the attendees came from, how they heard about it and whether they intend to return next year.
- The event sponsor may have other measures. Was the level of awareness of the product or service increased? What penetration did the advertising achieve? What media coverage was generated? What was the profile of the people who attended?
- Funding bodies will have grant acquittal procedures to be observed, and will usually require audited financial statements of income and expenditure along with a report on the social, cultural or sporting outcomes of the event.
- Councils and government departments may want to know what the impact was on their local, regional or national economies.
- Tourism bodies may want to know the number of visitors attracted to the area and what they spent, not only on the event, but also on travel, shopping and accommodation.

Quantified event outcomes can be very helpful to event organizers in promoting the profile and acceptance of the event. The City of Edinburgh Council, together with other stakeholders in the Edinburgh Festivals (including the organizers and the Scottish Tourism Board), use the economic impacts of the Edinburgh

Festivals very effectively in promoting support for, and acceptance of, the events. For example, in a press release announcing traffic and safety arrangements for Edinburgh's Hogmanay, the City of Edinburgh Council, noted that, 'Edinburgh's Hogmanay is now in the same league as the Edinburgh International Festival in terms of its position on the world's "must see" list, and the impact it has on the city's economy. For an outlay of around £1.4 million, including the cost of the safety measures, the economic return is in the region of £30 million' (City of Edinburgh Council, 2000c). Similarly, Bath and North East Somerset Council has used economic impact studies to underline the contribution of arts to the cultural economy of Bath and North East Somerset (B&NES, 2000).

Types of research

Primary research is original research undertaken directly in relation to a project or event. It involves many of the evaluation techniques, such as observation, questionnaires and surveys, which are discussed later in this chapter. Secondary research, undertaken by external organizations or agencies, is not conducted specifically for the purpose of the event, but may be of considerable value and assistance to the event manager. It includes research reports from previous events, information and statistics available from research bureaus, research journals and the Internet.

Secondary research

Secondary research can be useful throughout the life cycle of the event. However, it is particularly useful before the event in preparing feasibility studies, when existing information may assist the event manager in building up a picture of the event and predicting event outcomes. Some important sources of secondary research will now be discussed.

Research reports from previous events

If the event has been conducted before, then previous event reports and/or discussions with their organizers or staff may be of great assistance to the event manager. Each Commonwealth Games, for example, is required to provide a detailed post-games report, including the number of event participants and their partners, the number and type of competitions/functions that were conducted, the marketing strategies employed and detailed statements of income and expenditure of the event. The report from the 2002 Manchester Commonwealth Games has provided the basis for a useful online resource (www.gameslegacy.com) including the full reports, while a similar level of information is also available for Sydney Olympics (www.gamesinfo.com.au). By studying these previous event reports carefully, the event manager can form a fairly accurate profile of the event, including likely predictions of attendance figures and budgets. The specifics of the host city's planned event will need to be taken into account, including characteristics and aspects of the location that are likely to influence the event outcomes. If the event has not taken place before, studies of similar events, or discussions with their event managers, may prove rewarding. A new food and wine festival, for example, may be expected to have a similar profile to other existing food and wine festivals, allowing for differences of location, market, etc.

A conference for one industry group or association may be expected to behave in similar ways to previous conferences for similar groups or associations. By studying carefully what has gone before, an astute event manager may be able to develop a template that may need fine tuning and adjustment, but will provide valuable insights into the likely profile of a new event.

Research bureaus

There are many public and privately funded research organizations that will provide access to valuable data either free of charge or for a modest fee. The Office of National Statistics (www.statistics.gov.uk), for example, produces detailed information on a wide variety of topics, including social trends, census statistics and how British spend their leisure time. They also provide useful information on a range of social trends (Summerfield and Gill, 2005) which includes topics such as attendance at cultural events, reasons for attending the arts and children's participation in cultural and leisure activities.

Statistics on Tourism and Research, known as Star UK (www.star.org.uk), a site managed by VisitBritain on behalf of their UK Research Liaison Group partners Department of Culture, Media and Sport and the four national tourism organizations (VisitBritain, VisitScotland, Northern Ireland Tourist Board and Wales Tourist Board), contains annual national and international visitor surveys, which provide accurate data on visitor patterns and expenditure on a wide range of activities, including travel, accommodation and attendance at some types of events. The arts councils collect and disseminate data relating to arts-related events. The Business Tourism Partnership (www.businesstourismpartnership.com) produces and disseminates research, relating to aspects of business tourism and business-related events.

Web searches

A web search of similar events will produce a surprising amount of data, including how other event managers have approached the issues of programming, promotion and logistics. Some will even include research reports providing detailed information on event outcomes such as attendance and economic impacts.

Journal databases

Also found on the web are journal databases that will enable event managers to track down research articles in tourism, leisure, marketing and event-specific journals, which can be of great assistance in researching and planning an event. Some of these articles may be accessed directly from the web or through public and university libraries. Articles can be found on a wide range of event issues, including marketing, sponsorship, audience motivation and satisfaction, event impacts, risk management, harm minimization and event operations.

By undertaking a thorough scan of relevant secondary research, the event manager can proceed from an informed and knowledgeable position and can often save time and money in devising a primary research and evaluation plan for an event.

Primary research

An exact event profile and invaluable information for its future planning and improvement can only be obtained by close observation, and evaluation of the event. The evaluation of an event will usually be more effective if it is planned from the outset, and built into the event management process. Planning should include consideration of:

- what data is needed
- how, when and by whom it is to be gathered
- how it is to be analysed
- what format to use in the final reporting.

Data collection

The process of implementing the event may provide opportunities for useful data to be collected. For example, participants may be required to fill in an event registration form, which can be designed to capture useful information on numbers, age, gender, point of origin, spending patterns and so on. Ticketed events allow for a ready means of counting spectators, and the ticketing agency may be able to provide further useful information, such as the postcodes of ticket purchasers. For non-ticketed events, figures on the use of public transport and car parks, and police crowd estimates can be used in calculating attendance figures. Event managers should look out for and make use of all opportunities for the collection of relevant data.

Staff observation

An obvious but critical source of data collection is the direct observation of the event. Staff observation and reports may provide information on a number of aspects of the event, including performance quality, audience reaction, crowd flow and adequacy of catering and toilet facilities. However, staff will provide more accurate and useful data if they are trained to observe these issues and are given a proper reporting format, rather than being left to rely on casual and anecdotal observations. From the outset, staff should be made aware that observation and reporting on the event are part of their role, and should be given appropriate guidance and benchmarks. They may be given checklists to evaluate items, such as performance quality and audience reaction on a scale of one to five, or by ticking indicators such as below average, average, good, very good or excellent.

At outdoor events, stage managers should be required to complete a written report on each event, giving their estimates of attendance figures, weather conditions, performance standards and crowd reaction and commenting on any unusual occurrences or features. Likewise, security staff should be required to report on crowd behaviour, any incidents, disturbances or injuries and to estimate the size of crowds on the day assisted by photographs taken at regular intervals by security cameras at strategic locations throughout the event space. By compiling these reports with statistics from attraction operators, and assessing factors such as competition from other major events in the city, management is able to form profiles of individual events and to track trends over time.

Stakeholder observation

Other key players in an event such as venue owners, councils, sponsors, vendors, police and first-aid officers can often provide valuable feedback from their various perspectives.

- Venue owners may be able to compare the performance of the event with their normal venue patterns and comment usefully on matters such as attendance figures, parking, access, catering and facilities.

- Councils may be aware of disturbance to the local community, or of difficulties with street closures or compliance with health regulations.
- Sponsors may have observations based on their attendance at the event, or may have done their own surveys on audience reaction, awareness levels and media coverage.
- Vendors may have information on, for example, volume of sales and waiting time in queues that will be valuable in planning future catering arrangements.
- Police may have observed aspects such as crowd behaviour, traffic flow and parking, and may have constructive suggestions for future planning.
- First-aid providers may have statistics on the number and seriousness of treatments for injuries such as cuts, abrasions or heat exhaustion that will assist in future planning of safety and risk assessment.

All of these key stakeholders may have observations on general planning issues such as signage, access, crowd management, communication and the provision of facilities that will have implications for the improvement of the event. It is important that their observations are recorded and incorporated into the evaluation and planning stages of the event management process.

De-briefing meetings

All stakeholders should be made aware at the outset that they will be given an opportunity to provide feedback, and that this is a vital part of the event planning process. They should be encouraged to contribute their professional observations and assessment. This may be done at a single 'de-briefing' meeting or a series of meetings, depending on the complexity of the event. It is often useful for the date and agenda of this meeting to be made known to all parties early in the process, so that if it is not possible for them to communicate their observations during the heat of the event, then they are aware that a suitable forum will be provided during the finalization of the event. This meeting should ensure that neither congratulations nor recriminations overshadow the important lessons that are to be learnt from the event and the consequent changes to be incorporated into future planning. It is important that all parties are listened to and that their comments are taken into account in the future planning of the event.

The topics to be addressed at the meeting will be determined by the nature and size of the event. However, the checklist in Figure 14.2 is a useful starting point.

Questionnaires and surveys

Questionnaires can range from simple feedback forms targeting event partners and stakeholders to detailed audience or visitor surveys undertaken by trained personnel. The scale of the questionnaire will depend based upon the needs and resources of the event. Simple feedback forms can usually be designed and distributed within the event's own internal resources. They may seek to record and quantify basic data, such as the expenditure of event partners, the observations of stakeholders and their assessment of event management and outcomes. In their study of local authorities event-based tourism, Thomas and Wood (2003) found that visitor feedback/surveys were the most popular methods of evaluation undertaken by more than 60 per cent of responding authorities.

Surveys are used in order to ascertain reliable statistical information on audience profiles and reaction, and on visitor patterns and expenditure. They may be implemented by direct interviews with participants, or may rely on participants filling in written forms. They may be undertaken face-to-face, by telephone or by mail.

CHECKLIST FOR EVENT EVALUATION

Aspect	Satisfactory	Requires attention	Comments
• Timing of the event			
• Venue			
• Ticketing and entry			
• Staging			
• Performance standard			
• Staffing levels and performance of duties			
• Crowd control			
• Security			
• Communications			
• Information and signage			
• Transport			
• Parking			
• Catering facilities			
• Toilets			
• First-aid			
• Lost children			
• Sponsor's acknowledgement			
• Hosting arrangements			
• Advertising			
• Publicity			
• Media liaison			

Figure 14.2 Event evaluation checklist

Face-to-face interviews will usually generate a higher response rate, but techniques such as a competition with prizes as incentives for participation may improve the response rate of postal surveys. To undertake effective surveys requires expertise and the commitment of considerable organizational resources. For event organizers with limited in-house experience and expertise, professional assistance can be called upon for tasks ranging from the design of survey forms to the full implementation of the survey process.

In the case of repeat events, a single well-designed survey may satisfy the basic research needs of the event. Some event organizers may wish to repeat the survey each year, in order to compare successive events and to establish trends, or may want to embark on more ambitious research programmes in order to investigate other aspects of the event. Whatever the scale and approach that is decided on, experts such as Getz (2005), Veal (1997) and the publication by the UK Sport (1999c) suggest certain basic aspects that should be kept in mind:

- *Purpose*: identify clearly the purpose and objective of the survey. A clearly stated and defined purpose is most likely to lead to a well-targeted survey with effective results.
- *Survey design*: keep it simple. If too much is attempted in the survey, there is a danger that focus will be lost and effectiveness reduced. Questions should be clear and unambiguous, and should be tested by a 'trial run' before the actual survey.

- *Size of sample*: the number of participants must be large enough to provide a representative sample of the audience. The sample size will depend on the level of detail in the survey, the level of precision required and the available budget. If in doubt, seek professional advice on the size of the sample.
- *Randomness*: the methodology employed in the selection of participants must avoid bias of age, sex and ethnicity. A procedure such as selecting each tenth person to pass through a turnstile may assist in providing a random selection.
- *Support data*: the calculation of some outcomes will depend on the collection of support data. For example, the calculation of total visitor expenditure will require accurate data on the average expenditure of visitors as well as the number of visitors to the event. Then the spending pattern revealed by the survey can be multiplied by the number of visitors to provide an estimate of the total visitor expenditure for the event.

What to evaluate

Events have both tangible and intangible impacts. Surveys most commonly measure tangible impacts such as economic costs and benefits, as these can most easily be measured. However, it is also important to evaluate the intangible impacts of events, even if this evaluation needs to be more narrative based or descriptive. Some of the intangibles that are hard to measure include the impacts on the social life and well-being of a community, the sense of pride engendered by events, and the long-term positioning of a place or tourist destination.

The parade and events staged for the London gay and lesbian communities as Pride London, and its predecessor London Mardi Gras, have been a focus for Gay Rights and Pride. The Bradford Mela aims to celebrate Asian cultures and educate other residents, fostering a culture of racial tolerance. The Eisteddfod Festival, alternating between north and south Wales each year, has provided a strong focus for Welsh national identity. While events such as these have undoubted social worth, it may be difficult and perhaps even counterproductive to quantify this in anything other than descriptive terms. Nevertheless, their cultural meaning and social impacts would need to be taken into account in any serious evaluation of their community impacts.

Commenting on the publication of an evaluation report on A Quality of Light (an international visual arts festival held at various locations in West Cornwall during 1997), Graham Long, South West Arts Chief Executive, noted:

> A Quality of Light has defied geography. It has shown that it is possible to mount a major international arts event even in one of the most remote and rural parts of the country. It's been great for those who've seen the work – and for the economy and profile of Cornwall. A Quality of Light has generated £1.4 million for the economy of West Cornwall and people have been reading about it across the country and abroad. Most of that money came from outside Cornwall. That's an amazing return on the total investment of £300 000 in the project. The arts make economic sense (Chaloner, 1998).

Measuring visitor expenditure

All event managers will be familiar with constructing a simple financial balance statement of the income and expenditure of events. Until recent times, this form of reporting was considered sufficient, as most events were evaluated on the basis of their inherent social, cultural or sporting value to the local community. However, the growing involvement of governments, tourism and arts bodies, companies and sponsors has brought with it an increasing need to consider the wider impacts of events.

The impacts of events on the economy are based primarily on the expenditure of visitors to the event from outside the host community. UK Sport (1999c, p. 12) defines the economic impact as, 'the total amount of additional expenditure generated within a city, which could be directly attributable to the event'. They have published simple guidelines for measuring the economic impact of sport events, which can be applied to other events. Their publication outlines a basic methodology (illustrated in Figure 14.3), and includes sample questions for the visitor survey (Figure 14.4). This is discussed further below.

Phase 1: Pre-planning

This involves planning the data collection strategy, including the likely respondents. Points to consider include:

- How many of each respondent group will attend?
- When will they be arriving?
- Where will they be staying?
- When to conduct the survey?
- Any unique circumstances, for example children involved, therefore limited funds?

Phase 2: Primary data collection

This phase involves data gathering using the survey questionnaire. UK Sport highlights the fact that each event is unique, therefore the survey questionnaire

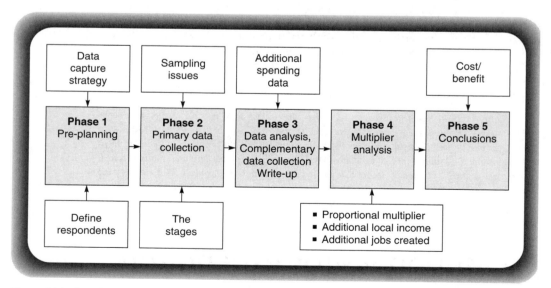

Figure 14.3 Five phase approach to economic impact evaluation
Source: adapted from UK Sport (1999c)

[*Event Name*] Visitors' Survey

We are asking for your help. We are looking to establish the economic importance of this event. We would be grateful if you could complete the following survey. Information provided will be treated in the strictest confidence. No individual responses will be identified.

1. Please state nationality [＿＿＿＿＿＿＿]

2. Where do you live? (please specify town or city) [＿＿＿＿＿＿＿]

3. Which of the following are you?

Athlete	1 ☐	Coach	2 ☐
Official	3 ☐	Journalist/media	4 ☐
Spectator	5 ☐		

   If you are a resident of Cityville thank you very much for your co-operation, however your assistance is no longer required. Please return this form to a research steward

4. Are you attending the event alone?

   Yes 1 ☐   No 2 ☐

   If YES: please go to QUESTION 5a

   If NO: How many other ADULTS (over 16) are there in your party today? [＿＿＿＿＿＿]

   If NO: How many CHILDREN (15 and under) are there in your party today? [＿＿＿＿＿＿]

5a. In which TOWN/CITY are you staying tonight?
   [＿＿＿＿＿＿]

5b. Is this -

At Home?	1 ☐
With Friends/Relatives?	2 ☐
A Guest House?	3 ☐
An Hotel?	4 ☐
A Camp Site?	5 ☐
Other?	6 ☐

   If Other: please specify ＿＿＿＿＿＿＿＿＿

For Official Use Only

Date
- ☐ 27th June
- ☐ 28th June
- ☐ 29th June

Gender
- ☐ 1   Male
- ☐ 2   Female

1. ☐ 1   British
   - ☐ 2   Other European
   - ☐ 3   North American
   - ☐ 4   South American
   - ☐ 5   African
   - ☐ 6   Asian
   - ☐ 7   Other
   - ☐ 99 Missing

2. ☐ 0   Sheffield
   - ☐ 1   Yorkshire
   - ☐ 2   North
   - ☐ 3   Midlands
   - ☐ 4   South
   - ☐ 5   Other UK
   - ☐ 6   Western European
   - ☐ 7   Central European
   - ☐ 8   Eastern European
   - ☐ 9   North America
   - ☐ 10 South America
   - ☐ 11 African
   - ☐ 12 Australia
   - ☐ 13 Other
   - ☐ 99 Missing

5a. ☐ 1   Sheffield
   - ☐ 2   Yorkshire
   - ☐ 3   North
   - ☐ 4   Midlands
   - ☐ 5   South
   - ☐ 6   Other UK
   - ☐ 7   Other
   - ☐ 99 Missing

Figure 14.4 Visitors survey
Source: adapted from UK Sport (1999c)

6. How many nights are you staying in CITYVILLE? ☐

If you are NOT STAYING OVERNIGHT in CITYVILLE, please go to QUESTION 8.

7. If you are STAYING OVERNIGHT in CITYVILLE:
   How much are you spending on ACCOMMODATION PER NIGHT? ☐

8. How much will you spend in CITYVILLE TODAY on the following -

Food & Drink?	£	☐
Entertainment?	£	☐
Travel?	£	☐
Programmes/Merchandise?	£	☐
Shopping/Souvenirs?	£	☐
Other? (Parking, petrol, etc.)	£	☐

9a. How much have you budgeted to spend in TOTAL during your stay in CITYVILLE?

Total Expenditure £ ☐

9b. Does this include expenditure on others?

Yes 1 ☐   No 2 ☐

If YES: How many others is this expenditure for? ☐

10. Is the EVENT the main reason for you being in CITYVILLE today?

Yes 1 ☐   No 2 ☐

11. Are you combining your visit to the EVENT with a holiday?

Yes 1 ☐   No 2 ☐

If YES: Where are you going? ☐

For how long? ☐

Can you provide us with a rough idea of your total budget for this part of your trip? £ ☐

Thank you for taking the time to complete this survey.
Please return this form to a research steward.

Figure 14.4 Continued

will need to be adapted in order to meet the objectives of the event and to achieve meaningful data. The objectives and stages of the research method are:

- To quantify the number of people from outside the host city who will be staying overnight in the host city and from this subsample to quantify how many are staying in commercially provided accommodation.
- To quantify how many nights those staying in commercial accommodation will spend in the city and how much per night such accommodation is costing.
- To quantify for both those staying overnight and day visitors, the amount spent per day on six standard categories of expenditure.
- To quantify how much in total people have budgeted to spend in a host city and on how many other people this expenditure will be made.
- To establish the proportion of people whose main reason for being in the host city is the event under investigation.
- To determine if any respondents are combining their visit to the host city with a holiday, so that the spending associated with the holiday, and the location of the spending, can be used to estimate any wider economic impact in other cities or regions due to staging of the event (UK Sport, 1999c, p. 12).

Phase 3: Data analysis, complementary methods and writing up

The data collected by the survey questionnaire should be analysed using a statistical package (e.g. SPSS), or a spreadsheet package (e.g. Microsoft Excel). The data should be analysed by using three filters. First, is the respondent a local or visitor? Second, which group do they belong to? Finally, based on their group type, are they a day visitor or staying overnight?

In addition to questionnaire analysis, it is useful to use complementary methods in order to understand the significance of the findings. This may take the form of observing the event or qualitative interviews with the event organizer and other stakeholders, including local hotels, restaurants and shops. The final area of data to collect, sometimes referred to as 'organizational spend', is additional expenditure in the host area directly attributable to the event but not collected by the questionnaire. Once the data is collected from the sources discussed above, the final write-up of the report can begin.

Phase 4: Multiplier analysis

The data collected may be analysed further, depending on the needs of the host organization or other stakeholders. Multiplier analysis involves calculating the amount of additional income retained in the city after allowing for 'leakage' from the local economy, for example, to suppliers or staff from outside the area. Using multipliers has been discussed by various authors, including Hall (1997) and Getz (2005), who warn that caution is required in calculating multipliers as it can lead to the impacts being exaggerated. UK Sport suggests that one of the most common methods used is the proportional income multiplier, illustrated in Figure 14.5.

Phase 5: Conclusions

The final phase involves an evaluation of the costs of staging the event, compared with the benefits. However, it should be remembered that events might make a direct

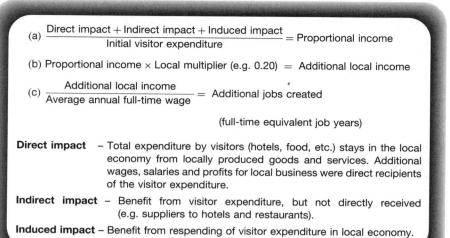

(a) $\dfrac{\text{Direct impact} + \text{Indirect impact} + \text{Induced impact}}{\text{Initial visitor expenditure}} = \text{Proportional income}$

(b) Proportional income × Local multiplier (e.g. 0.20) = Additional local income

(c) $\dfrac{\text{Additional local income}}{\text{Average annual full-time wage}} = \text{Additional jobs created}$

(full-time equivalent job years)

Direct impact – Total expenditure by visitors (hotels, food, etc.) stays in the local economy from locally produced goods and services. Additional wages, salaries and profits for local business were direct recipients of the visitor expenditure.

Indirect impact – Benefit from visitor expenditure, but not directly received (e.g. suppliers to hotels and restaurants).

Induced impact – Benefit from respending of visitor expenditure in local economy.

Figure 14.5 Economic impact equations
Source: adapted from UK Sport (1999c)

loss at the time of the event, with rewards achieved in the longer term. Data from studies such as this will allow stakeholders (such as local authorities or regional development agencies) to evaluate their economic development policies for growth in tourism, leisure and sports. For example, the World Student Games in 1991 left Sheffield with a political argument due to a direct loss of £10.4 million, however, in the longer term, Sheffield benefited from an investment of £147 million in new and refurbished facilities that are still providing income to the city today through major events (Bramwell, 1997).

The methodology takes into account the complexity of estimating the number of visitors from outside the region. It seeks to distinguish visitors attracted by the event or who have extended their visit because of the event, from those who would have visited the region anyway. In the case of an event that extends for more than one day or that has multiple events, it also takes into account the need to identify the number of days or events attended, and to weight this in calculating the results of the survey.

The survey form allows distinction between residents and non-local residents. This is important as it is generally accepted that local residents spending money at events does not usually lead to an increase in local income, as local residents would have spent money whether the event took place or not. This is sometimes referred to as 'deadweight expenditure' (UK Sport, 1999 c).

Calculating the economic impact of events is a complex task involving many factors. However, by applying the guidelines and the survey shown in Figure 14.4, a simple and useful snapshot of the economic impact of an event can be readily obtained.

Arts Council England has funded a range of projects relating to arts evaluation, which has application for festivals. Reeves (2002) provided an overview of arts impacts research based on the literature available, focusing on the economic and social aspects. One of the objectives of the study was to develop a practical resource to assist practitioners with effective evaluation. Further work commissioned as the 'National Arts Information Project: Evaluation Toolkit' (Comedia, 2003) includes an extensive practical overview of evaluation together with supporting evaluation tools developed in Microsoft Excel – participant and audience questionnaires and a project data template. The idea of the evaluation toolkit has also been explored by other arts organizations within the UK. Arts Council of Northern Ireland (Jackson, 2004) focus on the evaluation of social impacts on participants of arts groups working in community and voluntary sectors. Further, Scottish Arts Council (2003; Dean, Goodlad and Hamilton, 2001) have developed a pilot online toolkit for people and organizations to evaluate Scottish Arts Council funded arts projects, with using the toolkit a condition for grants.

Media monitoring and evaluation

Media coverage is an important aspect of an event. This coverage can be both positive and negative, depending on the event outcomes, the impact on the community and the kind of relationship built-up with the media. It is important to monitor and record this coverage as part of the documentation of the event. If the event is local, it may be possible to do this by keeping a file of newspaper articles and by listening and looking for radio and television interviews and news coverage. For larger events, a professional media-monitoring organization may need to be employed to track media coverage from a variety of sources. They will usually provide copies of print media stories and transcripts of radio interviews and news coverage. Audio and videotapes of electronic coverage can be obtained for an additional charge. This coverage provides an excellent record of the event, and can be used effectively in profiling the event to future potential sponsors and partners.

A further issue is content analysis of the media coverage as this is not always positive. Negative media coverage can impact on the reputation of the event, and by implication on stakeholders such as host organization and sponsors.

Some media monitors will attempt to place a monetary value on media coverage, usually valuing it at around three times the cost of equivalent advertising space, on the grounds that editorial coverage is likely to be better trusted by consumers and is therefore worth more. Such valuations should be regarded as approximate only, but may provide a useful comparative assessment of media coverage. For example, media coverage of the 2000 Love Parade in Leeds was valued by Yorkshire Tourist Board at £2.5 million. This included national radio coverage by Radio One (the organizer) and radio, television and newspaper reports covering the event.

Event evaluation reports and profiles

Once information has been collated from data collection, observation, feedback meetings and surveys, a final event evaluation report should be completed and distributed to all stakeholders. The information should give rise to a profile of the event, which can be included in the executive summary of the report. This profile can form the basis for a media release promoting the outcomes of the event, and can be used to begin planning for the next event and approaching sponsors. Figure 14.6 provides an example of a media release based on the profile of the Network Q Rally.

Press Release: 9914

MSA REPORT REVEALS ECONOMIC IMPACT OF WORLD RALLY CHAMPIONSHIP

A report commissioned by the Motor Sports Association (MSA) reveals that competitors and spectators at the 1998 Network Q Rally of Great Britain spent 11.1 million UK pounds in the area of the event. The world-wide television coverage of the event stimulated a further 17.25 million pounds of subsequent tourist spending in Wales alone.

An independent team measured the economic impact of the four-day rally on 7,814 businesses, employing 81,271 people in 20 counties. Their report concludes that the Network Q Rally 'is one of the largest spectator sporting events in Great Britain' and that the event 'would not happen at nearly this scale unless it was part of the FIA World Rally Championship'.

The study shows that 134,921 spectators paid to watch the 1998 event; 60% of them were visitors from outside the 10,503 square miles covered by the rally. Of the £11 million spent, 6.7 million pounds represented money flowing into the economies from outside. The main benefactors were hotels, motels and campsites (2.1 million pounds), eating and drinking establishments (3.3 million), retail stores (2.6 million pounds) and local transport services (2.2 million pounds).

The average spectator spent 83 UK pounds per day on tickets, parking, lodging, food, drink, entertainment and tourist purchases. Occupancy at local hotels reached 100%, at a time of year (November) when most establishments would otherwise be quiet.

'The rally created over 500 temporary jobs, notably at Rally HQ in Cheltenham and at the offices of the promoters, Silverstone Circuits.

MSA Chief Executive John Quenby commented: 'We already know from independent figures that the UK motor sports industry is a major contributor to our national economy, with at least 50,000 full-time jobs and an annual turnover of 1.3 billion pounds'.

'This report is the first systematic evaluation of the economic impact of a major rally. It shows that no fewer than 69 parliamentary constituencies gained direct employment benefits from the Network Q Rally of Great Britain.'

'What is particularly gratifying is that so much income flows into the area immediately surrounding the route and then remains in that area, strengthening the social fabric of the community.'

The 40-page independent report - 'The Economic Impact of the Network Q Rally of Great Britain'- was prepared for the MSA by American economic historian William Lilley III (former Staff Director of the US House of Representatives Budget Committee) and Laurence J DeFranco (an expert in geo-economics).

The complete report can be seen on the FIA website (http://www.fia.com).

Figure 14.6 Media release on economic impact of 1998 Network Q Rally
Source: Motor Sports Association (1999)

Finalization

Once the event is over, and before administration is disbanded or preparation for the next event is begun, it is important to tie up loose ends and to bring the event management process to a satisfactory conclusion. The following information is a useful checklist of tasks to be completed when finalizing the event:

- Hold a de-briefing meeting and provide an opportunity for feedback by all stakeholders.
- Settle accounts and prepare an audited financial statement.
- Ensure all contractual and statutory obligations have been fulfilled.
- Prepare and distribute to all key stakeholders, a full report on event outcomes.
- Make recommendations for future refinements and improvements to the event.
- Thank all staff, participants and stakeholders for their support of the event.

Chapter summary

Event evaluation is a process of measuring and assessing events throughout the event management cycle. It provides feedback that contributes to the planning and improvement of individual events and to the event industry's pool of knowledge.

Feasibility studies identify the likely costs and benefits of an event, and help to decide whether to proceed with it. Monitoring the event establishes whether it is on track and enables the event manager to respond to changes and adjust plans. Post-event evaluation measures the outcomes of the event in relation to its objectives. The exact nature of this evaluation will depend on the perspectives and needs of the stakeholders. The event manager needs to be aware of both primary and secondary research sources and techniques.

A range of techniques is used in event evaluation, including data collection, observation, feedback meetings, questionnaires and surveys. Good evaluation is planned and implemented from the outset of the event management process, with all participants made aware of its objectives and methodology. As well as tangible impacts, events have intangible benefits which cannot always be quantified, and may need to be recorded on a narrative or descriptive basis. These include social and cultural impacts on a community, and the long-term profile and positioning of a tourism destination. Calculating the economic impact of an event can be complex and expensive, but a simple methodology is available to carry out a basic study. A key factor in calculating this impact is the measurement of visitor expenditure through the use of visitor surveys. The media coverage of an event should be monitored in house, or by using professional media monitors. Once information is gathered from all sources, an event evaluation report should be compiled and distributed to all stakeholders. This report can provide the basis for media releases that promote the outcomes of the event, and can be used for future planning and seeking of sponsorship. In finalizing the event, it is important to tidy up loose ends and to feed lessons learnt from the event back into the event management process.

Questions

1. Imagine a fictional event that you would like to organize. Make a list of the secondary research sources that you would use in researching the event and make a detailed summary of one of these sources.
2. Identify an event that you are familiar with, or one that you are involved with in some capacity. Design an evaluation plan intended to provide a profile of the event, and to provide a basis of a report to key stakeholders.
3. Imagine that you are employing staff to work on a particular event. Design a report sheet for them to record their observations of the event. Decide what aspects you want them to observe and what benchmarks you want them to use.
4. Select an event that you are familiar with and identify the stakeholders that you would invite to a final evaluation meeting. Write an agenda for the meeting designed to encourage feedback on the event in an organized manner.
5. Imagine that you are a tourist officer for your region. Design a questionnaire for a major local event in order to evaluate the impact of the event on local tourism.
6. Obtain copies of three evaluation reports from libraries or direct from event organizations. Compare and contrast the methodology, style and format of the reports.
7. Identify a high-profile event in your region, and monitor, as closely as you can, the media generated by the event, including print media, radio and television coverage.
8. Choose an event that you have been associated with and assemble as much data as you can on the event. Using this data, create a written profile of the event. Using this written profile as a basis, draft a media release outlining the outcomes of the event and the benefits to the local community.

Case study 14.1

MTV Europe Music Awards 2003

The starring performance of Edinburgh in the 10th anniversary MTV Europe Music Awards won Scotland priceless world-wide exposure and an £8.9 million jackpot in direct economic benefit. Figures announced in March 2004 by Scotland's Tourism Minister, Frank McAveety, reveal that the rock and pop extravaganza delivered more than double the original estimate of economic benefit to the city and Scotland. It was anticipated when MTV Europe announced Edinburgh would host the 2003 'Oscars' of the music world that they would be worth £4.2 million to the economy. The real benefits are identified in an economic study of the event undertaken by independent consultants SQW on behalf of the public sector partners, Scottish Enterprise, City of Edinburgh Council and EventScotland, who supported the Awards with funding of £750 000.

The breakdown of where the benefits were realized in hosting the show, which attracted a galaxy of the world's hottest music talent, indicates:

- Edinburgh gained £6.4 million extra expenditure
- Lothians benefited by £300 000
- Scotland benefited from another £2.2 million of additional spend, giving a total of £8.9 million

MTV Europe's free performance in Princes Street Gardens, arranged as a thank you to Edinburgh and Scotland, and the first time MTV Europe has undertaken such a production, generated £1.3 million.

Television and media evaluation

The show, hosted by Christina Aguilera and featuring Beyoncé, Kylie Minogue, Justin Timberlake, Travis and a host of other stars, was beamed around the world in 77 hours of programming by MTV's global networks. MTV's viewing audiences showed a remarkable increase over the previous year. Even Spain, which was host to the show in Barcelona in 2002 increased its viewing figures. The UK audience was up 200 per cent, Sweden increased by 25 per cent, Spain increased by 45 per cent and America recorded a 38 per cent rise to its highest ever level for the show.

The study also identifies the value of television and print media coverage of the event.

- MTV's global networks screened 77 hours of coverage worth an estimated £8.6 million
- World-wide print media coverage in 2094 articles carried by 928 publications in 19 countries has an estimated value of £4.8 million.

Supplier evaluation

Hotels in Edinburgh received bookings valued at £2.2 million with 2360 more rooms being sold across the week of the event compared with the same week in 2002. Occupancy levels for the night of the event were 26 per cent up at 93 per cent while occupancy for the week rose by 9.4 per cent to 83 per cent compared with the same period in 2002.

During the show, the city and Scotland received 45 celebrity endorsements which the report says have 'a huge value' in reaching younger audiences and raising the profile of Edinburgh and Scotland as a tourist destination and place to live and work.

Retailers provided mixed feedback on the impact of the event with 37 per cent recording an increase in business, 37 per cent reporting no impact while 26 per cent said it had a negative effect on them. But 62.5 per cent said the Awards would provide long-term benefit.

Encouraging the use of local suppliers by MTV Networks Europe in supporting the production of the event was a key objective of the public sector's funding for the project. This resulted in more than 50 per cent of suppliers being Scotland-based, the highest involvement of local companies in the ten year history of the MTV Europe Music Awards. The study reveals that these companies between them earned a total of £1.883 million.

Evaluation of perceptions

Both MTV Europe and the public sector, commissioned reports on people's perceptions of the Edinburgh event. Those questioned for MTV placed the appeal of the event above the Brit Awards and the Oscars. Their report discovered that many attendees had been offered up to £1000 for their tickets. The public sector study found that among corporate guests, journalists and the stars' agents, 83 per cent rated the Edinburgh event the best they had ever attended. MTV Europe proclaimed the event their best ever and presented Edinburgh and Scotland with a special MTV Award, normally given only to the winning performers, in recognition of the support they received.

Views of key stakeholders

Commenting on the findings, Scotland's Minister for Tourism, Culture and Sport, Frank McAveety, said: 'Edinburgh and Scotland have benefited immensely by having the MTV Awards here. This was a hugely successful event, with the short term major economic benefits twice as high as was forecast. And we should not forget the long-term benefits we can expect as this occasion delivered a global profile for Scotland as a world class location for tourism and business. We can now look forward to building on this success to attract other world class events'.

Jim McFarlane, Chief Executive, Scottish Enterprise Edinburgh and Lothian, said: 'These results are a well earned tribute to the creativity, innovation and excellence of effort invested by everyone involved in the production of a star studded event that has promoted Edinburgh and Scotland around the world. The headline figures are really just the tip of the iceberg in measuring the value of the MTV Europe Music Awards 2003. The lasting impact will come from realizing the benefits of the exposure to a young, increasingly mobile global audience and the endorsement of the city, and Scotland as a world class location by universally recognized celebrities. The Awards were a challenge which we met. The standard has been set and the bar raised in terms of what we must seek to achieve in attracting international events of every nature. A prime lesson that can be learned from the success of the MTV Europe Music Awards 2003 is the effectiveness of real partnership working that has a "can do" attitude'.

Council Leader Donald Anderson said: 'It is a tribute to the huge success of the MTV Europe Music Awards that the economic findings have more than doubled from the original estimate. An £8.9 million boost to the Scottish economy, of which more than 70 per cent has gone directly to Edinburgh's economy, is a very significant return. It is clear from these findings that through MTV's visit to the city and the resulting world-wide media coverage we have reached new audiences, showing that Edinburgh is among the world's top destinations for visitors and conferences and events of this scale. MTV gave Edinburgh and one billion viewers worldwide, a fantastic party and it was an unforgettable experience that has left a lasting legacy for the city and its people'.

David Williams, Chief Executive, EventScotland added: 'These are very positive results reflecting the strength of both public and private sector partnerships, and the economic benefits associated with major events. We will use the example of the MTV Europe Awards 2003 when bidding for other events, to demonstrate Scotland's experience and capability of staging world class events'.

Richard Godfrey, Executive Producer, MTV Europe Music Awards, said: 'MTV Europe is delighted that Scotland has enjoyed such huge economic benefit as a result of the show coming to Edinburgh – this news duly caps the best ever MTV Europe Music Awards. Edinburgh was the perfect location for a show of this scale and the success, the show was built on our fantastic partnerships with Edinburgh and Scotland. Scotland is a world-class destination for high-profile events'.

Summary

Evaluation is key to ensuring that lessons are learnt from events and that the wider implications and impacts can be fully assessed. EventScotland, Scottish Enterprise Edinburgh and Lothian, City of Edinburgh Council and the Scottish Executive were keen to ensure that a range of perspectives on the MTV Music Awards were evaluated in order to gain an understanding of the true value in hosting events of this type and to inform the wider events policy for Scotland. Evaluating the 10th MTV Europe Music Awards provided some very useful insights and data, which have demonstrated the impact and also the capacity of Scottish suppliers to deliver world class events.

For further information about MTV, please visit www.mtveurope.com. To access the full impact evaluation report, please visit www.scottish-enterprise.com.

By Scottish Enterprise Edinburgh and Lothian, City of Edinburgh Council and EventScotland.

Questions

1. Identify the benefits of hosting an event such as this to Edinburgh and the wider region.
2. Discuss what activities the stakeholders in this event could undertake in order to maximize the benefits of hosting the event.
3. Identify which methods of evaluation were demonstrated in this case study.
4. Identify and discuss other methods of evaluation that may have been appropriate.
5. Investigate and discuss what support is available for attracting events to Edinburgh and Scotland.

Case study 14.2

T in the Park

From its beginnings at Strathclyde Country Park in 1994 to the twelfth festival at Balado in 2005, T in the Park has grown in size and influence to become one of the most important and critically acclaimed music events on the international festival circuit, as well as Scotland's most popular outdoor event.

Now attracting over 60 000 music fans from Scotland, the UK, and beyond each day, T in the Park is consistently a sell out success. This popularity can be attributed to the festival's unique atmosphere, legendary crowd, and an annual line-up that is one of the most exciting in the world. With over 120 artists performing across 8 stages over 2 days, T in the Park consistently attracts the finest homegrown talent, such as Franz Ferdinand, Idlewild and Biffy Clyro mixed with major international artists like REM, Oasis, Manic Street Preachers and Radiohead.

History

T in the Park was established when DF Concerts, one of the UK's leading concert promoters, teamed up with Scotland's favourite pint Tennent's Lager, who had a history of supporting the Scottish live music scene in the late 1980s. DF Concerts' founder Stuart Clumpas had for some time been considering the development of Scotland's first large scale, multi-stage music event to act as an annual focal point for the music scene, and Tennent's were keen to further increase its support of live music.

The first T in the Park took place at Strathclyde Country Park in 1994, with DF Concerts teaming up with MCD Promotions of Eire to create a sister company Big Day Out to promote the event. The festival was an artistic success, and while financially it was less successful, it fired the enthusiasm of the 17 000 fans that turned up each day, and subsequent years have been greeted with ever increasing popularity and acclaim.

Development

In 1997, when the festival's original site was developed as a supermarket, Balado Activity Centre, near Kinross, provided an excellent alternative at the very heart of Scotland. This relocation has made T in the Park more accessible for fans travelling from remote parts of Scotland – for example, Citylink, as official transport provider for the festival, provides 200 shuttle buses connecting Scotland's major towns and cities with Balado. The new location is also more convenient for all major cities and other parts of the UK – this is reflected in the increasingly diverse T in the Park audience, with 40 per cent of ticket buyers coming from outside Scotland, making the event one of the country's biggest annual tourist attractions. The scope of the event has increased over time with the NME Stage, the Slam Tent, the X Tent, the T Break Stage.

On-site activity at T in the Park has seen many changes over the years, with 85 per cent of the audience now opting for the 'true festival experience' of camping on-site for the whole weekend, compared to just 5 per cent in 1994 – making it the largest campsite in Scotland. The festival's main arena now measures over 42 acres with an additional 85 acres making up the campsite areas. The festival's appeal has also been boosted by the addition of a funfair, a global food village and a range of additional bars and entertainment – for example, 34 unique Multi-Dispense Units across the site pour 816 pints of Tennents a minute to keep up with the demand, while over 650 portaloos across the site cope with the aftermath. In total, around 4000 people work behind the scenes each year to bring T in the Park together, with some working all year round.

The festival will be covered extensively by the BBC again in 2005. BBC television will transmit exclusive coverage from T in the Park, with a continued commitment across the terrestrial and digital network planned for the event. Radio One is continuing its consistent support for the festival, with an increased programming commitment across the network.

Evaluation

Despite the large crowds that descend upon Balado each year, the event enjoys an extremely warm and positive reception from the local council and surrounding communities and recently became the only festival in the UK to have been awarded a three-year licence for the second time.

A recent survey also calculated that the festival generates upwards of £3 million, for the local and Scottish economies. This was recognized by the First Minister Jack McConnell who visited the event in its Tenth Year in 2003 and said: 'It is great to see so many young people enjoying themselves. The festival is very valuable to the Scottish economy and it symbolizes the modern Scotland we want to portray'.

The last two years of T in the Park have arguably been the festival's best to date. 2003 saw T celebrate its Tenth Year, which helped to generate the fantastic party atmosphere over the two days. Tickets for the event sold out weeks in advance, the sun shone over Balado, and major international names such as REM and The Flaming Lips performed alongside the UK's biggest acts including Coldplay and Idlewild. The success of 2003 led to the festival's earliest sell out ever in 2004. Despite an increase in capacity to over 65 000 each day, music fans snapped up tickets 10 weeks in advance to ensure that they secured their place at the festival.

There was some disappointment over the cancellation of headliner David Bowie, due to ill health, however, 2004 more than lived up to expectation with The Darkness stepping up to fill the slot alongside performances from The Strokes, PJ Harvey, Kings Of Leon and the Pixies. With the return of the new X Tent, the sultry sounds of the Bacardi B Bar, Scotland's best unsigned talent in the T Break stage and another sunshine filled weekend, T in the Park delivered yet another legendary weekend for music fans.

Tickets for the T in the Park 2005 went on sale for a limited period in 2004 when festival organizers Big Day Out Ltd., and founding partners, Tennent's Lager took the unprecedented move of putting 2005's tickets on sale just one day after 2004's event. During this month long limited buying period last summer, 33 per cent of event tickets were sold. This astounding figure, before the line-up had been revealed, remains a testament to the festival's consistent popularity and stature amongst global music fans. The remainder of event tickets was put on sale on Saturday 12 February 2005 at 9a.m. and took just 4 days to sell out completely, five months before the event and beating the previous year's record.

With over 120 acts playing across 9 stages to thousands of music fans from all over the world, this early sell out confirms the festival's consistent popularity and stature on the world musical calendar. The initial line up for T in the Park 2005, announced in February, included Travis, James Brown, Foo Fighters, New Order, Keane, Embrace, The Streets, Audioslave, Beautiful South, The Coral, Green Day, The Killers, Prodigy, Kasabian, Ian Brown, Kaiser Chiefs, Joss Stone, Snoop Dogg, Dizzee Rascal, Razorlight, Biffy Clyro, Athlete and Queen's of the Stone Age.

Summary

With a decade of success behind it and a further weekend of the very best music and unique atmosphere ahead in 2005, T in the Park can claim to be one of the British music industry's greatest success stories. T in the Park's development in both size and status has allowed DF Concerts to effectively combine the creative and business elements needed to produce an event with both financial stability and music industry prestige, ensuring it attracts the very best artists to Scotland each year.

Tennent's Lager's commitment and successful involvement in T in the Park has yielded many awards, amongst these the prestigious Hollis Award for Sponsorship Continuity in 2003, which not only saw a fitting tribute to T in the Park's Tenth Year, but saw the event beat Nationwide (Football Association and England Team), HSBC (ITV Drama Premieres), and Ford (UEFA Champions League) for the award. Finally, testament to the excellent event management of DF Concerts, T in the Park also won the award for Best Facilities and Organisation at the inaugural UK Festival Awards in 2004, as well as coming second in both the Best Major Festival and Most Memorable Live Moment categories (for Scissor Sister' Jake Shears donning a tiny tartan kilt on stage).

For further information about T in the Park, please visit www.tinthepark.com.

By DF Concerts and Tennent's Lager.

Questions

1. What do you see as the successful components of this festival which have seen it grow so quickly and result in tickets being sold out months before the event?
2. T in the Park has developed over the years to ensure that it can compete on the international stage. What evaluation methods would you propose the organizers undertake to ensure that T in the Park remains a must-see festival?
3. What criteria would you suggest for the success of the event to be measured from the organizer and other stakeholders' perspective?
4. What questions would you include in a visitor survey for T in the Park to obtain the data identified in question 3?

Section Four
Trends and issues

This final part looks at current and emerging topics in events management. It examines societal trends and their impacts on events, the growth of the event industry, the professionalisation of event management, event franchising, the use of events in skills development and training, information technology, transfer-of knowledge programmes, increased government involvement in events, and the adoption of environmental management practices by events.

Chapter 15

Issues and trends

Learning Objectives

After studying this chapter, you should be able to:

- list and discuss the major trends and issues in the event industry
- discuss the changes in society that are affecting the nature of events
- identify and discuss the major factors affecting the growth of the event industry
- list and discuss the factors in events management becoming recognized as a profession
- discuss the impact of information technology on the nature of contemporary events
- describe the impact of risk management on the events industry
- discuss the expansion of events education
- understand and describe the increased government involvement in events
- describe and discuss the factors influencing the adoption of environmental management practices by events.

Introduction

This chapter examines current trends and issues in the events industry. A trend is defined as a general direction in which a company or industry is moving. Issues are problems that are common across the industry. The solution to a number of related issues may result in a trend in the industry. The issues outlined in this chapter have a common thread: they are the growing pains of a young industry. As the industry grows, it absorbs older industries and redefines current ones.

Societal trends and their impact on events

Throughout the developed world, demographic changes are profoundly affecting societies and, consequently, the types of event and festival that will grow in popularity in the future. According to the World Bank (2004), these trends include the ageing of the population, a dramatic decrease in the birth rate, and a significant increase in migration from less developed countries to developed countries.

The ageing of the population is caused by people living longer as a result of improvements in health care (that is, a decrease in the death rate) and a decrease in the number of children born per woman (that is, a decrease in the birth rate). For example, the average family size has been falling since 1960s – in England the birth rate peaked at 2.95 children in 1964 and had fallen to a record low of 1.63 in 2001, though this is beginning to slowly rise. Alongside this, life expectancy rose to 67 for males and 69 for females, accompanied by a shift in population – in 1950 only 1 in 10 of the population was over 65, in 2003 this had risen to 1 in 6, while by 2007 there will be more people over 65 than under 16 (HM Government, 2005). This means family size has reduced and probably will continue to reduce, which increases the disposable income per household. Many other developed countries have experienced even more dramatic increases in the average age. In Japan, only 11.6 per cent of the population was 65 years or older in 1989, but over 25 per cent of the population is projected to be in that age category by 2030 (allrefer.com, 2005). The 'age pyramid' in developed countries is no longer a pyramid with the largest number of citizens being the youngest; rather, it is bulging around the middle years, as if to represent a stereotypical middle-age spread.

In many developed countries, as in the United Kingdom, increased immigration is used to ensure growth in the number of working-age residents. According to the National Statistics (2004), immigration was responsible for two-thirds of the population increase for the year to mid-2003 with higher levels of in- and out-migration.

These demographic changes will have several impacts on events produced in the future. As ethnic groups living outside their country of origin increase in number in host countries such as the UK, the number and scale of events that celebrate these cultures will increase. At the same time, events that celebrate (perhaps in reaction) the dominant or mainstream culture will also increase in importance. The VE (Victory in Europe) Day celebrations, for example, continue though it is over 60 years since the end of World War II. Other celebrations of the dominant culture that are expected to increase in significance are traditional sporting events (for example, test cricket), commemorations of historic events (for example, Battle of Trafalgar as part of the Sea Britain Festival in 2005) and long-standing events such as the Royal Welsh Show.

The demographic bulge (known sometimes as the baby-boom generation) will also affect future festivals and events. This generation's tastes and attitudes were formed in the 1960s and the music, lifestyle and values from that era, along with the events that celebrate them, will gain even more significance in years to come. An excellent example is the Cambridge Folk Festival, which gets larger each year.

People in developed nations are also becoming much better educated. Almost 30 per cent of school leavers now attend university, and this number is expected to grow with a government target of 50 per cent. This should ensure the market for more cerebral events grows as the proportion of university graduates in the population grows.

The growth of the Events Industry

A major trend worldwide over the past decade was the growth and expansion of the events industry. Having emerged as an industry in its own right through the 1990s, the events industry continues to grow, fuelled by economic growth and the increase in leisure spending in most western countries. In many of the UK's cities and towns, an almost bewildering array of public entertainment events is on offer each weekend, catering to almost every conceivable taste and interest group. Events have become an essential element of contemporary life, linked inseparably with tourism promotion, government strategies and corporate marketing. Major sporting events, along with the marketing campaigns and controversies that accompany them, feature almost daily in our newspapers and electronic media. Corporate use of event sponsorships and event marketing keep events at the forefront of our awareness. The term 'events', along with the associated management process and industry structure, has considerable currency and profile. Many other areas that were previously seen as distinct – such as meetings, conferences, exhibitions, festivals, major sporting fixtures and corporate functions – are now also perceived as part of a wider events industry.

Events have become so all encompassing and far reaching that it is almost impossible to accurately gauge the full size of the industry. If a major car company uses an event to launch a new model, it has no responsibility or even desire to notify anyone of this event other than the participants and guests. The event thus remains difficult to identify by anyone attempting to track and quantify the events industry. Nevertheless, evidence of the growth of the industry is overwhelming. The number of events listed by tourism organizations and 'what's on' entertainment directories, compared with the number of 10 years ago, indicates the extent of this increase.

Among the reasons for the virtual explosion of the events industry over the past decade are:

- rising levels of disposable income, combined with increasing time pressure, resulting in the demand for structured, high-quality leisure experiences.
- increased government awareness of the tourism and economic benefits of events, leading to further development of government event strategies and funding.
- growing corporate affluence and awareness of the marketing power of events, leading to increased use of events both for internal staff training and morale building, and as marketing and communications tools.
- increased awareness of event management as a cohesive discipline with the ability to focus resources and deliver specific objectives.

Increased demand and supply

This exponential increase in the number of events has created a demand for qualified event managers and for industry suppliers to fill the increasing need for event-related goods and services. The number of venues has increased, both at the level of publicly funded recreation spaces, conference and exhibition centres, and at the level of privately funded meeting facilities in hotels, stadia or arenas. The British Association of Conference Destinations (BACD) Investment Register provides a useful means of tracking some of these major developments across the UK (BACD, 2005). The need for unique and interesting event spaces has resulted in museums, historic houses, councils, universities and other property holders developing managed special event facilities as an additional revenue stream. A plethora of specialized hire companies, caterers, entertainment agencies, designers, publicists, technical producers, lighting and sound personnel, set builders and pyrotechnicians has also risen to meet the needs of this burgeoning new industry. A glance at the Yellow Pages directory (or online version Yell.com) under categories such as conference and event management and event suppliers will reveal the size and scope of this recent phenomenon. Event industry associations and directories have struggled to keep pace with this rate of expansion, and websites such as www.eventmagazine.co.uk and www.citmagazine.co.uk have taken an increasing role in tracking and communicating the growth and changes in the industry.

In a competitive marketplace, the supply of goods and services tends to rise to meet perceived demand; so far, the trend in the demand for event services continues to be upward. Whether this trend continues and how the industry might weather any future downturn in the economy remain the subject of speculation.

The growth of corporate events

One area strongly fuelling the expansion is the corporate sector. In the halcyon days of the 1980s boom, many companies became involved in event sponsorship, often tailored to the tastes and interests of senior management. With the recession of the late 1980s and early 1990s, there was a general cutback in spending on event sponsorships. As the financial climate improved through the late 1990s, many large companies re-entered the sponsorship market, but with a greater focus and rigour (Geldard and Sinclair, 2003). At a time when traditional advertising was perceived to be losing impact as a result of buyer cynicism and market clutter, events were perceived as a means of cutting through the clutter to reach consumers in terms of their own interests and the areas that were important to them. One sponsor might reach motor sport enthusiasts by sponsoring a car race, for example, or another sponsor might increase the profile of a youth-oriented product by sponsoring a rock concert.

Against the background of increasing corporate affluence, companies also expanded their internal use of events to train and reward staff, improve company morale, educate dealer networks and maintain customer relations. In many instances, the corporate sector wholeheartedly embraced events, but with a new rigour. Events were no longer the prerogative of senior management, but were selected and run by marketing departments or dedicated events teams, and subject to the same return-on-investment analysis used for marketing areas such as advertising and direct marketing. Figure 15.1 shows an example of an approval chain for a corporate event. (Chapter 10 also discusses control.)

Return On Investment (ROI) has been a subject of some discussion, with a need for clearer understanding identified. Industry magazines and association events have sought to address this with educating their markets about the tools and techniques available. For example, the Meeting Professionals International (MPI) Foundation have undertaken research and produced a number of articles on ROI, together with industry projects (visit www.mpifoundation.org for further details).

A major issue to arise over the past few years is the role of procurement/purchasing departments when putting business out to tender, which has lead to heated discussions at industry events and in the industry magazines. The tension has arisen due to a potential lack of understanding about the role that event management companies play in developing events and the differences in aims and terminology in use. In a bid to increase understanding of the roles of both parties, initiatives are being developed, for example, with the Chartered Institute of Purchasing and Supply (CIPS) working with Eventia with workshops to educate procurement officers about the best way to work with event management companies (and vice versa).

The growth of international event companies

As events became established as a significant component of the marketing mix, they became increasingly subject to rigorous evaluation of their outcomes, leading to the

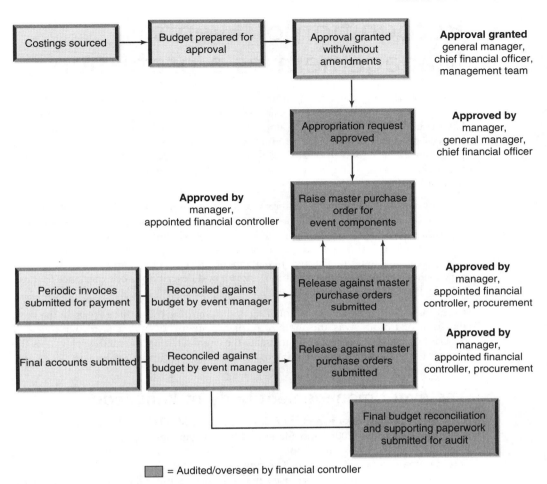

Figure 15.1 Corporate event financial management

need for standardized event management processes. Companies began to create event management teams, often within their marketing divisions. Global companies began to streamline their event production to ensure the delivery of a standard event product over different markets and locations. The launch of a new Mercedes Benz model, for example, would employ the same format and style whether conducted in Berlin, Tokyo, London or Sydney. To be able to deliver a standardized global event product to their clients, some of the larger event companies, particularly in the USA, bought out local event companies in different markets – for example, the large US company Jack Morton purchased the Communications Division of Caribiner International and rebranded to Jack Morton Worldwide to reflect their global presence. As this trend towards globalized event management continues, the question of local cultures and differences arises. The same event may not be able to be adapted from, say, Los Angeles to Hong Kong without taking careful account of the individual cultural nuances of each location. Arguably, local companies may sometimes be in a better situation to appreciate and respond to these cultural differences, although the process of standardization seems likely to continue in an increasingly globalized world.

Recognition of Events Management as a profession

When considering the events industry, it is easy to be misdirected and believe it is only about events. Events can be compared to any project-based industry. Civil engineering, for example, is not just about the product; it is a description of the process needed to create that product. Event management, therefore, is about the processes that are used to create and sustain the event. Recognition of this process is the basis for recognizing event management as a profession.

A profession is characterized by:

- *a body of knowledge* – this is the library of the profession. It is made up of information from other professions such as logistics, contract management and marketing. Journals and textbooks describe the body of knowledge and continually refine it.
- *a methodology* – this is made up of a series of processes or tasks, which can be described and taught. The risk management process is an example.
- *heuristics* – these are 'rules of thumb', stories and descriptions of experience that can be learned only 'on the job'.

Event management is gradually collating and describing these three areas. In the past, the 'rule of thumb' was the main way of organizing events. The recognition and description of the processes used to create the event – that is, the methodology – is the moment when event management progresses from a skill to a profession.

The event management body of knowledge

The event management body of knowledge (EMBOK) is being defined and developed. O'Toole (2002) and Silvers (2004a) began developing categories for the EMBOK, as described in Chapter 9, with the work further progressed by the International EMBOK Executive. The purpose of EMBOK is, 'To create a framework of the knowledge and processes used in event management that may be customized to meet the needs of various cultures, governments, education programmes, and organizations'. Figure 15.2 illustrates the EMBOK structure – for further definition of the knowledge domains, core values, phases, classes and processes, and to view how the EMBOK project is developing, please visit www.embok.org.

Standards

Combined with the advance of the EMBOK is the development of competency standards for event management. For example, in the United Kingdom, competency standards were developed for the National Vocational Qualifications, while comparable standards have also been developed in Australia, South Africa and Canada. A competency standard for event management gives the industry a benchmark to measure excellence in management. Previously, this benchmark was the success of the event; however, stakeholders cannot wait until the event to find out whether the event management is competent – by then, it is too late.

Linked to the development of standards is the interest in ethical standards for events. Many associations have codes of conduct, codes of ethics or standards which their members agree to abide by. These standards are designed to ensure best and honest practice in place throughout the industry. Although there are many

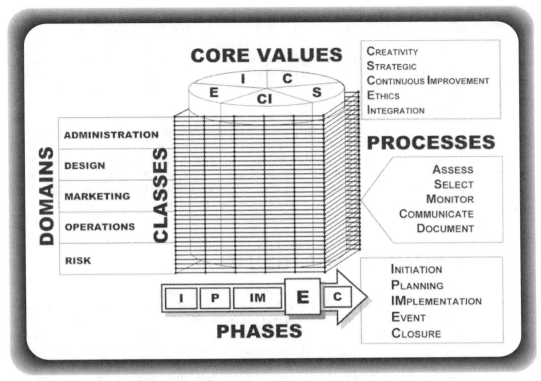

CORE VALUES

CREATIVITY
STRATEGIC
CONTINUOUS IMPROVEMENT
ETHICS
INTEGRATION

PROCESSES

ASSESS
SELECT
MONITOR
COMMUNICATE
DOCUMENT

DOMAINS

ADMINISTRATION
DESIGN
MARKETING
OPERATIONS
RISK

CLASSES

I C CI S E

INITIATION
PLANNING
IMPLEMENTATION
EVENT
CLOSURE

I P IM E C

PHASES

Figure 15.2 International EMBOK structure
Source: International EMBOK Executive (2005)

professional organizations operating within the events industry, there are still some examples of poor practice, for example, through the theft of ideas or poaching of clients/business, and ongoing discussions about the ethics of (hidden) commissions. Allen (2003), Goldblatt (2005) and Sorin (2003) provide a detailed discussion of this important issue.

The search for standards has led to the development of guidelines including outdoor events (BSI, 2004) and stewarding (BSI, 2003). With a constantly changing business environment, risk management is perceived as the way to handle the uncertainty. The requirement for accountability is behind the adoption of International Standards Organization (ISO) standards implemented in the UK through British Standards. Many government departments and large companies are investigating their events to see whether they can comply with ISO certification.

Management systems

When this need for standards and competency levels is integrated with the use of software, a management system emerges. PRINCE 2, for example, is a management system that some clients have requested their event management company or event office use. MS Project software is another. Both systems can create status reports. These work-in-progress reports are an example of the need for accountability of event management. They are a response to clients' and other stakeholders' demands to know how the organizing of an event is progressing.

A part of the trend of accountability is the need to measure success. The success of an event can be measured by the attitudes of the attendees surveyed after the event. However, attitudes are too intangible to be used in a business case for an event. Many event sponsors thus now regard the economic impact of an event as a key success factor. In the past, there was no accurate way to measure the economic impact, which was often exaggerated and more of a 'wish list'. More accurate methods of measuring this impact are being developed.

The introduction of methods to measure intangible benefits is another trend in the event industry. Consumer surplus is one such method, whereby the attendees are asked to assess the monetary value of the event to them. If this value exceeds the ticket price, the event is said to have a consumer surplus. The exhibition industry has a number of metrics to value an event. Other metrics include the generation of leads and sales directly attributed to the event. The measurement of intangibles is important in the feasibility study of an event and in the presentation of the business case.

Event franchising

With the development and recognition of a management system comes the ability to transfer this system to other events – that is, the ability to franchise. The successful event or festival becomes a model that can be developed into another event anywhere in the world. The value is not only in the single event, it is in the method used to organize the event. Event franchising is common in the sport industry and exhibitions. The Olympic Games is perhaps the largest example. Numerous sports races, such as the Formula 1 Grand Prix, 'fun runs' and rough water swims, are also franchised events. Further, some corporate events (such as seminars and conferences) are variations on an original model. An example of successful event franchising is the Night of the Ad Eaters. This started as a small event in France and now takes place in 160 cities across 47 countries, including Mongolia, Mexico and Japan.

Again, the value of a management system is illustrated. Without a system, there is nothing to pass on except personal experience.

The use of events in skills development and training

An unexpected opportunity has emerged from the trend towards standards and competency levels. In South Africa, the National Qualification Framework includes the experience and knowledge gained from working on events as credit points towards certification. This opens up a new use for events as vehicles for training.

With major events such as the Cricket World Cup, the South African Government had a platform to train volunteers: 'The National Skills Development Strategy Skills for productive citizenship for all has a mission to equip South Africans with the skills to succeed in the global market place' (ICC Cricket World Cup, 2003).

The Training of Volunteers 2003 programme was aligned to this skills development strategy. Once volunteers were registered, they were assessed for their current abilities by a process called 'recognition of prior learning'. As they worked on the event, they were trained in the national unit standards:

- caring for customers
- organizing oneself in the workplace
- maintaining occupational health and safety
- functioning as a team.

This innovative scheme now allows the South African Government to achieve maximum value from events: major events are used as a way to restructure the new South Africa. The result is that most of the volunteers are young. The skills they learn are not wasted, but rather used towards their careers. The 2002 Manchester Commonwealth Games used a similar approach, with the PGVP (discussed in Chapter 6) ensuring that volunteers can continue to use their skills.

Information technology

Any advance in information technology has an effect on events. Information technology permeates almost all areas of event management, from the sound system used at the event to the ticketing and attendee registration. The software used to manage events has become more sophisticated as the power of the microchip has increased. USI, one of the largest event software companies in the world, claims that the trend is towards 'thin client computing'. This means the software is not on the event management company's computer, but held on the software company's computer and accessed over the Internet by the event company when needed.

A further trend in computing is the growth of the Internet, which is used for research, marketing, communication and reporting. Any one of the knowledge areas of management outlined in Chapter 9 can benefit from the Internet. Being so pervasive, the Internet can no longer be described as only a trend.

The use of personal digital assistants (PDA), or hand-held computers, is also increasing at events. These pocket-sized devices can contain all the information about the event. The complete event manual can be placed into a PDA. Information can quickly be retrieved and new data can be entered. They can also be effectively deployed for visitor research with survey software such as SNAP.

Some events rely on the anonymity of the new media to exist. Rave parties are an example. By using SMS messages, these parties are kept exclusive.

Risk management

As mentioned earlier, the adoption of risk management is a strong trend in the event industry around the world. Reasons for this trend include the following:

- Event managers are increasingly obligated to produce a risk management plan to gain insurance cover, or to control premium levels.
- Internationally, various court cases and coronial inquiries have demanded to sight the risk management plans of the event companies involved.
- Government departments at various levels have adopted a risk management process and require their contractors do the same.
- Occupational health and safety codes recommend the use of risk management.
- Guidelines, such as The Event Safety Guide (HSE, 1999) and PAS 51 (BSI, 2004), call for the use of formal risk management.

- The event manuals published by local authorities, such as the City of Edinburgh and City of Westminster's event planning guides (City of Edinburgh Council, 2002; City of Westminster, 2005) ask event managers to produce a risk assessment, while City of Westminster provide specific guidance on preferred risk assessment practice (City of Westminster, 2000).
- Government funding bodies and authorities may request that a risk management plan be produced before giving a grant or approval.

Hannam (2004, p. 103) notes that there has been legal requirement to conduct risk assessments and make any changes required for over 20 years, with the Management of Health and Safety at Work Regulations 1999 detailing that the company must complete assessments on all activities and record any significant findings and that employees must be provided with relevant and suitable information about risks to themselves.

The above list constitutes the external pressure on event managers to use a risk management plan. However, there are internal reasons as well. A number of event companies have found that the risk standard improves their ability to manage an event. It is a formal way of looking for problems and solving them; it captures the whole process, so that process can be improved for each event. The case study in Chapter 11 demonstrates the effective use of risk management as part of general logistics management.

The increased threat to security

The changing world has introduced a new risk to public and private events – the threat of terrorism. Wars, the 11 September 2001 terrorist attacks in New York and Washington, the 7 July 2005 terrorist attack in London, the Bali bombings and the terrorist attack in Madrid have all affected events in UK and elsewhere. Major public events in UK are now subject to intense security, unheard of a few years ago. Simple matters, such as a car parked outside an event, can now take on an ominous meaning.

The expansion of events education

Over the past ten years, there has been significant growth in events-related courses. For example, in the United Kingdom, there are over 140 event-related undergraduate courses and seven postgraduate courses offered by over 41 colleges and universities. In Australia, the Event Educators Forum 2004 identified 212 registered training organizations and 23 universities with courses that include significant event management components. This pattern of course development is also being reflected in other countries, including Ireland, Germany, the Netherlands, India and America.

Important issues have been (1) where event courses sit in the overall pattern of further and higher education, and (2) what the content of such courses should be. Traditionally, the first generation of event courses comprised individual subjects within wider tourism, hospitality and leisure programmes. They often emphasized the meetings, incentives, conferences and exhibitions aspect of events and focused on the management of meetings and conferences in a tourism industry context. As the definition of events has broadened to include public and government events, new courses have been developed with a wider focus encompassing the full spectrum of event types. These courses sometimes sit within the broader framework of arts, sports and business management programmes. More recent courses have been developed as stand-alone programmes, for example, in events management, encompassing the full range of contemporary events.

The development of events education has been recognized through the development of the Events Management Educators Forum in the UK and the Event Educators Forum in Australia, with similar developments emerging elsewhere. In addition, formal recognition of events management as a subject area has led to the formation of AEME (Association for Events Management Education) as the subject association in the UK and acting as a vehicle for the future development of education and best practice in industry.

Transfer-of-knowledge programmes

Allied to the increase in event management programmes has been the identification of knowledge involved in the management of major events, and the formal and informal transfer of this knowledge to other events. The International Olympic Committee (IOC) paid $5 million to the Sydney Organizing Committee for the Olympic Games (SOCOG) for the intellectual property arising from the 2000 Olympics. This material was then made available to organizers of both the Salt Lake City Winter Olympics in 2002 and the Athens Summer Olympics in 2004. Known as the Transfer of Know-how (TOK) Program, the knowledge gained from the Sydney Olympic Games was transmitted via 90-plus individual guides and a debrief session by senior managers in Athens in November 2000. This knowledge will form the basis of a generic Olympics management guide, to which successive Olympic Games organizers will add. Olympic Games Knowledge Services, wholly owned by the IOC, has been formed to assist in tailoring the TOK Programme to the needs of individual Olympic Games and future bidding cities. It will also identify and credit Olympic Games experts and engage them to pass on their experience (Universitat Autònoma de Barcelona, 2005). The case study later in this chapter provides a detailed account of the development of transfer-of-knowledge programmes in relation to the Olympic movement.

The growth of events research

Paralleling the growth in events education and transfer of knowledge has been the growth of academic research on events, leading to a greater understanding of events' contexts, impacts and outcomes. Prior to 2000, event research was generally incorporated in wider fields such as tourism and hospitality, business and economics. In 2000, the Australian Centre for Event Management at the University of Technology, Sydney conducted the first dedicated international event management research conference, 'Events beyond 2000 – setting the agenda'. This conference has continued as a biennial conference with an increasing number of dedicated conferences now being developed, and event management has become increasingly recognized as a distinct field of study. The journal Festival Management and Event Tourism has been refocused as Event Management, Journal of Convention & Exhibition Management as Journal of Convention & Event Tourism and a new journal, International Journal of Events Management Research has joined the market. In addition, specialized event education and research websites such as WorldofEvents.net and discussion lists such as Event-Management (www.jiscmail.ac.uk/lists/event-management.html) have been developed to disseminate information. Further, event industry associations such as the International Festivals and Events Association, Meeting Professionals International and the International Special Events Society have developed academic research strands in their annual conference programmes or are actively encouraging the increasing participation of the academic community.

Much event research is still dispersed over a wide range of journals from allied fields, and some key topics remain under-researched. However, event research is continuing to expand and to provide valuable insights into the behaviour of events, and a better understanding of event management processes and outcomes.

Increasing government involvement in events

As the benefits and impacts of events have been increasingly recognized, governments at all levels have assumed a growing role in event creation, funding, management and regulation. Most major events – including the Olympic and Commonwealth Games, the Grand Prix and Expo circuits and international single-sport championships such as those in soccer, rugby union, athletics, tennis and swimming – are subject to bids by national associations. Given their costs and infrastructure needs, these bids are increasingly supported and/or underwritten by local or national governments or regional development agencies. The IOC has gone so far as to state that bids to host the Olympic Games will be considered only if they have the full and explicit backing of the host city government – for example, the successful London 2012 Olympic Games bid included messages of support from the Prime Minister Tony Blair and the Mayor of London, Ken Livingstone. Likewise, many homegrown festivals, community and cultural events seek the financial and organizational support of government. Major conferences and exhibitions also require government assistance through the provision of infrastructure such as convention and exhibition centres, and the support of convention bureaus, dedicated events teams or bidding units able to mount bids and orchestrate resources.

The creation of event strategies

Recognizing the social, cultural and economic benefits of these events, but aware of limited funds and conflicting needs, governments at all levels are increasingly devising event strategies to assist policy development and establish funding priorities. The number and extent of these strategies have grown in recent years, with an increasing number of local authorities and other agencies having a formal events or festivals strategy and providing event support (for example, EventScotland or Northern Ireland Events Company). This situation is mirrored globally, with Australia and Denmark among several countries to develop event strategies in the recent past. These strategies set out to identify the role of events in their country/region/city, and to provide policy guidelines and action plans for the funding, management, coordination, regulation and promotion of events. These strategies acknowledge the multiple roles of government as event host organizations, funding and regulatory bodies.

Event portfolio management

Most event strategies acknowledge the advantages of a region or city having a balanced portfolio of events spread across the annual calendar and including different types of event. Edinburgh has built on the success and reputation of the established International and Fringe Festivals and the Edinburgh Tattoo to build a year-round calendar, which also includes Hogmanay and the International Jazz and Blues, Science and Book festivals. Well-balanced and well-managed event portfolios have become an indispensable element of city marketing and tourism development, and are increasingly found in most urban and many rural centres.

The coordination of event infrastructure services

Staging major events successfully involves coordinating a wide range of infrastructure and support services, including venues, transport and communications, and public authorities such as police, fire, ambulance and emergency services. Many of these services are provided by government, so many event strategies include a 'one-stop shop' approach to their coordination and management. The staging of major events has increasingly underlined the importance of such coordination. The Edinburgh Event Planning and Operations Group (EPOG) is a best-practice example of such a coordination group. Working alongside a council established Event Management Team, EPOG consists of government and non-government agencies, including council pubic safety staff, emergency services, and other agencies. According to its terms of reference, the EPOG exists to:

- Coordinate the operational planning of all major events.
- Ensure a responsible person is nominated for each event, within or out with the Council, as appropriate.
- Liaise with the Emergency Services, Local Health Authority, Council Departments and any other appropriate bodies.
- Develop road closure/traffic management plans for all events.
- Produce event/area layout plans, as required.
- Ensure the production of Event Safety Plans, where appropriate (City of Edinburgh Council, 2002, p. 4).

The growth of government funding for events

As government involvement in events increased throughout the 1990s, the need for government financial support and funding became increasingly obvious. As a result, many governments at all levels now run funding programmes for events. In the UK, these programmes have ranged from national programmes (such as the Millennium Commission or UK Sport) to funding through national or regional organizations (such as EventsScotland or Highlands & Island Arts) and tourism boards/agencies, to local government funding through council event programmes. Issues raised by such funding programmes include the differing agendas of events, and the differing criteria for selection and evaluation.

At a regional level, funding programmes acknowledge the role of major events (which may be funded by events organizations, funding bodies or major events groups) and the more general needs of special interest groups, such as the arts, sport and ethnic communities (which may be funded by individual programmes). At the local government level, the need to create a portfolio of tourism events is often distinguished from the need for events that primarily serve community needs and objectives. In some areas, these two types of event are treated as separate funding programmes, each with its own set of objectives and selection criteria. Growing pressures on event funding and competition from other government programmes have resulted in an increasing emphasis on rigorous assessment and evaluation procedures. As requirements for funding increase and added pressure is placed on available resources, the need to predict event outcomes accurately and measure results is likely to continue to increase.

The adoption of environmental management practices by events

Many event organizers are now consciously seeking to manage the physical environmental impacts of their events, the Olympic Games being perhaps the most notable in this regard. The following discussion identifies a range of factors that have pushed event organizers in this direction.

Government adoption of the principles of ecologically sustainable development

The principles of ecologically sustainable development were adopted by 182 governments on the signing of the Agenda 21 document at the conclusion of the Earth Summit in Rio de Janeiro in 1992. While not legally binding, the adopted principles carry 'a strong moral obligation to ensure their full implementation' (United Nations, 1992, p. 3). Areas covered by this document included solid waste management, the protection of the atmosphere, the protection of the quality and supply of freshwater resources, and environmentally sound management of toxic chemicals. Perhaps not surprisingly, given the impact, size and international nature of Olympic Games, the IOC has been the most proactive of event-based organizations in embracing the principles of ecologically sustainable development. Cities seeking to conduct a winter or summer Olympic Games must now formally address environmental issues in their bid documents (IOC, 1999). The Olympic Movement has also developed its own version of Agenda 21 (based on the principles embodied in the more generic Earth Summit document) and has acted to make environmentalism the 'third pillar' of Olympism, the others being sport and culture (Tarradellas and Behnam, 2000).

Given the limited published material on the extent to which events (other than the Olympics) have engaged with the principals of ecologically sustainable development, it is difficult to be sure about the impact of these principles in the events area in general. Nonetheless, those organizations involved in the creation and conduct of events in signatory countries would be affected by the efforts of their government (at all levels) to pursue their responsibilities under this agreement. To some extent, the issue of waste management (discussed next) could be perceived as an example.

Government waste reduction efforts

Rapid economic and population growth in the post-World War period resulted in solid waste becoming a major environmental problem, with government increasing its focus over the last decade on ways in which to reduce waste. Events is an area that has been the subject of such attention because events often involve large numbers of people, and can result in the generation of significant volumes of solid waste. Waste Awareness Wales (2005), for example, has provided a useful events recycling guide offering useful information on potential event-related initiatives. They highlight the example of National Eisteddfod 2003 in Meifod which, through the support of Powys County Council Direct Services Organization (DSO) received free recycling from the event with funding support from the hosting budget and from the Sustainable Waste Grant. The Waste Awareness Wales events-initiative has been informed by the successful Resource New South Wales (Australia) Waste Wise Events project.

In the United States, there is also evidence that events are being actively targeted for waste reduction purposes. In the state of Wisconsin, for example, the recycling laws require event managers to make provisions for the recycling of:

- glass bottles and jars
- aluminium and steel/tin cans
- plastic containers
- newspapers
- corrugated cardboard
- office paper
- other items, depending on the community (Wisconsin Department of Natural Resources, 1998).

Cost savings

Increasingly, event organizers and event facilities are realizing the economic benefits that can result from the adoption of environmental management strategies. Publications such as Chernushenko's (1994) *Greening our games: running sports events and facilities that won't cost the earth* have been making the point for some time that financial savings or avoided costs can flow from the pursuit of environmental programmes and principles. An area of note in this regard is the reduction of disposal fees. Calculations by the Californian Showgrounds in 2000, for example, showed that the venue had realized savings of over US$5.5 million over the previous five years due to effective environmental management of its waste stream (Strauss, 2000). By recycling 410.44 tonnes of waste at Glastonbury Festival in 2004, organizers saved between £12 313 and £14 364 in waste disposal charges (Waste Awareness Wales, 2005). The SEXI project estimated that the total cost of waste to the exhibitions industry was £40 million per year, with over 60 000 tonnes of waste produced, much of which could be recycled or reduced (Midlands Environmental Business Club Limited, 2002). The decision to purchase reusable items, for example, reusable carpets in exhibitions or reusable cutlery instead of disposable, can also serve to reduce or eliminate disposal charges. The 1999 Pan American Games, for example, eliminated disposable plates and cups from its waste stream by purchasing crockery items. At the completion of the event, these items were sold, resulting in a total saving of an estimated $US30 000 over the alternative of disposal (Crawford, 2000).

Protection by sponsoring companies of their corporate image

The extent to which sponsors influence the environmental practices/policies of events is an area that has received little attention, yet sponsor expectations can be an important factor in the uptake by events of environmental programmes (Crawford, 2000). Goldblatt (2005), for example, notes that major corporations, being sensitive to criticism from consumers, will increasingly require that the events they sponsor meet or exceed certain environmental standards, for example, ISO 14001. He also suggests that companies involved in particular environmental strategies – recycling, for example – are likely to want recycling programmes to be in place at the event they sponsor. An example of the significance of 'green' policies in attracting sponsorship is the 2000 Sydney Olympic Games: Bonlac Foods, a large multinational corporation, stated that its decision to become an Olympic sponsor was directly influenced by SOCOG's environmental agenda (Green Games Watch, 2004).

Increasing consumer awareness of environmental issues

The trend towards increasing consumer awareness of environmental issues is well established and, in some contexts, supported by buyer behaviour findings (Minton and Rose, 1997; Schlegelmilch, Bohlen and Diamantopoulos, 1996). In the context of leisure-based products and services, however, there is little substantive research to indicate whether consumers are influenced by environmental concerns in their decisions to buy/participate in/attend leisure products or services such as events (Hjalager, 1996). Nonetheless, Crawford (2000) and others believe that this influence exists, and that event organizers need to ensure they reflect their market's concerns in this area if they are not to experience a consumer 'blacklash'.

The influence of environmental interest groups

Some events, particularly mega-events, have attracted the attention of environmental interest groups because they exhibit potential to have a negative impact on a community's physical environment, and because they can make significant demands on an area's resources. The first documented protest over the staging of a public event appears to have taken place in Denver, Colorado, when concerned local citizens successfully protested against the staging of the 1976 Winter Games (Chernushenko, 1994). Such concern over the impacts of large-scale events has persisted, as reflected in the establishment of Green Games Watch 2000 – a coalition of major state and national environment groups – to monitor the Sydney Olympics (Green Games Watch 2000, 2004) and initiatives undertaken at major events since Sydney.

The interest, or potential interest, of environmental groups in events focuses the attention of event organizers on environmental issues and pushes them to adopt a proactive stance on environmental matters. For example, as discussed in Chapter 2, London 2012 Olympic Games acknowledged that sustainable development was a key aspect of their bid (London 2012, 2004a). They worked with WWF and Bioregional Development Group to put together a 'One Planet Games' project with themes focusing on ensuring low carbon, zero waste, conserving biodiversity and promoting environmental awareness and partnerships (London 2012, WWF and BioRegional, 2005). Industry associations, such as the International Festival and Events Association are also now acknowledging in their annual industry awards the events that seek to embrace their environmental responsibilities.

Chapter summary

The common solutions to issues and challenges become the trends that help to define an industry. Some of the observable recent trends in the event industry include its rapid growth (particularly corporate events) and the increasing recognition of event management as a profession, as defined by a body of knowledge and the establishment of competency standards and management systems. Other observable trends are (1) event franchising, whereby the model established for an event is on-sold in other markets, (2) the use of events as vehicles for skills training, (3) the increasing interest in ethical business practice and standards, (4) the development and use of return on investment measures and (5) the role of procurement departments in the events industry and how the relationship can be developed to meet the needs of all parties.

Major influences on the industry include rapid advances in information technology, the changing climate of risk management and the increased international threat to security. In answer to the increasing demands of the industry, event education and research have expanded, and transfer-of-knowledge programmes have been developed to help build on the expertise gained from previous events. As awareness of the value of events has increased, governments around the world have become increasing involved in creating event strategies, establishing event portfolios, coordinating event infrastructure services and funding events. Events are increasingly adopting environmental management practices in response to growing awareness in the community and to pressures from governments and sponsors.

Questions

1. Do you think the number of events in your city or region is increasing? If so, what evidence can you offer of this increase?
2. Select an established profession and compare it with event management, using the characteristics of a profession outlined in this chapter. From this comparison, evaluate what you consider to be the progress of event management towards the status of a profession.
3. Identify an event that has been franchised and examine the method of the event. What aspects of the event can be franchised and transferred to a new location?
4. Choose a fairly large recent local event and interview the event manager to establish what risk management was undertaken. Evaluate the risk management of the event using the risk management procedures outlined in this book as a benchmark.
5. Choose a recent major event and investigate the security measures that the event had in place. How do you think increased threats to security might have influenced these measures?
6. Identify a situation in which a senior event manager has taken a position with a new event. What knowledge and skills was this manager able to transfer to the new event?
7. Identify a local or regional government body/agency in your region that has developed an event strategy. What are the major elements of this strategy? How is the strategy manifested in a portfolio of events?
8. Identify a body in your region that has been established to coordinate event infrastructure services. Who are the members of this body? With what issues does the body deal?
9. Identify an event in your region that has adopted environmental management practices, and outline the practices that they have adopted.

Case study 15.1

The Notting Hill Carnival

The Notting Hill Carnival takes place annually in the streets of Notting Hill, an area in West London. The carnival began in 1964 and provided an opportunity for West Indians to celebrate and commemorate their ancestors' 'freedom from slavery' which is celebrated every year in all parts of the Caribbean.

The first carnival had not been planned as a carnival. In the early 1960s in Notting Hill, there was an event called the Notting Hill Festival, which was a low-key street celebration attended by approximately 200 people, mostly children. In 1964 a Notting Hill social worker, Rhaune Laslett, being aware of the growing number of West Indian children in the area who were not taking part in the festival, decided to add some West Indian culture to the festival as an attraction. She invited a steel band, which was normally present at the Colherne pub in Earls Court, to play at the festival. When the steel band came onto the streets of Notting Hill, nearly every West Indian in the area, adults as well as children, came onto the streets and began to follow the steel band in a processional manner as they did back home, particularly in Trinidad the birthplace of steelpan, playing whatever makeshift instruments (dustbin lids, bottle and spoon, comb and paper) they could lay their hands on.

After that first event, the steel band became a feature of the Notting Hill Festival and the reputation of the festival grew as the only event at which West Indian culture was celebrated. Between 1964 and 1974, not more than 3000 people attended the festival which by then had a change in leadership and became exclusively a forum for West Indian culture, led by West Indians. However, the event was not widely known amongst West Indians from the different communities in London. The revellers tended to be exclusively Trinidadian because of the dominance of the steelpan music and its size was due to word-of-mouth transference of information within that community.

The first attempt to market the carnival on a London-wide scale came in 1975 with the advent of a new radio station in London, Capital Radio. That station had a community slot as part of its programming and announced the fact that there was a West Indian carnival being held in Notting Hill. One hundred and fifty thousand West Indians turned up from many different islands in the West Indies and not just Trinidad. A wider range of West Indian culture was present, most notably the influence of the Jamaican Sound System which brought a more contemporary edge to the carnival as black music was about to invade the English pop charts with Roots, Reggae and the Tamla Motown hits. The Sound Systems played that type of black music and so attracted younger black people to the carnival and they immediately identified with the ethos of the celebration.

In 1976, 250 000 young black people attended the carnival and the authorities, without warning, decided to stop the event and so sent in several thousand police officers. A riot ensued as the young people protested against the suppression of the event, with numerous casualties on both sides. This riot was the first public acknowledgement of ownership of the event by the West Indian community – the riot united the West Indian community in appreciation of their history and in celebration of their ancestors' 'freedom from slavery'. The riot characterized the event in the eyes of the press and British public as a violent affair and brought the Notting Hill Carnival to the attention of the press and, so, the world.

Until 2002, the Notting Hill Carnival was organized by the Notting Hill Carnival Trust, a registered charity established some ten years previous to pursue the development of the carnival and the safety of the people that are in attendance. In 2003 a new organization, London Notting Hill Carnival Limited was established to organize the carnival. The organization is assisted by the Metropolitan Police Service, the Royal Borough of Kensington and Chelsea, the City of Westminster, London Underground Limited, St John Ambulance Service, London Fire and Civil Defence Authority and London Ambulance Service.

Today, the Notting Hill Carnival boasts an audience of up to 1.5 million people over August Bank Holiday Sunday and Monday. It is probably the best known and one of the biggest carnivals in the world with numerous applications from other carnivals to participate in the event. The carnival has a strong multicultural character and is known for its capacity to cater for all age groups, the creativity of the designers, artists and communities that create the hugely attractive costumes, and the range of music available from top DJs and groups free of charge, hence its attractiveness to young people. Each year an increasing number of visitors and participants from Europe are attracted to the carnival.

The Notting Hill Carnival comprises a range of events that take place over a two-week carnival season:

- *Carnival Press Launch*: two hundred members of the press are invited to the Carnival Press Launch to get a taste of carnival culture and be positively cultivated by the carnival community.
- *Carnival Costume Gala*: this takes place the weekend before the carnival and is the event where the artistry of the Kings, Queens, Male Individuals and Females Individuals are judged. Two hundred costumes perform individually, portraying their themes through costume design and performance. The event is usually held at the Olympia Exhibition Centre and boasts an audience of 500 people.
- *The Calypso Monarch Competition*: this takes place on the Friday of the carnival weekend where ten Calypsonians compete for the title of Calypso Monarch. They compose and sing their own calypsos, which must be based on contemporary issues of politics and life generally.
- *The Steelbands Panorama*: this takes place the evening before the carnival procession where ten steel bands compete for the title of Champions of Steel. Each steel band has up to 100 players who perform innovative musical arrangements of calypsos of the season. It boasts an audience of 7000 people.
- *The Two Days of the Carnival*: this comprises a street procession on both days. At which costumes, steel bands, mobile and static sound systems perform in the streets to commemorate the 'freedom to walk the streets' which their ancestors had been denied during the period of slavery. The audience, 'Carnival revellers', are encouraged to join the procession. The emphasis is on the right of each individual to be part of the celebrations, *'Every spectator is a participant'*.

It would appear that the public has more than just an understanding of the event and identifies with its ethos, ensuring its assimilation into mainstream culture. The carnival has become more than just an event – it has become a way of life. The Notting Hill Carnival is now a major well-publicized event that is important to society on many different levels. While its economic impact has been recently quantified at around £93 million for a study undertaken for London Development Agency (2003) – its societal impact through education and the facilitation of better racial harmony is probably the most valuable outcome of its marketing strategies.

Given the recognized value and role of Notting Hill Carnival, together with its ability to attract a significant number of tourists to the region, and the potential impacts and safety issues caused by this number of people, the Mayor of London commissioned a study to evaluate the management, funding and safety of the event (Mayor's Carnival Review Group, 2004) and to make strategic recommendations for the future. The main recommendations from the study were:

- *Understanding and documenting the carnival*: increase awareness and appreciation of the history of the carnival and develop carnival archives to document this.

- *Listening to stakeholders, competing perspectives*: draw in the views and build on the support of carnival stakeholders including residents, Arts Council, Notting Hill Mas Band Association, artistic Arenas.
- *Achieving an effective communications strategy*: drive the news agenda, revise and adopt the Carnival Code for communicating key safety messages, greater use of directional signage.
- *Stewarding and policing*: ensure suitably qualified and sustainable group of stewards to ensure public and participant safety, develop multi-agency safety group, support for St Johns Ambulance.
- *Event management*: robust event planning and management framework adopted, contracts introduced for participants to comply with staging and performance protocols.
- *Waste management and recycling*: develop a sustainable carnival waste management and recycling strategy.
- *Public safety responsibility and accountability*: including considering changes to the route and an assessment of the entertainment arena, consideration, formalization and documentation of roles and responsibilities of organizations involved (for example, local authorities, police), greater accountability and transparency, consideration of the role of Health & Safety Executive.
- *Carnival management and leadership*: leadership development programme, limitations on length of service on board, broaden membership, include independent legal, finance, management, marketing, public safety and business skills and experience; distinction between development of London's carnival industry and event planning, management and delivery of Notting Hill Carnival.
- *The social, cultural and community value of carnival*: study required into education benefits, including mapping carnival arts and education initiatives, good practice in carnival and carnival arts development, contribution of carnival to development of communication and life skills; create Carnival Arts Education Officer, Carnival Arts Education Network, potential London Carnival School's Competition.
- *The business of carnival*: funding, finance and economic development: potential for establishment of Centre for Carnival Arts and Enterprise as a centre for excellence; LDA to consider implementing a Carnival Economic Development Strategy to ensure community benefits from impacts identified in study; develop carnival music policy and strategy; Caribbean-cuisine food and drink strategy.
- *Future vision*: the way forward: embrace Notting Hill Carnival and support politically and financially, strategic role for Mayor of London, implement London Carnival Development Plan to act as a catalyst for London carnival industry and focus on priority areas of:
  - Strategic management and leadership
  - Community outreach and development
  - Event operation and management
  - Fundraising and finance
  - Sustainable economic development
  - Marketing, branding and promotion (Mayor's Carnival Review Group, 2004, pp. 20–28)

For further details about Notting Hill Carnival, please visit www.lnhc.org.uk. For further details about the Mayor's Carnival Review Group, please visit: www.london.gov.uk/mayor/carnival.

Source: adapted from Holder (2001).

Questions

1. The above provides an extensive insight into the development of the Notting Hill Carnival, which has led to the culture, and ethos, of the event as it appears today. What are the main features of the Notting Hill Carnival? How has history influenced these?

2. Who are the stakeholders in the Notting Hill Carnival? What role do they play?
3. In evaluating the carnival, what are the long-term benefits for London and the host community?
4. How has London used the Notting Hill Carnival to create an identity for the area?
5. The above identified the main recommendations of the Mayor's Carnival Review Group. What implications do the recommendations have on the future of the carnival? Investigate what changes have been made as a result of these recommendations.
6. The case demonstrates the interest of the Mayor of London and other agencies in events. Why do politicians and local authorities taken an interest in the success of Carnival?

Case study 15.2

Managing the Knowledge of the 2000 Sydney Olympic Games

Event organizations need to effectively capture, share, manage, transfer, use and exploit their corporate information. By doing so, they can operate efficiently, reduce risk, coordinate their strategies, expedite policy implementation and not duplicate effort. Regrettably, managers have not understood the importance of knowledge management until recently; consequently, this facet of event management is often overlooked and underused. However, poor information and knowledge management at any stage can be a major source of risk for an event. Knowledge management is a multidisciplinary approach to achieving organizational objectives by making best use of knowledge. It involves the design, review and implementation of social and technological processes to improve the application of knowledge in the collective interests of the stakeholders (Standards Australia, 2003, p. 3).

The Olympic movement, in the lead-up to the 2000 Sydney Olympic Games, recognized the potential gap between professional event management and information/knowledge management. During the Sydney Games and since then, the International Olympic Committee (IOC) has understood that knowledge is too valuable a resource to be left to chance and has improved the management of its knowledge assets. The Olympic movement thus provides a rich case study of event knowledge management.

Every time the games are staged, both winter and summer, there is a new organizing committee, the host city and its culture are different, and technology and many other games-related procedures (such as security) have become more complex. Yet, until the 2000 Sydney Olympic Games, few standard operating methods, precedents or documentation – except the *official reports* produced after every games – were passed directly from the IOC or one organizing committee to the next. This lack of know-how about the organizational, operational and cultural aspects of past games can be problematic for each new organizing committee, which has the challenge of staging the world's most prestigious multi-sport event.

Added to this pressure is the fact that the event management team grows from a very small number of specialist staff to several thousand, and then rapidly closes down, all in about a seven-year time span (Halbwirth and Toohey, 2001). Toffler (1984) calls organizations that grow then shrink (such as the Olympic organizing committees) 'pulsating organizations'. Hanlon and Jago (2000) describe their main organizational characteristics as flexible, flat, highly formalized, decentralized (particularly during the peak stage of the event), having teams of people in functional units, innovative and regularly transforming their internal structure. An essential resource in such organizations is information. Its role is multidimensional in connecting and maintaining operational effectiveness and enhancing decision making.

The Sydney Organizing Committee for the Olympic Games (SOCOG) exhibited all of the characteristics of a pulsating organization. Additionally, its corporate governance was complex, embracing government and private sector agency interests. Its stakeholders included governments, sporting organizations, a range of corporate sponsors and broadcast rights holders, the public and the athletes who competed.

While commercial knowledge and sport management expertise were vital to SOCOG successfully staging the games, this achievement was underpinned by effective and innovative information and knowledge management strategies and leadership, including:

- a team of information professionals
- a corporate portal that ensured SOCOG staff had access to consistent, current and approved corporate, operational and public information
- research and retrieval services
- document and records management
- collaborative workspace for the authoring of key documents
- terminology and taxonomy management
- systems and processes to manage the flow of information to and from key stakeholders, such as sponsors and the public information call centre
- a knowledge-sharing culture, built-in part via staff social events, cross-functional teams, a corporate newsletter and so on
- induction and orientation sessions for new staff
- a test event for all sports and for a number of key functional areas ('learning from doing')
- debriefing sessions and actioned organizational learning from test events and the games.

In 1998, during a Coordination Commission visit, the IOC praised SOCOG for its progress in its games organization across its full range of functional milestones and activities. This marked the official beginning of the recognition that the Sydney Games might be a benchmark ('the best ever games') and might be able to provide many lessons for future event organizers. SOCOG agreed to develop a programme for collecting and transferring information and know-how to the IOC. In exchange, the IOC contributed $5 million to SOCOG's tight budget. This established, for the first time in Olympic history, a formal transfer of know-how (TOK) agreement. The transfer included the collection of data, information and story via the corporate portal, which was collated into 90 functional area manuals, video footage, face-to-face de-briefings with the IOC, Salt Lake City 2004 and Athens 2004 staff, work experience exchanges, and synthesis and analysis of documentation. The result of this process was the transfer to the IOC of hundreds of boxes of documents, electronic files and video footage, images and transcripts.

Each host city contract (which is signed by the IOC, the relevant national Olympic committee and the host city immediately after the games are awarded) contains an obligation to make available to the IOC, within two years after the games, a full and complete official report. Until the 2000 Sydney Olympic Games, this report was the only opportunity for the organizing committee and its management to document the success (or otherwise) of its achievements in various areas of games organization. The report also acted as a written legacy of the games which was available internationally. Sydney thus had a requirement to publish its report by October 2002. The result, the *Official report of the Games of the XXVII Olympiad*, contains three volumes: volume one explains the history and organization of the 2000 Olympic Games; volume two is an account of the 16 days of the sport competition of the games, life in the Olympic Village and Cultural Olympic activities; and volume 3 contains the official results of the sport competition. This results volume is in the format of a compact disc (CD) rather than the traditional book mode of reports of previous games (Toohey, 2001). The report is also more widely accessible than other previous reports, because it is available to the general public electronically at www.gamesinfo.com.au. This website also includes an electronic archive of public information related to the Sydney games.

The 2000 Sydney Olympic Games provided a number of information legacies – for example, transfer of know-how, the official report, www.gamesinfo.com.au and a comprehensive archive now managed by the State Records Authority of New South Wales. Post-Sydney 2000, the IOC had the issue of improving its own information and knowledge management as it took ownership of the TOK agreement resources. In 2001, it established the Olympic Games Knowledge Services, originally as a joint venture with Monash University but now wholly owned by IOC, to capitalize on Olympic know-how, create customized information packages for event organizers and continue a programme of know-how capture. The IOC also took on a new strategic intent, creating a new division in 2003 that coordinates its information and knowledge assets under the leadership of a director of information management. Further, the IOC recognized the need to include in future host city contracts the obligation for organizing committees to manage their information proactively and professionally through archives. All these initiatives have allowed the intellectual know-how and the historical legacy of Olympic material to be available for future use. The IOC is now active in managing its knowledge property.

While these activities have potential for positive outcomes for the IOC and other event organizers, there are ongoing issues and challenges in managing knowledge. Just as staging an Olympic Games requires complex organization and coordination, so too do the processes of collecting, documenting, disseminating and using relevant information. Before an Olympic Games, for example, staff in various functional areas are understandably more concerned about their own tasks and may not be willing to share their intellectual property or provide input into knowledge-sharing practices. The sheer enormity and complexity of the tasks of Olympic Games organization means processes are needed for harvesting key information from the vast knowledge bank. Organizers have to be able to sift through material to capture all vital information.

In a world where events are characterized by growing complexity in both their internal and external environments, information and knowledge management provide event managers with a multidisciplinary approach to ensure operational effectiveness, continuous improvement, the mitigation of risk and the streamlining of processes.

For further information about the 2000 Sydney Olympics, please visit www.gamesinfo.com.au. For further information about the Olympic Games Knowledge Services, please visit www.ogks.com.

By Kristine Toohey and Sue Halbwirth, University of Technology, Sydney.

Questions

1. Choose a specific event. List the key information resources, channels and processes that would be needed before, during and in the wind-down phases of the event.
2. What are the best ways in which to capture know-how in an event organization?
3. Why is it important to capture organizational information iteratively, rather than just at the end of the event?
4. How can event staff be encouraged to willingly contribute to knowledge sharing?
5. How does the 2002 Manchester Commonwealth Games knowledge transfer programme compare to the 2002 Sydney Olympics?

References

Abbot, J. (2000). The importance of proper crowd management and crowd control in the special events industry. In *Events Beyond 2000 – Setting the Agenda. Proceedings of the Conference on Evaluation, Research and Education, 13–14 July* (J. Allen, R. Harris, L. K. Jago and A. J. Veal, eds) Sydney, Australian Centre for Event Management, University of Technology.

Adams, J. S. (1965). Inequity in social exchange. In *Advances in Experimental Social Psychology* (L. Berkowitz, ed.) New York, Academic Press.

Advantage West Midlands (2004). *Motor Show Set To Boost Tourism by £5 Million.* (Internet) Press Release, 16 January. Available from <http://www.advantagewm.co.uk/news/motor-show-set-to-boost-tourism-by–5-million.html> (accessed 5 August 2005).

Aguilar-Manjarrez, R., Thwaites, D. and Maule, J. (1997). Modelling sports sponsorship selection decisions. *Asia-Australia Marketing Journal*, 5(1), 9–20.

All England Lawn Tennis Club (2005). *The All England Club In The Local Community 2005.* (Internet) Available from <http://www.wimbledon.org/en_GB/about/infosheets/AETLC_Community_2005.pdf> (accessed 2 August 2005).

Allen, J. (2000). *Event Planning: The Ultimate Guide to Successful Meetings, Corporate Events, Fundraising Galas, Conventions, Conferences, Incentives and Other Special Events.* Ontario, John Wiley & Sons Canada Ltd.

Allen, J. (2002). *The Business of Event Planning.* Ontario, John Wiley & Sons Canada Ltd.

Allen, J. (2003). *Event Planning Ethics and Etiquette: A Principled Approach to the Business of Special Event Management.* Ontario, John Wiley & Sons Canada Ltd.

Allen, J. (2004). *Marketing Your Event Planning Business: A Creative Approach to Gaining the Competitive Edge.* Ontario, John Wiley & Sons Canada Ltd.

Allen, J. (2005). *Time Management for Event Planners.* Ontario, John Wiley & Sons Canada Ltd.

Allen, K. and Shaw, P. (2001). *Festivals Mean Business: The Shape of Arts Festivals in the UK.* London, British Arts Festival Association.

Allrefer.com (2005). *Japan: Age Structure.* (Internet) Available from <reference.allrefer.com/country-guide-study/japan/japan67.html> (accessed 9 August 2005).

Allsop, K. (2004). How the Broncos "do" sponsorship. *Presentation at Queensland University of Technology*, 19 April 2004.

Andrews, J. (2001). *IEG Glossary and Lexicon: Ambush Marketing.* (Internet) Available from <http://www.sponsorship.com/learn/glossary.asp> (accessed 24 August 2005).

Anon (2000). *Rugby World Cup 1999 Economic Impact Evaluation: Summary Report.* Edinburgh, Segal Quince Wicksteed Limited and System Three.

Anon (2004). NPower ties with cancer charity. *Marketing*, August, 4, 8.

Anon (2005a). *IVCA Estimates Industry Worth £2.8 billion.* (Internet) *AVInteractive*, 21 July. Available from < http://www.avinteractive.co.uk/News.View.aspx?ContentID=1694> (accessed 3 August 2005).

Anon (2005b). *Tetley's 'Official Beer' Status of Super League Clubs.* 8 February (Internet) *Sponsorship News*. Available from <http://www.sponsorshipnews.com/svga/archive.cfm?id=1106> (accessed 3 August 2005).

Anon (2005c). *Tiger Beer to Sponsor Cult Asian Filmfest.* (Internet) *Event,* April. Available from <http://www.eventmagazine.co.uk/news/news_story.cfm?ID= 4082> (accessed 21 August 2005).

Ansoff, I. (1957). Strategies for diversification. *Harvard Business Review, September– October,* 113–124.

Arcodia, C. and Barker, T. (2002). A review of web-based job advertisement for Australian event management positions. In *Events and Place-making*: Proceedings of International Research Conference held in Sydney 2002 (L. Jago, M. Deery, R. Harris, A. Hede and J. Allen, eds). Sydney, Australian Centre for Event Management.

Armstrong, M. (2003). *A Handbook of Human Resource Management Practice.* 9th edn. London, Kogan Page.

Arnold, A., Fischer, A., Hatch, J. and Paix, B. (1989). The Grand Prix, road accidents and the philosophy of hallmark events. In *The Planning and Evaluation of Hallmark Events* (G. J. Syme, B. J. Shaw, D. M. Fenton and W. S. Mueller, eds), Avesbury, Aldershot.

Arts Council of England (1999). *Guidance Notes on Carrying out Audience/Visitor Surveys.* London, Arts Council of England.

Arts Development Service (2004). *Art Development Strategy 2005–2008.* (Internet) Bath, Bath and North East Somerset Council. Available from <http://www.bathnes. gov.uk/BathNES/lifeandleisure/leisure/artsdevelopment/ArtsDevelopment Strategy.htm> (accessed 3 August 2005).

Association of Exhibition Organizers, British Exhibition Contractors Association and Exhibition Venues Association (AEO, BECA and EVA) (2002). *The Guide to Managing Health and Safety at Exhibitions and Events,* Berkhamstead. AEO, BECA and EVA.

Australasian Special Events Magazine (2001). *Australian Tourism Recognised for Olympic Effort.* (Internet) 5th May. Available from <http://www.specialevents. com.au/archiveprev/2001/05may01/newsmay01/olympic.html> (accessed 24 August 2005).

Axelsen, M. and Arcodia, C. (2004). Motivations for attending the Asia–Pacific Triennial Art Exhibition. In *Paper presented at the 14th International Research Conference of the Council for Australian University Tourism and Hospitality Education,* 10–13 February, Brisbane.

Ayaya (2002). *At Tournament End, Converged Network Built by Avaya Scores FIFA World Cup Firsts.* (Internet) Press Release, 11 July. Available from <http:// www.avaya. com/gcm/master-usa/en-us/corporate/pressroom/pressreleases/ 2002/pr-020711.htm> (accessed 24 August 2005).

Backman, K. F., Backman, S. J., Muzaffer, U. and Sunshine, K. (1995). Event tourism: an examination of motivations and activities. *Festival Management and Event Tourism,* **3**(1), 26–34.

Baker, D. A. and Crompton, J. L. (2000). Quality, satisfaction, and behavioural intentions. *Annals of Tourism Research,* **27**(3), 785–804.

Ball, S. (2000). Thank you for the music. *Access All Areas,* May, 15, 32.

Bank of Scotland (2005). *Edinburgh International Festival: Bank of Scotland Connecting to Music.* (Internet) Edinburgh, Bank of Scotland. Available from <http:// www.hbosplc.com/community/edintfestival.asp> (accessed 21 August 2005).

Bank of Scotland Corporate (2005a). *Sponsorship Criteria.* (Internet) Edinburgh, Bank of Scotland. Available from <http://www.bankofscotland.co.uk/corporate/ sponsorship/criteria.html> (accessed 24 August 2005).

Bank of Scotland Corporate (2005b). *Corporate Sponsorship Request Form.* (Internet) Edinburgh, Bank of Scotland. Available from <http://www.bankofscotland.co.uk/ corporate/pdf/sponsorship.pdf> (accessed 24 August 2005).

Barclays Capital (2005). *Barclays Climbs the Leader Board in Golf Sponsorship*. (Internet) London, Barclays Capital Communications. Available from <http://www.barclaysscottishopen.co.uk/images/generic/sponsorship.pdf> (accessed 22 August 2005).

Barnes, P. (1999). Bournemouth makes Labour's part swing. *Access All Areas*, October, 44, 3.

Bath and North East Somerset District Council (B&NES) (2000). *Bath and North East Somerset Arts Impact Assessment*. (Internet) Bristol, Bath and North East Somerset District Council. Available from <http://www.bathnes.gov.uk/Committee_Papers/CCL/cl000124/14app.htm> (accessed 3 August 2005).

Bath Festivals Trust (2005). *About Us*. (Internet) Available from <http://www.bathmusicfest.org.uk/pages/about.php> (accessed 3 August 2005).

BBC (2004). *First Artists Announced for Beautiful Night*. (Internet) Press Release, 6 March. Available from <http://www.bbc.co.uk/pressoffice/pressreleases/stories/2004/03_march/06/beautiful_night.shtml> (accessed 6 August 2005).

BBC News (2002a). *The Golden Jubilee*. (Internet) *BBC News In Depth*, 8 October. Available from <http://news.bbc.co.uk/1/hi/in_depth/uk/2002/the_golden_jubilee/default.stm> (accessed 3 August 2005).

BBC News (2002b). *Palace Pop Spectacle Wows Jubilee Crowds*. (Internet) *BBC News UK Edition*, 4 June. Available from < http://news.bbc.co.uk/1/hi/entertainment/music/3116113.stm> (accessed 3 August 2005).

BBC News (2003). *Fans Go Wild for Robbie*. (Internet) *BBC News UK Edition*, 2 August. Available from <http://news.bbc.co.uk/1/hi/uk/2022995.stm> (accessed 3 August 2005).

BBC News (2005). *Dome to Reopen as Concert Arena*. (Internet) 25 May, *BBC News UK edition*. Available from <http://news.bbc.co.uk/1/hi/entertainment/arts/4578753.stm> (accessed 3 August 2005).

BDS Sponsorship Ltd (2005). *The Definition of Sponsorship*. (Internet) Available from <http://www.sponsorship.co.uk/in_sponsorship/in_sponsorship.htm> (accessed on 24 August 2005).

Bear Necessities of Golf (1998). *Electronic Telegraph*. (Internet) Issue 1310, 26 December. Available from <http://portal.telegraph.co.uk/html Content.jhtml? html= %2Farchive%2F1998%2F12%2F26%2Fsogile26.html> (accessed 8 February 2001).

Beardwell, I. and Holden, L. (2001). *Human Resource Management: A Contemporary Perspective*. 3rd edn. London, Pearson Education.

Beardwell, I., Holden, L. and Claydon, T. (2003). *Human Resource Management: A Contemporary Perspective*. 4th edn. London, Pearson Education.

Belfast City Council (2000a). *Events Unit Performance Improvement Business Plan*. (Internet) Belfast, Belfast City Council, 10 April. Available from <http://www.development.belfastcity.gov.uk/Press/performanceimpbusplan.pdf> (accessed 3 August 2005).

Belfast City Council (2000b). *Events Unit Strategic Vision*. (Internet) Belfast, Belfast City Council Development Department, 1 February. Available from <http://www.development.belfastcity.gov.uk/Press/eventsunitstratvision.pdf> (accessed 3 August 2005).

Belfast City Council (2005a). *Events*. (Internet) Belfast, Belfast City Council. Available from <http://www.development.belfastcity.gov.uk/ourwork/Events/index.asp> (accessed 3 August 2005).

Belfast City Council (2005b). *Supporting Sport*. (Internet) Belfast, Belfast City Council. Available from <http://www.belfastcity.gov.uk/supportforsport/> (accessed 3 August 2005).

Beniger, J. (1986). *The Control Revolution*. Cambridge, Harvard University Press.

Berlonghi, A. (1990). *Special Event Risk Management Manual.* Mansfield, Ohio, Bookmasters.

Birmingham Convention Bureau (2005). *Welcome to Birmingham Convention Bureau.* (Internet) Available from <http://www.birminghamconventionbureau.com> (accessed 9 August 2005).

Blakey, P., Metcalfe, M., Mitchell, J. and Weatherfield, P. (2000). Sports events and tourism: effects of motor car rallying on rural communities in mid Wales. In *Reflections on International Tourism: Developments in Urban and Rural Tourism* (M. Robinson, N. Evans, P. Long, R. Sharpley and J. Swarbrooke, eds) Sunderland, Centre for Travel and Tourism with Business Education Publishers.

Blicher-Hansen, L. (2003). *Event Denmark Strategy.* (Internet) Available from <http://www.danskturisme.dk/web/netserv.nsf/dok/event-danmark> (accessed 8 January 2004).

Blyth, A. (2003). Joining the throng. *New Media Age*, July, 31.

Bold, B. (2005). *CreditExpert Sponsors Bennett Arron's Edinburgh Show.* (Internet) *Brand Republic*, 4 August. Available from: <http://www.brandrepublic.com/news/search/article/489395/creditexpert-sponsors-bennett-arrons-edinburgh-show/> (accessed 16 August 2005).

Bond, C. (2005). *Showcase: Nokia Urban Music Festival.* (Internet) *Event*, May, p. 19. Available from <http://www.eventmagazine.co.uk/features/Features_story.cfm?ID=4102> (accessed 21 August 2005).

Boscombe Arts Festival (2005). *About Us.* (Internet) Available from <http://barfruit.co.uk/boscombeartsfestival/about.php> (accessed 1 August 2005).

Bowdin, G. A. J. and Church, I. J. (2000). Customer satisfaction and quality costs: towards a pragmatic approach for event management. In *Events Beyond 2000 – Setting the Agenda. Proceedings of the Conference on Evaluation, Research and Education, 13–14 July* (J. Allen, R. Harris, L. K. Jago and A. J. Veal, eds) Sydney, Australian Centre for Event Management, University of Technology.

Bradford Festival (2000). *Bradford Festival 2000 Review.* Bradford, Bradford Festival.

Bradner, J. (1995). Recruitment, orientation, retention. In *The Volunteer Management Handbook* (T. Connors, ed.) New York, John Wiley & Sons.

Bramwell, B. (1997). Strategic planning before and after a mega-event. *Tourism Management*, **18**(3), 167–176.

Brassington, F. and Pettitt, S. (2003). *Principles of Marketing.* 3rd edn. Harlow, *Financial Times*, Prentice Hall.

Britannica.com (2005). *Music Festival.* (Internet) *Encyclopedia Britannica Premium Service.* Available from <http://www.britannica.com/eb/article-9054427> (accessed 3 August 2005).

British Arts Festivals Association (BAFA) (2001). *New Research Shows that Festivals Mean Business.* (Internet) London, British Arts Festivals Association press release, March.

British Association of Conference Destinations (BACD) (2004). *The British Conference Venues Survey 2004.* Birmingham, British Association of Conference Destinations.

British Association of Conference Destinations (BACD) (2005). *BACD Investment Register.* (Internet) Birmingham, British Association of Conference Destinations. Available from <http://www.bacd.org.uk/default_frames.aspx?menu=rootandpage=investment registerandid=> (accessed 17 August 2005).

British Federation of Festivals for Music, Dance and Speech (BFF) (2005). *General Information.* (Internet) Macclesfield, British Federation of Festivals for Music, Dance and Speech. Available from <http://www.festivals.demon.co.uk/geninfo.htm> (accessed 3 August 2005).

British Standards Institution (BSI) (1999). BS 7960:1999. *Door Supervisors/Stewards — Code of Practice.* London, BSI.

British Standards Institution (BSI) (2002a). BS IEC 62198:2001. *Project Risk Management — Application Guidelines*. London, BSI.

British Standards Institution (BSI) (2002b). BS 7499:2002. *Static Site Guarding and Mobile Patrol Services — Code of Practice*. London, BSI.

British Standards Institution (BSI) (2003). BS 8406:2003. *Event Stewarding and Crowd Safety Services – Code of Practice*. London, BSI.

British Standards Institution (BSI) (2004). PAS 51:2004. *Guide to Industry Best Practice for Organizing Outdoor Events*. London, BSI.

British Tourism Authority (2005). *Business Tourism: International Marketing Opportunities 2005–2006*. London, British Tourism Authority.

Brody, R. and Goodman, M. (1988). *Fund-raising Events: Strategies and Programs for Success*. New York, Human Sciences Press Inc.

Brookes, F. and Landry, C. (2002). *Good Times: The Economic Impact of Cheltenham's Festivals*. Stroud, Comedia.

Brooks, I. and Weatherston, J. (2000). *The Business Environment: Challenges and Changes*. 2nd edn. Harlow, Financial Times, Prentice Hall.

Buckler, B. (1998). Practical steps towards a learning organisation: applying academic knowledge to improvement and innovation in business performance. *The Learning Organisation*, **5**(1), 15–23.

Burgan, B. and Mules, T. (2000). Event analysis — understanding the divide between cost benefit and economic impact assessment. In *Events Beyond 2000: Setting the Agenda — Event Evaluation, Research and Education Conference Proceedings* (J. Allen, R. Harris, L. K. Jago and A. J. Veal, eds) Sydney, Australian Centre for Event Management, University of Technology.

Burke, R. (2003). *Project Management: Planning and Control Techniques*. 4th edn. Chichester, John Wiley & Sons.

Business Tourism Partnership (BTP) (2005). *Business Tourism Leads the Way*. July. London, Business Tourism Partnership.

CACI (2004). *Acorn: The Smarter Consumer Classification*. London, CACI Limited.

Cake (2005). *19 More Reasons to be at V*. (Internet) Press Release, 8 March. Available from <http://www.vfestival.com/vfestival/pressreleases/oasis.pdf> (accessed 22 August 2005).

California Traditional Music Society (2005). *CTMS Volunteer Survey — 2005*. (Internet) Available from <http://www.ctmsfolkmusic.org/pdf/festival/VolunteerSurvey 2005.pdf> (accessed 24 August 2005).

Cambridge Policy Consultants (2002). *The Impact of the Manchester 2002 Commonwealth Games Executive Summary*. (Internet) Available from <http://www.manchester.gov.uk/corporate/games/impact.htm> (accessed 5 August 2005).

Canadine, I. C. (2001). *Transport, Logistics and All That!* (Internet) Corby, The Chartered Institute of Logistics and Transport (UK). Available from <http://www.ciltuk.org.uk/pages/whoweare> (accessed 7 April 2005).

Carling, P. and Seeley, A. (1998). *The Millennium Dome*. House of Commons Library Research Paper 98/32, 12 March. London, House of Commons Library Business and Transport Section.

Carlsen, J. and Millan, A. (2002). The links between mega-events and urban development: the case of the Manchester 2002 Commonwealth Games. In *Events and Place-making: Proceedings of International Research Conference Held in Sydney 2002* (L. Jago, M. Deery, R. Harris, A. Hede and J. Allen, eds), Sydney, Australian Centre for Event Management.

Carlsen, J. and Taylor, A. (2003). Mega-events and urban renewal: the case of the Manchester 2002 Commonwealth Games. *Event Management*, **8**(1), 15–22.

Carter, B. (2004). *O2 Sponsors Live Music to Boost Appeal to Youth.* (Internet) *Marketing,* 8 April. Available from <http://www.brandrepublic.com/news/article/207277/o2-sponsors-live-music-boost-appeal-youth/> (accessed 9 August 2005).

Cartwright, G. (1995). *Making the Most of Trade Exhibitions.* Oxford, Butterworth-Heinemann.

Catherwood, D. W. and Van Kirk, R. L. (1992). *The Complete Guide to Special Event Management: Business Insights, Financial Advice, and Successful Strategies from Ernst and Young, Advisors to the Olympics, the Emmy Awards and the PGA Tour.* New York, John Wiley & Sons.

Chaloner, H. (1998). *A Quality of Light Boosts Cornwall's Economy.* (Internet) Available from <http://www.southwesttourism.co.uk/prodev/light.htm> (accessed 8 January 2001).

Chartered Institute of Marketing (CIM) (2005). *Marketing Glossary.* (Internet) Maidenhead, Chartered Institute of Marketing. Available from <http://www.cim.co.uk/cim/ser/html/infQuiGlo.cfm?letter=M> (accessed 3 August 2005).

Chernushenko, D. (1994). *Greening Our Games: Running Sports Events and Facilities That Won't Cost the Earth.* Ottawa, Canada, Centurion.

City of Edinburgh Council (2000a). *Minutes: The City of Edinburgh Council: Appendix 1,* 24 August.

City of Edinburgh Council (2000b). *Edinburgh Launches Hogmanay Programme for 2000/2001.* City of Edinburgh Council Press Release, 23 November.

City of Edinburgh Council (2000c). *Edinburgh's Hogmanay Traffic and Safety Arrangements Announced.* City of Edinburgh Council Press Release, 15 November.

City of Edinburgh Council (2002). *Planning Guide: Events in Edinburgh.* April (Internet) Edinburgh, City of Edinburgh Council. Available from <http://download.edinburgh.gov.uk/events/planning%2Bguide%2B2.pdf> (accessed 9 August 2005).

City of Westminster (2000). *Preferred Practice Notes: Risk Assessment in Event and Filing Activities.* (Internet) London, City of Westminster. Available from <http://www.westminster.gov.uk/leisureandculture/artsandentertainment/events/upload/5711.pdf> (accessed 9 August 2005).

City of Westminster (2005). *Guidance Notes for Organisers Proposing Events in the City of Westminster on the Public Highway or in Council Managed Areas of the City.* (Internet) London, City of Westminster. Available from <http://www3.westminster.gov.uk/docstores/formsguidance_store/634-Major%20Event%20Guidance%20Notes%202005.pdf> (accessed 9 August 2005).

Comedia (2003). *National Arts Information Project: Evaluation Toolkit.* London, Arts Council of England.

Comfort, J. (1996). *Effective Meetings.* Oxford, Oxford Business English Skills.

Communications Agencies Federation (CAF) (2003). *The Client Brief: A Best Practice Guide to Briefing Communications Agencies.* (Internet) London, Communications Agencies Federation. Available from <http://www.cafinfo.com/documents/full_-client_brief.pdf> (accessed 3 August 2005).

Convention Industry Council (CIC) (2003). *APEX Industry Glossary.* (Internet) Available from <http://glossary.conventionindustry.org/> (accessed 10 July 2005).

Conway, L. (2000). *The Tobacco Advertising and Promotion Bill.* House of Commons Research Paper 00/97, 20 December (Internet) London, House of Commons Library. Available from <http://www.parliament.uk> (accessed 3 August 2005).

Cook, N. and Morse, P. (2004). *The Environmental Impacts of the Notting Hill Carnival 2004.* (Internet) Overview and Scrutiny Committee on Environmental Services, Environmental Health and Planning Policy, 1st November. London, The Royal Borough of Kensington and Chelsea. Available from <http://www.rbkc.gov.uk/NottingHill04/general/nhcreport2004.pdf> (accessed 3 August 2005).

Cordingly, S. (1999). *Managing Volunteers*. (Internet) Available from <http://www.fuel4arts.com.au> (accessed 22 August 2005).

Cornwell, T., Roy, D. and Steinard II, E. (2001). Exploring managers' perceptions of the impact of sponsorship on brand equity. *Journal of Advertising*, **30**(2), 41–51.

Couchman, N. and Harrington, D. (2000). Preventing ambush/parasitic marketing in sport. (Internet) *Sports and Character Licensing*, (4), March. Available from <http://www.townleys.co.uk/ambush%20marketing.htm> (accessed 31 January 2001).

Coulson, C. and Coe, T. (1991). *The Flatter Organisation: Philosophy and Practice*. Corby, Institute of Management.

Cravens, D., Merrilees, B. and Walker, R. (2000). *Strategic Marketing Management for the Pacific Region*. Sydney, McGraw-Hill.

Crawford, D. (2000). Environmental Accounting for Sport and Public Events: A Tool for Better Decision Making. (Internet) *Sustainable Sport Sourceline*, May. Available from <http://www.greengold.on.ca/newsletter/index.html> (accessed 3 August 2005).

Crofts, A. (2001). *Corporate Entertaining as a Marketing Tool*. Chalford, Management Books 2000 Ltd.

Crompton, J. (1993). Understanding a business organisation's approach to entering a sponsorship partnership. *Festival Management and Event Tourism*, **1**(3), 98–109.

Crompton, J. (1994). Benefits and risks associated with sponsorship of major events. *Festival Management and Event Tourism*, **2**(2), 65–74.

Crompton, J. and McKay, S. (1997). Motives of visitors attending festival events. *Annals of Tourism Research*, **24**(2), 425–439.

Crompton, J. L. and McKay, S. L. (1994). Measuring the impact of festivals and events: some myths, misapplications and ethical dilemmas. *Festival Management and Event Tourism*, **2**(1), 33–43.

Culture, Media and Sport Committee (2000). *Marking the Millennium in the United Kingdom: Eight Report from the Culture, Media and Sport Committee Session 1999–2000*. (Internet) London, HMSO. Available from <http://www.publications.parliament.uk/pa/cm199900/cmselect/cmcumeds/578/57802.htm> (accessed 9 August 2005).

Dale, M. (1995). Events as image. In *Tourism and Leisure – Perspectives on Provision* (D. Leslie, ed.) vol. 2. Brighton, LSA.

Davidson, H. (2004). *Manchester International Festival Proposal*. (Internet) Press Release, 12 January, Manchester, Manchester City Council. Available from <http://www.manchester.gov.uk/news/2004/jan/festival.htm> (accessed 9 August 2005).

Davidson, R. (2002). *Making the Most of Our Business Visitors*. (Internet) London, Business Tourism Partnership. Available from <http://www.businesstourismpartnership.com/pubs/makingthemost.pdf> (accessed 5 August 2005).

Davidson, R. and Cope, B. (2003). *Business Travel: Conferences, Incentive Travel, Exhibitions, Corporate Hospitality and Corporate Travel*. Harlow, Financial Times, Prentice Hall.

Day, J. (2002). Global sponsorship market soars. (Internet) *Media Guardian*, 15 January. Available from <media.guardian.ac.uk> (accessed 20 July 2005).

De Pelsmacker, P., Geuens, M. and Van den Bergh, J. (2004). *Marketing Communications – A European Perspective*. 2nd edn. Harlow, Financial Times, Prentice Hall.

De Smet, L. (1999). Enter the dragon. *Access All Areas*, September, 20–21.

Dean, J., Goodlad, R. and Hamilton, C. (2001). *Toolkit for Evaluating Arts Projects in Social Inclusion Areas: A Report to the Scottish Arts Council*. Edinburgh, Scottish Arts Council.

Deeley, P. (1998). Old Trafford in crackdown on rowdy element. (Internet) *Daily Telegraph*, 1 July. Available from <http://www.portal.telegraph.co.uk/

htmlContent.jhtml?html=/archive/1998/07/01/scdeel01.html> (accessed 9 August 2005).

Department for Culture, Media and Sport (DCMS) (1999). *Tomorrow's Tourism: A Growth Industry for the New Millennium*. London, Department for Culture, Media and Sport.

Department for Culture, Media and Sport (DCMS) (2005). *Creative Industries: Live Music Forum*. (Internet) London, Department for Culture, Media and Sport. Available from <http://www.culture.gov.uk/creative_industries/music/livemusicforum.htm> (accessed 9 August 2005).

Department of National Heritage and the Scottish Office (1997). *Guide to Safety at Sports Grounds*. 4th edn. London, HMSO.

Destination Sheffield (1995). *An Event-led City and Tourism Marketing Strategy for Sheffield*. Sheffield, Destination Sheffield.

Dibb, S., Simkin, L., Pride, W. M. and Ferrell, O. C. (2006). *Marketing: Concepts and Strategies*. 5th Euro. edn. Boston, Mass. Houghton Mifflin.

Dickman, S. (1997). Issues in arts marketing. In *Making It Happen: The Cultural and Entertainment Industries Handbook* (R. Rentchler, ed.) Melbourne, Centre for Professional Development.

Dinsmore, P. C. (1998). *Human Factors in Project Management*. New York, AMACOM.

Disability Rights Commission (DRC) (2002). *Code of Practice: Rights of Access: Goods, Facilities, Services and Premises*. Stratford-upon-Avon, Disability Rights Commission.

Disability Rights Commission (DRC) (2004). *Organising Accessible Events*. Stratford-upon-Avon, Disability Rights Commission.

Dolphin, R. (2003). Sponsorship: perspectives on its strategic role. *Corporate Communications: an International Journal*, **8**(3), 173–186.

Drucker, P. (1973). *Management*. New York, Harper & Row.

Duncan, T. (2002). *IMC: Using Advertising and Promotion to Build Brands*. Boston, McGraw-Hill Irwin.

Dyson, J. R. (2004). *Accounting for Non-accounting Students*. 6th edn. Harlow, *Financial Times*, Prentice Hall.

Edinburgh Festival Fringe (2002). *Edinburgh Festival Fringe Annual Report 2002*. Edinburgh, Edinburgh Festival Fringe.

Edinburgh International Book Festival (2005). *About The Edinburgh International Book Festival*. (Internet) Available from <http://www.edbookfest.co.uk/about/index.html> (accessed 23 August 2005).

Edinburgh International Festival (EIF) (2000). *Edinburgh International Festival Annual Review 1999*. Edinburgh, EIF.

Ellery, S. (2004). Hospitality — summer attractions. *PR Week*, March, 5.

Elstad, B. (2003). Continuance commitment and reasons to quit: a study of volunteers at a jazz festival. *Event Management*, **8**(2), 99–108.

English Sports Council (1999). Memorandum submitted by the English Sports Council. In *Fourth Report: Staging International Sporting Events. Volume II Minutes of Evidence* (Select Committee on Culture, Media and Sport). London, The Stationery Office.

English Tourism (1999). *Tourism and Sport in England*. Media brief, July. London, English Tourism.

European Dana Alliance for the Brain (2005). *Brain Awareness Week 14–20 March 2005*. (Internet) Available from <http://www.edab.net/BAWFrame.html> (accessed 9 August 2005).

Evans, G. (1996). Planning for the British Millennium Festival: establishing the visitor baseline and a framework for forecasting. *Festival Management and Event Tourism*, **3**(3), 183–196.

Event Assured (2005). *Risk Check List for Event Organisers – Risk and your Event.* (Internet) Event Assured Advice Centre, 28 April. Available from <http://www.event-assured.com/> (accessed 17 July 2005).

Event Marketing Support Unit (2002). *Achieving Our Potential: Event Marketing Support Scheme.* (Internet) Cardiff, Event Marketing Support Unit. Available from <http://www.wtbonline.gov.uk/30322/DOWNLOAD_LIST.html> (accessed 17 August 2005).

EventScotland (2005). *Regional Events Programme Overview & Objectives.* (Internet) Available from <http://www.eventscotland.org/supportprogrammes/regional-eventsprogramme.htm> (accessed 5 August 2005).

Events Tasmania (2003a). *Our Role.* (Internet) Available from <http://www.events-tasmania.com/subpage.cgi?pageID=2andsubsectionID=21> (accessed 9 August 2005).

Events Tasmania (2003b). *Events Tasmania Strategic Plan 2003–2008.* (Internet) Available from <http://www.eventstasmania.com/StrategicPlan2003-08.pdf> (accessed 9 August 2005).

Exhibition Audience Audits Ltd (2004). *UK Exhibition Facts*, Volume 15. North Seaton, Exhibition Venues Association.

Exhibition Audience Audits Ltd (2005). *UK Exhibition Facts*, Volume 16. North Seaton, Exhibition Venues Association.

Exhibition Liaison Committee (1995). *The Exhibition Industry Explained.* London, Exhibition Liaison Committee.

Farrelly, F. and Quester, P. (2003). The effects of market orientation on trust and commitment – the case of the sponsorship business to business relationship. *European Journal of Marketing*, **37**(3/4), 530–553.

Faulkner, B. (1993). *Evaluating the Tourism Impact of Hallmark Events*, Occasional Paper No. 16. Canberra, Bureau of Tourism Research.

Ferguson, B. (2005). Audiences to get a starring role with text rating, *Edinburgh Evening News*, 25 July (Internet) Available from <http://edinburghnews.scotsman.com/index.cfm?id=1679472005> (accessed 9 August 2005).

Flashman, R. and Quick, S. (1985). Altruism is not dead: a specific analysis of volunteer motivation. In *Motivating Volunteers* (L. Moore, ed.) Vancouver, Vancouver Volunteer Centre.

Fuller, M. (1998). *Basingstoke Arts Festival Feasibility Study: Report of the Director of Arts, Countryside and Community.* (Internet) Hampshire, Hampshire County Council Recreation and Heritage Committee, 15 January. Available from <www.hants.gov.uk/> (accessed 15 November 2000).

Gartside, M. (1999). Cornwall 'bungles' total eclipse. *Access All Areas*, September, 1–2.

Geldard, E. and Sinclair, L. (2003). *The Sponsorship Manual: Sponsorship Made Easy.* 2nd edn. Victoria, Australia, Sponsorship Unit.

Getz, D. (1991). *Festivals, Special Events and Tourism.* New York, Van Nostrand Reinhold.

Getz, D. (2005). *Event Management & Event Tourism*, 2nd edn. New York, Cognizant Communication Corporation.

Getz, D. and Wicks, B. (1994). Professionalism and certification for festival and event practitioners: trends and issues. *Festival Management and Event Tourism*, **2**(2), 108–109.

Getz, D., Neill, O. M. and Carlsen, J. (2001). Service quality evaluation at events through service mapping. *Journal of Travel Research*, **39**(4), 380–390.

Giddens, A. (1990). *The Consequences of Modernity.* Cambridge, Polity Press.

Giddings, C. (1997). *Measuring the Impact of Festivals* — Guidelines for Conducting an Economic Impact Study, Canberra, National Centre for Culture and Recreation Studies, Australian Bureau of Statistics.

Glastonbury Festivals Ltd (2000). *Recycling Crew: Information, Terms and Conditions.* Pilton, Glastonbury Festivals Ltd.

Goh, F. (2003). Irish Festivals, Irish Life: The Facts and How to Use Them. *Presentation at the 2003 Irish Festivals Association Conference.* (Internet) Available from <http://www.aoifeonline.com> (accessed 17 July 2005).

Goldblatt, J. (2000). A future for event management: the analysis of major trends impacting the emerging profession. In *Events beyond 2000 – Setting the Agenda. Proceedings of the Conference on Evaluation, Research and Education, 13–14 July* (J. Allen, R. Harris and L. Jago, eds) Sydney, Australian Centre for Event Management, University of Technology.

Goldblatt, J. (1997). *Special Events: Best Practices in Modern Event Management.* 2nd edn. New York, John Wiley & Sons.

Goldblatt, J. (2005). *Special Events: Event Leadership for a New World.* 4th edn. Hoboken, John Wiley & Sons.

Goldblatt, J. and Perry, J. (2002). Re-building the community with fire, water and music: the waterfire phenomenon. In *Events and Place-making: Proceedings of International Research Conference Held in Sydney 2002* (L. Jago, M. Deery, R. Harris, A. Hede and J. Allen, eds) Sydney, Australian Centre for Event Management.

Graham, S., Neirotti, L. D. and Goldblatt, J. J. (2001). *The Ultimate Guide to Sports Event Management and Marketing.* 2nd edn. New York, McGraw-Hill.

Gray, C. and Larson, E. (2000). *Project Management: The Managerial Process.* Boston, McGraw-Hill International.

Greaves, K. (1999). Tailor-made for business. *Marketing Event,* October, 45–50.

Greaves, S. (1996). Post Millennium Motivation. *Conference and Incentive Travel,* July–August, 46–48.

Green Games Watch (2004). *About Us.* (Internet) Available from <nccnsw.org.au/member/ggw/> (accessed 4 August 2005).

Grey, A. M. and Skildum-Reid, K. (2003). *The Sponsorship Seeker's Toolkit.* 2nd edn. Sydney, McGraw-Hill.

Gronroos, C. (1990). *Services Marketing and Management.* Lexington, Massachusetts, Lexington Books.

Gronroos, C. (1994). From marketing mix to relationship marketing: towards a paradigm shift in marketing. *Asia-Australia Marketing Journal,* **2**(1), 9–29.

Guinness World Records (2005). *Most Lucrative Charity Sporting Event.* (Internet) Available from <http://www.guinnessworldrecords.com/gwr5/content_pages/record.asp?recordid=52445> (accessed 2 August 2005).

Halbwirth, S. and Toohey, K. (2001). The Olympic Games and knowledge management: a case study of the Sydney Organising Committee of the Olympic Games. *European Sport Management Quarterly,* **1**(2), 91–111.

Hall, C. M. (1989). Hallmark events and the planning process. In *The Planning and Evaluation of Hallmark Events* (G. J. Syme, B. J. Shaw, D. M. Fenton and W. S. Mueller, eds) Aldershot, Avebury.

Hall, C. M. (1997). *Hallmark Tourist Events: Impacts, Management and Planning.* Chichester, John Wiley & Sons.

Hanlon, C. and Cuskelly, G. (2002). Pulsating major sport event organisations: a framework for inducting managerial personnel. *Event Management,* **7**(4), 231–243.

Hanlon, C. and Jago, L. (2000). Pulsating sporting events. In *Events Beyond 2000 – Setting the Agenda. Proceedings of the Conference on Evaluation, Research and Education, 13–14 July* (J. Allen, R. Harris, L. K. Jago and A. J. Veal, eds) Sydney, Australian Centre for Event Management, University of Technology, 93–104.

Hannagan, T. (2005). *Management Concepts and Practices.* 4th edn. London, *Financial Times,* Prentice Hall.

Hannam, C. (2000). *Sample Contract Terms and Conditions*. Kingston upon Thames, Production Services Association.

Hannam, C. (2004). *Heath and Safety Management in the Live Music and Events Industry*. Cambridge, Entertainment Technology Press.

Hansen, B. and Thomas C. (2005). *Off-Premise Catering Management*, 2nd edn. Hoboken, NJ, Wiley.

Hardman, R. (1995). *Youth Sets the Tone for Peace in Hyde Park*. (Internet) *Electronic Telegraph*, 8 May. Available from <http://www.telegraph.co.uk> (accessed 8 April 2001).

Harris, R. and Griffin, T. (1997). *Tourism Events Training Audit*. Sydney, Tourism New South Wales Events Unit.

Harris, R. and Jago, L. (1999). Event education and training in Australia: the current state of play. *Australian Journal of Hospitality Management*, **6**(1), 45–51.

Harrison, D. and Hastings, C. (2000). *High Spirits and Bright Lights Till Dawn*. (Internet) *Electronic Telegraph*, 2 January, Issue 1682. Available from <http://www.telegraph.-co.uk> (accessed 5 February 2001).

Harrison, P. (2004). *Sponsorship — Cutting Through the Hype*. (Internet) The Australia Council for the Arts, February. Available from <http://www.fuel4arts.com> (accessed 20 August 2005).

Harrogate International Festival (2004a). *Volunteer Event Steward Job Description*. (Internet) Harrogate, Harrogate International Festivals Ltd. Available from: <http://www.harrogate-festival.org.uk/jobs/volunteer_event_steward.doc> (accessed 5 August 2005).

Harrogate International Festival (2004b). *Volunteer Event Steward Application Form*. (Internet) Harrogate, Harrogate International Festivals Ltd. Available from <http://www.harrogate-festival.org.uk/jobs/volunteer_event_steward_application_form.doc> (accessed 5 August 2005).

Harrogate International Festival (2005). *Education and Community Programme*. (Internet) Harrogate, Harrogate International Festivals Ltd. Available from <http://www.harrogate-festival.org.uk/education/education.html> (accessed 5 August 2005).

Harrowven, J. (1980). *Origins of Festivals and Feasts*. London, Kaye & Ward.

Haymarket Land Events LLP (2005). *Town & Country Festival 05*. Stoneleigh Park, Haymarket Land Events LLP.

Health and Safety Executive (HSE) (1998). *Five Steps to Risk Management*. London, HSE.

Health and Safety Executive (HSE) (1999). *The Event Safety Guide*. Norwich, HSE Books.

Health and Safety Executive (HSE) (2000). *Managing Crowds Safely*. Norwich, HSE Books.

Health and Safety Executive (HSE) (2003). *Health and Safety Regulation. A Short Guide*. HSC13 (rev 1) 08/03. London, HSE.

Hede, A.-M., Jago, L. and Deery, M. (2003). Satisfaction-based cluster analysis of theatre event attendees: preliminary results. *Paper Presented at the 13th International Research Conference of the Council for Australian University Tourism and Hospitality Education*, 5–8 February, Coffs Harbour, New South Wales.

Hemmerling, M. (1997). What makes an event a success for a host city, sponsors and others? *Paper delivered* to The Big Event New South Wales Tourism Conference, 5–7 November, Wollongong, Australia.

Henderson, P. and Chapman, A. (1997). Thousands are left stranded. *Mail on Sunday*, April, 6, 2–3.

Hertzberg, F. (1968). One more time: how do you motivate employees? *Harvard Business Review*, **46**(1), 361–367.

Hicks, H. and Gullet, C. (1976). *The Management of Organisations*. Tokyo, McGraw-Hill Kogakusha Ltd.

Higgins, C. (2004). Edinburgh Festival faces new rival: Manchester to launch big-budget arts event. (Internet) *The Guardian*, 9 November. Available from <http://www.guardian.co.uk/arts/news/story/0,11711,1346606,00.html> (accessed 9 August 2005).

Hiller, H. and Moylan, D. (1999). Mega-events and community obsolesence: redevelopment versus rehabilitation in Victoria Park East. *Canadian Journal of Urban Research*, **8**(1), 47–81.

Hinch, T. and Higham, J. (2004). Sport tourism development. In *Aspects of Tourism* (C. Cooper, ed.) Clevedon, Channel View Publications.

Hjalager, A. M. (1996). Tourism and the environment: The innovation connection, *Journal of Sustainable Tourism*, **4**(4), 201–207.

HM Government (2005). *Opportunity Age – Opportunity and Security Throughout Life*. London, HMSO. (Internet) Available from <http://www.dwp.gov.uk/opportunity_age/> (accessed 9 August 2005).

HMSO. (2003). *Licensing Act 2003*. London, The Stationery Office Limited.

Holder, C. (2001). Case study: Notting Hill Carnival. In *Events Management* (G. Bowdin, I. McDonnell, J. Allen and W. O'Toole, eds) Oxford, Butterworth-Heinemann.

Home Office (2000). *Dealing with Disaster*. 3rd edn. London, Home Office Communication Directorate. (Internet) Available from <http://www.homeoffice.gov.uk/docs2/dwdrevised.pdf> (accessed 3 August 2005).

Howden, N. (2004). Extreme noise terror. *Access All Areas*, October, 7.

Howey, J. (2000). *Outdoor Events Policy – Royal Victoria Park*. (Internet) Bath and North East Somerset Council Community, Culture and Leisure Committee, 13 July. Available from <http://www.bathnes.gov.uk/Committee_Papers/CCL/cl000710/13events.htm> (accessed 3 August 2005).

Hoyle, L. H. (2002). *Event Marketing: How to Successfully Promote Events, Festivals, Conventions and Expositions*. New York, John Wiley & Sons Inc.

ICC Cricket World Cup (2003). *Volunteers 2003 Training Manual*. Johannesburg, South Africa, ICC Cricket World Cup Organising Committee.

Imaginate (2005a). *Welcome to Imaginate*. (Internet) Available from: <http://www.imaginate.org.uk/corporate/index.php> (accessed 9 August 2005).

Imaginate (2005b). *Bank of Scotland Children's International Theatre Festival*. (Internet) Available from <http://www.imaginate.org.uk/corporate/index.php> (accessed 9 August 2005).

International Chamber of Commerce (ICC) (2003). *International Code on Sponsorship*. (Internet) Commission on Marketing and Advertising, 17 September. Available from <http://www.iccbookstore.com/home/statements_rules/rules/2003/International%20Code%20on%20Sponsorship.asp> (accessed 3 August 2005).

International Congress & Convention Association (ICCA) (2004). *The International Meetings Market 2003*. Amsterdam, International Congress & Convention Association.

International Congress & Convention Association (ICCA) (2005). *The International Meetings Market 2004*. Amsterdam, International Congress & Convention Association.

International EMBOK Executive (2005). *Event Management Body of Knowledge (EMBOK)*. (Internet) Johannesburg, International EMBOK Executive. Available from <http://www.embok.org> (accessed 1 October 2005).

International Olympic Committee (1999). *Building a Positive Environmental Legacy Through the Olympic Games*. Lausanne, Switzerland, Commission on Sport and the Environment.

International Olympic Committee (IOC) (2005). *100 years of Olympic Marketing.* (Internet) Lausanne, International Olympic Committee. Available from <http://www.olympic.org/uk/organisation/facts/introduction/100years_uk.asp> (accessed 24 August 2005).

Jackson, A. (2004). *Evaluation Toolkit for the Voluntary and Community Arts in Northern Ireland.* Bath, Annabel Jackson Associates.

Jago, L. K. and Shaw, R. N. (1998). A conceptual and differential framework. *Festival Management and Event Tourism*, **5**(1/2), 21–32.

Jago, L., Chalip, L., Brown, G., Mules, T. and Ali, S. (2002). The role of events in helping to brand a destination. In *Events and Place-making: Proceedings of International Research Conference Held in Sydney 2002* (L. Jago, M. Deery, R. Harris, A. Hede and J. Allen, eds) Sydney, Australian Centre for Event Management.

Jago, L., Chalip, L., Brown, G., Mules, T. and Ali, S. (2003). Building events into destination branding: insights from experts. *Event Management*, **8**(1), 3–14.

Janiskee, R. (1996). Historic houses and special events. *Annals of Leisure Research*, **23**(2), 398–414.

Jobber, D. (2004). *Principles and Practice of Marketing.* Maidenhead, McGraw-Hill International (UK) Ltd.

Johnson, G., Scholes, K. and Whittington, R. (2005). *Exploring Corporate Strategy.* 7th edn. Harlow, *Financial Times*, Prentice Hall.

Joint Meetings Industry Council (JMIC) (2005). *Profile and Power: A Strategic Communications Plan for Building Industry Awareness and Influence.* Brussels, Joint Meetings Industry Council.

Jones, C. (2000). *It's Time for a Dressing Down at Stuffy SW19.* (Internet) *Evening Standard*, 7 June. Available from <http://www.findarticles.com/p/articles/mi_qn4153/is_20000607/ai_n11933808> (accessed 3 August 2005).

Jones, C. (2001). A level playing field? Sports stadium infrastructure and urban development in the United Kingdom. *Environment and Planning*, **33**, 845–861.

Jones, C. (2002). The stadium and economic development: cardiff and the Millennium Stadium. *European Planning Studies*, **10**(7), 819–829.

Judd, D. (1997). Diamonds are forever? Kipling's imperialism. (Internet) *History Today*, January. <http://www.britannica.com/magazine/article?content.id=17875> (accessed 2 January 2001).

Jura Consultants and Gardiner & Theobold (2001). *Millennium Festival Impact Study.* Edinburgh, Jura Consultants and Gardiner & Theobold Management Consultancy.

Kaless, S. (2003). *Looking at the Numbers Game.* (Internet) News, 24 November. Available from <http://www.rwc2003.irb.com/EN/Tournament/News/sk+24+11+stats.htm> (accessed 24 August 2005).

Kemp, C. (2000). *Music Industry Management and Promotion.* 2nd edn. Kings Ripton, ELM Publications.

Kemp, C. and Hill, I. (2004). *Heath and Safety Aspects in the Live Music Industry.* Cambridge, Entertainment Technology Press.

Keung, D. (1998). *Management: A Contemporary Approach.* London, Pitman Publishing.

Kirkwood, J. (2005). *Application for Occasional Public Entertainment Licence for Glastonbury Festival 2005.* (Internet) Mendip, Mendip District Council, 6 December. Available from <http://www.mendip.gov.uk/committeemeeting.asp?id=SX31F-A780B5E2> (accessed 17 July 2005).

Korman, A. (2000). *Basic Guide to Sponsorship Contracts.* (Internet) London, Townleys Solicitors. Available from <http://www.sponsorshiponline.com> (accessed 17 July 2005).

Kotler, P., Wong, V., Saunders, J. and Armstrong, G. (2005). *Principles of Marketing.* 4th Euro edn. London, Prentice Hall Europe.

Kotler, P., Bowen, J. and Makens, J. (1999). *Marketing for Hospitality and Tourism.* 2nd edn. Upper Sadler River, NJ, Prentice Hall International.

Kover, A. J. (2001). The sponsorship issue. *Journal of Advertising Research*, February, 5.

KRONOS (1997). *The Economic Impact of Sports Events Staged in Sheffield 1990–1997.* Destination Sheffield, Sheffield City Council and Sheffield International Venues Ltd.

Kyriakopoulos, V. and Benns, M. (2004). Passing the torch to Athens. *The Sun-Herald*, 22 February.

Lagae, W. (2005). *Sport Sponsorship and Marketing Communications: A European Perspective.* Harlow, *Financial Times*, Prentice Hall.

Lake District National Park Authority (1999). *Lake District National Park Management Plan.* Cumbria, Lake District National Park Authority.

Lee, S., Ryder, C. and Shin, H.-J. (2003). An investigation of environmental motivation factors among Minor League Baseball (MiLB) fans. (Internet) *The Sport Journal*, 6(3). Available from <http://www.thesportjournal.org/2003Journal/Vol6-No3/MiLB.asp> (accessed 9 August 2005).

Leeds Rugby (2005). *Welcome to Corporate Opportunities.* (Internet) Leeds, Leeds Rugby. Available from <http://www.atommedia.co.uk/leedsrugby/corporate/index.htm> (accessed 26 August 2005).

Lieberman, A. and Esgate, P. (2002). *The Entertainment Marketing Revolution.* Upper Saddler River, New Jersey, *Financial Times*, Prentice Hall.

Lilley III, W. and DeFranco, L. J. (1999a). *The Economic Impact of Network Q Rally of Great Britain.* Washington, D.C., InContext Inc.

Lilley III, W. and DeFranco, L. J. (1999b). *The Economic Impact of the European Grand Prix.* Washington, D.C., InContext Inc.

Litherland, S. (1997). Expose yourself live. *Marketing Event*, June, 41–42.

Live 8 (2005). *The Long Walk to Justice.* (Internet) Available from <http://www.live8live.com/whattodo/index.shtml> (accessed 2 August 2005).

Liverpool Culture Company (2005a). *Culture Uncovered – Your Questions Answered.* (Internet) Liverpool, Liverpool Culture Company. Available from <http://www.liverpool08.com/AboutUs/YourQuestions/index.asp> (accessed 9 August 2005).

Liverpool Culture Company (2005b). *Liverpool Culture Company 2004-5 Review: 2005-6 Delivery Plan.* Liverpool, Liverpool Culture Company.

Lloyds TSB Scotland (2005). *Lloyds TSB Scotland.* (Internet) Entry for Marketing Excellence Awards Scotland 2005. Available from <http://www.tunaweb.com/MarketingAwardsScotlandNominees/casestudies/Comms-SE-Lloyds.pdf> (accessed 24 August 2005).

Lock, D. (2003). *Project Management.* 8th edn. Aldershot, Gower.

London 2012 (2004a). *London 2012 Candidate File.* London, London 2012 Ltd.

London 2012 (2004b). *London 2012 Candidate File: Volume 3 Theme 12: Security.* London, London 2012 Ltd.

London 2012 (2004c). *London 2012 Candidate File: Volume 1 Theme 3: Legal Aspects.* London, London 2012 Ltd.

London 2012, WWF and BioRegional (2005). *Towards a One Planet Olympics: Achieving the First Sustainable Olympic Games and Paralympic Games.* London, London 2012 Ltd.

London Development Agency (2003). *The Economic Impact of the Notting Hill Carnival.* London, London Development Agency.

London Marathon (2005). *All in a Good Cause.* (Internet) Available from <http://www.london-marathon.co.uk/iframes/marathoninfo/goodcause.htm> (accessed 2 August 2005).

Lord Mayor's Show (2005b). *The Procession* (Internet). Available from <http://www.lordmayorshow.org/proc/index.shtml> (accessed 17 July 2005).

Lovelock, C. and Wirtz, J. (2004). *Services Marketing: People, Technology, Strategy.* 5th edn. Upper Saddle River, NJ, Pearson Prentice Hall.

Lyon, M. (2004). *A Planning Guide for Venue Finding Agencies, Meetings and Event Planners and Conference and Exhibition Managers.* Version 2. (Internet) Warwick, Write Style Communications Ltd. Available from <http://www.write-style.co.uk/pdfs/SiteInspectionHandbook.pdf> (accessed 2 August 2005).

Machiavelli, N. (1962). *The Prince* (Trans. L. Ricci). Chicago, Mentor Classics.

Made-Up Textiles Association (MUTA) (2001). *Code of Practice for Marquee Hiring Contractors and Code of Public Safety – Use and Operation of Marquees.* (Internet) Tamworth, Made-Up Textiles Association. Available from <http://www.performancetextiles.org.uk/downloads/codeMarquee1.pdf> (accessed 9 August 2005).

Made-Up Textiles Association (MUTA) (2005). *Marquee Hire – A Useful Guide.* (Internet) Tamworth, Made-Up Textiles Association. Available from <http://www.performancetextiles.org.uk/marquee1.asp> (accessed 9 August 2005).

Major Events Investigative Committee (2001). *Future Major Events In London: Final Report of the Major Events Investigative Committee.* March. London, Greater London Authority London Assembly.

Malouf, L. (1999). *Behind the Scenes at Special Events.* New York, John Wiley & Sons.

Manchester 2002 (2003). *2002 Manchester The XVII Commonwealth Games: Post Games Report.* London, Commonwealth Games Federation.

Mannell, R. and Iso-Ahola, S. (1987). Psychological nature of leisure and tourism experience. *Annals of Tourism Research*, **14**(3), 314–329.

Marketing Manchester (2004). *Northwest Conference Bidding Unit.* (Internet) Available from <http://www.conference.visitmanchester.com/conference/bidding.shtml> (accessed 3 August 2005).

Marsh, P. D. V. (1984). *Contract Negotiation Handbook.* 2nd edn. Aldershot, Gower.

Maslow, A. (1954). *Motivation and Personality.* New York, Harper & Row.

Masterman, G. (2004). *Strategic Sports Event Management: An International Approach.* Oxford, Elsevier Butterworth-Heinemann.

Masterman, G. and Wood, E. (2006). *Innovative Marketing Communications: Strategies for the Events Industry.* Oxford, Elsevier Butterworth-Heinemann.

Material Marketing & Communications Ltd (2005). *T In The Park.* (Internet) Entry for Marketing Excellence Awards Scotland 2005. Available from <http://www.tunaweb.com/MarketingAwardsScotlandNominees/casestudies/Comms-SE-TinthePark.pdf> (accessed 24 August 2005).

Matheson, C. (2005). *Firms Target Music Festival Goers.* (Internet) 23 May, *BBC News UK edition.* Available from <http://news.bbc.co.uk/1/hi/business/4438291.stm> (accessed 23 August 2005).

Maughan, C. and Bianchini, F. (2003). *Festivals and the Creative Region.* Nottingham, Arts Council England.

Mayor of London (2005). *Trafalgar Square Festival 2005.* (Internet) Available from <http://www.london.gov.uk/mayor/trafalgar_square/tsaf-05/index.jsp> (accessed 9 August 2005).

Mayor's Carnival Review Group (2004). *Notting Hill Carnival: A Strategic Review.* London, Greater London Authority.

McCarthy, E. and Perreault, W. (1987). *Basic Marketing.* Homewood, Illinois, Irwin.

McCarthy, E. J. (1971). *Basic Marketing: A Managerial Approach.* Homewood, Illinois, Irwin.

McCurley, S. and Lynch, R. (1998). *Essential Volunteer Management.* 2nd edn. London, Directory of Social Change.

McDuff, N. (1995). Volunteer and staff relations. In *The Volunteer Management Handbook* (T. Connors, ed) New York, John Wiley & Sons.

McKay, G. (2000). *Glastonbury: A Very English Fair.* (Internet) Gollancz. Extract Available from <http://www.uclan.ac.uk/facs/class/humanities/staff/mckaybook3.htm> (accessed 17 July 2005).

Meenaghan, T. (2001a). Understanding sponsorship effects. *Psychology and Marketing,* **18**(2), 95–122.

Meenaghan, T. (2001b). Sponsorship and advertising: a comparison of consumer perceptions. *Psychology and Marketing,* **18**(2), 191–215.

Midlands Environmental Business Club Limited (2002). *SEXI: The Sustainable Exhibitions Industry Project.* Birmingham, Midlands Environmental Business Club Limited.

Millennium Commission (2000). *Celebrating the Year 2000.* (Internet) Available from <http://www.millennium.gov.uk/lottery/festival.html> (accessed 24 August 2005).

Millennium Commission Press Office (2000). *August Bank Holiday Sees High Point for Millennium Festival.* (Internet) Millennium Commission Press Release, 23 August. Available from <http://www.millennium.gov.uk/cgi-bin/item.cgi?id=1286andd=11andh=24andf=46anddateformat=%25o-%25B-%25Y> (accessed 3 August 2005).

Mintel (2000). *Music Concerts and Festivals.* London, Mintel International Group Ltd.

Mintel (2004). *Music Concerts and Festivals.* London, Mintel International Group Ltd.

Minton, A. and Rose, R. (1997). The effects of environmental concern on environmentally friendly consumer behavior: an exploratory study. *Journal of Business Research,* **40**(1), 37–48.

Mintzberg, H. (1994). *The Rise and Fall of Strategic Planning.* New York, Prentice Hall.

Mintzberg, H. (2003). *The Strategy Process.* 4th edn. Harlow, Pearson Education.

Mohr, K., Backman, K., Gahan, L. and Backman, S. (1993). An investigation of festival motivations and event satisfaction by visitor type. *Festival Management and Event Tourism,* **1**(3), 89–97.

Mohr, K., Backman, K., Gahan, L. and Backman, S. (1993). An investigation of festival motivations and event satisfaction by visitor type. *Festival Management and Event Tourism,* **1**(1), 89–97.

Monmonier, M. (1996) *How to Lie with Maps.* 2nd edn. Chicago, University of Chicago Press.

Monroe, J. (2006). Art of the Event: *Complete Guide to Designing and Decorating Special Events.* Hoboken, NJ, Wiley.

Morgan, M. (1996). *Marketing for Leisure and Tourism.* London, Prentice Hall.

Morrow, S. S. (2002). *The Art of the Show.* 2nd edn. Dallas, IAEM Foundation.

Motor Sports Association (1999). *MSA Report Reveals Economic Impact of World Rally Championship (1999).* (Internet) Slough, Motor Sports Association press release, 19 November. Available from <http://www.ukmotorsport.com/networkq/1999/9914.html> (accessed 3 August 2005).

Motorsport Industry Association (MIA) (2003). *The Economic Impacts of the 2002 FIA Foster's British Grand Prix.* July. Stoneleigh Park, Motorsport Industry Association.

MPI (2005). *The Future is MPI Member Solutions.* (Internet) Available from <http://www.mpiweb.org/resources/pathways/default.asp> (accessed 1 August 2005).

Mules, T. (1993). A special event as part of an urban renewal strategy. *Festival Management and Event Tourism,* **1**(2), 65–67.

Mules, T. (1998). Events tourism and economic development in Australia. In *Managing Tourism in Cities* (D. Tyler, Y. Guerrier and M. Robertson, eds) New York, John Wiley & Sons.

Mules, T. (1999). Estimating the economic impact of an event on a local government area, Region, State or Territory. In *Valuing Tourism: Methods and Techniques*

(K. Corcoran, A. Allcock, T. Frost and L. Johnson, eds) Canberra, Bureau of Tourism Research.

Mules, T. and McDonald, S. (1994). The economic impact of special events: the use of forecasts. *Festival Management and Event Tourism*, **2**(1), 45–53.

Mullins, L. J. (2005). *Management and Organisational Behaviour*. 7th edn. London, Financial Times, Pitman Publishing.

Muthaly, S. K., Ratnatunga, J., Roberts, G. B. and Roberts, C. D. (2000). An event based entrepreneurship case study of futuristic strategies for Sydney 2000 Olympics. In *Events Beyond 2000 – Setting the Agenda. Proceedings of the Conference on Evaluation, Research and Education, 13–14 July* (J. Allen, R. Harris, L. K. Jago and A. J. Veal, eds) Sydney, Australian Centre for Event Management, University of Technology.

National Heritage Committee (1995). *Fifth Report Bids to Stage International Sporting Events, HC (1994–95) 493*. London, HMSO.

National Maritime Museum (2005). *What is SeaBritain 2005?* (Internet) Available from <http://www.seabritain.com/server.php?show=nav.00400q> (accessed 9 August 2005).

National Outdoor Events Association (NOEA) (1993). *Code of Practice for Outdoor Events: Other than Pop Concerts and Raves*. Wallington, NOEA.

National Outdoor Events Association (NOEA) (1997). *Code of Practice for Outdoor Events: Other than Pop Concerts and Raves: Amendments and Updates*. Wallington, NOEA.

National Readership Survey (NRS) (2005). *Top Line Readership: Daily Newspapers: Latest 12 Months – Apr04 – Mar05*. London, NRS Ltd. (Internet) Available from <http://www.nrs.co.uk/open_access/open_topline/newspapers/index.cfm> (accessed 9 August 2005).

National Statistics (2004). *Population Change*. (Internet) Available from <http://www.statistics.gov.uk/cci/nugget.asp?id=950> (accessed 9 August 2005).

Neal, C., Quester, P. and Hawkins, H. (2002). *Consumer Behaviour*. 3rd edn. Sydney, McGraw-Hill.

Neighbourhood Arts Unit (1991). *Community Festival Handbook*. Melbourne, City of Melbourne.

NetAid.org (1999). *Netaid.org Web Site Sets World Record for Largest Internet Broadcast; More than One Thousand Organizations Join Initiative to Fight Extreme Poverty*. 12 October. (Internet) Available from <http://www.cisco.com/netaid/pressroom.html> (accessed 4 May 2005).

New Leisure Markets (1995). *Festivals and Special Events*. New Local Authority Leisure Markets, 4. Headland, Cleveland, Business Information Futures Ltd.

Newcastle Gateshead Initiative (2005). *New £12m Cultural Programme Announced for the North East*. Press Release, 4 February. (Internet) Available from <http://www.visitnewcastlegateshead.com/mediacentre> (accessed 9 August 2005).

Newham Leisure Services (2000). *Reasons to be Cheerful: Newham's Local Culture Strategy*. London, Newham Leisure Services.

Nindi, P. (2005). *National Carnival Arts Strategy 2005–2007*. London, Arts Council England.

Noe, R., Hollenbeck, J., Gerhart, B. and Wright, P. (2003). *Resource Management*. 4th edn. New York, McGraw Hill.

Noise Council (1995). *Code of Practice on Environmental Noise Control at Concerts*. London, Chartered Institute Environmental Health Officers.

North West Arts Board (1999). *No Difference, No Future! Action for Cultural Diversity in Greater Manchester*. Manchester, North West Arts Board. (Internet) Available from <http://www.arts.org.uk/directory/regions/north_west/report_cult_div.html> (accessed 12 July 2000).

Northern Ireland Events Company (NIEC) (2005a). *Background*. (Internet) Available from <http://www.nievents.co.uk/about/default.asp> (accessed 9 August 2005).

Northern Ireland Events Company (NIEC) (2005b). *NIEC Major Events Fund*. (Internet) Available from <http://www.nievents.co.uk/funding/documents/majorevents.pdf> (accessed 9 August 2005).

Northern Ireland Tourist Board (NITB) (2003). *Tourism in Northern Ireland: A Strategic Framework for Action 2004-2007*. Belfast, Northern Ireland Tourist Board.

Northern Ireland Tourist Board (NITB) (2005). *Northern Ireland Conference Support Programme*. Belfast, Northern Ireland Tourist Board.

Northwest Development Agency (NWDA) (2003). *The Strategy for Tourism in England's Northwest*. (Internet) Warrington, Northwest Development Agency. Available from: <nwda-cms.amaze.co.uk/DocumentUploads/Tourismfinal.pdf> (accessed 9 August 2005).

Notman, S. (1999). *BEIC Topic Report: The Tourism Sector in Birmingham*. Birmingham, Birmingham Economic Information Centre.

Nurse, K. (2003). Festival tourism in the Caribbean: an economic impact assessment. In *Proceedings of the Fifth Annual Caribbean Conference on Sustainable Tourism Development*. Caribbean Tourism Organisation.

O'Neill, S. (2000). Geldoff fury as can't-do culture kills new year fireworks. (Internet) *Daily Telegraph*, issue 2006, 21 November. Available from <http://www.telegraph.co.uk> (accessed 6 February 2001).

O'Toole, W. (2000). Towards the integration of event management best practice by the project management process. In *Events Beyond 2000 – Setting the Agenda. Proceedings of the Conference on Evaluation, Research and Education, 13–14 July* (J. Allen, R. Harris, L. K. Jago and A. J. Veal, eds) Sydney, Australian Centre for Event Management, University of Technology.

O'Toole, W. (2004). *Event Project Management System*. Sydney, EPMS.net (Multimedia: CD-ROM).

O'Toole, W. and Mikolaitis, P. (2002). *Corporate Event Project Management*. New York, John Wiley & Sons.

Office for National Statistics (ONS) (2003). *All People Aged 16 and Over in Households: Census 2001, National Report for England and Wales – Part 2: Table S066 Sex and Approximated Social Grade by Age*. (Internet) London, Office for National Statistics. Available from <http://www.statistics.gov.uk/StatBase/Expodata/Spreadsheets/D7534.xls> (accessed 4 August 2005).

Office for National Statistics (ONS) (2004). *Socio-economic Classification of Working-age Population, Summer 2003: Regional Trends 38*. 1 March. London, Office for National Statistics. (Internet) Available from <http://www.statistics.gov.uk/STATBASE/Expodata/Spreadsheets/D7665.xls> (accessed 9 August 2005).

Office for National Statistics (ONS) (2005). *The National Statistics Socio-economic Classification User Manual*. London, Office for National Statistics. (Internet) Available from <http://www.statistics.gov.uk/methods_quality/ns_sec/downloads/NS-SEC_User.pdf> (accessed 9 August 2005).

O'Neill, M., Getz, D. and Carlsen, J. (1999). Evaluation of service quality at events: the 1998 Coca-Cola Masters surfing event at Margaret River, Western Australia. *Managing Service Quality*, **9**(3), 158–166.

O'Toole, W. J. (2002). *Competencies and Maturity Models for Events*: Towards the Integration of Event Management Best Practice by the Project Management Process. Sydney, Australia: ISES Conference for Professional Development.

Owen, J. and Holliday, P. (1993). *Confer in Confidence: An Organiser's Dossier*. Broadway, Worcester, Meetings Industry Association.

Oxford Interactive Encyclopedia (1997). *Folk Festival*. The Learning Company, Inc.

PA Cambridge Economic Consultants (1990). *An Evaluation of Garden Festivals.* London, HMSO.

Pagonis, W. G. (1992). *Moving Mountains Lessons in Leadership and Logistics from the Gulf War.* Boston, Harvard Business School Press.

Palmer, G. and Lloyd, N. (1972). *A Year of Festivals: British Calendar Customs.* London, Frederick Warne.

Parasuraman, A., Zeithaml, V. and Berry L. (1988). SERVQUAL: a multiple-item scale for measuring consumers' perceptions of service quality. *Journal of Retailing*, **64**(1), 22–37.

Peach, E. and Murrell, K. (1995). Reward and recognition systems for volunteers. In *The Volunteer Management Handbook* (T. Connors, ed.), New York, John Wiley & Sons.

Pearce, L. (2003). Open seeks new sponsor after Heineken decision. *The Age*, December, 31.

Pembroke Festival (2004). *Welcome to the 2004 Pembroke Festival Music Programme!* (Internet) Available from <http://www.pembrokefestival.org.uk/content/2004/index.htm> (accessed 10 May 2005).

Performance Research (2000). *British Football Fans Can't Recall Euro 2000 Sponsors.* (Internet) London, Performance Research. Available from <http://www.performanceresearch.com/euro-2000-sponsorship.htm> (accessed 24 August 2005).

Performance Research (2004). *Fourth Annual IEG/Performance Research Sponsorship Decision-Makers Survey.* (Internet) Available from <http://www.performanceresearch.com/sponsor-survey.htm> (accessed 21 August 2005).

Perry, M., Foley, P. and Rumpf, P. (1996). Event management: an emerging challenge in Australian education. *Festival Management and Event Tourism*, **4**(1), 85–93.

Pickett, B. (2002). *As Cingular Ads Parody, Not All Sponsorships Fit the Brandbuilding Bill.* (Internet) National Hotel Executive, September. Available from <http://www.brandchannel.com/images/papers/sponsorshipBC.pdf> (accessed 24 August 2005).

Policy Studies Institute (PSI) (1992). Arts Festivals. *Cultural Trends*, vol. 15. London, Policy Studies Institute.

Porter, M. (1990). *Competitive Advantage of Nations.* New York, Free Press.

PricewaterhouseCoopers (2001). *E-commerce Impact Study for the Exhibition and Conference Sector.* Final report, September 2001. London, DTI.

Project Management Institute (2000). *Guide to the Project Management Body of Knowledge 2000.* Philadelphia, Project Management Institute.

Rao, V. and Steckel, J. (1998). *Analysis for Strategic Marketing.* Reading, Massachusetts, Addison-Wesley.

Redmond, A. (2005). *Convention Bureau.* (Internet) Glasgow, Glasgow City Marketing Bureau. Available from <http://www.seeglasgow.com/convention-bureau> (accessed 9 August 2005).

Reeves, M. (2002). *Measuring the Economic and Social Impact of the Arts.* London, Arts Council of England.

Reid, F. (2001). *Staging Handbook.* 2nd edn. London, A. & C. Black.

Renault (2003). *Renault UK Sponsor of Cirque du Soleil's Saltimbanco Season.* (Internet) Press Release, 17 January. Available from <http://www.carpages.co.uk/renault/renault_sponsor_cirque_du_soleils_saltimbanco_season_17_01_03.asp?switched=on&echo=10757702> (accessed 22 July 2005).

Richards, G. and Wilson, J. (2002). The links between mega events and urban renewal: the case of the Manchester 2002 Commonwealth Games. In *Events and Place-making: Proceedings of International Research Conference Held in Sydney 2002* (L. Jago, M. Deery,

R. Harris, A. Hede and J. Allen, eds) Sydney, Australian Centre for Event Management.

Richmond Event Management (2005). *About Glasgow River Festival.* (Internet) Available from <http://www.glasgowriverfestival.co.uk/about.htm> (accessed 21 July 2005).

Ritchie, B. (2001). Turning 16 days into 16 years through Olympic legacies. *Event Management*, **6**(3), 155–165.

Ritchie, J. R. B. (1984). Assessing the impact of hallmark events. *Journal of Travel Research*, **23**(1), 2–11.

Robertson, D. and Pope, N. (1999). *Product Bundling and Causes of Attendance and Non-attendance in Live Professional Sport: A Case Study of the Brisbane Broncos and the Brisbane Lions.* (Internet) *The Cyberjournal of Sports Marketing*, 3(1). Available from <http://www.ausport.gov.au/fulltext/1999/cjsm/v3n1/robertson&pope31.htm> (accessed 24 August 2005).

Robinson, L. S. and Callan, R. J. (2001). The U.K. conference and meetings industry: development of an inventory for attributional analysis. *Journal of Convention and Exhibition Management*, **2**(4), 65–80.

Robinson, L. S. and Callan, R. J. (2002a). A qualitative gambit to formulate a foundation for the appraisement of service quality in the U.K. meetings industry. *Journal of Convention and Exhibition Management*, **3**(4), 1–16.

Robinson, L. S. and Callan, R. J. (2002b). Professional U.K. conference organizers' perceptions of important selection and quality attributes of the meetings product. *Journal of Convention and Exhibition Management*, **4**(1), 1–18.

Robinson, L. S. and Callan, R. J. (2005). UK conference delegates' cognizance of the importance of venue selection attributes. *Journal of Convention and Event Tourism*, **7**(1), 77–91.

Roche, M. (2000). *Mega-Events and Modernity: Olympics and Expos in the Growth of Global Culture.* London, Routledge.

Rogers, T. (1998). Conferences: *A Twenty-First Century Industry.* Harlow, Addison Wesley Longman.

Rogers, T. (2003a). *Conferences and Conventions: A Global Industry.* Oxford, Butterworth-Heinemann.

Rogers, T. (2003b). *Business Tourism Briefing: An Overview of the UK's Business Tourism Industry.* London, Business Tourism Partnership.

Rolfe, H. (1992). *Arts Festivals in the UK.* London, Policy Studies Institute.

Rose, D. and O'Reilley, K. (1998). *The ESCR Review of Government Social Classifications.* London, Office for National Statistics/Economic and Social Research Council.

Roy, D. and Cornwell, T. B. (2004). The effects of consumer knowledge on responses to event sponsorships. *Psychology and Marketing*, **21**(3), 185–207.

Royal Bank of Scotland (2003). *Royal Bank of Scotland Staff Turn up and Try it Themselves.* (Internet) Press Release 31 July. Available from <http://www.rbs.com/media03.asp?id=MEDIA_CENTRE/PRESS_RELEASES/2003/JULY/31_ED_FESTIVAL> (accessed 21 August 2005).

Royal Bank of Scotland (2004). *Royal Bank Lates - The Quintessential Festival.* (Internet) Press Release 1 April. Available from <http://www.rbs.com/media03.asp?id=MEDIA_CENTRE/PRESS_RELEASES/2004/APRIL/01_QUINTESSENTIAL> (accessed 21 August 2005).

Royal, C. G. and Jago, L. K. (1998). Special events accreditation: the practitioner's perspective. *Festival Management and Event Tourism*, **5**(4), 221–30.

Saleh, F. and Ryan, C. (1993). Jazz and knitwear: factors that attract tourists to festivals. *Tourism Management*, August, 298–297.

Salford Film Festival (2005). *Mission Statement and Aims.* (Internet) Available from <http://www.salfordfilmfestival.co.uk/about.asp?ID=24> (accessed 1 August 2005).

Schlegelmilch, B., Bohlen, G. and Diamantopoulos, A. (1996). The link between green purchasing decisions and measures of environmental consciousness. *European Journal of Marketing*, **30**(5), 35–55.

School of Volunteer Management (2001). *Rights and Responsibilities of Volunteers and Voluntary Organisations*. Sydney, School of Volunteer Management.

Scott, E. (2003). On the waterfront. *Australian Leisure Management*, February–March.

Scottish Arts Council (2003). *Evaluation Toolkit: The Scottish Arts Council E-Tool for Evaluation*. (Internet) Edinburgh, Scottish Arts Council. Available from <http://www.evaluationforall.org.uk> (accessed 9 August 2005).

Scottish Courage (2005). *The Strongbow Rooms*. (Internet) Entry for Marketing Excellence Awards Scotland 2005. Available from <http://www.tunaweb.com/MarketingAwardsScotlandNominees/casestudies/Comms-SE-StongbowRooms.pdf> (accessed 24 August 2005).

Scottish Executive (2002). *Scotland's Major Events Strategy 2003–2015*: Competing on an International Stage. (Internet) Available from <http://www.scotland.gov.uk/publications> (accessed 15 July 2005).

Scottish Exhibition and Conference Centre (SECC) (2005). SECC Successfully Hosts ERS. *Scene*, Issue 1, 4.

SeaBritain 2005 Press Office (2004). *SeaBritain 2005 – Take a Fresh Look at the Sea*. (Internet) Press Release 1 October. Available from <http://www.seabritain2005.com/server.php?show=ConWebDoc.116> (accessed 9 August 2005).

Select Committee on Culture, Media and Sport (1999). *Fourth Report: Staging International Sporting Events*. May. London, The Stationery Office.

Select Committee on Culture, Media and Sport (2001). *Third Report: Staging International Sporting Events*. London, The Stationery Office.

Shani, D. and Sandler, D. (1998). Ambush marketing: is confusion to blame for the flickering of the flame? *Psychology and Marketing*, **15**(4), 367–383.

Shimp, T. (2003). *Advertising, Promotion and Supplemental Aspects of Integrated Marketing Communication*. 6th edn. Ohio, Thomson.

Shone, A. (1998). *The Business of Conferences*. Oxford, Butterworth-Heinemann.

Shone, A. and Parry, B. (2004). *Successful Event Management*. 2nd edn. London, Thomson Learning.

Silvers, J. R. (2004a). Global knowledge domain structure for event management. In *Las Vegas International Hospitality and Convention Summit* (Z. Gu, ed) Las Vegas, Nevada, UNLV.

Silvers, J. (2004b). *Professional Event Coordination*. Hoboken, New Jersey, John Wiley & Sons Inc.

Silvers, J., Bowdin, G., O'Toole, W. and Nelson, K. (2005). *Towards an International Event Management Body Of Knowledge (EMBOK)*. Event Management (in press).

Skinner, B. E. and Rukavina, V. (2003). *Event Sponsorship*. Hoboken, New Jersey, John Wiley & Sons Inc.

Slack, N., Chambers, S. and Johnston, R. (2004). *Operations Management*. 4th edn. Harlow, *Financial Times*, Prentice Hall.

Slice (2000). *Creamfields 2000*. (Internet) London, Slice. Available from <http://www.slice.co.uk/creamfields00_sitemap.html> (accessed 2 February 2001).

Smith, A. and Jenner, P. (1998). The impact of festivals and special events on tourism. *Travel and Tourism Analyst*, **4**, 73–91.

Society of Motor Manufacturers and Traders (SMMT) (2004). *Motor Show Matters to the West Midlands*. (Internet) London, Society of Motor Manufacturers and Traders,

Press Release. Available from <http://www.smmt.co.uk/news/> (accessed 3 August 2005).

Sodexho Prestige (2004). *The National Corporate Hospitality Survey.* Alperton, Sodexho Prestige.

Sonder, M. (2005). *Event Entertainment and Production.* Hoboken, New Jersey, John Wiley & Sons, Inc.

Sorin, D. (2003). *The Special Events Advisor.* Hoboken, New Jersey, John Wiley & Sons Inc.

South East Arts (1998). *A Festival's Strategy for the South East.* London, England's Regional Arts Boards.

SponsorMap (2005). *SponsorMap.* (Internet) Available from <http://www.sponsormap.com/how.html> (accessed 20 July 2005).

Sponsorship Consulting Limited (2005). *Accenture – A Case Study.* (Internet) London, Sponsorship Consulting Limited. Available from <http://www.sponsorshipconsulting.co.uk/case_Accenture.htm> (accessed 23 August 2005).

Sponsorshiponline.co.uk (2005). *UK Sponsorship Statistics.* (Internet) Available from <http://www.sponsorshiponline.co.uk/images/headings//UK_Sponsorshipmarketplace_Stats04.pdf> (accessed 24 August 2005).

Sport Industry Research Centre (SIRC) (2005). *Tour of Britain Economic Impact Report.* Surrey, Tour of Britain.

SQW Ltd and TNS Travel and Tourism (2005). *Edinburgh Festivals 2004–2005 Economic Impact Survey Stage 1 Results.* Edinburgh, The City of Edinburgh Council, Scottish Enterprise Edinburgh and Lothian, EventScotland and VisitScotland.

Standards Australia (2003). AS 5037(Int)-2003. *Knowledge Management Standard* (Interim). Sydney, Standards Australia.

Stayte, S. and Watt, D. (1998). *Events: From Start to Finish.* Reading, ILAM.

Stephenson, G. (2005). *Arts and Culture in Northern Ireland: 2004 Baseline Survey.* Belfast, Arts Council of Northern Ireland.

Stone, R. (2002). *Human Resource Management.* 4th edn. Brisbane, John Wiley & Sons Australia.

Strauss, N. (2000). The last 10 per cent is the toughest. *BioCycle,* January, 35.

Sudhaman, A. (2004). Game, set and client match. *PR Week Asia,* 9, April.

Summerfield, C. and Gill, B. (2005). *Social Trends.* No. 35. (Internet) Basingstoke, Palgrave Macmillan. Available from <http://www.statistics.gov.uk/downloads/theme_social/Social_Trends35/Social_Trends_35.pdf> (accessed 9 August 2005).

Supovitz, F. (2005). *The Sports Event Management and Marketing Playbook.* Hoboken, New Jersey, John Wiley & Sons Inc.

Supply-Chain Inventory Management Forum (2003). *Glossary of Supply-Chain Inventory Management Terms.* (Internet) Corby, Chartered Institute of Logistics and Transport (CILT). Available from <http://www.ciltuk.org.uk/process/glossary.asp> (accessed 21 July 2005).

Tambe, R. (2004). *Corporate Hospitality.* London, Key Note Ltd.

Tarlow, P. (2002). *Event Risk Management and Safety.* New York, John Wiley & Sons Inc.

Tarradellas, J. and Behnam, S. (2000). *Olympic Movement's Agenda 21: Sport for Sustainable Development.* Lausanne, Switzerland, International Olympic Committee, Sport and Environment Commission.

The Association for Festival Organisers (AFO) (2004). *The Impact of Folk Festivals.* Matlock, The Association for Festival Organisers.

The Chambers Dictionary (1998). Edinburgh, Chambers Harrap Publishers Ltd.

The Comptroller and Auditor General (2000). *The Millennium Dome.* London, The Stationery Office.

The Guardian Hay Festival (2005). *Festival Sponsors*. (Internet) Available from <http://www.hayfestival.com/2005/sponsors.asp> (accessed 21 August 2005).

The NEC Group (2004). *Textile Show Gives Massive Boost to Region*. (Internet) Press Release, 16 March. Available from <http://www.necgroup-sport.com/media/PressRelease.asp?i=675> (accessed 3 August 2005).

The NEC Group (2005a). *The Lions Club*, The NEC Group Hall of Fame. (Internet) Available from <http://www.necgroup.co.uk/corporate/halloffame/lions-club.asp> (accessed 3 August 2005)

The NEC Group (2005b). *Factsheet 1 – The NEC Group – Introduction and Background*. (Internet) Available from <http://www.necgroup.co.uk/media/pdfs/facts1.pdf> (accessed 3 August 2005)

The Right Solution (2005). *UK Conference Market Survey*. Wellingborough, Meetings Industry Association.

The Scottish Traditional Boat Festival (2005). *Vision for the Second Decade*. (Internet) Available from <http://www.thebpl.co.uk/stbf/about_us.htm> (accessed 31 July 2005).

The Theatre Shop Conference (2002). *Panel Discussion: Programming Criteria Used By International Festivals*. (Internet) Available from <http://www.fuel4arts.com> (accessed 24 August 2005).

Thomas, R. and Wood, E. (2003). Events-based tourism: a survey of local authority strategies in the UK. *Local Governance*, **29**(2), 127–136.

Thompson, J. L. with Martin, F. (2005). *Strategic Management: Awareness and Change*. 5th edn. London, Thomson Learning.

Thrane, C. (2002). Music quality, satisfaction and behavioural intentions within a jazz festival context. *Event Management*, **7**(3), 143–150.

Toffler, A. (1984). *Future Shock*. New York, Bantam Books.

Toohey, K. (2001). *Official Report of the Games of the XXVII Olympiad*. Sydney, Sydney Organising Committee for the Olympic Games.

Torkildsen, G. (2005). *Leisure and Recreation Management*. 5th edn. Abingdon, Routledge.

Toulmin, V. (2002a). *Charter Fairs*. (Internet) Sheffield, National Fairground Archive, University of Sheffield. Available from <http://www.shef.ac.uk/nfa/history/charter/> (accessed 9 August 2005).

Toulmin, V. (2002b). *The HoppingShow Row*. (Internet) Sheffield, National Fairground Archive, University of Sheffield. Available from <http://www.shef.ac.uk/nfa/history/shows/newcastle.php> (accessed 9 August 2005).

Tourism Works (1996). *Economic Impact of the European Championships 1996 on the City of Leeds: An Image Volume Value Study*. Leeds, Leeds City Council.

Travers, T. (1998). *The Wyndham Report*. London, Society of London Theatre.

Tribe, J. (1997). *Corporate Strategy for Tourism*. London, International Thompson Business Press.

Tum, J., Norton, P. and Wright, N. (2006). *Managing Event Operations*. Oxford, Elsevier Butterworth-Heinemann.

Tynedale Council (2003). *New Events Grants for Hadrian's Wall Country*. (Internet) 30 April. Available from <http://www.tynedale.gov.uk/residents/news-viewsdetails.asp?menu=14andsubmenu=andnewsid=218> (accessed 17 August 2005).

UCAS (2005). *Course Search*. (Internet) Available from <http://www.ucas.com/search/index.html> (accessed 8 December, 2005).

UK Sport (1998). *Public Opinion Survey – Importance and Measure of UK Sporting Success*. London, UK Sport.

UK Sport (1999a). *A UK Strategy: Major Events – A 'Blueprint' For Success*. London, UK Sport.

UK Sport (1999b). Memorandum submitted by the United Kingdom Sports Council. In *Fourth Report: Staging International Sporting Events. Volume II Minutes of Evidence* (Select Committee on Culture, Media and Sport). London, The Stationery Office.

UK Sport (1999c). *Major Events: The Economics – A Guide*. London, UK Sport.

UK Sport (2000). *Major Events Blueprint: Measuring Success*. London, UK Sport.

UK Sport (2002). *Practical Environmental Guidelines*. London, UK Sport.

UK Sport (2005). *Major Sports Events: The Guide*. London, UK Sport.

Ukman, L. (1995). *Successful Proposals*. (Internet) Available from <http://www.sponsorship.com/forum/success.html> (accessed 25 April 2001).

United Nations (1992). *Agenda 21: Programme of Action for Sustainable Development*. New York, United Nations Department of Public Information.

Universitat Autònoma de Barcelona (2005). *Centre d'Estudis Olímpics*. (Internet) Available from <http://olympicstudies.uab.es/eng/> (accessed 24 August 2005).

Upton, M. (2004). Chapter 9: Crowd safety planning for major concert events. In *Health and Safety Aspects in the Live Music Industry* (C. Kemp, and I. Hill, eds), Cambridge, Entertainment Technology Press, pp. 143–161.

US Travel Data Centre (1989). *Discover America 2000*. Washington, DC, Travel Industry Association of America.

Uysal, M., Gahan, L. and Martin, B. (1993). An examination of event motivations. *Festival Management and Event Tourism*, **1**(1), 5–10.

Van Der Wagen, L. and Carlos, B. (2005). *Event Management for Tourism, Cultural, Business and Sporting Events*. 2nd edn. Frenchs Forest, Pearson Education Australia.

Vasey, J. (1998). *Concert Tour Production Management*. Boston, Focal Press.

Veal, A. (1997). *Research Methods for Leisure and Tourism*. 2nd edn. London, Pitman.

Verwey, P. (1999). *Sample Audience Survey Questions*. London, Arts Council of England.

ViewLondon.co.uk (2005). *What's On: BBC Henry Wood Promenade Concerts – Week Seven*. (Internet) Available from <http://www.viewlondon.co.uk/whats_on_31109.html> (accessed 22 August 2005).

Vignette (2004). *Vignette Powers Record-Setting Performance of Athens 2004 Olympics Web Site*. (Internet) Case Study: Publishing and Entertainment. Available from <http://www.vignette.com/Downloads/CS_Athens2004.pdf> (accessed 24 August 2005).

Virgin Radio (2004). *Wall's ice cream – Live to play*. (Internet) Available from <http://www.virginradio.co.uk/music/vfestival2004/walls.html> (accessed 23 August 2005).

Vroom, V. (1964). *Work and Motivation*. New York, John Wiley & Sons.

Waitt, G. (2003). Social impacts of the Sydney Olympics. *Annals of Tourism Research*, **30**(1), 194–215.

Wales Tourist Board (WTB) (2000). *Achieving Our Potential: A Tourism Strategy for Wales*. Cardiff, Wales Tourist Board.

Wallis, N. (2003). Analysis – festivals find their place in the sun. *Event*, November/December, 10.

Waste Awareness Wales (2005). *Events Recycling Guide*. Cardiff, Waste Awareness Wales.

Watt, C. (1988). *Event Management in Leisure and Tourism*. Harlow, Addison Wesley Longman.

Wells, W. D. and Gubar, G. (1966). Lifecycle concepts in marketing research. *Journal of Marketing Research*, **3**, 355–363.

Welsh, J. (2003). *Reinventing Sponsorship*. (Internet) Number 22 (Spring). Available from <http://www.poolonline.com/archive/issue22/iss22fea3.html > (accessed 24 August 2005).

Wendroff, A. L. (2004). *Special Events: Proven Strategies for Nonprofit Fundraising*. Hoboken, New Jersey, John Wiley & Sons Inc.

WIMFEST. (2004). *Our Vision*. (Internet) Available from <http://www.wimfest-liverpool.com/vision.php> (accessed 1 August 2005).

Windsor Festival (2005). *About Windsor Festival*. (Internet) Available from <http://www.windsorfestival.com/about/> (accessed 9 August 2005).

Wisconsin Department of Natural Resources (1998). *Special Events: Recycling and Waste Management*. (Internet) Available from <http://www.uwm.edu/Dept/besmart/festival/dnrspecial.html> (accessed 24 August 2005).

Wood, E. (2002). Events, civic pride and attitude change in a post-industrial town: evaluating the effect of local authority events on residents' attitudes to the Blackburn region. In *Proceedings of the Events and Place-Making Conference* (L. Jago, M. Deery, R. Harris, A. Hede and J. Allen, eds) Sydney, Australian Centre for Event Management, University of Technology.

Wood, H. (1982). *Festivity and Social Change*. London, Leisure in the Eighties Research Unit, Polytechnic of the South Bank.

Wood, J., Chapman, J., Fromholtz, M., Morrison, V., Wallace, J., Zeffane, R., Schermerhorn, J., Hunt, J. and Osborn, R. (2004). *Organisational Behaviour: A Global Perspective*. 3rd edn. Brisbane, John Wiley & Sons Australia.

Worcester Festival (2005). *Welcome to Worcester Festival 2005*. (Internet) Available from <http://www.worcesterfestival.co.uk/> (accessed 1 August 2005).

World Bank (2004). *Beyond Economic Growth*. (Internet) Available from <http://www.worldbank.org/depweb/english/beyond/global/chapter3.html> (accessed 24 August 2005).

Xerox Corporation (1998). *Guide to Waste Reduction and Recycling at Special Events*. New York, Xerox Corporation.

Yeoman, I., Robertson, M., Ali-Knight, J., Drummond, S. and McMahon-Beattie, U. (eds) (2004). *Festival and Events Management: An International Arts and Cultural Perspective*. Oxford, Elsevier Butterworth-Heinemann.

Yorkshire Tourist Board (2000). *Love Parade at Roundhay Park, Leeds: Event Evaluation*. York, Yorkshire Tourist Board Research Services.

Younge, G. (1999). New beat to saving the world from debt. (Internet) *Guardian Unlimited*, 15 February. Available from <http://www.guardianunlimited.co.uk> (accessed 15 April 2001).

Zeithaml, V., Parasuraman, A. and Berry, L. (1990). *Delivering Quality Service: Balancing Customer Perceptions and Expectations*. New York, Free Press.

Index